W9-BVQ-887

WITHDRAWN

BARRON'S

E-Z

AMERICAN HISTORY

William O. Kellogg
Former Head of History Department
St. Paul's School
Concord, New Hampshire

Past President
World Affairs Council of New Hampshire

Dedication
For the next generation—especially Matthew and Sarah Read Coburn, Rachel Ann and Emily Kay Blackwell, and Reid, Boden, and Alden Steele Kellogg. May they enjoy history as much as I have.

Better Grades or Your Money Back!

As a leader in educational publishing, Barron's has helped millions of students reach their academic goals. Our E-Z series of books is designed to help students master a variety of subjects. We are so confident that completing all the review material and exercises in this book will help you, that if your grades don't improve within 30 days, we will give you a full refund.

To qualify for a refund, simply return the book within 90 days of purchase and include your store receipt. Refunds will not include sales tax or postage. Offer available only to U.S. residents. Void where prohibited. Send books to **Barron's Educational Series, Inc., Attn: Customer Service** at the address on this page.

All inquiries should be addressed to:
Barron's Educational Series, Inc.
250 Wireless Boulevard
Hauppauge, NY 11788
www.barronseduc.com

Library of Congress Catalog Card No.: 2009015805

ISBN-13: 978-0-7641-4258-1
ISBN-10: 0-7641-4258-5

Library of Congress Cataloguing-in-Publication Data:
Kellogg, William O.
    E-Z American history / William O. Kellogg.—4th ed.
        p.   cm.
    Rev ed. of: American history the easy way. c2003.
    Includes bibliographical references and index.
    ISBN-13: 978-0-7641-4258-1
    ISBN-10: 0-7641-4258-5
    1. United States—History—Examinations, questions, etc.
2. United States—History—Outlines, syllabi, etc.
I. Kellogg, William O. American history the easy way.   II. Title.
III. Title: Easy American history.
E178.25.K39 2009
973—dc22
                                                    2009015805

PRINTED IN THE UNITED STATES OF AMERICA
9 8 7 6 5 4 3 2 1

CONTENTS

Foreword

This book was written to serve as an introduction to American History. It is designed to include the reader as an historian. Each chapter begins with a different "Approach to History" that historians pursue. There are questions raised within the text that invite the reader to consider issues of significance without being given "an answer." Chapters are divided into sections. At the end of each section are presented "Key Points to Remember," "Links from the Past to the Present," "People to Remember," and "Dates." Each summary includes two types of questions—identification and multiple choice—to help the reader recall important information. At the end of each chapter are open-ended, essay type questions to provoke thought and analysis of the content in the chapter. Many words important for understanding American History are defined at the bottom of the page where they are used. Maps are included in the text and in the Appendix. All these devices are meant to help the student of whatever age to grasp more readily and easily the content and significance of the history of the American people.

While my name alone is attached to this work and I am fully responsible for it, there are many people who have been influential in bringing my work to print. The book summarizes over 50 years of learning and teaching, and my many students and colleagues during those years greatly influenced my understanding of American History.

The St. Paul's School Research Librarian, Anne Locke, gave invaluable advice through the research process, and my typist, Elli Kellogg Blackwell, mastered my hieroglyphic writing to make a readable manuscript. My editors have all combined patience, criticism, and support in a wonderful mix that helped to make this endeavor an enjoyable one. Finally, I wish to thank Barron's Educational Series for providing me a rare opportunity to present my thoughts on the teaching and the meaning of American History. It has been a very rewarding experience. My hope is that others will benefit from what I have learned.

As in all of my writing, it could not have been accomplished without the support of my family particularly Ann. Thanks.

William O. Kellogg
Boulder, Colorado
April 1, 2009

Acknowledgments

Cartoon on page 24: Library of Congress

Painting on page 45: Library of Congress

Photographs on pages 85, 109, 177, and 223: Courtesy of the New Hampshire Historical Society, Concord, New Hampshire

Photographs on pages 103 and 115: Library of Congress

Drawing on page 130: Library of Congress

Photographs on pages 113 and 166: Courtesy of the Carnegie Branch Library for Local History, Boulder Historical Society Collection, Boulder, Colorado

Photograph on page 280: Courtesy of Dr. J. G. Whitesides

Cartoon on page 313: Reprinted with permission of Mike Marland, *Concord Monitor*, Concord, New Hampshire

Photograph on page 416: AP Photo/Louis Lanzano

Cartoons on pages 454 and 484: Courtesy of James Fenton and Rachael Blackwell, Australian High School students, Brisbane, Australia

Photograph on page 426: Associated Press

Photograph on page 457: Associated Press

A Nation of Immigrants

APPROACHES TO HISTORY

THE METHOD OF THE HISTORIAN

Many people think history is a set of facts, explaining what happened in the past, that everyone should learn. They believe that by memorizing this material, they will know history. Unfortunately, this is only partly true. The truth is that history is a record of the past, and consists of information historians have gathered to explain, as best they can, what occurred before the present. You might ask, "What is the difference between these two statements?" The answer is that the latter statement avoids the word *facts* and suggests the method historians use to gain an understanding of the past.

"Facts" come in all degrees of accuracy, something that can be hard for the inexperienced student of history to accept or understand. Part of the historian's method is to evaluate facts. For instance, you may be familiar with the statement "Columbus discovered America in 1492," and believe it to be a fact. Historians have considered the evidence and agree that Columbus came to the Americas in 1492—that is, 1492 according to the calendar used by most people in the United States but not 1492 according to the Jewish or Chinese calendars. Therefore, we must be clear what we mean when we state a "fact," because it may not be universally understood. More importantly, we know that there were Native Americans already in the Americas, and other Europeans had come here—they had all "discovered" America long before Columbus. So to be accurate, you need to rephrase the statement so it reads, "Columbus rediscovered America for the Europeans in 1492 A.D."

The historian's method begins with the collection and questioning of so-called factual information. Once historians have collected a good deal of information—often referred to as data—they study it and develop explanations of how these facts relate. These explanations are hypotheses[1], since there is no way we can be certain just how the events, the facts, of the past were understood and related to each other.

Underlying every explanation is the historian's personal values and biases. These affect the choice of and interpretation of the facts used. Some historians see economic issues as crucial in history; others emphasize the individual. There are innumerable perspectives and combinations that have been developed, and each reflects the personal perspective of the writer. Each chapter of this text will present a different perspective on how to view history, but all of them share the historic method.

The historian's method is very similar to the method used by scientists. Using the so-called scientific method, the scientist collects data, develops a hypothesis about why the observed data behaved the way it did, and then prepares experiments in the laboratory to prove the hypothesis by running the test over and over again to show the data will always perform the way the hypothesis states.

Unfortunately, once historians have developed a hypothesis as to why events occurred in a particular way, they cannot run an experiment over and over again to prove the hypothesis. Historians' hypotheses cannot be tested the way scientists' are. Therefore, there is always an element of uncertainty in what historians write and often differing hypotheses.

Historians must rely on careful research and analysis of information. They must be aware of their own personal views and try to keep their personal biases out of their interpretation, but it always is present.

Information such as the statement about Columbus is of little significance alone. As you study history, you must learn the facts (data), but a fact is meaningful only when it helps to support a hypothesis about how past events occurred. As a student of history, you need to understand the hypotheses the writer of history is supporting and judge how well they are proven by the facts presented. Then you need to ask if there are additional facts that might disprove the hypothesis.

In conclusion, historians do not think of history as a mere collection of facts but rather as a series of hypotheses or explanations of the past supported by factual evidence. Historians often disagree. Have you ever experienced a situation in which you and a friend, or you and your parents, disagreed and each presented an explanation with evidence that the other person would not accept? That can happen in history. As you read on, think what the hypotheses of the author are, and ask yourself how sound the evidence is to support the position presented.

---

[1] hypothesis   *A calculated guess; an unproved theory or explanation offered as a way to understanding.*

INTRODUCTION

We are a nation of immigrants. Some of you reading this book may be immigrants yourselves; most of you will know people in your communities from Asia, the Americas, Africa, or Europe, who recently came to America as immigrants. All of us have ancestors who were immigrants—some voluntary, some forced. The immigrant experience is one that all Americans have shared from the earliest to arrive—the Native Americans—to the most recent arrivals from Croatia, Sudan, or Iraq.

We will begin this study of American History with a brief look at the first immigrants, the ancestors of today's Native Americans, and those who followed before the arrival of Christopher Columbus. By realizing we all share in some way this immigrant experience and that it is still a current issue, the past will become closer and easier to understand.

I. Native American Immigrants

THE FIRST IMMIGRANTS

The first immigrants who came to the North American continent were the nomadic[2] ancestors of the Native Americans. Although new evidence and hypotheses are being developed all the time, the best estimate of historians is that sometime around 50,000 years ago, several related groups began crossing the Bering Sea over a land bridge between Siberia and Alaska. From there they moved south and east, and their descendants populated the North and South American continents.

> Native Americans arrive in North America over a land bridge. They were the first to "discover" the lands of the Americas.

These first groups were nomads who hunted animals and gathered fruits and berries. During the last Ice Age they moved south away from the cold. Later, as the ice receded, the land bridge over which they had come was flooded, cutting the new arrivals off from their places of origin.

This pattern of separation from home, from all that was familiar, has been repeated over and over again in the history of the Americas. Can you think what it would be like to be completely cut off from all familiar places? All immigrants share this experience.

What would such immigrants bring with them, either now or 50,000 years ago? Many have brought just what they could carry. Often that is not much, and in the case of the first immigrants it may have been little more than furs for clothing, some crude hunting tools, and perhaps baskets or fur sacks for gathering food.

The most important thing immigrants brought with them was what they knew— the skills they had developed. For these first Native American immigrants it was hunting and tracking skills, knowledge of fire, and tools of stone and bone.

They also had language. After thousands of years of separation from their relatives in Siberia, the languages of the Native Americans throughout the Western

---

[2] nomadic *Wandering; nomadic tribes are not settled and move from place to place usually in search of food or to find food for their animals.*

Hemisphere became greatly varied, with little resemblance to each other, and none with that of Siberia.

In spite of this separation, it is interesting to note that the descendants of these earliest inhabitants living in Siberia and North America developed similar ways of dealing with their environment. At a museum of the native peoples in Irkurst, Siberia, in Russia, you can see snow shoes and leather moccasins very much like those developed by Native Americans. It is doubtful that the idea for these items came to America with the first nomads, but peoples in similar circumstances developed similar ideas to deal with their environment.

DIFFERING CULTURES

All immigrants have had to adapt to their new environment. As the nomadic bands spread out to different parts of the two continents, they changed their ways of living and slowly developed different cultures[3]. By 5,000 years ago the beginnings of many such cultural groupings could be identified in the Americas, and several of these developed into highly complex civilizations. The most famous of these are the Aztec and Mayan civilizations in Mexico and Central America, and the Inca civilization in Peru. In the United States there were many different Native American cultures. The Pueblo culture of the southwest (Arizona, New Mexico, and Colorado) and the Algonquian culture of the northeast are significant examples. In each of these geographic areas, the Native Americans developed cultures and patterns of behavior that allowed for highly successful ways of life.

> Native Americans develop different cultures.

MAYAN, AZTEC, AND INCA

Mayan civilization was in decline by the time Spanish explorers arrived in the 16th century (1500s). It was an urban culture with cities dominated by large stone pyramid-temples. Large tracts of land were cultivated. Mayans had invented writing and a system of mathematics. The Aztecs, a more warlike civilization, had come to dominate Mexico and most of the areas of Mayan civilization by 1500. Their capital, Tenochtitlan (Mexico City is built on the site), was one of the great cities of the age. The gold and silver of the empire was collected there. In Peru the Incas had a flourishing urban-based civilization that controlled large areas of the Andes.

These civilizations, while extremely important for understanding the history of Mexico and all of the Americas, are not as directly related to United States history as the cultures of the Pueblos and Algonquians.

PUEBLO

The culture of the Pueblos revolved around their villages. Pueblos are villages of multi-storied buildings and were built with defense in mind. Some, such as Pueblo

[3] culture   *A set of beliefs and patterns of behavior developed by a group of people. These appear in their religious, artistic, social, and political attitudes and are supported by their material productions.*

Bonito, stand in valleys as large isolated structures with windowless solid walls facing out. Connected houses and rooms built against these outside walls face a yard where outdoor life centered safe from attack. Other pueblos were built on the sides of cliffs or, as with the Hopis, on mesas[4].

> Pueblo dwellers evolve very complex political, social, and religious organizations.

Often hundreds of people lived within one pueblo. Pueblo dwellers were dependent on agriculture, and not hunting, for survival. Men did this work while the women prepared the food and cared for children. Politically each pueblo was independent and was run by a man's council.

Religion centered around the cultivation of crops and there were elaborate ceremonies and rituals, often with dancing, to celebrate planting, harvesting, and to bring rain. Many of these ceremonies continue today as part of the rich culture of the various tribes who still live in pueblos in the southwest, and outsiders may attend these religious ceremonies.

As you watch the religious dances of, for instance, the Hopis, you are struck by the intricacy of the ritual, by the soberness and deep feelings of the participants, and by their great need for favorable conditions for their agriculture.

You can also appreciate how different these traditions seemed to the Spanish who entered the Southwest after 1500. Even today, when TV exposes us to all the cultures of the world, we often find it difficult to accept what is different. It is this experience of being different that all immigrants experience. The Spaniards found it difficult to accept the culture of the Pueblo peoples, yet it was a highly developed culture long before they came. That many pueblos still exist is a credit to the peoples of this earlier civilization in what became the United States.

ALGONQUIAN

The Native Americans who greeted the Europeans on the Atlantic coast also lived in villages. The villages of those tribes in the Algonquian language group were built of wood and other perishable materials, and little archaeological evidence remains of them. The villages were often surrounded by wooden posts forming a wall for defense. An extended family lived in a single house. The female members remained in the home in which they were born, and males joined their wife's families. This arrangement is referred to as matrilineal.

The way societies form families—matrilineally or patrilineally—is important because it reveals how important males and females are within the society, how social power is distributed, and often how political and economic power is held.

> The Algonquians live in a close relationship with nature.

For instance, Algonquian women did the agricultural work for the tribe, could become political leaders of the tribe, and often were the religious leaders.

The Algonquian peoples were hunters, gatherers, and farmers. They developed many tools to support their activities, built wigwams and longhouses, constucted birch bark and dugout canoes, used snowshoes, and domesticated wolves. However,

---

[4] mesas *Flat plateaus with steep sides.*

they did not use metal or the wheel. Since there were no animals in northeast America suitable for use as beasts of burden, the Algonquians relied on canoes and walking for transportation.

The religious beliefs of the Algonquians, as is natural with any agricultural people, focused on the crops. They worshipped the forces of nature involved with planting and harvesting. The Native Americans had an understanding of a close relationship between humans and their natural environment.

One Iroquois chief—the Iroquois are a tribe of the Algonquian group—remarked that the Iroquois planned for the "seventh generation," and not just for the next year or two. Planning for the seventh generation suggests a realization that actions have long-range effects that must be considered. As we face environmental crises, some scholars suggest we could have learned much if we had tried to understand the religious teachings of the agriculturally based Native American societies of the northeast, or of the Pueblos.

The Europeans did not understand, or appreciate, the complexity and significance to the Native Americans of their religious beliefs. The two cultures came into conflict, as often happens when two cultures meet or when immigrants from a different cultural tradition arrive. Usually the minority is persecuted by the intolerant majority, but as we shall see in the case of the Europeans coming to the Americas, the minority view triumphed. This was due to many factors and has meant the loss to us of ideas from which we might have learned.

EVIDENCE OF PRE-COLUMBIAN CONTACTS

There is now evidence to support the idea that many Native American cultures had contacts with Africans and Europeans long before the "discovery" of America by Christopher Columbus. These contacts appear to have been peaceful. There is no evidence for continual trade. What ideas were exchanged is not clear, but the appearance of clay figurines with distinctly Negroid features in Aztec art before 1500 A.D., and of inscriptions in Egyptian hieroglyphs and Celtic writing in New England prove there were contacts.

Another bit of information that is difficult to account for, except in terms of contact with Europe, is the fact that the arrangement of stars we call the Big Dipper was referred to as the Great Bear by the ancient Greeks, the Romans, and the Native Americans of New England. This is attested to by Cotton Mather, a minister in Boston in colonial days, who asked the natives in Boston what they knew of navigation. In their explanation they referred to the Big Dipper as the Bear, and described how they used the North Star and the Great Bear (Big Dipper) in finding direction. We can understand how different people would use the North Star but what makes this remarkable, and supports the idea of contacts, is the fact the stars in the Big Dipper are not arranged to look like a Bear except by the greatest stretch of the imagination.

Key Point to Remember
Native American peoples had developed sophisticated civilizations long before the arrival of European settlers or explorers.

Links from the Past to the Present

1. All Americans or their ancestors share the immigrant experience, giving us all something in common.

2. Native-American religious beliefs provide insights that can be helpful in the environmental crisis.

Dates

c.[5] 50,000 years ago—ancestors of Native Americans crossed from Siberia to North America.

c. 5,000 years ago—Native Americans developed urban-based civilizations.

c. 300–900 A.D.[6] Mayan culture developed in southern Mexico.

c. 1500 A.D.—Aztec culture flouished in Mexico; Inca culture thrived in Peru.

Questions
Identify each of the following:

Mayan	Pueblo
Aztec	Algonquian
Inca	Pueblo Bonito

Multiple Choice:

1. The Pueblos of the southwestern United States were built
   a. high up on mountains.
   b. on islands.
   c. on mesas and cliffs and in valleys.

2. The first Native-American immigrants to the Americas brought with them
   a. only the ability to communicate.
   b. fur clothing, hunting tools and baskets, hunting skills, fire, and communication.
   c. their relatives and their tents.

3. The religious beliefs of both the Pueblos and the Algonquians centered on
   a. the forces of nature involved in the production of crops.
   b. successful hunting expeditions.
   c. witchcraft involved in matrilineal descent.

---

[5] c. *An abbreviation for circa (about); it is used before a date to indicate the date is approximate and not exact.*

[6] A.D. *Designation of time in the Christian calendar, which begins counting with the birth of Jesus Christ. Thus,* A.D. *stands for the Latin* Anno Domini—*"in the year of our Lord."— Many nations today accept this system of dating even when not practicing Christians. The letters* C.E., *standing for the Common Era, are sometimes used in place of* A.D. *In the Christian calendar, time before the birth of Christ is designated as* B.C. *Sometimes* B.C.E., *before the common era, is used.*

4. The fact the Big Dipper is called the Great Bear by both Europeans and Algonquians suggests
   a. the Big Dipper can be seen by both groups at night.
   b. the North Star is important for navigation.
   c. there was contact between Europe and America before Columbus.

II. European Immigrants

The first European immigrants to the New World, of whom we have any clear evidence, came from northern Europe. They are usually referred to as the Vikings or Norsemen, and their visits and small settlements in Greenland, Nova Scotia, and New England are dated about 1000 A.D. Contacts between the Norsemen and the Algonquian groups lasted for the next 400 years. Recently evidence has been found that long before the Vikings, immigrants from the Celtic[7] lands of Europe had settled in the area of New England.

> The Celts and Vikings make contact with the New World.

THE CELTS

Two questions the historian would immediately ask on reading this last sentence are "What is the evidence?" and "Why is this information important?" The best way to answer the second question is to answer the first.

Evidence of settlements during the period of the Roman Republic (509–31 B.C.) by the Celtic peoples comes from inscriptions found at a number of locations in the northeast, from Algonquian tales of ancestors who came from "across the sea" rather than on the overland bridge, from circles of stones in North America that are similar to Stonehenge in England, and from the facial features of the Algonquians, which are as much like European features as they are like the features of the western Native-American tribes.

The latter point suggests that the Algonquians were a mixed group and not pure descendants of those who came across the land bridge from Siberia. They probably exchanged ideas with other peoples when both were at an early stage of civilization. The Algonquians may well have learned about navigation and the use of the North Star and of the Great Bear from the Celts.

THE VIKINGS

The story of the Vikings or Norsemen is more likely to be known by Americans than that of the Celts. It is often included in history textbooks because there is more evidence for their visits and settlements. There are written references to travel to North America in the archives[8] of Denmark.

---

[7] celtic *Civilization found in western France, southern England, and Ireland about 1000 B.C. Stonehenge in England was built by the Celts.*
[8] archives *Official records that are preserved.*

Eric the Red, who was exiled from Iceland, founded a settlement in Greenland about 1000 A.D. According to the *Sagas* or old stories of Scandinavia, his son, Leif Ericson, explored the coast of North America. Several settlements were established, with some evidence suggesting the Norsemen penetrated as far as Minnesota, either coming down from Hudson Bay or going west through the Great Lakes.

A Norseman, Leif Ericson, explores the coast of North America, and colonies are established.

Contacts with the Northeast continued for many years. A Danish court record states that in 1354 a search party was sent to locate a settlement on the coast of Greenland. Apparently the settlement had been destroyed, or there had been no contact with it for some time. After that time, contacts between the Norse settlements in North America and Europe appear to have ceased, and the next immigrants came from southern Europe.

WHY WAS CONTACT LOST?

Why did these contacts cease, and why were they not widely known throughout Europe? We do not know for certain, but historians have offered many hypotheses. These include the growth of new ideas and interests during the Renaissance[9], the rise and spread of Islam[10], and the drop in population as a result of the Black Death or plague. There is, however, no general agreement. Thus the answer, as so often in history, is hidden in mystery.

REESTABLISHING CONTACT

Slowly conditions changed and new views developed as they always do. The period we call the Renaissance replaced the Middle Ages. The Renaissance began in Italy around 1300 A.D. and slowly spread to northern and western Europe. Among the

Renaissance attitudes encourage new explorations.

many philosophical ideas of the Renaissance, new attitudes toward the individual, and the concept of a secular[11] nation state were most important. The former encouraged individual initiative, manifested in the individual exploits of discoverers, explorers, and conquerors. The latter encouraged the growth of what we consider a modern nation.

The Renaissance provided impetus for the explorations of the Portuguese and provided ideas and new sailing techniques, which Christopher Columbus used on his voyages. Another impetus to Portuguese exploration was a response to new economic conditions brought about by both the earlier Crusades and the Renaissance.

---

[9] Renaissance   *The period of time in Europe between the Middle Ages and the modern era. The dates of the Renaissance varied in different parts of Europe.*

[10] Islam   *The religion of which Mohammed is the prophet. Mohammed lived and heard the word of God as recorded in the Koran in Mecca and Medina, Saudi Arabia. From there the faith of Islam was spread by conquests from Spain to Indonesia. It is still the major faith in North Africa, the Near East, Pakistan, and Indonesia and is widespread throughout the world.*

[11] secular   *Having to do with worldly as opposed to spiritual or religious concerns.*

The Crusades had directed attention away from northern Europe toward the eastern Mediterranean. Although the Crusades failed, and Christian Europe could not dislodge the followers of Mohammed from the eastern Mediterranean, they did introduce new ideas and new goods from Asia to Europe. The Italians of Venice and Genoa traded with the Islamic peoples for goods like silks and spices, and developed a near monopoly[12] of the trade.

After 1400 the Portuguese rulers began to look for a route to Asia along the African coast, but they had no idea as to how large Africa would be.

New instruments—the magnetic compass and the astrolabe, which allows the sailor to determine latitude—helped navigators on these explorations. They were also aided by the development of a new type of ship, the caravel, which could sail against the wind.

As so often in history, inventions helped create change. Prince Henry the navigator, son of King John I of Portugal, is given credit for beginning these explorations, which became very profitable as the Portuguese brought African products to Europe. They introduced the first African slaves into Europe, thus beginning the era of African slavery. Eventually, in 1488 Bartolomeu Dias rounded the southern tip of Africa, and in 1498 Vasco da Gama sailed around Africa to India.

The Portuguese had found a new route to the riches of Asia. But this was not the only possible route. Christopher Columbus had another idea.

CHRISTOPHER COLUMBUS

Christopher Columbus was born in or near the Italian town of Genoa. His parents were wool weavers, but Columbus became a sailor and developed a vision that changed the course of history. Columbus' idea had been rejected by the Portuguese by whom he had been employed as a sailor. They were not interested in financing an expedition across the ocean because they were finding success along the African coast. Columbus therefore went to Ferdinand and Isabella rulers of Aragon and Castille in Spain.

After several years, the rulers of Spain agreed to help finance a voyage westward from Spain to Japan and on to India. The result is the famous first voyage of Christopher Columbus and his three sailing ships, the *Nina*, *Pinta*, and *Santa Maria*. He touched land, probably in the Bahamas, and named the first island he touched San Salvador.

While many others had already come to the Americas, his trip was followed by an ever increasing number of voyages, the stories of which spread throughout western Europe. Soon, the rapidly developing nation states of western Europe—Spain, France, and England—were involved in a race to find a way through the Americas and on to Asia.

To the Europeans it seemed that Columbus had "discovered a new world." It changed history. We know, however, that many immigrants and discoverers had

---

[12] monopoly   *Exclusive possession of anything; control of the supply of any commodity or service in a given market or area that permits the holder of the monopoly to set prices.*

already come to this new world of the Americas. It had already been "discovered" many times. Columbus came at a time in which many technical developments in sailing techniques and communication made it possible to report his voyages easily and to spread the word of them throughout western Europe. It was also at a time of growing economic rivalries between the developing nation states. They were all seeking new wealth, and this eventually led to a rivalry for the establishment of colonies in the Americas.

> Columbus is often credited with "discovering a new world," but he merely encountered what was already discovered by Native Americans and others.

SPANISH EXPLORERS

Columbus made four voyages to the west and explored the Caribbean and Latin American area extensively. He died in 1506, still certain he had arrived at the coast of Asia. His Spanish settlement in Santo Domingo became the base for many expeditions.

Two important Spanish expeditions were those led by Ponce de Leon, who conquered Puerto Rico in 1508–9 and explored Florida in 1513, and by Vasco Nunez de Balboa, who crossed the Isthmus of Panama and saw the Pacific in 1513. After extensive explorations along the coast, the Spanish began the conquest of Central and South America.

In 1519 Ferdinand Magellan, a Portuguese sailing for Spain, started on an expedition around the world. Although Magellan was killed, the expedition returned to Spain in 1522. Magellan's expedition proved that the earth was round, and that the lands visited by Columbus were not Asia.

JOHN CABOT

> English claims to North America are established by voyages of John Cabot.

The first voyage west not sponsored by Spain was that of John Cabot, an Italian who lived in Bristol, England. His two voyages, in 1497 and 1498, were supported by English merchants and by an agreement with the English King, Henry the VII. John Cabot sailed along the coasts of Newfoundland and New England and as far south as Delaware Bay, claiming this territory for England and providing the basis for English claims to North America.

SUMMARY

After the voyages of Christopher Columbus reacquainted the Europeans with the Americas, the nations of western Europe undertook many voyages to this "New World." Based on these expeditions, England, France, Spain, and the Netherlands all laid claim to large areas of the Americas in spite of the fact that the areas claimed were inhabited by Native Americans whose ancestors had come to the Americas as immigrants thousands of years before Columbus. The historian when writing history must create hypotheses based on evidence to explain the past. Evidence, such as the shared experience as immigrants by the ancestors of all Americans, needs to be included if the hypotheses are to be judged adequate.

Key Point to Remember

Christopher Columbus did not "discover" America. It had been discovered by the Native Americans and had been known to the Celtic peoples and Vikings. His voyages reacquainted Europeans with the American continent.

Links from the Past to the Present

1. The Renaissance inspired individualism, which has been a hallmark of American society.
2. Throughout history, inventions, ranging from the plow to the stirrup to the atomic bomb, have led to major historical changes.

People to Remember

Christopher Columbus   Italian explorer; reestablished regular contact between Europe and the Americas. His voyages from Spain to the Caribbean started in 1492.

Dates

Before 31 B.C.—Celts visited Americas.

c. 1000 A.D.—Norsemen visited Americas.

1492—First voyage of Columbus.

1519—Magellan's expedition circled the world.

Questions
Identify each of the following:

Crusades	Vasco de Gama
Middle Ages	Ferdinand and Isabella
Renaissance	Christopher Columbus
Islam	John Cabot

Multiple Choice:

1. Evidence of Celtic settlement in North America includes
    a. facial features of the Algonquians and inscriptions.
    b. circles of stones like Stonehenge in England.
    c. both of the above.

2. Viking contacts with America
    a. lasted for many years.
    b. were very limited.
    c. came only on the island of Greenland.

3. Portuguese explorations were helped by
   a. the Italians of Genoa and Venice.
   b. African slaves who sailed the ships.
   c. new instruments—the compass and astrolabe—and a new ship design—the caravel.

4. The rulers of Spain agreed to
   a. finance Christopher Columbus's voyage westward.
   b. repay Christopher Columbus for any expenses he had on his voyage.
   c. send immigrants to America.

Open-ended, Analysis Questions

The following questions require analysis and reflection. You are encouraged to bring to your answer information and ideas from many sources. The answers should be presented in composition or essay style but they may be used to initiate discussion. The questions put you in the role of the historian, gathering information to support your personal perspective on the question.

1. In what ways did the culture of the Pueblos differ from that of the Algonquians? How might these differences be explained?

2. With which immigrant group would you have preferred to come to the Americas? Why?
   a. Native Americans
   b. Celts
   c. Vikings

European Settlements in North America

APPROACHES TO HISTORY

EXPLAINING HISTORY BY MULTIPLE CAUSES

Usually the most satisfactory explanation of past events is one that includes many different reasons or causes. This approach to past events is known as a multi-causal approach. However, as we will see in future chapters, a historian will often concentrate on one explanation for past events.

The multi-causal approach is one that most of us use all the time in explaining events in our lives. For instance, if you tell friends from school that you will meet them at the movies, three miles from home, and you do not show up, your explanation the next day will often be multi-causal.

The story might include 1) you could not find your wallet and your mother would not lend you the money, 2) you could not call because the telephone wasn't working, and 3) you could not take the car because your license was in the wallet. Therefore, you could not get to the movie theater even though you knew your friends would pay for you if you got there.

That simple story involves three major categories of explanations—1) economics (no money), 2) fate (broken phone), and 3) ideology or belief (will not drive without a license).

We'll look at each of these explanations in greater detail in later chapters, but they provide reasons we often use to explain our own actions. These are also explanations used by historians to provide understanding of past events. All three explanations—economics, fate, ideology—have been used to explain the establishment of settlement by Europeans in North America.

I. The Spanish in the Americas—The Early Years

In the late 15th and throughout the 16th centuries, England and France were involved in domestic issues centering on nation building and a conflict over religion. While some exploration of the New World was done, no settlements were attempted by England and France until late in the 16th century. The Reformation[1] in Europe, which destroyed the unity of the Christian Church in western Europe, was the central concern of the northern Europeans in the 16th century. Spain, however, remained strongly Roman Catholic. Free of religious conflict in much of the 16th century, the Spanish were free to explore, conquer, and bring Roman Catholicism to the Americas.

> The Reformation disrupts the unity of the Christian Church.

SPANISH CULTURAL DEVELOPMENTS

The Spanish sought wealth and found it in Mexico, which was conquered by Ferdinand Cortez in the 1520s, and in Peru, which was conquered by Francisco Pizarro in the 1530s. The Spanish established their rule over these areas creating a huge empire that was kept under the tight control of the King of Spain.

Governors were sent to rule the new territories, and settlers, mainly males, came to exploit the riches. Much of the native population was either killed or died of disease, and those remaining were either enslaved to work in mines or made serfs on the land. The Spaniards later imported slaves from Africa. Some settlers married and/or had children with native women.

In their devotion to Christianity, the Spanish destroyed both written records and buildings of the Incas and Aztecs. They built Christian churches and worked to convert the natives to Roman Catholicism. They melted down most of the gold and silver artifacts[2] they seized into ingots for shipment to Spain. Their reasons for settlement are considered both economic and ideological, thus providing a clear example of a multi-causal explanation.

ST. AUGUSTINE, SANTA FE, AND SAN DIEGO

Spanish explorers traveled into Florida, explored the Mississippi River delta, and conquered several of the pueblos of the Southwest. These explorations later led to the founding of cities by the Spanish in what is now the United States. St. Augustine, Florida, the oldest surviving European settlement in the United States, was established in 1565 as a military fort to block the French exploration in Florida. The Spanish founded Santa Fe in New Mexico in 1609, just after Jamestown and Quebec had been founded, and San Diego in 1769, the first European settlement in

---

[1] Reformation *The religious movement in Western Christendom precipitated by Martin Luther in 1517 which resulted in the formation of various Protestant churches and which ended the unity of Europe under the Roman Catholic faith.*

[2] artifact *An object, product of human workmanship, such as carvings, bowls, etc. We often use* artifact *to refer to objects found by archaeologists while digging.*

California. As their names suggest, many of the early Spanish settlements were missions, established to bring Christianity to the natives.

NATIVE AMERICAN/SPANISH INTERACTIONS

The impact of Spanish conquest and settlement on the Native American culture was overwhelming. While a few Spaniards tried to preserve records, the majority were driven by dreams of wealth, and their leaders, by religious zeal. In establishing their control, they destroyed much of the culture of the Native American. This destruction of the material products of the culture, and the knowledge it represented, is a great loss for all people.

An even greater loss, however, was in the number of natives who died as a result of diseases introduced by European explorers and settlers throughout North and South America. The natives had no immunity to such European diseases as smallpox.

> The Spanish bring new diseases that kill many of the natives.

Natives everywhere died. One source estimates that of a million natives on the island of Hispaniola when Columbus arrived, 500 were left by 1550. Europeans did take a new, severe form of syphilis back from the Americas, and it spread throughout the continent but did not wipe out the European population.

One positive result of the opening up of the Americas was an exchange of products. Beans and potatoes were introduced to Europe, and cattle and horses, to the Americas. The horse totally changed the lifestyle of the Native Americans on the Great Plains. Tobacco, first grown in the Americas, likewise changed the life, wealth, and ultimately the health of the Europeans.

NON-SPANISH EXPLORATIONS

Despite their involvement in nation building and religious wars during the 16th century, northern Europeans did manage to send explorers to seek a water passage to Asia through the North American continent. A Frenchman, Jacques Cartier, explored the St. Lawrence River, the Great Lakes, and finally the Mississippi River area. The French made an attempt at a settlement in Florida but were stopped by the Spanish. It might have changed the history of the Americas if they had succeeded. The French also explored the coast of New England.

In the early 17th century Henry Hudson, sailing for the Dutch, explored the East Coast from Hudson Bay to the Carolinas. He gave his name to the Hudson River, which he hoped might be the long-sought passage to the Pacific Ocean. His voyages gave the Dutch a claim to what became New York.

The Englishman Sir Francis Drake explored the Pacific coast of the Americas, raiding Spanish ships and entering San Francisco Bay (1579), which he claimed for England. He went on to sail around the world—the second European expedition to do so. He is a hero to the English, but he was a pirate to the Spanish.

There were many other Spanish and non-Spanish explorers. We look back on these early explorers as great adventurers who opened up a new world. We often overlook the view Native Americans had of their exploits, or how peoples from other nations viewed them. They are the individuals who made later settlement possible.

They were daring and in many ways exciting people, but their activities need to be viewed from different perspectives. This is another aspect of a multi-causal approach. To the Native Americans, the Europeans were not explorers but conquerors.

Key Point to Remember

European nations explored and claimed lands in the Americas after 1492 even though the land was already inhabited by Native Americans.

Links from the Past to the Present

1. Spanish influence in the South and Southwest was established early in our history and is still important today.
2. Settlements by different European nationalities set the pattern for the diversity of people found in the United States.

Dates

1565—St. Augustine, Florida—oldest European city in U.S.—founded.
1609—Santa Fe, New Mexico founded.

Questions
Identify each of the following:

Jacques Cartier   Sir Francis Drake
Hispaniola   St. Augustine
Santa Fe

Multiple Choice:

1. In the Spanish colonies in the Americas
    a. governors were elected by the settlers.
    b. the settlers married both native women and slaves.
    c. the settlers quickly adopted the natives' religion.

2. The oldest surviving European settlement in the United States is
    a. San Diego.
    b. Santa Fe.
    c. St. Augustine.

3. The early European explorers made claims to areas such as
    a. Francis Drake's claim to San Francisco Bay for England.
    b. Jacques Cartier's claim to Hudson Bay for France.
    c. Henry Hudson's claim to the Hudson River for England.

II. European Colonies in North America

JAMESTOWN

Explorers set the stage for the period of rapid European colonization in the 17th century. The Spanish had already established the first colony in the future United States when the English made their first attempt at Roanoke Island on the North Carolina coast. This attempt organized by Sir Walter Raleigh failed, and the settlers all disappeared. The fate of this famous "lost colony" of 1584 has been the focus of many studies, but to this day no one is certain what happened to the first English immigrants in North America.

The first successful English settlement was established on an island in the James River in Virginia in 1607. Jamestown, named for the English king, James I, was founded by the London Company. Several of the original settlements were established by companies chartered by the king. Their goal was to make money.

> English settlers establish the colony of Jamestown in Virginia in 1607.

The settlers at Jamestown suffered greatly at first until they learned to grow tobacco and ship it to England. Tobacco became the source of wealth for Virginia and affected its history.

The first African Americans to arrive in North America were brought to Jamestown as bound or possibly as indentured servants[3] in 1619 to help raise tobacco. By 1680, it is estimated, there were roughly 3,000 Africans in bondage in Virginia.

The majority of workers were English, many of whom came over as indentured servants. Passage to the colonies was expensive so many signed contracts to work for a set number of years, usually seven, in return for passage and board. Bound servants, on the other hand, were committed to work for life, but they could buy out of the contract. Slavery in America began as a system of bondage that grew more and more harsh over the years. While Virginia is remembered for the introduction of tobacco and the arrival of the first African Americans, it should also be remembered for having the first elective legislature in North America, thus establishing our tradition of democracy. Twenty-two Burgesses[4]—two chosen by each town or plantation—met in 1619 to establish the tradition of an elected house of representatives.

The House of Burgesses played an important but varied role throughout colonial history and particularly at the time of the Revolution. It was traditions of this type that laid the foundation for our nation.

NON-ENGLISH COLONIES

In 1608 the French established their first permanent settlement in North America at Quebec. Again the purpose was to make money, in this case by developing the trade

---

[3] indentured servant   *One who signs a contract or agrees to labor (work) for a set period of time in return for some commitment, such as free passage across the ocean. The length of labor was often seven years.*

[4] Burgess   *A citizen or freeman living in an English borough (a town and its surrounding lands). The English colony of Virginia in 1619 had 11 boroughs and each elected two citizens to represent the borough in the legislature.*

in furs with the Native Americans. There was a large market for fur in Europe, and along with the fish caught in the Gulf of St. Lawrence and the North Atlantic, this trade brought some prosperity to the French settlers.

The Dutch followed up on the explorations of Henry Hudson in the area of New York by founding a colony. Companies were formed in Holland to further the exploration and settlement of the area. After buying the island of Manhattan in New York Harbor from the local Indian tribe for $24 worth of goods, the Dutch established the settlement of New Amsterdam there in 1624. Later the Dutch worked with some Swedish investors to establish a settlement at what is now Wilmington, Delaware.

> French settle in the St. Lawrence Valley, Dutch in New York, and Swedes in Delaware.

By 1640 there were Spanish, English, French, Dutch, and Swedish colonies established along the coast of North America. The latter four nations had established their first colonies for economic reasons, and while the Spanish established a fort at St. Augustine for military reasons, they were also motivated by economics.

While this suggests a single cause for settlement, members of each colony had different reasons for being there. Many settlers were interested not only in making money but in converting the native population to Christianity. Some were there to escape conditions at home, and others had very personal reasons for leaving their homelands.

THE PILGRIMS AT PLYMOUTH

The later English colonies were founded for several different reasons. The second English colony, that at Plymouth Bay in Massachusetts, was founded by an English company, but the settlers, the Pilgrims, had religious (that is, ideological) reasons for coming.

During the reign of Queen Elizabeth I, the Protestant Church of England was firmly established as England's official religion. Immediately, differing groups began protesting. Each of these wished to change the newly established church in some way. With the death of Elizabeth I in 1603 and the accession of James I, protest grew.

One group, the Pilgrims, also known as Separatists as they wished to separate from the Church of England, went to Holland but did not wish to bring their children up as Dutch. Their leaders arranged with the Virginia Company to go to America. They joined a group of non-Pilgrims and sailed on the *Mayflower,* landing on Cape Cod.

Before landing and settling in Plymouth, 41 adults on the Mayflower signed an agreement, the Mayflower Compact. This plan of government, drawn up by a few and agreed to by all, formed the basis of the government of the colony. This concept of government by compact or written agreement became a cornerstone of our democracy.

> The Mayflower Compact is signed and establishes a plan of government for Plymouth colony.

THE PURITANS AT MASSACHUSETTS BAY

Other colonies were soon established in the Massachusetts Bay area. The most important was the Massachusetts Bay Colony founded in 1629. It was founded by another group of religious reformers, the Puritans, whose ideas have been very important throughout our history.

The founders had a company charter, taken to America, and annual meetings were held there. This provides a third idea (the first being the elected House of Burgesses and the second the compact theory) that influenced our democratic ideas and that appeared early in the English-speaking colonies.

Annual meetings allowed America to develop its own Parliamentary tradition and later led the colonists to reject offers from the English that would allow the colonists to send representatives to England's Parliament.

The first Bay Colony governor, and one of its most distinguished citizens, was John Winthrop, a devout Puritan. He helped make Massachusetts Bay a "Bible Commonwealth," which he believed would serve as a "shining city on the hill"—that is, as an example for all people.

Massachusetts Bay Colony flourished as King James I increasingly enforced on his subjects conformity to the Church of England. Many protesting Puritans fled to America for freedom of worship. This has occurred many times in our history as different governments have persecuted their subjects for their religious beliefs. In fact, it happened several times in New England. Massachusetts' Puritans prosecuted Roger Williams and exiled him. He founded a colony at Providence in Rhode Island, which was noted for religious toleration and fair treatment of the Native Americans. Anne Hutchinson, another religious leader, was also forced to leave the colony. She not only challenged the religious teachings but also the male dominance in both religious and political leadership.

One of the more tragic examples of persecution occurred in Salem, Massachusetts in 1692. Fear of the devil led to hysteria and panic. Nineteen men and women were judged guilty and hung after accusations of witchcraft were brought against them by young women. Judge Samuel Sewall presided over these Salem Witch Trials and gave them the stamp of government approval. The trials are an example of hysteria, generated by fear of others and the power of individuals to exploit this fear. It was the first but not the last time in American history where this occurred.

Settlements in Connecticut and New Hampshire were also established before 1640. These settlers had religious as well as economic motives for settlement.

THE OTHER ENGLISH COLONIES

The Puritan protesters wished to move the Church of England even further from the Roman Catholic position. Meanwhile, the Catholics in England also suffered under the policies of King James. The Catholic Lord Baltimore acquired from the king the right to establish a colony in what is now Maryland. He was named the proprietor, or owner, of the colony in the charter, which did not state what church had to be set up as the official church of the settlement. Lord Baltimore encouraged Catholics to come to Maryland to escape religious persecution.

Pennsylvania was given to William Penn, a Quaker, as his personal property. It became a refuge for those of the Quaker religious persuasion as well as a place for those who wished to prosper economically.

Thus from the start America became a refuge for individuals wishing to escape persecution for their beliefs, regardless of what they were. The country has remained a haven for the persecuted to this day.

The last colony, Georgia, was founded as a military buffer between the Spanish in Florida and the other English colonies, and as a penal location for English criminals. It soon became an area of plantations.

By 1740 the English had established thirteen distinct colonies along the North American coast. It should be clear they were established for different reasons, and the settlers had various personal reasons for coming, ranging from a desire to worship as they wished to making money quickly. Some settlers were forced to come, as were the African-Americans and the criminals who were sent to Georgia instead of being put in English jails.

Key Points to Remember

Settlements in the Americas were established by the Spanish, English, French, Dutch, and Swedish primarily for economic and religious reasons. Individuals, however, had many other motives for coming.

Links from the Past to the Present

1. Many democratic ideas incorporated in the United States system of government have their roots in the governments of different colonies.

2. Many colonists were intolerant of those who held a different religious belief, and this attitude has surfaced often in United States history.

People to Remember

John Winthrop   Puritan; first Governor of Massachusetts Bay Colony; tried to build the perfect Christian community based on the Bible.

William Penn   Quaker; Proprietor of Pennsylvania; established religious toleration in the colony.

Roger Williams   Persecuted by Massachusetts Bay Puritans; founded Providence in Rhode Island on the basis of religious toleration and fair treatment of the local inhabitants.

Dates

1607—Jamestown, Virginia founded by English.

1608—Quebec founded by French.

1619—First African Americans brought to Virginia.
     First meeting of House of Burgesses.

1620—Plymouth, Massachusetts settled by English.

1624—New York settled by Dutch.

Questions
Identify each of the following:

Lord Baltimore   Quebec
William Penn   New Amsterdam
Plymouth

Multiple Choice:

1. Settlers at Jamestown suffered until they learned to grow
   a. corn.
   b. cotton.
   c. tobacco.

2. The Dutch established a colony in
   a. Manhattan, New York.
   b. St. Augustine, Florida.
   c. Plymouth, Massachusetts.

3. Roger Williams established a colony in
   a. Rhode Island.
   b. Connecticut.
   c. New Hampshire.

Founding of Colonies in North America
Date of First National Settlements

Date	Name	Founding Country	Primary Reasons For Founding	Important Leader
1565	St. Augustine, FL	Spain	Military Fort & Missionary base	—
1607	Jamestown, VA	England	Missionary base to convert Indians, to make money	Capt. John Smith
1608	Quebec, Canada	France	Export Fur Trade	Samuel de Champlain
1624	Manhattan, NY	Holland	Develop Farming & Trade	Peter Minuit
1638	Wilmington, DE	Sweden/Holland	Develop Farming & Trade	—

Date of First English Settlement in Each of the Thirteen States

Date	State	Reason for Settlement	Important Leader
1607	Virginia (Jamestown)	Economic & Religious	John Smith
1620	Massachusetts (Plymouth)	Religious	Wm. Bradford
1631	Connecticut	Religious & Economic	Thomas Hooker
1634	Maryland	Religious & Economic	Lord Baltimore
1636	Rhode Island	Religious	Roger Williams
1638	New Hampshire	Economic	John Wheelwright
1654	North Carolina	Economic	—
1664	New York—Conquered from the Dutch	Economic Military	Duke of York

Date	State	Reason for Settlement	Important Leader
1664	New Jersey—Conquered from the Dutch	Economic Military	Sir George Carteret
1680	Pennsylvania	Religious & Economic	Wm. Penn
1680	South Carolina	Economic	Anthony Cooper
1682	Delaware—Conquered from the Dutch in 1664—separated from Pennsylvania in 1682	Economic & Military	—
1732	Georgia	Penal colony, Economic & Military	James Oglethorpe

Question

On the basis of the preceding information, how important was religion in the founding of colonies in the southern half of the eastern seaboard?

III. The English Colonies to 1763

IDEAS FROM THE PAST

Whenever we tell a story, we must decide what to include and what to leave out. We do this all the time. When someone asks you, "What happened at school or work today?" you pick certain things to tell. You leave out many details and sometimes major events. Historians must do the same when writing the story of the past. The information is so extensive, some must be left out. This had to be done in writing this account of American history. We made decisions about what is important. In determining what to include from the history of the English colonies to 1763, we decided that three points are particularly important:

- first, experiences or traditions shared by all the colonies;
- second, geography and how it influenced the development of different lifestyles;
- third, developments that established ideas or principles that have become the foundation of the independent American nation and still affect us today.

In the previous section we indicated three colonial developments that became important foundations of the American nation:

- first, the idea of a written compact or constitution as the basis for government, which was first done by the Pilgrims when they signed the Mayflower Compact;
- second, the idea of a legislative body elected by the people living in an area, which would make laws for governing those people;
- third, annual meetings of the legislative body to make laws for the territory.

This connection between the colonial past and today is the most important point to understand about this 170-year period of our history.

GEOGRAPHIC DIFFERENCES

For purposes of analysis, the thirteen English colonies are often grouped into three divisions: first, the New England colonies of New Hampshire, Massachusetts, Rhode Island, and Connecticut; second, the Mid-Atlantic colonies of New York, New Jersey, Pennsylvania, and Delaware; third, the Southern colonies of Virginia, Maryland, North Carolina, South Carolina, and Georgia.

This division is based on geographic variations that led these colonies to develop in different ways. Geography is an important tool of historians because geography affects so many parts of our lives. In fact, some historians view geography as the all-important factor in history.

Consider how important where you live is to you. How does your neighborhood, your geographic location in this world, affect what you can and cannot do?

LAND AND CLIMATE

The geography of each of these three regions helped determine the area's lifestyle. The Southern colonies were blessed with rich soil, warm climate, and many rivers that were navigable far inland. This combination of geographic factors helped the South

> An area's geography helps determine its agricultural and economic life.

become a major agricultural area. At first tobacco was the cash-producing crop, and later indigo, rice, and cotton became important.

Tobacco cultivation was best done on large farms or plantations. It would not grow easily in the rocky soil and colder climate of Massachusetts. However, New

Join or Die Cartoon by Benjamin Franklin
First Published May 9, 1754 in the Pennsylvania Gazette, *to urge the colonies to unite in opposition to the French and Indians during the war. It became one of the most popular cartoons in the period prior to the Revolution.*
Courtesy: Library of Congress

England was covered with fine forests that provided lumber for ship building, and the ocean off the coast was full of fish. Therefore, a seafaring lifestyle developed quickly. New England farmers raised food for the area near them, but there was no large agricultural export crop, and the farms in New England remained small.

In the Mid-Atlantic colonies, especially Pennsylvania, there was good soil but a cooler climate than that of Virginia. The Pennsylvania settlers, especially the Germans, developed large farms and raised staple crops such as wheat and corn for all the colonies.

CITIES AND TOWNS

Cities and towns, an important part of the trade and life of New England, grew up first along the seacoast and later throughout New England. Boston with its excellent harbor became a thriving seaport. The cities of Philadelphia and New York—both located on rivers—became important trade centers and harbors for the Mid-Atlantic colonies. The produce from the immediate inland area came to those cities and was transported overseas or shipped to other colonies. The tidal rivers of the South allowed ships to go far inland to pick up tobacco at the docks of the plantations. There was thus no need for commercial cities in the South, and before the Revolution, Charleston and Savannah, the largest cities of the region, were still small towns compared with Boston, New York, and Philadelphia. Thus geography affected the development of the colonies and helped establish the lifestyle of the three regions.

ECONOMIC GROWTH

Close to 170 years elapsed between the establishment of the first permanent English colony at Jamestown and the signing of the Declaration of Independence by the thirteen English colonies. In those years many changes occurred in the colonies and in the relations between them and the "Mother Country," England.

Each colony grew in population, and several had immigrants who were not from England. Germans came to Pennsylvania. African-Americans were brought especially to the Southern colonies.

The government structure of each colony underwent changes. By 1763 all thirteen colonies were Royal Colonies under the supervision of the king or were under the supervision of private proprietors or owners. Life in the colonies ranged from the rather austere, church-focused life of Massachusetts merchants to the more relaxed, plantation-centered life of the Virginia aristocracy.

Prosperity grew for all the colonies, although not at an even rate. Trade increased, and each colony or region developed its own specialties just as today. New England developed her forests and fisheries as well as some manufacturing such as the making of rum. The Mid-Atlantic colonies developed agriculture, and people on the frontier in that region relied on the fur trade. Virginia and North Carolina relied on tobacco, and the lower Southern colonies added indigo and rice as sources of wealth. By the middle of the 18th century there were thirteen distinct colonies, but they shared many points in common.

TRADE

Although the colonies were all under the supervision of the King or their proprietors, the colonists all shared the rights and privileges that the citizens of England had won over the years. The colonies all followed English law, and while each had an appointed governor, each also had some form of elected legislative body to check his power. The English Parliament, following the theory of mercantilism[5], passed laws to control manufacturing and trade in the colonies, but from the 1650s when the first Acts of Trade and Navigation were passed until the end of the French and Indian War in 1763, the colonists largely ignored—and the British only fitfully enforced—these laws. This neglect benefitted both the English merchants and colonists, and this 100-year period has been referred to by historians as the period of "salutory[6] neglect."

> Following mercantilist theory, the Acts of Trade and Navigation set controls on colonial trade.

New England merchants were able to develop a triangular trade system in which molasses made from sugar cane grown in the French and English colonies in the West Indies (Caribbean) was brought to New England, distilled into rum, shipped to Africa, sold for natives who were in turn sold as slaves in the West Indies in order to purchase more molasses or sugar. There were many other opportunities for trade such as selling dried fish or furs in the European market and buying manufactured goods—fancy cloth, furniture, china—to sell in the colonies.

The Southern colonies sold their agricultural products in England and bought manufactured goods there, so the Southern colonies were much more closely tied to England in their trade.

The English Acts of Trade stipulated what could be manufactured and traded. They also required that all goods go to England before being shipped to other countries. When the British began to enforce these laws after 1763, thus ending the period of "salutory neglect," they antagonized the colonists who had grown accustomed to little control by the English government.

MILITARY CONFLICT

During the 150 years after the founding of the Jamestown colony, the thirteen colonies also shared several military experiences. All the colonies shared the frontier experience of opening up new land for European settlement. This created conflicts with the Native Americans and led to several bloody encounters in different colonies. Also, all the colonies were threatened directly or indirectly by the Spanish colonies in Florida and the French colonies in Canada.

> Wars provide shared experiences for the colonists.

In the 18th century the French, Spanish, and English were all interested in gaining control of the area west of the thirteen original English colonies. These three nations were also in conflict in Europe, and they fought a series of wars between 1689 and 1763, each of which involved the American colonies to some extent. Fortunately for the English colonies, the English either won or fought to a draw in all these conflicts.

[5] mercantilism   *A system of economic organization based on the theory that gold is wealth. A mother country attempted to control its trade with its colonies so that it achieved a greater amount of gold than the colonies. Acts of Trade and Navigation controlled trade relationships.*
[6] salutory   *Bringing beneficial or helpful results.*

These shared experiences of trade, language, English law, and military activity laid the foundation for the union of the colonies in 1776.

EDUCATION IN THE COLONIES

The connection with the colonial past that probably most directly affects you at this moment is the importance placed upon education in society. Schooling was a major concern of the Puritans of Massachusetts. To ensure that the church members could all read the Bible, the colony's legislative body passed a law, "Ye Olde Deluder Satan Act," in 1642 requiring that each town provide schooling for its youth. The college of Harvard was founded in 1636 to ensure an educated leadership, especially clergy, for the colony. In New York and Pennsylvania laws encouraging schooling were passed in the late 17th century, and apprentices were generally required to be given a certain level of formal education, which was then referred to as "book learning." Today we believe education is essential in order for our citizens to participate in democratic government.

RELIGIOUS TOLERATION

Another important link to the colonial past is our religious toleration, which can be traced back to the Act of Toleration in Maryland in 1649 and the New York Chapter of Liberties of 1683, granting freedom of religion to all Christians. Pennsylvania's laws were also very tolerant. However, other colonies such as Massachusetts were intolerant of religious diversity, and the government enforced a particular religious worship. This view was overcome in the course of our history, and our Bill of Rights established a separation of church and state.

LINKS TO THE BILL OF RIGHTS

Another right found stated in our Bill of Rights is that of bearing arms. Throughout colonial history the colonists were under continual military threat from other European nations and from the Native Americans. As they pushed westward into the land of the native inhabitants, the colonists had to be prepared to fight.

> American rights "to bear arms and freedom of the press" are rooted in colonial traditions.

Thus an attitude was developed about self-defense that was written into the Bill of Rights as the Second Amendment. United States citizens were guaranteed the right to bear a weapon as a member of a "well-regulated militia." (See page 58.)

Another right incorporated in the Bill of Rights and based on colonial experience is freedom of the press. In a famous trial in New York in 1735, Peter Zenger, a publisher, was acquitted of seditious[7] libel against the government. His paper, *The Weekly Gazette*, had published articles criticizing the government of the colony, and Zenger was arrested. His acquittal was a landmark in the history of the free press—a right we often take for granted but which is considered basic to a democratic and free society.

[7] seditious   *Attempting to undermine or overthrow a government; opposition to government power.*

CONTROL OF THE PURSE

Another very important connection with the colonial past is summed up in the expression, "the legislative power of the purse." This phrase means that the legislative body chosen by and/or representing the people of the colony has control of the government's budget. It appropriates money and passes tax laws. Almost all colonial legislators worked on this basis, particularly the Virginia House of Burgesses. When the English government curtailed the "power of the purse" in Virginia, the struggle for independence was not far away.

CONCLUSION

All of these important ideas that affect us today grew out of the tradition of English Common Law. Common Law was and is based on the tradition of past cases and experiences. The English have never written a Constitution, but at times they forced the king to sign documents [Magna Carta (1215), Petition of Right (1628), Bill of Rights (1689)] giving specific rights to his subjects. All the English colonists believed these rights extended to them—rights such as trial by a jury, bearing arms, and regular meeting of Parliament to allow the people's voice to be expressed. When the French and Indian War ended in 1763, the English government began to change its policies toward the colonies, and many colonists believed these changes threatened their traditional rights as Englishmen. This finally led to the revolt of the English colonies in America. There were multiple causes for this revolt, all of which are interrelated.

Important Connections Between Colonial History and the Present

1. The importance of education.
2. Religious toleration.
3. The right to and need for self-defense.
4. Freedom of the press.
5. The power of the people to control the purse, i.e., taxation and the budget.
6. The rights of Englishmen as seen in the English Bill of Rights and Petition of Right, for example, trial by jury.
7. The concept of a contract or written agreement as the basis of government.
8. An elected legislature chosen by the people in an area.
9. Annual meetings of the legislative body.

Key Point to Remember

There are important connections or links between colonial times and today especially in education, the Bill of Rights, and governmental structure.

Links from the Past to the Present

1. The shared experiences of the colonists tied them together; shared experiences still tie people together today.

2. The rights stated in the Bill of Rights, which we all share, are based on colonial experiences.

Dates

1642—"Ye Olde Deluder Satan Act."

1649—Maryland Act of Toleration.

1650s—First Acts of Trade and Navigation.

Questions
Identify each of the following:

Mercantilism	Peter Zenger
Boston	"Ye Olde Deluder Satan Act"
"Power of the Purse"	Maryland Act of Toleration

Multiple Choice:

1. The Mid-Atlantic colonies included
    a. Massachusetts, New York, Delaware.
    b. Pennsylvania, New York, Delaware.
    c. Virginia, Maryland, Connecticut.

2. By 1763 all thirteen colonies were either controlled by proprietors or were under the supervision of the king as
    a. his private estate.
    b. economic centers of royal power.
    c. royal colonies.

3. All thirteen colonies had in common
    a. good harbors with large port cities.
    b. the frontier experience.
    c. rich soil.

Open-ended, Analysis Questions
The following questions require analysis and reflection. You are encouraged to bring to your answer information and ideas from many sources. The answers should be presented in composition or essay style, but they may be used to initiate discussion. The questions put you in the role of the historian, gathering information to support your personal perspective on the question.

1. For what reasons did Europeans wish to settle in the Americas during the colonial period?

2. How did the English colonies along the eastern coast of North America differ from each other? What factors caused these differences?

3. From the box on page 28 titled "Important Connections Between Colonial History and the Present" pick the one item you believe is most important to you personally. In a brief essay explain why you believe it is most important.

The American Revolution

APPROACHES TO HISTORY

UNDERSTANDING THE PAST THROUGH CAUSE AND EFFECT ANALYSIS

We in the western tradition of civilization are continually seeking the causes of actions. We understand the past—that is, our history—as a series of happenings, each with causes and each having an effect. Just as in personal relations we believe you are who you are because of your past, so we believe the United States as a nation is what it is because of past events, all of which had effects that in turn became the causes for other events. It is for this reason that history textbooks start far in the past and trace the cause and effect of events to the present.

Students sometimes are uninterested in the distant events and fail to understand there is a chain connecting all of the past to the present. Some would rather study more recent or current events, but because of the cause-effect relationship, you cannot understand the present without looking at the past causes.

In our own lives we all seek causes for events, sometimes more consciously than at other times. For instance, if we lose a game, we often seek the causes—lack of practice, poor conditioning, a better coached opponent—and we plan ways to avoid our mistakes the next time. The historian does the same with the past, seeking the causes of events and trying to determine how one event led to another.

In the last chapter we saw that an event, colonization, had several different causes. In this chapter we will consider an event, the American Revolution, and trace how one event led to another in a series of actions and reactions.

The historian, looking back at events and putting them in order, can create what appears to be an inevitable series of causes and effects, of actions and reactions, that led in this case to American independence. However, while history may seem inevitable as described in the textbook, the progression of events was not inevitable since at any time people could have reacted differently than they did and the historian's hypothesis as to why they acted as they did may be incorrect.

I. Steps Leading to the American Revolution

FRENCH AND INDIAN WAR

The French and Indian War (1754–63) was one of a series of four wars fought between England and France, and their different European allies between 1689 and 1763. These wars involved fighting both in Europe and overseas as the

> The English and French fight a series of wars between 1689 and 1763.

Europeans struggled for hegemony[1] in Europe and control of an overseas empire. America was involved to some extent in all the wars, as the colonists fought the French in Canada and repulsed attacks on frontier settlements. The English prevailed in the first four wars and the treaties ending them either restored the status quo[2] or granted new territories to England.

The French and Indian War, called the Seven Years War in Europe (1754–63), was the fourth of these wars. For Americans the most famous battle in this war was the capture of Quebec in Canada by the English General Wolfe, whose British troops successfully assaulted the cliffs of Quebec and defeated the French General Montcalm at the Citadel. The most important event of the war, however, was the ambush and defeat of the English General Braddock by combined French and Indian forces near modern Pittsburgh. George Washington, a member of the Virginia militia and a surveyor who knew the area, helped save the British forces in their retreat and thus gained a wide reputation—to say nothing of a lesson in tactics. It was largely because of this reputation that Washington was chosen to lead the colonial forces in the Revolution.

The French and Indian War was very costly for the English. Besides fighting in the Americas, there was fighting in India and on the European continent. At the start of the war, the English suffered several defeats, but under the leadership of William Pitt, the king's first minister, they finally won. In the Peace of Paris signed in 1763, the French ceded to England its claim to Canada, Cape Breton, and the islands in the St. Lawrence River, as well as all territory east of the Mississippi River except the city of New Orleans. Spain, who had fought as an ally of France, ceded East and West Florida to the English, who in turn restored Cuba to Spanish rule.

The French and Indian War thus ended with the English in control of North America east of the Mississippi from Hudson Bay to the Florida Keys. The English became the dominant power in the world, but domestically they faced a huge war debt. How to pay the debt and how to govern the newly acquired territory of Canada became pressing problems for the English government. The steps they adopted to

---

[1] hegemony *Domination or control over another area by one country.*
[2] status quo *A situation remaining the same without change.*

handle these two issues became the first steps in the series of events that led to the Revolution.

Wars Between England and France—1689 to 1783

Dates	Name of the War in the Americas and (Europe)	Name of Treaty	Main Terms of Treaty
1689–1697	King William's War (War of the League of Augsburg)	Treaty of Ryswick	Status quo
1702–1713	Queen Anne's War (War of the Spanish Succession)	Treaty of Utrecht	England gains Newfoundland, Acadia, Hudson Bay
1739–1748	King George's War (War of the Austrian Succession)	Treaty of Aix-La-Chapelle	Status quo
1754–1763	French & Indian War (Seven Years War)	Treaty of Paris	England gains Canada and land east of the Mississippi
1775–1783	American Revolution (War of the American Revolution)	Treaty of Paris	13 colonies gain independence

PROCLAMATION LINE OF 1763

The first step taken by the English after the war was the issuing of the Proclamation Line of 1763, declaring that there was to be no English settlement west of the Appalachian Mountains. This included the Northwest Territory from which Ohio, Indiana, Illinois, Wisconsin, and Michigan were later created.

> The Proclamation Line of 1763 forbids colonial settlement west of the Appalachians and antagonizes the colonists.

The English believed conflict over this area had brought the Native Americans to the side of the French in the war. Many of the native inhabitants had followed Chief Pontiac of the Ottawa Tribe in attacks on English forts in the frontier area.

To the English, the Proclamation seemed a good solution to the problem of Indian rights. To the colonists, who had already begun to settle the area in small numbers, it appeared an infringement of their rights. Men such as George Washington and Benjamin Franklin—both of whom became important leaders of the Revolution—were involved in plans for land development in the Northwest Territory.

The Proclamation also stated that English law would prevail throughout the territory, including Quebec. This annoyed the French.

The effect of the Proclamation was thus to antagonize important colonial leaders, those colonists who were already settled in the area, and the French settlers of Quebec. These effects later became important causes of unrest, which led to revolution.

PAYING FOR THE WAR

The English next faced the problem of how to pay their war debt. The war had been expensive. English taxes were already high, and the government had to keep an army in the colonies to protect the frontier and control their new Canadian possessions. The government, led by the Chancellor of the Exchequer, i.e., treasury, George Grenville, decided to raise money in the colonies by means of import duties on a number of items including molasses and sugar. The law quickly became known as the Sugar Act—the first act passed by the English Parliament[3] for the specific purpose of raising tax monies in the colonies.

Parliament also passed a Currency Act, which forbade the issuing of paper money in the colonies and required the use of gold in business transactions. The Acts of Trade and Navigation, first passed in the 1650s, had regulated trade using import duties, but their purpose had not been to raise money, and the acts had never been strictly enforced. Now the English government was prepared to enforce the Acts of Trade as well as the Sugar and Currency Acts.

The colonists were shocked by these measures. They were suffering from a business recession and believed the new import duties, the required payment in gold, and the enforcement of the trade acts would further deflate their business opportunities. A town meeting in Boston denounced the laws as "taxation without representation," a slogan that became the rallying cry of colonial opposition.

> The colonists react with the cry, "no taxation without representation."

Boston proposed united action. Protest spread to the other colonies. This protest took the form of nonimportation agreements in which colonists agreed not to use certain goods imported from England, such as lace, and to wear only colonial-made clothes. A nonimportation agreement is similar to an embargo and is meant to have an impact on the economic life of a nation.

The British did not respond directly to the colonial protest but rather passed two more acts designed to alleviate their domestic economic problems. The first act, the Quartering Act of 1765, required the government of the colonies to provide barracks and supplies as needed by the English forces in the colonies. In 1766 the act was extended to require putting the soliders in inns or taverns, where they would be paid for by the colonists. The colonists saw this as an invasion of their personal privacy and of their homes. The Quartering Acts angered many colonists not affected by the revenue acts.

THE STAMP ACT OF 1765

The second act of 1765, the Stamp Act, affected almost everyone in the colonies. To raise money to be used for the defense of the colonies, the Stamp Act required that every paper document from newspapers to playing cards carry a stamp on it. The stamps were to be purchased from colonists who were designated as stamp agents. Any lawbreakers were to be tried in vice admiralty courts, where there were no juries.

The reaction of the colonists to the Stamp Act was immediate. The act broadened the base of the opposition to England—lawyers, land speculators, publishers, merchants, tavern owners, everyone was affected—and all feared this would be only the first of many direct taxes on the colonists. The colonial economy was still

[3] Parliament   *The legislative, i.e., lawmaking, branch of the English government.*

suffering from the war, and leaders believed they should pay no new taxes—a cry that still resounds in American political life and that is deeply rooted in our past. Some feared that the use of vice admiralty courts would change the colonial legal system based on the traditional right of Englishmen to a trial by a "jury of one's peers"[4] to a system of trial by judges without juries.

In reaction to these laws, several leaders of colonial opposition attacked the English in written statements incorporating new political theories on the relationship between the colonies and England. Some argued that the English Parliament could not tax the colonists but could levy import duties. Other leaders, such as Patrick Henry, turned to speech making. Patrick Henry of Virginia led a successful fight in the House of Burgesses to pass resolutions stating the English king had always acknowledged Virginia's right to govern her internal affairs and supporting the concept of no taxation without representation.

Another effect of the laws was the formation of secret organizations, usually called the Sons of Liberty, in many towns. They often turned to violence, as they did in Boston, where the records of the vice admiralty courts were burned.

A third reaction was the calling of an intercolonial meeting, the Stamp Act Congress, which met in New York in October of 1765 with eight colonies represented. They passed a "Declaration of Rights and Grievances," claiming for the colonists all the rights of English citizens and declaring that taxation without representation in the legislature was a violation of these rights.

Nonimportation gained further support, and English merchants whose exports had suffered called for repeal of the Stamp Act. Yielding to the pressure, the English government repealed the act in March 1766. At the same time Parliament passed the Declaratory Act, which claimed Parliament had the authority to pass laws for the colonies "in all cases whatever." This proved that in spite of the effect of the Stamp Act on the colonies and their reactions, the English were not ready to admit the need for a change in the relationship between colony and Mother Country. The progression of actions and reactions continued.

Key Point to Remember
The English after the French and Indian War had a large war debt and sought ways to get the colonists to pay some of it.

Links from the Past to the Present
America's attitudes toward taxes, as illustrated in the pre-Revolution slogan "no taxation without representation," reflects a basic distrust of taxation and government power that runs throughout our history, including George H. W. Bush's 1988 campaign pledge, "No new taxes."

People to Remember
Benjamin Franklin   Inventor, businessman, diplomat; a resident of Philadelphia. Franklin had interest in western lands, represented the colonies in London before the Revolution, and was considered a senior statesman at the Constitutional Convention.

---

[4]peer   *A person of equal rank with you.*

His *Poor Richard's Almanac* is full of wisdom that has appealed to Americans throughout history.

Dates
See page 47.

Questions
Identify each of the following:

Proclamation Line	Quartering Act
Sugar Act	Stamp Act
Currency Act	Sons of Liberty
Nonimportation Agreements	Declaratory Act

Multiple Choice:

1. The French and Indian War ended by a treaty signed at
   a. Ghent.
   b. Vienna.
   c. Paris.

2. The colonial response to the Sugar and Currency Acts and the enforcement of Acts of Trade and Navigation was to adopt
   a. nonimportation agreements.
   b. the Quartering Act.
   c. payment in gold for all debts.

3. To the English the Proclamation Line seemed a good way to
   a. gain the support of Benjamin Franklin and George Washington.
   b. support French law in Quebec.
   c. solve the problem of Indian rights.

II. The Beginning of Violence

THE TOWNSEND ACT

The English government still felt the need to raise revenue in the colonies. During this period in English history, the government leadership changed quite often, and the next acts bear the name of Chancellor of the Exchequer, Charles Townsend. While Townsend denied the latest argument of some colonists that Parliament could not place internal taxes[5] on the colonists but could place external taxes[6], the Townsend Acts of 1767 were all external taxes—import duties on glass, lead, paints, paper, and tea. The income was to be used for the defense of the colonies and in

[5] internal taxes   *Taxes paid by the citizens within a country, for example, income or sales tax.*
[6] external taxes   *Taxes paid on goods imported to a country and paid at the point of importation; import duties.*

"support of the civil government." New vice admiralty courts, again without trial by jury, were established to enforce the Townsend Acts.

Massachusetts led the way in protesting against the acts. A circular letter[7] written by Samuel Adams was sent to the other twelve colonies telling of their opposition to the Townsend Acts and calling for a renewal of nonimportation agreements. English customs officials in Boston were attacked after they had seized a ship belonging to John Hancock, a merchant they suspected of not paying the duties. The custom officials requested protection, and English troops were sent to occupy Boston.

> British troops are sent to Boston to protect customs officials after violence breaks out over the Townsend Acts.

Throughout 1768 and 1769 support grew for nonimportation in every colony except New Hampshire. In 1769 Virginia, again led by Patrick Henry, adopted a strong nonimportation agreement—the Virginia Association—and in reaction the Royal Governor dissolved the House of Burgesses.

The colonies were quite united in their opposition to the Townsend Acts. There was general agreement that the English Parliament had no right to raise revenue in the colonies in any way. Finally, in April 1770, responding to the economic pressure, Parliament repealed the Townsend duties except for the tax on tea. Again, acts of the English met with strong reactions from the colonists, and the cause-and-effect pattern continued.

VIOLENCE IN NEW ENGLAND

As a result of the English action, the nonimportation agreements were all abandoned by mid 1771. Agitation against the British quieted. It appeared the crisis might be over, but three incidents in New England showed it was not. On March 5, 1770, an English soldier seeking part-time work and a colonial worker got into a fight. That evening bands of colonists roamed the streets in protest. Feeling threatened by these colonists, British troops fired on a crowd and five colonists died, including Crispus Attucks, a mulatto[8] and one of the leaders of the protest.

> The Boston Massacre and Gaspee incident increase tensions.

This incident, known as the Boston Massacre, raised tensions. The English soldiers, including their leader, Captain Thomas Preston, were put on trial and were defended by John Adams and Josiah Quincy, both of whom were strong patriots but who also were strongly committed to the rule of law in the struggle against England. All but two of the soldiers were acquitted. The two were found guilty of manslaughter, branded on the hand, and released. Bostonians accepted the verdict but tensions remained.

The next incident occurred in June 1772. The customs schooner *Gaspee* ran aground in Naragansett Bay. That night, armed men from Providence, Rhode Island, boarded the *Gaspee,* wounded the captain, and after removing the crew, burned the boat. It was announced that any suspects in the incident would be sent to England for trial. Soon thereafter the Governor of Massachusetts announced that he and the colony's judges would be paid by the English government and not by the colonial assembly.

[7] circular letter   *A letter that is circulated or sent to several recipients.*
[8] mulatto   *An individual of mixed white and African-American parentage.*

The Boston Massacre, the *Gaspee* incident, the threat of trial without a jury of peers, and the loss of the "power of the purse" that gave colonial legislatures some control over the royal governors all struck at the traditional rights of Englishmen and colonial rights. Samuel Adams, a leader of the patriots' cause in Massachusetts, called for meetings to discuss this loss of rights and to establish Committees of Correspondence in each town and colony to keep the colonists informed of what was happening. Today cell phones and the Internet fill this function when protests are undertaken. The English response to the Committees of Correspondence was to pass still another act that agitated the colonists.

BOSTON TEA PARTY

In 1773 the only duty remaining from the Townsend Acts was the tax on tea. As the chief English supplier of tea, the East India Company was important to the government because it had extensive influence in India, but the company was close to bankruptcy. To save the company, parliament decided to take several measures. They dropped the tax on tea paid in England but kept the import tax on tea in the colonies. Then they allowed the company to sell tea directly to agents at a set price rather than at public auction.

Colonial merchants saw these actions as arbitrary. They believed that with no public auction to set the price of tea, the East India Company had in essence been given a monopoly. They also believed their profits had been undercut.

Reaction was immediate. The Committees of Correspondence spread the word quickly. Meetings in New York and Philadelphia condemned the Tea Act. In December 1773, when the Governor of Massachusetts refused to send recently arrived tea ships back to England, men dressed as Native Americans boarded the ships and dumped 342 chests of tea into the harbor.

The English in turn reacted strongly with a series of Coercive Acts referred to by the colonists as the Intolerable Acts of 1774. These acts were meant to punish the Bostonians for the "Tea Party." One act, the Boston Port Bill, closed the port of Boston by forbidding the unloading of all ships in the harbor. Another act changed the government of Massachusetts to bring it more under the king's direct control. Finally, the Quebec Act set up a permanent, highly centralized government for Canada in which Parliament was given the power to tax Quebec and the border of Canada was extended south to the Ohio River.

> The English close the port of Boston after the Boston Tea Party.

The colonists believed the Quebec Act threatened both their claim to "no taxation without representation" and their claims to the Northwest Territory. The stage was set for further action to unite the colonies. The cause and effect, action and reaction, pattern continued.

FIRST CONTINENTAL CONGRESS

Rhode Island, New York, and Pennsylvania called for a meeting or congress of all the colonies, and Massachusetts suggested that a meeting take place in Philadelphia in September 1774. At this first Continental Congress, fifty-six leaders from twelve colonies (Georgia was not represented) gathered. Some, like Patrick Henry and Richard Henry Lee of Virginia, Sam and his cousin John Adams of Massachusetts, and Christopher Gadsden of South Carolina, were considered radicals[9] and were the leaders of the patriot[10] cause. There were, however, many outstanding conservatives[11] like Joseph Galloway of Pennsylvania, who desired to heal the growing division between England and the colonies and who later became a leader of the Loyalists[12].

The delegates decided to keep their deliberations secret and to allow each colony only one vote. These two decisions set the pattern for later colonial meetings. The Patriots introduced a series of resolutions, the Suffolk Resolves from Massachusetts, which called for the people to arm, not to obey the Coercive or Intolerable Acts, and to collect their own colonial taxes. The conservatives countered with a plan of union between England and the colonies written by Joseph Galloway.

Debate followed; Galloway's plan was defeated six to five with one abstention. A modification of the Suffolk Resolves was then adopted. The Declaration and Resolves that the congress passed declared the Coercive Acts and Quebec Act illegal and called on the colonies to reinstate the nonimportation agreements until Parliament repealed the acts.

An association to enforce nonimportation was established, and the delegates agreed to meet the following May if Parliament had not changed the laws.

The colonists had resorted to an economic boycott to make Parliament change its policy, but their reaction was still peaceful.

During 1774 Thomas Jefferson in a pamphlet, *Summary View of the Rights of British America,* and John Adams in his "Novanglus" letters developed the concept of a dominion status or relationship between England and the colonies. They argued that the colonies should have their own government, and simply acknowledge the king as the head of state. This concept was later adopted by England in dealing with other colonies—Canada, South Africa, and India—but the idea was too radical at the time.

The English government offered a plan of conciliation in 1775, but it was rejected by the House of Lords, the upper house of the English Parliament. Parliament then declared Massachusetts to be in rebellion. In the meantime, Massachusetts colonists had begun to arm themselves and to organize special groups of militia, the Minutemen, who would be prepared to defend the colony at a minute's notice.

FIGHTING: LEXINGTON AND CONCORD

In April 1775 General Gage, commander of the English forces occupying Boston, decided to seize the weapons the Minutemen were gathering at Concord, twenty-one miles west of Boston. On the night of April 18, he secretly sent forces to seize these

---

[9] radical   *One who favors major changes in the structure of society.*

[10] patriot   *Those colonists who supported the cause of opposition to England and eventually supported the concept of independence.*

[11] conservative   *In politics, one who wishes to keep conditions basically as they are with little or no change.*

[12] Loyalist   *Those colonists who remained loyal to the king and Parliament of Great Britain throughout the war.*

stores, but his plan was discovered. Paul Revere and William Dawes rode out from Boston to alert the Minutemen. Some gathered on the village green in Lexington, where they confronted the English troops. There was considerable confusion, shots were fired, and eight colonists were killed and one English soldier wounded. The British went on to Concord, where some supplies were destroyed. Then the British began the march back to Boston.

The colonists were now fully alerted, and there was fighting along the return route. Seventy-three British were killed; the Minutemen's losses were considerably less. A war had begun. Massachusetts was truly in rebellion.

> The Revolutionary War begins at Lexington and Concord in April 1775.

The English attempt to have the colonists help pay for the costs of the French and Indian War, which seemed so logical to them, had had a devastating effect on English colonial relations and had led to another war. None of the events was inevitable, but as we look back at the period 1763–75, we can see how colonial reactions to specific English acts, and vice versa, led in a cause-and-effect progression to war. It is this logical progression of events that the historian seeks to discover when writing history. As a student, if you look for this progression, you will become your own historian and events should be easier to understand.

ORGANIZING FOR WAR

The Second Continental Congress met on May 10. On the same day, a band of Green Mountain Boys under the leadership of Ethan Allen seized Fort Ticonderoga on Lake Champlain. They captured a large number of cannons and other supplies from the English. The war was under way. The Congress quickly agreed to put the colonies in a state of defense and sent an appeal to the people of Canada to join them. On June 15, at the suggestion of John Adams of Massachusetts, Congress named George Washington of Virginia, who had gained a military reputation in the French and Indian War, as chief of the continental forces and called for soldiers to join him.

Washington accepted the post and headed for New England to take command of the Massachusetts Minutemen, who had now become part of the Continental Army. Before Washington could arrive in Boston, General Gage declared the Americans to be in arms and rebels and offered amnesty to all who would surrender except Sam Adams and John Hancock. Instead, the Americans moved to occupy heights overlooking Boston Harbor. On June 17 General Gage attacked the colonists on Breed's Hill (known through history as the Battle of Bunker Hill) and dislodged them, but at the loss of over 1,000 men.

Although hostilities had begun, the Continental Congress made one more effort at reconciliation with the king. They sent a petition, the Olive Branch Petition. The Congress rejected a proposal of the British government that still asserted the supremacy of the English Parliament over the colonies, and moved rapidly to set up a government. A post office department was established, and a commission to negotiate with Native-American tribes. The nonimportation agreements were changed to allow importation of arms from other countries.

In September delegates from Georgia joined the Congress. The king rejected the Olive Branch Petition and declared the colonies to be in rebellion. The Congress authorized a navy, and in December, Virginia and North Carolina militia defeated the Governor of Virginia and his Loyalist forces at Great Bridge, Virginia, and later destroyed his base at Norfolk.

INDEPENDENCE

The rebellion had begun in 1775, but the goal of the colonists was not yet determined. In January 1776 a pamphlet, *Common Sense,* written by Thomas Paine, called for independence as the goal and claimed it was ridiculous to have such a little country

> **The Continental Congress votes for independence on July 4, 1776.**

as England ruling such a large area. Thomas Paine also blamed the king for all the problems between Mother Country and colonies. The pamphlet became very popular. By June the move for independence was strong, and the Continental Congress appointed a committee to draft a Declaration of Independence. Congress voted for independence 12–0, with New York abstaining. On July 4 the Continental Congress approved the Declaration essentially as written by Thomas Jefferson. The united colonists now had a goal for the war.

ARTICLES OF CONFEDERATION

A form of governmental organization was needed. The Continental Congress appointed a committee to draft a frame of government, an idea that finds its roots in the Mayflower Compact. The Committee's report, the Articles of Confederation, was not adopted by Congress until November 1777. The Articles were then sent to the individual colonies—now states—for ratification. Final approval did not come until March 1781, so throughout most of the Revolution, the Americans had no officially approved government.

This did not prevent the Continental Congress from waging a full-scale war, including gaining allies. France recognized American independence in December 1777 and signed a Treaty of Alliance in 1778. Soon after, England and France were at war again, greatly helping the American cause. The War of American Independence thus became another in that long series of wars between England and France for world domination. In that series, it became the only war the English lost.

Document
Declaration of Independence: The Unanimous Declaration of the Thirteen United States of America
The Declaration of Independence can be divided into three sections. The first is a statement of philosophy, which is based on John Locke's theory of government. The second part is a list of grievances against the King of England, which provided the reasons for taking action and declaring independence. The third part is a declaration that the thirteen colonies are independent states. All Americans should be familiar with the statement of philosophy and the declaration. These

> **The Declaration of Independence is based on John Locke's theory of government.**

form the basis of our national philosophy. They are presented here. They are followed by a set of questions to help you identify the important points in the document.

"WHEN IN THE COURSE OF HUMAN EVENTS it becomes necessary for one people to dissolve the political bands which have connected them with another, and to assume among the powers of the earth the separate and equal station to which the laws of nature and of nature's God entitle them, a decent respect to the opinions of mankind requires that they should declare the causes which impel them to the separation. We hold these truths to be self-evident: (1) that all men are created equal, (2) that they are endowed by their Creator with certain inalienable[13] rights, that among these are life, liberty, and the pursuit of happiness; (3) that to secure these rights governments are instituted among men, deriving their just powers from the consent of the governed, (4) that whenever any form of government becomes destructive of these ends, it is the right of the people to alter or to abolish it and to institute a new government, laying its foundation on such principles, and organizing its powers in such form, as to them shall seem most likely to effect their safety and happiness.

The Declaration of Independence assumes the existence of self-evident truths and inalienable rights.

"Prudence, indeed, will dictate that governments long established should not be changed for light or transient causes; and accordingly all experience hath shown that mankind are more disposed to suffer, while evils are sufferable, than to right themselves by abolishing the forms to which they are accustomed. But when a long train of abuses and usurpations[14], pursuing invariably the same object, evinces a design to reduce them under absolute despotism, it is their right—it is their duty—to throw off such government and to provide new guards for their future security.

The Declaration of Independence states the "right of revolution."

"Such has been the patient sufferance of these colonies, and is now the necessity which constrains them to alter their former systems of government. The history of the present King of Britain is a history of repeated injuries and usurpations, all having in direct object the establishment of an absolute tyranny over these states. To prove this, let facts be submitted to a candid world . . ."

[a list of grievances follows]

"In every stage of these oppressions we have petitioned for redress in the most humble terms; our repeated petitions have been answered only by repeated injury. A prince [King of England] whose character is thus marked by every act which may define a tyrant is unfit to be the ruler of a free people.

"Nor have we been wanting in attentions to our British brethren. We have warned them, from time to time, of attempts by their legislature to extend an unwarrantable jurisdiction over us. We have reminded them of the circumstances of our emigration and settlement here. We have appealed to their native justice and magnanimity[15]; and we have conjured[16] them, by the ties of our common

[13]inalienable   *Incapable of being surrendered or transferred.*
[14]usurpations   *The illegal seizure of political power or authority.*
[15]magnanimity   *Quality of being honorable or exhibiting nobleness.*
[16]conjured   *To charge or call upon in a solemn manner.*

kindred, to disavow these usurpations, which would inevitably interrupt our connections and correspondence.

"They, too, have been deaf to the voice of justice and consanguinity[17]. We must, therefore, acquiesce in the necessity which denounces our separation, and hold them, as we hold the rest of mankind, enemies in war, in peace friends.

"We, therefore, the representatives of the United States of America, in general congress assembled, appealing to the Supreme Judge of the world for the rectitude of our intentions, do, in the name and by authority of the good people of these colonies, solemnly publish and declare that these united colonies are and of right ought to be FREE AND INDEPENDENT STATES; that they are absolved from all allegiance to the British crown, and that all political connection between them and the state of Great Britain is and ought to be totally dissolved; and that as free and independent states they have full power to (1) levy war, (2) conclude peace, (3) contract alliances, (4) establish commerce, and (5) to do all other acts and things which independent states may of right do. And for the support of this declaration, with a firm reliance on the protection of Divine Providence, we mutually pledge to each other our lives, our fortunes, and our sacred honor."

Questions

1. What are the four self-evident truths stated in the Declaration?

2. What are the three inalienable rights listed in the Declaration?

3. When does it become the "duty" of a people "to throw off" a government?

4. What is stated as the object of the acts of the King of England?

5. What do the colonists claim they have done in response to the King's "oppressions?"

6. What five powers do the "free and independent states" claim they now have?

7. Upon whom does the writer call for protection?

8. Why were the colonists concerned about the "opinions of mankind"?

Answers

1. The four truths are numbered one through four in paragraph two.

2. "Life, liberty, pursuit of happiness."

3. "When a long train of abuses and usurpation reveals a design or plan to reduce or bring them (meaning the people) under absolute despotism or tyranny."

4. The establishment of an absolute tyranny over the states.

5. "Petitioned for redress," meaning begged or asked for a change in the policy.

6. The five powers are numbered in the last paragraph.

7. "Divine providence," meaning some concept of a higher being or a god.

8. The document was both a statement of philosophy and a propaganda piece, and the colonists wanted support from as many people as possible.

[17]consanguinity   *Blood relationships or any close relation or connection.*

Key Point to Remember
Neither the English nor the colonists truly understood the other's views or concerns, and the actions and reactions of each side steadily escalated until they found themselves at war.

Links from the Past to the Present

1. Throughout American history there has been a distrust of monopolies and the control of business opportunities by one company or group of companies, as seen in the opposition to the tea tax, antitrust legislation, and regulation of industry.

2. The philosophy expressed in the Declaration of Independence concerning equality, inalienable rights, the purpose of government, and the right of revolution and dissent forms the core of America's beliefs and, while questioned at times during the past 225 years, still provides the basic ideology of the nation.

Dates
See pages 47 and 48.

Questions
Identify each of the following:

Townsend Acts	Coercive or Intolerable Acts
Internal Taxes	Quebec Act
External Taxes	Continental Congress
East India Company	Olive Branch Petition

Multiple Choice:

1. At the first Continental Congress the delegates
   a. were all radical leaders of the Patriots' cause.
   b. decided to keep deliberations secret and to allow each colony one vote.
   c. voted to approve Galloway's Plan of Union.

2. The English repealed the Townsend Acts as a result of
   a. the request of English and French merchants.
   b. the urging of the East India Company.
   c. the effectiveness of the nonimportation agreements.

3. John Adams and Josiah Quincy defended the English soldiers accused of killing colonists in the Boston Massacre because
   a. they were forced to do so by the British.
   b. they were both supporters of the English.
   c. they were committed to the rule of law in the struggle against England.

4. In the fighting on Lexington Green, the Minutemen
   a. killed the English commander.
   b. had been alerted the English were coming.
   c. fled before the English troops arrived.

III. The American Revolution

To make the study of the American Revolution simpler, we will divide the conduct of the war into three regions; New England, the Mid-Atlantic States, and the South. We will mention only the most important battles in each region.

THE FIGHTING IN NEW ENGLAND

We have mentioned the fighting at Lexington and Concord, where, according to tradition, the war began, and at Breed's Hill, which is traditionally called Bunker Hill. Both these battles occurred outside Boston. The battle at Breed's Hill provided the first real test of the ability of the colonial militia to stand up to regular English forces, which they did well. The army under Washington laid siege to Boston, and on March 17, 1776, the British withdrew their forces, sending them to New York. Washington moved his army to New York but could not stop the English from occupying the city. Washington escaped with his army across New Jersey into Pennsylvania. Matters were bleak for the Americans at that point, but the fighting had moved out of New England.

THE FIGHTING IN THE MID-ATLANTIC STATES

A victorious surprise attack on the British at Trenton, New Jersey, in December 1776 and another victory at Princeton in January 1777 gave hope to the Americans who spent the rest of the winter camped near Morristown, New Jersey. The British planned a major attack for 1777 to cut New England off from the other states. The plan was to have three armies meet at Saratoga, New York. One army was to come up from New York City, one army was to move east from Lake Erie, and one army was to move south from Canada under General Burgoyne. The British General Howe, who was now the British Commander in New York, decided to first attack Philadelphia, the American capital. Although Washington lost battles, he delayed Howe's move north to Saratoga, and the Americans defeated General Burgoyne at the Battle of Saratoga.

> After the Battle of Saratoga, the French sign a treaty with the colonists.

This was the turning point of the war. Although the British had occupied Philadelphia, when the French heard of the victory at Saratoga, they recognized America's independence, signed a Treaty of Alliance, and joined the war the next year. This was decisive for America.

Meanwhile, Washington spent the winter of 1777–78 at Valley Forge in Pennsylvania. The conditions were miserable in his camp, while the British enjoyed the pleasures of Philadelphia and New York, but the British withdrew from Philadelphia to New York in June of 1778 upon hearing that a French fleet was heading for New York.

For the next several years fighting in the Mid-Atlantic States focused on New York and on the frontier, where the English, allied with Native American tribes, perpetuated several massacres. These frightened the American frontiersmen, who organized successful attacks on British forces in the Northwest Territory. These victories allowed the Americans to claim the area at the peace conference.

Disbanding the Continental Army, November 3, 1783
This wood engraving by H. A. Ogden was published in Harper's Weekly, *October 20, 1883, as part of the one hundredth anniversary of the winning of the Revolution. You can identify General Washington. Note how well uniformed the army appears, suggesting the liberty an artist may take, particularly when recalling an event years later. It is important to realize all paintings are not accurate and that the victors often glorify their heroes.*
Courtesy: Library of Congress

THE FIGHTING IN THE SOUTH

Fighting in the South had begun in Virginia in 1775 and continued in the different Southern states until the last major battle of the war at Yorktown, Virginia, in October 1781. Lord Cornwallis, the English commander in the South, had been fighting in the Carolinas but was unable to defeat the Americans, who got supplies and recruits from Virginia. So Lord Cornwallis moved his attack into Virginia. Washington then moved south from New York, joined by a French army that had been in Newport, Rhode Island. These two armies joined the Southern army led by General Lafayette, the most famous European to join the American cause, and General Von Steuben.

> General Cornwallis surrenders to Washington's forces at Yorktown on October 19, 1781, bringing the war to an end.

Lord Cornwallis established a base at Yorktown, where the English fleet could supply him. Fortunately the American and French land attack was coordinated with the French fleet, which sailed into Chesapeake Bay blocking escape or reinforcement from the sea for Lord Cornwallis. After several successful American attacks on his lines, including one led by the young Alexander Hamilton, aide-de-camp[18] to Washington, Lord Cornwallis surrendered his army to Washington's forces on October 19, 1781.

Several British defeats by the French in the West Indies followed the American victory at Yorktown. In March 1782, the English House of Commons voted to no

[18] aide-de-camp   *A military term for a person of rank who assists a higher ranking officer.*

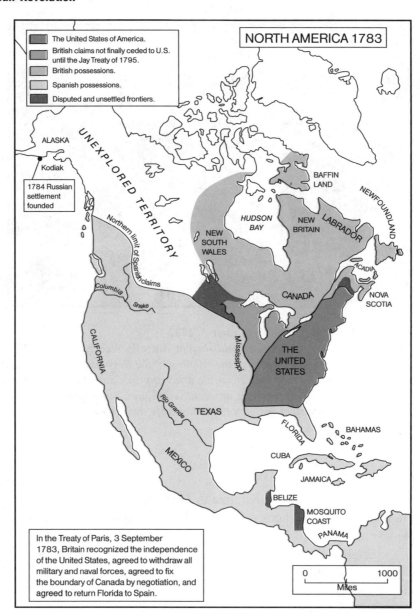

NORTH AMERICA 1783

The United States of America.

British claims not finally ceded to U.S. until the Jay Treaty of 1795.

British possessions.

Spanish possessions.

Disputed and unsettled frontiers.

In the Treaty of Paris, 3 September 1783, Britain recognized the independence of the United States, agreed to withdraw all military and naval forces, agreed to fix the boundary of Canada by negotiation, and agreed to return Florida to Spain.

longer pursue the war in the colonies, and the government of Prime Minister Lord North, which had run the war, resigned. Peace negotiations began, and the terms of the Peace of Paris were finally agreed upon in January 1783, ending the American War for Independence.

TERMS OF THE PEACE OF PARIS, 1783

The terms of the Peace of Paris were very generous for the Americans. The English recognized the independence of the thirteen colonies, gave the United States rights to fish off Newfoundland and to dry fish there, and agreed to withdraw all troops as quickly as possible. The boundaries were generous also: the United States received all the land east of the Mississippi River, south of the Great Lakes and the watershed of the St. Lawrence River, and north of Florida, which was returned to Spain. Debts owed by citizens of the two countries were recognized, and it was agreed the Congress would ask the states to return properties seized from any Loyalists and restore their rights. The English were to give their forts in the Northwest Territory to the United States.

SUMMARY

The Peace of Paris of 1783 ended twenty years of conflict and created a new nation with a very large territory to rule. The early years of the conflict were nonviolent and centered on issues of the rights of the colonists as Englishmen and on taxation without representation. Because neither side truly understood the other, the action escalated into violence by 1775 and full-scale war when the colonists declared independence in 1776. With aid from the French, the United States finally forced the English to recognize their independence in 1783. The steps leading from the Peace of Paris in 1763 to the Peace of Paris in 1783 can clearly be traced in a cause-and-effect relationship of action and reaction.

Key Point to Remember

The French recognized the United States' independence and joined the war after the Battle of Saratoga in 1777, and the war ended through the combined French and American victory over Lord Cornwallis at Yorktown.

Links from the Past to the Present

1. Successful military operations are complex and require extensive planning, as illustrated at Yorktown.

Steps Leading to American Independence
Action and Reaction—Cause and Effect

1763—Proclamation of 1763

1764—Sugar Act and Currency Act

1764–65—Non-Importation Agreements

1765—Stamp Act

1765 and 1766—Quartering Act

1765—Sons of Liberty Organizations

1766—Repeal of the Stamp Act
     Declaratory Act

1767—Townsend Acts

1769—Virginia House of Burgesses dissolved

1770—Boston Massacre

1772—Committees of Correspondence
     Gaspee Incident

1773—Boston Tea Party

1774—Coercive or Intolerable Acts

Quebec Act

Summary View of the Rights of British America and "Novanglus" Letters

First Continental Congress

1775—Battle of Lexington and Concord

Declaration and Resolve of the Continental Congress Second Continental Congress

Battle of Breed's Hill

1776—*Common Sense* published

July 4, 1776—Declaration of Independence

1777—Battle of Saratoga

1777–78—Winter at Valley Forge

1778—Treaty of Alliance with France

1781—Battle of Yorktown

Surrender of Lord Cornwallis

1783—Peace of Paris recognizes the independent United States.

People to Remember

George Washington   Virginia planter; Commander of Colonial forces in the Revolution, victor at Yorktown; later President of the Constitutional Convention and first President of the United States under the Constitution; most noted of the "Founding Fathers" of the United States.

Lord Cornwallis   British general, Governor General of India, Viceroy of Ireland; opposed taxation of North American colonies but later fought against the colonies on Long Island and in New Jersey; led the Carolina Campaign and was defeated by Washington at Yorktown; his surrender ended the American Revolution; held important political positions in India and Ireland after Yorktown.

Questions
Identify each of the following:

Battle of Lexington and Concord	George Washington
Battle of Breed's Hill	Lord Cornwallis
Battle of Saratoga	General Lafayette
Battle of Yorktown	General Burgoyne

Multiple Choice:

1. The American Revolution was fought in the following regions:
   a. only the south and New England.
   b. New England, the Great Lakes, and the Mid-Atlantic States.
   c. New England, the Mid-Atlantic States, and the south.

2. The British plan for the campaign that led to the Battle of Saratoga was to have
   a. three armies meet at Saratoga, splitting the colonies.
   b. General Howe lead General Washington away from Saratoga.
   c. the French withdraw from the war.

3. The victory at Yorktown demonstrated close cooperation between
   a. the English fleet and General Lafayette.
   b. the French fleet, the Colonial forces, General Washington, and General Lafayette.
   c. the French and English fleets.

Open-ended, Analysis Questions

The following questions require analysis and reflection. You are encouraged to bring to your answer information and ideas from many sources. The answers should be presented in composition or essay style, but they may be used to initiate discussion. The questions put you in the role of the historian, gathering information to support your personal perspective on the question.

1. Many believe *the* cause of the American Revolution can be summarized as "unfair taxation." Would you agree or disagree? Explain your view giving specific reasons and/or examples.

2. To what extent was the colonists' victory in the American Revolution due to the leadership of George Washington? Use specific examples of events and/or leadership to support your opinion.

3. Pick three consecutive events from the period 1763–1783 (see pages 47 and 48), and show how one event led to or caused the next event.

4

The Constitution and the Establishment of the New Nation

APPROACHES TO HISTORY

THE INFLUENCE OF INDIVIDUALS

When we consider who we are and how we got that way, one factor we must consider is the influence of individuals on our lives. From our births we are influenced by other people—sometimes positively, sometimes negatively.

Think about people who have influenced you—parents, teachers, and friends you know personally; or sports heroes, political leaders, or rock and roll stars. Some of these you would like to know and be like, while others you detest and wish they would drop dead. All these people have helped to make you who you are.

The same is true in the history of a nation. There are always people, individual men and women, who influence a nation's history and have a positive or a negative impact. Some historians explain all history as the result of the influence of men and women—individuals like us. What do you think? Have individuals been important in your life? Can you relate this to your study of history?

So far we have mentioned many individuals whose actions were important in the history of the United States, like John Cabot sailing to North America for England or George Washington at Yorktown. Without them, our history would have been very different.

In the first years of United States independence, the nation benefited from the leadership of many great men who have been referred to as "The Founding Fathers." These men wrote the Constitution and provided the leadership of the nation during its first twenty years of independence. If we think of them as individuals like us with similar strengths and weaknesses, passions and concerns, it may be easier to appreciate their contributions to United States history.

I. Post-Revolution Government Under the Articles of Confederation

The Articles of Confederation[1] provided the first government for the independent United States. The Articles were written in 1777 but were not finally approved by all the states until 1781. Maryland delayed ratification until each state that claimed land in the Northwest Territory agreed that the area would not be controlled by any existing state.

> A method of government, with a plan for entrance into the union, is designed for the Northwest Territory.

Designing a method of government for the Northwest Territory was, after the winning of the war, the greatest success of this government. The Land Ordinance of 1785 required that the Northwest Territory be surveyed and divided into six-square-mile townships and that these be subdivided into thirty-six sections each. This pattern of surveying and eventual settlement can still be seen, especially in Ohio, where the rural roads follow the straight township lines surveyed after 1785, and it now seems strange to find a right angle turn in a road in the midst of a cornfield.

It was this pattern that the United States followed throughout the westward expansion. Sections were sold and the proceeds went to the United States treasury.

The Northwest Ordinance of 1787 required that three to five new states be created from the territory. Each state was to be given self government when the population reached 5,000 free adult males. When there were 60,000 free inhabitants, the new state would be admitted to the union "on an equal footing with the original states." Thomas Jefferson (as with the Declaration of Independence) was the individual behind the Northwest Ordinance, which established the policy the United States followed as it grew from thirteen to fifty states, all equal in rights. This far-sighted policy eliminated the Mother Country–Colony relationship that had plagued the English colonies until independence in 1783.

WEAKNESSES OF THE ARTICLES

Despite that success, the Articles of Confederation proved to be a weak and ineffective frame of government. In fact, the time during which they were in operation was called the "critical period" by an early American historian, John Fisk, and the name has stuck. The writers of the Articles of Confederation, reacting against the power of the English king and Parliament, wanted to be certain the central government would be weak compared to that of each of the thirteen states.

[1] confederation   *A body of independent, separate states loosely united for joint action.*

The central government was given no power to tax or to control commerce—powers the colonies had objected to in Parliament. There was no court to enforce federal laws. Executive authority was exercised by a committee of the legislature. It was difficult for the central government to conduct foreign policy. For example, it was impossible for the central government to get the states to honor the debts owed to the Loyalists. As a result, the English refused to withdraw from some of the forts in the Northwest Territory as required by the Treaty of Paris. The central government had no way to force the states to obey its orders; the states could only be requested to provide militia and monetary contributions.

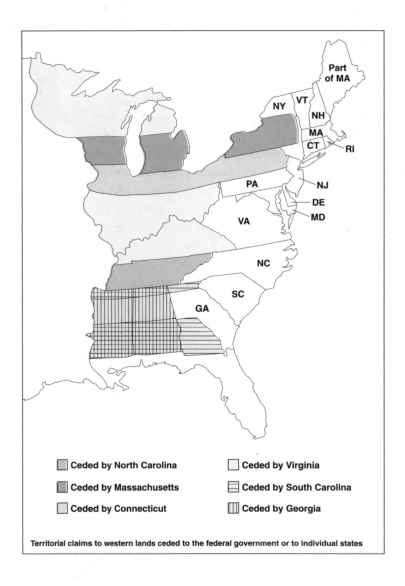

Part of MA

NY VT
NH
MA
CT — RI

PA   NJ
            DE
VA   MD

NC

SC
GA

☐ Ceded by North Carolina   ☐ Ceded by Virginia

☐ Ceded by Massachusetts   ☐ Ceded by South Carolina

☐ Ceded by Connecticut   ☐ Ceded by Georgia

Territorial claims to western lands ceded to the federal government or to individual states

RESPONSES TO ECONOMIC PROBLEMS

The economic situation in the United States had deteriorated badly during the war and continued to decline after 1783. Again the central government was powerless, as each state developed

Shays' Rebellion reveals the economic distress of farmers.

policies for its own benefit. The frontier farmers were particularly hard hit. To avoid bankruptcy, many banks were forced to foreclose on their mortgages. Finally, in 1786, disgruntled farmers led by Daniel Shays rose in rebellion against the government of Massachusetts. While Shays' Rebellion was crushed, it frightened many people in the United States and encouraged a movement toward revision of the Articles of Confederation.

Just as during the American Revolution the country had split into Loyalists and Patriots with many individuals undecided, so did the country split over support for the Articles of Confederation.

Responding to economic problems between Virginia and Maryland, in 1785 James Madison and George Mason of Virginia arranged for a conference hosted by George Washington at his home, Mount Vernon. These individuals led the way in finding solutions to some immediate economic problems between Virginia and Maryland, and they also suggested that all the states gather at Annapolis, Maryland, in September 1786, to discuss commercial problems. Meanwhile, in Congress, Charles Pinckney of South Carolina proposed a reorganization of the federal government.

Many men who had been Patriot leaders were speaking out on the need for changes in the Articles. Only twelve individual delegates arrived at Annapolis so they could not accomplish much, but they sent a proposal, drafted by Alexander Hamilton, to all the states proposing a convention in Philadelphia in May 1787 to discuss commercial and all other matters. The Congress of the Confederation government finally endorsed the proposal, and the stage was set, thanks to the work of these individuals, for a major revision in the frame of government of the United States.

CONSTITUTIONAL CONVENTION

The convention officially opened on May 25, 1787, in Philadelphia. Fifty-five delegates, many already famous for their contributions to American independence and government, eventually participated in the Convention. George Washington was elected president. His fairness and patience contributed greatly to its success. Some of the delegates wanted merely to revise the Articles of Confederation, but Edmund Randolph introduced a plan, the Virginia Plan, which would create a new central government with a bicameral[2] legislature with membership determined by population, an executive[3] elected by the legislature, and a separate judiciary[4]. In Randolph's plan, representation in the bicameral legislature would be based on each state's population. This raised concern among the smaller states. William Paterson then introduced a plan, the New Jersey Plan, which basically retained the Articles of Confederation and gave the states equal power in the legislature but added a supreme court.

[2]bicameral   *A legislature (lawmaking body) that has two chambers or houses. The United States Congress is bicameral with the Senate and the House of Representatives making up the two chambers.*
[3]executive   *The branch of government that is responsible for executing the laws.*
[4]judiciary   *The branch of government responsible for judging the laws and those accused of breaking them.*

Debate was long. We can follow the debates of the Convention through the invaluable notes taken by James Madison. The Convention operated in secrecy, which allowed delegates to discuss their opinions openly and to change their position without publicity—something no longer possible in the U.S. government. Madison's notes were not published until 1840, four years after his death.

> Through compromises a new federal Constitution is written.

Debate on the Virginia and the New Jersey Plans continued until Roger Sherman of Connecticut offered a compromise, which is often referred to as the Great or Connecticut Compromise. Sherman's plan was accepted by both the large and the small states because it had something for each. His plan called for a bicameral legislature: in the upper house of the legislature, to be called the Senate, each state would have equal representation; in the lower house, to be called the House of Representatives, each state would have representation based upon its population. Another crucial compromise involved the establishment of the Electoral College for the election of the president (Article II, Section 1). A third important compromise involved the election of representatives for the House (Article I, Section 2). The article states, "Representation and direct taxes will be apportioned among the several states according to respective numbers determined by adding to the whole number of free persons including those bound to service for a set number of years and excluding Indians not taxed three-fifths of all other persons." This compromise satisfied the southerners who were able to count their slaves—the "other persons"— as three-fifths of a person in determining their population and thus they would have stronger representation in the House of Representatives.

It was through many compromises of this type that the delegates were finally able to agree upon a new frame of government for the United States—the United States Constitution. An entirely new federal[5] system of government was set forth to replace the confederation established in the Articles approved by Congress in 1777. The new system distributed powers between the state and federal government and set the Constitution as the "supreme law of the land." The powers of government were separated and distributed among the three branches. A committee of five individuals—William Johnson as Secretary of the Convention, Alexander Hamilton, James Madison, Rufus King, and Governeur Morris—actually wrote the document, incorporating all the compromises and points that had been approved in the three and one-half months of debate. Finally thirty-eight of the fifty-five convention members signed the Constitution. The Convention sent the new document to Congress, which in turn submitted it to the states with the recommendation that special ratifying[6] conventions be called in each state.

RATIFICATION DEBATE

> The Federalist Papers explain the new Constitution and win votes for ratification.

Debate immediately began on the merits of the Constitution. Those supporting the Constitution were called Federalists and

[5] federal *A form of government in which a group of states join and establish a central governing body, which they recognize as superior, but that allows the states to retain certain designated powers.*
[6] ratify *To approve or confirm formally.*

those opposed were called Anti-Federalists. Many were undecided, and how they voted would determine the future of the United States.

To help persuade them, James Madison, John Jay, and Alexander Hamilton wrote a series of papers, *The Federalist Papers,* which explained and analyzed the Constitution. *The Federalist Papers* are considered the best analysis of our Constitution and of the process of democratic government ever written. These three men helped to win votes in several states such as New York and Virginia, where the debate over ratification became intense. In Virginia, Patrick Henry, the patriot and hero of attacks on the power of the English Parliament, led the Anti-Federalists while James Madison, who because of his many contributions at the Convention has been called the "Father of the Constitution," led the Federalists.

One of the strong arguments of the Anti-Federalists was that the Constitution did not protect the individual rights of the people—those same rights that had been at the heart of the struggle against England. Virginia finally ratified the Constitution 89–79 but only after a proposal to add a Bill of Rights to the Constitution was agreed to.

In New York, where Alexander Hamilton led the Federalists, defeat appeared certain. However, George Clinton, the Anti-Federalist leader, was out-maneuvered by Hamilton, and New York approved the Constitution 30–27.

Before Virginia's and New York's ratification, the required nine states had ratified the Constitution. With the approval of nine states, the Constitution was to go into effect. However, the government could never have functioned effectively if New York and Virginia had not joined the Union. The work of Hamilton and Madison was crucial for establishing the new government.

> Narrow victories in New York and Virginia bring those states into the new government.

Delaware was the first state to ratify the Constitution, doing so in December 1787; Rhode Island was the last. Rhode Island first rejected the Constitution in a popular referendum[7]. However, after the other twelve states ratified and the new government was functioning, Rhode Island reconsidered and entered the Union in May 1790. The vote was 34–32 and with that close vote, the Union of the thirteen states was complete.

Key Point to Remember
Through a series of compromises, the Founding Fathers were able to agree on a new frame of government, the Constitution of the United States of America.

Links from the Past to the Present

1. We still live under the Constitution, and if we did not, we would not be the United States we have been known as for over 200 years.

People to Remember
James Madison Virginian, called "Father of the Constitution"; his notes give us invaluable information on the Convention; later he was one of the authors of *The Federalist Papers,* which is one of the finest analyses of constitutional republican

---

[7]referendum *The process of referring measures passed by a legislature to the voters for their approval or rejection in a general election.*

government; he introduced the amendments known as the Bill of Rights in Congress in 1789 and served as President of the United States from 1809 to 1817.

Dates

1785—Land Ordinance.

1787—Northwest Ordinance.
      Constitutional Convention.

1788—Constitution ratified.

Questions
Identify each of the following:

Founding Fathers	Critical Period	John Jay
Daniel Shays	Virginia Plan	Roger Sherman
Alexander Hamilton	Federalist Papers	Edmund Randolph
Northwest Ordinance	Anti-Federalists	William Paterson

Multiple Choice:

1. After the winning of the war, the greatest success of the government under the Articles of Confederation was
   a. writing the Constitution.
   b. creating five new states.
   c. designing a method of government for the Northwest Territory.

2. Edmund Randolph's Virginia Plan called for
   a. a bicameral legislature based on population.
   b. a Senate with equal representation for each state.
   c. no judiciary.

3. The Great or Connecticut Compromise called for
   a. an executive of five individuals.
   b. a Senate with equal representation for each state and a House of Representatives with representation based on population.
   c. the convention to operate in secrecy.

II. The New Government

Once the Constitution was ratified by nine states, it was to go into effect. The old congress of the Articles set the dates when the new government would begin to function and chose New York City as the temporary capital. The first elections for the House of Representatives and the Senate were held in February 1789, and at the same time the presidential electors cast their ballots. George Washington was unanimously elected President and John Adams, Vice President. George Washington was inaugurated as the first President on April 30, 1789, in New York City.

Several executive departments were quickly created. Thomas Jefferson was named Secretary of State; Henry Knox, Secretary of War; Alexander Hamilton, Secretary of the Treasury; Samuel Osgood, Head of the Post Office; and Edmund Randolph, Attorney General. According to the Constitution it was the responsibility of the Congress to establish a court system under the Supreme Court, which they did in the Judiciary Act of 1789. John Jay was named the first Chief Justice of the Supreme Court.

These men, all of whom had been active in state and national government, worked together to set the basic policies for the new government. Many precedents were established that still apply today. For instance, the Constitution does not mention a presidential cabinet[8] but, by regularly meeting with his department heads, George Washington established the idea of a cabinet.

BILL OF RIGHTS

During the ratification of the Constitution, four states, in addition to Virginia, indicated the need for amendments to the Constitution to protect individual rights. Constitutional amendments to form a Bill of Rights was one of the first issues considered by the newly elected House of Representatives. Again it was James Madison who led the debate. The Federalists did not want to go through another Constitutional Convention so they responded quickly to the suggestions of the Anti-Federalists. Twelve amendments were offered to the states and ten were ratified by the requisite nine states by December 15, 1791.

> The Bill of Rights, the first Ten Amendments to the Constitution, is adopted.

These ten amendments formed the United States Bill of Rights. They are the guarantee of our liberty. For over 200 years they have been interpreted by the Supreme Court. These interpretations have extended our original rights. These decisions have extended the freedoms guaranteed in the Bill of Rights to incorporate inventions such as the telephone, which was never anticipated by the Founding Fathers. The Supreme Court has said that freedom of speech forbids wire tapping. Of course, there are limits and times when wire tapping would be legal, just as there are some limits to the freedom of speech. But these limits have been carefully guarded by the court.

> The Supreme Court's interpretation of the Bill of Rights keeps it a living document.

Because of such careful decisions, the Bill of Rights of 1791 is a vital and living document, which provides Americans with freedoms and rights enjoyed by few other nations in the world. James Madison and the other individuals who worked for the adoption of these ten Constitutional Amendments deserve our respect and admiration. It is important to note that the rights guaranteed require a sense of responsibility on the part of citizens to uphold them and to act in civil ways. There is no "Bill of Responsibilities" attached to the Constitution. What do you think some of those responsibilities might be?

---

[8] cabinet   *The leaders of executive departments who meet regularly and share responsibility of government. They give advice to the President who makes final decisions.*

Document

The Bill of Rights: The First Ten Amendments to the Constitution

The first ten amendments adopted by the states in 1791 guarantee our individual rights as United States citizens. They reflect the period of colonial opposition to England when the colonists believed many of these rights were threatened by English action. One reason for opposition to the Constitution by the Anti-Federalists was its lack of a statement of rights. The first congress under the leadership of James Madison wrote and sent to the states these ten articles, and the states ratified them quickly. These amendments and their interpretation by the Supreme Court are important to all United States citizens. Which ones are most important to you personally?

ARTICLE I

Congress shall make no law respecting an establishment of religion, or prohibiting the free exercise thereof; or abridging the freedom of speech, or of the press; or the right of the people peaceably to assemble and to petition the government for a redress of grievance.

> **Basic Liberties: Religion, Speech, Press, Assembly, Redress**

ARTICLE II

A well-regulated militia being necessary to the security of a free state, the right of the people to keep and bear arms shall not be infringed.

> **Right to Bear Arms**

ARTICLE III

No soldier shall in time of peace be quartered in any house without the consent of the owner, nor in time of war but in a manner to be prescribed by law.

> **Quartering of Troops**

ARTICLE IV

The right of the people to be secure in their persons, houses, papers, and effects against unreasonable searches and seizures shall not be violated; and no warrants shall issue but upon probable cause, supported by oath or affirmation, and particularly describing the place to be searched and the persons or things to be seized.

> **Search and Seizure: Warrants**

ARTICLE V

No persons shall be held to answer for a capital or otherwise infamous crime unless on a presentment or indictment of a grand jury, except in cases arising in the land or naval forces or in the militia, when in actual service in time of war or public danger; nor shall any person be subject for the same offense to be twice put in jeopardy of life or limb, nor shall be compelled in any criminal case to be a witness against himself, nor be deprived of life, liberty, or property without due process of law; nor shall private property be taken for public use without just compensation.

> **Rights of the Accused**

ARTICLE VI

In all criminal prosecutions the accused shall enjoy the right to a speedy and public trial by an impartial jury of the state and district wherein the crime shall have been committed, which district shall have been previously ascertained by law, and to be informed of the nature and cause of the accusation; to be

> **Protection for the Accused in Criminal Trials**

confronted with the witnesses against him; to have compulsory process for obtaining witnesses in his favor; and to have the assistance of counsel for his defense.

ARTICLE VII

In suits at common law, where the value in controversy shall exceed twenty dollars, the right of trial by jury shall be preserved; and no fact, tried by a jury, shall be otherwise re-examined in any court of the United States, than according to the rules of the common law.

Suits at Common Law

ARTICLE VIII

Excessive bail shall not be required, nor excessive fines imposed, nor cruel and unusual punishments inflicted.

Bails and Punishments

ARTICLE IX

The enumeration in the Constitution of certain rights shall not be construed to deny or disparage others retained by the people.

Other Rights

ARTICLE X

The powers not delegated to the United States by the Constitution, nor prohibited by it to the states, are reserved to the states respectively, or to the people.

Powers Reserved to the States or to the People

Questions

1. Can Congress make a law limiting the freedom of the press?
2. Under what conditions may soldiers be housed in a person's house?
3. Under what conditions may a search warrant be issued?
4. When may private property be taken for public use?
5. What type of trial is guaranteed to all citizens?
6. Do people have any rights not listed in the Bill of Rights?
7. Who holds the powers not delegated to the federal government?

Answers

1. No, see Article I.
2. Only with the consent of the owner or in time of war as prescribed by law.
3. Only upon probable cause when the cause is supported by an oath and the place to be searched and the person or things to be seized are described.
4. Only when just compensation or payment is given.
5. All citizens are guaranteed a speedy and public trial by impartial juries.
6. Yes. Over time, responding to new ideas, understandings, and technology, the Supreme Court has interpreted the Bill of Rights and the Constitution to extend the legally protected rights of the American people. Therefore, just because a right is not listed in the Bill of Rights does not mean it is not held by the people today.
7. The powers not delegated to the federal government or denied to the states are held by the states or the people.

HAMILTON'S ECONOMIC PROGRAM

The greatest failures under the Articles were in the area of commercial and financial matters. The Constitution gave the new government the power to both tax and regulate commerce. Alexander Hamilton, as Secretary of the Treasury, developed a financial program for the new nation. He proposed that the United States pay at par[9] both the foreign and domestic debt acquired by the central government under the Articles and that the state's war debts be taken over and paid by the federal government.

> Hamilton's economic program is designed to encourage national unity and provide security for economic activity.

Hamilton's goal was to encourage a sense of national unity and support for a government that was financially reliable and responsible. He believed such responsibility would improve business and commerce and would ultimately help the new nation.

Opposition to Hamilton's plan came from southern states that had made arrangements to pay off their debts and from those individuals who had sold their government bonds[10] at less than par value. Support came from New England states that had large debts and from those people who had bought government bonds. The House of Representatives, led by James Madison, voted down the proposed assumption of state debt by the federal government. Government was at a standstill and some resolution of the crisis was needed.

What occurred illustrates how individuals can change history. Thomas Jefferson arranged a dinner party for Madison and Hamilton. At the dinner Madison agreed to support the assumption of state debts, and in return Hamilton agreed to support the establishment of a new capital city on the Potomac. Both had to give up something, but both gained—Hamilton, who was from New York, lost the national capital, but he got his economic plan accepted; Madison got the capital in his area of the country but had to accept the fact that the federal government would pay the states' war debts. It is through compromises of this type, often arranged in a personal way, that the federal government has operated since that date. The House of Representatives voted in favor of both measures.

Southerners led by Patrick Henry still objected, but Hamilton's economic plan went into effect. To provide money to pay off the debt, the plan included a tariff on many imports. Later in 1791, in order to collect more money, Hamilton imposed an excise tax on domestically produced whiskey.

> Farmers rebel over whiskey tax and are crushed by the federal government.

Whiskey was important especially on the frontier to farmers, who turned their excess grain into whiskey that could then be sold or saved for later consumption. The whiskey was easier to move to market than the grain from which it was made. As a result, there was considerable opposition to the whiskey tax on the frontier and there were cases of violence. In Pennsylvania the federal government used the state militia to crush the opposition to the tax in what has been termed the Whiskey Rebellion. The action established the authority of the federal government over the state militias.

---

[9] par   *Equal to the value stated on a bond.*
[10] bond   *Any interest-bearing certificate issued by a company or government.*

The farmers who objected to the tax later strongly supported Thomas Jefferson in his disagreements with Hamilton.

ARGUMENTS OVER THE BANK OF THE UNITED STATES

The next proposal of Hamilton's was for the establishment of a Bank of the United States. Congress approved the proposal, and before signing the bill, George Washington asked his cabinet members to give him their written opinions on whether the Bank of the United States was constitutional or not. The responses represented two interpretations of the Constitution—two interpretations that still divide Americans. The first, articulated by Thomas Jefferson, supported "strict construction." This view emphasizes the 10th Amendment, which states that powers not delegated to Congress are held by the states. Nowhere in the Constitution is a bank mentioned. Therefore, according to Jefferson's view of strict constructionism, a national bank is not constitutional.

The second view, stated by Alexander Hamilton, supported "loose construction" and the idea of "implied powers." This view of the Constitution emphasizes that every idea could not be anticipated by the Founding Fathers, and therefore everything could not be listed in the Constitution. The Constitution does give the federal government the power to tax. According to Hamilton's interpretation, implied in the power to tax is a place to keep the tax money. Therefore, a national bank is constitutional because it provides that place to keep the tax money and is thus needed in order for the government to exercise one of its stated powers.

Washington accepted Hamilton's argument. The disagreement between Jefferson and Hamilton is one base upon which the American two-party system of government is built. These two conflicting views toward government and the Constitution still guide the view of Americans. They have been combined in different ways over our history, but the attitudes of the Jeffersonians and Hamiltonians that developed during Washington's first term are still with us.

What are your opinions about government? Would you have followed Jefferson or Hamilton in 1791?

Two Views of Government—Jeffersonian and Hamiltonian

Jeffersonian

Jeffersonians distrusted strong central government. Their sympathies were with the debtors and the agrarian (farming) order, based on individuals who own their own farms. They supported a broad distribution of wealth and disliked industrialism and organized finance. They believed in the perfectability of man and that the people using representatives knew best how to govern themselves. In summary, Jeffersonians believed that the less power the federal government has, the better.

Hamiltonian

Hamiltonians supported a strong and active central government, which would encourage industry, commerce, and finance. Their sympathies were with creditors and business interests. They distrusted the people's ability to govern themselves and supported a powerful executive with an elite following. In summary, Hamiltonians believed in a strong and active government, which acted to benefit certain interests.

THE START OF POLITICAL PARTIES

In spite of their differences, both Hamilton and Jefferson supported George Washington for a second term. It was clear, however, that their differences on government policy were leading to a personal feud. George Washington tried to reconcile the two individuals but failed. After George Washington and John Adams were reelected, Jefferson resigned from the government. In the vice presidential election of 1792, George Clinton, the old Anti-Federalist, had won fifty votes. The Federalist, John Adams, was reelected with seventy-seven votes. This vote, the resignation of Jefferson, and the disagreements over the role of government between Jefferson and Hamilton mark the beginning of the two-party system in the United States. The first two parties that developed under the government of the Constitution were known as the Federalists and Democratic-Republicans.

IMPORTANCE OF WASHINGTON'S FIRST TERM

During George Washington's first term the basic structure of the U.S. government was put into place. It included executive departments, a cabinet, and the judicial structure. The Bill of Rights was added to the Constitution. The basis of the two-party system can be found in the disagreements between Alexander Hamilton and Thomas Jefferson over the Bank of the United States, their understanding of the role of government, and their interpretation of the Constitution. The main concerns of George Washington's first term were the financial issues of war debt payment and a Bank of the United States. During his second term foreign policy issues became the major concern.

Key Point to Remember

Under the presidency of George Washington, precedents such as the cabinet were established, arguments over loose and strict construction of the Constitution were developed, and a written Bill of Rights guaranteeing individual rights was adopted.

Links from the Past to the Present

1. The basic theories of loose and strict construction are still referred to in political debate, although these terms are not always used.
2. The Bill of Rights still guarantees Americans' basic liberties.
3. The structure of the government of the United States, such as the executive cabinet and departments, the powers of Congress and the states, as it was written in the Constitution or established during Washington's presidency, is still in place.

People to Remember

Alexander Hamilton   New Yorker, aide-de-camp to George Washington at Battle of Yorktown; argued for stronger central government at Constitutional Convention; first United States Secretary of the Treasury, whose economic plans, including a Bank of the United States, supported a strong government and loose construction of the Constitution; he was killed in 1804 by Aaron Burr in a duel over political disagreements.

Dates

1789—George Washington inaugurated as first President.
      Judiciary Act.
1791—Bill of Rights approved by states.

Questions

Identify each of the following:

Judiciary Act of 1789   Loose Construction
Bill of Rights   Strict Construction
Bank of the United States   Hamiltonian View of Government
Cabinet   Jeffersonian View of Government

Multiple Choice:

1. Among the actions taken in George Washington's first term were
   a. the establishment of several executive departments.
   b. a declaration of war against France.
   c. the passage of the Judiciary Act of 1801.

2. Hamilton's economic plans included
   a. a tax on cigarettes and gasoline.
   b. a tax on whiskey.
   c. forcing the states to pay their war debts.

3. The beginning of the two-party system in the United States can be seen in
   a. the vote over the Bill of Rights.
   b. the resignation of Jefferson from Washington's cabinet and his disagreement with Hamilton over the role of government.
   c. the Anti-Federalists' dislike of Washington's authority.

III. The French Revolution's Impact on America

UNITED STATES REACTION TO THE START OF THE FRENCH REVOLUTION

The French Revolution began in 1789, and most Americans seemed to support it. The Revolution appeared modeled on our own revolutionary fight for individual rights. The French Revolution began with protests but gradually grew more violent. In 1792 the French established a republican government and in January of 1793 beheaded their king, Louis XVI. In February, France declared war on Great Britain, Spain, and Holland. The final war in the 150-year series of wars between the English and the French had begun.

American attitudes toward the French Revolution began to change. Again Thomas Jefferson and Alexander Hamilton represented the two opposing views. Thomas Jefferson, who had served as United States representative to France supported the revolution and viewed it as a fight to extend individual rights. Alexander Hamilton saw the revolution as a threat to established government. He sympathized with the English and supported economic ties with our former enemy. Neither Jefferson nor Hamilton wanted the United States to become involved in the war. Both supported American neutrality[11].

As you recall, however, in 1778 the United States had signed a treaty of mutual support with France. France had supported the

> **Washington declares United States neutrality.**

United States in the war for independence. This treaty was still in effect. Technically it had been signed with the Royal Government of France, which had been overthrown. George Washington used this technicality to proclaim United States neutrality, stating that we were at war with neither England nor France. United States citizens were warned not to support either side.

It was a wise move for the young republic not to become involved in the war, yet it clearly indicated how national needs often take precedent over written documents when individual leaders make decisions affecting national policy. Commitments to another nation, such as a treaty, are often disregarded by later leaders.

NEGOTIATIONS WITH ENGLAND AND SPAIN

Actions of both the English and the French during the War of the French Revolution affected the United States. First, the French government's representative to the United States, Citizen Genet, commissioned privateers to attack English shipping. Washington asked for his recall to France, but Genet remained in America as a private citizen and married a daughter of George Clinton.

Second, the English issued orders in council in 1793 whose enforcement led to the impressment[12] of United States ships and sailors. We were close to war with England, yet George Washington's government needed the trade with England to maintain its financial stability. Import duties on imported English goods were the main source of revenue for paying off the national debt.

There were other disagreements with the English, such as the British failure to evacuate their forts in the Northwest Territory as was stated in the Peace of Paris. Washington decided to send a special envoy[13], John Jay, then Chief Justice of the United States, to England to negotiate the issues and avoid war. The result, Jay's

---

[11] neutrality   *The state of being neutral or uncommitted, not taking sides.*

[12] impressment   *The practice of the British forcing American sailors into service on British warships under the assumption that they were escaped British seamen and not accepting the fact that they were American citizens.*

[13] envoy   *An official representative from one country to another.*

Treaty of 1795, was not popular. Jeffersonian Republican members of the House of Representatives attempted to block the treaty, but Washington established another important precedent for later presidents when he refused to provide the House with all of the legal papers involving the treaty negotiations.

By the terms of Jay's Treaty the British agreed to withdraw from the Northwest forts, opening the area to United States settlement and giving the United States control over the area's valuable fur trade. Other issues of concern, such as impressment, were to be resolved by commissions or were not mentioned. Alexander Hamilton strongly supported the treaty and wrote papers arguing for its passage. The Jeffersonian Republicans opposed it, but it was ratified by the Senate.

The United States also had continuing disagreements with Spain over the terms of the Peace of Paris of 1783. By the efforts of Thomas Pinckney, United States Minister to England, these were resolved in Pinckney's Treaty. In Pinckney's Treaty, Spain and the United States reconfirmed the Mississippi River and the 31st parallel as the United States boundary.

The Treaty also granted the United States free navigation on the Mississippi and the "right of deposit"[14] in New Orleans. This allowed settlers in the area west of the Appalachians to have a water route to ship their produce abroad. It was an important development for the West, whose population was growing. It also tended to tie the West to the South. This alignment remained until the Erie Canal and railroads made it possible for those in the Northwest Territory to ship their produce east.

By the end of Washington's second term, the terms of the Peace of Paris were honored, and the United States had established her neutrality in the War of the French Revolution.

WASHINGTON'S "FAREWELL ADDRESS"

In September 1796 a Philadelphia paper published what has become one of the most often quoted documents in United States history, Washington's "Farewell Address." In it Washington explained why he would not seek a third term as president, a precedent followed until World War II and now incorporated into the United States Constitution as Amendment XXII. He also gave three other often quoted bits of advice to the American public based on his own individual perceptions.

First, he argued the dangers of political parties as a potentially divisive force in the nation, particularly if they were to follow geographic divisions. The nation has ignored his advice on parties only once. In 1860, just before the Civil War, our parties divided on strictly geographic lines. Washington's advice was good.

Second, he urged the nation to rely on "temporary alliances for extraordinary emergencies" and to avoid permanent alliances with foreign powers. Again, the policy was followed until after World War II. Some people still believe we should not join alliances as we did in the postwar period but instead remain isolated.

---

[14] right of deposit   *The privilege that allows a nation to deposit goods temporarily in a port or place controlled by another nation without paying import or export tariffs on the goods deposited. The goods are in transit and merely deposited temporarily.*

Third, Washington argued that the credit or reliability of debt payment by the United States must be cherished. We still acknowledge this concept, but since World War II we have had more and more difficulty controlling the debt of the United States.

Washington's advice is still quoted by political leaders. It again illustrates the important role an individual can play in history and illustrates what an important contribution George Washington made to the history of the United States— Commander of the Revolutionary Army, President of the Constitutional Convention, and first President of the United States.

The Presidential Election of 1796

The Presidential Election of 1796 illustrated how divided the country had become and how the party system, deplored by Washington, was already established. John Adams, the Federalist, was elected president with 71 votes in the Electoral College[15] and Thomas Jefferson, whose followers would soon be designated as members of the Democratic-Republican party, was elected vice president with 68 votes. Thus we had a president and vice president from different political parties.

> John Adams is elected the second President.

The main issues of John Adams' presidency dealt with foreign policy and United States attempts to avoid involvement in the European war between France and England.

XYZ Affair

In reaction to Jay's Treaty and the apparent closeness of the United States to England, the French began interfering with United States shipping. In 1797 President John Adams sent three envoys to negotiate the United States-French differences. In Paris the French Foreign Minister, Talleyrand, delayed negotiations and sent three representatives, who were later designated as X, Y, Z, to seek bribes and a loan for France. Two American envoys immediately returned home.

> The XYZ Affair splits the Federalist Party.

A record of the French actions, which became known as the XYZ Affair, was made public early in 1798. There was a strong reaction against France and talk of war. Defense measures were taken including the establishment of the Department of the Navy. There were several naval skirmishes between 1798 and 1800. The Federalist Party split into two factions—one antiwar group led by Adams and a

---

[15] Electoral College   *The Electoral College elects the president and vice president of the United States. It was established in the Constitution to avoid direct elections of the president. Every state has as many electors in the Electoral College as it has senators and representatives combined. The process by which electors are chosen has shifted over the years. The electors were originally voted for by state legislatures. Today they are voted for by the people in the general election in November every four years. The electors together make up the Electoral College. They vote for president and vice president. Today they vote as the people in their state voted but at the beginning of United States history they voted for whomever they wished. The original idea was to take the election of the president out of the control of the masses and put it in the control of specially elected state leaders who would be able to pick the best person for the presidency.*

prowar group led by Alexander Hamilton. Adams decided to negotiate with France. The resulting Convention of 1800 ended the Treaty of 1778. The Senate approved the Convention, which ended the threat of war.

Alien and Sedition Acts

The threat of war with France had led to a fear of foreigners. Many leading Democratic-Republican writers were foreign born, and they were pro-French. The Federalists, feeling threatened by the Democratic-Republican writers and fearing France, in 1798

> The Alien and Sedition Acts reflect American fear of foreigners.

passed four laws known collectively as the Alien and Sedition Acts. These Acts increased from five to fourteen years the period of residence required to become a citizen and allowed the president 1) to send from the country aliens considered dangerous, 2) to arrest aliens in case of war, and 3) to punish anyone forming groups to oppose national laws or publishing writings that brought disrepute on the government or congress. The latter provisions would stifle opposition to the government, and the Democratic-Republicans attacked the laws as unconstitutional and an infringement on the Bill of Rights.

As an individual, how would you have reacted to the Alien and Sedition laws?

Kentucky and Virginia led the attack on the Alien and Sedition Acts. Both state legislatures (Kentucky had become a state in 1792) adopted resolutions in late 1798 calling the acts unconstitutional.

Thomas Jefferson wrote the Kentucky Resolutions and James Madison the Virginia Resolutions. Both the Kentucky and Virginia Resolutions argued that the Constitution was a contract between states, and when laws passed by the federal government were unconstitutional, it was the duty of the states to stop the evil and to nullify the law. This argument is known as the Theory of Nullification[16].

The Theory of Nullification was resorted to on several other occasions before the Civil War to object to federal government actions that some groups felt infringed upon the rights of the states. The Theory of Nullification formed an important part of the concept of states rights. States rights are still invoked by many American leaders. The basis of the nullification argument is the idea that the states created the union, and as the Tenth Amendment states, powers not "delegated to the United States. . . are reserved to the states respectively or to the people."

The Theory of Nullification and the concept of a strict construction of the Constitution form the cornerstone of the states' rights argument. They were both firmly stated by Thomas Jefferson, who believed in the rights of the individuals and the states over the rights of a powerful federal government.

PRESIDENTIAL ELECTION OF 1800

The Alien and Sedition Acts became a major issue in the presidential election of 1800. The Electoral College vote ended in a tie between Thomas Jefferson and Aaron Burr. Both were Democratic-Republican candidates, and each had 73 votes. John Adams had 65; C. C. Pinckney, 64; and John Jay, 1.

[16] nullification   *Making invalid or inoperative.*

The Federalists controlled the House of Representatives, where the final decision between the leading candidates had to be made. In spite of his personal feud with Thomas Jefferson, Alexander Hamilton supported Jefferson, who won the election on the 36th ballot cast in the House of Representatives. Aaron Burr became the vice president. Burr, who was also from New York, never forgave Hamilton, with dire consequences. In 1804 Aaron Burr shot Hamilton in a duel.

After the election of 1800, Congress proposed the Twelfth Constitutional Amendment, which established separate voting by the electors for president and vice president.

Before leaving office John Adams had the opportunity to appoint a Federalist, John Marshall, Chief Justice of the Supreme Court. His leadership and decisions over the next years provide another important example of the role of the individual in shaping history. Also in 1801 a Judiciary Act was passed, enabling Adams to appoint a number of new judges. He appointed Federalists to these posts. This meant that the Federalist Party would have considerable power even though the new president was from the Democratic-Republican party.

These two acts, the appointment of Marshall and the appointment of federal judges, illustrate the significance of the federal court system in our nation. Today it is as important as it was in 1801, and a president's appointments to the courts can assure a continuation of his, or his party's, policies long after he is out of office.

SUMMARY

The period of United States history from 1783 to 1801 particularly illustrates the theory that history is made by individuals. These two decades were dominated by our Founding Fathers. The individual contributions of these men to our history is so great and so complex that it cannot be calculated. Their understanding of human nature, their philosophy of government, their reactions to crisis, and their feuds and disagreements helped shape the nation we have today. What kind of a country would have developed if there had been no George Washington, Thomas Jefferson, Alexander Hamilton, John Adams, James Madison, or Edmund Randolph?

That no women have been mentioned in this chapter may seem unfortunate but reflects the realities of political and economic life of the period. The wives, Martha Washington and Abigail Adams particularly, played important roles but not on the center stage at that time in history.

Key Point to Remember
During the first twelve years under the Constitution, ideas were developed—such as states' rights—and a philosophical foundation of individual rights was established, all of which are still part of our government and affect each of our lives today.

Links from the Past to the Present

1. The tension between national interests and treaty obligations must always be considered in foreign policy decisions.

2. The advice of George Washington in his "Farewell Address" has been quoted throughout our history to support isolation and to deplore partisan politics.

3. Supreme Court justices often remain on the court for many years and so have a great influence on the nation.

4. The argument for states' rights as dominant over the power of the federal government (the basis of the Theory of Nullification) is still used today although some of the arguments have changed since the Civil War.

People to Remember

John Adams   Massachusetts Patriot and lawyer; defender of English troops accused of the Boston Massacre; first vice president and second president (1797–1801) of the United States; avoided United States involvement in wars of the French Revolution.

Dates

1795—Jay's Treaty and Pinckney's Treaty.

1797—XYZ Affair.

1798—Alien and Sedition Acts.
   Kentucky and Virginia Resolutions.

1801—John Marshall appointed Chief Justice of the Supreme Court.

Questions

Identify each of the following:

Jay's Treaty

Twelfth Amendment

Washington's "Farewell
   Address"

Aaron Burr

Kentucky and Virginia
   Resolutions

Alien and Sedition Acts

Convention of 1800

John Adams

Multiple Choice:

1. The theory of states rights includes
   a. a strict construction of the Constitution.
   b. the idea that the Constitution is a compact between the states.
   c. both of the above.

2. During the Washington and Adams administrations the United States
   a. almost went to war with England and then with France.
   b. was not affected by the French Revolution.
   c. proclaimed neutrality, which was respected by both the French and English.

3. The Alien and Sedition Acts
   a. allowed the government to punish anyone forming groups to oppose national laws or publish writings bringing disrepute on the government.
   b. decreased the period of residence required for citizenship from fourteen to five years.
   c. were directed at Federalists and their friends.

Open-ended, Analysis Questions

The following questions require analysis and reflection. You are encouraged to bring to your answer information and ideas from many sources. The answers should be presented in composition or essay style, but they may be used to initiate discussion. The questions put you in the role of the historian, gathering information to support your personal perspective on the question.

1. James Madison is sometimes referred to as the "Father of the Constitution." Does he deserve this title? Why or why not?

2. Many individuals played important roles in the early development of the United States. Pick two individuals from the following list, and explain how the ideas and actions of each of the two were important in the establishment of the government of the United States.
   a. John Adams
   b. Alexander Hamilton
   c. Thomas Jefferson
   d. George Washington

3. The rights guaranteed to Americans in the Bill of Rights as well as those added through the interpretation of the Constitution by the Supreme Court all require some degree of responsibility in the exercise of those rights. Create a Bill of Responsibilities that would support proper exercise of the rights found in the Bill of Rights. Then pick one of those responsibilities and describe how it would lead to a sound use of one of the rights guaranteed to Americans.

4. The expression, "Founding Fathers," illustrates the concept of the "great men" interpretation of history. In an essay address two issues:
   a. To what extent is it fair to say that the Constitution and the establishment of the new nation was the result of the actions of a few great individuals?
   b. Why are no women mentioned as leaders in this time period?

Sectionalism and Nationalism: 1801–1850

APPROACHES TO HISTORY

MANIFEST DESTINY OR THE CONCEPT OF BEING A SPECIAL OR CHOSEN PEOPLE

Another way of looking at history is to consider your nation as particularly blessed and deserving. Most people at some time in their lives feel this way about themselves. Whether it was a close call in an accident or a good grade when you didn't study, you can probably recall a moment when you felt lucky or blessed. Some people, unfortunately, have few such times but still a feeling can persist that they deserve a better deal; that they really are as good and deserving as others who seem to have "all the luck."

The same sense of being deserving and just as good as some other individual can also apply to nations. All citizens of a nation share a sense of belonging to their country. This sense is called nationalism. Nationalism is defined as devotion to the interest and prestige of your country.

All peoples at some point in their history experience a sense of nationalism and pride in their country. Usually nationalism or love of country is a valuable trait. It is normally a healthy concept, but it can be carried to extremes. Political leaders may encourage a nationalistic feeling among their followers in order to achieve personal goals or to divert their nation's attention from domestic issues, or they might single out a religious or ethnic group within their nation to attack as different and rally their supporters for a crusade of ethnic cleansing against them proclaiming this is for the benefit of the nation. This is nationalism carried to the extreme.

The rhetoric of nationalism often includes references to the special qualities of one's nation and how these are the result of being "chosen" or singled out by God or Providence to fulfill a particular mission or goal on earth. The national seal of the United States illustrates this with its phrase "In God We Trust," as do the many references in presidential speeches to God and His protective role for America. Many other nations have this same view.

In the 19th century several famous American historians wrote histories of the United States assuming the young nation was particularly blessed. The idea is still a popular way of looking at the history of the United States. As we grew as a nation, it certainly seems we were unusually blessed or lucky, whether it was in establishing the original colonies, winning the American Revolution, or writing the Constitution. Good fortune generally continued to bless the American nation in the first half of the 19th century.

In spite of various crises, most Americans still consider their nation to be blessed, "a shining city on a hill," as Ronald Reagan described it quoting the Bible. This concept underlies the interpretation of United States history written by many historians. Can you identify with this approach? Can you identify the bias when reading a text?

I. The Revolution of 1800 and Jefferson's Presidency

The election of Jefferson as President in 1801 has been considered by some a peaceful revolution. After twelve years of Federalist rule, a new party, the Democratic-Republicans, moved into power. In his inaugural address, Jefferson spoke of continuity and reconciliation after the prolonged voting procedure in the House of Representatives. The Judicial Act of 1801 was repealed and attempts were made to remove Federalist judges, but the country weathered the transition of power easily. The Constitution worked. There was a lot to be proud of as an American.

> Jefferson's election marks a peaceful revolution.

BARBARY PIRATES

In spite of the foreign policy successes of John Adams, the United States was not fully respected by other nations. For years, pirates had disturbed commerce along the Barbary Coast of North Africa, which includes modern Algeria, Morocco, Tripoli, and Tunisia. Safety could be purchased through paying tribute or bribes to the pirate states. Washington and Adams had done so. In 1801 the Pasha of Tripoli increased his demands and declared war on the United States.

Jefferson had opposed a navy and wanted peace, but he was determined to confront the pirates of Tripoli to defend American commerce. This support of the free passage of all ships on the open seas has been a continuing policy throughout United States history.

A blockade of the pirates proved successful. A treaty, which freed United States commerce from the payment of tribute, was signed with Tripoli in 1805, although we continued to pay tribute to the other Barbary states. This incident gave a boost to national pride and provides an important line in the United States Marine Hymn: "From the Halls of Montezuma (in Mexico) to the shores of Tripoli."

In this situation, Jefferson had gone against his party's sentiments for peace in order to pursue what he perceived to be the good of the nation. He thus provided a precedent for strong presidential leadership.

THE LOUISIANA PURCHASE

In another incident of nationalism, Jefferson again went against his former ideas. He was given the opportunity in 1803 to purchase the Louisiana Territory from France, which had recently acquired it from Spain. The territory included all the area between the Mississippi River and the Rocky Mountains. Jefferson supported the purchase.

> The Louisiana Purchase doubles the size of the nation.

Jefferson believed French control of the territory and particularly of the city of New Orleans, which could block transport on the Mississippi River, was a threat to the United States. Jefferson believed American control of the Mississippi River would provide an opportunity for the yeoman[1] farmers, whom he supported, to move further west and have free transport to the sea.

Such a purchase was not mentioned in the Constitution, so Jefferson had to abandon his "strict construction" on this issue. Such flexibility was deplored by some of his supporters, but Jefferson's purchase greatly increased the size of the United States and removed a potential French threat. It provides another precedent for presidential leadership and an example of flexibility in response to different situations.

Much of the Louisiana Territory was unknown to Europeans when it was purchased. To develop relations with the Native Americans and to develop routes to the west, Jefferson sent Merriwether Lewis and William Clark on a three-year, very successful exploratory trip through the northern part of the territory. Lewis and Clark's trip opened the territory for settlement and inspired future explorers. In turn, these added to the United States sense of nationhood.

Since the first settlements in Virginia and Massachusetts, there had always been individuals moving west. Life on the frontier was always a challenge. Men led the movement westward, and the few women who came were "quickly married." Life was often lonely and quite isolated, but those on the frontier moved quickly to establish communities. By 1803, with the admission of Ohio, the union had grown to seventeen states—Vermont, 1791; Kentucky, 1792; Tennessee, 1796; Ohio, 1803. By 1821 there were twenty-four states. These new states were to play an important role in the development of national policy.

---

[1]yeoman   *A free and independent farmer.*

NAPOLEONIC WARS: NON-IMPORTATION AND EMBARGO

After a brief peace in 1802, the English-French conflict in Europe—known during its first years as the War of the French Revolution and, after Napoleon took power, as the Napoleonic War—broke out again in 1803. Unable to defeat the other nation decisively, both sides turned to attacks on commerce of noncombatant[2] nations. In spite of attempts by Jefferson and his successor, James Madison, to remain neutral, American commerce was affected.

The English again impressed American sailors. A legal precedent, the "broken voyage," which allowed goods from the West Indies to be landed in the United States, go through customs, and then be shipped to France as American goods, was reversed by an English judge in 1805. After the judge's decision, ships carrying such goods were seized by the English in their blockade of the French ports. The United States retaliated with a Non-Importation Act listing many goods that were not to be imported from England. An attempt to negotiate with the English failed.

In June 1807 a British warship in United States territorial waters attempted to take four sailors from a United States navy frigate, the *Chesapeake.* When the United States officers refused, the British fired on the ship, killing three Americans. The nation was close to war, but Jefferson avoided it and retaliated with an embargo to be effective in December 1807.

View of Boulder, Colorado, 1872
Boulder was founded in 1859 as a supply town for gold miners. The rather desolate, treeless background identifies it as a western settlement, but the general layout is typical of frontier settlements since the founding of the country.

[2]noncombatant   *A neutral nation or person not involved in the war or conflict.*

The Embargo of 1807 won Jefferson support in the West and the South but upset many East Coast merchants. The embargo stopped all trade of United States ships with any foreign nation, and restricted our coastal shipping. Smuggling quickly began, and Napoleon, suggesting he was aiding the United States, began to seize all United States ships, saying that because the embargo forbade them to leave the United States, they must actually be English ships. United States trade suffered greatly and opposition to the embargo grew, particularly in New England. The sense of national unity was threatened.

FIGHTING ON THE FRONTIER

Westward expansion and the frontier area added another dimension to the growing national tension. Two Native-American leaders, Chief Tecumseh and his twin brother, the Prophet, realized that the white settlers would keep coming and want more land in spite of treaties. Chief Tecumseh organized tribes in the old Northwest Territory in a defensive alliance.

Settlers were certain the English supplied weapons and encouraged Tecumseh's attacks. New leaders in Congress, particularly Henry Clay from Kentucky and John C. Calhoun of South Carolina, helped stir up sentiment against England. This created a greater regional split. The West wanted war with England, while New England disliked the embargo against England and wished to open up trade. Both regions believed they were supporting what was best for the national interest. Those congressmen who supported a war with England were referred to as War Hawks—the term *hawk* has been used often in United States history to describe individuals who want to use military strength in a crisis.

Taking preemptive action, General William Henry Harrison, in 1811, attacked Tecumseh's forces at Tippecanoe, burned his village headquarters and ended the immediate threat, but the attack did not stop the anti-English sentiment of the westerners.

ECONOMIC WARFARE

In the meantime, opposition to the embargo had grown, and it was repealed in 1809 by the Non-Intercourse Act because Jefferson still wished to pursue an economic policy against England. The Non-Intercourse Act opened trade with all nations except England and France. The Act stated that if either England or France stopped harassing United States shipping, trade would be opened with that nation. At this point James Madison became president. Jefferson, following Washington's precedent, refused to seek a third term. Madison continued Jefferson's attempts to avoid war through economic pressure just as the colonists had used it against England in response to the Stamp Act.

> Economic measures appear to fail, and the War Hawks from the west push Madison to ask Congress to declare war on England.

In the next three years, 1809–12, both England and France agreed verbally to change their policies toward United States shipping but failed to follow through. The War Hawks scored election victories in November 1810, and Henry Clay was elected Speaker of the House of Representatives. Continued impressment, which was viewed as an outrage on the national honor, and the Native-American threat on the frontier, played into the hands of the War Hawks. Finally, Madison asked Congress to make defense preparations.

He still continued to negotiate with the English, who insisted the United States interpretation of French actions was wrong. The English were facing economic distress and on June 16, 1812 finally agreed to accept the United States' position. Unfortunately Madison had asked Congress for a declaration of war on June 1, 1812, and war was voted on June 18. The War of 1812 had begun.

Diplomacy and economic pressure appeared to have failed, yet if there had been faster communication across the Atlantic, it would have been otherwise. The War of 1812 should never have been fought, because the English had accepted the United States position two days before war was voted by Congress. The war, as do wars generally, created strong nationalist sentiment among some Americans. The West and South strongly supported the war; however, New York and New England were not as enthusiastic.

THE WAR OF 1812

There were three major areas where fighting took place during the war. The United States mounted an unsuccessful attack on Canada (Quebec) but did win some successes on the Great Lakes; the English attacked Baltimore, Maryland (an attack described in our National Anthem), and burned the capitol, Washington, in a raid; the United States fought successfully in the Southwest, where the great hero of the war, Andrew Jackson, defeated the English at the Battle of New Orleans on January 8, 1815.

Unfortunately, this battle was fought two weeks after the United States and England had signed the peace treaty. Thus, in the war that should not have been fought, the greatest United States victory came after the war was over. Again we have an illustration of the slowness of communication in the era.

> Andrew Jackson wins fame at the Battle of New Orleans.

TREATY OF GHENT

The terms of the Treaty of Ghent signed in December 1814 restored the prewar conditions. Prisoners were released, territory restored, and a commission of arbitration established to settle the United States-Canada boundary. No mention was made of impressment or other matters of maritime law that had been the major cause of the war.

Some historians have referred to the war as the second American War of Independence. The United States fought the English to a draw and lost no territory. The war confirmed the integrity and viability of the new nation. It enhanced the sense of nationalism in most of the country. The Federalists of New York and New England who opposed the war lost their national support and died as a political party.

THE HARTFORD CONVENTION

The final act of the Federalists, one that sealed the fate of the party, was the calling of the Hartford Convention, which met from December 1814 into January 1815. The Convention was called because the Federalists were upset by the use of economic warfare and the declaration of war in 1812.

While its proposals for change were not radical, the meetings were held in secret, following the tradition of the Constitutional Convention. This made the Convention appear a secret plot to destroy the nation. The Democratic-Republican opponents accused the members of the Hartford Convention of sedition and treason. In reality, its program was a restatement of Jefferson's and Madison's ideas expressed in the Kentucky and Virginia Resolutions calling for the nullification of "infractions of the Constitution."

Thus a truism of American political life was established—those out of office call those in office to strict accountability to the Constitution, while those in office, for example, Jefferson making the Louisiana Purchase, will stretch the meaning of the Constitution.

Key Point to Remember

The United States under Presidents Jefferson and Madison used economic measures to avoid being pulled into the Napoleonic War.

Links from the Past to the Present

1. Freedom of the seas has always been one of the United States's foreign policy goals.
2. The United States has resorted to a hawkish approach to solving international problems many times from the War of 1812 to the War on Terrorism in 2001.
3. Economic boycott as a way to force other nations to change their policy has been used by Americans from the nonimportation agreement of the pre-Revolutionary period to the United States support of the United Nations sanctions against Iraq invoked after the first Gulf War to the sanctions against Iran's nuclear programs starting in 2006.
4. Usually the party in power has supported loose construction, and the party out of power has supported strict construction.

People to Remember

Thomas Jefferson   Virginia planter and gentleman; author of the draft of the Declaration of Independence and of the Land Ordinance for the Northwest Territory; Washington's first Secretary of State; supporter of strict construction of the Constitution and Theory of Nullification (Kentucky Resolutions); third president of the United States (1801–9); arranged for the Louisiana Purchase and sent the Lewis and Clark expedition to explore the territory; founder of the University of Virginia; author of Virginia Statute for Religious Freedom.

Dates

1801—Thomas Jefferson elected president.
　　　Judiciary Act repealed.

1803—Louisiana Purchase.

1807—Embargo.

1809—Non-Intercourse Act.

1811—Battle of Tippecanoe.

1812—War of 1812.

1814—Treaty of Ghent.

1815—Hartford Convention.

Questions
Identify each of the following:

Pirates of Tripoli	Chief Tecumseh
Louisiana Territory	Henry Clay
Embargo of 1807	James Madison
Battle of New Orleans	Treaty of Ghent
War Hawks	Hartford Convention

Multiple Choice:

1. Which one of the following opened United States trade to all nations except England and France?
   a. Non-Intercourse Act of 1809
   b. Embargo of 1807
   c. Non-Importation Act of 1806

2. Leaders of the War Hawks were
   a. James Madison and Thomas Jefferson.
   b. Merriwether Lewis and William Clark.
   c. Henry Clay and John C. Calhoun.

3. The War of 1812 need never have been fought because
   a. the Treaty of Ghent basically reaffirmed the status quo.
   b. the British government accepted United States' terms before the Congress declared war.
   c. the Battle of New Orleans was fought after the treaty was signed.

II. The Era of Good Feelings and the Jackson Presidency

With the demise of the Federalist Party, James Monroe was overwhelmingly elected to the presidency in 1816. It took time for new political combinations to be developed. This period immediately after the War of 1812 has been called the Era of Good Feelings. In 1820 when James Monroe was reelected to a second term, he won by 231 votes to 1 in the Electoral College.

Domestic issues during the so-called Era of Good Feelings focused on the need for a Bank of the United States, since the first bank's charter was due to expire, on tariffs, and on improvement of internal transportation. These three issues eventually led to conflict over sectional needs and Constitutional interpretation. The southern states preferred low tariffs because they imported many goods while exporting agricultural products. The East desired higher tariffs to protect its growing industries and, in general, supported a national bank in order to make business exchanges easier. The West desired better transportation routes, particularly between the West and the growing markets in the East.

DOMESTIC AFFAIRS

During Monroe's presidency the Republicans reversed their stand from Jefferson's original view on the bank and voted to recharter it in 1816. However, President Monroe would not accept the loose interpretation argument that the phrase in the Preamble of the Constitution, to "promote the general welfare," permitted the federal government to build roads, even if they would aid military defense. Monroe vetoed several road-building bills pushed through Congress by the new leaders from the West. A tariff was voted in 1816, which helped the manufacturers of the Northeast. Henry Clay, congressman from Kentucky, in 1824 coined the expression "the American System" to refer to the combination of high tariffs and internal transportation improvements in roads and canals that he and his fellow westerners supported.

MONROE'S FOREIGN POLICY

Between 1816 and 1824 President Monroe had several foreign policy successes that established our national borders and gave the nation a sense of unity and strength. Under the leadership of Secretary of State John Quincy Adams from Massachusetts, after the War of 1812 the United States quickly negotiated the Rush-Bagot Agreement and the Convention of 1818 with England and the Adams-Onis Treaty with Spain. The English treaties established the United States' border with Quebec and set the precedent for a nonfortified border with Canada by reducing the number of warships on the Great Lakes. The Convention of 1818 established a joint occupation of the Oregon Territory—the land west of the Rockies north of the 42nd parallel to the 54°42′ line. In the Adams-Onis Treaty, Spain ceded eastern Florida to the United States, and the United States renounced its claims to Texas. The border of the Louisiana Territory was also finally set.

> Treaties with England and Spain adjust United States borders with Canada, Florida, and Mexico.

At the same time in the Far West, Russia was claiming the California coast as far south as San Francisco Bay. Adams contested the Czar's attempt to exercise Russia's control, and a treaty was signed by which Russia withdrew north of the 54°42′ line but kept her claim to Alaska. This treaty eliminated Russia's claim to the Oregon Territory.

THE MONROE DOCTRINE

There had been revolutions in the Spanish colonies of South America during the Napoleonic War, and they had all declared independence. With peace reestablished in Europe, there was talk after 1815 of reestablishing Spanish rule in the area. The British were opposed, as they enjoyed trade benefits with the newly independent countries. The English asked Adams to join them in preventing European interference with the new states. Adams and President Monroe preferred to handle the matter without the English.

In his 1823 message to Congress, Monroe stated four principles which, since that time, have been known as the Monroe Doctrine—a doctrine honored by every United States President since then. The Monroe Doctrine is the cornerstone of United States policy toward Central and South America. The four points Monroe made were:

1. The American continents were no longer available for colonization.
2. In the Americas there was a political system different from that of Europe.
3. The United States would consider dangerous to its peace and safety any interference by European powers in the Americas.
4. The United States would not interfere with existing colonies nor interfere in internal affairs of Europe nor take part in European wars.

While the European nations paid little attention to the Monroe Doctrine in 1823, they did not interfere in the Americas. The English government made it clear they would oppose the restoration of Spanish rule in the Americas. The United States Navy was too small to enforce the Doctrine but it was followed because of the English stand. These apparent foreign policy successes of John Quincy Adams reinforced an American sense of nationhood and gave her greater national pride.

PANIC OF 1819

Henry Clay's American System was an attempt to unite the nation and encourage nationalism. It was not successful in doing so because the American System included nothing of appeal to southern interests. The election of 1824 reflected growing sectional interests that had been brought into focus by two earlier events: the Panic[3] of 1819 and the Missouri Compromise of 1820.

> The United States experiences its first major economic recession in the panic of 1819.

The Panic of 1819 was the first of many in United States history. During the 19th and early 20th centuries, the American capitalist system experienced major economic difficulties approximately every twenty years. The causes were often similar, and those who suffered were the same groups.

The Panic of 1819 was brought on mainly by the rapid westward expansion, which led to extensive land speculation that forced up land prices, combined with a Congressional act that required the repayment in specie[4], rather than paper money, of

[3] panic   *A sudden, widespread fright concerning financial matters, which results in a drop in value or scarcity of specie.*
[4] specie   *Coined money, usually gold or silver.*

any loans or mortgages involving the purchase of public lands. Because specie was in short supply in the West, land speculators and farmers were frightened and the panic resulted.

The second Bank of the United States enforced this act, which led Senator Thomas H. Benton of Missouri to refer to the bank as "the Monster." Specie was never in great supply for farmers. Farmers often had to borrow from banks to get funds for spring planting and were dependent on fluctuating crop prices to get funds for repayment; frontiersmen struggling to establish new farms seldom had cash. When farmers and land speculators could not pay on loans, the bank had to foreclose[5] on them.

Several western states passed laws against mortgage foreclosures, but still the economy suffered. Manufacturers suffered because as farmers and banks went bankrupt, there was less money to buy manufactured goods. The worst of the crisis passed in 1819, and the economy slowly recovered, but a deep resentment toward "the Monster" persisted in the West and agricultural South.

THE MISSOURI COMPROMISE

The Missouri Compromise of 1820 was the first of many attempts to resolve the issue of the expansion of slavery into new states. The Constitutional Convention had sidestepped the issue of slavery. The Founding Fathers compromised. First, they allowed each slave to be counted as three-fifths of a person in determining a state's population for representation in Congress. Second, they postponed action on the slave trade for twenty years.

> Growing sectional interests are reconciled in the Missouri Compromise of 1820.

During those years slavery was abolished in some northern states, but southern agriculture became more dependent on slave labor. Congress outlawed the slave trade in 1807, but smuggling continued. As settlers moved West, those from the South took their slaves with them. As new states wanted to enter the union, slavery became an issue. Southern leaders wished to keep their number of votes in the Senate equal to that of the northern states.

Slavery had been outlawed in the Northwest Territory under provisions of the Northwest Ordinance of 1787, passed under the Articles of Confederation. This meant that each of the five states created in that area would enter the union without slavery. This set a precedent for the federal government to outlaw slavery in a territory. In 1820 Missouri applied for admission as a state to the union.

The acceptance of slavery in Missouri immediately became an important issue. It had the potential for splitting the nation. A compromise was needed. There was much negotiation in Congress. Henry Clay, with his strong national feelings, led the way in resolving the problem.

Henry Clay became known as the Great Compromiser because during the next thirty years he worked out several compromises between sectional interests that threatened to destroy the union. The Missouri Compromise of 1820 stated:

---

[5] foreclose   *To take mortgaged land when the owner can no longer make payments on the mortgage (loan).*

The United States in 1821 after the Missouri Compromise

1. Maine, separated from Massachusetts, would enter as a free state (state number 23).

2. Missouri would enter as a slave state (state number 24). This kept the balance in the Senate.

3. Slavery would be excluded from the territory of the Louisiana Purchase north of 36°30'.

This solution postponed the resolution of the issue of slavery for another generation.

THE ELECTION OF JOHN QUINCY ADAMS

The Era of Good Feelings had been slowly dissolving as these sectional interests arose. No new party had yet emerged by the 1824 presidential election, but there were several strong individual candidates representing different views within the Republican Party.

Traditionally, members of the party in Congress had nominated the party's presidential candidate. Now, with divisions within the Republican Party, several state legislatures nominated candidates. Tennessee and Pennsylvania nominated Andrew Jackson, the military hero of the Battle of New Orleans. Kentucky nominated Henry Clay, the Great Compromiser. Massachusetts nominated John Quincy Adams, the successful Secretary of State. Congress nominated William H. Crawford.

In the Electoral College voting, Jackson received 99 votes, Adams 84, Crawford 41, and Clay 37. Calhoun received 182 votes as vice president and was elected, but because no one running for president had a majority, the House of Representatives had to pick the next president from the three top candidates. An illness made Crawford's candidacy unimportant, so the race was between Jackson and Adams.

Adams had supported Clay's American System. Clay threw his support to John Quincy Adams, who was elected president to the dismay of Andrew Jackson. Henry Clay was then appointed Secretary of State by Adams. Jackson supporters suggested that a corrupt bargain had been struck, but there is no proof. The supporters of Jackson became known as the Democrats, while Clay's supporters were referred to as National Republicans. Thus, the old Jeffersonian Democratic-Republican Party split, creating two new parties.

ANDREW JACKSON BECOMES PRESIDENT

In the election of 1828, the Democratic candidate was Andrew Jackson. Jackson was nominated for the presidency by the Tennessee legislature in October 1825, three years before the next election. He resigned from the Senate to organize his campaign. Jackson's support came from the South and the West, where he was a war hero and a supporter of the American System of internal improvements. He was also billed as a "common" man, a symbol of the new American—not an aristocrat from an old Virginia or Massachusetts family. Actually, Jackson was wealthy and owned a fine plantation, the Hermitage, in Tennessee, but campaign slogans emphasized other aspects of his background.

In the years prior to 1828, many states had extended the vote to all white males and not just property owners. In the presidential election of 1828, 22 of 24 states allowed the people to vote directly for the electors rather than have them chosen by state legislatures. This move toward greater democracy was reflected in the election of that symbol of the common man—Andrew Jackson.

The election of 1828 was a mudslinging election—the first but not the last in American history. Mrs. Jackson died before Andrew Jackson's inauguration, and it has been suggested her death was in part due to accusations made against her in the

> Andrew Jackson wins the mudslinging election of 1828.

campaign. The country was quite sectionally divided in the election, with the South and West plus New York and Pennsylvania supporting Jackson, and New England supporting Adams.

In his inaugural address Jackson made no reference to what became the major issues of his presidency: the tariff, national unity, internal improvements, and the second Bank of the United States. In the eight years Jackson was president, sectional issues threatened national unity. Through his decisive acts, Jackson emphasized national unity and strengthened the presidency.

To assure that his party's policies would be followed by government agencies, Jackson used the spoils system[6] extensively to place his supporters in government offices, replacing Federalist office holders. This policy was one further manifestation of the growing democratic ideas in the country.

> The spoils system is used by Jackson to assure his policies will be followed by the bureaucracy.

The spoils system is based on the idea that anyone can govern—no experience is necessary in a democratic society where all are equal.

---

[6] spoils system   *The awarding of government jobs or the granting of favors by government officials to political supporters and workers.*

The spoils system was first used by Jefferson, and it remained an important part of American political life until Civil Service Reform at the end of the 19th century. Today, many political leaders use the spoils system as much as the law allows since it permits them to reward their supporters and to get advice from people who think as they do. It assures that their party's policies will be followed.

Jackson also relied on friends, his "Kitchen Cabinet," rather than the cabinet of the heads of government agencies. This policy of relying on personal friends for advice has been followed in varying degrees by all presidents.

THE TARIFF ISSUE, NULLIFICATION, AND NATIONAL UNION

The struggle over the tariff issue began before Jackson became president. In 1828, a tariff raising import rates on many goods was passed. It was quickly dubbed the "Tariff of Abominations" by its southern opponents. The South Carolina legislature adopted resolutions calling the tariff oppressive and issued the *South Carolina Exposition,* written by the vice president of the United States, John C. Calhoun.

In the *South Carolina Exposition,* Calhoun argued the right of nullification by one state. It was the same theory advanced by Thomas Jefferson and James Madison in the Kentucky and Virginia Resolutions of 1798. In 1832, a new tariff reduced some import duties but still maintained the principle of protection, which the South opposed.

A state convention in South Carolina met, nullified the Tariff Acts of 1828 and 1832, and forbade the collection of duties in South Carolina or any appeal of the issue to the Supreme Court. The state threatened to secede if the federal government were to use force. South Carolina issued a call to the other states for a national Constitutional Convention but received no support.

Jackson asked Congress for authority to enforce the tariff laws, which was given in the Force Bill of 1833. Secession and war seemed imminent when Henry Clay introduced in the House of Representatives a compromise tariff. At its passage, South Carolina suspended its nullification decree on the tariffs but nullified the Force Bill, which was, by then, unnecessary.

The crisis over tariffs and possible secession was averted, and national unity was preserved. Jackson was clearly a strong and national president. He had held the South in line, but the issue of secession and nullification would return in the future.

The second major issue of Jackson's presidency involved nationalism and internal improvements. It first took the form of debates in the Senate on the question of the nature of the union. Was it a compact between states or a popular government created by the people? The debate moved to the issue of union versus liberty. Daniel Webster of Massachusetts spoke firmly for the union of the states and made an often quoted statement—"Liberty and Union, now and forever, one and inseparable"—in concluding one of his speeches. Senator Robert Y. Hayne from South Carolina spoke for the southern view and emphasized state sovereignty and liberty over union.

Jackson became involved after these Hayne-Webster debates when he appeared at a dinner honoring Jefferson. In a famous toast Jackson made his position clear, stating, "Our union, it must be preserved." In spite of this nationalistic viewpoint, Jackson vetoed several measures that would have allowed for internal improvements

View of State St., Portsmouth, New Hampshire
This print of the main street of Portsmouth, New Hampshire in the 1830s illustrates the building style, the Greek Revival, that was popular. It went with the Jacksonian period with its emphasis on democracy. Athens in ancient Greece was the first democracy recorded in history, and its temples were built with columns in front as are two of the buildings in this scene. The print also illustrates the condition of the streets, the dress, and the style of transportation. How would the streets be lit at night?
Courtesy: The New Hampshire Historical Society, Concord, New Hampshire

in the states. However, he did support harbor and river improvements paid for by federal funds.

THE END OF THE BANK OF THE UNITED STATES

The third major issue, the rechartering of the Bank of the United States, arose in 1832. The charter was not to expire until 1836, but the head of the bank, Nicholas Biddle, requested a renewal of the charter in 1832 as a political move. The Bank had been quite successful in helping business and controlling the currency, but opposition was widespread. Debtors, again largely in the South and West, opposed the strict monetary policies of the Bank; state banks wanted to have some, or all, of the federal government deposits that went to the Bank of the United States. Many southerners believed the Bank was unconstitutional. Nicholas Biddle's policies of support for business and his strong personality worked to his disadvantage as many viewed him as an arrogant supporter of an elitist minority. Congress voted to recharter the Bank, but Jackson vetoed the measure, and the Senate failed to override the veto.

Jackson's arguments against the Bank reflect a limited understanding of banking, but a strong dislike of monopoly. It is the same American viewpoint that was seen in the colonists' opposition to the English support of the East India Tea Company's monopoly. The Bank became an issue in the election of 1832, which Jackson won easily.

Beginning in 1833 Jackson ordered the government to begin depositing government money in selected state banks that were quickly called "pet banks." These pet banks were not controlled by any regulations, and many loaned the money for speculation. Land speculation, especially, grew dramatically in the next four years.

In 1836, concerned about the situation, Jackson issued the Specie Circular, which required payment for public land to be made in specie. This curtailed land speculation but put a strain on the pet banks and eventually, just as in 1819 when specie was demanded for payment of western lands, led to the second major panic of United States history, the Panic of 1837. Jackson's intentions with the Specie Circular were sound, but there was not enough specie available to keep the entire economy working smoothly.

> The Specie Circular is issued to curtail land speculation in the West, but it leads to the Panic of 1837.

Jackson also supported the removal of the Native-American populations to reserved areas west of the Mississippi. The forced march to the West of the Cherokees from South Carolina has been called "The Trail of Tears," a suitable name for the tragedy it brought. The South gave him strong support for this policy, which opened up large areas of valuable land to white settlement. Jackson ignored Supreme Court decisions favorable to the Native Americans in pursuing this nationalistic policy.

PERSONALITY CONFLICTS AND THE EMERGENCE OF VAN BUREN

During Jackson's presidency there were personality conflicts that provide an interesting background to many of the political decisions. Jackson discovered that Vice President Calhoun, as Secretary of War in 1818, had not supported his attack on the Cherokee Nation. This, combined with Calhoun's views on nullification, led to his resignation as vice president. Jackson's attempts to force Washington society to accept Peggy Eaton, a former barmaid and the second wife of his friend the Secretary of War, ended in a standoff. Cabinet intrigues led to the resignation of all but one cabinet member in 1831. Finally, Martin van Buren of New York emerged as Jackson's closest political ally and logical successor as President.

Following the precedent they had set in 1832, in 1836 the Democrats held a party convention to nominate their candidate for president. The convention nominated Martin Van Buren. Party nominating conventions became the accepted method and are still used today.

> Political parties adopt nominating conventions as the method for choosing presidential candidates.

Opposition to the Democrats was offered by the former National Republicans now loosely grouped as the new Whig Party. The Whigs backed several candidates. The first organized third party in American history, the Masonic Party, also offered opposition.

Van Buren easily won election but no vice presidential candidate won a majority of electoral votes. Following the Constitution, the Senate then voted and elected Richard Johnson vice president.

Key Point to Remember

Sectional differences were balanced by a sense of nationalism during the 1820s and 1830s, and the issues of Andrew Jackson's presidency reflected both of these concerns.

Links from the Past to the Present

1. Use of the spoils system to reward political supporters has been a common practice.
2. Party conventions to nominate presidential candidates evolved to become an established part of American politics.
3. Americans have opposed the formation of monopolies since before the Revolution.
4. The Monroe Doctrine has been a cornerstone of United States foreign policy since 1823 and was invoked often in the early years of the 20th century.

People to Remember

Andrew Jackson   Lawyer and general; commanded United States forces at Battle of New Orleans, 1815, and in attacks on Native Americans; lost presidential election of 1824 in the House of Representatives; seventh president of the United States, 1829–37; vetoed Second Bank of the United States recharter bill and countered South Carolina Tariff nullification, 1832, with show of force.

Dates

1818—Adams-Onis Treaty and Convention of 1818 with Great Britain.

1819—First economic panic.

1820—Missouri Compromise.

1823—Monroe Doctrine.

1828—Jackson elected president.
        "Tariff of Abominations."

1828—South Carolina Exposition.

1832—Tariff of 1832.
        Veto of Bank of the United States.

1833—Force Bill.
        Compromise Tariff.

1836—Specie Circular.

Questions
Identify each of the following:

The American System	Monroe Doctrine
Panic of 1819	John Quincy Adams
Compromise of 1820	Daniel Webster
Era of Good Feelings	*South Carolina Exposition*
Democratic-Republicans	Specie Circular
Second Bank of the United States	"Trail of Tears"

Multiple Choice:

1. The Monroe Doctrine, the cornerstone of United States policy toward Central and South America, stated that
   a. any colonization in the Americas had to be approved by the United States.
   b. the United States was available to fight in European wars.
   c. the Americas had a political system different from Europe.

2. The American System proposed by Henry Clay consisted of
   a. high tariffs and internal transportation improvements paid for by the national government.
   b. roads built for American defense.
   c. high tariffs and subsidies for southern farmers.

3. The Missouri Compromise of 1820 stated that
   a. both Maine and Missouri would enter the union as free states.
   b. slavery would be excluded from land north of 36°30′ in the Louisiana Purchase.
   c. slavery would be excluded in the Northwest Territory.

4. The *South Carolina Exposition,* written by John C. Calhoun,
   a. nullified the Tariffs of 1828 and 1832.
   b. argued the right of nullification by one state.
   c. was declared illegal by the Force Bill of 1833.

III. Nationalism and Territorial Expansion

Van Buren's presidency was hampered by the panic of 1837 and tensions with England. Some of Jackson's pet banks were among the many state banks that failed, and by 1840 the government established an Independent Treasury for the deposit of federal funds. The Democrats would not support another Bank of the United States but accepted this compromise measure, which meant the end of pet banks and their speculation with federal funds. While not as effective as a bank would have been, the Independent Treasury provided adequate control over federal finances. The tensions with England centered on the failure to pay debts, issues of copyright, and the Maine boundary. These led to strong anti-English feelings, but war was avoided in spite of strong provocations in Maine.

One aspect of the growing democratic spirit (see Chapter 6) of the Age of Jackson was the issue of slavery abolition. Congress was receiving many petitions to abolish slavery and the slave trade in Washington, D.C. Debates were heated, and in 1836 southerners in the House led by John Calhoun got the leadership to adopt a rule effectively ending Congressional debate on abolition. This "Gag Rule" was renewed yearly to 1844. Slavery would become the major issue in the 1850s after a decade of westward expansion under Van Buren's successors.

THE NONISSUE ELECTION OF 1840

The Whigs in 1840 nominated William Henry Harrison, a war hero with no political experience, and James Tyler, a states' rights Democrat who had turned against Jackson over the issue of nullification in 1832–33. They easily won in a nonissue campaign based on hype and personality—what may be considered a rather typical presidential campaign of the 19th century. The Whigs chanted "Tippecanoe and Tyler too"—General Harrison had defeated Chief Tecumseh at the Battle of Tippecanoe in 1811. The parties held parades complete with slogans, campaign hats, and torches. They eulogized the log cabin background of Harrison. Van Buren could not overcome the effects of the Panic of 1837 and he lost 234–60 in the Electoral College, winning only 7 of the 26 states.

JAMES TYLER SUCCEEDS TO THE PRESIDENCY

President Harrison died of pneumonia one month after his inauguration, and James Tyler succeeded, the first vice president to do so. Because Tyler had been put on the Whig ticket to gain

> James Tyler, succeeding to the presidency on Harrison's death, frustrates the Whig Party leadership.

southern votes, and because his sentiments were with the Democrats, his four years in office were not productive for the Whigs. They wanted to establish a new Bank of the United States, but President Tyler twice vetoed bills doing so. As a result, the Whig members of his cabinet resigned. Henry Clay, the most prominent Whig, resigned from the House of Representatives to prepare his campaign for the presidency in 1844. The most important achievement of Tyler's presidency was the signing of the Webster-Ashburton Treaty with Great Britain, which finally set the United States-Canada border from Maine to Lake of the Woods in Minnesota.

SUFFRAGE IN RHODE ISLAND

An incident in Rhode Island may be the most interesting development of Tyler's presidency. The Constitution of Rhode Island was the charter that had been issued by King Charles II in 1663. The charter greatly restricted the suffrage[7]. In 1842 those who were disqualified from voting wrote a new charter, or state constitution, and put it into operation. This gave the state two functioning governments, and the new government included the right to universal male suffrage.

Tyler was prepared to use federal troops to support the old government because of Article IV, Section 4 of the Constitution, which upheld the validity of charters. The new government collapsed, but in 1843 a new state constitution was written extending the suffrage as was being done in many states.

The incident illustrates Tyler's strict construction of the Constitution even if it went against the program, in this case the extension of the suffrage to all males, supported by the Democratic Party.

[7]suffrage *The right to vote.*

THE FIRST DARK HORSE CANDIDACY

The election of 1844 was a contest between the Whigs, who nominated Henry Clay, and the Democrats, who nominated James K. Polk, the first "dark horse"[8] in our political history. A third party, the Liberty Party, carried enough votes in New York to deny the state to Henry Clay, and Polk became President. All three parties used party nominating conventions to pick their candidates, and they thus became an established part of American political life.

The main domestic goal of President Polk and the Democrats was to reestablish the Independent Treasury system, which had been repealed by the Whigs. It was achieved in 1846. They campaigned heavily on foreign policy issues calling for the annexation of Texas and a claim to all of the Oregon Territory, which they phrased as "54°40′ or fight." 54°40′ was the northern boundary of the Oregon Territory, which was jointly administered with Great Britain.

POLK'S FOREIGN POLICY

President Polk's major contribution to history is in the international arena. Under his administration we fought a war with Mexico, and we settled a dispute with England over control of the Oregon Territory. These two events completed, except for the small Gadsden Purchase the United States made from Mexico in 1853, the acquisition of the adjacent territories that make up the 48 connected or lower states.

> Polk embodies the concept of Manifest Destiny as he settles the Oregon boundary dispute and fights a war with Mexico.

MANIFEST DESTINY

The steps leading to the Oregon settlement and the War with Mexico are complex. They illustrate the concept of Manifest Destiny. The term *Manifest Destiny* was first used in an editorial stating that foreign nations were blocking the annexation of the Republic of Texas by the United States to stop "the fulfillment of our manifest destiny to overspread the continent allotted by providence for the free development of our... millions (of inhabitants)." This statement provides an illustration of American nationalism and the feeling that the United States was a "chosen" nation with a particular destiny to fulfill. This is the essence of Manifest Destiny.

President Polk in his first message to Congress enlarged the Monroe Doctrine by stating that the people of the Americas had the right to decide their own destiny, and European powers could not block the union of the United States with any independent state on the American continent. This was a response to the situation that had developed in Texas in the 1830s.

[8]dark horse   *A candidate for political office, particularly the presidency, who was not considered a likely candidate for the office, and therefore the nomination is a surprise to many people.*

THE UNITED STATES IN TEXAS

United States involvement in Texas, then a part of Mexico, began in 1821 when Stephen F. Austin took possession of land grants made to his father by the government of Mexico. In the following years, more Americans settled in Texas. A new Mexican government in 1830 restricted American immigration and outlawed slavery in Texas. Six years of tension, attempted negotiation, and government instability in Mexico led to war in 1836 between the American settlers and the Mexican government. After losing the Battle of the Alamo in San Antonio, the settlers won a victory and achieved recognition as an independent, sovereign nation. President Jackson finally recognized the independence of Texas. Her formal petition for annexation by the United States was rejected by the Senate in 1837 because anti-slavery members of Congress objected. Negotiations, which included the threat by Texans that they would ally with England and France, went on for several years.

John C. Calhoun, Secretary of State in President Tyler's cabinet, finally negotiated a treaty of annexation with the Republic of Texas, but the Senate rejected it also. Northern abolitionists[9] saw the possible annexation of Texas as a plot to extend slavery. Southerners saw it as an area of economic opportunity and feared English influence on an independent Texas.

In signing the treaty, Tyler had promised to send federal troops to defend Texas from a possible attack from Mexico. In spite of the Senate's rejection of the treaty, troops and ships were moved to defend Texas from possible attack by Mexico. This issue of the annexation of Texas as well as the Oregon boundary dispute became major issues in the election of 1844.

After the election of Polk in 1844, Tyler asked Congress to accept the Texas treaty by a joint resolution of both houses. This would require only a majority, and not the two-thirds vote required by the Constitution for the ratification of treaties. This

> Congress accepts Texas as a state, and this leads to war with Mexico.

ploy to get around the Constitution was successful. By this treaty, Texas became a state without going through a period as a territory. The slavery issue was addressed by extending the Missouri Compromise line of 36°30′ thus allowing slavery in Texas.

Polk in his inaugural address said the issue of the annexation of Texas was between Texas and the United States alone and did not involve other nations. Mexico disagreed and broke off diplomatic relations, claiming Texas was Mexican territory. There were other issues of dispute with Mexico, such as Mexico's desire to stop United States immigration into their territory of California. President Polk sent John Slidell to Mexico to negotiate, but negotiations stalled, and the Mexican government was overthrown in a coup d'état[10].

Independent Texas and Mexico had not agreed on the southern border of Texas, with Texas claiming the Rio Grande as the border and Mexico the Rio Nueces, farther north. With negotiations at a standstill, troops were moved into this disputed territory on the Mexican-Texas border. No resolution of the border dispute was in

[9] abolitionists   *Before the American Civil War, one who believed in the abolition or ending of slavery.*
[10] coup d'état   *A sudden forceful overthrow of a government.*

sight. President Polk asked for a declaration of war, which Congress voted on May 13, 1846. Many voted against this war, which lasted for two years.

THE MEXICAN WAR

The Mexican War (1846–48) was fought in several areas: first, in California, where United States settlers gained control of the area with aid from Captain John Charles Fremont of the United States Army and Commodore Robert Stockton of the United States Navy; second, in the New Mexico territory, where a United States expedition occupied Las Vegas, Taos, and Santa Fe, securing this large area for the United States; third, in Mexico, which United States forces invaded, capturing Monterrey, seizing the port of Vera Cruz, and finally capturing the capital, Mexico City, in September 1847. The war was then quickly brought to a successful military conclusion. Several famous generals of the Civil War, including Robert E. Lee, gained experience in these various campaigns.

While the fighting was progressing, Congress fought over war aims. The Wilmot Proviso, an attempt by Whigs to exclude slavery from the conquered territory, was defeated but focused attention on the issue of the expansion of slavery to new territories. John C. Calhoun led the Southern opposition to any restriction on slavery in the territory.

Polk began secret negotiations to end the war, which led to the Treaty of Guadalupe Hidalgo. By its terms the United States acquired Texas as far south as the Rio Grande River, the territory of California, and the New Mexico territory, which included present New Mexico and parts of Arizona, Utah, Colorado, and Nevada. The United States agreed to pay Mexico $15,000,000 and to pay the claims of all United States' citizens against the government. Some opposed the treaty because they wished to annex all of Mexico; others opposed it on the slavery issue. However, the treaty was accepted by the Senate in March 1848, adding the last great block of territory to the continental United States, thus achieving—in some people's eyes—another step in our Manifest Destiny.

> The United States expands its territory in the Treaty of Guadalupe Hidalgo.

SETTLEMENT OF THE OREGON BOUNDARY

While the Mexican War was starting, a peaceful solution to the Oregon boundary dispute was achieved through negotiation with England. While the compromise did not satisfy the expansionists and forced Polk to reject his party's campaign slogan of "54°40′ or fight," it avoided war with Britain. The Oregon Territory was divided at the 49th parallel, which was the border between the United States and Canada from Lake of the Woods to the Oregon border. England got all of Vancouver Island. With the Senate's approval, the territory, later divided into the states of Washington, Oregon, and Idaho, was added to the United States, which now stretched from coast to coast. According to American nationalists, this was the Manifest Destiny of the United States, and for many the culmination of God's plan for the nation.

The agreement helped persuade England to remain on the sidelines during the Mexican War in spite of her earlier support for an independent Texas. It also illustrates the benefits from negotiation and treaty making in international affairs, as one can thus gain the support of nations in time of need. England's action was also a sign of the importance to both nations of the United States-English trade relationship, which had been growing since independence.

SLAVERY IN THE TERRITORIES

With the acquisition of new territory, the question of slavery in the territories became a crucial issue for the nation. The question was very complex. At its core was disagreement over whether Congress could outlaw slavery in the territories or whether the inhabitants should have control of the matter. This latter view was dubbed popular sovereignty or "squatter"[11] sovereignty.

The question of slavery had been a potentially divisive issue from the time of the Constitutional Convention. After much debate the Oregon Territory was organized, and slavery was outlawed. President Polk signed this bill, stating it upheld the Missouri Compromise line of 36°30′ because Oregon was north of that line. After the Treaty of Guadalupe Hidalgo was signed, President Polk tried to get both California and New Mexico organized as territories, but his proposals failed because of the slavery issue (both territories were below the 36°30′ of the Missouri Compromise).

President Polk had said he would serve a single term. In the election of 1848 the Whig candidates, General Zachary Taylor, hero of the Battle of Buena Vista in the Mexican War, for president, and Millard Fillmore of New York for vice president, defeated the Democratic candidates. Slavery was a major issue of the campaign. A new third party, the Free Soil Party, which opposed popular sovereignty on the slavery issue, was the deciding factor because it took votes away from the Democrats. President Taylor died in office in 1850, the second president in ten years to do so. Millard Fillmore became the 13th president.

THE COMPROMISE OF 1850

Congress was badly split on the issue of slavery in the territories. In 1849 when California applied for admission as a state, there were fifteen slave and fifteen free states in the union. The population of California had grown rapidly as a result of the discovery of gold in 1849, which started a great "Gold Rush" to California. The territory moved quickly toward statehood. Californians organized a state government and wrote a constitution outlawing slavery.

The growing controversy over slavery alarmed both moderates and conservatives in Congress. Henry Clay again stepped forward with a compromise solution, which quieted matters briefly but proved to be the last compromise before the slavery issue tore the nation apart in the Civil War. Clay's compromise included five acts,

> The Compromise of 1850 provides something for each sectional interest.

---

[11] squatter *A term used to describe settlers in new territories who moved on to the land. It has a negative connotation that they are there temporarily and are not solid citizens of the territory.*

and the five together are known as the Compromise of 1850. The Compromise had something for each sectional interest:

1. California entered as a free state.

2. New Mexico was organized as a territory with no mention of whether it would be slave or free. But it was understood that popular sovereignty would prevail when the territory applied for admission.

3. The organization of Utah as a territory was approved, and it would enter free or slave as determined by its written constitution.

4. The prohibition of the slave trade in Washington, D.C., and the noninterference by Congress with slavery in Washington, D.C., was established.

5. A strong Fugitive Slave Law, which called for the return of run away slaves to their owners at federal government expense, was passed.

The union was saved, but many Northerners were prepared to hinder the enforcement of the Fugitive Slave Law. It was a compromise all could accept for the moment because it had something for each interest.

SUMMARY

National and sectional issues maintained an uneasy balance between 1801 and 1850. While there were many sectional issues dividing the nation, there were always compromises that preserved the union, and the nation grew in strength and national spirit. Many saw the expansion of the nation to the Pacific Ocean as the working out of the nation's Manifest Destiny as planned by a Providence that had chosen the United States to be great. This spirit of Manifest Destiny allowed the nation to prosper and avoid being torn apart by its sectional interests.

Key Point to Remember

The Oregon settlement and the Mexican War illustrate the concept of Manifest Destiny or the idea that "Providence" or God has "chosen" your nation to fulfill a particular role in history.

Links from the Past to the Present

1. Whole political campaigns, from local to presidential, have been based on hype and personality, though this is regularly deplored by historians and the press.

2. The benefits of compromise and negotiation in international affairs can be found in our history from the Oregon dispute to disarmament treaties.

People to Remember

Henry Clay   Senator from Kentucky; coleader of the "War Hawks" in 1812; became known as the Great Compromiser because of his work on the Compromises of 1820 and 1850 and the Compromise Tariff of 1833; ran unsuccessfully for president in 1824, 1832, and 1844.

John C. Calhoun   Senator from South Carolina; coleader of the War Hawks in 1812; vice president under John Quincy Adams and Andrew Jackson until he resigned in 1832; author of *South Carolina Exposition* explaining nullification and states rights; strong supporter of southern rights in his later years.

Daniel Webster   Congressman, senator from Massachusetts, lawyer, noted orator, Secretary of State; won fame in winning the Dartmouth College and *McCulloch* v. *Maryland* cases before the Supreme Court; noted for his Congressional speeches supporting federalism and the Union; opposed Mexican War; supported Henry Clay in Compromise of 1850; negotiated Webster-Ashburton Treaty settling U.S.–Canada border.

James K. Polk   Lawyer, congressman, governor of Tennessee, 11th president of the United States; leading Jacksonian Democrat, the first "dark horse" presidential candidate; nominated for president when 1844 Democratic Convention deadlocked; hardworking, achieved his four stated goals as president—tariff reduction, reestablish Independent Treasury System, settle Oregon boundary, acquire California; waged the Mexican War after the annexation of Texas by the United States provoked the Mexicans.

Dates

1836—Battle of the Alamo.
     Independent Texas.

1844—James K. Polk elected president.
     Texas annexed.

1846—Oregon Boundary Settlement.

1846–48—Mexican War.

1848—Treaty of Guadalupe Hidalgo ended Mexican War.

1849—California Gold Rush.

1850—Compromise of 1850.

Questions
Identify each of the following:

"54°40′ or fight"   James K. Polk
The Battle of the Alamo   Martin Van Buren
Treaty of Guadalupe Hidalgo   James Tyler
The Gag Rule   Millard Fillmore

Multiple Choice:

1. Popular or "squatter" sovereignty meant
   a. the people in a territory had to follow the Missouri Compromise.
   b. squatters who just arrived could decide what were the most popular political issues.
   c. those living in a territory could vote on whether to have slaves when the territory became a state.

2. The Compromise of 1850 consisted of five bills that included the provision that
   a. California entered the union as a slave state.
   b. a strong fugitive slave law.
   c. New Mexico and Utah were organized as free territories to enter the union later as free states.

3. The Webster-Ashburton Treaty finally set the United States-Canada border
   a. from Maine to Lake of the Woods in Minnesota.
   b. in Oregon and Washington.
   c. in Idaho.

Open-ended, Analysis Questions

The following questions require analysis and reflection. You are encouraged to bring to your answer information and ideas from many sources. The answers should be presented in composition or essay style, but they may be used to initiate discussion. The questions put you in the role of the historian, gathering information to support your personal perspective on the question.

1. Pick three of the following events and briefly explain how each of the three can be used to illustrate the concept of the "Manifest Destiny" of the United States.
   a. Louisiana Purchase
   b. Defeat of Tecumseh
   c. Monroe Doctrine
   d. Mexican War
   e. Oregon Boundary Dispute

2. To what extent were the causes of the Mexican War and the War of 1812 similar? Illustrate your answer with specific examples. *(Note: Essay questions can often be worded to ask for one perspective in the answer—in this case similarities. In spite of the wording, the best answer will include other perspectives. In this question, the differences between the causes of the two wars seem more obvious and important than the similarities. This may be noted in the answer and some differences mentioned.)*

3. Which president—Andrew Jackson, Thomas Jefferson, or James K. Polk— appears to have been most nationalistic during his presidency? Explain your view using specific illustrations. *(Note: Be sure to include in your answer your understanding or definition of the word* nationalistic. *Make a habit of defining key terms in your answers.)*

A Growing Nation–
Social Change:
1800–1860

APPROACHES TO HISTORY

LAW AND SOCIETY

All people need rules guiding behavior in order to function effectively. Without such rules, individuals who wish to change society or even rebellious individuals cannot function effectively since they cannot know what to rebel against. This can be illustrated in home life where certain guidelines or unwritten laws are followed—who does the dishes, what can be eaten in the refrigerator, what TV may be watched, who makes financial decisions. These guidelines are usually established by the adults based on their beliefs and assumptions about life, but in some families all members contribute to the creation of the rules. Sometimes we don't like the rules and don't obey. Then judgments are made and decisions, including punishment, are handed out.

A nation operates the same way. So far in the text we have mentioned several laws—which are the same as rules—that were passed by Congress. In regard to the tariffs of 1828 and 1832, one state (South Carolina) objected and announced it would disobey the law by nullifying it. The federal government judged the situation and forced South Carolina to obey the tariff laws.

In the United States during the years from 1800 to 1850, just as today, there were many laws and situations to which people objected. Their recourse was to go to the courts and ultimately to the Supreme Court for judgment and decision on the meaning of the law. The decisions of the Supreme Court in these cases shaped the future of the United States, just as the decisions of the Court do today. It is important to understand what the Supreme Court said in several crucial cases during these early years because those decisions have provided the rules by which the nation has operated since then.

In some situations it was impossible then, just as it is now, to develop a legal case around a desired change. Objectors often form organizations to work for reform of accepted rules and patterns of behavior. Many reform groups over the years have achieved success. The growing diversity in American life has supported many movements for change in behavior and ultimately the law. The laws of a nation are based upon the nation's core beliefs that include a society's attitudes toward and treatment of others. Some historians view history as an interplay between these three factors— law, changing core beliefs, and reform. In the United States in the 1830s and 1840s these three factors—law, beliefs, religion—interacted in a forceful and meaningful way. The results of this interplay have been referred to as Jacksonian Democracy, a major period of change and reform in United States history. It is merely one such period that the historian of social change emphasizes in seeking an understanding of history.

I. Early Supreme Court Decisions

As one of his last acts as president, John Adams appointed and the Senate confirmed John Marshall as Chief Justice of the United States Supreme Court. John Marshall was a Virginia Federalist, a wise lawyer and politician who followed the Hamiltonian view of government. As Chief Justice between 1800 and 1835, the Court he led handed down decisions that strengthened the federal government and the business community. The latter decisions helped develop the American economy and supported the capitalist system.

> Chief Justice John Marshall upholds the Federalist viewpoint.

Even when the presidents were Jeffersonian Republicans or Jacksonian Democrats, the Court supported the Federalist position under Marshall's strong leadership. This fact clearly illustrates the power of the Supreme Court and explains why there has been such controversy over the appointment of judges to the Supreme Court in recent years.

"THE SUPREME LAW OF THE LAND"—*MARBURY V. MADISON*

The Constitution stated it would be "the supreme law of the land," but it did not clarify just how this would be enforced if a law passed by Congress or a state was contrary to the Constitution. There had developed a tradition in the Colonies and in England of courts making such determinations, but this concept of judicial review[1]

[1]judicial review   *The power of a court to accept appeals concerning laws passed by the legislature, actions of the executive, or decisions by lower judicial courts with the possibility of modifying or nullifying such laws, actions, or decisions because they are unconstitutional.*

was not written into the Constitution. Marshall, in the case of *Marbury* v. *Madison* in 1803, decided the case in a way that gave the Supreme Court the power to review and declare unconstitutional laws passed by Congress.

The case involved Marbury, who had been appointed Justice of the Peace by President Adams just before Adams left office. President Jefferson's Secretary of State, James Madison, refused to give Marbury his commission, and Marbury asked the Supreme Court to issue a Writ of Mandamus[2] that would force Madison to give Marbury the commission.

While Marshall's sympathies may have been with the Federalist Marbury, as a wise politician he realized that the court could not force Madison to act. He therefore looked at the Judiciary Act of 1789, which gave the Supreme Court the power to issue writs, and at the Constitution, which in no place gave the court that power. He and the Supreme Court decided the Judiciary Act of 1789 contradicted the Constitution, the "supreme law of the land," when it gave the Supreme Court the power to issue Writs of Mandamus. The Supreme Court decided, therefore, it could not issue the writ requested by Marbury.

Thus Marbury lost his case and did not become a Justice of the Peace, but John Marshall took upon the court the power of judicial review over laws passed by Congress—a great power for the court and a great tool for supporting national unity. There were many objections to the decision, but it has stood throughout our history to give the court this power of judicial review.

OBLIGATION OF CONTRACT

In 1810 in the case of *Fletcher* v. *Peck,* the court invalidated a Georgia state law as contrary to the United States Constitution. The Georgia legislature in 1795 had been bribed into granting a contract to land speculators. At a later session of the state legislature, the contract was revoked. The Supreme Court held this was a violation of the Constitution's clause upholding the "obligation of contract" (Article 1, Section 10). Even though the original contract had been obtained by bribes, it was valid as law. The Supreme Court declared it could not investigate the motives or methods of the legislature in passing the law. It only could read what the law said. The *Fletcher* v. *Peck* decision was the first in which the Supreme Court declared a state law unconstitutional. It also gave the business community support by assuring them the court would uphold contracts made with state governments.

In the Dartmouth College Case in 1819, the Court extended the *Fletcher* v. *Peck* concept to private contracts. Dartmouth College had been established by a royal charter (contract) by King George III. The New Hampshire legislature passed a law making Dartmouth a state institution with a new charter and a new Board of Trustees. The original trustees sued the state, whose Supreme Court upheld the state law. The trustees then

> The Dartmouth College Case decision states private contracts are protected by the Constitution.

---

[2]Writ of Mandamus   *Written orders (writs) handed down by a court ordering a public official or lower court to do a specific task.*

appealed[3] to the United States Supreme Court. Marshall and the Court held that the state law violated the original contract and was invalid. The original charter was honored.

Private contracts thus were understood to be under the protection of the Constitution and outside the control of the states. This encouraged business growth since businesses could count on the court to uphold contracts they made.

In 1837 the court under the new Chief Justice, Roger B. Taney, modified this position slightly in the *Charles River Bridge* v. *Warren Bridge* case. The Charles River Bridge Company chartered by Massachusetts sued the Warren Bridge Company, claiming the latter broke the Charles River Bridge Company's right to exclusive bridge building over the Charles River in Boston. This point was not specifically in the contract, and Taney held that ambiguous clauses in the contract must be interpreted to benefit the people of the state. This idea of the state representing the public's interest in business contracts made possible later legislation controlling business in the public interest.

THE COMMERCE CLAUSE: *GIBBONS* V. *OGDEN*

Another decision of Chief Justice Marshall interpreted the commerce clause of the Constitution very broadly. New York had given a monopoly to Robert Fulton to operate steamboats on New York waters. Thomas Gibbons had received a federal

> In *Gibbons* v. *Ogden* Congress's power over commerce is clarified.

license to operate a boat from New York to New Jersey across the Hudson River. Fulton's successor, Aaron Ogden, sued Gibbons for violating his monopoly of transport on New York waters. In his decision in the *Gibbons* v. *Ogden* case, Marshall defined commerce as including "every species (type) of commercial intercourse" including navigation. He declared the federal government's power over interstate and foreign commerce did not stop at state borders and took precedence over state control of commerce within their borders. States could control intrastate commerce, that is, commerce strictly within the state, but Congress had an overarching control so Gibbon's federal license prevailed over the state monopoly.

The case thus strengthened Congress' power over commerce and added to the power of the federal government. At the time of the *Gibbons* v. *Ogden* decision in 1824, internal improvements in transportation were a major political issue. While the president vetoed national transportation measures, Marshall held the states could not monopolize the building of the system.

LOOSE CONSTRUCTION: *McCULLOCH* V. *MARYLAND*

Marshall's strongest statement of the Federalist position came in the 1819 case of *McCulloch* v. *Maryland.* He used Hamilton's "loose construction" argument to uphold the constitutionality of the Second Bank of the United States, claiming that while limited in its powers by the Constitution, the federal government is supreme in its designated areas and must have the powers needed to carry out its work. The

[3]appeal *A process in which a case is moved from a lower to a higher court for reexamination or review.*

decision said, "Let the end be legitimate, let it be within the scope of the Constitution, and all means [are constitutional which] are appropriate, [and] which are plainly adapted to that end and which are not prohibited. . . . " The case involved a Maryland law taxing the Bank of the United States. The Bank refused to pay the tax, and the state sued McCulloch, a branch cashier.

> Marshall supports Hamilton's idea of loose construction in *McCulloch* v. *Maryland.*

The issues of the case as Marshall saw them were, "Was the bank constitutional?" "Was the tax legal?" Having declared the bank constitutional in the argument quoted above, Marshall declared the tax illegal since "taxing involves the power to destroy" and no state had the right to destroy a legitimate federal institution. This strong statement of the loose construction theory antagonized many people, and controversy followed.

Throughout its history the Court has not always followed Marshall's position, but the case of *McCulloch* v. *Maryland* stands as a precedent for those who wish to expand the power of the federal government. The Marshall Court by 1835 had established rules that still guide our nation. Many people objected at the time, and some still object to the exercise of judicial review by the Court and to its power over commerce and contracts. However, the interpretation of the constitution made by the Marshall Court gave a strong foundation to the nation. Later Supreme Court decisions also greatly affected our nation.

Key Point to Remember

Supreme Court decisions under Chief Justice John Marshall strengthened the power of the federal government and supported the growth of American business.

People to Remember

John Marshall   Virginia lawyer, member of the Virginia Assembly, Federalist congressman, secretary of state under President Adams and Chief Justice of the Supreme Court for 34 years; wrote most of the Court's decisions, many of which gave greater power to the federal government, especially the Supreme Court, and to business.

Links from the Past to the Present

1. Supreme Court decisions interpret the Constitution and thus are of crucial importance to Americans.
2. The Supreme Court's power of judicial review has been exercised to both extend and limit the power of federal, state, and local governments.

Dates

1803—*Marbury* v. *Madison.*

1810—*Fletcher* v. *Peck.*

1819—Dartmouth College Case.
      McCulloch v. *Maryland.*

1824—*Gibbons* v. *Ogden.*

1837—*Charles River Bridge* v. *Warren Bridge.*

Questions
Identify each of the following:

Judicial Review   *Marbury* v. *Madison*
Supreme Law of the Land   *Fletcher* v. *Peck*
McCulloch v. *Maryland*   Dartmouth College Case

Multiple Choice:

1. Although there was a tradition of judicial review in the colonies and in England,
   a. it was not accepted by Congress.
   b. it was not written into the Constitution.
   c. Chief Justice Marshall did not support the idea.

2. The case of *Marbury* v. *Madison* illustrates that a new interpretation of the law can be established even if the defendant
   a. loses the case.
   b. is found guilty but not punished.
   c. has no valid argument.

3. *McCulloch* v. *Maryland* stands as a precedent for those who support
   a. strict construction.
   b. no judicial review.
   c. expansion of the power of the federal government.

II. Religion and Reform: 1800–1850

Religion, like laws and judges, provides individuals with rules or guidelines for behavior. Religion has played an important role in this country since the arrival of the Puritans in New England. Although the First Amendment of the Bill of Rights required the separation of church and state, religion has, in both our personal and public lives, continued to provide guidelines for conduct.

> In spite of the First Amendment, religion plays an important role in the United States.

Often these have provided the stimulus for very positive, creative, and beneficial acts. At other times, when one religious denomination or group has tried to enforce its viewpoint on others or when a group of Americans have reacted with intolerance to the views of a religious group, the result has been very negative, creating dissension and division. We see such a division in the United States today in the controversy over gay rights, which is partly rooted in different religious viewpoints. Both the positive and negative influence of religious attitudes are reflected in United States history.

THE FIRST GREAT AWAKENING

We have mentioned 17th-century Puritanism and its continued importance in New England. In the 1740s there was a major revival of religious concerns in New Jersey and Pennsylvania, which spread throughout the Colonies and is known as the Great

Henry Joseph Adams Family, 1846
This Daguerreotype family portrait is an early example of what became the art of photography. No longer was it necessary to rely on an artist's interpretation of what one looked like. It also illustrates the clothing style of the period.
Courtesy: Library of Congress

Awakening. Stimulated by preachers from England, ministers emphasized personal revelation and the reading of the Bible. The Methodist church, founded in England, was brought to America as part of this first Great Awakening. One of the longest lasting results of the Great Awakening was the founding of several colleges such as Princeton, the University of Pennsylvania, Columbia, Brown, and Rutgers—all for the training of ministers.

The Great Awakening of the 1740s was the first of many such religious revivals that emphasize one's ability to be "born again" to God's way.

This Great Awakening was only the first of several periods of revivals in American history, all of which had a major impact on the nation. Each period of revival has emphasized the individual's personal relationship to God, thus reinforcing

American individualism. Revival religion has emphasized that no one's fate is predetermined, as some religious teachings suggest, but instead, that by changing yourself or being "born again" to God's ways, you can determine your own fate and be saved. This has given a great sense of security and of mission to those who have been "saved" or "born again" as Christians.

This sense of mission played a very important role in United States' history in the 1820s and 1830s, leading to many reform movements. Revival religion also had an element of fundamentalism, holding that the Bible contains the specific words of God and must be followed. This in turn has put an emphasis on education and the ability to read the Bible.

THE SECOND GREAT AWAKENING

A second Great Awakening began in western New York State in 1821 when Charles G. Finney had a religious conversion. His preaching emphasized revival religion and that Christians by making the right choices could find salvation.

His preachings and those of his followers had particular appeal to women on the frontier, where women's lives were often isolated, and in urban centers. They enjoyed the community activity of meetings with visiting preachers, going to church, and participating in church-sponsored activities out of the home. They appreciated the message of individualism and redemption.

> Revival religion of the Second Great Awakening provides impetus to many reform movements.

The Great Awakening's impact, however, was not just on women. New religious groups such as the Latter Day Saints, commonly called the Mormons, founded in 1830, grew out of the atmosphere created by the Second Great Awakening. The message of revival religion—individualism, a community of chosen people, the potential worth of each individual in God's eyes—reinforced the growing democratic attitudes of Americans. It gave support to and provided a base for many of the reform movements that developed in the 1830s and 1840s. These reforms are often lumped together under the phrase "Jacksonian Democracy." The Second Great Awakening also reinforced the concept of Manifest Destiny.

REFORMS IN EDUCATION

> Education is seen as a way to attack problems of poverty and crime.

The reform aspects of Jacksonian Democracy that probably most affect you, the student, are those that took place in education. Horace Mann, who served as secretary of the newly created Massachusetts Board of Education from 1837 to 1848, is considered the leader of the movement for educational reform. He established the first minimum school year requirement: six months of school. He saw the first training college for teachers established and fifty new high schools built in the state. Curriculum changes instituted by Horace Mann included less emphasis on religion and more on "useful skills" and on making the students into good citizens. This latter included the teaching of American history and you, as you read this work, are following in that line.

Mann and his fellow education reformers of the pre–Civil War era were convinced that education was the best way to attack problems of poverty and crime. It was an optimistic message, reflecting the optimism of revival religion. Connecticut soon followed Massachusetts in instituting educational reforms, and in the years following these reforms spread around the nation.

Some of these reforms were directed at the education of women. In 1821 the first women's high school in the nation was opened in Troy, New York, by Emma Willard. Oberlin College in Ohio became the first coed college in the country in 1833, and Mount Holyoke, the first women's college, was established in Mount Holyoke, Massachusetts, in 1836.

Another related area of reform was work done to improve conditions in insane asylums and to educate the public as to the causes of insanity. Dorothea Dix was a leader of this movement—another aspect of what came to be known as the period of Jacksonian Democracy.

SUFFRAGE

It was also during these years of reform that the suffrage was greatly extended so that by the time of Jackson's election to a second term in 1832 most white males were able to vote. Over the years the separate states lowered or abolished their property (or wealth) requirements for voting. Free African-Americans could vote in some states, but there was no discussion of voting rights for slaves, and very little discussion of voting rights for women until after the Seneca Falls Convention. Even then it took seventy years for a Constitutional amendment to pass giving the vote to women. The extension of the vote to all white males helped make the election of Jackson possible and reinforced the idea of equality upon which Jacksonian Democracy was based and which was reinforced by the Great Awakening.

THE WOMEN'S MOVEMENT

Another reform that may seem very contemporary centered on feminism. Its roots were complex and include women's involvement in the Second Great Awakening. Women's leadership roles in reform efforts such as temperance and abolition and their growing role in the workforce helped train leaders for these reform efforts. A growing realization that the legal status of women was demeaning, since many state laws gave wives no individual rights over money or property and denied them the vote, provided a catalyst for the pre-Civil War feminist movement.

Among the early organizers of the movement were two sisters, Angelina and Sarah Grimke, who began lecturing against slavery but came to realize the status of women was not greatly different from that of slaves. The movement was not as successful as other reforms of the Jacksonian period. Few men joined or supported the women's movement.

An important meeting at Seneca Falls, New York, in 1848 issued a proclamation modeled on the Declaration of Independence listing women's grievances and calling for action. The Seneca Falls Convention was led by Elizabeth Cady Stanton and Lucretia Mott, who became the leaders of the movement for women's rights. In the years after 1850, the women's movement focused more and more on gaining the vote for women, believing this to be the first step toward gaining equal rights. Susan

B. Anthony, who began her career as a teacher, became a leader of the temperance movement in New York State and later focused her attention on the Women's Suffrage and National American Women Suffrage Associations. Her name is always linked to the movement that won the right to vote for women. However, after 1850, the nation as a whole became more and more focused on another immediate reform movement: abolition.

ABOLITION

While throughout United States history some individuals and groups such as Quakers had expressed opposition to slavery and the first state, Pennsylvania, to abolish slavery did so in 1780, the movement for total abolition of slavery in the United States did not gain momentum until the 1830s. The American Colonization Society, formed in 1816, had as its goal the resettlement of freed slaves in Africa. Free African-Americans in the North worked for immediate abolition. A few whites worked for gradual abolition.

Then, in 1831, matters changed with the publication of the *Liberator* by William Lloyd Garrison. He had been a gradualist, but in the *Liberator* called for "immediate and complete emancipation" of slaves. Garrison's leadership, the moral and ethical climate established by the Second Great Awakening, and the political and economic ramifications of the possible spread of slavery into the western territories, such as Louisiana, and later, Texas, California, and the New Mexico territory, combined to create strong support for the abolitionists. Harriet Tubman, known for her efforts on the Underground Railway[4], and Frederick Douglass, a self-educated, articulate former slave, were outstanding African-American leaders of the abolition movement.

Feeling threatened by abolitionist publications, southern states seized the literature and attacked abolitionists, actions many northerners saw as a threat to individual civil rights. Slave owners also felt threatened by possible slave insurrections stirred up by the abolitionists. Throughout the period of slavery, there were insurrections or rebellions organized by slaves. One of the most significant was led by Nat Turner, an African-American preacher, in Virginia in August 1831. Over 50 whites were murdered, and over 100 African-Americans were killed in hunting down the leaders. Nat Turner was tried and executed along with his coleaders. In Virginia a debate was held on the future of slavery. The idea of emancipation lost narrowly. From then on the South was committed to maintaining the institution of slavery. Slave codes restricting slave rights were tightened, and laws were passed curbing owners' rights to emancipation.

In Congress the Gag Rule was passed in 1837. It blocked the petitions of abolitionists to Congress and cut out debate in Congress on the issue of slavery.

At first, the abolitionists were not united in their programs, but the activities of the proslavery forces, particularly in calling for the return of escaped slaves, slowly brought them together. The Compromise of 1850 attempted to reconcile the political differences between pro- and antislavery forces. It could not last, as the abolitionist forces became more united in the 1850s. They saw the political developments of the

[4]Underground Railway   *An escape route for slaves organized by abolitionists so slaves could travel North, often to Canada, by night and be hidden by day.*

decade (see Chapter 7) as a threat to individual rights and a move to force on the nation the extension of slavery. Their attacks, based on moral and ethical objections, made the abolition of slavery a major political issue of the 1850s. For the abolitionists there could be no compromise with slavery, which was immoral, against their religious principles, and in opposition to their understanding of the American ideals expressed in the Declaration of Independence and Bill of Rights.

TEMPERANCE

Temperance, the reform movement aimed at the banning of alcohol, also had a strong moral and ethical base. The consumption of alcohol was widespread in America. Frontiersmen drank in saloons, city dwellers in public houses, and "respectable" women drank alcohol-based patent medicine at home. Drinking crossed class lines. Revivalist preachers and their followers viewed it as the destroyer of family life. Factory owners saw it as the destroyer of good work habits. Christians saw it as an attack on the holy Sabbath as bars and taverns were open for business on the working man's one day off.

These elements combined to create a movement against alcohol consumption. At first, workers for temperance urged individuals to abstain, but as the movement grew, prohibition of both the sale and manufacture of alcohol became their goal. Under the pressure of temperance groups, alcoholic use dropped dramatically, and in 1846 Maine passed the first state prohibition law.

> The temperance movement gains support from different groups and achieves success when Maine passes a prohibition law.

Temperance was one of the more successful reform movements of the period of Jacksonian Democracy. The temperance movement remained an important fact in American life throughout the 19th century and had strong political impact. The Anti-Saloon League, formed in 1895, finally achieved the temperance movement's goal of prohibition nationally in 1919 with the ratification of the Eighteenth Amendment to the Constitution. That amendment was repealed in 1933. The concept of prohibition and temperance continues to be a force in America, where its utopian[5] dream of an alcohol-free or drug-free society appeals to many.

UTOPIAN COMMUNITIES

Another result of the Second Great Awakening on American life was the growth of utopian thinking. The idea that life on Earth can be improved, that it can, by human efforts, approximate a perfect situation, has many roots but a particularly strong one is its religious root. Revival religion emphasized that by human action one's life can be made better and that one can be saved. If one believes that, then by extension, one can design a community with rules that will make life better or lead to perfection on Earth.

Utopianism had appeared in America prior to the Second Great Awakening. One example is the religious communities of the Shakers whose founder, the Englishwoman Ann Lee, taught that sin entered the world through sexual intercourse.

[5]utopian *A visionary who believes in the perfectibility of human society.*

Shakers established several communities in New England and New York where they lead celibate lives, hoping to improve the world through human action.

Several utopian communities in United States history have focused on ways to improve the lot of the factory worker. The first was organized at New Harmony, Indiana, by Robert Owen in 1825. Unfortunately, when the workers attempted to run the textile mill, it failed, and New Harmony collapsed. Later in the century, George M. Pullman created a supposedly ideal community where Pullman railroad cars were manufactured. It too collapsed over economic disagreements between workers and Mr. Pullman. In spite of such failures, utopian communities have continued to be established throughout our history. A large number were established during the Vietnam era of the 1960s and early 1970s.

> Utopians attempt to improve life for workers.

BROOK FARM AND TRANSCENDENTALISM

The most interesting utopian community of the Jacksonian era was Brook Farm, founded in West Roxbury, Massachusetts in 1841. Its founders were Unitarians and Transcendentalists. The teachings of Unitarianism were introduced in Boston by W. E. Channing in 1819. Unitarian faith emphasized both individualism and brotherhood. Transcendentalism was not a systematic philosophy, but Transcendentalists held that each person's individual understanding of experience was unique and sacred, that humans had a divine spark, and, in a mystic relation to nature, could discover truth. Brook Farm brought together in a community of shared work the greatest literary figures of the first sixty years of United States history. Sharing a belief in Transcendentalism, these authors—Nathaniel Hawthorne, Ralph Waldo Emerson, Henry David Thoreau, Herman Melville, Margaret Fuller (the editor of the *Dial*, the journal of Transcendentalism)—shared their ideas and farmed together. The farm experiment proved unsuccessful, but the sharing of ideas helped establish an American literary tradition. The writers emphasized nature, self-reliance, and the individual. These factors formed the basis of the Romantics' view of life. Romanticism[6] has been an important element in the arts in America throughout our history and can be seen especially in painting and literature.

American themes had earlier been introduced into literature by Washington Irving (*Sketch Book*, which includes *The Legend of Sleepy Hollow*) and James Fenimore Cooper (*The Last of the Mohicans*). While few people read these early American authors today, their works had important impact on succeeding generations. Ralph Waldo Emerson's essays reflect many of the values associated with Jacksonian Democracy. Henry David Thoreau in *Walden* described his voluntary existence in a cabin beside Walden Pond. He emphasized the individual and nature. His comment about each man marching "to his own drummer" was widely quoted during the Vietnam protests. It is a strong statement for individualism

> Emerson, Thoreau, and Melville help establish an American literary tradition.

[6]Romanticism   *A literary movement, but one also seen in the fine arts; the Romantic movement of the 19th century emphasized the importance of imagination and sentiment against the rules and formality of classicism. There was strong emphasis on individualism in both thought and expression.*

The Willey House, 1838
In this 1838 print by E. Benjamin and W. H. Bartlett of The Willey House, *the American interest in nature and the romantic is seen. It can be found in many of the art works of the pre-Civil War period. The Willey House was located in a notch in the White Mountains of New Hampshire. The area was soon to be a center for vacationing wealthy Americans, and it was works such as this that made these resorts famous. Would you like to spend a vacation at the Willey House?*
Published for the Proprietors by George Virtue, London, 1838.
Courtesy: The New Hampshire Historical Society, Concord, New Hampshire

and civil disobedience. Herman Melville's major work, *Moby Dick,* published in 1851, relates a struggle of power, of good versus evil, in the story of the obsessed sea captain, Captain Ahab, and his battle with the white whale, Moby Dick.

These three authors, as well as others, reflect the society of which they were a part. Religious works were the most popular reading. There were many popular novelists during the time including women who had large followings. By reading these works, the historian can gain important insights into the thought patterns of an age and learn what were the expected rules and guidelines for behavior. The works of these early American writers all suggest the importance of the individual and the choices he or she must make. The writers accept rules of conduct that are grounded in ethical understanding—Christian, Unitarian, or Transcendental.

They and the leaders of the various reform movements—education, feminism, temperance, utopian communities—all reflect the good side of revival religion. They reflect different aspects of Jacksonian Democracy. Unfortunately, there were other movements in the 1830s through the 1850s also grounded in religious conviction that were negative and reflect a less positive aspect of commitment to a particular viewpoint. These are considered in the next section.

Key Point to Remember
The Second Great Awakening reinforced a growing interest in democracy and reform in the nation, and many leaders pursued reform especially in education, women's rights, and temperance. The reforms are grouped together under the name of Jacksonian Democracy.

People to Remember

Frederick Douglass   African-American abolitionist, writer, and orator; born a slave of a white father, he escaped and became a spokesperson for the Massachusetts Anti-Slavery Society; wrote *Narrative of the Life of Frederick Douglass,* edited an abolitionist newspaper, lectured on abolition, and served as United States Consul General to Haiti.

Harriet Tubman   Abolitionist leader; born a slave, escaped, and worked on the Underground Railway leading slaves north to freedom; known as "Moses" to the movement members.

William Lloyd Garrison   Abolitionist, editor, publisher; an outspoken supporter of abolition to be achieved through moral persuasion; his newspaper, the *Liberator,* was noted for its uncompromising stand for abolition; while extremely vocal and supported in New England, his impact on the entire nation is subject to debate.

Emma Willard   Education reformer; opened in her home in Vermont a school for girls where college level courses were offered; later with support from New York State opened the Troy Female Seminary where a high school/college education could be obtained by girls.

Ralph Waldo Emerson   Poet, essayist, Congregationalist minister, lecturer; graduated from Harvard at 18, attended Harvard Divinity School, was minister of the Old North Church in Boston for three years, retired over a dispute about doctrine; traveled in Europe, settled in Concord, Massachusetts, became a member of a group interested in transcendentalism—considered the first American intellectual movement; attracted national attention with his 1837 Phi Beta Kappa oration, *The American Scholar,* in which he urged American independence from European culture.

Henry David Thoreau   Poet, naturalist, essayist; was a member of the Transcendentalist group in Concord, Massachusetts; sought a logical, individualist, satisfactory life; his essay, *Civil Disobedience,* in which he championed the individual versus the organized group, was very influential in the 20th century, inspiring M. L. King, Jr.

Links from the Past to the Present

1. Temperance, education, and women's rights are still important issues today.
2. The influence of revival religion and "born again" Christians is seen in reform movements and government policy, from the first Great Awakening to the presidency of George W. Bush and the election campaign of 2008.
3. Concern for equality, freedom, and the individual has been expressed in many ways throughout our history from the abolition movement to federal laws to Supreme Court decisions to anti-war movements.

Dates

1821—Second Great Awakening began.

1825—New Harmony, Indiana, founded.

1831—William Lloyd Garrison started publication of the *Liberator*.

1848—Brook Farm established.
　　　 Seneca Falls convention.

1851—*Moby Dick* published.

Questions
Identify each of the following:

Great Awakening	Horace Mann
Second Great Awakening	Angelina and Sarah Grimke
Revival Religion	Harriet Tubman
Seneca Falls Convention	Ralph Waldo Emerson
The *Liberator*	Henry David Thoreau
New Harmony, Indiana	Herman Melville
Brook Farm	Transcendentalism

Multiple Choice:

1. In *Walden*, Henry David Thoreau described
   a. his experiences fighting Walden, a white whale.
   b. Walden, the ideal community combining intellectual and physical labor.
   c. his solitary existence in a cabin beside Walden Pond.

2. Abolition became an important issue in American life because of the
   a. ending of the slave trade.
   b. concern over the spread of slavery as an accepted institution in the territories.
   c. breakdown of the Underground Railway.

3. Temperance became an important issue because
   a. factory owners saw drinking as the destroyer of good work habits.
   b. revivalist preachers saw it as a destroyer of family life.
   c. both of the above.

III. Social Changes in America

AMERICAN NATIVISM

One movement grounded in both religious conviction and a sense of nationalism and uniqueness was the Native American Association formed in Washington, D.C., in 1837. The name is very interesting, since with our current use of the term *Native American,* we might think it was an Indian tribal organization but it was not. The members of the Native American Association were white Europeans, most of whose ancestors had immigrated to America before the American Revolution. They believed they were the native Americans and resented and feared the new immigrants.

In the 1830s there was increased Irish immigration and many of the new immigrants were Catholic. The focus of the association became, therefore, anti-

Catholic and anti-Irish immigration. The Native American Association entered the political arena in 1845, creating the Native American Party. Its program called for changes in the naturalization laws and restricting the voting rights and office-holding privileges of Catholics. Violent conflict between Catholics and Protestants occurred in Philadelphia in 1844, and twenty people were killed.

The intensity of commitment to one's own religious faith and fear and hatred of others is a reflection of the negative aspect of revivalist religion. Strong feelings of belief are important but can become intolerant of other's beliefs.

The Native American Party was unsuccessful. A new party, the Know-Nothing Party, was organized in the 1850s and had as its major purpose agitation against Catholics. The intolerance of

> Intolerance is a negative aspect of Nationalism.

these two political parties, with their strong sense of righteousness rooted in their own religious beliefs, has returned at other times in our history. This intolerance is one example of the negative side of American Nationalism and Jacksonian Democracy. As we have seen, Jacksonian Democracy itself was a very diversified movement reflecting the great diversity that had developed in American life by the 1830s.

DIVERSITY IN WEALTH AND LABOR

Some of the more interesting examples of this diversity can be found in the division of wealth and labor, the contrast between urban and farm life, the changes in American economic life, and the increasing number of immigrants in the period between 1830 and 1850. Many families became wealthy during the Colonial period, and many continued to be wealthy by carefully investing in new enterprises ranging from canals to mills. A few Americans, such as John Jacob Astor in the western fur trade, made fortunes in the early 19th century. It is estimated that by 1860 the wealthiest ten percent in the United States owned seventy percent of its wealth. Even more extreme figures for the distribution of wealth are present in the United States today.

At the other extreme from this ten percent were the urban poor who lived in slum areas of the cities, as do our poorest citizens today. These urban poor were paid low wages, lacked job security, and, in retrospect, provide a negative side to industrial growth. There was a growing middle class of working men and housewives whose economic position was precarious and who were threatened by every economic crisis, such as the panics of 1819 and 1837. As manufacturing enterprises increased, the division between rich and poor widened in many urban centers. The first labor unions to protect workers' rights were formed in the 1830s but proved quite ineffectual. Conditions in factories for most industrial workers were often poor, hours were long, and wages were low.

In the Age of Jackson, which was an age of growing democracy, the country had a distinct class division of slaves, poor, middle class, and wealthy. As industrial growth developed and cities grew, the work done by men and women diverged from the old agricultural life where couples worked the farm together.

> Industrialization redefines the role of men and women, and reinforces class divisions.

Men tended to leave the home to work in businesses or factories; women tended to stay home to care for children and do the household chores. There were exceptions,

Altoona One-Room Schoolhouse, Boulder County, Colorado, c. 1882
This building is typical of the thousands of one-room schools found throughout the country in the 19th and early 20th centuries. Note the outhouse, the clothes worn, the single teacher, the range of ages of the students, and the fact that the sexes are separated in the photograph as they would have been in the classroom.
Courtesy: Carnegie Branch Library for Local History, Boulder, Colorado

and some women were employed in factories and retail shops, but the majority of employed single women held positions related to the home—cooks, servants, or boarding house managers. As public schools increased, some women found employment there as they do today. The pattern of the distribution of wealth continues today but the distribution of jobs changed drastically during and after World War II.

The Lowell factory girls provide a precursor of the role women were to play in factories during and after World War I. The Lowell system was first established in Waltham, Massachusetts in the 1810s where Francis Cabot Lowell built the first American factory for converting raw cotton into finished cloth based on his observations of developments in England. Large factories were built along the river to house the new water-driven power looms for weaving textiles. Workers, largely young girls from local farms, were employed, providing them with an opportunity to earn a living and help support the family. It provided some independence for the young women. The system was developed further in the factories of Lowell, Massachusetts, named for Francis Cabot Lowell after his death. The hours were long and the pay low, but the factories were clean and the girls lived under careful supervision in boarding houses designed and controlled by the owners. Their parents were thus much happier letting their young daughters go to the growing city.

The Lowell system brought some women into the workforce, encouraged the manufacture of textiles in New England, and reflected the moral and ethical attitudes of revival religion, which taught concern for the individual poor. The paternalistic approach to their workers by Lowell and other factory owners in the era reflects both concern for their well-being and a way to make good profits. The girls could be employed at low wages. However, when immigrant labor could be employed at even lower pay in the early 1850s, it was no longer necessary to maintain the expenses of the boarding houses, and profits could be increased.

DIVERSITY IN URBAN AND FARM LIFE

Cities grew rapidly in the first half of the 19th century, and business patterns and lifestyle changed dramatically as a result. Retail shops became specialized, as did business functions; factories needed workers, and

> Cities offer many opportunities but also many problems, while farms are often isolated.

farmers and immigrants came to fill the jobs. Slum areas developed where the poor lived; pleasant areas were planned and inhabited by wealthy citizens. Smells—there were few sewers and little garbage collection—were everywhere; crime flourished. Boston, in 1837, organized the first city police force in the country. As today, there were many opportunities in the city. The cities teemed with life. Entertainment became business. By contrast life on the farm was more traditional and often isolated and lonely. Entertainment had to be created and often took the form of a trip to the nearest village, where men could gather at the local tavern and women could visit. Barn raisings, a community effort to help a farmer improve his land, quilting bees, or similar events also supplied social life for the farmer.

Changes, however, were taking place in farm life as new machines such as the McCormack reaper, patented in 1834, were invented. The Eastern farms, particularly those small rock-strewn farms in New England, were not suited to the use of the new machinery. Many New Englanders went west or to the city and the amount of cultivated land declined as one can learn by viewing the stone walls that today are found in pine forests throughout New England. Those that remained adapted to dairy and vegetable farming. The farms in the old Northwest Territory prospered using the machinery, and with the Erie Canal and later railroad lines, they were able to ship their produce to ever larger markets.

Today, with TV, telephones, and automobiles, the contrast between farm and urban life may not be as great, but there still exists a sharp contrast between these two lifestyles. It was particularly obvious in the pre-Civil War period.

DIVERSITY OF PEOPLES: IRISH AND GERMAN IMMIGRANTS

As we learned in Chapter 1, all inhabitants of the Americas arrived as immigrants. In the United States in 1800 the majority of European immigrants were English, Scotch-Irish, Scottish, or Welsh, from the British Isles. There were settlers from other countries, but after the English victories in the 18th-century wars, the future territory of the United States became effectively English and Protestant although there was usually toleration of other faiths. After 1800 the United States expanded both geographically and industrially, and more people were needed. Immigration increased. Some states that were building railroads or canals in the pre-Civil War period even advertised for immigrants to come to take jobs. The first non-English, non-Protestant group to arrive in large numbers were the Irish. They settled largely in New York and Boston, whose population reached 35 percent foreign born. The Irish who arrived were Catholic and largely from rural areas. As was true of most

White Cotton, Black Pickers, c. 1915
This segment from a photograph could have been taken at almost anytime after cotton became "king" in the south. It illustrates one continuing aspect of life in the cotton growing south. Realizing the power of the photographic image, one wonders what the reaction might have been if such photographs were available during the era of slavery.
Courtesy: Library of Congress

19th-century immigrants, at first they found the adjustment difficult. It was made harder by the rise of American nationalism and intolerance described earlier, which was spurred on by the differences, particularly religious, between the Irish immigrants and the majority of Americans. Irish immigration reached its peak around 1850 when over a million Irish arrived in a period of five years.

Germans also came. They too found the adjustment difficult. Many continued to speak German and were Catholic, which separated them from the majority of the American population. Their celebration on Sundays, with dancing and beer drinking, drew the wrath of Protestants who saw the Germans as profaning God's day, and of the temperance leaders who opposed beer drinking. No immigrant group has found adjustment easy, but they all brought diversity and made great contributions to American life. Gradually the Irish and Germans were integrated into mainstream American life. Antagonism was directed at other immigrant groups who arrived in large numbers between the Civil War and World War I.

In the years between 1800 and 1850 many changes in American economic life increased the diversity of opportunities available to all people. As people moved west, transportation was needed and this led to improvements and new inventions that in turn speeded the westward movement of the frontier. The frontier ran from Ohio through Kentucky and Tennessee to western Georgia in 1800, but by 1850 it was the area between the Mississippi and the Rockies with areas of settlement in Texas, California, and Oregon.

The first of many inventions that changed transportation was the steamboat, patented in 1791. By 1807 Robert Fulton had a truly successful model, and he was given the monopoly for transportation on the Hudson River mentioned earlier. By 1848 the English Cunard Company began regularly scheduled steamboat travel between New York and Liverpool, England. The time of passage was approximately two weeks. Transatlantic travel by steamboat made immigrant travel to the United States much easier.

The first railroad opened in 1830, and by 1850 railroads were the chief means of heavy transport between the old Northwest Territory and the East, replacing the Erie Canal. The Erie Canal, an example of an internal improvement built by a state, had opened in 1825 to connect the Hudson River with the Great Lakes. It helped tie the Northwest Territory to the East economically and provided a route west for many New England farmers. The canal and the railroads realigned the political commitments as the westerners could send their produce to the large urban markets of the East and were no longer dependent on the river traffic down the Ohio and Mississippi Rivers.

The telegraph, invented by Samuel F. B. Morse in 1844, made almost instant communication possible and tied the nation even closer together. The invention in 1793 of the cotton gin by Eli Whitney set a pattern for American manufacturing. The development of standardized or interchangeable parts made possible the manufacture of many identical items. Colt revolvers used on the frontier to help conquer the West and McCormack's reapers used in the expanding farmlands of the Midwest used this concept, making many machines all the same, with parts that could be exchanged or replaced. Later Henry Ford used this concept in manufacturing the Model T Ford.

> The concept of standardized or interchangeable parts revolutionizes American manufacturing.

Specialization, standardization, and interchangeable parts made possible the rapid growth of American industry in the period before 1850. These developments in transportation, communication, and manufacturing increased the diversity of opportunities available to Americans and changed America's way of living. In the first half of the 19th century America grew dramatically.

SUMMARY

During the period 1800–50 America grew as a nation. A strong sense of nationalism was reinforced by the decisions of the Supreme Court under Chief Justice Marshall. The Second Great Awakening laid the foundation for reform movements that affected the American way of life. The increase in the numbers of immigrants with different religions created some urban difficulties. The developments in manufacturing, communication, and transportation also created a greater diversity in the American nation. However, the sense of national unity rooted in the Constitution as interpreted by the Supreme Court and in beliefs expressed through religion during the Second Great Awakening held the nation together.

Key Point to Remember

Between 1800 and 1850 the United States became much more diverse:

a. large numbers of new immigrants, especially Irish, arrived;

b. the gap between rich and poor and the contrast between urban and rural life grew;

c. inventions aided the growth of manufacturing and provided new opportunities for many;

d. a series of reform movements grouped as Jacksonian Democracy changed American life.

Links from the Past to the Present

1. Fear of and antagonism toward "foreigners" and immigrants has appeared many times and in many forms, ranging from the Alien and Sedition Acts to anti-Irish political parties to immigration legislation.

2. There has been a continuing struggle to provide jobs and other opportunities for women since the 1830s.

3. Changes in manufacturing and transportation transformed the country in the 19th century and changes continue.

People to Remember

Francis Cabot Lowell   Industrial innovator, cotton manufacturer; visited England, observed the new cotton manufacturing technology, returned to the United States, and copied it, building the first cotton mill in the nation in Waltham, Massachusetts; hired farm girls to work in the factory and thus began what came to be known as the "Lowell System" where the mills provided housing and supervised the life of the young workers.

Dates

1793—Cotton gin invented.

1807—Steamboat.

1820s—Lowell System established.

1825—Erie Canal opened.

1834—McCormack reaper invented.

1837—Boston Police force established.

1845—Native American Party founded.

1848—Cunard Company steamship service to England.

Questions
Identify each of the following:

Native American Association
Lowell factory girls
McCormack reaper

Standardization and
    interchangeable parts
Cunard Company

Multiple Choice:

1. The Native American and the Know-Nothing Parties
   a. had a strong sense of righteousness rooted in religious beliefs.
   b. encouraged immigration of Irish Catholics.
   c. were successful third parties.

2. As manufacturing grew, most men left the home to work during the day and most women
   a. found jobs in retail shops.
   b. stayed home to care for the children and do the household chores.
   c. became schoolteachers.

3. The contrast between farm and urban life widened as farms continued to be
   a. centers of entertainment and intellectual stimulation.
   b. places where new machinery was never used.
   c. isolated and lonely places.

Open-ended, Analysis Questions

The following questions require analysis and reflection. You are encouraged to bring to your answer information and ideas from many sources. The answers should be presented in composition or essay style, but they may be used to initiate discussion. The questions put you in the role of the historian, gathering information to support your personal perspective on the question.

1. In what ways did the Supreme Court decisions under Chief Justice John Marshall strengthen the power of the federal government? In what ways did they support the growth of American business?

2. To what extent were the reforms grouped together under the heading of "Jacksonian Democracy" based on attitudes, values, and ideas that are usually considered religious? Use specific information to support your view.

   (Note: In your answer you need to:

   a. explain what you mean by religious
   b. explain what attitudes, values, and ideas you believe several specific reforms of Jacksonian Democracy were based upon
   c. evaluate how the ideas discussed in b. relate to your understanding of religion
   d. present your conclusion)

3. Explain how the growth in population and economic diversity changed life in the United States in the period between 1800 and 1860.

Slavery and the Civil War

APPROACHES TO HISTORY

ECONOMICS AND HISTORY

There is one group of historians who believes all human actions are the result of economic conditions. They believe that all social standing and political power is based on one's level of prosperity, that economic forces drive us to be who we are and what we are. These historians believe that the desire for material goods and well-being drives all people and determines history.

Historians who believe in economic determinism look for the economic motives that they believe underlie all political and social developments. It is certainly clear that having money and material goods is important in American society. You must realize this whether you have, or do not have, much material wealth. Money allows you to enjoy things you cannot otherwise have, such as health insurance or the latest electronic device. You may also realize how hard it is to work and save enough money for a major purchase such as a car.

If you do not have money or material goods to begin with, you can easily believe your future is determined. This is what drives economic determinists to see economics as the driving force of history. Karl Marx[1], the German philosopher, first expressed the theory of economic determinism and the historians who follow his interpretation of history are called Marxist historians. As we study the history from 1850 to 1876, it may be easier to understand if we think of the economic needs and motivations of the leaders and people of that time. To what extent were they driven by economics?

---

[1] Karl Marx   *A German philosopher and economist who believed that the forces driving history are material, i.e., economic. In* Das Capital *he critiqued capitalism as an economic system and presented an alternative, communism.*

I. The Failure of Compromise

THE INSTITUTION OF SLAVERY

The Southern way of life in the years before the start of the Civil War in 1861 was rooted in the institution of slavery. While over two-thirds of the homes in the South had no slaves, the social and political leaders of the South did. Slaves worked the larger, wealthier plantations, and even a few yeoman farmers had a slave or two to help on their small farms.

After the invention of the cotton gin in 1793, cotton became the great cash crop of the South. Growing it required heavy labor, which was supplied by slaves. Southern spokesmen believed that without the slaves they could not grow cotton and their economic prosperity would collapse. While there were many yeoman farmers on the Southern frontier who lived independent and sufficient lives without slaves and there were a

> The economic welfare of the South depends on expanding the growth of cotton, the South's major cash crop, which is cultivated by slave labor.

number of free African-Americans and mulattoes, their economic impact on the South was negligible. These groups, except for the free African-Americans, endorsed the wealthy leaders who set the political and social goals for the South.

Thus at the root of any discussion of slavery, its merits or its horrors, its expansion into new territory or its abolition, was its economic necessity for the South as seen by the Southern leadership.

Unfortunately, this issue was never directly confronted nor solutions offered to make an economic shift in Southern lifestyle possible. Instead, slavery became an issue in political arguments over power and territory and in moral arguments over the treatment of slaves and the need for abolition. The true interests and needs of the South were never addressed, and viable

> An economic alternative to cotton production and slavery is never seriously explored.

economic solutions were never offered that might have compensated Southerners for their freeing of the slaves.

Political power and the extension of slavery to new territories were important issues for United States history, but the economic determinist would declare all these arguments missed the true point, the economic importance of slavery to the Southerner.

In recent years a lot of study has been done on the institution of Southern slavery. While the number of slaves grew prior to the Civil War, the percentage of Southerners owning slaves dropped. While the image of large plantations with many slaves still persists, just over ten percent of those owning slaves owned more than twenty. The majority of slaves worked on farms with fewer than five fellow slaves. Life was harsh for all slaves, food was monotonous, clothing was scarce, and housing was inadequate. Slaves were viewed paternalistically as inferior beings who needed to be protected.

> The attitude that views African-American slaves as inferior beings establishes race, not class, as the divider between white and black.

This attitude permeated Southern thinking and established race rather than economic class as the divider between groups, setting whites against blacks. Yet the racial division was rooted in the economic need for slave labor. The purpose of a plantation was to make money, and slaves were worked by overseers from dawn to dusk and in all seasons. A few slaves had it easier, doing jobs within the house. Often planters who had children by slave mistresses treated their offspring well and even educated them. Several of the well educated former slaves became leaders in the post-Civil War reconstruction.

On the whole, life for the slaves was bleak. Although some historians suggest many slaves were treated better than northern workers, they all lacked that prized possession of Americans—freedom. However, the slaves were able to maintain a sense of identity and build on their African traditions, which are seen in everything from their clothing style to musical instruments. Many slaves adopted Christianity, which for them was a religion of hope and salvation for all, a point missed by many whites. Slaves maintained a sense of family in spite of the fact families could be split by slave auctions.

Slaves were property. The reason for owning them was to make money. Slaves did greatly affect the social and political life of the South, but the reason they did so was because of their economic importance.

SLAVERY ISSUES BEFORE 1850

Slavery was a factor in American life since the first colony. African-Americans were brought to Jamestown in 1619 to help create wealth by working in the tobacco fields. While these first African-Americans probably arrived as indentured servants, the system of slavery was soon established. When the English colonies declared independence and proclaimed that "all men are created equal . . . ," a moral dilemma was also created. The abolitionists expressed one side of the dilemma. The slave owners, who used passages from the Bible to prove God established slavery, expressed the other side. While compromises were attempted, the moral issue could not be compromised.

The slavery issue periodically became an important matter after independence: at the Constitutional Convention the Founding Fathers accepted compromises permitting slavery but never used the word *slave* or *slaver*; the slave trade was abolished in 1807; the Missouri Compromise, which banned slavery north of 36°30′, was adopted in 1820; the *Liberator* was first published by William Lloyd Garrison in 1831, and as a result the abolition movement gained life; Congress avoided the slave issue by adhering to the Gag Rule after 1837; antislavery forces opposed the annexation of Texas and the Mexican War of 1846–48. Finally, the Great Compromise of 1850 included a strong anti-fugitive slave law. The political leaders hoped the Compromise of 1850 would satisfy pro- and antislavery forces and put the question to rest. It did not.

SLAVERY AND TERRITORIAL EXPANSION

The slaves did constitute a powerful interest that the South had to defend. As the nation expanded in the 1840s to reach its Manifest Destiny, it became clear that these new territories would someday enter the Union. If they entered as free states, the South, which had a smaller population than the nonslave states and so had a smaller representation in the House of Representatives, would lose its parity[2] or equality with the North in the number of Senators it had. This loss of political power through loss of representation could have grave consequences at a time the Abolitionists were agitating. The South saw the necessity that some of the new territories be slave territories.

> The South sees a need to expand slavery to new territories in order to maintain the balance of slave and nonslave states.

The Compromise of 1850 maintained the balance in the Senate and introduced a new concept, popular sovereignty, into the organization of the territories. The New Mexico territory was organized without restriction on slavery and with the proviso that when it applied for statehood it would enter free or slave depending on what the state constitution said at the time. Leaving the decision up to the people in the territory would give more power to the people and give them more control over their future, according to the theory.

Previously, Congress had indicated when organizing territories whether they would be free or slave. Questions had been raised as to whether Congress had this power. Popular sovereignty[3] seemed to its supporters to be a fair and democratic way to determine the future of slavery in the territories. (The idea of popular sovereignty was another side of the movement for greater democracy begun under Andrew Jackson. States had been adopting universal male suffrage, and letting the males in the territories vote on slavery furthered this idea.)

THE FUGITIVE SLAVE LAW AND *UNCLE TOM'S CABIN*

A good illustration of the complexity and contradictory nature of the conflict over slavery is the Fugitive Slave Law, approved as part of the Compromise of 1850. While Senators voted to let the inhabitants of the territories vote on whether to adopt slavery, they voted to use federal money to help capture and return escaped slaves to their owners. Again we see the economic importance placed on slaves by the South. They demanded their human property be returned to them.

The Fugitive Slave Law backfired. While few slaves escaped and were captured, those that did received such publicity in the North that Northerners were exposed to a particularly cruel aspect of slavery and were morally repulsed. A book, *Uncle Tom's Cabin,* strengthened this repulsion through its description

> *Uncle Tom's Cabin* stirs the conscience of the North and crystalizes antislavery sentiment.

of slavery and slave conditions. Written by Harriet Beecher Stowe, an abolitionist sympathizer, and published in 1852, *Uncle Tom's Cabin* in its first year sold over a quarter million copies in a nation of just over 21 million people. *Uncle Tom's Cabin* was one of the most influential books in history as it helped to crystallize Northern opinions about slavery. It is an excellent illustration of both the power of a free press and the influence an individual can have on history.

[2]parity *Equality; often used when comparing the currency of two nations.*
[3]popular sovereignty *Sovereignty is the power to rule, and popular means the people. Popular sovereignty put the decision of who was to rule or how ruling was to be done in the hands of the people in the area concerned. In the specific case of slavery extension, popular sovereignty meant the people in the territory would decide the slavery question.*

THE KANSAS-NEBRASKA TERRITORY AND POPULAR SOVEREIGNTY

In 1854 attention in Congress turned to the organization of the Kansas-Nebraska territory. This area was north of the Missouri Compromise line of 36°30′ and so, according to that law, should have been organized without slavery. Stephen A. Douglas from Illinois, a Democrat with presidential ambitions who needed Southern support, introduced a bill, the Kansas-Nebraska Act, to organize the territory incorporating the idea of popular sovereignty. The South, as Douglas hoped, saw this as a chance to spread slavery into an area previously closed to it.

The bill was passed; the Missouri Compromise was specifically abandoned by Congress. The question now became who would control Kansas. There was fighting in Kansas, which was dubbed "bleeding Kansas" as a result. Pro- and antislavery governments were established. Manipulations in Congress prevented either government from being accepted as legitimate.

The Kansas-Nebraska Bill backfired, and Stephen Douglas lost the 1856 Democratic nomination for President. Partly in reaction to the Act, a new party, the Republican Party, was formed in 1854 to oppose the extension of slavery. Kansas

> The Republican Party is formed to oppose the extension of slavery.

finally entered the Union as a free state in 1861 after the Southern states had seceded. Popular sovereignty did not prove successful as a way to deal with the slavery issue.

THE SUPREME COURT ON SLAVERY: *DRED SCOTT* V. *SANDFORD*

The Supreme Court next offered a solution to the slavery issue in the *Dred Scott* v. *Sandford* case in 1857. The case involved Dred Scott, a slave, who had been taken by his owner to a free state, Illinois, and a free territory, Wisconsin. Scott sued for freedom in the Missouri courts and appealed its decision to the Supreme Court. Hoping to resolve the issue of slavery in the territories, the Court entered the political arena with its decision. Chief Justice Taney and the Court held that Scott was not a citizen of the United States or of Missouri and could not sue in federal courts. Then the Court went on to say that Dred Scott's temporary residence in a free state did not make him free, and the Congress could not outlaw slavery in the territories since it deprived persons of their property, which was unconstitutional under the Fifth Amendment. This interpretation made the Missouri Compromise unconstitutional.

The *Dred Scott* decision was a sweeping victory for the South and its institution of slavery. The North and the newly formed Republican Party would not accept it. Instead of healing the nation by its decision, the Supreme Court split the nation more than ever over slavery. In the next three years many Southern leaders, especially in the lower South, insisted the nation respect the *Dred Scott* decision.

In 1858, the year after the *Dred Scott* decision, in a famous debate between Abraham Lincoln and Stephen Douglas in their campaign for a United States Senate seat from Illinois, Douglas, the Democrat, repudiated the *Dred Scott* decision,

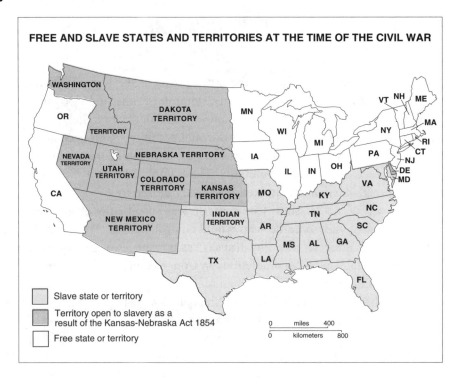

FREE AND SLAVE STATES AND TERRITORIES AT THE TIME OF THE CIVIL WAR

☐ Slave state or territory

☐ Territory open to slavery as a
result of the Kansas-Nebraska Act 1854

☐ Free state or territory

arguing that a territory could exclude slavery by popular vote. He won the Senate seat but lost Southern support by this step backwards from the *Dred Scott* decision. Douglas' loss of Southern support was to prove fatal for his Presidential ambitions and a peaceful solution to the slavery issue.

THE USE OF VIOLENCE: HARPER'S FERRY

While the events just described may all appear political, behind each was a concern over slavery and the future of this economic institution. However, more and more Northerners were taking a stand against slavery based on ethical standards and moral repulsion. One extreme moralist and abolitionist, John Brown, believed one should fight the evil. John Brown organized a raid on the federal arsenal at Harper's Ferry, Virginia, in October 1859, hoping to seize weapons to arm slaves and start an uprising.

> John Brown attacks the federal arsenal at Harper's Ferry as the first step of a planned slave uprising.

John Brown was captured, tried, and executed, but his action epitomizes the growing split in the nation. He became a martyr in the North, and verses and songs were written about his attempts to end slavery. Meanwhile, Southerners had expanded their rhetoric in defense of the institution of slavery. They used the Bible to justify it just as abolitionists quoted the Bible to condemn it.

The important political events of the decade 1850–60 were all related to slavery. The events culminated in the war that split the nation. Abraham Lincoln summarized the situation of the 1850s well in his second inaugural[4] address delivered in 1865. He said:

[4] inaugural (inauguration)   *Pertaining to the formal installing into office of an individual.*

One-eighth of the whole population were colored slaves, not distributed generally over the Union, but localized in the southern part of it. These slaves constituted a peculiar and powerful interest. All knew that this interest was, somehow, the cause of the war. To strengthen, perpetuate, and extend this interest was the object for which the insurgents would rend the Union, even by war; while the government claimed no right to do more than to restrict the territorial enlargement of it.

THE ELECTION OF ABRAHAM LINCOLN

By 1860 the nation was in a severe crisis. Leaders of the lower South had been speaking of secession if their "rights" were not allowed. Virginians still voiced the hope that sectional differences could be settled within the Union. The political parties nominated candidates during the summer, and Abraham Lincoln won the new Republican Party's nomination. Many believed Abraham Lincoln was opposed to slavery. From his public statements it was not clear what his personal views were. However, in 1858, Lincoln delivered a speech that has become famous as the "House Divided" speech. He declared a house divided could not stand and that the nation would have to be all free or all slave.

In the election of 1860 Southerners were convinced Lincoln would abolish slavery and establish an all-free Union. It was clear Stephen Douglas controlled the Democratic Convention and that he would only support Congressional nonintervention in the territories. The South wanted a guarantee for slavery in the territories. Douglas won the nomination and eight Southern states withdrew from the Democratic Party Convention and nominated John C. Breckinridge of Kentucky as their candidate. A

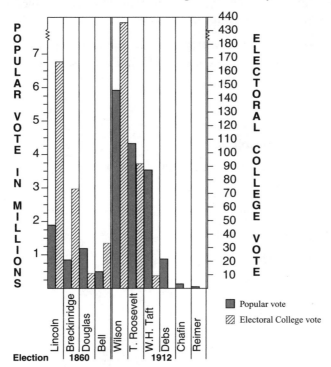

Two Key Election: 1860 and 1912.

fourth candidate, John Bell of Tennessee, was nominated by a new party, the Constitutional Union Party, which was ready to compromise to save the Union.

In the election Lincoln won in the Electoral College but received a minority of the popular votes. Breckinridge won in the South, Lincoln in the North, but Douglas and Bell combined had almost as many votes as Lincoln or Breckinridge alone, which suggests the many voters were still satisfied with the Union. However, the danger that George Washington had warned against of a nation split into political parties along geographic lines had come about. The result was to be disaster for the Union.

> In a four-candidate election, Lincoln receives a minority of the popular vote but wins in the Electoral College.

Key Point to Remember

In the decade before the Civil War the major issue of political concern was the question of the extension of slavery to the territories. Northerners objected on moral and ethical terms; Southerners saw the extension as an economic necessity and as the only way they would be able to maintain political parity with the North. The slavery issue split the nation, and war resulted.

People to Remember

Harriet Beecher Stowe   Author, abolitionist; wrote *Uncle Tom's Cabin* first published in serial form 1851–52; as a book it sold over 300,000 copies the first year and is credited with focusing antislavery sentiment in the North.

Links from the Past to the Present

1. Social and political issues, whether slavery, temperance, or homelessness, often have economic roots that must be considered.

2. The Supreme Court has at times tried to settle political issues by handing down a decision such as *Dred Scott* v. *Sandford,* which did not settle the issue but merely made it worse.

Dates

1852—*Uncle Tom's Cabin* published.

1854—Kansas-Nebraska Act incorporated popular sovereignty.

1857—Dred Scott Decision.

1858—Lincoln-Douglas Debates.

1859—John Brown raided Harper's Ferry.

1860—Abraham Lincoln elected President.

Questions
Identify each of the following:

Economic determinism	*Dred Scott* v. *Sandford*
Uncle Tom's Cabin	Harper's Ferry
Kansas-Nebraska Act	Stephen A. Douglas

Multiple Choice:

1. In the pre-Civil War period in the South
    a. two-thirds of the homes had no slaves.
    b. most slaves lived on large plantations with 20 or more slaves.
    c. there were no free African-Americans.

2. According to Abraham Lincoln
    a. popular sovereignty was the correct solution to the slavery issue in the Territory.
    b. the Fugitive Slave Law should not be enforced.
    c. a house divided against itself cannot stand.

3. In the election of 1860
    a. John Brown and John Bell were abolition candidates.
    b. Stephen Douglas was the Democratic Party candidate.
    c. Abraham Lincoln won a majority of the popular vote.

II. The Civil War

THE CONFEDERATE STATES OF AMERICA

With the election of Lincoln, the conflict sharpened. The Lower South insisted on a guarantee of the right to slavery in the territories. Lincoln insisted on holding to the Republican platform, which stood for no extension of slavery to the territories. The average Republican voter may have been willing to compromise, but Lincoln could not afford to compromise. That would antagonize the party congressional leadership, many of whom were strong abolitionists. This leadership later became known as the Radical Republicans. This same division in the party later haunted the party's postwar efforts at reconstruction.

There were attempts at compromise in the Senate, but they failed. The days of the Great Compromiser, Henry Clay, were over. South Carolina seceded from the Union in December 1860. Extremists in Mississippi, Florida, Alabama, Georgia, Louisiana, and Texas called conventions, and all six state conventions voted to secede. No Southern state asked the citizens to vote on the issue of secession. The Union was dissolved by the actions of these state conventions.

> South Carolina secedes, followed by the states of the Deep South.

By February 1861, the Confederate States of America (CSA) were organized as a new nation. Jefferson Davis was chosen as President, and Montgomery, Alabama, as the capital. The Upper South—Virginia, North Carolina, Tennessee, and Arkansas—did not secede until hostilities had begun.

LINCOLN'S RESPONSE

Lincoln was faced with a dilemma: how to restore the Union, his primary goal, without provoking a conflict. Restoration of the Union remained Lincoln's goal throughout the war. Lincoln moved slowly looking for a solution. He determined to hold federal lands in the seceded states, thus maintaining the concept of Union with federal authority operating in all the states. The CSA could not accept this if they were to be a sovereign nation.

THE WAR BEGINS

The clash came on April 12, 1861, when the Confederate States of America attacked the federal fort, Fort Sumter, in the harbor of Charleston, South Carolina. After two days of shelling, the garrison surrendered and was allowed to leave. War had begun.

The four states of the Upper South seceded to join the Confederacy. The capital was then moved to Richmond, Virginia. Robert E. Lee, graduate of West Point, accepted the command of the army of his home state, Virginia, having turned down command of the Union army. Several states that had been considered Southern did not secede. Kentucky, Maryland, and Delaware remained in the Union, and what is now West Virginia broke off from the state of Virginia during the war to form a new state.

Compromises on the issue of slavery had failed. Slavery was ultimately too important for the South to compromise on, and the Northern Republicans had come to see its extension to new territories as incompatible with the avowed beliefs of a democratic society. As Lincoln had said in 1858, a house divided could not stand. The question in April 1861 was whether the house could be made whole again. There were no goals at that time on the future of slavery, there was only a war to be fought and, in the eyes of Lincoln, a Union to be saved, but the origin of the war lay in attitudes toward slavery and the way of life it made possible economically.

> Lincoln has no plan for the future of slavery as the war begins.

With the outbreak of war Lincoln's constitutional role as Commander-in-Chief of the military forces gave him almost unlimited powers to act. Before Congress could act he asked for volunteers to join the army and declared a naval blockade of the Confederate ports. His most controversial act was the suspension of the writ of habeas corpus[5], an action permitted in the Constitution only in cases of rebellion or invasion. Citizens were arrested on suspicion of disloyalty and confined in military prison. Lincoln declared that persons resisting the draft would be tried by court martial under martial law[6]. Such actions went against the principles for which the Union stood but are typical leaders' responses to wartime situations.

THE UNION WAR STRATEGY

The Civil War was bloody—one million casualties in a population North and South of approximately 31 million; expensive—the estimated cost of over $20 billion, perhaps a small sum today in terms of governmental expenditure, was five times the

[5]Writ of habeas corpus   *Developed in England over centuries as a safeguard against illegal imprisonment, it is one of the rights of Englishmen fought for by the colonists. A writ is an order from a judge; in this case an order to someone detaining another person to bring that person before a judge where specific charges against the person must be made and the judge determine if the charges are justified, thus making it illegal to detain the person without a charge or due process.*

[6]martial   *of, or pertaining to, war and military affairs.*

total expense of the federal government between 1789 and 1860; and long—it lasted four arduous years. The South's strategy was to hold on and wear the North down. The North's strategy had three parts.

1. Blockade the South in order to isolate it from markets and potential allies.
2. Capture the capital of the Confederate States of America, Richmond.
3. Split the South into two parts along the Mississippi River and then by a thrust through Georgia to the sea to split it further into three units.

THE BLOCKADE

The blockade was put into effect immediately. The Confederate States of America hoped for some European support especially from England, whom they believed needed Southern cotton for their cotton mills. But England also needed wheat from the Northwest and had long been opposed to slavery. While there was some help from blockade runners, and some Confederate ships, such as the *Alabama,* were built in England, the English basically honored the blockade. The French became involved in an attempt to conquer Mexico and stayed out of the conflict.

SPLITTING THE CONFEDERACY

The campaign to split the South was very successful. General Ulysses S. Grant captured Forts Henry and Donelson on the Cumberland and Tennessee Rivers in Tennessee in 1862. This opened a path to the interior of the Confederacy. New Orleans,

> The capture of Vicksburg splits the Confederacy in half.

near the mouth of the Mississippi River, was also captured in 1862. The campaign continued into 1863, and with the capture of Vicksburg, Mississippi, on July 4, the Confederacy was split.

Attacks were then directed at Chattanooga, Tennessee, and after its capture, at Atlanta, Georgia, which fell in September 1864. General Sherman then led his Union forces on a "march through Georgia," destroying homes and supplies. Sherman captured Savannah, Georgia, in December 1864, splitting the South further.

The tactics Sherman followed were those of total war. Southerners referred to Sherman as "the brute." The argument in favor of such tactics is that the destruction of supplies meant for

> Sherman wages total war.

soldiers will shorten the war and destruction of homes and families will weaken the will to fight. Sherman's tactics have become familiar in the 20th century, and his often quoted comment that "war is hell" proven true too many times.

THE FIGHTING IN THE EAST

It took four years to capture Richmond. There were many battles fought in Virginia, beginning with the First Bull Run in 1861 and ending with the siege of Petersburg from June 1864 until its capture April 2, 1865. Richmond was abandoned and fell to the Union forces on the same day. General Robert E. Lee, who had commanded the Army of Northern Virginia for four years, surrendered to General Ulysses S. Grant, who had taken command of the Union Army of the Potomac in 1864. Lee's

View from the Summit of Little Round Top, Battle of Gettysburg, July 2, 1863
This pencil sketch done by E. J. Forbes as General Longstreet's Corps advanced on the Union 5th Corps captures the feel of the battle, unlike the photographs that required a stop in the action for the film to capture the image. Thus, many of the famous photographs of the war, we now know, were posed after the action. The artist's notes describe the actions and read in part, "Sketch of the fighting of Thursday evening from Rocky Hill to the left of . . . Meade's / position . . . The enemy was beaten yesterday afternoon. . . . I went out to the cemetery after I had finished the first two sketches. I could not take a sketch, it was too hot . . . I shall go there this morning. I have just been out near the line of skirmishes. We hold the field."
Courtesy: Library of Congress

surrender at Appomattox Court House on April 9, 1865 essentially ended the war although a few skirmishes continued until May.

The Virginia campaign was the bloodiest of the war. In a few hours on June 3, 1864, Grant lost 12,000 men. In the month of June his losses were equal to the size of Lee's army, but new recruits from the North kept coming, and eventually Grant's tactics of pounding away with his overwhelming numbers at Lee's army gained success.

Lee's greatest asset was his ability to outmaneuver the Northern forces. In 1863 he actually invaded Pennsylvania until stopped at Gettysburg, one of the most famous battles of the war. The Battle of Gettysburg not only marked the high point of the Confederacy's attack, it provided Lincoln an opportunity, when dedicating the Union cemetery at Gettysburg, to deliver one of the most memorable and sincere tributes ever given to those who are asked to fight for their country.

In the Gettysburg Address, Lincoln said, "The world will little note nor long remember what we say here. . . ," but he was wrong. The opening and concluding lines of his very short Gettysburg Address set forth the idea Lincoln had come to as the goal of the war. He said:

Fourscore and seven years ago our fathers brought forth on this continent a new nation, conceived in liberty, and dedicated to the proposition that all men are created equal. Now we are engaged in a great Civil War, testing whether that nation, or any nation so conceived and so dedicated, can long endure. . . . We here highly resolve that these dead shall not have died in vain; that this nation, under God, shall have a new birth of freedom; and that government of the people, by the people, for the people, shall not perish from the earth.

EMANCIPATION PROCLAMATION

Previously, in September 1862, Lincoln had acted on the slavery issue. Lincoln had not wanted to antagonize the border states by abolishing slavery but he finally accepted the views of the Radical Republicans and agreed to abolish slavery in those areas in rebellion. A war strategy was also involved in the decision as it was hoped slaves would disrupt the Southern war effort and

> The Emancipation Proclamation frees slaves in those states in rebellion on January 1, 1863.

join military units for the North. During the war African-Americans fought with distinction for the Union, but they fought in segregated regiments.

In the Emancipation[7] Proclamation Lincoln stated that as of January 1, 1863, those slaves held in states in rebellion against the United States would be free. It did not free slaves in the border states or in those areas of the South occupied by Northern armies. It was not until the Thirteenth Amendment to the Constitution was adopted in 1865 that slavery throughout the United States was abolished.

THE SOCIAL AND ECONOMIC IMPACT OF THE WAR

The impact of the war on society in both the North and South was enormous. With the loss of the Southern market, Northern industry slumped. The war effort encouraged certain industries—coal, iron, cloth for uniforms—and great profits were made by a few. More machines were introduced into factories as men went off to fight. While many people lived frugally and suffered economic distress as inflation ate up raises, others displayed their new wealth openly. The contrasts were great, and these intensified later in the century.

With the South out of the Union, Congress revived Henry Clay's old American System concept and, catering to the manufacturing East, raised the tariff in 1864 to almost twice its pre-war rates. In 1861–62 Congress chartered two railway companies, the Union Pacific and Central Pacific, to build a cross-country line from Omaha, Nebraska, to Sacramento, California. The railroad would open up the West. The effort was supported by huge government grants of money and land. Another company, the Northern Pacific, was chartered in 1864 to build a line. It had been impossible for the Congress to agree on a location for the transcontinental line until the South had seceded.

Aiding Western settlers was the Homestead Act of 1862, which granted settlers 160 acres of surveyed public land if they were citizens or intended to be, were over 21, lived on the land continuously for five years, and paid a registration fee of approximately $30. Until the Homestead Act, public lands

> A cross-country railroad and free homesteads for settlers open up new territories in the West to settlement.

had been sold as a source of revenue. Now a new economic policy was introduced:

[7]emancipation *Act or process of setting or making free; freeing, especially applied to slaves.*

make land cheap so more land would be settled. This would increase the market for goods and provide cargo for railroads. Economics played an important part in determining Northern policy on these three issues—tariffs, railroads, and land.

The war was not universally popular in the North, and there were draft riots in New York in 1863. Some opposed Lincoln's power and saw the war as unjustified. The impact of the war on the North, however, was not as severe as on the South. The South began from scratch, in 1861, to form a government. An administrative bureaucracy had to be built at a time when men were called upon to fight. Women took over many positions in teaching and in the bureaucracy. The South had been an agricultural economy, heavily dependent on exports, and it suffered from the North's blockade. It lacked the railway system of the North and, while advocating states' rights philosophically, was forced to centralize its efforts in order to run the war machine. This antagonized some of its supporters, and the Confederate States of America resorted to martial law to maintain authority.

Inflation, which was over 7,000 percent by the end of the war, destroyed businesses. Fearing a slave revolt, the Confederate States of America passed a law permitting any male supervising over twenty slaves to avoid serving in the army. Because only the wealthy had this many slaves, it made the war appear a war for the rich's economic advantage but fought by the poor. Economic differences between groups became an important issue in both the North and the South during the Civil War.

Key Point to Remember

The Civil War was a bloody, expensive war that had a great impact on the economic, social, and political life of both the Union and the Confederate States of America.

People to Remember

Robert E. Lee   Virginian; graduate of West Point; gained military experience in the Mexican War; was offered the command of the Union Army by Abraham Lincoln but rejected the offer and remained loyal to Virginia when it seceded; commanded the Army of Northern Virginia and finally surrendered to General U. S. Grant at Appomattox Court House in April 1865, ending the Civil War.

Jefferson Davis   General, planter, U.S. Senator from Mississippi, Secretary of War under Pierce, President of the Confederate States of America (CSA); served with distinction in Mexican War; strong supporter of Southern rights and expansion of slave territory; elected President of Confederacy; forced by war to centralize power in contrast to his personal philosophy of states' rights.

Abraham Lincoln   Frontiersman, lawyer, Illinois State Legislator, member of U.S. Congress, 16th President of the United States; born in Kentucky and raised on the frontier in Indiana, Lincoln was self-educated and attended formal school for less than a year; joined the new Republican Party in 1856; gained national attention through Lincoln-Douglas Debates in race for Senate in which he stated "A house divided cannot stand"; his election as president in 1860 precipitated Southern secession; his war aim was to preserve the Union; Lincoln's plans for reconstruction were not popular among Radical Republicans; he was assassinated by John Wilkes Booth, a Southern sympathizer, just as the war ended and after his election to a second term.

Links from the Past to the Present

1. The long-term economic and social cost of war are always great—a fact often overlooked as we focus on the cost in lives and material.

2. Growth of bureaucracy and centralization of power has occurred over and over again during wars from the Civil War to Vietnam to the War on Terrorism.

Dates

1861—Confederate States of America established.

1862—Pacific Railway Act.
   Homestead Act.

1863—Capture of Vicksburg split confederacy.
   Emancipation Proclamation took effect.
   Battle of Gettysburg.

1864—Fall of Atlanta.

1865—Surrender of General Robert E. Lee at Appomattox Court House.

Questions

Identify each of the following:

Confederate States of America
Fort Sumter
Robert E. Lee
Ulysses S. Grant

Appomattox Court House
Battle of Gettysburg
Emancipation Proclamation
Gettysburg Address

Multiple Choice:

1. The military phase of the Civil War began with
   a. firing on Fort Sumter.
   b. the Battle of Bull Run.
   c. the fall of Petersburg.

2. The Northern strategy for winning the war included a blockade and
   a. the capture of Richmond, Virginia.
   b. the splitting of the South into two parts.
   c. both of the above.

3. In his Gettysburg Address, Lincoln declared the war was testing whether
   a. "government of the people, by the people, for the people" shall perish.
   b. Gettysburg was a beautiful site for a cemetery.
   c. the South had legitimate reason for seceding.

4. Once the South had seceded, the Congress passed
   a. the Gettysburg Address.
   b. the Homestead Act.
   c. the Anti-inflation Act.

The Civil War Amendments to the Constitution

Amendments XIII, XIV, and XV are referred to as the Civil War Amendments. The Southern states were forced to adopt them as a condition for their acceptance back into the Union under the Radical Republican plan for reconstruction. The three together were designed to give civil and political rights to the former slaves, but they were subject to interpretation by the Supreme Court. By 1896 the Court was very restrictive in its interpretation of the guarantees granted in these three amendments.

Amendment XIII. Prohibition of Slavery   *Adopted 1865*

1. Neither slavery nor involuntary servitude, except as a punishment for crime whereof the party shall have been duly convicted, shall exist within the United States, or any place subject to their jurisdiction.

2. Congress shall have power to enforce this article by appropriate legislation.

> Slavery is declared unconstitutional, but jail sentences depriving one of freedom are legal.

Amendment XIV. Civil Rights for Former Slaves   *Adopted 1868*

1. All persons born or naturalized in the United States, and subject to the jurisdiction thereof, are citizens of the United States and of the State wherein they reside. No State shall make or enforce any law which shall abridge the privileges or immunities of citizens of the United States; nor shall any State deprive any person of life, liberty, or property, without the due process of law; nor deny to any person within its jurisdiction the equal protection of the laws.

> Citizenship is defined and the rights of United States citizens are stated—the "due process of law" is meant to guarantee these rights.

2. Representatives shall be apportioned among the several States according to their respective numbers, counting the whole number of persons in each State, excluding Indians not taxed. But when the right to vote at any election for the choice of Electors for President and Vice-President of the United States, Representatives in Congress, the executive and judicial officers of a State, or the members of the legislature thereof, is denied to any of the male inhabitants of such State, being twenty-one years of age and citizens of the United States, or in any way abridged, except for participation in rebellion, or other crime, the basis of representation therein shall be reduced in the proportion which the number of such male citizens shall bear to the whole number of male citizens twenty-one years of age in such State.

> Ex-slaves are now to be counted as full citizens in determining Congressional and electoral representation, but if an ex-slave is denied the vote, the state's representation will be reduced. This latter clause was never enforced.

3. No person shall be a Senator or Representative in Congress, or Elector of President and Vice-President, or hold any office, civil or military, under the United States, or under any State, who, having previously taken an oath, as a member of Congress, or as an officer of the United States, or as a member of any State legislature, or as an executive or judicial officer of any State, to support the Constitution of the United States, shall have engaged in insurrection or rebellion against the same,

> Confederates who had held office under the U.S. and then served in the Confederacy are denied the right to hold office under the United States unless Congress by a two-thirds vote allows the person to serve again. This was meant to remove from positions of political influence the leaders of the Confederacy.

or given aid or comfort to the enemies thereof. But Congress may, by a vote of two-thirds of each house, remove such disability.

4. The validity of the public debt of the United States, authorized by law, including debts incurred for payment of pensions and bounties for services in suppressing insurrection or rebellion, shall not be questioned. But neither the United States nor any State shall assume or pay any debt or obligation incurred in aid of insurrection or rebellion against the United States, or any claim for the loss or emancipation of any slave; but all such debts, obligations, and claims shall be held illegal and void.

5. The Congress shall have power to enforce, by appropriate legislation, the provisions of this article.

Amendment XV. Voting Rights for Blacks　　　　　*Adopted 1870*
1. The right of citizens of the United States to vote shall not be denied or abridged by the United States or by any State on account of race, color, or previous condition of servitude.

2. The Congress shall have power to enforce this article by appropriate legislation.

> The debt of the Confederacy is repudiated, but the southern states must pay their proportional share of the Union debt.

> Because of this section, if Confederate soldiers were to receive pensions, states had to pay them, not the federal government.

> Because the right to vote cannot be denied on the basis of color or slavery, all male ex-slaves are to have the vote.

III. The Period of Reconstruction

CONFLICT OVER RECONSTRUCTION PLANS

Reconstruction, the name given to the process of reestablishing the Union to again include the seceded states, began during the war and lasted until 1877. Opinions differed as to the process to follow, and your opinion depended on your answers to two questions:

1. Were the states in rebellion out of the Union?
2. Who should be in charge of the process of reconstruction?

Abraham Lincoln believed secession was unconstitutional, and so legally, the Southern states were still in the Union. He believed the executive branch, particularly the president, should establish the process of reconstruction and the terms should be generous. As the Union Army gained control of seceded states such as Tennessee, Lincoln appointed military governors and was prepared to recognize a new state government once 10 percent of the state's 1860 voting population swore allegiance to the Union.

Members of Congress in 1864 presented their own much less generous plan, but Lincoln did not sign the bill, angering the radical or extreme Republicans in Congress. The Radical Republicans, led by Senator Charles Sumner and Congressman Thaddeus Stevens, had been a force in Congress since before the war. They were intolerant of slavery, strong abolitionists, and prepared to make the South "pay" for the war. With their plan for reconstruction blocked by the President, the stage was set for confrontation.

Before Lincoln's plan was fully operative, he was shot by John Wilkes Booth, just five days after Lee's surrender at Appomattox. Lincoln died on April 15, 1865, and Andrew Johnson became president. Johnson followed Lincoln's plan welcoming the Southern states into the Union.

> Lincoln is assassinated before his Reconstruction plan is fully in operation.

The Radical Republican Senators were not pleased. They resented the growth of executive power during the war. They were concerned by the restriction of the rights of the freed slaves by the Black Codes passed by the former Confederate states. While these law codes, which applied only to former slaves, guaranteed the right to sue, to be sued, and to own property, they restricted many basic rights—the right to bear firearms and the right to testify in trials (freed slaves could only testify in law cases involving African Americans)—and in South Carolina they were excluded from practicing skilled trades. When Alexander Stephens, the Vice President of the Confederacy, was elected as a Senator from Georgia, Thaddeus Stevens and Charles Sumner believed the situation had become intolerable and offered their own plan for reconstruction.

Their plan was embodied in Amendment XIV, which made the ex-slaves citizens. Slavery had been made unconstitutional by Amendment XIII adopted in 1865. Amendment XIV guaranteed all citizens due process in defense of their rights. This was meant to combat the Black Codes. The Amendment also repealed the three-fifths rule of the Constitution so ex-slaves were now counted in determining state representation in Congress. The Amendment provided that if the vote was denied a citizen, the state would lose representation in Congress. This was an attempt by the radicals to assure that ex-slaves would vote in the South, hopefully for the Republican Party that had fought the war to free them.

President Johnson could have compromised his views to work with the more moderate Republicans in Congress and thus maintain some of his and Lincoln's more lenient policies. He failed to do so. Amendment XIV was rejected by the South in the election of 1866 in which the Republicans won a large majority in Congress. There had been little progress in reconstruction in one and a half years. Congress in 1867 focused on the issue.

IMPEACHMENT OF PRESIDENT JOHNSON

The entire Senate-President struggle over reconstruction was tied up in issues of political, not economic, power. Republicans feared the return of the Southern Democrats to Congress. The Congress resented presidential power, and the president believed reconstruction was an executive matter. The political power struggle became intense and culminated in impeachment[8] proceedings against President Johnson.

> The Radical Republican Congressional leadership impeaches President Johnson, but he is acquitted.

[8]impeach   *To indict a public official for misbehavior. The case is then tried before a jury assigned to the case, and the indicted official is found guilty or not guilty. In impeachment proceedings against the President of the United States, the Senate serves as the jury and the House of Representatives must prepare the charges against the President.*

Behind the impeachment was the belief held by the Radical Republican Congressional leadership that the President was blocking Congressional reconstruction. The impeachment case centered on Johnson's dismissal of his Secretary of War, Edwin M. Stanton, in 1867. This violated the recently passed Tenure of Office Act, which stated the President could dismiss government appointees who had been confirmed by the Senate only with the consent of the Senate. This law changed the established precedent, followed since George Washington, that the president could dismiss executive appointees at his pleasure even if they had been confirmed in their office by the Senate.

Indictments were brought against Johnson in 1868, and impeachment proceedings began. Johnson was impeached by the House of Representatives. The Senate vote on conviction fell one vote short of the two-thirds required under the Constitution. Johnson finished his term in office but was able to exert no power over the radicals in spite of his acquittal.

Ulysses S. Grant, the winning General of the Army of the Potomac, received the Republican nomination in 1868 and was elected President. Military heroes continued to have appeal to the voting public even if they had no political experience.

THE CONGRESSIONAL PLAN FOR RECONSTRUCTION

After the South rejected Amendment XIV in 1866, Congress adopted a new policy of military reconstruction, which went into effect in 1867. The new plan abandoned all that had been done in the two years since the war. Troops were to stay in the South until states adopted new constitutions, agreed to emancipation, and approved Amendment XIV. The states slowly complied and re-entered the Union, but the last military forces were not withdrawn until 1877.

Many of the Southern states' new constitutions incorporated quite liberal ideas and eliminated property qualifications for voting, made more offices elective, gave more property rights to women (but not the vote), and required the building of schools and special institutions for the deaf, the blind, and orphans.

African-Americans served in the state legislatures under these new constitutions until disenfranchised after the end of military reconstruction. Many of them that served had been well educated. Some were relatives of the white representatives—a point rarely discussed.

In 1865 Congress established the Freedman's Bureau. This temporary bureau was to help defend the rights of the freedmen and to look after the abandoned lands in the South. It was authorized to distribute up to 40 acres of abandoned land and to provide food, clothing, and education to white refugees and to freedmen. The Freedman's Bureau built schools and churches and arranged for the teaching of reading to many African-Americans.

> The Freedman's Bureau is established to aid the freed slaves, but essentially they are given no economic support.

While there was discussion of economic support to help the ex-slaves buy farms, essentially nothing was done. Reconstruction ignored the economic problems inherent in emancipation, and this led to problems that are still with us today.

The military reconstruction plan of the Radical Republicans provided the African-Americans with access to the political process. This worked while the military occupation forces remained in the South, but when they were withdrawn, African-Americans were slowly eliminated from the political process by disenfranchisement.

LIFE FOR THE FREEDMAN

Reconstruction had also ignored the traditional power structure and social structure of the South while concentrating on political reform. While Southern economic life had been disrupted, many families were able to rebuild their wealth. The land was still held by the former owners, and few of them had changed their opinion of African-Americans. Without land of their own, many African-Americans worked as sharecroppers[9], and this made them still dependent on the whites. Neither their social status nor economic power had been changed by the war or reconstruction.

In fact, not only did Southern states turn to Black Codes during reconstruction to keep the freedmen "in their place," but the Ku Klux Klan was organized in 1867. The Klan used terror

> **Black Codes and the KKK are used to keep the freedmen "in their place."**

and violence and was denounced in the North. The KKK was officially disbanded in 1869, but its policies continued to be used and the Klan was reorganized later in the century. The KKK Acts passed by Congress in 1870 and 1871 attempted to curtail the use of violence and to enforce Amendments XIV and XV. In spite of the KKK Acts, the Ku Klux Klan has emerged at several times in United States' history as an organization of intimidation.

CIVIL RIGHTS ACT OF 1876

As one of its last acts during the reconstruction era, Congress passed a Civil Rights Act in 1876 to provide equal accommodation in public places like hotels. No enforcement provisions were included, however, and without federal enforcement provisions, the Act was a failure. This failure discouraged Congress from making further attempts to secure civil rights by legislation. When the Civil Rights Movement[10] got Congress to act in the 1960s, enforcement measures were included in the Civil Rights Act.

For those who lived through reconstruction, it was a hard time. Change is never easy to accept, and the members of the federal government were so involved in their own power struggles that they failed to provide direction for the creation of a new South. In the 20th century a new social and political power relationship finally emerged after the struggles of the Civil Rights Movement.

The final blow to Congressional reconstruction and the effort to provide African-Americans with access to the political process came in the Supreme Court decision

---

[9] sharecropper   *One who shares the crops he raises with the owner of the land in return for the right to farm the land. It provides a tenant relationship without exchange of cash, as crops are used instead.*

[10] Civil Rights Movement   *A movement in the 1950s and 1960s that, through the use of civil disobedience, obtained civil rights—the right of equal access to lunch counters, hotels, education, etc.—legislation by the federal government. Among many leaders, Martin Luther King, Jr., is the most prominent.*

in the Civil Rights cases. The Court interpreted Amendment XV as a limited statement of how the right to vote could not be denied and not as a guarantee of voting under all conditions. Southern states soon found ways to deny the vote to ex-slaves, such as a Grandfather Clause that simply said if your grandfather had not voted, you could not. Obviously, no slaves had grandfathers who had voted. By the end of the century, most African-Americans were disenfranchised[11] in the South. Reconstruction had even failed to provide the freedmen with access to the political process.

> Southern states move to deny the vote to former slaves after the Supreme Court decisions in the Civil Rights cases.

ECONOMIC EXPLOITATION AND DEVELOPMENT

The South was split politically during reconstruction, but economic issues tended to unite different elements. Carpetbaggers[12], Northerners who came South, exploited economic situations and worked to keep the Republican Party in power by not allowing ex-Confederates to vote and by supporting the voting rights of ex-slaves. Scallywags[13], white Southerners who cooperated with the Republicans, worked with the yeoman farmers who had not been slave owners to re-establish the farm lands and to stimulate industry. These two groups profited economically from the post-war conditions. Also, the new Southern state governments encouraged economic growth by loans and by providing tax exemptions in certain cases. These again benefited certain groups within the South, but not the ex-Confederates.

> Economic recovery comes slowly to the South.

There was some corruption in the new state and local governments, but overall they ran well. Corruption was a national problem in the 1870s. There had been a breakdown in the values and ethics of society during the war, and the corruption was as much a result of this breakdown as it was a result of incompetency on the part of Southern leaders of the new governments.

Most historians agree there were some benefits in reconstruction. They cite expanding educational opportunities and an improvement of property rights for women, which were included in the new state constitutions.

THE ELECTION OF GENERAL ULYSSES S. GRANT

Grant easily won the election of 1868, but when he ran for re-election in 1872, liberal Republicans, who favored a more lenient reconstruction policy, lower tariffs

---

[11] disenfranchise   *To remove the right of one to vote. Franchise is used in political science and history to refer to the right to vote.*

[12] carpetbagger   *A Northerner who traveled to the former Confederacy during the reconstruction period to participate in the political and economic reorganization of the South with the goal of profiting from the situation. The name originated among Southerners who claimed the carpetbaggers arrived with all their possessions in a carpetbag. In the mid-19th century many suitcases were made from carpet.*

[13] scallywag   *A contemptuous name for a Southern white who cooperated with Northerners and African-Americans during reconstruction.*

to help the South, and civil service[14] reform, banded together. They were opposed to the widespread corruption in government, broke from the party, and nominated Horace Greeley, editor of the *New York Tribune,* as candidate for President. The Democratic Party, still attempting to re-establish itself as a national party and not just a party of the South, also nominated Horace Greeley. Grant easily won reelection, however, and the Congressional reconstruction continued.

> **Corruption becomes widespread in government.**

Grant's second term is noted for the Panic of 1873 (see Chapter 9) and scandals. Corruption in the federal government was exposed in two scandals—the Credit Mobilier and the Whiskey Ring. In the former, Congressmen were accused of profiting from and giving political influence to the promoters of the Union Pacific Railway Company. In the latter, members of Grant's administration, including his private secretary, were involved in defrauding the government of tax money.

Corruption appeared widespread in the era and reflects the breakdown of ethics and morality that so often follow a war. There was corruption in city government, as in New York City, where the Tweed Ring—the associates of the city's political boss, William M. Tweed—milked money from the city to make themselves rich. Behind this corruption was the desire to get rich without work. Marxist historians see this as another example of economics as the driving force of all history.

Can you relate to this concept of economics being the driving force for these illegal actions?

ELECTION OF 1876: THE END OF RECONSTRUCTION

The national political balance began to shift, and in 1874 the Democrats gained control of the House of Representatives. In the presidential election of 1876, they nominated Samuel J. Tilden of New York. The Republicans nominated Rutherford B. Hayes of Ohio. Neither man won a majority in the Electoral College. Tilden had a majority of the popular vote with 51 percent, but he needed one more electoral vote to win a majority. Nineteen electoral votes from Florida, Louisiana, and South Carolina were

> **The era of reconstruction ends after Rutherford B. Hayes is named President by a congressional commission following the disputed election of 1876.**

disputed, and one from Oregon was undecided. A Congressional commission was created to resolve the issue of who won the election by determining the validity of the contested votes. The fifteen-member commission, with eight Republicans, voted 8–7 in favor of Hayes on each of the nineteen contested votes. Tilden had needed only one of them to be elected President, so the final electoral vote was 185–184 for Hayes. The Democrats, quite unhappy, decided to accept the result rather than threaten another war or more uncertainty about the future.

---

[14] civil service   *The administrative side of government, which includes bureaucrats, except those connected with or members of the armed forces or the legislative and the judicial branches. Those who run the executive branch of government are members of the civil service.*

After his inauguration, Rutherford B. Hayes ordered the withdrawal of troops from the South, ending reconstruction. For years it was suspected a "deal" had been arranged to pay for this "stolen election," but recent research has found no clear evidence for such a deal. The nation was again united twelve years after the end of the Civil War. Reconstruction had finally recreated the Union, but beyond that, what had been achieved? This is a question we each need to answer for ourselves.

Key Point to Remember

The Radical Republicans in Congress and Presidents Lincoln and Johnson each had plans for reconstruction and the former plan was implemented from 1866–77 with the result the ex-slaves achieved temporary access to the political process but little social or economic power.

People to Remember

Thaddeus Stevens   Lawyer, abolitionist, founder of Republican Party in Pennsylvania, Congressman, leader of Radical Republican faction in House; opposed Lincoln's plans for Reconstruction; introduced 14th Amendment; led impeachment proceedings against President Andrew Johnson.

Charles Sumner   Lawyer, abolitionist, organizer of Republican Party in Massachusetts, senator, leader of Radical Republican faction in Senate; believed Congress should control Reconstruction; appeared vindictive toward Southern slave owners; worked hard to obtain conviction of President Andrew Johnson.

Andrew Johnson   Congressman, senator, military Governor of Tennessee, Lincoln's Vice President, 17th President; in Congress, he supported legislation for free western homesteads, remained in Senate when Tennessee seceded; supported Lincoln's Reconstruction plans; impeached by Radical Republican leadership but acquitted by one vote.

Ulysses S. Grant   Ohioan; West Point graduate; served with distinction in the Mexican War; resigned to farm and work in real estate; returned to service as a Colonel of Illinois volunteers in 1861; won victories at Forts Henry and Donelson, Shiloh, Vicksburg, and Chattanooga; appointed Lt. General in command of Union forces; defeated Robert E. Lee; elected 18th President; presidency tarnished by Credit Mobilier and Whiskey Ring scandals and Panic of 1873.

Links from the Past to the Present

1. Since the Civil War the United States has been subjected to the periodic recurrence of corruption in the federal government.

2. War has an impact on the ethics and values of members of society, as can be seen in both public and private actions, ranging from the scandals of Grant's administration to the widespread flaunting of the prohibition laws in the 1920s.

3. Presidential impeachment, while rarely used, is always a possibility, especially when there are deep disagreements between parties and between the President and Congress.

Dates

1865—President Lincoln assassinated.
Amendment XIII.
Freedman's Bureau.

1867—Congressional Plan for reconstruction.
Ku Klux Klan founded.

1868—President Johnson impeached.
Amendment XIV.

1870—Amendment XV.

1876—Civil Rights Act.

1877—End of reconstruction.

Questions
Identify each of the following:

Black Codes   Radical Republicans
Tenure of Office Act   Tweed Ring
Freedman's Bureau   Election of 1876

Multiple Choice:

1. Amendment XIV
   a. was gladly accepted by the former Confederate States of America.
   b. granted citizenship to ex-slaves.
   c. was designed to aid the growth of American corporations.

2. The Freedman's Bureau was
   a. a temporary bureau designed to help the former slave in education and economic matters.
   b. a social club where former slaves were able to get an education.
   c. the cornerstone of Radical Reconstruction.

3. Southern whites had not changed their basic view of African-Americans as inferior by 1870 as can be seen by their setting up the
   a. Black Codes.
   b. Civil Rights Cases.
   c. Congressional Commission on Election Fraud.

IV. Foreign Policy Issues

UNITED STATES AND LATIN AMERICA

While the attention of the nation focused on the domestic issues of slavery, Civil War, and reconstruction in the period 1850–77, there were several foreign policy decisions that have had long-term effects on the United States. All of these had important economic consequences. The first was the Clayton-Bulwer Treaty with England, signed in 1850. There was interest in a canal between the Atlantic and Pacific Oceans, and this treaty guaranteed that if one were built through Nicaragua, there would be equal access to the canal for both England and the United States. It guaranteed the United States would enjoy a canal if the British built one but meant we could not build one we controlled. Later negotiations with England nullified the treaty before the United States built the Panama Canal.

In the 1840s and 1850s there was interest in annexing Cuba or other areas in Latin America. Americans led expeditions south, and there was talk of our Manifest Destiny to control the Caribbean. Such plans were frustrated by antislavery groups, who believed any annexation of territory in the Caribbean or Latin America would provide more territory for slavery.

In 1853 the United States bought a small piece of territory from Mexico, the Gadsden Purchase. Congress had been debating the transcontinental railway line and one route, the far southern route, would have benefited from going through this small piece of Mexican territory. The land was purchased, but Congress could not agree on what route to use until the South seceded, and then the route went through the center of the country. Whatever route was taken, south, north, or central, that area would greatly benefit economically from the railroad.

> The Gadsden Purchase in 1853 completes the territory of the lower 48 United States.

PERRY OPENS JAPAN

> Trading contacts are established with Japan.

One of the more interesting foreign policy events of the 1850s was Admiral Matthew C. Perry's trip to Japan in 1853 and the treaty he signed the next year. The Treaty of Kanagawa opened Japan to Western trade and influences. Since then United States relations with Japan have gone through many phases, all of which have had important economic implications. If Perry had not gone to Japan, some other individual or nation no doubt would have. It would have been impossible for Japan to remain isolated from the rest of the world throughout the 19th and 20th centuries. Yet that is what Japan, the Island Kingdom, had been able to do for over 200 years. With the opening of Japan and the market in China, with which the United States had been trading for years, there were many economic opportunities available to American citizens in Asia. These became more and more important and helped determine our Asian policy over the next 150 years.

MAXIMILLIAN IN MEXICO

During the Civil War the Monroe Doctrine was put to a test when Emperor Napoleon III of France attempted to establish Maximillian, Archduke of Austria, as Emperor of Mexico. There was little the United States could do while the war was on, but in 1866 the United States delivered an ultimatum[15] demanding the withdrawal of France and sent troops to the United States-Mexican border. Napoleon III

---

[15]ultimatum *A final proposition, conditions, or terms offered by either side in a negotiation between two nations or states; an ultimatum is the final offer, and, in disputes between nations, suggests that if it is not accepted, the next step will involve military force.*

withdrew his troops, and in 1867 Maximillian was shot by Mexican forces. The United States was prepared to keep European powers out of the Americas.

Also during the war, England permitted the building of several Confederate ships in English shipyards. These ships raided Northern shipping. After the war the United States and England submitted to arbitration[16] claims for damages. The settlement of these Alabama Claims—one Confederate raider was named the *Alabama*—was one step in the development of closer ties between England and the United States.

THE UNITED STATES GROWS BEYOND ITS BORDERS

Lincoln and Johnson's Secretary of State, William H. Seward, had dreamed of a United States empire that stretched from Canada to Panama. While his dreams were not realized, he did

> Midway Island and Alaska are acquired.

make two territorial acquisitions that have proven of great importance to the United States. In 1867 the island of Midway in the Pacific was occupied by the United States. It had been discovered in 1859 by the United States and became an important naval and shipping base as our economic interests in Asia increased in the later 19th century. Also in 1867 Seward arranged for the purchase of Alaska from Russia for $7,200,000, and after a propaganda campaign the Senate approved the purchase. Alaska was referred to as "Seward's Folly," but it has proven a great bargain. The economic and strategic importance of Alaska today is testimony to how one man's vision can affect history.

SUMMARY

Foreign policy issues were of minor importance during the period 1850–77, although several events occurred that have had important effects on our history. The issue of slavery and its extension to new territories dominated the 1850s. When no compromise could be reached, the nation split into two nations—the Union and the Confederate States of America. After four years of intensive fighting, the Union won and faced the issue of how to bring the seceded states back into the Union. There were several plans for this reconstruction of the Union and the congressional, Radical Republican plan was adopted. It failed to deal with economic and social problems but did provide the ex-slaves, for a short time, with access to the political process. With the withdrawal of Northern troops from the South after the disputed election of 1876, Southern whites slowly re-established their control over the political, as well as the social and economic, life of the South. While slavery is often suggested as the cause of the Civil War, the more inclusive issue of economic power must also be considered as the dominant issue in the period from 1850 to 1877.

Key Point to Remember

During the period 1850–77 while foreign policy issues did not dominate, the United States was involved in creating new markets in Asia, in enforcing the Monroe

---

[16]arbitration　*Settlement of a dispute by means of an impartial hearing before one or more persons chosen by the parties in conflict.*

Doctrine, and in adding to the United States the first territory that did not border on the previous states, thus setting precedent for overseas expansion.

Links from the Past to the Present

1. Economic relations between Japan and the United States have been important from the signing of the Treaty of Kanagawa in 1854 to present tensions over imports and exports.

2. United States involvement in the Caribbean and Central America began before the Monroe Doctrine and continue, as illustrated by our concern over drug trafficking and illegal immigration across the Mexican border.

Dates

1850—Clayton-Bulwer Treaty.

1853—Treaty of Kanagawa.

1867—Maximillian, proclaimed Emperor of Mexico, shot.
      Alaska purchased from Russia.

Questions
Identify each of the following:

Clayton-Bulwer Treaty   Alaska
Gadsden Purchase   Commodore Matthew C. Perry
Midway Island

Multiple Choice:

1. The Clayton-Bulwer Treaty guaranteed that
   a. there would be equal access to a canal for England and the United States.
   b. no canal should be built through Nicaragua.
   c. there would be no later negotiations.

2. France supported Maximillian's attempt to become Emperor of Mexico until
   a. the Mexicans captured him.
   b. the English threatened to declare war.
   c. the United States delivered an ultimatum demanding troop withdrawal.

3. Alaska was referred to as Seward's Folly but
   a. it has proven to be a great bargain.
   b. it shows how one man's vision can affect history.
   c. both of the above.

Open-ended, Analysis Questions
The following questions require analysis and reflection. You are encouraged to bring to your answer information and ideas from many sources. The answers should be presented in composition or essay style, but they may be used to initiate discussion.

The questions put you in the role of the historian, gathering information to support your personal perspective on the question.

1. To what extent were the events that led to the Civil War rooted in the economic needs of the North and the South? Analyze specific events in presenting your view.

2. What, if any, advantages did the North have over the South at the outbreak of the Civil War? (*Note: You should consider different types of advantages. They might be considered under different headings such as economic, political, etc. or under specifics such as industrial base, population, etc.*)

3. What part did economics play in determining the course of events referred to as "Reconstruction"? (*Note: In your answer be sure to explain the terms* economics *and* reconstruction, *to describe several events of Reconstruction and to discuss any connection of these events to economics.*)

4. "The overseas expansion of the United States in the years immediately after the Civil War was driven by the economic needs of the growing United States business community."

Do you agree or disagree with this statement? Explain your reasons.

Changing Lifestyles: 1865–1914

APPROACHES TO HISTORY

THE EFFECT OF THE FRONTIER ON AMERICAN CHARACTER

Throughout history a few historians have proposed hypotheses to explain history that have introduced an important new idea that has affected the way we see the past. In the 1890s a famous American historian, Frederick Jackson Turner, argued that the American character was formed on the frontier. He believed that the ideas and traditions brought to America by the Europeans were changed by the frontier experience, and the "striking characteristics" of the American intellect were the products of the frontier. These characteristics were "that coarseness and strength combined with acuteness and inquisitiveness: that practical inventive turn of mind . . . ; that masterful grasp of material things lacking in the artistic but powerful to affect great ends; that restless, nervous energy; that dominant individualism, working for good and for evil . . . with exuberance that comes from freedom." Turner wrote *The Significance of the Frontier in American History* in 1893, three years after the census bureau announced that a frontier line no longer existed in the United States—that the frontier was closed. If the frontier had formed the American character and the frontier no longer existed, then Turner wondered, what would happen to the American character, how would it change?

Turner's thesis was based on the idea of challenge and man's response to it. He believed the frontier presented unique challenges to Americans who, in meeting them, developed a unique character that distinguished them from other nationalities. Are these assumptions correct? Is his description of the American character accurate? For 1893? For 2009? Are Americans unique? Might other challenges have been as important as the frontier? These are the questions one must consider in evaluating Turner's thesis, and similar questions must be raised concerning any interpretation of history. The frontier certainly played an important part in American life from the time the first settlers arrived on the Atlantic coast. The frontier experience has been written about at length in novels and short stories, varying from Mark Twain's *Adventures of Huckleberry Finn* to Owen Wister's *The Virginian*, which established the image of the western cowboy. Advertisements, television programs, and movies have used the theme of challenge and conflict in the West. This is what Turner saw in the frontier experience, a challenge to the easier, accepted way of life of Europe or the settled areas of the United States. The individual had to struggle against the unexpected on the frontier—unexpected challenges of weather, geography, and native inhabitants.

Challenges are a part of life. We have all met and overcome challenges. It is often these challenges and the way we meet them that helps to form our character. This is what Turner's thesis says. However, did Turner ignore other important challenges of the 19th century? We have already considered a number of different challenges to Americans. In the fifty years after the Civil War, in addition to the frontier, the growing urbanization of life, industrialization, new waves of immigration, and overseas growth gave special challenges to Americans.

Can you relate to character forming challenges? Have you had challenges from natural conditions or from other people in your life? Does Turner's thesis appear a valid analysis of American development? What other factors might you consider in explaining the development of the United States in the 19th century?

I. The Frontier and American History

CHANGING FRONTIERS

In the 250 years between the first English settlements and the end of the Civil War, the frontier line gradually moved westward, first to the Appalachian Mountains and then slowly on across the country. We have discussed the significance of Manifest Destiny and the march west as it related to the spread of slavery and the Civil War. Before the war the discovery of

> The westward movement of the frontier is quickened by the discovery of gold and silver.

gold in California in 1849 and of gold and silver in the Rockies brought boom towns and new settlers to these regions. This mining frontier was a rough frontier of great challenges where a few individuals made fortunes but most did not. Companies with Eastern money were more likely to strike it rich, which frustrated the prospectors[1]. Other natural resources such as oil and lumber were also exploited on the frontier and presented their own challenges to Americans. After the Civil War, the pace of the westward movement increased.

The cattle frontier provides the material for most of the legends and stories of the West. At first, cattle were raised in the Southwest for their hides. When the

[1] prospector   *Someone who hunts for gold, silver, or other valuable minerals.*

THE WALL OF THE MARTYR.

"THERE IS NO GEETTING O-ON WITH LO! ALL I DID WAS TO WITHHOLD HIS FOO-FOOD
AND BLANKETS, KICK HIM OUT OF HIS RESER-V-VATION, SELL HIM SAND FOR FLOUR, KEEP
HIM DRUNK ON CHEAP WHI-HISKEY, AND NOW, JUST BECAUSE HIS PEOPLE ARE STARVING
AND THERE IS NO REDRESS, HE GETS MA-MAD AND THER-REATENS TO STRIKE ME!"

Indian Wars continued until 1886. Helen Hunt Jackson's A Century of Dishonor *published
in 1881 aroused concern over the treatment of Native Americans. What view is expressed
concerning relations between the white men and the Native Americans by the artist, J.A.M.,
in this cartoon?*
Published in Life, *March 27, 1884.*

transcontinental railroad made it possible to get cattle closer to
markets, they were raised for their meat. The proverbial cowboy,
an individual alone with his horse on the plains, drove great herds
of cattle north on "long drives" to railheads so the cattle could be
taken by the railroads to meat processing plants. The cattle
frontier, consisting of open range ranching with no fences marking
ownership, turned America into a nation of meat eaters. The cattle frontier gave us a
folklore and mythology that is still used today in advertising everything from beer to
automobiles. Americans, over 100 years after the end of the cattle frontier, still find the
experience appealing and relate to the qualities of character it brought forth.

> The cattle frontier leaves
> a great impression and
> continues to be an
> important aspect of
> American culture.

NATIVE AMERICANS AND THE FRONTIER

The white man's frontiers all were developed at the expense of
the Native Americans. Treaties were signed and then ignored as
lands became valuable because of natural resources or railroad
building. Americans tended to think of all natives as the same,

> Westward expansion
> displaces Native
> Americans who fight to
> preserve their lands.

but there were great differences between the tribes, which worked to the tribes' disadvantage. The Native Americans were often provoked into action, and fighting resulted. These outbreaks are referred to as the Indian Wars.

The most famous battle in the Indian Wars after the Civil War took place at the Little Big Horn River in southern Montana in 1876. There, Chiefs Sitting Bull and Crazy Horse of the Sioux Tribe annihilated Colonel Custer's troops. The Battle of the Little Big Horn has gone into history as "Custer's Last Stand." It was more pointedly one of the last stands of the tribes, who were finally overwhelmed by the greater supplies and the persistence of the United States Army.

Until 1887 the United States' policy was to gather Native Americans on reservations. The Dawes Severalty Act reversed the policy, dissolving community-owned tribal lands, giving the land to individual families and citizenship to those who accepted this land. Assimilation into American society rather than separation on reservations became the new policy of the United States' government. The change in policy was in part due to violence between whites and those on reservations. In part it was the result of a book, *A Century of Dishonor* by Helen Hunt Jackson, published in 1881. Helen Jackson told a sorry story of broken treaties, massacres, and forced movement to reservations. America's conscience and sensitivity to the needs of others was raised. The Dawes Act was the result.

> The Dawes Severalty Act attempts to address the needs of Native Americans but fails.

Unfortunately, the Dawes Act created new problems, and the United States' treatment of the native population continued as a blemish on the American nation and as an example of American intolerance for those who are different. The challenge of and commitment to equality could not be made by the frontiersmen whose material needs and expedient solutions to challenges came first. We still see as part of the American character an intolerance of those different from ourselves and a desire to fill material needs and use expedient solutions to attain them. The nation's treatment of Native Americans improved somewhat with the Civil Rights Movement in the late 20th century, but for most of our history the Native American has not been accepted as a full member of the American democratic society.

THE FINAL FRONTIER

The final frontier was the farming frontier. Stimulated by the railroad and wartime demand for food and aided by the Homestead Act of 1862, farmers moved westward. They came from the eastern states or Europe. Some were enticed westward by promises of a new life by railroad companies, which needed produce to haul to market to make the lines more profitable.

Life on the farming frontier was harsh. With little lumber, homes had to be built of sod. Water was scarce on the Great Plains west of 100° longitude, where rainfall averaged less than 28 inches per year, not enough for growing wheat. New machinery aided the farmers and increased productivity, but farmers often cultivated lands that were unsuitable for farming in an attempt to make money to pay for the machinery. The results were disastrous for both the land and the farmers.

Because farm allotments were 160 acres under the Homestead Act, homes were isolated. Lives were lonely, and church and club meetings provided the few social times available. The Grange (see page 152) helped to address the issue of loneliness, but the Sears Roebuck and Montgomery Ward mail order catalogues did more as they made the latest fashions and inventions available on the farms. The extension of rural free delivery by the United States Post Office provided another link to the outside world. Wind-up phonographs brought entertainment by the end of the century.

RAILROADS CHANGE AMERICAN LIFE

Railroads transformed American life in the 19th century, just as automobiles did in the 20th century. By the Civil War the old Northwest Territory and the East were linked by rails, and the rail

> The railroads transform American life.

network of the North gave it a great advantage over the Confederate States. Before the war no agreement could be reached on a transcontinental rail route, but after the South seceded, the central route from Omaha, Nebraska, to Sacramento, California was voted by Congress, with large federal government subsidies in both cash and land given to the builders, the Union Pacific and Central Pacific companies.

Throughout United States history the federal government has been prepared to subsidize industries deemed important to the national interest either directly or through tariffs. The railroads in the mid-19th century benefited from such government subsidies.

The building of the railroads presented many challenges, which greatly affected the West. First, labor was needed to lay the rails and blast the route through the Rockies. Chinese immigrants, among the first from Asia, came to work on the Central Pacific. As the Asian population grew in California, they met increasing hostility from the white inhabitants. Finally in 1882 Chinese immigration to the United States was banned in spite of the Chinese workers' contribution to the linking of the two coasts.

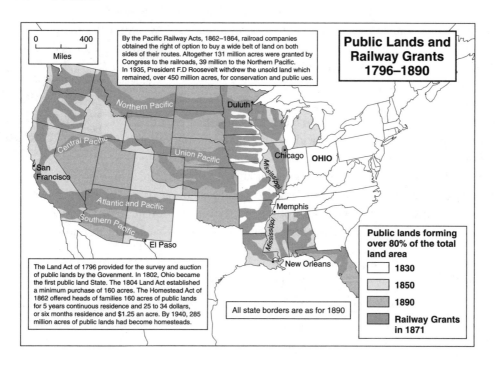

0 — 400 Miles

By the Pacific Railway Acts, 1862–1864, railroad companies obtained the right of option to buy a wide belt of land on both sides of their routes. Altogether 131 million acres were granted by Congress to the railroads, 39 million to the Northern Pacific. In 1935, President F.D Roosevelt withdrew the unsold land which remained, over 450 million acres, for conservation and public ues.

Public Lands and Railway Grants 1796–1890

The Land Act of 1796 provided for the survey and auction of public lands by the Govenment. In 1802, Ohio became the first public land State. The 1804 Land Act established a minimum purchase of 160 acres. The Homestead Act of 1862 offered heads of families 160 acres of public lands for 5 years continuous residence and 25 to 34 dollars, or six months residence and $1.25 an acre. By 1940, 285 million acres of public lands had become homesteads.

All state borders are as for 1890

Public lands forming over 80% of the total land area

☐ 1830
▨ 1850
▨ 1890
■ Railway Grants in 1871

A second challenge was the herds of buffalo that roamed the Great Plains. The herds interfered with railroad building and operation. They could knock a train off the track. The railroads wanted the herds destroyed, and the army supported their desire for destruction of the herds as a way to starve the Native Americans into submission. The life style of the nomadic tribes was based on the buffalo.

. A third challenge was to make money. The availability of railroads created the long drive in the cattle frontier. Later the railroads encouraged farmers to settle, ending the cattle frontier and replacing it with the farming frontier. The railroads became the target of farmers' anger when they abused their power and used rebates and the long- and short-haul agreements to increase their profits. The railroads made a few men millionaires, such as Leland Stanford and James J. Hill, and provided jobs for hundreds even if at fairly low wages. The building of the railroads stimulated the steel and other industries. Steel rails became the norm, as did a standard gauge[2]. The challenges of transcontinental railroad building were met with ingenuity. The rail lines helped destroy the last frontier and linked America together as a united nation.

RAILROADS AND THE FRONTIER

The railroads encouraged settlement, but once they had a guaranteed source of produce to carry to market, they often raised freight prices and exploited the farmers, who were at their mercy. The anger of farmers at this situation grew when prices fell both domestically and abroad as a result of overproduction and increased competition from other farming nations such as Canada. The Patrons of Husbandry, known as the Grange, which at first was formed as a social and self-help organization, began to organize farmers and apply political pressure. Several states like Illinois passed laws controlling railroads' rights to set fares. At first the Supreme Court upheld the laws but later reversed itself, saying the Constitution gave the federal government, and not the states, control over commerce. Federal action followed, but the Interstate Commerce Commission of 1887, a first step from the laissez-faire[3] business philosophy of the age, proved ineffective.

As had happened previously in the nation when groups were disaffected with the major parties or had a particular issue to pursue, the disaffected farmers joined with some disaffected laborers to organize a new political party. The resulting People's or Populist Party became the high point of farmer activism to improve farm conditions through political activity. It made a strong showing in the election of 1892, and its Omaha Platform[4] provides an excellent summary of reform ideas (see page 178). In 1896, the Populist Party also nominated the Democratic Party nominee, William Jennings Bryan, and with his defeat by the Republican,

> The People's or Populist Party becomes the vehicle for farmers' political protest.

[2] standard gauge *For railroads, the gauge is the distance between the rails. Once a standard was agreed upon, railroad cars could move from one line to another, creating a national railroad network.*

[3] laissez-faire *Noninterference by government in private enterprises; a hands-off policy.*

[4] platform *A declaration of principles and policies concerning their views on governing issued by a political party.*

William McKinley, the Populist Party was no longer a contender on the national level. Farmers have not formed another national political party since then. Throughout the 20th century a farm lobby, or bloc, in Congress has labored to protect farmers and the quality of farm life, which Thomas Jefferson viewed as the basis of a democratic society. With the passing of the frontier in 1890, industrial activities as exemplified by railroads, steel, and oil became the focus of most American's lives.

To deal with the farming frontier, people had to have certain traits of character. Were the same traits needed in an industrialized nation, or did American character change after 1890 as business interests came to dominate the nation?

INVENTIONS

The steel industry is just one example of the growth of United States industry after the Civil War. The war effort in the North also gave impetus to some industries such as cloth- and cannon-making. The population grew rapidly after the war, providing both a market and labor for new industrial developments. Inventions came rapidly and transformed American life.

Thomas Edison, a famous inventor, organized his work of invention and centered it around the use of electricity. He produced both the first light bulb and the phonograph. Think what life would be like without them. Singer's sewing machine and Bell's telephone had an equal impact on American lifestyles. The sewing machine speeded clothing manufacture, and the phone created a new lifestyle. Together with the typewriter, they provided many opportunities for women in the workforce. Advertising, including billboards, entered the American scene. Special incentives to retailers and easy financing for purchasers became part of the way American business was done. By the end of the century, people were working on ideas for the automobile, the airplane, and other inventions that drastically affected our life in the 20th century.

CAPITALISM AND PROFIT

Business needs to make profits and cuts wages to do so.

The guiding principle of business capitalism was to make profits. There were many opportunities to do so as new inventions were made and new machinery became available. New machinery was expensive and needed to be fully used, but increased production meant more produce. In order to sell the added produce, prices had to be reduced, and then profits would fall. The cost of running machines and bank payments on loans were both fixed costs. Wages were not. Factory owners would often cut wages to maintain profits. A growing population provided new workers in case the old ones quit or went on strike when wages were reduced.

BUSINESS ORGANIZATION

To make profits even more secure, new types of business organizations were adopted. The first organizations used were pools, which were informal arrangements

This page of advertisements from Harper's Weekly *is similar to what one finds in many magazines today. Advertising became a growing business at the end of the 19th century as new products became easily available. One can learn a great deal of history by looking at old ads. What items are advertised? Would you find similar ads today? Do you recognize the items such as the item advertised by H.C. Curtis and Company?*

Answers to these questions will give you a good deal of information about life in the United States at the end of the 19th century. For instance, there are two bicycle ads and one for the New York Central Railroad in this time before the automobile. There are ads for socks and underwear, furs, tobacco, soft drinks, perfume, olive oil, life insurance, and other items that would be advertised today. One item that would not be advertised today is stiff collars for men's shirts—see H. C. Curtis and Company ad. Harper's Weekly, *October 24, 1896.*

to divide the market among several companies rather than rely on the free market operation. In prosperous times these informal pools worked well, but in times of recession, a more powerful and legally constituted arrangement was needed as companies broke their pooling agreements.

John D. Rockefeller from Cleveland, Ohio, had entered the oil industry in 1865, six years after oil was first discovered in Pennsylvania. He and his brother established an oil refining company, the Standard Oil Company. The company absorbed many rivals. In 1879 John D. Rockefeller organized his company as the Standard Oil Trust. To form a trust, different companies turn control of their stock, which represents ownership, over to a Board of Trustees who then run all the companies. The trust does not own but merely manages the company for the supposed benefit of all the companies and to obtain higher profits. Trusts worked much more effectively than pools because they were binding agreements.

> John D. Rockefeller develops a new form of business organization, the trust.

A final idea for company organization in order to increase profits and to control the market was the holding company. New Jersey was the first state to allow one company to own or hold stock in other companies and to own property in other states. John D. Rockefeller again took the lead in trying a new organizational form. He used the New Jersey law to turn the Standard Oil Trust into the Standard Oil Company of New Jersey, a new company that included forty previous companies. It was the first large holding company.

> The holding company becomes a tool for creating monopolies.

Holding companies could own companies that did various jobs. For instance, an oil holding company could own a drilling company, the pipelines, the refinery, and the distribution centers or gas stations. Such an arrangement is called vertical integration and gave the company great control over the market from the raw material production to retail sale. In other cases a holding company would own all or almost all the companies doing one step in the manufacturing process, and this is called horizontal integration.

Trusts and holding companies became tools of industrialists wishing to create monopolies, that is, to exercise complete control over a particular industry. Such control would allow a company to set prices and thus to make higher profits, very often at the expense of the consumer and worker.

SOCIAL DARWINISM

Some manufacturers were concerned about the working and living conditions of their employees. George Pullman built a model village for his workers in the Pullman Sleeping Car plant, but he insisted on running the village in his own way and cut wages to maintain profits. His plan for a utopian working society collapsed with the Pullman Strike of 1894. Many business and social leaders of the age were less interested in their workers and more concerned about their profits. They followed the tenets of Social Darwinism.

Social Darwinism loosely applied Charles Darwin's Theory of Evolution to economics. Taking Darwin's suggestion of the survival of the fittest as the determinant in evolution, Social Darwinists believed that the state should not interfere in economic life. They believed those on top in the business world were there because they were the fittest. They had survived the battle of the marketplace because they were the best. Any interference in the free market operation would wreck the economy and upset its natural evolution. This view of economics is referred to as laissez-faire. Social Darwinists believed any person with ability could rise to the top, and laborers were where they were because of natural selection.

This philosophy of Social Darwinism dominated the thinking of many American business leaders in the late 19th and early 20th centuries. The fact the federal government aided businesses through high tariffs and subsidies, such as those for the railroad, was overlooked or ignored. In *Santa Clara County* v. *Southern Pacific Railroad* the Supreme Court extended the protection and rights of the 14th Amendment to trusts thus giving them "corporate personhood"—a controversial interpretation of the amendment. Recent correspondence between Chief Justice Waite and the Court Reporter suggest there was a deliberate misinterpretation made of the decision—a decision that has greatly affected the development of American business and the capitalist system in the nation.

THE GOSPEL OF WEALTH

By the end of the century one millionaire, Andrew Carnegie, a brilliant Scots immigrant who created Carnegie Steel and sold it to the banker J. P. Morgan, added a twist to Social Darwinism in a speech "The Gospel of Wealth," in 1889. Carnegie argued that wealth was essential for civilization and by the natural law of competition only a few could achieve it. However, what these few did with their wealth was crucial for society. They could leave their wealth to their children, but this was "injudicious" and undermined the natural law of acquisition because their children began life with an advantage. Secondly, the rich could bequeath their wealth for public purposes after their death, but they would have no control over its use. Carnegie then argued that the rich should administer their wealth through their lifetime to benefit society. Andrew Carnegie did so, spending over $350,000,000 he got from the sale of Carnegie Steel to establish libraries and endow the Carnegie Endowment for International Peace and the Carnegie Foundation for Advancement of Teaching.

Following Carnegie, charitable contributions and philanthropy[5] became the way followed by many of the great entrepreneurs of the age. The railroad builder, Leland Stanford, founded and endowed Stanford University. John D. Rockefeller of Standard Oil Company endowed the University of Chicago and established the Rockefeller Institute of Medical Research and the Rockefeller Foundation. Rockefeller money was used to buy large tracts of land that later became national parks, and his descendants helped purchase the site for the United Nations in New York City. Such philanthropy is a vital part of American economic and cultural life today and separates us from other nations where the government supports many artistic and other endeavors. We all benefit from the philanthropy of individuals in

---

[5] philanthropy   *The spirit of active goodwill toward one's fellow men as shown in efforts to promote their welfare through gifts or the building of institutions.*

different ways either enjoying museums, libraries, hospitals, schools, orchestras, or special charities supported by philanthropically minded individuals.

While "The Gospel of Wealth" supported philanthropy, Social Darwinism supported an economic system that benefited a few at the expense of many. The wealth that philanthropic entrepreneurs spent was often accumulated by the exploitation of workers and natural resources. Some was made through trade, including selling opium in China. Workers' wages were kept low and working hours long, which encouraged slum conditions. As a result discontented workers organized but with limited success. By the end of the century "progressive" leaders were calling for reforms in urban government and living conditions as well as in the organization of American business.

Some of the qualities of the American character which Turner ascribed to the frontier experience could also be ascribed to competition in the business world—coarseness, acquisitiveness, a grasp of the material, dominant individualism, and exuberance of life. The question is, Were these qualities born on the frontier and applied to business, or did they arise from economic competition? There is no agreed on answer. What do you think?

BEGINNING OF LABOR ORGANIZATION

The first unions or organizations of workers came during the era of Jacksonian Democracy and were local. In the post-Civil War period attempts were made to organize workers on a national basis. The National Labor Union was organized in 1866 with the goal of establishing the eight-hour day. In 1868 Congress passed an eight-hour day for mechanics and laborers who worked for the United States government, but progress elsewhere was slow. Unsuccessfully turning to national politics in 1872, the National Labor Union quickly collapsed. After the Panic of 1873 there was labor unrest, but labor unions were unsuccessful in organizing support. Until the 1930s union strength and influence dropped during times of depression or panic.

> The first attempts at a national labor union fail.

In 1878 the Knights of Labor was organized as a national union of both skilled and unskilled workers. Their platform called for the eight-hour day, boycotts not strikes, a graduated income tax, and consumer cooperatives. The Knights forced some concessions from several railways but collapsed after a general strike for an eight-hour day failed in Chicago and the Haymarket Massacre occurred in 1886 (see page 158). One inherent weakness of the Knights of Labor was bringing together all workers, skilled and unskilled, in one union. The wage level and concerns of the two groups differed.

The next national union to be founded, the American Federation of Labor (AFL), was formed in 1886. It concentrated on organizing skilled workers. It continues today as the important AFL-CIO. The organizational approach used by the AFL under its first President, Samuel Gompers, was to recognize the autonomy of each specialized trade, such as carpenters or cigar makers. The AFL formed the coordinating group for these separate trades. Membership in the AFL grew. Its program under Samuel Gompers included laws curbing immigration in order to protect jobs, relief from technological unemployment created by the introduction of new machines, and labor legislation to include the eight-hour day and workmen's compensation.

Unskilled workers remained largely unorganized after the collapse of the Knights of Labor. The Industrial Workers of the World (IWW) was formed in 1905 to organize the unskilled workers. It was considered very radical by many Americans and was never very successful as a union. It died after World War I in a period of political and economic reaction.

STRIKES: A TOOL OF LABOR ORGANIZATION

Industrialization created new working conditions and new relationships between the employed and employers. As large textile factories replaced weaving done in homes, workers became just another factor to reckon with in analyzing costs and making profits. The personal relationship of the small shop where the boss knew his employees as individuals was replaced by large impersonal factories where the workers seldom if ever met the owner. As the workers were treated like another machine to be used, they became alienated from their job. Employers in seeking profits often cut wages, and if a worker did not accept the cut, there were others who needed the job. It was a situation in which factory owners, the capitalists, were in control and held the power.

Unions were a way of uniting the workers to give them power equal to the owners. The major tool used by unionized workers to force their program or wishes on the employers was the strike. How to organize strikes and make them effective was the great challenge. It required as much ingenuity and skill as did organizing business or struggling with the challenges of the frontier.

> Unions give workers power.

Workers could rarely count on the support of government when on strike. Most city and state governments were under the control of successful businessmen who used their political influence to break or end strikes and destroy unions. Also the theory of Social Darwinism worked in favor of the owners who had "made it," they would claim, on their own, overlooking the help of the tariffs. Unionization seemed to be against the individualism that was so highly respected in America. Many workers were recent arrivals in the United States and appeared different from earlier arrivals. Middle class Americans often saw strikes as threats to the stability and security that they had achieved. Some union members did hold radical ideas for reforming American life, but they were a tiny minority.

One incident, the Haymarket Massacre in Chicago in 1886, was falsely linked to an anarchists'[6] plot, and it frightened the middle class and destroyed the Knights of Labor, which was seen as the organizer of the incident. The Haymarket Massacre occurred just after the Chicago police had broken up an anarchist/communist meeting. A bomb exploded and seven police were killed. The remaining police opened fire on the crowd. Eight anarchists were later arrested, accused of the bombing, and tried. Four were found guilty and hung, yet no one was found guilty of

---

[6] anarchist   *One who advocates anarchy—a society in which there is no law or supreme power—and who advocates violence or terrorism to achieve this goal.*

throwing the bomb. When a new governor of Illinois was elected, he released those prisoners still in jail, but the action hurt his political career.

Both political and business leaders were frightened by the incident, and the average American citizen followed their lead in seeing a threat to the traditional standards of society in the actions of the unions. The incident reflects the problems faced by labor protesters and organizers.

GOVERNMENT INTERVENTION IN STRIKES

The federal government intervened in the Pullman Strike in 1894. In that strike workers in the Pullman, or sleeper, cars on the railroads went on strike to gain higher wages and better working conditions. Train service was blocked by their work stoppage. The Democratic President, Grover Cleveland, sent in federal troops to end the strike so the United States mail would not be stopped. Both Republicans and Democrats put the delivery of the mail and the operation of the railroads above the needs of workers for better pay and improved working conditions.

It was not until the progressive Republican President Theodore Roosevelt intervened in the Anthracite Coal Strike in 1902 and appointed a commission to set the settlement terms that strikers received any help from the federal government. The coal strikers won a 10 percent pay rise, but the union was not recognized. The incident was unusual in the pre-World War I period, but suggested times would change.

The strike is the final threat used by workers to get employers to hear their demands. It had limited success in the prosperous 1920s but became an effective tool of laborers in the New Deal period. While few industrial workers ever saw the frontier, the traits Turner said developed on the frontier—coarseness and strength, practical, inventive nervous energy, and an ability to effect great ends—were helpful in labor's efforts to organize and improve working conditions.

IMMIGRATION

Another matter that hurt the industrial workers and made the establishment of unions difficult was the increasing number of immigrants who came to America after 1880. While most pre-Civil War immigrants came from the British Isles or northern Europe, after 1880 more and more came from southern and eastern Europe. By 1910 almost two-thirds of immigrants came from Russia, Italy, and the Austro-Hungarian empire. Most were unskilled workers from farms who came seeking a better life and settled in the cities. Conditions in the cities were difficult. Immigrants were eager to find work and willing to work for low wages. This hurt the efforts of workers to organize and gain higher wages.

During this time period, unlike today, no immigrants were coming from Asia and almost none were arriving from areas other than Europe. In 1882, Congress passed the Chinese Exclusion Act, prohibiting immigration of Chinese. In 1907, the Gentleman's Agreement with Japan stopped Japanese immigration.

By the end of the 19th century, many of the older immigrants from western and northern Europe came to resent the new immigrants from southern and eastern

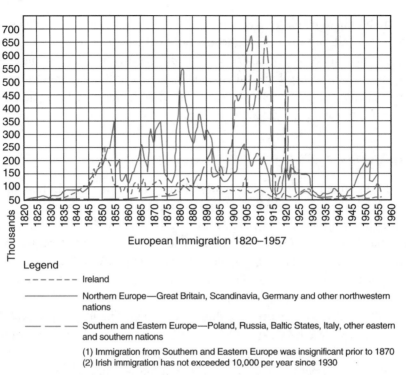

European Immigration 1820–1957

Legend

– – – – – – – Ireland

————— Northern Europe—Great Britain, Scandinavia, Germany and other northwestern nations

— — — — Southern and Eastern Europe—Poland, Russia, Baltic States, Italy, other eastern and southern nations

(1) Immigration from Southern and Eastern Europe was insignificant prior to 1870
(2) Irish immigration has not exceeded 10,000 per year since 1930

This line graph illustrates the immigration to America from Europe from 1820 until 1960. It clearly shows when immigration reached its highest levels and the areas of Europe from which immigrants came. Note that Irish immigration peaked in the 1850 period, that from Northern Europe at the end of the last century, and that from Southern and Eastern Europe in the early years of the 20th century. A line graph of this type can present a great deal of information easily and quickly. Why do you think there was an increase of immigration from Northern Europe after 1945?
Source: U.S. Bureau of the Census, Historical Statistics of the U.S., Colonial Times to the Present.

Europe. There were occasional clashes. There were language, religious, and social differences. As the children of immigrants went to public schools and learned English, they became more American but lost some contact with their own culture, creating tensions within the new immigrant groups. Many of the new immigrants were Roman Catholic, and the difficulties Catholics faced in pre-Civil War America continued for them. Some immigrants were Greek Orthodox and others Jewish, which added both to diversity in America and to tensions.

Most of these new immigrants settled in urban areas, which grew rapidly in the late 19th century. Major coastal cities had their centers of immigrant culture, and all had a high percentage of foreign-born or first-generation Americans. The rapid growth of cities illustrates perhaps the greatest change in lifestyle in post-Civil War America, as the nation changed from a rural to an urban culture.

Key Point to Remember

The fifty years after the Civil War was a period of rapid changes on the frontier, in the development of industry and business, and in the labor force and its organization.

People to Remember

Samuel Gompers   Labor leader; founder and first president of the American Federation of Labor (AFL).—1886

John D. Rockefeller   Businessman; philanthropist; founder of the Standard Oil Trust—1879—and the Standard Oil Company of New Jersey, a holding company.

Andrew Carnegie   Business leader; philanthropist; Scots immigrant who founded Carnegie Steel; presented "The Gospel of Wealth"—1889—idea, which argued that the rich should spend their money on philanthropic enterprises during their lifetime.

Thomas Edison   Inventor; had a laboratory establishment at Menlo Park, New Jersey, where the lightbulb, phonograph, electric voting machine, and motion pictures were developed.

Chief Sitting Bull   Native-American leader; Sioux chieftain who organized his tribe to stop the westward movement of the whites onto the Great Plains; he defeated General Custer.

Links from the Past to the Present

1. The image and legend of the frontier is used in everything from political speeches to movies to commercial advertising to gain Americans' support.
2. Large corporations are still important under the capitalist system of the United States.
3. The philosophies of laissez-faire and Social Darwinism still have strong support in the United States.
4. Philanthropy has been crucial to the improvement of the quality of life in America.
5. Unions still play a significant role in labor-management relations.
6. New inventions continue to change American lifestyle (iPods, cell phones).

Dates

1862—Homestead Act.
   Pacific Railway Act.

1866—National Labor Union formed.

1876—Battle of the Little Big Horn.

1878—Knights of Labor formed.

1879—Standard Oil Trust formed by Rockefeller.

1886—Haymarket Riot.
   American Federation of Labor organized.

1887—Dawes Act passed.
   Interstate Commerce Commission established.

1889—Carnegie's "The Gospel of Wealth" speech.

1893—Panic of 1893.

1902—Anthracite Coal Strike; T. Roosevelt intervened.

Questions

Identify each of the following:

Frederick Jackson Turner	Social Darwinism
A Century of Dishonor	"The Gospel of Wealth"
Singer Sewing Machine	Knights of Labor
Standard Oil Trust	American Federation of Labor

Multiple Choice:

1. Thomas Edison is noted for his work with electricity and especially for his invention of the
   a. sewing machine.
   b. telephone.
   c. lightbulb.

2. Social Darwinism is based upon the theory of
   a. laissez-faire.
   b. management efficiency.
   c. evolution.

3. The American Federation of Labor organized
   a. unskilled workers.
   b. skilled trade workers and unskilled laborers.
   c. skilled trade workers such as carpenters and cigar makers.

4. Older immigrants resented the new immigrants because
   a. they would accept low wages.
   b. they were highly skilled.
   c. they could fight better.

II. Reform Movements

THE SOCIAL GOSPEL

Late 19th century cities had many of the same problems as cities today. There were pockets of poverty, crowded living conditions, rampant crime, and often political corruption. Reared in the tradition of the Puritan work ethic and Social Darwinism, many American leaders and the voting middle class believed poverty to result from a lack of effort and to reflect poor character. While social workers began to realize environment also had an effect on poverty, American voters were not prepared to help the poor.

Help did come from many quarters. After a trip to England where she saw settlement houses that had an impact on life in the cities, Jane Addams founded Hull House in Chicago in 1889. This first settlement house in the United States became famous as a model way to improve community and civic pride. Jane Addams was awarded the Nobel Peace Prize in 1931 for her work on behalf of the urban poor.

In churches preachers of the Social Gospel encouraged the establishment of settlement homes and the use of the city churches as centers of learning and recreation. Walter Rauschenbusch in New York and Washington Gladden in Columbus, Ohio, were leaders of the Social Gospel movement.

They called upon their churches to heed the Sermon on the Mount[7] and other teachings of Jesus and to act accordingly, giving to the poor and needy. They thought that socialism might be a better way than capitalism if the poor and laborers were not helped by capitalists. Their preaching in the 1880s prepared the way for the reforms of the Progressives early in the 20th century. The Social Gospel helped focus attention on life in the cities.

LIFE IN THE CITIES

Cities grew rapidly after the Civil War. While the number of buildings increased, the population grew even faster. As wages went up, some were able to purchase homes, and as street cars and trolleys were developed, suburbs became the place to go if you could afford it. Many, particularly immigrants, could not afford to buy property. They had to rent from landlords. Often the only places they could rent were in tenements[8]. In tenements families of immigrants and the poor often lived in one room and shared kitchens and bathrooms. Many tenements did not have indoor plumbing. To make a living, the parents sometimes sewed or rolled cigars in the one room. There were efforts at reform in different cities, but America's commitment to free enterprise prevented the building of public housing to replace tenements.

Such living conditions encouraged crime, which was often blamed on the immigrants rather than the conditions. Gangs made up of both old and recent city dwellers were a common element of city life. Theft, feuds, and organized vice were the most prevalent crimes. One form of vice was prostitution, which literally enslaved young girls from rural states or from immigrant families. Prostitution, gambling, and other activities were often given police protection in return for a slice of the profits. As more African-Americans from the South began to move to northern cities after the turn of the century, race riots occurred in many of those cities. Discrimination against Asians and Mexicans increased. In San Francisco, Dennis Kearney, an immigrant from Ireland and founder of the Working Man's Party, led the attack on Chinese immigrants. His slogan was "The Chinese Must Go!" In 1877, twenty-five Chinese laundries were burned in the city and in Truckee, California, a railroad town, 1,000 Chinese who had built the railroad were driven from town. Intolerance was a fact of life in American cities.

[7] Sermon on the Mount   *Preached by Jesus as reported by Matthew in the New Testament of the* Bible. *Among the most famous passages are "Blessed are those who show mercy," "Blessed are the peacemakers," "Blessed are those who have suffered persecution for the cause of right," "Blessed are you when you suffer insults and persecution for my sake, you have a rich reward in heaven," "You are a light to the world . . . and must shed light among your fellows."*

[8] tenement   *A dwelling house where separate apartments are rented to families; usually occupied by the lower classes.*

But not everything in cities between the Civil War and World War I was bad. Street lighting was introduced after Edison's invention of the incandescent lightbulb in 1879, which made the streets much safer. Fire-fighting equipment became a regular part of city life. A clean water supply and sewage disposal made life more bearable and reduced the stench of the city. Streetcars made travel easier. The growth of suburbs allowed escape from the crowded conditions of the inner city, and in the 20th century this opportunity was incorporated in the "American Dream," in which a house of your own in the suburbs became an important element. Cultural offerings—theater, concerts, opera—made urban centers attractive for those who could afford to attend. Free libraries and museums added a welcome diversion for poor and wealthy alike.

THE CITY POLITICAL BOSS

In many cities where the government was unable to cope with the complexity of problems, political bosses emerged. Bosses controlled political machines[9], which in turn controlled the city. Machine politics were often corrupt, and bribery was used to stay in power, but they had to have the support of the people

> Corrupt political machines run many cities, but they provide benefits for immigrants.

who voted. For voting purposes cities were subdivided into wards and the political machine had people working in each ward who knew the residents and could help with their problems. The ward workers would help their constituents[10] find jobs or housing, deal with the police or city administration, and solve many of the problems presented by urban living.

While the boss and his close associates were often driven by greed and power, political machines and their ward workers did make the lives of many immigrants and poor more tolerable. The bosses distributed city business, everything from garbage collection to printing, to those who would help them stay in power. The boss system, while often corrupt, did make the cities function quite efficiently for the poorer residents. Bosses supplied in a personal way many of those needs that are now supplied by an impersonal government agency.

URBAN REFORM

The corruption and the ever-rising taxes to pay for it and the new city services like sewage and lighting upset many voters, particularly in the middle class. At the end of the century, urban reformers emerged in many cities. They formed part of the Progressive Movement (see page 182). These urban reformers offered plans to reorganize and streamline city government in the same way large American businesses were reorganizing and streamlining. New forms of city government—the city manager and the city commission—were introduced to replace the mayoral

[9] political machine   *A group, usually from the same political party, organized to control the political life of a city, or other political unit. Political machines are usually under the control of an individual called the boss.*

[10] constituents   *Those citizens who are qualified to vote for a legislator and to whom the elected legislator is responsible for his or her actions.*

system, which was more easily controlled by the political machine. In the mayoral system one person, the mayor, had the executive power and could be bribed. In some cities reformers supported city ownership of electric and gas companies and streetcar lines to prevent bribery. Some worked to provide better jobs and living conditions.

The reformers made government more efficient, but the new efficient governments often lacked the contact with the people that gave bosses their power. Most reform movements were short lived, and machine politics soon returned. Americans wanted their cities to have effective government and to be livable places without crime and poverty, but few reformers or their followers were prepared to work for the city. Therefore, periodic reform efforts followed by a return to old ways became the norm for urban political life.

Many reformers were from the middle and upper classes of the cities. As industrialization continued, a class of very wealthy people emerged in the United States, and most of them lived in the cities. For instance, in New York City, Fifth Avenue was

> The gap between rich and poor in the cities grows steadily.

lined with mansions built by the wealthy. These mansions along Fifth Avenue overlooked the new Central Park, an extensive open area in the center of Manhattan that was preserved to provide open space, grass, and trees for all those living in the crowded city. The expenditures of the rich were often extravagant, and the gap between the rich and the poor in the cities steadily widened. Even though wages climbed, industrial profits grew even more rapidly for the few millionaires. Many of the rich did social work, helping the poor as suggested in Carnegie's "The Gospel of Wealth." For instance, Eleanor Roosevelt, born into an upper class family, niece of President Theodore Roosevelt and wife of President Franklin Roosevelt, did social work in New York prior to her marriage, as did many of her class. Other people worked in or contributed monetarily to reform movements or philanthropic organizations.

ENTERTAINMENT

Middle class America grew in size, and as new types of jobs and the eight-hour day became more prevalent, leisure time increased. This greatly changed the American lifestyle. There were new products to consume and fun to pursue. Entertainment became an industry. Vaudeville shows, in which a series of acts

> As some Americans gain leisure time, entertainment becomes a major industry.

including everything from acrobats to yodellers, were presented on stage were very popular. William (Buffalo Bill) Cody and his Wild West Show was particularly popular. Movies, developed toward the end of the 19th century as slot-machine peep shows, quickly developed into a major mode of entertainment. By World War I movies were an important form of artistic expression and a new American industry. Movies have had a tremendous impact on American culture and attitudes, providing dreams for the young and homogenizing experiences so we all share certain visions or nightmares.

Eldorado Springs Resort, Colorado, 1908
In the post-Civil War era, as leisure time became available for more citizens, recreation became a focus for many. A variety of resorts were started from the mountains of New England to this one in Colorado that had swimming and hot springs. Note the clothing on the women and on the men in the pool, and that the men are wearing suits but a few have removed their coats. This was typical summer, recreational attire a hundred years ago. Also note there are no women in the pool.
Courtesy: Carnegie Branch Library for Local History, Boulder, Colorado

Professional sports also emerged as a major industry. The first World Series game was played in 1903. Football, first played between Rutgers and Princeton Universities right after the Civil War, became popular. The mania for winning football games cost eighteen lives in 1905 and was condemned by President Roosevelt. Individuals also participated in sports such as bicycling and croquet. While the latter has faded in popularity, America's interest in sports continues as a major aspect of the American character, perhaps rooted in the need for an active life, which was necessary on the frontier.

LITERATURE

After the Civil War, cheaply bound books called dime novels sold in great numbers to an increasingly literate public. Adventure stories laid in the West were replaced by detective

Authors reflect the values of society in their works.

stories as the most popular reading as the 20th century dawned. Horatio Alger published 130 books, all on the same "rags to riches" theme of the poor boy who becomes wealthy because of honesty, ambition, and thrift. Horatio Alger's works were widely popular and reinforced the teachings of the Social Darwinists. These popular books were important in forming the thought patterns of young Americans.

There were also a number of works produced that are considered classics and reveal different sides of American life. The most popular author was Mark Twain,

Rogers makes a comment on the newspapers of the late 19th century when the term, "yellow press," first came into use. Papers turned to stories of crime and scandal to attract readers. What does Rogers see as the role of the "Paterfamilias" (father of the family) in dealing with these stories?
Published in Life, *February 7, 1884.*

the pen name for Samuel Clemens, whose short stories of the West and great novels, *The Adventures of Tom Sawyer* (1876) and *The Adventures of Huckleberry Finn* (1884), revealed the comic and tragic side of life. Edith Wharton and Henry James wrote about upper class Americans while some, like Theodore Dreiser in *Sister Carrie*, explored realistically the struggles of slum life, sexuality, and violence.

NEWSPAPERS

Newspapers were popular in the post-Civil War period. Analytical, in-depth reporting made good reading, but it could antagonize readers. Such reporting was often replaced by features in order to avoid offending advertisers upon whom the papers depended for their profits. What the reader pays for a newspaper has never covered the cost of publishing. Advertising has been the great source of money in the publishing business.

Joseph Pulitzer, who began with a St. Louis newspaper and moved to New York, introduced the idea of the "yellow press," which was named for the "yellow kid" in his colored comic page in the *New York World*. Yellow journalism is based on sensationalism and exposures in order to sell papers. Papers battling for more readers and more advertising struggled to outdo each other in reporting scandals. The public bought the papers suggesting an aspect of the American character different from the clean cowboy image of frontier legend. William Randolph Hearst in the *San Francisco Examiner* was another noted practitioner of yellow journalism. Both he and Joseph Pulitzer built large publishing empires.

> Yellow journalism is developed to sell more papers.

Editors' competition for readers led to emotional reporting on the international situation in Cuba in the 1890s. The press had a major role in bringing the United States into the Spanish-American War. The press, and more particularly magazines such as *Harpers*, *Scribner's Monthly*, and *The Nation*, published well-researched stories of corruption in cities and business. Influential leaders of business and education read these accounts. The revelations published led to the urban reforms mentioned previously and encouraged others who saw the need to reform America in other areas.

How powerful do you think the press or TV news are today in forming our opinions and attitudes?

THE TEMPERANCE MOVEMENT

> The temperance movement succeeds with the passage of Amendment XVIII.

Among the concerns of reform-minded citizens in the post-Civil War period were several concerns that continued from the era of Jacksonian Democracy. Foremost of these was the temperance, or anti-alcohol, movement. Drinking had increased during the Civil War, and many immigrants came from cultures where drinking was an accepted part of life. A National Prohibition Party was formed in 1869 and ran candidates for office in many elections. Women's Christian Temperance Union (W. C.T.U.) was founded in 1874. Under the leadership of Frances Willard and Carrie Nation, who gained fame for smashing bottles in bars with her hatchet, the organization grew, and in 1893 the Anti-Saloon League was formed.

Agitation for reform by these two groups was widespread. Several states passed prohibition laws. The peak of the temperance movement was reached in 1919, when Amendment XVIII to the Constitution was ratified.

Amendment XVIII prohibited the sale and consumption of alcohol, and Congress was empowered to make laws to enforce it. The acceptance of prohibition by the Congress was tied in with support for World War I because prohibition would save grain for food rather than using it for alcohol. Prohibition became national policy and lasted for fourteen years. Amendment XVIII was repealed in 1933. Prohibition reveals one aspect of American character, the idea of fighting for a good cause.

WOMEN'S SUFFRAGE

The fight for women's suffrage began in the era of Jacksonian Democracy and continued after the Civil War. In 1869 the Wyoming Territory granted the vote to women. In some states and territories women were allowed to vote for school board members but not for candidates for political office. In 1890 the National American Woman Suffrage Association was organized. Elizabeth Cady Stanton, who had been a leader of the Seneca Falls Convention in 1848, and Susan B. Anthony were among the leaders. Increased agitation during the Progressive Era at the turn of the century brought some success as several states extended the suffrage to women.

Finally, Congress acted, and Amendment XIX was ratified by the states in 1920. Amendment XIX guaranteed women the right to vote in federal elections, but the states controlled who could vote in state elections. The right of women to vote quickly spread to all the states after the Nineteenth Amendment was adopted. After almost a hundred years of reform agitation, women achieved equality at the ballot box. The good aspects of the American character, fighting for a good cause and support of the individual, overcame negative arguments, and the suffrage reform cause was won.

Opportunities for women to work grew greatly after the Civil War. The telephone and typewriter opened many new opportunities for employment, as did the sewing machine. Many poor women had to work to supplement the family's meager income. In World War I women took some positions previously held only by men. Smaller families became the norm in urban centers, and this gave women more opportunities to be out of the home. All of these factors helped create widespread support for the granting of the suffrage to women.

OTHER SOCIAL CHANGES

Hull House, mentioned earlier, became a model for providing help to immigrants and the urban poor. Hull House began in one building but grew to 13. It operated as a welfare agency for the needy and provided recreation and other opportunities for young people as an alternative to juvenile delinquency in the slums. Settlement houses provided meeting rooms, gyms, day care nurseries, arts and crafts, and adult education, especially in simple skills and English language for foreign-born urban dwellers. Hull House and other settlement houses were financed by voluntary contributions and grants from other welfare organizations. They made life for the urban poor more bearable and prepared many immigrants for productive lives as U.S. citizens.

With the New Deal and Great Society, the federal and state governments took more responsibility for issues handled by settlement houses. However, many organizations still struggle to meet the needs of the urban poor and of immigrants. Hull House Association continues to be one of these.

There were many other areas where changes and reforms were introduced in the late 19th and early 20th century. One change of particular significance for all of us today occurred in the area of medical and emergency relief. Clara Barton, who had nursed Union soldiers in the Civil War, founded the American Red Cross in 1881. She saw the need for better treatment by and better standards for nurses. Her work has saved hundreds of lives and affects us today.

> The American Red Cross is founded.

CIVIL SERVICE REFORM

The reform movement in the cities has already been mentioned. Another political concern of reformers was civil service reform. The spoils system had been an accepted part of United States politics at least since Thomas Jefferson's presidency. It was based on the belief we were all created equal and in a democratic society every citizen could be president or run an office of the government. However, as business turned to greater specialization and efficiency, reformers began to think of ways to apply the same principles to government. While the spoils system was democratic, the rapid turnover of untrained government workers appointed by the winners of elections was inefficient and often led to corruption. The solution reformers offered was to create an effective civil service of trained workers who would run the government bureaucracy as professionals. They could not be replaced by newly elected officials. After a disgruntled office seeker, who expected a reward under the spoils system, assassinated President Garfield in 1881, Congress finally passed the Pendleton Civil Service Reform Act in 1884.

> The spoils system is modified by the Pendleton Civil Service Reform Act.

The issue of efficient and noncorrupt people in the government workforce continued to be an issue after the passage of the law, which many thought did not go far enough. Today workers in the government bureaucracy have to pass entrance tests. The bureaucracy has grown greatly, but it is no longer filled solely by the political whims of elected officials. The first civil service laws made government a much more efficient operation.

SUMMARY

All of the reform movements mentioned reflect American values and character, and those characteristics and values are still with us. Whether they were formed on the frontier can be debated, but there is no doubt that working for good with exuberance and working for practical, inventive ways to solve problems, often in materialistic ways, are part of the American approach to problems and reforms. These reforms, as well as the many changes brought on by industrialization, immigration, the building of the railroads, and the closing of the frontier, drastically changed America's life style between 1877 and 1914.

Many of the qualities and characteristics one identifies with post-Civil War Americans are still seen in America today. Whether they were born on the frontier or simply emerged as responses to the challenges of the era, is a debatable question. What do you think?

Key Point to Remember
Urban changes and growth led to reform movements in several areas, among them voting rights for women, city government, and prohibition.

Links from the Past

1. The needs of the urban poor are still of great concern in this country.

2. Leisure-time activities, especially athletics and movies, remain important in American life.

3. Concern over the use of alcohol, as seen in the prohibition movement, and drugs continues today.

People to Remember

Mark Twain   Author, newspaper writer; pen name of Samuel Clemens; widely read popular author of short stories of the West and novels such as *The Adventures of Tom Sawyer* and *The Adventures of Huckleberry Finn.*

Jane Addams   Social worker, humanitarian; founder of Hull House, Chicago, the first settlement house in the United States built to improve community and civic life for the poor; leader of the National Progressive Party (1912) and in women's peace movement during and after World War I; winner of the Nobel Peace Prize in 1931 for her work on behalf of the poor.

Susan B. Anthony   Reformer, feminist; one of the leaders of the National American Woman Suffrage Association, which finally succeeded in obtaining the vote for women with the passage of Amendment XIX in 1920.

Elizabeth Cady Stanton   Reformer, feminist; leader and founder with Lucretia Mott of the 19th century feminist movement; the two organized the Seneca Falls Convention in 1848; Elizabeth Stanton went on to head the National American Woman Suffrage Association and was co-editor of *Revolution*, a publication of the feminist movement.

Joseph Pulitzer   Newspaper publisher; born in Hungary, Pulitzer came to the United States, served in the Union Army, and entered the newspaper business in St. Louis, Missouri with the *Post Dispatch*; bought the *N.Y. World* and in a rivalry with the *N.Y. Journal* in the late 1890's the two papers pursued "yellow journalism" to sell papers; Pulitzer left funds to found the School of Journalism at Columbia University, which in turn established the annual Pulitzer Prizes for excellence in journalism.

Dates

1869—Wyoming Territory gave vote to women.

1874—Women's Christian Temperance Union formed.

1881—Red Cross formed by Clara Barton.

1884—*Adventures of Huckleberry Finn* published.
     Pendleton Civil Service Reform Act.

1889—Hull House founded by Jane Addams.

1893—Anti-Saloon League formed.

1903—First World Series baseball game.

1919—Amendment XVIII—Prohibition—adopted.

1920—Amendment XIX—vote for women—adopted.

Questions
Identify each of the following:

Social Gospel	Amendment XVIII to the Constitution
Political Boss	Amendment XIX to the Constitution
Yellow Journalism	Pendleton Civil Service Reform Act

Multiple Choice:

1. The leadership of institutions such as Hull House, and urban political machines both worked
   a. to help the living conditions of the urban poor.
   b. to increase the political power of a political boss.
   c. to provide an escape from unsanitary conditions.

2. Examples of changes in city living which benefited everyone are
   a. the development of a clean water supply and sewer systems.
   b. street lighting and street cars.
   c. both of the above.

3. Examples of leisure-time activities, which were available to all by 1900, were
   a. movies.
   b. vaudeville shows.
   c. World Series baseball games.

Open-ended, Analysis Questions

The following questions require analysis and reflection. You are encouraged to bring to your answer information and ideas from many sources. The answers should be presented in composition or essay style, but they may be used to initiate discussion. The questions put you in the role of the historian, gathering information to support your personal perspective on the question.

1. Consider the reforms of the period 1865–1914. Then pick one that you believe would reinforce the idea of American individualism and pick one that you believe would reinforce the idea of American equality. In an essay, explain your choices. Be sure to include specific information about each reform and statements explaining your understanding of individualism and of equality.

2. How do you account for the many reform movements that developed in the period 1865–1914?

3. Pick four of the following individuals, and briefly explain how the actions of each of the four did or did not reflect those "striking characteristics of the American character" Fredrick Jackson Turner believed were developed on the American frontier. See "Approaches to History," page 147 for a description of these "striking characteristics." *(Note: Remember, even though an essay question includes ideas stated as factual, a student may take exception to the statement and argue against the statement's assumption. In this question you may see no connection between Turner's thesis and these individuals.)*
   a. Jane Addams
   b. Susan B. Anthony
   c. Andrew Carnegie
   d. Thomas Edison
   e. Samuel Gompers
   f. Joseph Pulitzer
   g. John D. Rockefeller
   h. Elizabeth Cady Stanton

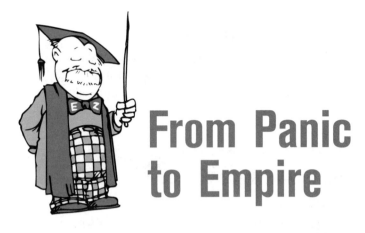

From Panic to Empire

APPROACHES TO HISTORY

THE CYCLICAL VIEW OF HISTORY

One way of looking at history is that it follows certain patterns or cycles. Just as season follows season in a never-ending cycle, so some historians see history not as repeating itself but as following a similar pattern, which is repeated over and over. How often in your life do you see patterns repeating? From the daily routine of brushing teeth in the morning to the celebration of holidays—Thanksgiving, Christmas, Yom Kippur, birthdays—we usually repeat the cycle, yet each repetition is different— no two holiday celebrations are the same. So it is with history. There are cycles or patterns, but no two cycles are the same.

The origin of this view goes far back into Greek and Roman history, when philosophers discussed natural laws that guided both nature and human life. This concept of life following laws of nature was reinforced in the 19th century by Charles Darwin's work on evolution. At that time some individuals looked at events and said they were inevitable; they were simply following the natural progression. They concluded that we should not interfere with what was natural.

This viewpoint was used especially to respond to the business cycles of periodic panics or depressions alternating with good economic times. It was also used to describe the movement toward overseas expansion and empire as a natural step in the growth of a nation. According to this cyclical, biological, and evolutionary view, each nation went through the same cycle. Writers described this cycle in human terms and talked about the childhood, adolescence, and young manhood of the United States. In this analogy, growth was natural and not to grow would be to die.

This concept of inevitable, natural growth following messages encoded in your hormones should be familiar to all young students. Do you think the same growth pattern is followed by nations? Many at the end of the

19th century did view history in this way. They saw the United States as a young adolescent emerging from the trauma of the Civil War. They viewed our history as following natural laws. We were going to follow the same cycle of growth and greatness that previous nations had followed.

I. Business Cycles

By the time of the Civil War, the United States had already experienced two major economic depressions, the Panics of 1819 and 1837. By 1873 post-war expansion, especially of railroads, a drop in European demand for United States farm produce, speculation and market manipulation by a few individuals, and the failure of the large banking house of J. Cooke brought on a depression that lasted from 1873 to 1878. The government's concern over the debt payment and desire to maintain strong credit rating prolonged the crisis, which began with a fall in security prices, what today we call a "plunge," on Wall Street.

The stages of this depression—overexpansion, speculation, bankruptcy, recovery—make a pattern that has repeated itself throughout United States history, but in each case the details are somewhat different. After the New Deal in the 20th century, the federal government has been actively involved in attempts to avoid or control the ups and downs (i.e., cyclical movement of the business cycle), but the cycle continues to move up and down. However, the 19th century business philosophy of laissez-faire, supported by the attitudes of the Social Darwinists, called for no government interference in the economic cycle, which was considered "natural" and part of the law of nature.

THE MONEY SUPPLY

Some people did want help from the federal government in controlling the business cycle. These people suggested the government should increase the money supply either by adding coins of silver to those of gold in order to increase the specie supply or by issuing paper money. Throughout the 19th century

> The money supply has an impact on panics and depressions.

and until the United States abandoned gold as the basis of its money supply in 1933, there were many proposals for coining silver and issuing "greenbacks," that is, paper money. At times these requests were accepted. For instance, the Union issued large numbers of greenbacks to help pay for the Civil War. When these greenbacks were recalled, and only specie became correct currency, there was a major impact on the money supply that helped precipitate the depression of 1873.

The details of the many acts involving the money supply, and silver and greenbacks need not concern us, but the reasoning behind it does. The arguments for and the groups that support the two policies have been similar throughout the natural cycles of boom and bust. The arguments are still used today as we face the economic concerns—inflation, stagnation, boom, and recession.

There are two basic economic approaches to, or arguments about, money. One view, the hard money view, believes that the money supply should be restricted or limited. In the 19th century hard money supporters believed the money supply should be linked to something of value—gold—whose availability would naturally limit the supply. The hard money view is a deflationary view, or one that tends to deflate prices. The other view, the cheap money view, believes that the money supply should be flexible and should continually grow. This is an inflationary view, or one that tends to inflate prices. Advocates of hard money are creditors, bankers, those who loan money, and in many cases businessmen who fear inflation. Advocates of cheap money are debtors, farmers, and those who borrow money.

> **What is the difference between "hard" and "soft" or "cheap" money?**

Why would someone want either hard or cheap money? Take this example. You have bought a new bicycle for $300. You borrowed the money. Your interest payment over the three years will total $30 so you must repay $330. You have a job selling ice cream that pays $5 per hour. To pay back the money you must work 66 hours. Now if money becomes cheaper, there will be inflation. Prices and wages rise. Your pay goes to $6 per hour, but your loan and the interest rate remain the same at $330 over three years. You now need to work only 55 hours to pay back the loan. As a debtor, cheap money or inflation helps you. Of course, prices are rising and your cost of living rises, which may hurt you, but if your biggest expense is paying debts—mortgages on houses or farms, loans for purchases of major equipment, etc.—then you will be happy with inflation brought about by cheap or easily available money. Too much inflation would make it hard for you to both pay your debts and live decently, but just the right amount would be wonderful.

But what of the banker who loaned you the $300? As you pay it back in cheap money, he can buy less with the money since prices have risen. He has had to increase the wages of his workers just as you got a raise. Although you pay the money back with interest, it still isn't worth as much as when he loaned it. He would prefer a deflationary or hard money situation in which wages and prices dropped. If your pay went to $4, you would need to work 82.5 hours to pay back your loan. The banker would be able to buy more with the money you pay him since prices as well as wages would have dropped. He is happy but you aren't—you must work harder to pay the loan.

This is the essence of the hard money/cheap money, deflationary/inflationary monetary policy that has been argued in the United States through all the business cycles. When farm prices drop, farmers must work harder and sell more produce to pay back loans, just as you would need to work longer to pay back a loan when your wage drops. In the business cycle the same factors occur over and over, but the causes and outcome are different each time. However, the views on hard and cheap money have remained the same through all the cycles. In the years after the Civil War until the New Deal, those who supported the hard money view argued that the U.S. currency should be based on gold. Those who supported the cheap money view argued that the U.S. currency should be based on silver and gold, and the government should issue paper money, or greenbacks.

During the New Deal, gold was abandoned as the sole basis of our money supply.

THE PRESIDENCY

In the period 1876–1914 the major issues of the day related to business growth and the economic situation of the nation. The Republican Presidents—Hayes, Garfield, Arthur, Harrison, and McKinley—generally supported hard money, a hands-off laissez-faire attitude toward business and high tariffs. Grover Cleveland, the only Democrat to hold the presidency between 1860 and 1912, supported the same laissez-faire approach. The Presidents between Grant and William McKinley were elected to single terms. None of the Presidents exercised strong leadership, and until McKinley, none were elected to two consecutive terms.

> Post-Civil War Presidents follow a laissez-faire approach to business.

THE FARMER AND THE ECONOMY

One continual concern in the post-Civil War years was the economic position of the farmer in America. The nation slowly emerged from the 1873 depression only to suffer another cycle of recession in 1884–85. A major factor was declining farm prices. With increased production in other agricultural nations, prices for wheat and other farm products began a decline in 1884 that continued for a dozen years. Hurt further by a bad drought in 1887, discontented farmers organized protest groups that merged into regional bodies—the Southern Alliance and the National Farmer's Alliance of the Northwest. They replaced the Grange as the farmer's spokesman against Eastern bankers, railroads, and the rapidly growing industrial monopolies, all of whom set prices. These latter groups supported hard money and advocated the gold standard, that is, gold as the base of the money supply with no silver coinage or greenbacks. The farmers argued for silver coinage to inflate the currency.

THE ICC

Farmer protests and public anger over railroad abuses finally led the Congress to pass the Interstate Commerce Act in 1887. The Supreme Court's decision in the Wabash case, in which a state law controlling rates charged by interstate railroads was declared unconstitutional because only the federal government could control interstate commerce, was the act that finally led Congress to abandon the laissez-faire view toward business.

The Interstate Commerce Act created the Interstate Commerce Commission, the first of many regulatory commissions created by the United States government. Its purpose was to regulate the railroads. The ICC was given power to investigate railroad management, but its orders were not binding. It had to get the federal courts to issue the orders, and the judges were often quite conservative and would not cooperate with the ICC. The Act prohibited pooling and rebates[1] and made it illegal

[1] rebates   *When a bill is paid at the full price, a company can give the payer a rebate after the bill is paid. The rebate is money paid back to the payer.*

Abbot–Downing Co. built the Concord coach that was widely used by Stage Coach companies, such as Wells Fargo, on their routes throughout the west. The coach had standardized parts, but there was a lot of individualized work that went into them, including hand-painted decorations. The company was locally owned, and the owners had offices in the building complex with the workers. Compare these conditions with those you would find on an assembly line where workers repeated the same simple task over and over.
Courtesy: New Hampshire Historical Society, Concord, New Hampshire

to charge more for a short haul than for a long haul[2] on the same line, a practice that hurt farmers. Railroads were required to post their rates, which were to be reasonable and just. The act worked quite well at first, but with disagreements over its interpretation and with changing economic conditions in the 1890s, ways were found by many railroad owners to avoid obeying the law.

THE GROWTH OF TRUSTS

The growth of trusts is another example of business growth. The trust issue finally led to another abandonment of laissez-faire. After John D. Rockefeller had established the Standard Oil Trust in 1879, trusts were established in many other industries such as beef (Armour), sugar (E.C. Knight and Co.), and tobacco (American Tobacco Company). Concern and protest over this apparent growth of

[2]short haul and long haul   *When railroads had a monopoly between two locations, they could charge whatever price they wished for the haul between stops along that line. When there was competition between two locations, they would often charge a lower fee even if the distance was longer. Therefore, sometimes farmers needed to pay more for a short haul between two places on a line where there was a monopoly than they would have had to pay for a long haul where there was competition.*

business monopolies led several states to pass laws controlling trusts, but no state could control a trust engaging in interstate commerce.

In 1890 the federal government passed the Sherman Anti-Trust Act to regulate trusts. The act declared illegal any "combination in the form of a trust…in restraint of trade or commerce." By the law the federal government could use the courts to dissolve illegal trusts. Since the act had ambiguous phrasing and terms were not clearly defined, the conservative federal courts interpreted the law to apply to all combinations from labor unions to railroads. The labor unions were brought to court as much as businesses. In 1895 in the case of the *United States* v. *E.C. Knight Co.,* the Supreme Court restricted the ICC law, deciding that manufacturing was not commerce and so could not be regulated by Congress, which had power to regulate commerce but not manufacturing. This was considered by many to be a very narrow interpretation of business and a very strict interpretation of the Constitution. Although the E.C. Knight Co. controlled 95 percent of the sugar refining in the United States, according to the Court it was not restraining trade.

TARIFFS

Another issue relating to the economic situation in the post-Civil War period was high tariffs. Business wanted them and they were supported by Congress. The tariff issue was addressed by President Cleveland in his annual message to Congress in 1887. He had supported the high tariff but changed his mind and in the annual message called for a lower tariff. Congress failed to pass a tariff, and the issue split the parties in the 1888 election, which Cleveland lost to Benjamin Harrison.

In 1890 Congress passed the McKinley Tariff, which raised duties an average of over 48 percent. It was a boost for manufacturers, and the Republicans hoped to help the distressed farmer by raising some duties on agricultural products. This did not help farmers because the United States imported few agricultural products. Instead, higher import duties added to the cost of manufactured products and hurt the farmers. This has been the essence of the tariff issue throughout American history: High tariffs hurt farmers, help some manufacturers, and force the general public and workers to pay higher prices.

The backlash to the McKinley Tariff was great, and half the Republicans in the House of Representatives lost in the 1890 election. Discontent with established policy was growing.

THE POPULIST PARTY

The 1892 presidential campaign included a new party, the People's Party, popularly known as the Populist Party. It was organized by farmers and laborers as a protest against the two established parties' continued adherence to high tariffs and hard money. Meeting in Omaha, Nebraska, the Populists chose James B. Weaver of Iowa as their candidate. Their platform, the Omaha Platform, called for the free and unlimited coinage of silver and an increase in the money in circulation, which were cheap money policies. Other planks called for a graduated income tax, government ownership of railroads and telegraphs and banks operated by the post office. The

Omaha platform contained suggestions for changes that reformers pursued during the next 35 years.

The Populists were plagued by the issue of race relations. While discontent was widespread in the South, farmers there did not support the Populist cause as was hoped. The white farmers feared losing political power to the African-Americans, many of whom could still vote, if the whites did not vote for the Democratic candidate. After 1892, more restrictions were placed on African-Americans to assure they would not attain political power.

Grover Cleveland, the Democrat who had previously served as President from 1884 to 1888, was reelected, defeating the Populist Weaver and the incumbent Republican President, Benjamin Harrison. President Harrison was hurt both by the McKinley Tariff and the brutal way Pinkerton detectives broke a strike at Carnegie's Homestead Steel Plant in Homestead, Pennsylvania. Seven strikers were killed, and the union was broken. No steel union was formed until the 1930s. Republicans were identified with businesses such as Carnegie Steel. However, the Democrat Cleveland was not inclined to enforce the recently passed Interstate Commerce Act and Sherman Act, so there was little change in business operation.

Soon after Cleveland's election, another panic in the apparently inevitable business cycle of boom and bust occurred. The 1893 panic was precipitated by the failure of an English bank. Banks then called in loans, which were payable only in gold, and as businesses and farmers needed gold to pay their loans, the United States government's gold supply dropped. Panic then hit Wall Street. The result was again a cry for cheap money from those who needed gold to pay back loans. The resulting recession appeared to be a great boost to the program of the Populist Party. And the party looked forward to the election of 1896.

> The Panic of 1893 appears to help the Populist Party's struggle for power.

To counteract the Panic of 1893 Cleveland asked Congress to pass a lower tariff in 1894, but when the Senate finished the bill, duties were dropped less than 8 percent. The tariff continued as a major issue between Republicans and Democrats. The Democrats achieved a major reduction in 1913 with the Underwood Tariff, but Republicans raised the duties to their highest level ever in 1930 when they were back in power. With the enactment of the Reciprocal Trade Agreements Act under the New Deal in 1934, duties slowly declined, leveling off at just over 10 percent after World War II. Reciprocal agreements permit negotiation on duties with different countries to the mutual benefit of each.

> The tariff continues to be a major political issue.

Tariff and trade policies changed greatly after World War II and tariffs were not a major issue through most of the latter half of the 20th century. Since the early 1990s, there has been more talk of tariffs and tariff policy. Some business and labor leaders see advantages in tariffs: business in order to guarantee the home market for United States' products and labor as a way to keep prices of foreign made goods high. This, they believe, will keep prices for American manufactured goods high, which in turn will allow the laborers to demand a share of the profits by getting higher wages. In 1994 with the signing of NAFTA—North American Free Trade Agreement among Mexico, Canada, and the United States—and GATT—General Agreement on Tariffs and Trade—it appears the United States is heading toward free trade without tariffs.

However, the nation has not heard the last of tariffs, which helped to make and break presidents in the 19th century. Then tariff debates occurred with cyclical regularity; each tariff was different, but the basic arguments were always similar, and the same arguments are used today.

THE WATERSHED ELECTION OF 1896

The election of 1896 offered the electorate a choice between two very different political views of the future. It was one of the most important elections in United States history.

Republicans nominated William McKinley, author of the high McKinley Tariff. His campaign manager, Mark Hanna, was an Ohio millionaire who followed the Hamiltonian view of government. (See page 61.) He believed government should aid business. The Republican platform praised high, protective tariffs, blamed the hard economic times on the Democrats, and made a gesture toward cheap money by calling for an international gold and silver monetary system, something other nations would not accept.

Most Democrats were disillusioned with Cleveland, who had not vetoed the 1894 tariff. He had broken the Pullman Strike of 1894 by sending in federal troops to keep the United States mail moving, and he had upheld hard money. He made a deal with J.P. Morgan, a New York banker, to avoid a depletion of the government gold supply. Cleveland appeared to many Democrats to be more Republican than many Republicans.

There was, however, no clear choice of a leader to replace Cleveland. Then William Jennings Bryan of Nebraska, a brilliant orator who advocated the unlimited coinage of silver to achieve cheaper money, delivered one of the most momentous speeches in American history. His "Cross of Gold" speech captivated his audience. In the "Cross of Gold" speech Bryan described the conditions in the country and declared cities were dependent on the farm, not vice versa. He argued that prosperity worked its way up from farmers and laborers when they had money to spend; it did not trickle down from the wealthy to the workers as Republican theory implied. Bryan ended his speech with the phrase, "You shall not press down upon the brow of labor this crown of thorns, you shall not crucify mankind upon a cross of gold."

> Democrats find a champion of cheap money in William Jennings Bryan.

Bryan's message overwhelmed the Democrats at the convention. They adopted a platform in favor of silver and gave Bryan their nomination for President.

Democratic supporters of hard money nominated their own candidate in 1896. The Populist Party, whose program had been taken over by the silver Democrats under Bryan, also endorsed Bryan as their candidate. Bryan appealed to the debt-laden farmers of the West and the South; McKinley, to the business interests of the East. The campaign began well for Bryan, but Mark Hanna's careful spending of large campaign funds and the Republican's attack on cheap money's inflationary impact on prices won the vote of many factory workers to the Republicans.

In the election Bryan carried the South and the Plains states, but McKinley carried all the states from North Dakota to Massachusetts plus Oregon and California. The nation voted for business and hard money. The Populist Party died. The call for reform in American economic and political life was taken up at the turn of the century by a new group known collectively as the Progressives.

Key Point to Remember

Business prosperity was cyclical throughout the 19th century with panics occurring regularly; the government between 1877 and 1900 officially maintained a laissez-faire attitude toward business, except for tariffs, the Interstate Commerce Act, and the Sherman Anti-Trust Act.

People to Remember

William Jennings Bryan   Lawyer, noted orator, populist, political leader, three-time Democratic candidate for president, W. Wilson's first Secretary of State; Bryan gained fame for his "Cross of Gold" speech at the Democratic Convention in 1896 in which he advocated the unlimited coinage of silver; although never president he dominated the Democratic Party for 20 years as many reforms he supported—income tax, prohibition, women's suffrage, direct election of senators—became law; as a spokesman for religious fundamentalism, he opposed evolution and was a witness at the Scopes trial.

Links from the Past to the Present

1. Alternating economic recession and prosperity have been the pattern of the American economy from the Panic of 1819 to the financial crisis of 2008–2009.
2. Cheap versus hard money arguments have been expressed throughout our history from the time of Shays' Rebellion to today's arguments over interest rates.

Dates

1873—Panic of 1873.

1890—McKinley Tariff.
     Sherman Anti-Trust Law.

1892—Populist Party ran first candidate.

1893—Panic of 1893.

1895—*United States* v. *E.C. Knight Co.*

1896—"Cross of Gold" speech by William Jennings Bryan.

1913—Underwood Tariff.

1934—Reciprocal Trade Agreement.

1994—North American Free Trade Agreement and General Agreement on Tariffs and Trade.

Questions
Identify each of the following:

Greenback	"Cross of Gold" Speech
Interstate Commerce Act	Election of 1892
Sherman Anti-Trust Act	Cheap Money

Multiple Choice:

1. The Interstate Commerce Act of 1887
   a. was passed because the Supreme Court ruled states could control interstate commerce.
   b. established the Interstate Commerce Commission.
   c. made it legal to charge more for a short haul.

2. The idea behind the cry for coinage of silver was
   a. the creation of cheap money.
   b. the creation of hard money.
   c. neither of the above.

3. Presidents Hayes, Garfield, and Arthur supported
   a. cheap money and silver coinage.
   b. high tariffs and a laissez-faire policy.
   c. hard money and low tariffs.

II. The Progressive Movement

THE PROGRESSIVE PROGRAM

The Progressives of the early decades of the 20th century wanted to clean up and reform government and to use government to advance human welfare. They were opposed to the abuse of power by political machines and monopolies. They wanted to apply scientific management to government just as it was being applied to business and to use it to solve urban problems. Many Progressives had an aversion to party politics. Unlike the Populists whose leadership came from the West and South and whose support came mainly from farmers and some workers, Progressives could be found in all economic groups—laborers, farmers, businessmen, intellectuals—and among all immigrant groups. However, Progressives shared little interest in the African-American population, whose place in American society at this period was reflected in the *Plessy* v. *Ferguson* decision of the Supreme Court, which accepted the "separate but equal" philosophy (see page 188). Many Progressives were concerned by the increase in immigration, which they perceived as a negative force in American cities.

Progressives were repulsed at the corruption and injustice revealed in the writings of investigative journalists like Lincoln Steffens, who put the spotlight on many urban problems in his book, *The Shame of the Cities.* President Theodore Roosevelt referred to these reporters as muckrakers, a figure in the English poet John Bunyan's *Pilgrim's Progress* who was so busy raking manure he did not see the crown overhead.

In spite of his condemnation of their zeal, Theodore Roosevelt responded as a Progressive would and during his presidency attacked monopolies and called for reform inspired by the muckrakers. For instance, Upton Sinclair in a novel, *The Jungle,* published in 1906, attacked the meat-packing industry. Horrified by the accusations of Sinclair, Theodore Roosevelt appointed a commission to investigate the meat-packing industry. The commission uncovered clear evidence that rats and rope were included in canned ham. The commission found many other abuses by the industry. President Roosevelt pressed Congress to pass the Meat Inspection Act in 1906. The act established federal inspection from the farm to the finished product of all meat sold in interstate commerce. A government seal of approval assured the public of the quality of meat purchased. We still benefit from this act every time we eat meat. Look on meat you buy for the government seal of approval.

Muckrakers directed their attacks at everything from the Standard Oil Trust to the "white slave" or prostitution trade to the voting allegiance of United States Senators to trusts and railroads. Senators were often supported in their campaigns by the trusts and railroads, and they in turn often voted to help their benefactors rather than the people they were supposed to represent. Progressive reform at the urban level (see page 164) was extensive. Governor Robert LaFollette of Wisconsin made a reputation as a reform governor, introducing the direct primary[3] for the nomination of political candidates rather than party conventions, more equitable taxes, and railroad rate regulation. Other states followed Wisconsin's lead, and later, as United States Senator, Robert LaFollette supported reforms at the national level.

> Reforms are instituted by all levels of government.

THEODORE ROOSEVELT

Theodore Roosevelt had become president of the United States on the assassination of William McKinley in 1901, soon after McKinley's election to a second term. Theodore Roosevelt is one of those individuals who have had a great impact on history. A rather weak, asthmatic child, his father sent him west to live and study on the theory that the West would toughen him. A graduate of Harvard, he read law, wrote history, and lived on a ranch in North Dakota before becoming a Civil Service Commissioner and later Police Commissioner in New York City. He served as Assistant Secretary of the Navy from 1897–98 and helped prepare for the Spanish-American War. He organized the first United States Volunteer Cavalry, referred to as the "Rough Riders," and led a charge up San Juan Hill in Cuba during the Spanish-American War. Returning in 1898, he was elected Governor of New York and was put on the Republican ticket as vice president in 1900 because his moves toward reform worried the political bosses in his state. When McKinley was assassinated on September 6, 1901, Theodore Roosevelt became president. He used the presidency as a "bully pulpit" to argue both the cause of reform and expansion.

One example of reform legislation besides the Meat Inspection Act is the Pure Food and Drug Law, which President Theodore Roosevelt pushed through Congress in 1906. The Pure Food and Drug Law provides each of us with a sense of security when we buy our medicines. He used the presidency to support the labor movement and give it a "square deal"[4] along with business. In the Anthracite Coal Strike of 1902, he forced arbitration on the owners and the miners. While accepting the growth of

[3]direct primary   *An election in which voters elect their party's candidates for office. The winners of the primary are the party's nominees in the general election for office.*
[4]Square Deal   *The slogan used to describe the domestic program of President Theodore Roosevelt.*

American business and trusts as an inevitable part of growth, he distinguished between good and bad trusts and had the government use the Sherman Anti-Trust Law to attack the ones he considered bad. In one such case in 1904, the Supreme Court ruled that the Northern Securities Company, a huge holding company created by J.P. Morgan to monopolize the railroads of the northwest, violated the Sherman Anti-Trust Law. It was a shock to big business and a victory for those who felt the government had a role in the economic life of the nation.

> Roosevelt is an active President and pushes for a Square Deal for all Americans.

CONSERVATION EFFORTS

Perhaps Theodore Roosevelt's most memorable efforts from a current perspective were directed at conservation. He set aside 125 million acres of forests in Federal Reserves and did the same for both coal and water resources. The Newlands Act of 1902 authorized the government to use money from the sale of western land for irrigation projects. In 1908 a conference on conservation at the White House helped encourage governors to follow Roosevelt's lead, and forty-one states set up conservation commissions. He appointed Gifford Pinchot, an active conservationist, head of the Federal Division of Forestry. Theodore Roosevelt stimulated interest in our natural resources by such acts as climbing in Yosemite Valley, California, with the most famous naturalist-conservationist of the day, John Muir. Theodore Roosevelt was the embodiment of an active, reform-minded President who would lead the nation. He provided a sharp contrast to the Presidents of the previous thirty years.

PANIC OF 1907

In 1907 another of the periodic panics hit the United States. It was less severe than the previous ones and hurt businesses more than the average worker, but nevertheless it illustrated the cyclical nature of prosperity. The panic was centered on Wall Street and had as one cause worldwide economic trends. Thus, the first panic of the 20th century illustrated the increasingly worldwide nature of the American economy and the growing position of America in the world.

THE TAFT PRESIDENCY

Roosevelt had antagonized business but was very popular in the nation. Having served almost eight full years, he decided not to seek a second term of his own. William Howard Taft of Ohio, Secretary of War in Theodore Roosevelt's Cabinet and a moderate Progressive, won the Republican nomination and the presidency against William Jennings Bryan, making his third and final try for the presidency on the Democratic ticket. Theodore Roosevelt went on a trip to Africa.

President Taft has always suffered by comparison to the flamboyant Roosevelt, yet his record of reform is a solid one. In 1912 Congress passed Amendment XVII to the Constitution, establishing the direct election of senators by the people rather than by state legislatures where business interests often manipulated elections.

Progressives saw this amendment as a way to make the senators responsive to the people. Taft continued Theodore Roosevelt's trust busting, gaining Supreme Court decisions against Standard Oil Company and the American Tobacco Company. He got legislation through Congress to remove acres of coal lands from exploitation and established a Bureau of Mines to safeguard resources.

However, his Secretary of the Interior, Ballinger, following the law, allowed certain water power sites that Theodore Roosevelt had arbitrarily set aside to be developed by private interests. Gifford Pinchot of the Forestry Department objected. Pinchot was dismissed by Taft, who believed in administrative order and thought Pinchot had been insubordinate. A furor erupted that alienated the Progressives and Roosevelt's followers from President Taft.

> **Disagreements over conservation issues create a split between Taft and Roosevelt.**

A split in the Republican party developed, and a National Progressive Republican League was formed in 1910 under Robert La Follette, who appeared a likely candidate for the presidency. However, in 1912 Theodore Roosevelt reversed himself and decided to seek the presidency again. After losing the Republican nomination for President to Taft, Roosevelt accepted the nomination of the Progressive Republican Party, which was nicknamed the "Bull Moose" Party. His program for progressive reform was called the "New Nationalism." Roosevelt accepted the existence of trusts

THE EMPLOYMENT AGENT.
—Kirby in the New York *World*.

What is Kirby commenting on in this cartoon? In spite of civil service reform, when Wilson was elected President in 1912, the Democrats used the spoils system to reward deserving party members. William Jennings Bryan, the party leader since 1896 and presidential candidate in 1896, 1900, and 1908 was Wilson's Secretary of State. Kirby is commenting that Bryan rewarded Democrats who had supported him since his first presidential candidacy. From the New York World *reprinted in* The Literary Digest *of January 30, 1915* and advocated "bad" trusts be controlled by the government. The Democrats, after a long convention battle, nominated the Progressive Governor of New Jersey, Woodrow Wilson, as their candidate. In the campaign Wilson's program was designated "New Freedom." He wanted government regulation of trusts, reform in banking, and the direct election of senators—all to help the people control their lives.

WOODROW WILSON

Woodrow Wilson was an intellectual, a historian, a Virginian, and had served as president of Princeton University before becoming Governor of New Jersey. Son of a Presbyterian minister, he inherited the clergyman's power of expression and commitment to what is right. Raised in the Jeffersonian tradition, he believed in the masses and in government for and by the people. A fine orator, his eloquence could inspire, but he was a private person who appeared cold and reserved in public—a great contrast to the outgoing, jovial Theodore Roosevelt. Wilson had lived in war-ravaged Georgia, and this experience, combined with his Christian training, made him hate war. He was a scholar whose field was government, and he firmly believed in a strong presidency that led the Congress into action.

In the three-party race of 1912 Wilson won overwhelmingly in the Electoral College but received less than 42 percent of the popular vote. However, the two Progressive candidates, Roosevelt and Wilson, had won an overwhelming majority of the popular vote. It appeared the nation was committed to reform just as it had been in the era of Jacksonian Democracy. This pattern of recurring periods of reform is another illustration of the cyclical aspect of history. The United States experienced another period of reform in the 1930s and a fourth in the 1960s—each was different, but each had a profound effect on United States history.

Upon the election of Wilson, the second Democrat to occupy the White House since the Civil War, Democrats sought office in spite of civil service reforms. William Jennings Bryan, three times presidential candidate, a teetotaler and pacifist, was named Secretary of State. As the cartoon on page 185 suggests, many old Democrats sought government positions through their previous contacts with Bryan, and they got jobs, a blemish on the Democrat's reform record.

PROGRESSIVE REFORMS OF WILSON

In other areas Wilson's leadership addressed major issues in need of reform. He first addressed the issue of monetary policy. Congress established the Federal Reserve Banking System in 1913. It was a complicated answer to America's banking and monetary problems. The system was under the control of an appointed Federal Reserve Board in Washington. Under the board were twelve Reserve Banks in different parts of the country. They served as banks for bankers. The Federal Reserve Banks could receive government deposits, could move money to areas in need, and could issue greenbacks, or paper money, called Reserve Notes. Reserve Notes were the Progressive Democrats' answer to the demand for cheap money.

Wilson next turned to monopolies and, in the Federal Trade Commission Act and the Clayton Anti-Trust Act of 1914, strengthened the government's ability to control monopolies. While neither was perfect, the Trade Commission Act provided for a commission to investigate unfair business practices and stop them before they became a problem. The Clayton Act tightened the Sherman Anti-Trust Act. It forbade business practices that lessened competition, set unfair prices, or created monopolies. It outlawed interlocking directorates, a business device that strengthened monopolies by having directors serve on the Board of Trustees of several companies.

Labor unions were specifically excluded from the provisions of the Clayton Act. The Sherman Anti-Trust Act had been more successful in destroying unions than in destroying business monopolies. The Clayton Act permitted peaceful picketing and strikes and prohibited court injunctions in labor disputes. While there were still many restraints on labor, the Act helped put unions on an equal footing with business. Business leaders accepted the laws; courts punished only the most extreme cases of restraint of trade.

The issue of trusts faded from the public view as World War I drew closer. During the war business production was essential, and antitrust prosecution was dropped. By then the Progressive movement was over, but these three acts—the Federal Reserve Act, the Clayton Act, the Federal Trade Commission Act—were major contributions to the reform of American business and banking and important steps in addressing the issue of cyclical boom and bust.

AID TO FARMERS AND WORKERS

In other legislation the Democrats under Woodrow Wilson addressed the needs of American farmers and workers. A Federal Farm Loan Act made low interest loans available to farmers, the Seamens Act required decent food and wages for seamen (which helped the sailors but almost priced American shipping out of business), the Workingmen's Compensation Act gave help to federal civil service employees when they were disabled, and the Adamson Act set an 8-hour day for all employees on interstate trains. The days of laissez-faire appeared to be over. The federal government was acting on behalf of laborers and farmers, and acting to put effective limits on business monopolies.

In 1916 Wilson was again the Democrat's candidate for President. He won in a very tight race by carrying the state of California. World War I had begun in 1914 in Europe. One of Wilson's campaign slogans was "He kept us out of war." The war was to become the primary concern of America in the next two years, and the movement for reform died as reform movements had died before and have since.

One act of Wilson's that won Progressive support and helped maintain a Progressive voice in one branch of government in the postwar years was his appointment of Louis D. Brandeis, the first Jew so appointed, to the Supreme Court in 1916. While usually in dissent, Louis Brandeis provided a liberal view on the Court until his retirement in 1939. Finally, in the next period of reform in the 1930s, Louis Brandeis' voice became that of the majority, but not until after the Supreme Court had declared unconstitutional many of the reform efforts of the New Deal.

> Louis D. Brandeis is appointed to the Supreme Court and supports the liberal view during the conservative 1920s.

SUPREME COURT DECISIONS: 1873–1908

The Supreme Court as interpreter of the Constitution has a major impact on United States society and history. Through most of its history before the 1930s, the Court upheld a more conservative position than society or the other branches of government would endorse. Occasionally, as in the Dred Scott decision, it attempted to establish social policy and to resolve a political issue, but this approach has been rare. From the Slaughterhouse Cases in 1873 until *Muller* v. *Oregon* in 1908, the Court's decisions essentially upheld the status quo.

> The Supreme Court in the post-Civil War years upholds the status quo.

Several cases in addition to those mentioned earlier were of major significance and illustrate how the Court either blocked what we consider today as reasonable and progressive reform or upheld very conservative legislation. In 1883 the Court declared the Civil Rights Act of 1875 invalid, because it upheld social not political rights. The Civil Rights Act had forbidden discrimination in hotel accommodations. The decision stopped federal civil rights legislation under the Fourteenth Amendment until the 1960s. In the same area of race relations, *Plessy* v. *Ferguson* in 1896 upheld a Louisiana law segregating railroad facilities. The court held that if the facilities were separate but equal, the African-American was not deprived of equal protection of the law under the Fourteenth Amendment; separate was not unequal according to the 1896 Court and this concept of "separate but equal" remained the "law of the land" until reversed by the *Brown* v. *Board of Education* decision in 1954.

In *Lochner* v. *New York* in 1905 the Court declared a law limiting the hours of labor in a bakery as an unconstitutional interference in the right of free contract. This was a view held by supporters of the free enterprise, laissez-faire system that was being challenged by the Progressive movement. In *Muller* v. *Oregon* decided in 1908, the Court reversed itself and upheld a law limiting the hours of work for one group—women.

The Supreme Court plays a major role in United States history and must always be considered when seeking social or economic reforms. Any attempt to change the perceived natural order such as the growth and power of trusts or cyclical nature of business life had to gain the approval not only of the Congress, especially the Senate, but of the Supreme Court.

Key Point to Remember
Theodore Roosevelt and Woodrow Wilson were Progressive Presidents whose presidencies are noted for reform in the areas of conservation, health, banking, and business.

People to Remember
Theodore Roosevelt   New York lawyer and government worker; as Assistant Secretary of the Navy, he helped prepare for the Spanish-American War and was a hero of the war; 26th president of the United States, worked for reform legislation to benefit the people including suggestions to control gifts to political candidates, won Nobel Peace Prize for making peace at end of Russo-Japanese war, a flamboyant and

activist President whose approach to foreign policy is summed up in his phrase, "Speak softly but carry a big stick."

William Howard Taft   Lawyer and judge of Superior Court of Ohio, Civil Governor of the Philippines 1901–1904, T. Roosevelt's Secretary of War, 27th President of the United States, Yale University law professor, Chief Justice of the United States 1921–1930; considered opposed to labor unions as a judge; while president he continued T. Roosevelt's trust busting and supported railroad regulation, the Payne-Aldrich Tariff, and "Dollar Diplomacy"; as Chief Justice his record was conservative; he voted to overturn laws against child labor and minimum wages for women.

Links from The Past to The Present

1. Efforts at getting legislation and other reforms to benefit workers and farmers have been pursued at many different times in our history.
2. Supreme Court decisions on civil rights issues continue to have a major impact on our society.
3. The Meat Inspection and Pure Food and Drug Laws, passed to protect the health of the American people, were only the first of many such laws designed to protect the public.

Dates

1883—Civil Rights case.

1896—*Plessy* v. *Ferguson.*

1901—President McKinley assassinated; T. Roosevelt succeeds.

1902—Anthracite Coal Strike.
    Newlands Act.

1904—Northern Securities case.

1905—*Lochner* v. *New York.*

1906—Pure Food and Drug Act.
    Meat Inspection Act.

1907—Panic of 1907.

1908—W. H. Taft elected President.
    Muller v. *Oregon.*

1912—Amendment XVII—direct election of senators.
    W. Wilson elected President.

1913—Federal Reserve System.

1914—Clayton Anti-Trust Act.
    Federal Trade Commission established.
    World War I began in Europe.

1916—President Wilson reelected—"He kept us out of war."

Questions
Identify each of the following:

William Howard Taft
Muller v. *Oregon*
Meat Inspection Act
Federal Reserve Board

Pure Food and Drug Law
Plessy v. *Ferguson*
Theodore Roosevelt
Woodrow Wilson

Multiple Choice:

1. Among the important legislation passed under Theodore Roosevelt were the
   a. Pure Food and Drug Act and Meat Inspection Act.
   b. Clayton Anti-Trust Act and Federal Reserve Act.
   c. Newlands Act, and Adamson Act.

2. The Supreme Court declared the federal government could not protect social rights under the Constitution
   a. in the Slaughterhouse cases.
   b. in *Plessy* v. *Ferguson.*
   c. in the Civil Rights cases.

3. In *Muller* v. *Oregon* the court upheld a law in which the state of Oregon
   a. limited the hours of labor for bakery workers.
   b. established separate but equal railroad cars for blacks and whites.
   c. limited working hours for women.

4. The *Jungle* and *The Shame of the Cities* were
   a. inspirations for Progressive reform legislation.
   b. both written by Upton Sinclair.
   c. both repudiated by President Theodore Roosevelt.

III. Foreign Policy: 1877–1914

While domestic concerns dominated United States history from 1877 to 1914, issues of foreign policy were always in the background. They briefly took center stage in the late 1890s and again after 1916. Presidential and Congressional decisions of any

> Foreign policy issues continue to be important.

type had to take these foreign policy issues into account. America expanded overseas in these years, and just as business cycles were seen as natural, this expansion was seen by many as the natural growth from the "adolescence" of the pre- and immediate post-Civil War period to the era of "young manhood" of the Spanish-American War. Some historians today still find parallels between human growth and the growth of nations.

IMPERIALISM

The last half of the 19th century was a time of imperialism[5]—of great expansion by European powers, who divided Africa among themselves at the Berlin Congress in 1878 and established spheres of interest in China later in the century. Following the

> Social Darwinism is applied to foreign policy.

teachings of Social Darwinism, the white leaders of Europe and America believed they were chosen to civilize the world. Their nations were the most advanced militarily and commercially, and to them this was the way progress and civilization were to be judged. Competition for overseas possessions was rampant among the European powers, and the United States was not to be left out.

OVERSEAS INVOLVEMENT: 1877–1898

Between 1875 and 1898 the United States continued to be involved in both the Pacific and Caribbean-Central America area. In the former we acquired rights to a naval base in Pago Pago, Samoa, in 1878, keeping the Germans from acquiring full control of the Samoan Islands. Interest in the Hawaiian Islands developed in these years as Americans bought property and became settlers in the islands. In 1893 a revolution planned by these American settlers overthrew the ruler of Hawaii, but President Cleveland blocked annexation by the United States. Five years later Hawaii was annexed to America's growing Pacific empire when we were involved in the Spanish-American War. In the Caribbean area interest in Cuba and Central America predated the Civil War. Under President Garfield, Secretary of State Blaine encouraged United States economic involvement in Latin America and called for the first Pan-American conference in 1881. His successor in office immediately canceled the invitations. These two actions rather symbolize the United States' attitude toward our neighbors—at one moment friendly and supportive, at the next moment antagonistic or indifferent. A Pan-American conference was finally held in 1889, but the delegates rejected a United States proposal for a customs union and machinery for the arbitration of disputes between the countries. One wonders what United States-Latin American relations would have become if the two proposals had been adopted.

PROBLEMS IN CUBA

An insurrection against Spanish rule began in Cuba in the early 1890s. The treatment of the rebels by the Spanish, who confined them in concentration camps, seemed intolerable to the United States. After United States protests, Spain made concessions, but the United States yellow press whipped up sentiment against Spain, and with the sinking of the battleship *Maine* in the harbor of Havana in February 1898, matters reached a crisis. Demand for war seemed to sweep the United States and President McKinley in April 1898 asked Congress for permission to use "forcible intervention" in Cuba. Congress responded with recognition of Cuban

[5]imperialism   *A policy followed by governments in which they annex territory by force or political pressure, thus gaining control of weaker countries.*

independence, a disclaimer of any desire to annex Cuba, and an authorization to use force to achieve these ends. The United States had embarked on an imperialistic war that was to change the United States and, in the view of some historians, make the United States mature into a young adult.

SPANISH-AMERICAN WAR

The Spanish-American War lasted eight months. Some 5,500 Americans died, but of these only 379 were battle casualties. Theodore Roosevelt, as Assistant Secretary of the Navy, had ordered Commodore George Dewey of the Pacific Fleet in Hong Kong to attack Manila in the Spanish colony of the Philippines in case of war. Dewey did, and Manila fell on August 13, 1898. Cuba was invaded, but it was the defeat of the Spanish fleet outside Santiago that decided the fate of Cuba. United States naval superiority had been assured when the country began building a steel fleet in the 1880s. The United States won the war, and in the process occupied Wake Island and annexed Hawaii, both of which provided good harbors for the fleet.

THE TREATY OF PARIS, 1898

The terms of the Treaty of Paris, which ended the Spanish-American War, stated that Spain would free Cuba and cede Puerto Rico and Guam to the United States. Spain also agreed to cede the Philippines to the United States in return for $20 million. President McKinley had decided to demand the Philippines for economic (a fine market), strategic (a naval base in the Far East), and humanitarian (we could civilize the natives) reasons. The arguments were those of all imperialist nations. The Senate battle over ratification became a forum for expression of ideas that would be echoed over and over again in the 20th century.

> Americans argue over the acceptance of an imperialist position.

As in the election of 1896, the Senate debate was another time when a decision as to the future of the United States had to be made. The debate was between imperialists and anti-imperialists. Some of the arguments used were the same as those used to support the idea of Manifest Destiny in the 1840s.

Imperialist arguments focused on economic and strategic advantages, national prestige, and our "civilizing" mission. Imperialists argued that if we did not take the Philippines, another European power would. Anti-imperialists argued that acquisition of the Philippines was contrary to the United States' principles of democratic government and our own arguments in our struggle for independence and contradicted the United States' commitment to isolation from Europe. They argued that the assimilation into United States society of the different population of the Philippines would be impossible. William Jennings Bryan, himself a pacifist, persuaded some Democrats to vote for the treaty in order to end the war. He argued that the future of the Philippines, whether independent or a United States colony, could be decided in the 1900 presidential race.

The treaty was adopted by two votes more than the necessary two-thirds of the Senate. Bryan ran for President against McKinley in 1900, and Philippine independence was a major issue. Bryan lost and the Philippines became a United

Uncle S.: WILLIAM, I CAN NEVER DIGEST THAT MESS WITHOUT STRAINING MY CONSTITUTION.

In this cartoon the artist Attwood comments on the aftermath of the Spanish-American War and American Imperialism. He makes clever use of the word constitution. *"Uncle S.'s" reference to constitution is both to the United States Constitution and to his own personal constitution or digestion. What is the waiter (President McKinley) offering Uncle Sam? Why would it be hard on his Constitution to accept the food (Puerto Rico—the wine; Cuba—under the food cover; the Philippines—on the platter) offered?*
Published in Life *November 24, 1898.*

States colony for 45 years. The United States had grown up, according to those who see nations following human biological growth patterns. We had joined the European Imperialist Club. We had expanded overseas. On learning that the Philippines were to be annexed by the United States, a nationalist leader, Emilio Aquinaldo, led a rebellion against United States control. The Filipinos were defeated by the United States Army but fighting continued until 1902.

The issues raised in the arguments over the Treaty of Paris and the annexation of the Philippines get at the heart of imperialism. Are some nations more advanced than others, giving them the right to rule others? How do you measure advanced societies? Are some people inherently less good than others, or are "all men (and women) created equal," as the Declaration of Independence says? Some people believe we do have a "God-given right" to rule others. What do you think? The United States as a nation must still wrestle with these questions domestically and in foreign policy.

THEODORE ROOSEVELT AND BIG STICK DIPLOMACY

During the 19th century, the Monroe Doctrine was accepted by presidents of all parties as United States policy. President Johnson, following the Doctrine, saw to it that the French-supported Archduke Maximillian was forced out of Mexico after the Civil War. In 1895 President Cleveland interjected the United States into a long-standing dispute between Venezuela and England over the boundary between British Guiana and Venezuela. In bringing the dispute to arbitration, Cleveland's Secretary of State said, "Today the United States is practically sovereign on this continent . . ." and claimed the right under the Monroe Doctrine to force arbitration on the two nations. President Theodore Roosevelt based his foreign policy on the assumption that the United States had a special role to fill in world affairs. In 1904 he added a further interpretation to the Monroe Doctrine, usually called the Roosevelt Corollary. It stated:

> Chronic wrongdoing or an impotence which results in a general loosening of the ties of civilized society may in the Americas, as elsewhere, ultimately require intervention by some civilized nation, and in the western hemisphere the adherence of the United States to the Monroe Doctrine may force the United States, however reluctantly, in flagrant cases of such wrongdoing or impotence, to the exercise of an international police power.

In other words, the United States would be the policeman of the Western Hemisphere. The United States statement came as a reaction to the desire of several European powers to collect debts owed them by the Dominican Republic. The Dominican Republic signed an agreement giving the United States the right to run the customs houses. The Senate rejected it, but Theodore Roosevelt went ahead anyway. The use of the Monroe Doctrine to justify forcing United States views and values on the Americas is another example of imperialism. It is an example of what has been called Theodore Roosevelt's "big stick diplomacy."

Do you believe the United States has the right to be a policeman in the Caribbean?

Another example of Theodore Roosevelt's "big stick" diplomacy can be seen in his dealings with Colombia and the establishment of Panama. For years there had been talk of a canal connecting the Atlantic and Pacific Oceans through a Central American country. A French company began such a canal in Colombia's province of Panama. The company failed. United States Navy and business interests wanted to build a canal, but the Clayton-Bulwer Treaty signed with England in 1850 stated the United States would not build a canal alone. A new treaty was negotiated with England and ratified in 1900. The United States agreed to keep any canal built neutral. The United States bought the French rights to the canal, and then Colombia balked when the United States demanded perpetual control over the canal zone through which the canal would be dug. President Theodore Roosevelt was not to be blocked. In 1903 the province of Panama revolted from Colombia. Theodore Roosevelt immediately recognized it as a nation; he signed a treaty with the new government leasing the canal zone for 99 years; he ordered United States warships to guarantee Panama's new status. Big stick diplomacy had been exercised again in the Americas. The canal was built—a great benefit to world shipping.

Roosevelt expands the original meaning of the Monroe Doctrine.

Panama's independence is assured by the actions of Roosevelt.

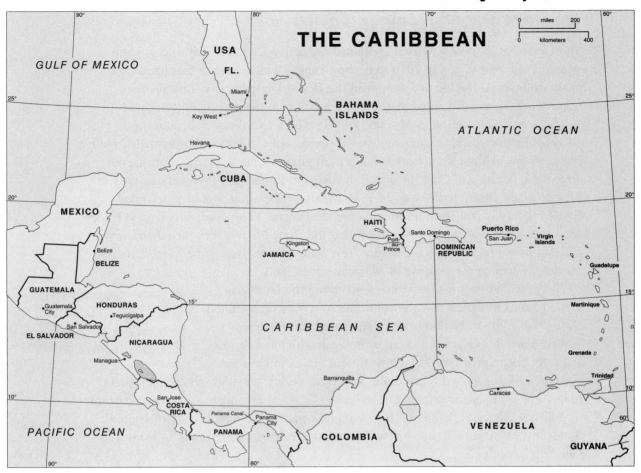

TAFT'S DOLLAR DIPLOMACY

President Taft was not as flamboyant in his Central American
policy, although he maintained the same spirit, sending troops
into Nicaragua in 1912 to protect American banking interests.
The Nicaraguan government had fallen behind in payments on

> Taft pursues a policy of
> Dollar Diplomacy in
> Central America and Asia.

bank loans. Taft's policies of encouraging economic development in Central America
and also in Asia has been called Dollar Diplomacy[6]. As United States investments
grew in the Americas, any threat to them would bring in the United States Marines
to protect business interests.

In 1912 Senator Henry Cabot Lodge introduced a resolution in the Senate
expressing concern over Japanese negotiation with Mexico to lease land for a
possible naval base. Senator Lodge's resolution extended the Monroe Doctrine to
include non-European powers and any foreign corporation that had close connections
with its government.

---

[6]Dollar Diplomacy   *A type of economic imperialism whereby the United States sought to*
insure its investments abroad.

WILSON'S LATIN AMERICAN POLICY

The Democrat Woodrow Wilson continued the active United States role in Latin America. He sent troops in 1916 to occupy Santo Domingo when that nation was again in financial trouble and continued the Dollar Diplomacy of Taft, using or threatening the use of United States military power to aid and support business.

There was a revolution in Mexico in 1910, which overthrew a dictator. In the succeeding four years, the situation was unstable. An incident with unarmed United States troops in Tampico almost led to war to protect United States' interests, but Argentina, Brazil, and Chile mediated the dispute. Further revolutionary activity in Mexico again almost led to war. In 1916 Mexico reluctantly agreed to a United States military expedition into Mexico to stop Pancho Villa, a self-proclaimed leader who opposed the Mexican government that the United States recognized and who had conducted raids across the border. The United States was going to have its way in Mexico even at the expense of Mexican sovereignty.

Party commitment made no difference when the issue was United States influence and control in the Americas. The United States was going to be dominant on this continent. This was United States imperialism. One must understand United States–Latin American relations during this time if one is to have any understanding of United States–Latin American policy, tensions, and cooperation today. The cycle of troop intervention and withdrawal to enforce American economic or political interests continues—for example, consider the long history of United States involvement in Haiti—but was suspended briefly during Franklin Roosevelt's Good Neighbor policy.

> Revolution in Mexico almost provokes a second war with Mexico.

THE UNITED STATES IN ASIA

The United States had important trade relations with Asia throughout the 19th century. They became more important after the opening of Japan by Commodore Perry in 1854. After the middle of the century, European nations began to establish spheres of influence in China, and by the end of the century, the United States felt such spheres would close areas of China to free and open trade. The United States solution was for an "open door" into China for all trading nations. This would mean that all nations would have equal access to the China trade.

> The United States works to maintain open trade and peace in Asia.

Not all European nations were pleased with the idea, especially because the acquisition of the Philippines gave the United States a foothold in Asia. However, by 1900 European nations reluctantly agreed to the Open Door Policy. Although the agreement could not be strictly enforced, the United States proclaimed it as policy.

Asia at the time was undergoing major political upheavals. War broke out between Russia and Japan in 1905, and President Theodore Roosevelt was concerned that if either side won, it would upset the balance of power in Asia and threaten the Open Door in China. Theodore Roosevelt made several proposals for mediation, and Japan and Russia accepted. A peace treaty was negotiated at Portsmouth, New

Hampshire, which ended the war and won the Nobel Peace Prize for Theodore Roosevelt.

United States-Japanese relations after 1906 were strained because of growing opposition over immigration to the United States of Japanese laborers and over the fear of Japanese military strength. In 1907 a "gentlemen's agreement" with Japan led to restriction of Japanese immigration. To intimidate Japanese military leaders, Theodore Roosevelt sent the United States fleet on a world cruise to emphasize the United States naval power. Tensions between the United States and Japan were always there, under the surface if not formally stated, until they finally erupted into World War II. It was clear the United States was to be an important player in the affairs of Asia.

THE ALGECIRAS CONFERENCE

Theodore Roosevelt also helped settle a dispute over the future of Morocco in North Africa. During the last half of the 19th century, through a series of wars, Germany became unified and emerged as an important industrial, political, and military power in Europe. By 1904 the traditional European enemies, England and France, felt threatened and concluded an entente or agreement for cooperation and defense. Germany, the newcomer, having been united as a nation only in 1871, felt excluded. At a Congress in Berlin in 1878, agreements between the European powers divided up Africa into spheres of influence. Following the Berlin Congress, France worked to establish a protectorate[7] over Morocco. Germany, angered by the French and English Treaty (Dual Entente of 1904), declared support for Moroccan independence and asked for an international conference on Morocco's future. Germany asked Roosevelt's support in getting France and England to the conference.

> Roosevelt interjects the United States into the negotiations of European nations.

Roosevelt, fearing a war in Europe might grow out of the Morocco crisis, intervened. The conference was held at Algeciras, Spain. Roosevelt persuaded Germany to accept the settlement, which affirmed Moroccan independence, guaranteed equal commercial opportunities to all nations, yet put the Moroccan police under the control of France and Spain. War was averted.

The Algeciras meeting was a major break in traditional United States foreign policy. We had become involved in a European dispute. The Monroe Doctrine, the cornerstone of our Latin American policy, was ignored. The United States was ready to participate in the affairs of Europe, although we were not actively involved in other European disputes until the outbreak of World War I in 1914.

PEACEKEEPING

Theodore Roosevelt was an active participant on the world stage as a peacemaker. Besides the Treaty of Portsmouth and the Algeciras Conference, he urged the Czar of Russia to call the Second Hague Peace Conference to consider the establishment of a World Court of Justice. Such a court would work to solve international disputes.

[7]protectorate   *A country protected by a more powerful state that shares in its government.*

A concern for international peacekeeping has been one prong of United States foreign policy since that time. It manifested itself in Woodrow Wilson's proposal for a League of Nations, in the United Nations, and in the permanent international court of justice. It is most recently seen in the establishment of an international war crimes tribunal. It illustrates an aspect of the American character, a desire to do good, which has had a great impact on world history.

Another important prong of United States policy has been a commitment to isolation, first expressed in Washington's "Farewell Address." However, with the 20th century, United States history has become entwined with world history. Isolation has not been possible even though many Americans have supported the concept, particularly in the 1920s and 1930s. We hear calls for isolation today, but the United States more often acts as the international peacekeeper.

What policy do you think would be best for the United States?

SUMMARY

Panics and economic crises occurred in regular succession during the 19th and early 20th century. To some they seemed inevitable, and in spite of a few attempts by government to change the economic order, crises continued. Toward the end of the 19th century the United States became more involved with overseas economic investments, and these in turn led to more political and military involvement. Just as a child matures into an adult, so the United States appeared to be maturing into a nation just like other nations. In 1898 we joined the imperialistic nations of the world and annexed Puerto Rico and the Philippines. In the early 20th century, with our large navy and Progressive Presidents, we played an important role on the world stage as befit a strong, powerful, yet young individual.

Some historians have interpreted these developments of 1877–1916 in terms of natural law, inevitable cycles, and biological growth. Do such interpretations help your understanding of this period?

Key Point to Remember

While domestic issues dominated United States history between 1877 and 1914, several foreign policy developments were of great significance, including the Spanish-American War, the annexation of the Philippines, the "policing" of debt-ridden Latin American countries, and business investments in Latin America and Asia.

Links from The Past to The Present

1. The Monroe Doctrine and its various interpretations continue to underlie United States policy toward Latin America.

2. Tensions in relations with Japan have surfaced many times and are still a concern as seen in the recent discussions about trade.

3. Business investments in Latin America and Asia have been important throughout our history.

Dates

1878—Pago Pago naval base annexed.

1889—First Pan-American Conference met.

1895—Venezuela-British Guiana boundary dispute settled.

1898—Peace of Paris ended Spanish-American War.

1900—Open Door Policy for China.

1903—Panama recognized.

1905—Russo-Japanese War ended by Treaty of Portsmouth.

1907—Gentlemen's Agreement with Japan.
        Algeciras Conference.

1910—United States troops sent to Nicaragua.

1916—United States troops sent into Mexico to capture Pancho Villa.

Questions

Identify each of the following:

Imperialists   Dollar Diplomacy
Anti-Imperialists   Treaty of Portsmouth
Open Door Policy   Spanish-American War

Multiple Choice:

1. President Theodore Roosevelt was not to be blocked in his desire to build a canal across Panama so he
   a. asked Mexico to help persuade Panama to lease the United States the land.
   b. signed the Clayton-Bulwer Treaty.
   c. ordered United States warships to protect the new Republic of Panama.

2. The belief that "the United States is practically sovereign on this continent" was first exemplified in President Cleveland's
   a. handling of the British Guiana-Venezuela boundary dispute.
   b. forcing Archduke Maximillian out of Mexico.
   c. sending of marines to the Dominican Republic.

3. The Anti-Imperialists in the debate over the Treaty of Paris argued that
   a. the United States had a civilizing mission to fulfill in the Philippines.
   b. acquisition of the Philippines was contrary to United States principles of democratic government.
   c. there was a strategic advantage to holding the Philippines.

4. Investments in Dollar Diplomacy were made especially in
   a. Latin America and Asia.
   b. Latin America and Africa.
   c. Asia and Africa.

Open-ended, Analysis Questions

The following questions require analysis and reflection. You are encouraged to bring to your answer information and ideas from many sources. The answers should be presented in composition or essay style, but they may be used to initiate discussion. The questions put you in the role of the historian, gathering information to support your personal perspective on the question.

(Note: The essay questions at the end of each chapter have, so far, required information only from that chapter or time period. Often essays will require the student to use information from a more extensive time period than that covered in a single chapter. For instance, question 1 below requires information found in chapters 6, 8, and 9. In the open-ended question section in the remaining chapters at least one question will require information from several chapters. Therefore, these questions can serve as a good review of the history you have studied and for major tests. Also, on major examinations, essay or open-ended questions will usually not be restricted to a narrow time period.)

1. In what ways were the reforms of the period referred to as Jacksonian Democracy similar to the reforms established in the period 1865–1914?

2. T. Roosevelt and W. Wilson are referred to as *Progressive Presidents*. What does the word *progressive* mean in this context? What actions by each president earned him this label?

3. How might the pattern of economic boom and bust have affected each of the following in the years 1865–1914?
   a. an average business owner
   b. an industrial worker
   c. a midwestern farmer

Turmoil of War and Depression

APPROACHES TO HISTORY

IDEOLOGY AND HISTORY

"What do you believe?" is a question one hears often. According to some historians, it is the most important question one can ask about a people or nation. These historians suggest that what a nation believes and what values it cherishes determine a nation's actions. They believe a nation's beliefs or ideology distinguishes it from other nations, and when the ideology is abandoned, the nation fails.

Often there are tensions and conflicts between values a nation holds. Citizens of the United States express belief in both equality and freedom, yet we know that if we try to make all men and women equal, our individual freedom to choose different paths of action will be hampered. The situation is made more complex if we consider the conflicting views of the meaning of equality held by Americans—equality of opportunity as opposed to absolute equality.

While such tensions exist, the ideology of the United States provides the nation with a sense of national identity and guides the leaders in decisions they make for action. Sometimes the decisions are painful because of the tensions between two good points of view, and then action is delayed, but according to these ideological historians, in order to maintain integrity and attain greatness, a nation must follow its ideology.

Individuals also have beliefs or an ideology that guides them. You may not articulate or discuss what you believe very often. Most people do not, but they have certain values varying from "Don't kick a dog" or "Never cheat on a quiz or test" to "All life is sacred." Believing these statements, you will act in certain ways when confronting situations. For instance, if a wet dog jumps on you and you really believe you should not kick a dog, you won't kick the dog down. You will accept getting your legs wet.

We are continually acting upon our beliefs, and so do nations. In the period between 1914 and 1941 the United States confronted three major crises—two World Wars and a great economic depression. While slow to act in all three situations, the nation, under strong presidential leadership, did address each crisis in keeping with avowed American beliefs. Ideological historians believe the only way to understand America's response to these three crises is to look at America's traditional values, such as freedom, individual rights, and democracy.

As we have seen, other historians believe other forces such as economics or natural cycles drive history and must be followed in making decisions. What do you think is most important?

I. World War I and the Peace

BACKGROUND

The fighting in the World War[1] began in Europe in August 1914. While many Americans were shocked at the outbreak of war, the crisis precipitated by the assassination on June 28, 1914 of Archduke Francis Ferdinand, heir to the throne of the Austro-Hungarian empire, was only the last in a series of crises among the European nations. Solutions to the other crises had been successfully negotiated. Negotiations also followed the assassination, but this time no solution except military action could be found.

In the preceding years the European nations had split into the two alliances that fought World War I. On one side were the Central Powers—Germany and Austria-Hungary and later Turkey and Bulgaria—and on the other side were the Allied Powers—England, France, and Russia and later Japan and Italy (who had originally been allied with Germany). Alliances had been formed by each nation to gain support for its claims to territory in Africa, for markets in Asia, for spheres of influence in China, for security of its borders in Europe, and out of fear.

After the Napoleonic Wars ended in 1815, there were no continent-wide conflicts in Europe during the 19th century, although there was a brief war—the small German states became unified, and they defeated France in 1871—and there was plenty of tension. French fear of Germany and a desire for revenge, German fear of France and England and a desire to be a world power, English fear of losing markets to a growing Germany and a desire to maintain control of her huge empire, Austria-Hungary's fear of breaking into separate nations as a result of nationalism and a desire to remain a power—all these made a compromise impossible in 1914.

At the start of the war, Germany invaded neutral Belgium without warning in order to attack France, and this act brought forth great sympathy for the Belgians by the Americans, who believed in fair play. British propaganda made the most of this attack, categorizing the Germans as barbarians. Following United States tradition and

[1] The World War   *Until the Second World War, the first was referred to as The World War or The Great War.*

Copyrighted. 1914. by John T. McCutcheon.
BRITANNIA MUST BE MORE CAREFUL HOW SHE WAVES THE RULES.
—McCutcheon in the Chicago *Tribune*.

John T. McCutcheon uses a clever play on the expression—"Britannia rules the waves"—to illustrate his view of England's use of the Blockade of Germany in 1915. What does he suggest is happening to neutral shipping?
From the Chicago Tribune *reprinted in* The Literary Digest *of January 16, 1915.*

the Monroe Doctrine's statement that we would not interfere in European affairs, President Wilson immediately proclaimed United States neutrality, but there was a great deal of support for the Allied cause. Many Americans had English ancestors and had sentimental feelings for the French who had fought with us in 1778. In spite of the many Americans with German background, there was a lot of anti-German feeling in the United States, and when Germany began using submarines to sink merchant ships, this feeling grew.

SUBMARINE WARFARE

At the start of the war, the English announced a blockade of German ports and stopped neutral ships to search them. (See cartoon above.) In 1915 the Germans retaliated by declaring the seas around the British Isles a war zone and announcing that any enemy merchant ship within this zone would be sunk on sight without providing for the passengers or crew. Any neutral ship in the war zone waters was there at its own risk.

> The submarine changes naval warfare.

The Germans used a new weapon, the submarine with underwater torpedoes, to enforce their declaration. Submarines were a dangerous threat to the English because merchant vessels, even if armed, were essentially defenseless against them. Convoys of ships escorted by navy vessels gave limited protection, but even then the submarines could get through and sink ships. President Wilson protested the German submarine warfare and declared the German action "an indefensible violation of neutral rights." We were again defending the rights of neutrals to use the high seas as we had against the Barbary Pirates in 1805 and the English in 1812.

> Wilson protests the German infringement on neutral rights.

On May 7, 1915, a German submarine sank the English passenger ship, *Lusitania*, and 1,198 died, including 128 Americans. Several Americans had been killed in previous torpedoings. President Wilson again protested. The Secretary of State, William Jennings Bryan, resigned, as he was a pacifist and believed Wilson's language was too strong. But Wilson was always a strong spokesman for what he believed was right. The Germans responded by agreeing to stop sinking ships without warnings. The United States entry into World War I had been delayed.

WILSON WINS REELECTION

Wilson ran for reelection and defeated the Republican candidate, Supreme Court Justice Charles Evans Hughes. The Progressive Party (Bull Moose Party) again nominated the pro-war, pro-English Theodore Roosevelt, but he declined and campaigned as a Republican for Hughes. Until the California vote was counted, it appeared Hughes had won the election, but California went for Wilson and he won. Wilson's support of the eight-hour day and other progressive legislation, combined with the slogan, "He kept us out of war," appeared to be the deciding factors in the election.

UNITED STATES INVOLVEMENT THROUGH TRADE

Although we were not in the war, Americans were profiting from it. American munition companies sold weapons to the Allies, and banks loaned them money. The Germans believed this violated the neutrality position. The United States' response was to welcome purchases of arms from either side, but because of the English blockade, the Central Powers were unable to carry goods from the United States to Germany. Thus, America's commitment to neutrality, equality, and business opportunities for all aided the Allies while it upheld our ideology.

There were overtures toward peace from the Germans in late 1916, and Woodrow Wilson made attempts to bring the parties together but was unsuccessful. Wishing to end the war and unable to do so on the battlefield in France, in February 1917, the Germans announced they would again practice unrestricted submarine warfare.

In January 1917, the British Naval Intelligence Service intercepted and deciphered a message, the Zimmerman Note, from the German government to their ambassador in Mexico. It informed him of the renewal of submarine warfare and instructed him to offer an alliance to the Mexicans in which they would get Texas, Arizona, and New Mexico in return for fighting the United States. Publication of the Zimmerman Note helped to solidify popular opinion against the Germans and won support for Wilson's decision to declare war.

On April 2, 1917, Wilson asked Congress to declare war on Germany. German submarine warfare, he declared, was "warfare against mankind," and the United

States would fight to make the world "safe for democracy." American ideology or belief in democracy, a common humanity, equality, and individual freedom were all invoked in our move to war. We were fighting for what we believed.

THE UNITED STATES ENTERS WORLD WAR I

The United States entered the war on April 6, 1917, the month in which English merchant marine losses to the German submarines peaked. 1917 was a bad year for the Allies. The Germans launched a successful attack on Russia; the Bolshevik Revolution in Russia overthrew the Czar; a French attack failed to break the German line in France; the British lost a great number of soldiers in an ineffective summer and fall attack; the Italians lost the northern section of their country to the Germans.

The United States passed a Selective Service Act (the draft) and immediately began to increase the armed services from about 200,000 to over 4,500,000. An American Expeditionary

> Americans fight in Europe.

Force (AEF) was sent to France under command of General John J. Pershing, and by November 1918 almost 1,500,000 Americans had seen combat in the battles of Belleau Wood and the Marne and in the Somme and Meuse-Argonne offenses. These offenses finally brought an end to the war. The heaviest fighting of the war had been in Europe, but there had also been fighting by the Allies in German colonies in Africa, in the Turkish Empire in the Middle East (modern Jordan, Iraq, Syria), and against German spheres of influence in Asia.

ORGANIZING THE UNITED STATES GOVERNMENT FOR WAR

The war had profound effects on society at home. The nation was highly organized for its war effort. A War Industries Board headed by a millionaire, Bernard Baruch, coordinated the effort to supply the military needs of both the United States and the

> The United States organizes for war.

Allies. Antitrust laws were suspended. Business leaders came to Washington as "dollar-a-year" men to help the war effort, and the power of the government bureaucracy grew. A Food Administration headed by Herbert Hoover, a young engineer who had organized food relief for the Belgians, worked to improve food production and distribution, and encouraged "victory gardens" planted in suburban yards, and meatless days—all done voluntarily in keeping with America's commitment to the individual.

The Committee on Public Information headed by George Creel was charged with uniting public opinion behind the war effort and did so through everything from news releases to movies. The Committee's charge was to bring Americans together, ignoring differences and individual interests in order to give full support to the war effort. While this seemed to work against American individualism, the Committee emphasized equality based on conformity to a common idea. Other committees added to the government's control over economic life and to the growth of the bureaucracy.

The war created job opportunities, and many African-Americans left the South to find work in steel mills and railway yards in northern cities. Opportunities for women also increased, but the gains for women faded when the men returned after the war. African-Americans throughout the country continued to meet with discrimination. Segregation was the law even in the armed services, and the Ku Klux Klan was reborn. A movie, *Birth of a Nation*, respected and renowned for its breakthrough in technique had a racist message in its story of the KKK.

> The war increases opportunities for women and encourages intolerance.

As hatred of the Germans was encouraged, it helped create intolerance in other areas. An Espionage Act and Sedition Act further limited individual liberty, making it unlawful to obstruct the draft, to use disloyal or abusive language against the armed services, the government, or the flag. The mobilization of the nation was effective in winning the war, but it strained America's ideological commitments to the individual and democracy.

WILSON'S PEACE PLAN

President Wilson led the war effort and mobilized America for victory. He had made a move toward peacemaking in 1916. During 1917 there was talk of a negotiated peace and the need to state war aims. In January 1918 Wilson addressed Congress and stated fourteen points "as the only possible program" for peace. The Fourteen Points held out the promise of a new world order supervised by a League of Nations. The Fourteen Points appealed to many of the belligerents as promising a peace without victory and the recognition of self determination by peoples so each could create their own nation state.

> Wilson introduces The Fourteen Points as a plan for peace.

Although many of the Allies opposed certain points, which would not give them the spoils of victory they wished, by the time Germany signed an armistice on November 11, 1918, and the Kaiser had fled to Holland, the Fourteen Points had been accepted as the basis for a treaty. The English had insisted, however, on reservations[2] on freedom of the seas, and the French had insisted on reparations[3]. The latter created great problems in the 1920s.

PEACEMAKING: THE TREATY OF VERSAILLES

World War I was very costly. The United States suffered over 110,000 dead and eventually paid over $75 billion in benefits to veterans but experienced no destruction on her soil. European nations lost many more soldiers (see chart), the costs to them were higher, and they also suffered heavy damage to roads, cities, and countryside. They wanted revenge, yet Wilson's Fourteen Points presented an idealistic, very Wilsonian approach to the peace, based on American ideology.

Woodrow Wilson had been a college professor before entering politics. He often used scholarly experts for advice. When it came to creating the delegation to attend

---

[2] reservations *Special clauses or qualifications.*
[3] reparations *Payments made by a defeated nation to the victor in a war. Reparations may be in goods, services, or money.*

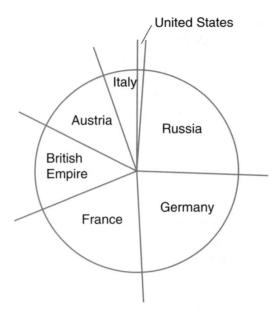

Information helpful to the historian is often presented in charts and graphs. Graphs can present a large amount of information quickly to those trained in reading them. This pie graph compares the losses of the nations fighting in World War I. While it does not tell you the number of men each nation lost, it quickly gives you information about the comparative losses. The United States lost 110,000 dead in World War I. Which nation had the largest losses? Approximately how many times greater were their losses than those of the United States?

the peace conference at Versailles, France, he called on experts from various areas to assist him. He decided to go to Europe, the first President to do so while in office, to attend the Versailles Conference. He took with him no member of the United States Senate, which by law would have to ratify the treaty, nor did he take with him any prominent Republican in spite of the fact the Republicans had won a majority in the Congress in the November 1918 election.

When the leaders of the four major powers—Clemenceau of France, Orlando of Italy, Lloyd George of England, and Woodrow Wilson—met at Versailles, Wilson was the only one who did not have the backing of a legislature. The Democratic Party had lost the majority in the Congress, and in a parliamentary democracy modeled on England, this would have meant the resignation of the Prime Minister or leader. It does not work that way within the United States government, but the loss of his party's control of Congress weakened Wilson's position.

During the war the Allies had made a number of secret agreements about the peace terms. Wilson was aware of these but ignored them in pushing for his Fourteen Points. The clash of ideas came at Versailles, when the tradition-minded, imperialistic allies looked for their spoils of victory as Wilson

> **Secret alliances undermine the Fourteen Points.**

defended his idealistic new vision of a world order. Wilson was a fine spokesperson for America's ideological idealism, but he was not prepared to deal with the realistic views of the Allies.

At the heart of Wilson's plan was the League of Nations. The purpose of the League was to prevent future wars. After intense debate and intrigue, the Versailles

Conference accepted the League of Nations as part of the Treaty of Versailles. It went on to write a treaty in which many of Wilson's points were amended. The Allies were to receive reparations, or payments from Germany for war damage. German colonies were given to the Allies under League of Nations mandates[4], as were Middle Eastern lands formerly within the Ottoman (Turkish) Empire. Imperialism, under a new name, triumphed in these mandates. The Saar Basin, heart of German industrialism, was to be ruled under League of Nations supervision for fifteen years, and then it would vote on its future. This was to provide France with security and economic power but was directly against Wilson's ideal of self-determination.

American idealistic ideology was compromised by Wilson at Versailles, but he believed the League of Nations would be able to discuss and resolve any problems growing out of the treaty. President Wilson believed that with the United States in the League of Nations, it would maintain the peace.

THE SENATE REJECTS THE TREATY OF VERSAILLES AND LEAGUE OF NATIONS

Woodrow Wilson had miscalculated. The Senate, led by Republican Senator Henry Cabot Lodge, rejected the Treaty of Versailles and membership in the League of Nations. There was a personal antagonism between Henry Cabot Lodge and Woodrow Wilson—another example of the role individuals play in history. This disagreement, some say, was the cause of Senator Lodge's strong stand against the League. However, the issues were complex.

A clash of ideology emerged in the debates over the League. Many Americans saw the League as violating George Washington's advice of no permanent alliances and the Monroe Doctrine's commitment to staying out of Europe. These people, known as isolationists, wished to preserve America as a unique nation and to remain isolated from the traditional problem of European politics and international diplomacy. Their ideological commitments stressed traditional American values. They believed in the uniqueness of America, that it had been called to a special role in world history, and that isolation from Europe was needed to fulfill this role.

> After debate, ideological differences cannot be resolved, and the Senate rejects the Treaty of Versailles.

Woodrow Wilson and his followers, the Internationalists and League supporters, stressed other American values: the brotherhood of man (all men are created equal), the interdependence of nations, and the need for open trade and freedom of the seas. Wilson represented a new interpretation of Jefferson's belief in the common man. As

---

[4] League of Nations mandate *An order from the League of Nations to a member nation to establish a responsible government over former German colonies or land taken from the defeated Central Powers. Such governments were to be under the review of the League of Nations. The territories so governed were referred to as mandated territories and were not considered possessions as colonies were. The idea was that eventually they would become independent nations.*

he had during the war, Woodrow Wilson appealed to the American people to support his program. He traveled by train throughout the country. Unfortunately, the stress of office became too much, and he suffered a stroke and returned partially paralyzed to Washington in September 1919. Although he remained in office until the election of Warren G. Harding, his power to persuade others was at an end.

THE UNITED STATES AND THE SOVIET UNION

When the United States entered World War I, Russia had just had a democratic revolution. Russia was an ally, but after the Bolshevik Revolution of October 1917, the Soviet Union withdrew from the war. In March 1918 the Soviet Union signed the Treaty of Brest-Litovsk with Germany. The Soviet Union did not participate in the Versailles Conference, and the new government was ignored by the victors. It was not recognized by the United States as the legitimate government of Russia until 1933. In fact, the United States joined the Allies in sending an army to the Russian port of Archangel in an attempt to keep supplies located there from going to the Germans.

> The United States joins the Allies in sending troops into the Soviet Union.

The United States also sent almost 10,000 soldiers to Siberia, ostensibly to keep Japan from taking control of the area and to rescue some Czechoslovakian soldiers who were fighting the Soviet forces. Since Russia was in the throes of a civil war and the Bolsheviks were struggling to control Siberia, they viewed the invasion very differently. For years American textbooks ignored and few Americans knew much about this invasion of the Soviet Union, which was taught to every student in the Soviet Union—a clear indication of differences in viewpoint and ideology. In spite of domestic fear of communism and a growing sense of the Soviet Union as an enemy, the United States withdrew the troops from the Soviet Union after the Bolsheviks established their control of the country. The United States suffered several hundred casualties in this expedition.

ATTEMPTS AT DISARMAMENT

The United States did not join the League of Nations but did participate in many League-sponsored events or meetings endorsed by the League. A disarmament conference, the first of several in the 1920s, was held in Washington and hosted by the United States. At this Washington Disarmament Conference of 1922, several disarmament treaties were signed limiting navy building and setting a ratio on the number of large ships. The ratio formula was 5 for the United States and Great Britain, 3 for Japan, and 1.75 for Italy and France. The navies of the five powers were to remain in this ratio to each other. Eventually Japan saw the ratio as an insult to her status as a great power. Other treaties defined great power relations, particularly in the Pacific. In 1927 the United States and France sponsored the Kellogg-Briand Pact to outlaw war, and eventually 62 nations signed it. Disarmament and the attempt to outlaw war illustrate that America's idealistic ideology and commitment to peace and lasting security continued in the 1920s even if the dominant philosophy of the nation was isolation.

AND SO ON, AND ON—
—Doyle in the Philadelphia *Record*

What is Doyle suggesting about the success of disarmament conferences?
From the Philadelphia Record *reprinted in* The Literary Digest *of November 25, 1933.*

REPARATIONS

In Europe the reparations demanded of Germany proved too much to pay, and the United States took the lead in developing revised payment plans. The United States was particularly eager that payments continue because the Allies used them to pay their huge war debt to the United States. With the depression of 1929, reparation payments ceased. So did payment on the foreign debt owed to the United States. Throughout the 1920s the United States continued to exercise its power in the Caribbean. Thus the United States was involved internationally in the 1920s in spite of the rejection of the League of Nations and the Treaty of Versailles.

> The United States remains active internationally.

Key Point to Remember
The United States entry into World War I reflected an ideological commitment to freedom and equality, peace, and democracy, which, although the nation voted to remain out of the League of Nations, continued in a commitment to disarmament and the outlawing of war in the 1920s.

People to Remember
Woodrow Wilson   Virginia-born college professor and Progressive, reform-minded Governor of New Jersey; 28th President of the United States; activist in domestic and foreign affairs; reform legislation included the Federal Reserve System and Clayton Anti-Trust Act; his idealism is reflected in the Fourteen Points, which provided the framework for the German surrender and the Treaty of Versailles in 1919; the Treaty including his plan for a peace-keeping League of Nations was rejected by the United States Senate; nevertheless, he was awarded the Nobel Peace Prize.

Links from the Past to the Present

1. Defense of neutral rights on the sea has been United States policy since the issue of impressment in the 1790s.

2. Ideological commitment to peace, democracy, and the equality of peoples has been expressed by Presidents over and over again.

3. Disarmament agreements were sought throughout the 20th century.

Dates

1914—Archduke Francis Ferdinand assassinated.
   World War I began.

1915—*Lusitania* sunk.

1917—United States entered World War I.

1918—United States troops sent to Soviet Union.
   Armistice ended World War I.

1919—Treaty of Versailles and League of Nations signed.

1920—Senate rejected Treaty of Versailles.

1922—Washington Disarmament Conference.

1927—Kellogg-Briand Peace Pact.

1929—Reparations ended.

1933—United States recognized the Soviet Union.

Questions
Identify each of the following:

Washington Disarmament Conference	Treaty of Versailles
League of Nations	Committee of Public Information
Isolationist	American Expeditionary Force (AEF)
Internationalist	Belleau Wood
Lusitania	Fourteen Points

Multiple Choice:

1. United States forces participated in the following battles in World War I:
   a. the Marne, and San Juan Hill.
   b. the Somme and Meuse-Argonne offensives and Belleau Wood.
   c. Belleau Wood and Bunker Hill.

2. The major European Allies in World War I were
   a. Germany, Austria-Hungary, Turkey, and Bulgaria.
   b. Italy, Russia, England, and Turkey.
   c. Italy, Russia, England, and France.

3. After the Bolshevik Revolution the United States joined the Allies in sending troops to
   a. Siberia and Moscow.
   b. Archangel and Siberia.
   c. Archangel and Brest-Litovsk.

4. Examples of the growth of the bureaucracy and the concentration of power in Washington during World War I are
   a. dollar-a-year men and the War Industries Board.
   b. Food Administration and the Committee on Public Information.
   c. both of the above.

II. The Coming of World War II

In 1931 the first aggressive step toward World War II was taken when Japan invaded Manchuria, a province of China, in violation of the League covenant, the Kellogg-Briand Pact, and numerous other treaties. It was the beginning of a series of military actions the League of Nations was unable to control. The World War I Allies proved powerless to halt them.

The roots of these actions were deep. The actions of Germany were partly motivated by frustrations created by the Treaty of Versailles; Japan's were rooted in its belief that it should have a major role in the Pacific and China, a belief that had been frustrated by the European powers and the Open Door policy in China. With

Salt on the Dragon's Tail

—"The Evening Times" (Glasgow).

Two years after Japan invaded Manchuria, Davidson in this cartoon makes a comment about the League of Nations. The League had been established to preserve the peace and prevent aggression. How effective was it in preventing Japanese aggression in Manchuria according to Davidson?

From the Glasgow Evening Times *reprinted in* The Literary Digest *of February 25, 1933.*

the coming to power of Benito Mussolini in Italy in 1922 and Adolf Hitler in Germany in 1933 and the growing strength of the military in Japan under Emperor Hirohito, leaders were in power in three nations who were prepared to reject the new order of peace through the League of Nations and to revert to the old order of power through military action. In 1931 Japan invaded Manchuria and annexed it in 1932. The League of Nations did nothing. What became World War II began in Asia in 1937 when Japan invaded China. Actions taken by Germany and Italy during the 1930s led to war in Europe in 1939. After the bombing of Pearl Harbor in December 1941, the United States declared war on Germany and Japan linking the Asian and European wars in what is known as World War II.

HITLER'S AGGRESSION IN EUROPE

Hitler's steps to war and the appeasement[5] practiced by the European Allies in Europe in response has haunted Americans since the end of World War II. Adolf Hitler in many ways was an opportunist who seized on issues of emotional appeal. He

> Hitler rejects the Treaty of Versailles.

used the Jews as the scapegoat for Germany's ills and killed six million Jews in pursuing his "final solution." Gypsies, homosexuals, and many eastern Europeans were also forced into slave labor camps, and over five million were killed at Auschwitz and other death camps. The Holocaust[6] illustrates the worst tendencies of human nature. Hitler attacked the Treaty of Versailles, which blamed Germany for the war, demilitarized her, and included some Germans within the borders of the newly created European nations of Austria, Czechoslovakia, and Poland. This went against Woodrow Wilson's concept of self-determination expressed in the Fourteen Points.

Once in power Hitler moved to right these "wrongs." In 1935 he rejected the military restrictions of the Treaty and began building a navy. England accepted this and signed a naval treaty with Germany. In 1936 Hitler occupied the Rhineland, German

> England and France negotiate with Hitler at Munich.

territory along the Rhine River that had been demilitarized and was to serve as a buffer between France and Germany under League of Nations supervision. England and France did nothing and neither did the League. After a failed attempt in 1934, in March 1938 a coup d'etat in Austria opened the country to German annexation, which Hitler called a reunion of German peoples. It was the third time the Allies ignored Hitler's violation of a clause in the Treaty of Versailles. In September 1938 Hitler was ready to seize the lands in Czechoslovakia along the German border,

[5] appeasement *The policy of giving concessions to potential military opponents in order to maintain peace.*
[6] holocaust *The word in religious terms means a burnt offering. It has come to mean a great or massive destruction of human life to achieve "ethnic cleansing," i.e., the elimination of members of another tribe, race, or religion within the borders of a nation. Since Hitler's attempt to destroy certain ethnic groups, especially the Jewish population of Europe, the word capitalized has been used to refer specifically to that attempt. However, it has also been used to refer to other recent attempts to destroy ethnic groups in Cambodia, Uganda, Rwanda, Yugoslavia, and Sudan.*

where over three million Germans lived. After some negotiation, the leaders of France, Italy, Germany, and England met at Munich, Germany, where English Prime Minister Neville Chamberlain agreed to a policy of appeasement of Hitler. Hitler was allowed to seize the Czechoslovakian territory of the Sudetenland where most of the Germans lived. Hitler promised no further aggression, and Chamberlain claimed he had achieved "peace in our time." It was the high point of the appeasement policy, and the word *Munich* has stood for appeasement ever since.

OUTBREAK OF WAR IN EUROPE

In March 1939 the rest of Czechoslovakia split in two over internal differences. Hitler occupied half of the nation. The Allies did not act in spite of having guaranteed Czechoslovakia's borders at Munich. When Hitler approached Poland in May 1939 concerning his desire to annex the free city[7] of Danzig, England and France assured Poland they would end appeasement and provide aid in case of an invasion.

> Hitler invades Poland, and World War II begins in Europe.

Danzig was a free city with a large German population created by the League of Nations to give Central Europeans an outlet to the Baltic Sea. To provide Poland with her own outlet on the sea, a corridor of land was given to Poland separating East Prussia from the main part of Germany. In order for Hitler to seize Danzig, he would have to move across this Polish corridor. To achieve his goal, Hitler next turned to the Soviet Union. Hitler, opportunist that he was, had used the German fear of communism to aid his rise to power. But in August 1939 he was ready to negotiate a nonaggression treaty with the Soviet Union. The secret terms of the Soviet-German Treaty stated that in case of an attack on Poland, the Soviet Union and Germany would divide Poland between them.

On September 1, 1939, having signed the treaty with the Soviet Union, Hitler invaded Poland, and Soviet troops immediately entered to occupy the eastern region of Poland. England and France honored their commitments. World War II had begun.

Americans since then have understood the cause of the war to have been the appeasement of Hitler. On many occasions since then, Presidents have justified foreign policy actions by saying the United States cannot appease a potential aggressor. They often refer to Munich and make comparisons to Hitler and the 1930s as President George H. W. Bush did in August 1990 after Iraq seized Kuwait. It has become imbedded in our ideology that appeasement is wrong and force must be used to stop any threat of or use of force by an aggressor.

UNITED STATES NEUTRALITY

Other events in Europe and Asia in the 1930s had led the United States to pass neutrality acts. In 1935 Benito Mussolini invaded Ethiopia in Africa. King Haile Selassie made a plea for help before the League of Nations, but the League did not act. Ethiopia was conquered and absorbed by Italy in 1936. The United States passed

---

[7] free city   *An independent city not ruled by any nation; often there will be special trade agreements set by the city to encourage economic activity.*

two neutrality acts (1935 and 1936) aimed at keeping the country out of the war. They were a reaction to our entry into World War I. The acts prohibited loans or credits to belligerents—some believed the United States had entered World War I to protect

our loans to the Allies. The neutrality acts also prohibited arms sales or travel by United States citizens on belligerent ships except at their own risk—some believed the United States had entered World War I because of the sale of arms and/or of the loss of Americans killed while sailing on English ships. Civil War broke out in Spain in 1936. Italy and Germany aided the Fascist[8] General Franco, but the Allies and the United States did not support his democratic opponents. Neutrality was the United States official policy and was confirmed in a new act in 1937. When Japan invaded China that year, Roosevelt did not invoke the full act but he forbid transport of war goods on United States ships. This actually benefited Japan as she had a larger merchant fleet than China and could import goods.

The United States reaction to the outbreak of war was the same as it had been to the Napoleonic War and World War I—neutrality. The proclamation of neutrality in European wars had deep ideological roots in United States history. President Franklin Roosevelt himself was not in favor of this stance, but he signed the law. In 1937 he suggested that an international quarantine of aggressors was the only way to preserve the peace. Public opinion was not yet ready for this stand in spite of the aggressive actions of the German and Italian dictators and of the Japanese militarists. Japan was embarked on a policy of domination of the western rim of the Pacific. Hitler and Mussolini were ignoring the League of Nations and pursuing aggressive policies, yet Americans desired to remain isolated and uninvoled.

GOOD NEIGHBOR POLICY

With his election in 1933, Franklin D. Roosevelt introduced a new policy toward Latin America, called the Good Neighbor Policy. It improved relations, led to less United States economic and military control over Latin America, and created an

atmosphere of cooperation that was helpful in World War II. Also, Roosevelt led the United States to consider changes in colonial policy. In 1933 independence was voted for the Philippines, to take effect in 1945. Statehood for Hawaii was first considered in 1937. These actions suggested a move away from "Big Stick" and "Dollar Diplomacy" toward a greater respect for other people, more in keeping with the United States ideological commitment to democracy and equality.

COOPERATION WITH THE ENGLISH: 1939–1941

When war began in 1939 in Europe, Roosevelt moved cautiously to support England and France. In November the arms embargo aspect of the Neutrality Act was replaced with a cash-and-carry policy that allowed nations to buy arms for cash and carry them

[8] Fascism   *The political philosophy of dictatorship first developed by Benito Mussolini in Italy. All interest groups—labor, business, etc.—are organized under the control of a central government that is controlled by a single political party. Interests of all these groups are subordinated to the interests of the state.*

away in their own ships. The English were able to buy and carry the arms in their large merchant fleet, but the Germans were unable to do so. Negotiations with the English established joint defense measures and finally in 1941 a Lend Lease Act made it possible for nations the president deemed vital to the United States defense to receive arms by sale, lease, or transfer. Roosevelt used the act to aid the English.

In his annual message to Congress in January 1941, President Roosevelt described Four Freedoms—freedom of speech and expression, freedom of religion, freedom from want, freedom from fear—the achievement of which should guide United States policy. The Four Freedoms were deeply rooted in America's traditions and ideology. When the United States entered the war, the Four Freedoms became our war goal; they formed the ideology we proclaimed to the world. Should they still be our goals in international affairs?

> The Atlantic Charter illustrates how strongly the United States supports the Four Freedoms and other democratic values.

In August 1941 President Roosevelt met with Prime Minister Winston Churchill, the new English prime minister[9], on a cruiser off Newfoundland, and they signed an agreement called the Atlantic Charter. Although the United States was not in the war at that time, the Atlantic Charter stated the postwar goals of the United States and Great Britain. These included national self-determination, free access of all people to economic opportunity, freedom from want and fear, and freedom of the seas. It indicated how far we had moved from neutrality in the two years since the war in Europe had begun. The Atlantic Charter also showed how deeply committed the United States was to certain values and ideologies.

However, not all Americans agreed with Roosevelt's policies. While Roosevelt made preparations for defense and worked closely with the English and French, others opposed any European involvement.

OPPOSITION TO ROOSEVELT'S POLICIES AND THE 1940 ELECTION

Charles A. Lindbergh Jr., a popular American folk hero who had won America's heart when he became the first to fly solo from the United States to France, supported an America-first movement and Hitler's position on a greater Germany. Many other individuals and groups did the same. They were encouraged when in the spring of 1940 Hitler won a series of victories and France surrendered in June. Roosevelt then decided to run for a third term, the first president to do so. The Republicans nominated Wendell Wilkie, who had been an anti-New Deal Democrat. Roosevelt promised not to send Americans to war, and with this promise, similar to Woodrow Wilson's in 1916, he won reelection easily.

The United States Enters the War: Pearl Harbor

United States interests in Asia were threatened by Japanese aggression in China. In the war between China and Japan, the United States remained neutral, but there was great

[9] prime minister   *The first minister and thus the actual head of government in parliamentary governments.*

sympathy for China. When France fell to Hitler in June 1940, Japan signed a treaty with the Vichy government, the German puppet government of France, which gave Japan bases in the French colony of Indo-China. The United States warned Japan not to invade Indo-China. When Japan did so in July 1941, the United States froze Japanese assets in the United States, which brought United States-Japanese trade to a halt.

During the remainder of the year relations deteriorated in spite of active negotiations. The United States put the Philippine army under command of General Douglas MacArthur, and President Roosevelt appealed to Emperor Hirohito of Japan for peace but on December 7, 1941, Japanese military forces attacked the United States naval base at Pearl Harbor and other installations in Hawaii. On December 8, 1941 President Roosevelt asked Congress to declare war on Japan. Congress immediately voted for war against Japan and then, on December 11, after Germany and Italy had declared war on the United States, declared war on those two nations. The United States thus entered World War II as one of the Allies fighting the Axis Powers of Germany, Italy, and Japan. To what extent was America's entry into the war driven by America's ideological commitment to freedom, equality, and the self-determination of nations? Or were other factors more important?

Key Point to Remember

Adolf Hitler of Germany, Benito Mussolini of Italy, and Emperor Hirohito and the military leaders of Japan began a series of aggressive moves in 1931 that led to the outbreak of war in China in 1937 and in Europe in 1939. The League of Nations and the World War I Allies failed to react, and this "appeasement of aggressors" has greatly affected the United States view of foreign relations since that time.

Links from the Past to the Present

1. A negative reaction to appeasement of aggression as symbolized by Munich has been an important element of United States policy since then as illustrated by Vietnam and the 1990 Persian Gulf War.
2. Commitment to neutrality in affairs of Europe was a goal of early foreign policy, incorporated in the Monroe Doctrine, adhered to in the 1930s, and still supported by some Americans.
3. Values incorporated in the Four Freedoms and the Atlantic Charter come from United States ideology.
4. Concern over a major power controlling Southeast Asia has guided our policy in that region since the Spanish-American War.

Dates

1931—Japan invaded Manchuria.

1935—Mussolini invaded Ethiopia.

1936—Hitler seized the Rhineland.
    Spanish Civil War.

1937—Neutrality Act reconfirmed.

1938—Munich Agreement.

1939—Soviet-German Pact.

Germany invaded Poland.

1941—Lend Lease Act.

Four Freedoms speech.

Atlantic Charter.

Japan attacked Pearl Harbor; United States entered World War II.

Questions
Identify each of the following:

Emperor Hirohito	Neville Chamberlain
Munich	Ethiopia
Holocaust	Spanish Civil War
Adolf Hitler	Benito Mussolini

Multiple Choice:

1. Examples of Hitler's breaking of clauses of the Treaty of Versailles are
   a. rejection of military restrictions and the invasion of Manchuria.
   b. the occupation of the Rhineland and the annexation of Austria.
   c. seizure of the Sudetenland and the attack on Ethiopia.

2. Civil war broke out in Spain in 1936 and
   a. the Allies of World War I immediately sent aid to the democratic forces.
   b. General Franco agreed to the Four Freedoms as the goal of the civil war.
   c. Hitler and Mussolini aided their fellow Fascist, General Franco.

3. After the fall of France to Germany in 1940, the Japanese
   a. signed a treaty with the Vichy government of France for bases in Indo-China.
   b. invaded China.
   c. began negotiations with the United States for bases in the Philippines.

III. Domestic and Social Issues: 1918–1932

THE RED SCARE AND PALMER RAIDS

After the Bolshevik Revolution in Russia, the Soviet Union began an intensive propaganda campaign against the west hoping to precipitate the world revolution predicted by Karl Marx. In a reaction of fear, the Department of Justice undertook a number of raids against political and labor leaders who were suspected of having Communist or leftist sympathies. Over 3,000 people were arrested in raids organized by the Attorney General Mitchell Palmer against what he claimed was a Red or Communist threat. The Palmer Raids in late 1919 and 1921 mark the beginning of 70 years of the use of America's fear of communism by ambitious politicians to further their personal goals. Palmer had presidential ambitions but failed to obtain the nomination. At the time of

> The Palmer Raids are an illustration of America's fear of communism.

the raids, President Wilson had suffered a stroke and was incapacitated. Americans' willingness to accept the Red Scare as real and to prosecute those arrested reveals a continuing aspect of intolerance rooted in American history.

ELECTIONS OF 1920 AND 1924

The war had centralized political and economic power in Washington. Wilson began the decentralization of the wartime concentration of power. Railroads, which had been under government control, were returned to private control on March 1, 1921. In the 1920s government policy became again one of laissez-faire. Warren G. Harding was nominated for President in 1920 and was elected over a Democratic ticket of James Cox and Franklin Delano Roosevelt. Women voted in the 1920 election for the first time. Calvin Coolidge from Vermont became president on Harding's death in 1923 and was nominated by the Republicans in 1924.

The Democrats were in disarray. Torn between southern Fundamentalists[10] and northern Internationalists[11], between urban wets[12] and depressed farmers, they nominated John Davis, a New York conservative on the 102nd ballot at their convention. Calvin Coolidge easily won the election. Nicknamed Silent Cal, he took an inactive role, letting prosperity and the Roaring '20s roll along.

THE HARDING SCANDALS

In 1924 a number of scandals in the government were disclosed. They involved the Departments of Justice, Interior, and the Navy, and the Veterans Bureau. They were reminiscent of the post-Civil War scandals under President Grant. The major scandal involved the Teapot Dome Oil Reserve, which had been set aside for the use of the Navy but was leased illegally to oil magnate Harry Sinclair by Secretary of the Interior Albert B. Fall. The Secretary had been "loaned" money by Sinclair. The implication was there had been a private deal. Both Fall and Sinclair served jail terms as a result.

LIMITING IMMIGRATION

The Red Scare and the Harding scandals were only two examples of intolerance and corruption in the 1920s. The Ku Klux Klan returned in strength, and over 40,000 members marched in Washington in 1925. Lynchings of African Americans continued in spite of their contributions to the war effort in World War I. Many immigrants had come to America immediately after the war. Having rejected the League of Nations, Americans were ready to turn inward in isolation and to preserve

[10] Fundamentalist   *A person who believes in fundamentalism—the militantly conservative movement of American Protestants that hold the Bible to be literally true in every respect and the only source of ethical standards.*
[11] internationalist   *A person who supports Internationalism—the concept of cooperation among nations to promote the good of all—as opposed to Nationalism—the concept of devotion to the needs and goals of one nation, often to the detriment of other nations.*
[12] wets   *Those opposed to prohibition.*

what was theirs. They saw a threat from the immigrants and feared they might be radicals or Communists.

The Sacco-Vanzetti case illustrates this fear. Sacco and Vanzetti were Italian born and adhered to the philosophy of anarchism. They were accused of killing a paymaster and guard in South Braintree, Massachusetts, in 1920. The evidence was slim, but they were convicted and sentenced to death—many thought because of their names and philosophy. There were appeals and a special commission headed by President Lowell of Harvard University investigated the case. The commission confirmed the verdict, and Sacco and Vanzetti were executed while still claiming their innocence. The Sacco-Vanzetti case is a striking illustration of political intolerance and fear of immigrants.

In 1882 the Chinese Exclusion Act had restricted immigration from China, and immigration from Japan had been restricted in 1907, indicating Americans' fear and prejudice against Asians. Then, in 1921, Congress passed an Immigration Act, the Emergency Quota Act, the first across-the-board restriction on European immigration passed by the United States Congress. In 1924 and again in 1929 laws were passed restricting immigration further. These laws created quotas for the number of immigrants who could come from each country. These quotas were based on the number of United States' citizens claiming ancestors from the country according to the 1890 (later the 1910) United States census[13]. The 1890 date gave larger quotas to the Irish and English because immigration from southern Europe increased greatly between 1890 and 1910. The 1890 date reflected America's prejudice against eastern and southern Europeans.

The restriction of immigration marked a great shift in American ideology. No longer were we the land of opportunity for all oppressed people.

We ignored the fact that we were all immigrants. The National Quota System was eliminated in 1965, and many refugees have come to the United States since World War II, but the immigration quotas reflect 1920s isolation, intolerance, prejudice and fear. But there was another side to the 1920s.

UNITED STATES INDUSTRY

After a minor post-war economic recession, business boomed. New industries centering on electricity and oil flourished. The automobile industry led the way. Henry Ford had introduced the assembly line for the making of his Model T car in 1913. His Rouge River Plant produced a new car every 10 seconds. The automobile industry stimulated the steel, oil, and rubber industries. Road building and gas stations were needed. As travel and vacations by car became more popular, guest houses and cabins for overnight travelers developed as a business. The automobile provided young people independence and changed dating habits as couples could find privacy away from their home in their cars. A full analysis of the way the car changed American business, values, and life style would fill a large volume. Advertising for all the new products stimulated that industry. Prosperity continued for seven years and the stock market reflected this prosperity.

[13] census *An official count of the number of people living in a country.*

CHANGES IN AMERICAN CULTURE

Another new invention, the radio, created a complex industry and added a new dimension to entertainment. With the first talking motion picture, Al Jolson's *The Jazz Singer* in 1927, movies experienced a tremendous growth. It is estimated that by 1930 almost four-fifths of the United States population was going to movies weekly. As a result both vaudeville and legitimate stage performances declined.

> **Movies and literature reflect American values and concerns.**

American authors of the 1920s and 1930s created literature of high quality reflecting American life and values. T. S. Eliot, F. Scott Fitzgerald, Ernest Hemingway, and Gertrude Stein established residence in Europe. Gertrude Stein, better known as a critic and lecturer than as writer, referred to them as the "Lost Generation"—a name which has stuck. She held a salon or regular gathering at her apartment in Paris where theories of modernism were expressed and explored by many artists and writers. In her *Autobiography of Alice B. Toklas* (1933), her lifetime companion, Stein discusses her theories. T. S. Eliot chose England not France for his residence. He became the most important poet of the generation and won the Nobel Prize for Literature in 1948. In the *Lovesong of J. Alfred Prufrock* (1915) he anticipated his work and style of the next forty years, which affected all poets of the first half of the century. In *The Waste Land* (1922) Eliot reflected the disillusionment of the 1920s and inspired many poets and writers. Eliot, like Stein, was a noted literary critic and contributed to the quarterly review *Criterion*. F. Scott Fitzgerald in *This Side of Paradise* (1920) and *The Great Gatsby* (1925) caught the spirit of the success-oriented generation in which "all gods were seen as dead, all wars fought, all faith in man shaken." Ernest Hemingway wrote brilliantly of the war experience and disillusionment in *The Sun Also Rises* (1926) and *A Farewell to Arms* (1929). William Faulkner, while he did not become an expatriate in Europe, is linked with the Lost Generation. Faulkner created a fictional county in the South and revealed the restricted souls of its inhabitants in *The Sound and Fury* (1929) and *As I Lay Dying* (1930). There are parallels in his portrayal of the decaying South with the disillusionments expressed by Eliot, Fitzgerald, and Hemingway. Faulkner won the Nobel Prize for Literature in 1949. His reputation has grown, and he now ranks as one of the finest American authors.

In Harlem, New York, there was a great renaissance of African-American culture. The Harlem Renaissance, led by authors Langston Hughes and Claude McKay and jazz musician Louis Armstrong, encouraged African-American artists and produced some of the finest literature of the decade.

> **African-American culture thrives in the Harlem Renaissance.**

Eugene O'Neill emerged as the greatest American playwright. In *Mourning Becomes Electra* (1931), he turned to Greek tragedy for inspiration and wrote a compelling drama of suppression and revenge. He won the Nobel Prize in 1936. O'Neill used ideas from the works of the Austrian psychiatrist, Sigmund Freud, in his plays and helped introduce Freudian principles and understanding of sexuality to Americans.

THE ROARING TWENTIES

The 1920s, often referred to as the Roaring '20s, were a time of great change and experimentation for some Americans. There was prosperity for many in urban centers, but the prosperity was not evenly distributed. There were poor in the cities and few African-Americans shared in the good times.

Prohibition changes America's habits and provides a background for the Roaring '20s.

There were many changes in Americans' attitudes in the years after World War I. The war had disturbed the lives of over 4 million young men, taking them from their homes and exposing over 2 million of them to Europe. Women had gained new places in the workforce. The prohibition amendment, banning the sale of alcoholic beverages, had passed in 1919. America would never be the same again. The distilling of liquor went underground and quickly came under the control of criminal elements in the cities. The era of urban gangsters like Al Capone in Chicago was born. Alcohol could be purchased at speakeasys[14], where men and women drank cocktails and discussed Freud's views on sex.

The age of the vamp—a female vampire introduced in the movies—and the flapper—symbol of a devil-may-care, independent young woman—had arrived. The ideal woman of the mid-1920s was the flapper. She smoked cigarettes, wore her hair and skirt short, flattened her breasts, used lipstick, and rouged her face. The flapper replaced the Gibson Girl image of the turn of the century, when the ideal was a slim-waisted, willowy young woman with bouffant hair, long dress, and large hat. Each type reflected an age and to a large extent was created by advertisers.

Since the 1920s, movies and later television have provided us with ideal types for both women and men. Ideal women have ranged from the innocent Mary Pickford of silent movies to Betty Grable, the pin-up girl of World War II, to Marilyn Monroe, the sex symbol of the 1950s, to the singer/actress

Advertisers and the movies create male and female sex symbols.

Madonna noted for extremes in dress and action in the 1980s to, in the early years of the 21st century, Jennifer Aniston and Angelina Jolie—actresses but also the favorite subject of paparazzi and gossip magazines who cover their every action—positive and negative. For men, the idols have included Rudolph Valentino, the sultry romantic hero of the silent screen; Clark Gable—with his famous line at the end of *Gone With the Wind* (1939), "Frankly, Scarlett, I don't give a damn"—the sensitive and rebellious James Dean and the macho John Wayne in the 1950s; Harrison Ford and Paul Newman in the 1980s to actors Tom Cruise and Brad Pitt who have talent but whose private lives are publicized and followed by the public. Such models from Hollywood and advertising have set the standard not only for the way people want to look but also for the way many, especially young people, think men and women should behave.

Flappers and their young beaus danced to jazz bands and explored the new views of sex in darkened movie houses or in parked cars. The sexual revolution had begun, and "petting" and "necking" were added to the American vocabulary. Margaret

---

[14] speakeasys   *Illegal bars where liquor could be purchased. They were often controlled by gangsters.*

Sanger, wishing to limit the births of "undesirables," led an organized movement for birth control, which eventually provided women with greater control over their lives. Talk of an equal rights amendment to the Constitution began. But the new ideas were not popular everywhere.

THE SCOPES TRIAL

Religious Fundamentalists in Tennessee brought to trial in 1925 John C. Scopes for breaking a Tennessee state law forbidding the teaching of evolution. These Fundamentalists advocated traditional values and condemned Darwin and evolution as against the Bible's story of creation in seven days. They saw a breakdown in the traditional attitudes on sex and morality and

> Religious fundamentalists reject the new and support the "traditional American values."

believed these had been brought about because Darwinian philosophy made people doubt the truths of the Bible. The Scopes trial (nicknamed the Monkey Trial by the press because evolution suggested humans were descended from monkeys and not created by God) attained national prominence. William Jennings Bryan, Fundamentalist and three-times presidential candidate, testified as an expert on the Bible. Scopes was found guilty, but the trial lawyers made Bryan appear ridiculous, and the Fundamentalist cause was temporarily set back nationally.

Photograph of Farmhouse in Acworth, New Hampshire, about 1900
The residents of this New England farmhouse paid $75 a year rent for the house and farm about the turn of the century. The house is typical of New England farmhouses of an earlier era. The scene illustrates the starkness, yet dignity, of farm life. What is the main characteristic of the style of the house?
Courtesy: The New Hampshire Historical Society, Concord, New Hampshire

THE FARMERS

World War I had again brought prosperity to American farmers. Food was needed to feed the armed forces as well as the Allies, whose food production had been interrupted by the war. The good times for the farmers peaked in 1920. As the rest of the world went back into food production, the demand for United States produce dropped, and prices fell dramatically. Just as in the 19th century, increased demand had led to more land under cultivation, and new machinery had helped to increase production. A surplus resulted.

> As agricultural prices fall, farmers do not share in the prosperity of the 1920s.

What to do with farm surplus in order to raise prices and increase farm income became the farm problem of the 1920s and has continued, with few exceptions, as a problem to the present. It can be viewed in two ways. If the problem is overproduction, then the solution is to cut production. However, if it is viewed as a problem of underconsumption[15], then the solution is to find ways to enable more people at home and abroad to consume the food.

In the 1920s one out of every four farmers abandoned farm work, and a bloc representing the interests of those who remained on the farms emerged in Congress. The Farm Bloc's solution was based on underconsumption as the cause of surpluses. The Farm Bloc wanted the government to buy surpluses and sell the produce abroad. Congress passed such legislation twice, but President Coolidge vetoed it. In 1929, under President Hoover, Congress passed the Agricultural Marketing Act that established a Farm Board to loan money to cooperatives[16], which would buy up the surplus and then sell it when prices rose. With the start of the Depression, surpluses grew rapidly, and the Farm Board was overwhelmed.

In an attempt to guarantee themselves a market and higher prices, farmers turned to the tariff. Under President Wilson the Underwood Tariff brought duties down to their lowest level in years. In 1922 they had been raised to roughly 39 percent in the Fordney-McCumber Tariff as part of the Republican support for business. While generally designed to help business, tariffs had always included duties on some agricultural products such as sugar but tariffs did not help many farmers. The United States could produce more products more cheaply and efficiently than other nations and farmers depended on exports for much of their income. President Hoover supported some limited changes in the tariffs to help farmers, but when the 1930 Hawley-Smoot Tariff was finally passed, it had made significant changes in the tariff arrangements and had raised duties to an average of just under 60 percent.

> The Hawley-Smoot tariff raises duties, and as other nations raise their tariffs, international trade slows.

Higher tariffs made it difficult for foreign countries to sell in the United States. Lacking dollars, they could not buy farm products. This proved to be a short-sighted move as other nations retaliated by raising their tariffs, and international trade suffered. These artificial trade barriers hurt business worldwide at a time when all

---

[15] underconsumption   *An inability to use up all the goods and services produced.*
[16] cooperatives   *A business or association that is owned jointly by those who use its services or facilities.*

nations were suffering from the effects of the Depression precipitated by the Wall Street Crash of 1929.

THE STOCK MARKET CRASH: 1929

During the years of business prosperity in the 1920s, the value of stock on the New York stock market climbed steadily. Many people bought "on margin," investing a small amount of cash and borrowing the rest to be paid back when the stock price went up, as everyone came to believe it was bound to do. For example, if a share of stock sold for $100, you the buyer might put up $10 in cash and borrow $90. When the stock rose to, say, $120, you could sell, pay back the borrowed $90 (with interest), and still pocket a comfortable profit on your $10 investment. But what if stock prices dropped? If the share you bought at $100 dropped to $80, you not only lost your $10 investment but could not pay back the full loan. You lost your investment, the person from whom you borrowed lost, and both of you were headed for bankruptcy.

This is what happened in October 1929. Stock prices dropped. Individuals lost their investments. Then banks began to fail. As banks and businesses went bankrupt, business slowed as the market for goods shrank and there was less money to borrow, and unemployment rose. A recession began and by 1931 had turned into America's worst recession to that point. It greatly challenged America's ideological

Disarmament Needed Here, Too

—Cowan in the Boston "Transcript."

In this cartoon Cowan illustrates his view on tariffs. What does he see as the relationship between tariffs, world trade, and war? How did these three relate to the depression? From the Boston Transcript *reprinted in* The Literary Digest *of May 20, 1933.*

commitment to capitalism. While history does not repeat itself in perfect cycles, there are many similarities to previous periods of business growth and later panic. As the housing/financial crisis of 2008 worsened, many scholars were suggesting certain similarities to the 1929 situation and the possible need for reforms in the economic structure that would again challenge America's ideological commitments.

> A number of factors contribute to the stock market crash.

Why did the stock market crash? A number of factors contributed. They ranged from the frenzy of speculation and the overpriced nature of stocks to the unevenness of prosperity and the farmers' depressed status. A rise in interest rates in England, designed to attract investment money away from Wall Street and to England, also had an effect as investors moved money from stocks to English bonds to get these higher earnings. Perhaps the most important factor was psychological—a desire to get rich quick, which led to gambling with borrowed money, which is one way of looking at buying "on margin." This psychological factor has always been important in the operation of the stock market.

The United States also suffered from chronic underconsumption of its production both of goods and farm produce. This was another cause of recession. New products were available in abundance. They could not all be purchased because of the unevenness of prosperity and the disparities between wages. Many workers were paid subsistence[17] wages making them underconsumers. The farmers, suffering from eight years of declining income, were not a good market for manufactured goods. With the great drop in prices on the stock market, margin loans could not be paid. To get cash for their depositors, banks called in other loans. When these loans could not be paid, banks failed. Business activity slowed, and layoffs of workers began. With no income, workers could not purchase goods, and this increased inventories of unsold goods. Businesses then had to cut back their production. This meant more lost jobs and less purchasing of raw materials. The downward spiral of economic depression had begun.

It was not confined to the United States. Europe, to whom the United States had loaned millions of dollars for post-war rebuilding and to help nations pay their reparations, was soon affected as United States banks called in these loans or failed.

> The depression becomes worldwide.

The depression became worldwide and was one of the reasons for Adolf Hitler's rise in Germany and the growing strength of Japanese militarists, who looked outside of Japan to help economic conditions at home.

HOOVER'S RESPONSES TO DEPRESSION

Herbert Hoover, a successful engineer and businessman, had won the Republican nomination in 1928. The Democrats nominated Governor Al Smith of New York. Smith was the first Roman Catholic to win a major party nomination for president. Religion and prohibition became campaign issues but the apparent national prosperity allowed Hoover to win easily.

---

[17] subsistence   *Having enough to survive without having any extras or luxuries.*

The American economic system had worked for Hoover, and he was committed to preserving that system as he knew it. He had explained his views on the American system and "rugged individualism" during the 1928 campaign, saying the system demanded "economic justice as well as political and social justice" and was "no system of laissez-faire." He also extolled liberalism as "a force truly of the spirit, a force proceeding from the deep realization that economic freedom cannot be sacrificed if political freedom is to be preserved."

> **President Hoover supports the American system of "rugged individualism."**

By thus tying economic freedom to political freedom, when faced with the recession, Hoover firmly believed he could not act to control or infringe the freedom enjoyed by business and business interests. Yet he believed in economic and political justice and that the government was "an umpire instead of a player in the economic game." He believed that the government could have a role in economic activity, but only as an insurer of fair play. With his contradictory beliefs, Hoover was torn as to what the government should do.

Hoover's cabinet contained six conservative millionaires. Others of his advisers believed they could apply to government the scientific efficiency that had been applied to business in recent years. While Hoover recommended more government involvement than had ever occurred before, he also vetoed several economic measures passed by Congress because he saw them as infringements on state and individual rights. Farm conditions continued to deteriorate, and the Hawley-Smoot Tariff was a response but it worsened the economic situation.

By 1930 unemployment had risen, but Hoover was opposed to direct relief (i.e., payments) to the unemployed because he believed such payments would undermine the American ideology of rugged individualism. Instead he proposed a national voluntary effort under federal government leadership. The government could be an umpire. Money was appropriated for public works to be built by the unemployed under state and local supervision. In early 1932 Congress adopted Hoover's proposal for a Reconstruction Finance Corporation (RFC), which would loan money to banks and railroads on the theory that they would supply employment and the benefits of the government loan would "trickle down" to the unemployed workers. When unemployment reached over 10 million in 1932, Hoover accepted the extension of the RFC allowing it to lend money to state and local agencies for funding of public works to provide employment.

Hoover was a compassionate man. He had organized the feeding of Belgians in World War I, but he would or could not abandon his commitment to rugged individualism and lead the government into adopting measures of direct relief for the unemployed. It was up to his successor to do this.

THE ELECTION OF 1932

The Republicans had lost control of the House of Representatives in the 1930 election. Economic conditions continued to worsen. In the presidential election of 1932, the Republicans renominated Hoover. Their platform called for no new economic programs. The Democrats nominated Franklin Delano Roosevelt, Governor of New York. Franklin Roosevelt flew to the convention and delivered his acceptance speech before it, the first nominee to do so. It was the type of attention-getting, encouraging move that Roosevelt relied on to instill confidence in the people. In his speech he spoke of reconstructing the economy and pledged "a new deal for the American people." The Democratic Party platform called for unemployment and old age insurance, banking reforms, and regulation of securities and stocks.

> Franklin Delano Roosevelt pledges "a new deal for the American people" and defeats Hoover for the presidency in 1932.

Both parties supported changes in Amendment XVIII, the Prohibition Amendment—the Democrats were for repeal; the Republicans, for revision. The Amendment had clearly failed to eliminate the consumption of alcohol and had created a whole new criminal element in society.

The 1932 campaign was vigorous. Roosevelt spoke of both reduced expenditures and new programs without addressing the issue of paying for them. He spoke of the forgotten man and of direct relief to the unemployed. Hoover spoke on his old theme of the American system and rugged individualism and said the election was "a contest between two philosophies of government."

The American people voted for a new philosophy. Roosevelt won by over 7 million votes and carried 42 of the 48 states. The Democrats controlled the Senate with 60 of the 96 seats and the House of Representatives with 310 to 117. The nation was ready for the New Deal.

New Deal legislation was extensive and very different from past policies of laissez-faire. The goals of the New Deal, however, were deeply rooted in American ideology. In the 1790s

> The New Deal is rooted in American ideology.

these goals—justice, equality, and a fair deal for all people—were emphasized by Jefferson. An active government aiding a group or groups of citizens was emphasized by Hamilton. Franklin Roosevelt combined these ideas in the New Deal, but whereas Alexander Hamilton advocated government support for business and the wealthy, Roosevelt directed the government's involvement toward the worker and the middle class.

Key Point to Remember

In the Roaring '20s new industries created prosperity for many, but it was not evenly distributed, and this contributed to the severity of the Depression, which began with the stock market crash of 1929.

People to Remember

Herbert Hoover   Engineer, millionaire, and government servant; organized the food relief program for Belgium in 1914, ran the Food Administration under Woodrow Wilson in World War I, and served as the 31st president; his belief in the American ideology of rugged individualism made it difficult for him to find new approaches to solving the problems of the Great Depression, which followed the stock market crash in 1929.

Links from the Past to the Present

1. Cycles of prosperity and recession have continued since the Panic of 1819.

2. Overproduction and/or underconsumption of farm produce has created problems for farmers ever since the Great Plains were opened to farming.

3. Intolerance and government corruption have occurred with cyclical regularity throughout United States history.

4. Politicians exploited the American fear of communism from the time the Bolsheviks established the Soviet Union. With the fall of the Soviet Union, such fear has been directed toward China, Cuba, and North Korea.

Dates

1919—Palmer Raids.

1920—Warren G. Harding elected President.

1921—Emergency Quota Act.

1924—Teapot Dome Scandal.

1925—Scopes Trial.

1927—*The Jazz Singer.*

1928—Herbert Hoover elected President.

1929—Stock Market Crash.

1930—Hawley-Smoot Tariff.

1931—*Mourning Becomes Electra* presented.

1932—Reconstruction Finance Corporation.
　　　Franklin Delano Roosevelt elected President.

Questions
Identify each of the following:

Teapot Dome Oil Reserve
Palmer Raids
The Vamp and the Flapper
Rouge River Plant

Reconstruction Finance Corporation (RFC)
Emergency Quota Act
Hawley-Smoot Tariff

Multiple Choice:

1. Symbols of the 1920s were
   a. the gangster, the flapper, and the vamp.
   b. the gangster, the Gibson Girl, and the automobile.
   c. the gangster, the Gibson Girl, and Sigmund Freud.

2. The stock market crash of October, 1929 had among its varied causes
   a. the unevenness of prosperity and the depressed status of farmers.
   b. the lowering of interest rates in England.
   c. the end of buying "on margin."

3. Herbert Hoover used the federal government to combat the recession by having Congress pass
   a. the Reconstruction Finance Corporation Act.
   b. the Emergency Quota Act and the Hawley-Smoot Tariff.
   c. both of the above.

4. Examples of corruption and intolerance in the 1920s include
   a. the return of the Ku Klux Klan and advertisements for X-rated movies.
   b. the Teapot Dome Scandal and Red Scare.
   c. the restriction of immigration and hate messages on the radio.

IV. The New Deal

FRANKLIN DELANO ROOSEVELT

Franklin Delano Roosevelt was not new to politics. He served in the New York State Senate and then as Assistant Secretary of the Navy during World War I under Woodrow Wilson. A graduate of Harvard, he had studied at Columbia Law School. In 1921 he was stricken by polio and was partially paralyzed in his legs for the remainder of his life. In spite of his handicap, he was elected Governor of New York

WHAT'S THE NEXT PLAY GOING TO BE?
—Knott in the Dallas *News*

In this cartoon what point is the artist Knott making about the reaction of the business community to the NRA?
From the Dallas News *reprinted in* The Literary Digest *of November 11, 1933.*

in 1928 and president in 1932. He went on to be elected again in 1936, 1940, and 1944—the only president in our history to break with George Washington's tradition and serve more than two terms.

Roosevelt led the nation as a strong and active president through the later years of the Great Depression and through World War II. In his first inaugural address he set a tone for the nation, balancing optimism with the reality of the harshness of the Depression. In a voice never forgotten once heard, Roosevelt said, "Let me assert my firm belief that the only thing we have to fear is fear itself—needless, unreasoning, unjustified terror which paralyzes needed efforts to convert retreat into advance." He acknowledged Republican attempts to address the Depression but deplored their values based on "monetary profit." Roosevelt called the American people to "apply social values more noble than mere monetary profit." It was a reemphasis on the ideological position of Jefferson and Wilson. He outlined a program that would include first, putting "people to work" and treating the task as we would "the emergency of a war"; second, a "better use of the land"; third, "strict supervision of all banking"; and fourth, a "good neighbor" policy in world affairs, especially toward Latin America. He called for an immediate special session of Congress.

> An optimistic Roosevelt says in his inaugural, "The only thing we have to fear is fear itself."

Since 1929 many banks had failed. There was fear that the Democrats would make matters worse, and there were rushes to get savings out of banks. Many states closed their banks to avoid possible failure due to lack of funds. Roosevelt's first act as president was to declare a four-day national bank holiday, during which all banks were closed. On March 9 Congress passed the Emergency Banking Relief Bill. Its terms provided that all banks connected with the Federal Reserve System would be allowed to open only if licensed by the Treasury Department. This meant that any opened bank had been checked by the government and depositors need not fear that they would lose their deposits because the banks were sound or safe.

On March 12, a Sunday evening, Roosevelt addressed the American people in his first "fireside chat," which became a hallmark of his presidency. Listening on their radios, Americans heard Roosevelt's soothing voice assure them that the banks were safe and the money crisis was over. The people believed. A corner was turned, and although the Depression continued, the mood of the nation began to shift. Roosevelt had addressed the question of fear, and the public responded.

THE ONE HUNDRED DAYS

The Emergency Banking Relief Bill was the first of many important measures passed in the three months following Roosevelt's inauguration, a time period that has been referred to as the One Hundred Days. Roosevelt had gathered a Brain Trust to advise him. They were men with many talents, and they decided that bigness was part of American life and business. What was needed was some central planning and regulation by the government. The Brain Trust recommended legislation to address problems in agriculture, business, and banking and to make reforms. Roosevelt and the Democrats were ready to give direct aid to the unemployed in the form of relief and to help business recover from the depths of depression.

Some historians have grouped all the New Deal measures under these three headings: relief, recovery, and reform. While it is helpful to think of the New Deal as working in these three areas, the measures proposed often overlapped the three divisions. Some measures were tried and abandoned; others were modified and continued; a few are still in effect. Some of the ideas that guided the New Deal legislation were rejected in the 1980s during the presidency of Ronald Reagan, but the lives of all Americans have been affected by the New Deal legislation.

RELIEF: SUPPLYING JOBS

So much important legislation was passed in the first One Hundred Days it often seems overwhelming. It is not necessary to understand all the details of New Deal legislation, but it is important to understand its purpose and the basic approach of the New Deal to the reforming of American economic life. One goal was to supply jobs for people of different talents.

The Civilian Conservation Corps took unemployed young men from the cities and put them to work in rural areas, building roads and working on preventing soil erosion and on

> Relief legislation supplies jobs for the unemployed.

reforestation. A re-establishment of the CCC has been discussed in recent years as a response to present environmental concerns. During the New Deal several agencies, including the Public Works Administration (PWA) and the Works Projects Administration (WPA), were established to supply unemployment relief through work projects that ranged from bridge building to mural painting in post offices.

RECOVERY: HELPING BUSINESS

The major piece of legislation relating to business was the National Industrial Recovery Act (NIRA). Its premise accepted bigness in industry and asked business and labor to develop fair trade codes of conduct, which would apply self-regulation to the

> Business is to be self-regulated under the administration of the NRA.

industry. These codes would be administered by the National Recovery Administration (NRA). The government was given power to develop codes for industries that did not do so. Section 7-A stated certain rights that each code had to guarantee to labor. The NRA began well, but the complexity of organizing and regulating all industry became overwhelming. The Supreme Court in 1935 in *U.S.* v. *Schechter Poultry Corporation* declared the law unconstitutional as it delegated Congressional power to legislate to an agency of the executive branch of government. It was declared in violation of the separation of powers.

RECOVERY: HELPING THE FARMER

Democrats saw the farm problem as one of overproduction, not underconsumption. In the Agricultural Adjustment Act they introduced the principle of subsidies to cut production. The subsidy principle established by the AAA set cash benefits to be paid to farmers who voluntarily did not grow certain products, thus reducing acreage and production. The cash for the benefits was obtained by a tax on the processors of agricultural goods. The Supreme Court said this was an illegal use of the tax power and declared the first AAA unconstitutional.

A second AAA was passed in 1938 and continued the subsidy principle but without the taxes on processors of agricultural goods. This New Deal approach to the reduction of farm production remains the government's basic approach to overproduction.

RECOVERY AND REFORMS: BANKING AND ELECTRIC POWER

Other reforms that affect us today include the Federal Deposit Insurance Corporation (FDIC), which insures individual bank deposits so individual depositors will not lose their money if their bank fails, and the Securities Exchange Commission (SEC), created to oversee the stock markets. The Tennessee Valley Authority (TVA) was established to plan the regional development of the Tennessee River Valley with everything from flood control projects to protect the environment to hydroelectric plants. In the 1940s the hydroelectric power created by the TVA supplied the energy needed for the building of the first atomic bombs. The New Deal in its first One Hundred Days had addressed many concerns and developed new approaches to old problems. However, many old problems continued, and the New Deal addressed many of them in later legislation.

> Other New Deal legislation affects us today.

REFORM: THE SECOND NEW DEAL—SOCIAL SECURITY

The election of 1934 showed the nation's support for the New Deal. The Democrats won seven new seats in both the Senate and the House of Representatives, an unusual event because traditionally the party in power can expect to lose seats in Congress in nonpresidential election years. With the economy still depressed, Roosevelt launched what has been called the Second New Deal in 1935. The Second New Deal emphasized social security. The industrialized countries of western Europe had had social security legislation for over thirty years, but the American ideology of individualism and self-help had worked against the adoption of such a program. The major legislation of the Second New Deal was the Social Security Act of 1935, which provided unemployment insurance, old age insurance, and grants to the states for relief for the blind and for homeless children.

REFORM: HELPING THE WORKER

Two acts greatly helped workers. The National Labor Relations Act of 1935, known as the Wagner Act, established workers' rights to join unions and to bargain collectively. The Fair Labor Standards Act of 1938 established the first minimum hourly wage ($.40) and maximum hours (40 per week) for workers in industries engaged in interstate commerce. These had been the goals of labor unions for many years, and they were finally achieved through New Deal legislation.

THE CIO

At the start of the Depression, unions were ineffective in keeping jobs in companies that were hurting economically. Most major industries—coal, steel, automobile, rubber—were not unionized at all. The AFL was a union of crafts and skilled workers, few of whom worked in major industries. Labor provisions of the NRA encouraged growth in union membership. There were disagreements within the AFL as to whether it should organize unskilled workers in major industries. The AFL decided against it. However, John L. Lewis of the Coal Miners Union and others organized the Committee for Industrial Organization (CIO) within the AFL to organize these unskilled industrial workers. The CIO's goal was to organize unskilled workers on an industry-wide basis. The United Automobile Workers Union of the CIO introduced a new technique, the sit-down strike, when fighting for recognition by General Motors, Chrysler, and Ford. In a sit-down strike workers remain in the plant at their jobs but do not work. General Motors called in the police and obtained a court order to force the evacuation of the plant, but the workers stuck together and finally General Motors recognized the union. By the end of the decade, the CIO, which had been expelled from the AFL, had won recognition from most major industries.

> The CIO organizes unskilled workers in major industries.

WOMEN AND THE NEW DEAL

The number of employed women increased in the 1930s although women still suffered from job discrimination. Women were often the only employed member of a family. This antagonized some men, who suggested that if the women stopped working, there would be no unemployment as all the men would have jobs.

What do you think of that type of reasoning? Is it compatible with America's ideology based on equality and individual rights?

Eleanor Roosevelt, wife of the President, worked hard to change attitudes. She was a close advisor to her husband and often traveled where he could not, bringing back reports on conditions. When the Daughters of the American Revolution refused to let the African-American opera star, Marion Anderson, sing in their Washington headquarters auditorium, Eleanor Roosevelt arranged for her to sing at the Lincoln Memorial. The concert inspired many leaders of the later Civil Rights Movement.

The first woman ever to serve in the Cabinet, Frances Perkins, served as Roosevelt's Secretary of Labor. She had worked with Roosevelt in New York State and was a friend of Eleanor's. Together, Eleanor Roosevelt and Frances Perkins formed the center of a network of women in government—women who supported each other and attempted to make the government more sensitive to women's issues.

> Eleanor Roosevelt and Frances Perkins further the cause of women in government.

Although they laid foundations for future action, they had limited success at the time. For example, federal relief agencies seemed to emphasize finding jobs for men, the Social Security Act did not protect low-income workers (many of whom were women), and the CCC excluded women.

AFRICAN-AMERICANS AND THE NEW DEAL

Segregation remained the rule, and race relations remained tense throughout the 1930s. There were outbreaks of racial violence in several cities. Roosevelt had African-Americans as advisors and appointed several to positions in government, including Mary McLeod Bethune in the National Youth Administration and Robert C. Weaver in the Department of the Interior. Roosevelt ordered an end to segregation in the government offices in the Capitol; however, much New Deal legislation was not color blind. Both the TVA and CCC were segregated, and federal mortgages were not available to African-Americans who purchased homes in white neighborhoods.

> African-Americans benefit from Roosevelt's Executive Order Number 8802.

As World War II neared and more jobs became available, African-Americans still did not get many of them. A threat of a march on Washington made by A. Phillip Randolph, the African-American President of the Brotherhood of Sleeping Car Porters Union, forced President Roosevelt to issue Executive Order Number 8802, setting up the Fair Employment Practices Committee. The Committee was to address the issue of segregation and discrimination in employment. It was a welcome step, but there was still a long way ahead for minorities to achieve recognition and equality in the American workplace.

CRITICS OF THE NEW DEAL

The New Deal won the support of the farmers, the unemployed, the aging, and the workers with its legislative program, but there were also critics. Conservative businessmen who still believed in rugged individualism worried about the government giving direct relief to the unemployed, while some workers thought the NRA was too supportive of business. Other critics deplored the growing bureaucracy needed to run the New Deal programs. Some believed the legislation limited freedom unnecessarily, and others thought the deficit financing[18] used to pay for the programs would require higher taxes in the future and might bankrupt the government. A few critics saw a danger in the increased power of the presidency. Today we hear similar concerns expressed over the size of the bureaucracy, the use of the Social Security surplus to pay current costs, and the power of the president.

> Some critics suggest the New Deal has abandoned America's values; others say it has not done enough to reform the nation.

Some reformers believed the New Deal had not gone far enough in helping the people. For instance, Huey Long, United States Senator and former governor and political boss of Louisiana, presented a simple idea to solve the Depression and help

---

[18] deficit financing   *The concept of deficit financing originates in the economic philosophy of John Maynard Keynes. The theory is that in times of prosperity, governments will raise taxes to slow the inflation, and in times of recession, money will be spent on government programs to "prime the pump" to get business working again. If there is not enough money in the treasury, the programs are financed through borrowing, which creates a deficit. Thus deficit financing means paying for programs when you do not have the funds to do so and must borrow.*

the unemployed. His Share Our Wealth program called for the government to tax all income over $1 million and give each family an income of $2,500 per year with the money. Supposedly close to seven million members joined Long's Share Our Wealth program. Huey Long was a demagogue[19], an astute politician, and ambitious. He was assassinated in 1935. If he had not been shot, he would have been a strong contender in the presidential race of 1936. As it was, Roosevelt won renomination and the presidency.

THE SUPREME COURT AND THE NEW DEAL

The Supreme Court declared two important acts of the New Deal, the AAA (*United States* v. *Butler*) and the NIRA (*Schecter* v. *United States*), unconstitutional. Roosevelt offered a plan, referred to as "court packing," to increase the size of the Supreme Court, thus allowing him to appoint judges who would approve the New Deal legislation. There were strong objections to the plan in Congress, and it was not passed. However, the Supreme Court upheld the Social Security Act in 1937 while the battle over Roosevelt's proposal was still raging in Congress.

Some believe the Court shifted its position under this threat, but most believe the Supreme Court justices were carefully interpreting the Constitution. Because of natural attrition on the Court, Roosevelt was able to appoint seven justices of his choice by 1941. The change in the Court's view of New Deal legislation made possible a permanent shift in American ideology.

END OF THE NEW DEAL

During the decade of the 1930s, Europe was moving toward war. The New Deal program was developed against a background of world depression and growing aggression. American neutrality, proclaimed in 1935, emphasized the public's desire for isolation. Roosevelt, however, was inclined to become involved, and from 1937 on foreign policy issues required more and more of his attention. A slight business downturn in 1937–39 ended as United States industry responded to United States government mobilization efforts and the military needs of those opposing Hitler's Germany and Mussolini's Italy.

When the United States declared war against Japan on December 8, 1941, the New Deal was over. America's war effort finally ended the Depression. By 1944 unemployment was down to roughly 1 percent from its height of over 25 percent in 1932.

SUMMARY

Historians agree the New Deal legislation did not end the Depression, but it did provide a more optimistic outlook than the nation had when Roosevelt was first elected, and it avoided a revolution, which might have ended democracy as happened

---

[19] demagogue   *One who appeals to the lowest interests of the people, stirring them up to support a program by emotional speeches.*

in Germany. The New Deal had its roots in American's belief in equality and justice. It advanced the rights of labor, improved the income of farmers, and provided old age security for the elderly, and unemployment compensation for the unemployed. These changes began in the United States what has been called the Welfare State. These changes had been introduced into the industrialized nations of Europe before World War I, and while introduced in some states, they had not been accepted nationally until the New Deal. The New Deal ended a period of laissez-faire government with an emphasis on individualism, which had been practiced by Herbert Hoover and the Republican leaders of the 1920s. Individualism and a fear of government are also an important aspect of America's ideology. They were not the focus of the New Deal, which greatly expanded the government bureaucracy and the power of the executive branch, especially the president, which reflects Alexander Hamilton's view of government. The New Deal made permanent changes in United States society and, in spite of the efforts of the Republican Party under Ronald Reagan to reverse many of the New Deal changes, ideas introduced in the New Deal remain an important part of life.

The New Deal was the most intense and important period of reform and change in American history, a history that has periodically had movements of reform. Yet the reforms and changes were all rooted in different expressions of America's ideology.

Many of the ideas found in the Populist Party Platform in 1892 were incorporated in the New Deal program, suggesting there is a continuity in America's concern for reform to create greater equality and improve the life of the people. This belief in equality and the idealism that believes conditions can be improved runs through America's ideology. It clearly was behind the United States actions in the New Deal and in World War I. Herbert Hoover and the leaders of the 1920s had emphasized other parts of America's basic beliefs in leading the nation in that period.

Key Point to Remember
The New Deal was a major effort to solve the problems created by the Depression by having the federal government take action and intervene in the business cycle, reversing the laissez-faire policy of the 1920s.

People to Remember
Franklin Delano Roosevelt   New York lawyer and politician; State Senator, Assistant Secretary of the Navy, vice-presidential candidate, Governor of New York, and 32nd president; although paralyzed in his legs by polio, he provided vigorous presidential leadership through the Depression and World War II. Elected president four times, he instituted the New Deal to help fight the Depression and bring about relief, recovery, and reform; in spite of neutrality legislation, he provided support to England and France before the United States entered World War II. He died in office just before the war ended. His wartime conferences with the Allies determined the postwar future including the United Nations.

Two Views of Government at the Time of the New Deal

Laissez-faire

This view of no government intervention in the business cycle is rooted in the classical economic ideas of Adam Smith presented in the *Wealth of Nations* (1776). Smith believed that economic conditions are regulated by natural forces referred to as "an invisible hand"—a phrase often quoted in economic discussions—and people should not attempt to change economic conditions but rather should leave them alone to work their natural course. Intervention only upsets the natural balance and makes the situation worse. Economic and social issues should be left to individual initiatives.

Interventionists

Many who supported government intervention in the business cycle to combat the Great Depression followed the theories of the economist, John Maynard Keynes. Keynes believed government had the responsibility to tax heavily in times of prosperity to provide funds for economic relief and support including unemployment payments in times of recession. These interventionists believed there was a role for government in economic policy. They believed, quoting the Constitution, that government was responsible for the "general welfare" and, by intervening in the business cycle, could alleviate, if not fully control, the extreme fluctuations of the business cycle.

Links from the Past to the Present

1. Environmental concerns have been important to some Americans since the time of Theodore Roosevelt and are reflected in the CCC and in the environmental legislation since the 1970s.

2. Farm subsidies as a way to solve the farm surplus problem began with the New Deal and are still used.

3. Labor unions in the United States have played an important role since the Civil War, and the CIO in the 1930s is one example.

4. Cycles of reform occur regularly in American history from the 1830s on.

Dates

1933—New Deal began—One Hundred Days Legislation includes NIRA, AAA, FDIC, TVA, and Emergency Banking Relief Bill.

1935—Social Security Act.
National Labor Relations Act.
Schecter v. *United States* invalidated NIRA.

1936—*United States* v. *Butler* invalidated first AAA.

1937—Court Packing Plan.

1938—Fair Labor Standards Act; Second AAA.

Questions

Identify each of the following:

Emergency Banking Relief Bill	Tennessee Valley Authority (TVA)
Civilian Conservation Corps (CCC)	Congress of Industrial Organization (CIO)
National Recovery Administration (NRA)	Executive Order Number 8802
	Share Our Wealth Program
Agricultural Adjustment Administration (AAA)	Federal Deposit Insurance Corporation (FDIC)
	Social Security Act

Multiple Choice:

1. Franklin Delano Roosevelt before his election to the presidency had been
    a. Secretary of State under Woodrow Wilson.
    b. Vice President of the United States.
    c. Governor of New York.

2. Over 2 million young men were employed by the New Deal in
    a. reforestation work under the CCC.
    b. painting murals in post offices under the PWA.
    c. farm rehabilitation under the AAA.

3. Some people did not believe the New Deal had gone far enough and offered their own solutions to the recession such as
    a. Huey Long's Share Our Wealth program.
    b. John Maynard Keynes' deficit financing.
    c. both of the above.

4. Which of the following New Deal legislation attempted to restructure American business practices?
    a. TVA and AAA
    b. CIO and FDIC
    c. NIRA and SEC

Open-ended, Analysis Questions

The following questions require analysis and reflection. You are encouraged to bring to your answer information and ideas from many sources. The answers should be presented in composition or essay style, but they may be used to initiate discussion. The questions put you in the role of the historian, gathering information to support your personal perspective on the question.

1. In the New Deal, the federal government became actively involved in the regulation and control of economic activity, thus abandoning the traditional American value of laissez-faire. Why did the government do this? What values or attitudes were being emphasized by the New Deal leadership? In your answer, make specific references to values and attitudes and to government actions.

   (Note: The values you discuss may be taken from any time period in American history.)

2. What were the causes of the Stock Market Crash of 1929?

3. What actions of the New Deal addressed the needs of:
   a. Business
   b. Industrial workers
   c. Farmers

   How successful was each of these actions? Present specific information in your answer.

4. In Washington's Farewell Address (see pages 65 and 66) he gave advice on foreign policy. Did the United States follow this advice regarding:
   a. World War I?
   b. The League of Nations?
   c. The coming of World War II?

Do you believe the United States acted wisely? Why or why not?

World War II and the Early Years of the Cold War

APPROACHES TO HISTORY

THE SIGNIFICANCE OF WAR IN HUMAN ACTIVITY

In the study of history, war has had a major role. Some historians seem to suggest in their writings that peace is merely that brief period of time between wars. They emphasize in their works the causes of war, the strategies employed, and the results. By the emphasis they place on war, other human activities fade in significance. Also, the concept of war as a struggle has had particular appeal to both historians and political leaders in recent years. Politicians have used the image of war and possible victory as a device to rally the public behind programs and actions from the "War on Poverty" of Lyndon Johnson to the "War on Terrorism" of George W. Bush to the unending "War on Drugs" of all recent presidents.

After World War II several anthropologists gave support to the perception of war as the primary activity of human history. These anthropologists emphasized the evolutionary connection of humans to animals, whose primary drive after reproduction is for territory and tribal dominance. Animals will fight to defend both territory and tribe. Robert Ardrey identified these drives as the "territorial imperative" and saw them as the root cause of war and conflict among humans.

Long before Ardrey's concept became popular, some historians had presented their version of it in the texts they wrote. While many recent texts place less emphasis on war-centered history, it is still appealing to many authors as a way to explain history, and it is interesting to many readers. Certainly war greatly affects the history of nations and the lives of all those involved in it. As military activity became "total war" over the past 200 years, no one—man, woman, or child—can escape its impact, whether directly as the victim of bombings of a city or indirectly as a sufferer from food shortages or industrial losses. As we begin a War on Terrorism in the 21st century, new issues of the impact of war on civilians will be faced. War has an impact on us all, as these war-centered historians emphasize.

While war has many negative effects on the citizens of the nations involved, it can also be exciting and stimulating. War is violent, raises the adrenaline level, and brings forth great moments of heroism as well as moments of terrible degradation. Why? Does it appeal to the basic nature of humans? Are war, violence, and protection of territory a part of being human? Are they important enough to be the explanation of human history? How important are they to you? How have you reacted to moments of verbal or physical violence? How do you react when challenged?

Many who have experienced war know that it brings those involved close together and that it leads them to noble acts and sacrifices. War and violence can bring out the best in humans, but they also bring out the worst. War creates extraordinary challenges to which the people and the leaders must respond. Both World War II and the Cold War that followed produced such challenges and dominated the history of the middle of the 20th century as many historians have indicated.

I. WORLD WAR II

The Japanese attack on Pearl Harbor presented great challenges to the American nation. A major portion of the Pacific fleet was damaged or destroyed. When Germany and Italy declared war on the United States on December 11, 1941, the war became worldwide. Because the Allies' resources were limited, a decision was soon made to concentrate on the war in Europe. While forces in the Pacific were slowly strengthened and attacks launched, the challenge of Hitler and Mussolini received major attention.

> The War in Europe is given top priority.

THE WAR IN EUROPE

By the time the United States entered the war, Hitler had conquered France, the Netherlands, Belgium, Luxemburg, Denmark, and Norway. The Atlantic coast of France and the French colonies in North Africa had been occupied by the Germans, and England had been subjected to intensive bombing raids in the Battle of Britain. Failing to force England's surrender, Hitler made his greatest mistake. He invaded the Soviet Union, which immediately became England's ally. When the United States entered the war, the Soviet Union became our ally also in spite of our long antagonism to Communism.

The Soviet Union was hard pressed and desired her allies to open a "second front" to draw German forces away from the Russian front. Churchill feared the loss of life

WORLD WAR II IN EUROPE

Arctic Ocean

ICELAND

Norwegian
Sea

SWEDEN

FINLAND

NORWAY

Gulf
of
Bothnia

0   miles   250

0   kilometers   500

Leningrad

**Siege of
Leningrad**

USSR

ESTONIA

North
Sea

LATVIA

Moscow

DENMARK

Baltic
Sea

LITHUANIA

EAST PRUSSIA

IRELAND

GREAT
BRITAIN

NETHERLANDS

**Battle of
Berlin**

**Battle of
Warsaw**

**Battle of
Stalingrad**

ATLANTIC
OCEAN

London

Berlin

Warsaw

Stalingrad

BELGIUM

GERMANY

POLAND

**Normandy:
Utah and Omaha
Beaches**

Paris

LUX.

**Rhine
Crossing**

CZECHOSLOVAKIA

**Ardennes Forest:
Battle of the Bulge**

FRANCE

SWITZERLAND

AUSTRIA

HUNGARY

Bay of
Biscay

ROMANIA

Black Sea

PORTUGAL

ANDORRA

SPAIN

**Invasion of
Southern
France**

ITALY

Rome

Adriatic
Sea

YUGOSLAVIA

BULGARIA

TURKEY

**Invasion
of Italy**

ALBANIA

GREECE

Aegean
Sea

**Invasion of
North Africa**

M E D I T E R R A N E A N

Ionian
Sea

S E A

**Invasion
of Sicily**

CRETE

**Battle of
El Alamein**

MOROCCO

ALGERIA

TUNISIA

LIBYA

EGYPT

☐ **Germany, her allies, and
occupied territory at
its greatest extent**

involved in an invasion along the Atlantic coast. He also was worried about the
future of Europe and feared Soviet domination of Europe. Churchill wanted
American help first in repulsing a German attack on Egypt and the Suez Canal. Then
he wanted to invade Europe through the Balkans to be able to contest postwar
control of that area with the Soviet Union. Roosevelt agreed on the first point, and in
November 1942 as the English launched from Egypt an attack against the German

General Rommel, United States forces invaded German-occupied North Africa in the west. The North African campaign was a success, and in July 1943 Sicily was invaded and captured. In September an invasion of Italy rather than the Balkans was launched.

In the meantime, the Soviets broke the 17-month-old siege of Leningrad (St. Petersburg) and stopped the German advance into the Soviet Union at the Battle of Stalingrad. This battle was the turning point of the war in the Soviet Union and probably of the entire European war. A German army surrendered at Stalingrad on February 2, 1943, proving the Germans were not invincible. Hitler's challenge had been met by the Soviet Union, and although civilian and military casualties were huge, the Soviets went on the attack and crossed into Poland in January 1944.

The American Air Force based in England began massive bombings of German industrial and rail centers in early 1944 in preparation for an invasion. The Germans had failed to defeat England through air attacks. While heavy damage was done, Germany did not capitulate because of air raids either.

> The Allies invade France on D-Day.

On June 6, 1944, D-Day[1], United States, British, and Canadian forces under the supreme command of General Dwight David Eisenhower invaded the Normandy peninsula of France. After heavy fighting on the beaches, the United States Third Army under command of the flamboyant General George S. Patton broke out at St. Lo. The French capital, Paris, was captured on August 25. Another Allied army invaded southern France on August 15. By September, American forces entered Germany.

The Germans counterattacked in December, when they attempted to break through the Allied line in Belgium, drive to the coast, and cut the Allied supply line. After Americans gave up a "bulge" of territory, they were able to stop the German advance. In this Battle of the Bulge, fighting was heavy and losses high.

The Allied offensive continued through the winter and spring. Auschwitz and other death camps where Hitler's Nazis had killed millions of Jews and Eastern Europeans in the Holocaust were liberated. They revealed to a disbelieving world the worst horrors of the Nazi movement.

The Russians advanced from the east. On May 1, 1945, Hitler committed suicide in Berlin. On May 8, V-E Day[2], General Eisenhower signed with the new German government a document of unconditional surrender[3].

> Hitler commits suicide and the Germans surrender.

Italy had surrendered to the Allies in 1943, only to be occupied by the Germans. Mussolini was killed by Italians in April 1945 as the Allied forces moved quickly northward, having been blocked for a long time south of Rome. They linked with the victorious armies in Germany. The Axis Powers in Europe had been defeated. The challenge of war had been met but at a terrible price.

---

[1] D-Day   *D-Day was the designation for the day allied forces invaded Europe across the English channel.*

[2] V-E Day   *V-E Day signified the day victory was won in Europe in World War II.*

[3] unconditional surrender   *Unconditional surrender became the terms decided upon for victory in World War II by the Allies. It was applied to Italy, Germany, and Japan.*

THE WAR IN ASIA

While the Allies had determined to concentrate first on the war in Europe, there were campaigns in Asia throughout World War II. The Japanese had attacked China in 1937, and fighting continued on the mainland—with major United States aid after December 7, 1941—until the Japanese surrendered. The Japanese attack plan after Pearl Harbor was masterfully executed. Guam, Wake Island, and Hong Kong fell quickly. Malaysia, the Philippines, and, after the fall of Singapore, the Netherlands East Indies (now Indonesia) were all invaded. The Philippines fell after a gallant defense by American and Philippine forces on the Bataan Peninsula, which forms one side of Manila Bay.

The only attack on the United States mainland occurred when a submarine shelled an oil refinery near San Francisco. Two great sea battles—Coral Sea in May 1942, the first sea battle fought entirely by aircraft from ships, and Midway in June, considered the turning point of the Pacific war—stopped the Japanese advance and prevented an invasion of Australia.

The United States went on the offensive in August 1942 with the invasion of the island of Guadalcanal. It was the first in a series of island invasions across the Pacific that finally brought

> **The United States goes on the offensive.**

United States air-power close enough to bomb Japan. A campaign in Burma opened up a supply route to China. Indonesia was recaptured. After the Battle of Leyte Gulf in October 1944, which destroyed most of the remaining Japanese naval forces, the Philippines were invaded in January 1945. They were quickly recaptured and General Douglas MacArthur, the supreme commander of the army forces in the Pacific, returned to the Philippines where he had been commander before the attack on Pearl Harbor, fulfilling the promise, "I shall return," he had made when he had fled the Philippines.

The United States mounted a series of air raids on major Japanese cities. In the fire bombing of Tokyo in May 1945, over 80,000 civilians were killed by the fires set by napalm bombs. Still the Japanese would not surrender.

THE ATOMIC BOMB

Throughout the war the United States worked on improving old and developing new weapons. The most important of these was the atomic bomb. As early as 1942 President Roosevelt created a secret project, called the Manhattan Engineer District, and referred to as the Manhattan Project, to explore the possibility of creating such a weapon. In 1945 a weapon was tested at Alamogordo, New Mexico. The new President, Harry S. Truman, decided to use it against Japan.

There were many arguments over its use, but the deciding argument then seemed to be that it might save the lives of many Americans if the bomb forced Japan into surrender without an invasion of the islands. On August 6, 1945, a bomb was dropped without clearly informing the Japanese of the potential power of the weapon. The city of Hiroshima was destroyed in a matter of seconds with well over 150,000 people killed or wounded. Two days later a second bomb destroyed

World War II in the Pacific

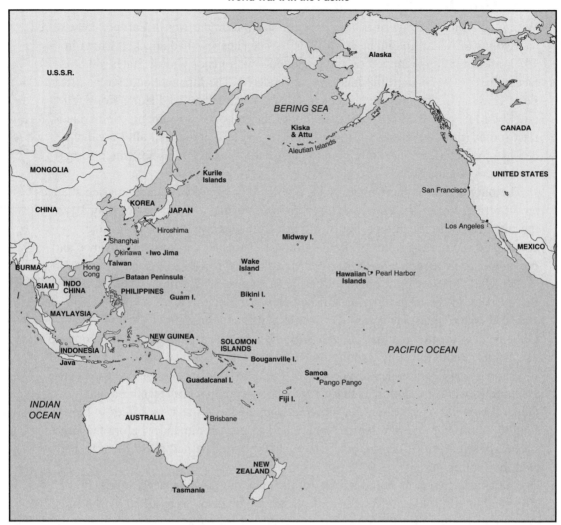

Nagasaki. On August 15, V-J Day[4], the Japanese surrendered, and on September 2 aboard the battleship *Missouri* in Tokyo Bay, General Douglas MacArthur, Commander in Chief of the Allied forces, signed a formal document of Japanese surrender. World War II had ended.

CHALLENGES OF WAR

Reading about the military planning and efforts of World War II or seeing movies of the heroism displayed by young men in the war can be exciting. Both clearly illustrate the challenges war presents to humans—challenges that often bring out the finest in individual emotions but that also allow for horrible incidents.

The cost of World War II in human lives and human suffering was staggering. The United States alone had over 800,000 wounded and over 300,000 dead, and our

---

[4] V-J Day   *V-J Day signifies the day Japan was defeated.*

losses were among the smallest of the participating nations. In the Holocaust, six million Jews were killed by the Nazis in gas chambers and concentration camps as Hitler waged genocide against the European Jewish population. Over five million

gypsies, homosexuals, and Eastern Europeans were also killed in the Nazi concentration camps. Millions of civilians lost their lives in Europe and Asia. The economic costs to the world were huge. The United States is still paying some of those costs in veteran's benefits and pensions. While meeting the challenges of war, the Allies began to address the challenge of creating a postwar world.

WARTIME CONFERENCES

Even before the United States entered the war, President Roosevelt had met with the English Prime Minister, Winston Churchill, to discuss military plans and postwar possibilities. The resulting Atlantic Charter outlined the war aims. Conferences involving Cabinet level officials continued throughout the war. At one, the policy of unconditional surrender[5] was accepted as the condition for ending the war, and this was accepted by the Allied leaders. In two important conferences—Teheran in November 1943 and Yalta in February 1945—Winston Churchill, Franklin Roosevelt, and Joseph Stalin (the leader of the Soviet Union), referred to as the Big Three, met to make decisions about war policy and the postwar world.

At Teheran agreements were reached on a second front and on the future of Iran. At Yalta, the Soviet Union, in return for several Japanese islands and a sphere of influence in Korea, agreed to enter the war against Japan after the war in Europe

ended. Free elections were set as the way to reestablish governments in the occupied nations of Europe, but the Western Allies, and the Soviet Union, a totalitarian state, later differed as to what this meant and how it should be implemented. This made it possible for the Soviets to control those nations in Eastern Europe that it had conquered or "liberated" as the war ended. Finally, at Yalta the United Nations Security Council voting procedures were agreed upon. In essence they gave the "Big Five"—England, France, China, United States, and the USSR—veto power over Security Council resolutions. Previously, in the Connally-Fulbright Resolutions in 1943, the United States Congress endorsed membership in a United Nations organization reversing the position taken on the League of Nations after World War I.

Later some Americans saw the Yalta agreements as a sell-out to Stalin. They believed an ailing President Roosevelt had been duped. At the time the agreement seemed wise. The atomic bomb had not yet been tested, postwar tensions and disagreements had not surfaced and the conference participants were just about to conclude successfully a war in Europe in which they had cooperated. From a later Cold War perspective, the agreements do not appear as wise, yet they did lead to the

---

[5] unconditional surrender   *The demand that your opponent in a military confrontation give up without any guarantees as to what the future peace and security arrangements will be.*

successful establishment of the United Nations at the San Francisco Conference in April 1945 when 50 nations subscribed to the Charter.

Modeled on the League of Nations, the United Nations was to have a Secretariat, a Security Council of 11 (later increased to 15 as UN membership grew) members including the Big Five permanent members, and a General Assembly open to all nations, in which each nation regardless of size or economic strength would have one vote. There was also a Trusteeship Council to oversee Trust Territories, an Economic and Social Council to deal with human welfare and freedoms, and an International Court of Justice. This time the United States joined the international organization. The United Nations has played an important role in the postwar world.

The final wartime conference was held at Potsdam, Germany, after Germany surrendered. Stalin still represented the USSR, but Clement Atlee had replaced Winston Churchill as leader of England, and Harry Truman had replaced Franklin Roosevelt. The new Allied leadership was not comfortable together. However, they agreed draft treaties were to be prepared for the defeated enemy, war criminals were to be tried, and no monetary reparations were to be paid. The USSR was given the right to remove factory equipment from Germany.

These wartime conferences set the pattern for summit diplomacy, which was practiced throughout the Cold War years and continues as regular meetings are scheduled among world leaders. While these major wartime conferences set the outline for the postwar world, much of the work was done by lower-level officials of the Allied Powers. The leaders provided directions, but the real challenges of war and peace were met by hundreds of hard-working staff members.

THE WAR AT HOME

Long before Pearl Harbor, private industry began slowly turning to production for war. As soon as the United States entered the war, the federal government organized the war effort. A War Production Board (WPB) and many other organizations were established to oversee the transformation of a civilian economy into a full military economy. Anti-trust suits were stopped, and cost/payment arrangements were made to benefit war industries. When labor disputes threatened, a National War Labor Board (NWLB) was established to control disputes. It was given broad powers to set 30 day cooling off periods before strikes and to seize and operate plants. Both labor and industry came under strict government supervision.

> The War Production Board and other organizations are established to run the war effort.

An Office of Price Administration (OPA) set prices and supervised rationing of goods in short supply. Americans were issued coupon books with coupons that could be turned in for one's share of gas, sugar, and other scarce commodities. New industries, ranging from synthetic rubber to replace the rubber lost when the Japanese occupied Malaysia and Southeast Asia to the atomic bomb, were developed.

By 1943 full employment had returned to the United States, and the Great Depression had ended. The challenge and stimulation of war had achieved what government legislation could not. With over 12 million in the armed services, there was a shortage of industrial workers. This created many opportunities for minorities, and more African-Americans left the South for the North and West, where industries were growing. Women joined the work force in large numbers, both in offices and factories. "Rosie the Riveter" became a famous wartime symbol—a woman working in heavy industry riveting airplanes or ships needed in the war

> Full employment returns to the United States, and the Great Depression is considered over.

effort. The armed services all opened their ranks to women in noncombat support services. The Army's WACs (Women's Army Corps) and the Navy's WAVES (Women Accepted for Volunteer Emergency Service) served in many positions on the mainland and overseas.

WARTIME INTOLERANCE

While new opportunities opened for women in the armed services, African-Americans still served in segregated units. Intolerance still plagued minorities, and there were race riots on several military bases and in several cities where African-Americans had come to take advantage of new jobs. Military service provided African-Americans opportunities to exercise leadership and to gain self-esteem. Many African-Americans who served in the armed services were not willing after the war to accept the segregated conditions of prewar American life and became supporters of the Civil Rights Movement. America met the challenges defeating oppression overseas; in the postwar years the United States would need to meet the challenge of ending oppression at home.

War breeds intolerance as the people are taught to hate the enemy. Intolerance, always a part of American life, intensified during World War II. Besides manifesting itself in race riots, there was intolerance in the actions of the Committee on UnAmerican Activities, first organized to keep communists out of government. This committee of the House of Representatives was chaired by Martin Dies and had as its charge the maintenance of loyalty in government. It recommended over 3,500 government officials be dismissed, of whom, after investigation, only 36 were. These numbers suggest the type of hysteria that was rampant in the country.

While the general persecution of those suspected of connections to the enemy was less than during World War I, the government put Japanese Americans on the west coast into camps. This clearly was an infringement of the Bill of Rights, but it was done in the name of national security. Panicked by the attack on Pearl Harbor and the fleet losses that seemed to make the west coast vulnerable to attack and not knowing where the

> Japanese Americans are placed in camps to protect the nation's security—one example of wartime intolerance.

Japanese might attack, the government ordered all Japanese Americans to leave their West coast homes. They were settled in relocation centers throughout the West. Almost two-thirds of the resettled Japanese Americans were American citizens. Not one of them was ever accused of a crime. They were simply identified on the basis of race as a threat to American security. Many lost their property—homes, businesses, furniture, possessions. They were released at the end of the war, but the Supreme Court upheld the internment. Finally in 1982 the government recommended that those interned be compensated for their losses, and Congress appropriated money for compensation and apologized.

The internment of the Japanese Americans illustrates how easily war can lead people into acts of intolerance and persecution. It is just one illustration of the horror war can inflict on the innocent; in modern warfare everyone in a society can become a combatant or a victim.

FRANKLIN ROOSEVELT'S FOURTH ELECTION: 1944

In 1944 Roosevelt was elected to an unprecedented fourth term, defeating Republican Governor Thomas E. Dewey of New York. Roosevelt had picked Senator Harry Truman of Missouri as his vice president. Roosevelt died April 12, 1945, of a massive cerebral hemorrhage. He did not live to see either the end of the war or the establishment of the United Nations, both of which occurred within weeks of his death. While Roosevelt was disliked by many for his attempted solutions to the problems of the Depression, it is generally agreed he was a great president who successfully led the United States through depression and war. He was not as successful in preparing Harry Truman for the presidency. As a result, recent presidents have worked closely with their vice presidents, keeping them informed of all policies.

Truman succeeded Roosevelt knowing nothing about the atomic bomb research and several other matters of significance. Truman quickly mastered the intricacies of the government and led the nation through the first postwar years. During these years Allied wartime cooperation gave way to the Cold War between the Communist East led by the Soviet Union and the Democratic West led by the United States.

TRANSITION TO PEACETIME

In 1944 the war effort was proving successful, and Congress addressed the issue of demobilization[6] of the armed forces. The Serviceman's Readjustment Act, known as the GI[7] Bill of Rights, passed in 1944 to make the soldiers' transition to civilian

> The nation begins to plan for peace with the passage of the GI Bill.

life easier. The GI Bill included several provisions: it provided mustering-out pay[8], unemployment pay for up to a year, and low interest loans for homebuilding. There were special advantages offered in the Civil Service, and the bill guaranteed the rehiring by former employers and seniority in those jobs. The GI Bill also made available money for education and apprenticeship training. Using these funds, over a million returning GIs entered college—the greatest single boost to higher education in American history. Within a year of the end of the war, over 9 million servicemen had returned to civilian life.

---

[6] demobilization   *Returning to civilian status of those serving in the armed forces at the end of a war.*

[7] GI   *GI is the term applied to the soldiers in the American army. It comes from the term General Issue (GI). The uniform and other equipment for the average soldier came under the category of General Issue. Officers often received Special Issue items, which separated them from the common foot soldier.*

[8] mustering-out pay   *Pay given to a soldier when he leaves service. Mustering out means returning to civilian life.*

The country feared the impact demobilization would have on the economy. There was a sharp rise in unemployment in 1946. The Unemployment Act of 1946 set deficit spending as a government policy to combat such unemployment and established the Council of Economic Advisors to help the president determine economic policy. Prices rose dramatically when price controls were ended, and inflation became a concern. Truman acted firmly against labor strikes, seizing the coal mines and threatening to draft into the army any striking workers. The built-up demand for goods such as cars, stoves, refrigerators, and homes stimulated the economy and opened job opportunities for many returning soldiers. Overall, the new President, Harry Truman, presided over a successful return to a peacetime economy, but the scars of war throughout the world took longer to heal.

Key Point to Remember
World War II was a very costly worldwide conflict that required great organization and sacrifice to win; the use of atomic bombs brought the end of the war against Japan.

Links from the Past to the Present

1. Intolerance and fear of foreigners continued to be seen during World War II and is still seen today.

2. Every war has a high cost in both lives and money.

3. Use and control of nuclear weapons has been a concern since the atomic bomb was used at Hiroshima.

Dates

1941—United States entered World War II.

1942—Invasion of North Africa.
   Manhattan Project.
   Battles of the Coral Sea and Midway.

1943—Battle of Stalingrad.
   Invasion of Sicily and Italy.
   Italy surrendered.

1944—GI Bill.
   D-Day.
   Battle of the Bulge.

1945—Philippines invaded.
   Yalta Conference.
   F. D. Roosevelt died.
   United Nations Charter.
   Germany surrendered.
   Atomic bomb dropped.
   Japan surrendered.
   Potsdam Conference.

Questions
Identify each of the following:

Pearl Harbor
D-Day
Battle of Stalingrad
The Manhattan Project
Battle of the Coral Sea

Yalta Conference
Battle of Midway
War Production Board
Battle of the Bulge
GI Bill

Multiple Choice:

1. The Battle of the Bulge was the
   a. most successful attack on Germany by United States forces.
   b. the last German counterattack.
   c. the final attack on Italy.

2. Two great sea battles of the Pacific war were
   a. the battles of St. Lo and the Coral Sea.
   b. the battles of Midway and the Coral Sea.
   c. the battles of Midway and Guadalcanal.

3. The Japanese signed a document of surrender on the battleship *Missouri* with the supreme commander in the Pacific
   a. General Dwight Eisenhower.
   b. General George S. Patton.
   c. General Douglas MacArthur.

4. The United Nations was established by 50 nations meeting in the spring of 1945 at the
   a. San Francisco Conference.
   b. Yalta Conference.
   c. Potsdam Conference.

II. The Early Years of the Cold War

BACKGROUND

Throughout the war the Allies had met to plan and reach agreements on the makeup of the postwar world. Like all international agreements, these were all based on certain assumptions about power, security, government, and human behavior. Unfortunately, the assumptions of the western Allies and the Soviet Union were not always the same, yet the differences were not fully explored under the military pressures of the time. In the immediate postwar period these differences surfaced as attempts were made to put agreements into operation.

> Differences between the Western Allies and Soviets surface after the end of the war.

In the West, and particularly in the United States, there had always been a great distrust and fear of communism since the establishment of the Soviet Union. The Soviets, following the teachings of Karl Marx, believed capitalism was doomed.

During the 1920s and 1930s they established international communist organizations to work to speed the downfall of capitalism. While the Soviets claimed to have abandoned such organizations, the fact of their former existence frightened Americans and colored their interpretation of Soviet activities. Likewise the Soviets' assumptions about capitalistic exploitation of workers and the imperialistic ambitions of Western nations colored their views of the Allies' activities.

Also, the Soviets had suffered great losses in the war, and much of European Russia had experienced the presence of occupation armies. The Soviets had suffered invasions from the west under Napoleon and in World War I by the Germans. Their primary goal in Eastern Europe was to prevent another invasion. They wished to be certain the nations on their borders were friendly. Although wartime agreements had called for democratic elections in these countries, the election process and the definition of "democracy" were very different in the Soviet Union and in the West. Since the Soviet armies had liberated and occupied the states of Eastern Europe in the last year of the war, the Soviet armies were in a position to enforce their ideas on these nations.

The result was the split of Europe into two blocks, and the Cold War between them lasted forty-five years. In 1946 Winston Churchill in a speech at Fulton, Missouri, said an "Iron Curtain" had descended on Europe separating East and West. The concept of an Iron Curtain became the symbol of postwar separation between the two blocks. This separation of Europe into two blocks—one Democratic in the West and the other Communist in the East—was the background for the Cold War[9].

> Winston Churchill describes an "Iron Curtain," which separates the Soviet bloc of eastern Europe from the West.

PEACE CONFERENCES AND OCCUPATION OF GERMANY

Peace negotiations were to be conducted by the foreign ministers of England, the United States, and the Soviet Union. At the first conference in September 1945, no agreement could be reached. England insisted on including France in the negotiations. Finally, in 1946 agreement was reached on treaties for Italy, Hungary, Bulgaria, Romania, and Finland, and the treaties were signed in 1947. No agreement was achieved on the future of Japan, Austria, or Germany.

Germany had been split into four separate Occupation Zones administered by England, the United States, France, and the Soviet Union. Berlin, the German capital, was within the Soviet zone, but it was divided into four Occupation Zones also. Determining the future of Germany was one of the great challenges of the Cold War. The Soviets wanted a united Germany that they could control. The West wanted a federal Germany with power shared among the several German states.

> Germany and Berlin are divided into Occupation Zones, and the first crisis of the Cold War in Europe centers on Berlin.

[9] Cold War *The struggle between the Communist philosophy and the Democratic philosophy for control of nations in Europe and throughout the world, which began at the end of World War II and continued until the fall of the Berlin Wall in 1989. The Soviet Union led the Communists, and the United States and her allies, especially those in NATO, led the Democracies.*

Berlin presented the first major crisis of the Cold War in Europe when the Soviets rejected a proposal for a unified Berlin and the West rejected the Soviet insistence that Soviet Zone money be used throughout Berlin. When the West went ahead and issued its own new currency in Berlin, the Soviets in June 1948 closed all roads and rail lines between the West's three Occupation Zones and their sections of the city of Berlin. The land blockade was successful, but the Allies responded with an airlift that kept western Berlin supplied with food.

A year later the Soviets ended the blockade and treaty negotiations began again, but with little success. The Western Allies then combined their Occupation Zones and established a government, the Federal Republic, usually referred to as West Germany, with its capital in Bonn. The Soviet Union then created the German Democratic Republic from its Occupation Zone with the Soviet Zone of Berlin as its capital. Berlin remained divided.

Another crisis in Berlin in 1961 resulted in the building of the Berlin Wall to further isolate the West from Eastern Europe. This confirmed the Iron Curtain concept. The Berlin Wall became a sign in concrete of the division of Eastern and Western Europe. When the Berlin Wall fell in November 1989, it marked the end of the Cold War.

> The Berlin Wall is built in 1961.

CONTAINMENT POLICY

The first confrontation of the Cold War involving military deployment occurred in Iran in 1946. Iran occupies a strategic location in the Middle East, bordering the Soviet Union and the Persian Gulf, and Iran has large oil resources. The Soviet army had occupied the northern part of the country, and the English the southern part. Wartime agreements had called for withdrawal of the English and Soviet forces. The Soviets did not withdraw. Iran complained to the United Nations, which considered the matter. An agreement including concessions on the right to oil exploration by the Soviets was signed between Iran and the Soviet Union. The troops were withdrawn. During the next year the United States persuaded the Iranians to cancel the oil exploration agreement. Such actions added to the distrust on both sides.

One of the most significant events illustrating the separation between the Soviet Union and its former allies occurred in Greece. In some analyses, it is noted as the first event of the Cold War. It was precipitated by the economic situation of Western Europe, which was deteriorating rapidly. In 1947 England announced she could no longer support the Greek government the English had been subsidizing. A civil war was raging in Greece between the government and Communist forces. President Truman decided Greece and Turkey should be helped. Announcing the Truman Doctrine, he asked Congress for funds to aid Greece and Turkey, replacing the aid from England. The Truman Doctrine declared the United States would aid any free peoples who resisted armed minorities attempting to overthrow an established government. With this support from the United States, the Greek government defeated the Communist guerrillas. Throughout the conflict there was no evidence of direct Soviet support for the Greek Communists. The acceptance

> Crises in Iran and Greece lead to the Truman Doctrine.

of the Truman Doctrine illustrates the fear of communism, an important factor in Cold War decisions.

Soon after the Truman Doctrine was announced, George F. Kennan, the leading expert on the Soviet Union in the United States Foreign Service and the director of the policy planning staff of the State Department, published in the magazine *Foreign Affairs* an article that has become known as the "X" Article because the author was simply identified as "X." The "X" Article set forth what became United States policy for the Cold War. The policy is known as containment. In the article Kennan said the way to deal with the Soviet Union was to contain it with force—economic or political or military—applied to counter Soviet influence wherever it encroached "upon the interests of a peaceful" world. Kennan then believed the two powers should negotiate.

> The "X" Article presents the concept of containment, which becomes official United States Cold War policy.

For the next forty years the United States applied force in varying degrees to counter Soviet pressure. There were periods of some cooperation and times of dangerous confrontation during these years. To better prepare for the latter, the United States defense establishment was changed and a new Cabinet position, the Department of Defense, was established, replacing the Departments of the Army and Navy. The Central Intelligence Agency (CIA) was established and the National Security Council organized to advise the President and to plan for any international emergency, i.e., to plan how to apply force against any Soviet force.

The CIA became a very controversial body as its role changed from collecting information to carrying out policies. For example, in Guatemala in 1954 the CIA overthrew the elected government, which had confiscated lands of the United Fruit Company, a United States private concern. The United States government claimed a Communist threat existed, but no proof had been uncovered. The new Guatemalan government returned the lands to the United Fruit Company. Later the CIA overthrew the government in Iran and plotted the unsuccessful assassinations of Fidel Castro and several other international leaders. In later Cold War years there were major discussions as to what the role of the CIA should be. They continue today.

THE MARSHALL PLAN AND NATO

Along with the Truman Doctrine, 1947 saw the introduction of the Marshall Plan, designed to aid the recovery of the economies of the Western European nations still suffering from the war. The dollars supplied through the Marshall Plan to the European nations were to be spent in the United States, which helped business at home. The Marshall Plan, named for President Truman's Secretary of State, George C. Marshall, who had served as Chief of Staff of the United States Army during World War II, revitalized the European economy. In doing so it provided one example of a "counter force" to the Soviets since capitalist or socialist prosperity in Western Europe reduced the attractiveness of communism as an economic system. Under George Marshall's original invitation, Eastern European nations could have joined the Marshall Plan, but none did so at the insistence of the Soviet Union. It is now

> The Marshall Plan is presented to revitalize the European economy.

Europe and NATO–1982

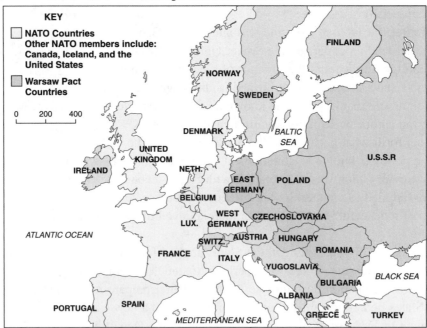

clear that there were weaknesses in the Marshall Plan approach to rebuilding the economy of Western Europe. It did not push European integration, which developed slowly in the following forty years. However, overall it is a fine example both of America's help for others and a response to a Cold War challenge. It is an example of how war can bring out the best in human beings.

Another response following the policy of containment was the establishment of NATO—the North Atlantic Treaty Organization—in 1949 after the ending of the Berlin Blockade. Breaking with the precedent set by George Washington of not signing peacetime alliances, the United States joined NATO. United States troops were to be stationed in Europe, guaranteeing that the United States was prepared to counter a military thrust by the Soviet Union into Western Europe. Concern was expressed that the NATO alliance could involve the United States in war without a declaration of war. That was not to be the case in Europe, even though the Soviet Union organized her allies into a military alliance, the Warsaw Pact, to counter the strength of NATO.

> NATO is organized to combat Soviet aggression in Europe.

NUCLEAR PROLIFERATION

At the end of the war as the only nuclear power, the United States offered to turn its nuclear secrets over to United Nations supervision with no vetos allowed. The United States' offer was not accepted. The Soviets objected to international control and particularly to inspection. Soviet espionage agents gained access to American secrets. In 1949 the Soviet Union detonated an atomic bomb. These two events heightened Cold War tensions and provided the

> The Soviet Union rejects international control of nuclear energy and develops its own nuclear weapons.

background for the activities of Senator Joseph McCarthy. (See page 266.) The United States and the USSR soon developed hydrogen bombs, and both powers tested their nuclear weapons, polluting the atmosphere. This led to many protests. In 1958 the Russians unilaterally announced no more testing. The United States followed. Tests were resumed in 1961. Finally, a test ban treaty was negotiated. However, under George W. Bush's unilateralist approach to foreign policy, the United States withdrew from the treaty so it could develop and test a new generation of weapons.

Meanwhile, a nonproliferation[10] treaty was passed by the United Nations General Assembly, but not before England, France, and China had all developed atomic weapons. In spite of the nonproliferation treaty, India and Pakistan both developed nuclear weapons. Israel is believed to have built a limited number of atomic bombs. Libya and South Africa began research on weapons but abandoned their programs under pressure from the United States who promised help in developing nuclear power in those nations. Under pressure from its neighbors and the United States, North Korea in 2008 agreed to stop their nuclear weapons program that had successfully tested a weapon and built several bombs. There are questions concerning North Korea's compliance with the agreement and whether it will be successful. In 2008, the United Nations adopted sanctions against Iran to force the abandonment of a nuclear program that the United States and UN believed was directed toward development of a bomb. To date, it is not clear if the sancitions will achieve their desired effect. Iran has been defiant claiming they have the right to develop nuclear power. All of these nations saw nuclear weapons as a way to protect their territory and maintain their security.

With the breakup of the Soviet Union at the end of the Cold War, the Soviet arsenal came under the control of Russia and the newly independent states of Ukraine, Kazakhstan, and Uzbekistan. United States–Russian agreements have brought all these weapons under Russian control and slight reductions in the number of weapons have been negotiated.

The United States and the USSR developed many different nuclear weapons—everything from battlefield artillery shells to ICBMs (Intercontinental Ballistic Missiles) for the firing of nuclear weapons across thousands of miles. The nuclear arsenals grew rapidly giving each side enough power to destroy the earth several times—an indication of the madness that war creates. The history of the Cold War thus unfolded against the background of potential nuclear war. Negotiations over nuclear arms limitations finally led to the first SALT (Strategic Arms Limitation Treaty) agreement in 1972.

BRINKMANSHIP

In 1952 General Eisenhower defeated the Democrat Adlai Stevenson for the presidency. Eisenhower's Secretary of State, John Foster Dulles, added a new dimension, brinkmanship, to containment. Dulles believed in pushing the Communists to the "brink" of nuclear

> Secretary of State Dulles proposes brinkmanship as United States policy, and the Soviets agree to a summit meeting.

---

[10] nonproliferation   *Nonproliferation means not spreading. The nonproliferation treaty was designed to limit the spread of nuclear weapons to other nations.*

war in order to preserve the free world. It was a frightening concept. Some claim it brought the Soviet Union to the first summit meeting since Potsdam.

In 1955 a slight thaw in the Cold War occurred as happened several times as the intensity of the Cold War confrontations varied. The leaders of France, England, and the United States met at Geneva with the new Soviet leader, Nicolai Bulganin, who emerged as leader of the Soviet Union after the death of Joseph Stalin in 1953. Little was achieved, but negotiations began on arms limitations. In 1960 a summit with the new leader of the Soviet Union, Nikita Khrushchev, was set. Two weeks before the meeting the Russians shot down a United States U2 spy plane. Spying was a major part of the Cold War, but Khrushchev cancelled the summit when the United States refused to apologize for flying over Soviet airspace.

John Foster Dulles exercised brinkmanship in offering no apologies. It was meant to illustrate American toughness against the perceived Communist threat. It was a policy with potential danger for human survival. However, it was not fully followed.

In 1956 the Hungarian people attempted to overthrow the Communist government of their country. They thought the United States, under the brinkmanship policy, might aid them if the Soviet Union sent in troops. The Soviets did send troops to crush the revolt, but the United States did not intervene. There were limits to brinkmanship and containment when events occurred behind the Iron Curtain.

> The Soviets crush the attempt of the Hungarians to establish a non-Communist government.

THE UNITED NATIONS

The policy of brinkmanship was one extreme articulation of Cold War attitudes. Other attitudes manifested during the Cold War are seen in the work of the United Nations. At the end of the war, hope had been high that the United Nations would function effectively to maintain the peace. Unfortunately, the divisions between the communist and capitalistic views of the world and the veto power of the Big Five in the Security Council made united action on the international political scene impossible.

However, the United Nations did operate effectively in other spheres, with its agencies helping war refugees, organizing health campaigns, and monitoring labor conditions. It also served as a forum for discussions of opposing views. A major success of the United Nations General Assembly was the agreement reached on a Universal Declaration of Human Rights.

The success of this was largely the result of the work of Eleanor Roosevelt, widow of the president, whom President Truman appointed as a United States delegate to the United Nations. Eleanor Roosevelt had already acquired an international reputation as a spokesperson for the oppressed and downtrodden. As chair of the Committee on Human Rights, Eleanor Roosevelt was able to bring together opposing views, and the final declaration contains both individual rights such as free speech, press, and trial, advocated by the capitalistic Western nations, and economic rights, such as those to a job, a house, and education, supported by the communist nations.

The Universal Declaration of Human Rights was accepted in 1948. It has served as a guide to new nations as they write constitutions. The United Nations General Secretary, U Thant, called it "the Magna Carta of mankind." The United Nations has no power to enforce the Declaration, but it stands as a hope for humanity and a standard by which to judge the actions of governments. It and the other actions of international cooperation showed there was a place for the United Nations in international affairs.

THE MIDDLE EAST

Brinkmanship was not the only international policy of the Eisenhower presidency. In 1955 the USSR and the United States finally agreed on a peace treaty with Austria. In 1956 they cooperated in forcing England, France, and Israel to withdraw from the Suez Canal, which the three powers had seized from Egypt.

The background to the Suez Crisis was involved and reveals the many pressures at work in the Cold War. In 1948 the United Nations had established a Jewish state, Israel, in the Middle East on land claimed by both Arabs and Jews. War broke out, and Israel won. A coup in Egypt brought an Arab nationalist, General Nasser, to power. This began the long history of the United States involvement in the Middle East, caught between the interests of both Arabs and Israelis.

The United States offered to help General Nasser build a dam at Aswan to provide electric power for Egypt's development. When Nasser declared neutrality in the Cold War, Secretary of State Dulles withdrew the offer of help in building the dam. General Nasser then seized the English-owned Suez Canal to gain its revenues. Fearing loss of their oil supply—much of their oil reached Europe through the canal—England, France, and Israel attacked. Eisenhower essentially told them to get out, and the USSR supported his stand. The three nations withdrew, and Egypt gained control of the canal.

> The establishment of the nation of Israel by the United Nations precipitates war in the Middle East.

It was a rare moment of cooperation between the two great powers. In spite of this cooperation, John Foster Dulles feared the extension of Communist influence into the Middle East. He also believed that no nation could be neutral in the Cold War. It was this viewpoint that led him to withdraw the aid from the building of the Aswan Dam.

Following Secretary of State Dulles' views of brinkmanship in the Cold War, in a Congressional address in 1957, President Eisenhower asked for permission of Congress to use United States armed forces to aid any nation that asked for United States support against aggression by any country under the control of international communism. This became known as the Eisenhower Doctrine. Soon after, the President of Lebanon sent a request to the President to send United States troops to Lebanon to help crush a rebellion. Troops were sent and the Lebanese rebellion crushed. However, it precipitated a coup d'etat in nearby Iraq, in which the royal family was overthrown and the Baathist Party came to power. Eventually Saddam Hussein emerged as leader of the party and ruler of Iraq. Cold War action

> Proclaiming the Eisenhower Doctrine, the president sends troops to Lebanon.

by President Eisenhower led to events that came to dominate the history of the Middle East.

Before the Eisenhower Doctrine, the CIA had been instrumental in overthrowing a popular but anti-American government in Iran and establishing the autocratic Shah (King) on the throne. Behind these Cold War moves were the West's

> The CIA supports the Shah of Iran.

need to have access to the oil of the Middle East and fear of Communist expansion into the area. To United States policy makers it seemed an appropriate application of containment and a logical reaction to the Cold War challenges. It provides the background for the later rise of Islamic extremism in Iran under Ayotollah Khomeni and for the United States reaction to the Iran-Iraq War in the 1980s, the two Iraq wars, and the War on Terrorism. After the fall of Soviet communism, the access to oil, defense of Israel, and reaction to Islamic extremism drove United States policy in the region. However, Cold War concerns began the involvement.

THE COLD WAR IN JAPAN

World War II began in Asia with the Japanese attack on China. With the Allied victory, the United States occupied Japan. General Douglas MacArthur headed the occupation forces. Following the Yalta Agreement, the Russians occupied North

> The United States signs a separate treaty with Japan.

Korea and half of Japan's Sakhalin Island. The island of Taiwan, called Formosa by the Japanese occupiers, was returned to China. Cold War disagreements between the United States and the USSR delayed a peace treaty with Japan until 1951, when the United States signed a separate treaty establishing Japan as a non-nuclear, non-military, democratic monarchy and ending the occupation. The United States and Japan signed a defense treaty that allowed United States troops to remain in Japan, an agreement still in effect. But peace did not come to China.

THE PEOPLE'S REPUBLIC OF CHINA

In China throughout the 1920s and 1930s there had been conflict between the Nationalist government led by General Jiang Jieshi (Chiang Kai-shek) and Communist forces led by Mao Zedong (Mao Tse-tung). Mao had escaped defeat by leading his forces from the coastal cities on a "long march" inland, where his urban soldiers were transformed into a peasant army. A wartime truce between the two groups proved very shaky but allowed the Nationalists and Communists to fight the Japanese. With the end of World War II, the conflict between the two Chinese factions again turned violent. The United States made several attempts at mediation but stopped the efforts in 1947. Both Jiang Jieshi's Nationalists and Mao Zedong's Communists share the blame for atrocities that occurred in the conflict and for the failure of mediation. The United States sent supplies to the Nationalists; the USSR sent supplies to the Communists.

Finally, in December 1949, Mao Zedong triumphed, and Jiang Jieshi and his army fled to the island of Taiwan, where a Nationalist government was established. Mao Zedong ruled the People's Republic on the Asian mainland with its capital in

Beijing. There were two Chinese governments each supported by one of the Cold War antagonists.

There were outcries in the United States that China had been lost. The Republican Conservatives claimed that Mao's victory was a result of the inept foreign policy of the Democrats under Truman. A strong China lobby in Congress supported Jiang Jieshi for years. There had always been a sentimental attraction for China in the United States, but this was not transferred to Mao and his Communist forces. After fleeing to Taiwan, Jiang Jieshi continued to control China's permanent United Nations Security Council seat over the protests of the Soviet Union. The Soviets boycotted the Security Council from January to August 1950 in protest and thus were not present to veto the United Nations resolution calling for force to combat North Korea's invasion of South Korea.

THE KOREAN WAR

How to restore occupied Korea as an independent, united nation was another Cold War challenge. United States forces occupied the south, and Soviet forces the north, as a result of agreements made at Yalta. With no progress on the issue as a result of the Cold War differences, the United States established the Republic of Korea, usually referred to as South Korea, with Syngman Rhee as President. The Soviets countered, establishing a Communist Peoples Republic, referred to as North Korea. The United Nations tried to resolve the issue but failed.

In a speech, Dean Acheson, Secretary of State under Truman, mentioned that Korea was not essential to the defense of Asia from the Communists. Reading this as a statement of no interest in Korea, on June 25, 1950, the North Koreans turned the Cold War hot by invading South Korea.

The United Nations Security Council adopted a resolution asking the United Nations members to "furnish such assistance to the Republic of Korea as may be necessary to repel the armed attack." The Russians were boycotting the Security Council because of its refusal to accept the Communist government of China as the holder of the Security Council seat assigned to China, so they were unable to veto the resolution. President Truman responded and ordered United States troops into action without a declaration of war by Congress—a precedent followed by presidents throughout the Cold War, most recently in Iraq by George W. Bush. The Korean War, under United Nations auspices, had begun. Over 30,000 Americans lost their lives in this undeclared war, which successfully halted the military aggression of a Communist nation. Unlike the League of Nations, the United Nations had stood up to aggression.

The United Nations forces were put under Command of General Douglas MacArthur. The North Koreans swept through the south, occupying almost four-fifths of the country and confining the United Nations troops to the region around the southern port of Pusan. The United Nations mounted an offensive, landed forces at Inchon behind the North Korean battle line, and swept through the north almost to the Yalu River, the border between Manchuria, a province of the People's Republic of China, and Korea.

The Chinese, concerned over the motives of the United Nations and fearing the presence of United States forces on its borders, entered the war in October 1950.

General Douglas MacArthur threatened China, an ally of the USSR with atomic attack and was removed from his command by President Truman. It was not United States government policy to use atomic weapons. Truman and the United States

> **The Chinese Communists join the war in support of North Korea.**

were not ready to turn the Korean War into another world war by attacking an ally of the USSR. The Chinese Communists forced the United Nations' troops to retreat until a line was finally stabilized along the 38th parallel, the old dividing line between North and South Korea.

The war became a stalemate. It was an issue in the presidential election of 1952, when General Eisenhower promised to "go to Korea" if elected. He was elected and went. Finally, in late 1953 an armistice was negotiated, but United States forces remained in Korea. While the Republic of Korea (South Korea) has prospered economically since the armistice, the nation is still not united and tensions exist between North and South Korea and between North Korea, her neighbors, and the United States especially concerning the development of nuclear power, the secretive nature of the government, and the abuse of human rights. The Korean War confirmed for United States policy makers the aggressive intentions of Communist nations and the value of the containment policy and the use of counter force to block Communist expansion.

FOREIGN AID

Monumental changes took place elsewhere in Asia in the early years of the Cold War. In 1947 the English withdrew from India, establishing the new independent nations of India and Pakistan,

> **Former colonies in Asia gain independence.**

and in 1948 England withdrew from Myanmar (Burma) and Sri Lanka (Ceylon), making them independent. The Dutch granted independence to the United States of Indonesia in 1949. The United States met its commitment to the Philippines, and they became independent in 1946. The old world of imperialistic powers was changing. Similar changes were to come about in Africa in the 1960s.

As the Cold War continued, one issue for the United States foreign policy makers was how to gain the support of these newly independent nations or to keep them from joining the Communist side. This created a polarized view of the world made famous by Secretary of State John Foster Dulles' view that if you are not with us, you are against us.

One solution the United States found to the problem was the development of foreign aid as a tool to win support of newly independent nations. It began with President Truman and his "Point Four" Program in 1949. Under the Point Four program, Truman offered economic aid to undeveloped areas around the world. By 1960 the United States had spent almost $73 billion in foreign economic and military aid. Some Americans believed it was money well spent; others believed it would have been better spent taking care of domestic concerns. War, cold or hot, was costly and provided challenges and stimulation to those who fought.

A breadth and clarity of view was lost by these people who saw the world in black and white, we and they, terms only. They often failed to understand or appreciate the complexity of issues and forces driving nations and people. It became easy to see Communists behind every action with which Americans disagreed. It was easy to use economic aid to bribe nations to support American views. Later, foreign aid became more heavily military aid. The "with us or against us" approach to foreign policy led the United States to support with economic and military aid many leaders who were anti-Communist but not democratic and did not support American values.

Key Point to Remember

The World War II Allies soon fell into disagreement over the structure of the postwar world, and the resulting conflicts and tensions between the West, or democracies, and the East, or communist states, was called the Cold War.

People to Remember

Douglas MacArthur General, Superintendent of West Point Military Academy and Army Chief of Staff, advisor to Philippine government; at start of World War II evacuated from Bataan Peninsula to Australia to command Southwest Pacific Area Theater; appointed Supreme Commander over occupied Japan, led U.S. and UN forces in Korean War, relieved of command by President Truman; a flamboyant, outspoken military hero, he tested the concept of civilian control of the military; his leadership skills have come under increasing scrutiny.

George Marshall General, Secretary of State, Secretary of Defense; gained notice in World War I, became Army Chief of Staff at the start of World War II and was responsible for planning the war strategy; Truman appointed him special ambassador to China and then Secretary of State after the war; organized the European Recovery Program (Marshall Plan) for which he won the Nobel Peace Prize in 1953.

Dwight Eisenhower General, adviser to Philippine government, Supreme Commander of Allied Forces in Europe, Commander of U.S. occupation forces in Germany, President of Columbia University, Supreme Allied Commander, Europe (NATO), 34th president of United States; in World War II, he rose rapidly to Five-Star General status and led the D-Day invasion of Normandy; negotiated truce to end Korean War; continued Truman's anti-communism policies and established Eisenhower Doctrine of aid to Middle East to block communism; supported conservative domestic agenda but sent troops to Little Rock to support integration; warned of power of a military-industrial complex in the United States.

Eleanor Roosevelt Humanitarian, First Lady, U.S. delegate to the UN; wife of the 32nd president; a very active First Lady—held the first press conference, wrote a news column, *My Day*, traveled widely; served as Assistant Director of the Office of Civilian Defense in 1941–1942; chaired the UN Commission on Human Rights, which produced the Universal Declaration on Human Rights; was an activist supporting women's organizations, civil rights, and youth movements and opposing unemployment and inadequate housing.

Links from the Past to the Present

1. The black and white, we versus they, oversimplified view of complex international issues has been a characteristic of American foreign policy.

2. The division of Korea and tensions in that area continue today.

3. Arab-Israeli tensions and disagreements still prevent the acceptance of peace in the Middle East.

4. Issues relating to the unification of Germany and Berlin were an important part of the Cold War and are a concern still because Germany is now the single strongest economic power in Europe.

5. The origins of the Cold War and the split of Europe into East and West are important for understanding Europe today in spite of the end of the Cold War.

Dates

1946—Churchill's "Iron Curtain" speech.

1947—Truman Doctrine on Greece.
United States signed treaties with Italy, Hungary, Bulgaria, Romania, and Finland.
Marshall Plan.

1948—Nation of Israel established.
Berlin Blockade began.
UN Universal Declaration of Human Rights.

1949—Soviet Union exploded an atomic bomb.
Point Four foreign aid program began.
NATO formed.
People's Republic of China established.

1950—Korean War began.

1951—United States signed peace treaty with Japan.

1953—Korean War armistice.

1954—CIA overthrew government of Guatemala.

1955—First Cold War summit meeting in Geneva.

1956—Suez Crisis.

1957—Eisenhower Doctrine.
United States troops sent to Lebanon.

1960—U2 plane incident.

Questions
Identify each of the following:

Berlin Wall	"X" Article
Truman Doctrine	United Nations Universal Declaration
The Iron Curtain	of Human Rights
Brinkmanship	Marshall Plan
Korean War	Mao Zedong

Multiple Choice:

1. Among the reasons for the start of the Cold War were
   a. basic ideological differences over capitalism and socialism.
   b. the fact the Soviets had suffered so little in World War II.
   c. Russian desire for revenge on Napoleon.

2. The changes made in the United States defense establishment to better conduct the Cold War included
   a. the CIA and the National Security Council.
   b. separate Cabinet level posts for the army and navy departments.
   c. both of the above.

3. Nuclear proliferation in the postwar period included
   a. the United States giving atomic secrets to all United Nations members.
   b. the development of hydrogen bombs by NATO.
   c. the development of atomic and hydrogen bombs by the USSR.

4. The United Nations could respond to the invasion of South Korea with military action and without a Security Council veto because
   a. President Truman was ready to send troops.
   b. the USSR was boycotting the Security Council.
   c the USSR and the United States agreed it should be done.

III. Domestic Affairs: 1945–1960

DOMESTIC IMPACT OF THE COLD WAR

The American people first reacted to the international divisions of the Cold War by looking for possible Communist infiltration into government. The Smith Act of 1940, enacted against the Nazi threat, had made it illegal to advocate the overthrow of the United States government or to belong to any organization that did. President Truman used the act to jail leaders of the Communist party in the United States. He established a Loyalty Review Board in 1947 to review the loyalty of government employees. The House UnAmerican Activities Committee, the Dies Committee mentioned earlier, also turned its investigations toward possible Communist infiltration into government. The committee gained extensive publicity for its efforts, which included accusing Truman of being "soft on communism."

> Concern grows over possible Communist connections of government employees.

In 1948 Whittaker Chambers, an editor of *Time* magazine and a former Communist spy, accused Alger Hiss, the president of the Carnegie Endowment for International Peace, of being a Communist agent. The implications for government security were great. Alger Hiss had been a member of the State Department and a close advisor to President Roosevelt. Hiss had been with Roosevelt at the Yalta Conference, which the Republicans were calling a "sellout" of Europe to the Communists. Alger Hiss denied the charges. The case received much publicity and scared many people. They thought that if Chambers was correct, the entire planning for peace by the United States and the USSR could have been controlled by Communists. Because the legal statute of limitations had run out and Hiss could not be convicted on spying charges, charges of perjury[11] were brought against him for his conduct in the preliminary hearings. He was tried on the perjury count and was found guilty. Hiss claimed his innocence until his death. In 1950 Julius and Ethel Rosenberg were found guilty of giving atomic secrets to the Soviets. They were executed for treason in 1953.

Congress responded to the Cold War with the McCarran Internal Security Act of 1950, which required any Communist front[12] organization to register with the government and prevented the organization's members from working in defense companies or from traveling. It was a restriction on individual liberty and reflects the national mood of fear and uncertainty. It clearly illustrates the impact of fear of others on society. Throughout the United States history the federal government has curtailed the liberties and rights of citizens when confronted by a powerful enemy. This was seen in the Alien and Sedition Acts during the French Revolution, in the Palmer Raids after World War I, and in the actions of the Department of Justice after the September 11, 2001, destruction of the World Trade Center's Twin Towers and attack on the Pentagon by al-Qaida terrorists.

McCARTHYISM

In 1950 Republican Senator Joseph McCarthy from Wisconsin used the national mood to project himself onto the political stage as a major player. In a speech he claimed he had the names of 205 Communists in the State Department. He never produced the names and kept changing the numbers, but he captured national attention. McCarthy and his accusations became a campaign issue. Eisenhower, after his election, did nothing to stop McCarthy, who expanded his accusations to include scholars and the United States Army. His accusations against the Army led to a Senate hearing. It was televised nationally—the first Senate hearing to get such publicity.

> Senator Joseph McCarthy claims he has evidence of Communist infiltration into the State Department and army.

McCarthy's tactics at the hearing disgusted many viewers, who responded favorably to the Army's Chief legal counsel, Joseph Welch. The hearings backfired. No clear proof of misdeeds by the army was produced, so McCarthy's case was destroyed. In 1954 the Senate censored McCarthy for discrediting the Senate. The Senate never condemned McCarthy for the methods he used, which violated the Bill of Rights. McCarthy's activities and their acceptance for four years by the people and the government again illustrate the challenges of the Cold War and the impact they had domestically. It also illustrates that tendency toward intolerance so often seen in American history.

---

[11] perjury   *The deliberate and willful giving of false or misleading information when under oath in a criminal proceeding whether in court or in an affidavit.*

[12] Communist front   *A front organization is an organization that is designed to hide the activities of its members. Therefore, a Communist front organization is one in which the organization is not stating it is Communist but is working quietly for Communist causes.*

Joseph McCarthy gave a new word, *McCarthyism*[13], to the language. Fortunately for the nation, Senator McCarthy lost all credibility after his censure. He died in 1957. However, his actions frightened many government civil servants, some of whom quit government service, and silenced others who remained. McCarthyism made many young scholars decide not to enter government service for fear of being falsely accused, and it reduced the effectiveness of the Foreign Service for a number of years. It was an unfortunate period, but in many ways it resembles the breakdown of ethics that followed both the Civil War and World War I.

CIVIL RIGHTS

The policy and practice of segregation contradicted the United States' position in the Cold War as a champion of free peoples. Foreign diplomats from newly independent Asian and later African nations were subjected to situations that proved embarrassing to the United States. The time had finally come for federal action to change segregation and to guarantee the civil rights of all Americans. It

> Foreign diplomats encounter segregation in the United States.

took time, and although racist attitudes and discrimination remain in the nation, great changes were made in the 1950s and 1960s.

During World War II segregation prevailed in military units, but the exposure to leadership positions and the experience of visiting other countries created a cadre of future African-American civil rights leaders. Also in wartime, African-American workers worked alongside white workers in war industries as members of those CIO industrial unions recognized in the 1930s, and some African-Americans moved into the middle class. These people joined leaders like A. Philip Randolph of the Pullman Porters Union who had been working for civil rights for years.

The cause of civil rights was aided by the changing urban voting pattern created by the migration of African-Americans to urban areas in the North. Their votes were important and made members of the government more responsive to civil rights needs.

The National Association for the Advancement of Colored People (NAACP) had been working through the courts for years to improve the situation for African-Americans. The Supreme Court declared in 1944 that Democratic Party primaries, which permitted only whites to vote, were unconstitutional, and in 1946 the court declared segregation on interstate buses unconstitutional.

President Truman, a student of American history, had a personal commitment to civil rights. In 1946 Truman appointed a Committee on Civil Rights whose report, *To Secure These Rights*, set the goals of the Civil Rights Movement for the next thirty years. The Committee recommended a civil rights division in the Department of Justice, voting rights legislation, and the end to segregation. In 1948 Truman moved to end racial discrimination in government and ordered the start of desegregation of the military, which Eisenhower completed.

The Supreme Court decision in *Brown* v. *Board of Education* in 1954 is often considered the start of the postwar Civil Rights Movement, but it had already begun.

---

[13] McCarthyism   *"Smearing" people with unsupported accusations, usually of disloyalty.*

The case however, is very important. In *Brown* v. *Board of Education* the Supreme Court declared "separate but equal," the formula the Court first declared in the *Plessy* v. *Ferguson* case in 1896, unconstitutional in schools. The Court accepted the arguments of psychological damage done by segregation and ordered its end in schools. In a follow-up decision in 1955 the Court ordered desegregation of educational facilities with "all deliberate speed."

> The *Brown* v. *Board of Education* decision reverses the "separate but equal" doctrine of *Plessy* v. *Ferguson*.

Since education is a local concern in America and controlled by local governments and school boards, each community with segregated schools had to determine how to integrate them. The struggle was fought throughout the South and later in northern cities, where housing patterns created all or nearly all African-American urban schools. Since the 1950s, federal courts have played an important role in desegregation and in the protection of individual rights. School integration has not come easily, and there are still examples of de facto segregation in schools. An early example of a failed attempt to integrate schools in the South is Little Rock, Arkansas.

Arkansas, on the edge of the South, does not have as large an African-American population or as strong a tradition of segregation as states further south, but when in 1957 the city school board selected nine outstanding young African-Americans to enter the white high school, rioting occurred. At first Governor Orville Faubus ordered in the Arkansas National Guard to stop the students' entry. When one teenage African-American girl alone tried to enter the school, a mob was ready to lynch her, but a white woman got her away safely.

President Eisenhower was slow to act. His personal stance on civil rights and his style of presidential leadership opposed strong federal intervention. Finally, however, Eisenhower sent in federal troops; the Little Rock Nine completed the year with the troops protecting them. The public schools, however, were closed for the next two years rather than continue with integration.

Public schools were closed in Virginia and other parts of the South in order to avoid integration. Eventually they were opened as integrated institutions. Many private, often church-sponsored,

> Much of the South resists the integration of schools.

all-white schools opened in the South. School desegregation was finally accepted by most Americans, but there are still problem areas in both southern and northern cities.

CIVIL DISOBEDIENCE

In Montgomery, Alabama, in December 1955, the Civil Rights Movement took a new direction away from the courts and into direct action. Rosa Parks, a tired seamstress who had worked for the NAACP, refused to give up her seat to a white man on the city's segregated private bus line. Local African-American leaders had been waiting for an opportunity to make a case against segregated buses. When Rosa Parks was arrested, they began court proceedings, and at the same time a bus boycott was organized by African-Americans in Montgomery. African-Americans, who far outnumbered whites as riders, stayed off the buses for almost a year. A young minister, Martin Luther King, Jr., emerged as the spokesperson for the boycott and went on to become a leader and hero of the Civil Rights Movement until his assassination in 1968. The United States Supreme Court in 1956 declared segregation on local buses unconstitutional under the Bill of Rights and Amendment XIV. The Montgomery bus boycott was ended, and the buses were integrated.

In the Montgomery boycott the idea of civil disobedience was first used by the Civil Rights Movement. Articulated by Martin Luther King, Jr. and the other African-American ministers who led the boycott in Montgomery, civil disobedience combined the teachings of Jesus and other religious leaders, the teachings and practices of the American transcendentalist thinker Henry David Thoreau, the practices of Gandhi's civil disobedience movement (which led to India's independence from England), and the experiences of African-Americans.

> Martin Luther King, Jr. introduces civil disobedience into the struggle for integration in the Montgomery Bus Boycott.

Civil disobedience was used to draw attention to legal injustices by breaking the law and going to jail. No violence was used against the forces of the law. Those breaking the law appealed to a higher moral and ethical code than that supported by the local law. By making this appeal, attention was drawn to injustices. It was hoped that correction of these injustices would follow.

Civil disobedience required the support of the people who were oppressed. It required leaders to organize the protests, and the charismatic Martin Luther King, Jr. and other religious leaders founded the Southern Christian Leadership Conference (SCLC) to provide this leadership. Another organization, the Student Non-Violent Coordinating Committee (SNCC) was organized in 1960. SNCC provided more grassroots leadership for the movement, not relying on nationally known figures. It was people, young and old, African-American and later their white supporters, and not the leaders, who made civil disobedience work.

For example, in 1960 four African-American students from North Carolina Agricultural and Technical College sat down at a white lunch counter in Greensborough, North Carolina, and refused to leave until served. The sit-in[14] technique of civil disobedience was born. The sit-in technique was applied to bring about desegregation of buses, lunch counters, and other facilities in the South.

> The sit-in technique is used to integrate lunch counters.

PRESIDENTIAL ELECTIONS: 1948–1956

In 1946 in the first postwar election, the Republicans made large gains and took control of Congress for the first time since the start of the Depression. It appeared the nation was ready to toss out the Democrats and perhaps return to a period similar to that of the Harding post-World War I years. In 1948 Southern Democrats, concerned over maintaining segregation and upset by the Democratic Party's platform plank on civil rights, formed their own party, the States' Rights Democratic Party (Dixiecrats). The Dixiecrats ran Senator Strom Thurmond of South Carolina

---

[14] sit-ins *Demonstrations in which protesters occupy seats and refuse to move until they are recognized and/or their demands are met. It was used by the Civil Rights Movement to break down segregation in public places.*

for president. However, in spite of this third party and the nation's concerns over postwar inflation and other domestic issues, in 1948 Harry Truman won a term of his own as president by narrowly defeating Republican Thomas Dewey of New York.

In 1952 Senator Robert Taft of Ohio, son of President William Howard Taft, was the leading Republican contender for the nomination. After some uncertainties it became clear that General Dwight Eisenhower, World War II leader of Allied forces in Europe, postwar head of NATO, and president of Columbia University, would run as a Republican if nominated. He received the Republican nomination, and Richard M. Nixon, a young congressman from California who had made a reputation as both a conservative and a strong anti-Communist, was named his vice presidential candidate. At the start of the campaign a question was raised over Nixon's campaign financing in California. In a memorable television speech Nixon appealed to the people using his dog Checkers as a prop and won Eisenhower's strong endorsement.

The Democrat's candidate, the scholarly, clever, and witty Governor Adlai Stevenson of Illinois, was overwhelmingly defeated by the popular "Ike." Eisenhower's campaign slogan, "I like Ike," his aura as a military hero while the Cold War raged, and his promise, if elected, to "go to Korea" and speed an end to the fighting made him unbeatable. He and Nixon again defeated Stevenson in 1956.

DOMESTIC LEGISLATION IN RESPONSE TO THE COLD WAR

Several pieces of important domestic legislation came as responses to Cold War events. In 1946 when the United Nations failed to agree on international control of atomic energy, the Atomic Energy Commission was established to control domestic nuclear developments. The legislation gave the president sole power over the use of the atomic bomb. In 1954 the Atomic Energy Act authorized the building of private nuclear power plants under supervision of the commission. The military reorganization and the McCarran Act mentioned earlier were passed in response to the Cold War.

> The Atomic Energy Act and the National Defense Education Act are passed in response to Cold War tensions.

In 1957 the Soviet Union launched into space the first satellite, known as Sputnik, the Russian word for satellite. After the launch of Sputnik, there was fear the American educational system was not preparing students for the challenges of the Cold War. There was fear American engineering and science was inadequate to protect the nation's integrity. In reaction, Congress passed the National Defense Education Act to improve American education in foreign languages, mathematics, and science. The act provided federal funding for what had traditionally been funded only by state and local governments. Again, the impact of war on society is seen.

THE TAFT-HARTLEY ACT AND THE FAIR DEAL

In 1947 the Republican Congress passed the Taft-Hartley Labor Act over President Truman's veto. The Taft-Hartley Act put certain limits on unions, which had benefited greatly from the New Deal legislation. The Act made illegal a closed shop[15] and required, under specified conditions, an 80-day "cooling-off" period[16] before a union could call a strike. Truman was a supporter of the New Deal and wanted to extend legislation to create a "fair deal" for every American including health care. Congress failed to act on his requests, but it did not abandon any major New Deal concepts except those repealed by the Taft-Hartley Act. Truman did achieve passage of a Government Reorganization Act, which he used to make government operations more efficient.

DYNAMIC CONSERVATISM OF EISENHOWER

President Eisenhower, although a Republican, also supported the New Deal legislation. He claimed he was a conservative in economics, but a liberal in human affairs. His approach to government has been dubbed "dynamic conservatism." There was little social legislation passed, but Congress did pass a Civil Rights Act in 1957, which established a Civil Rights Division in the Department of Justice and a permanent Civil Rights Commission. These two agencies gave the federal government a way to investigate infringements of civil rights and to enforce adherence to them. During Eisenhower's presidency social security coverage was extended to 10 million more people.

President Eisenhower deserves the title "Transportation President" for two measures. The first, the building of the St. Lawrence Seaway, opened the Great Lakes to ocean-going ships through a series of canals and the development of the St. Lawrence River. The second, the Federal Aid Highway Act, called for a massive interstate highway system, with the federal government paying 90 percent of the cost. The act was a great boon to the automobile industry but helped make the United States dependent on autos and oil. It hurt the railroads. The Federal Aid Highway Act had a major impact on American industry and on the infrastructure[17] of the nation.

NEW INDUSTRIES

Between the end of World War II and the election of John F. Kennedy, the United States' economy grew rapidly. Military spending in response to the Cold War stimulated old industries, and military research created new ones, especially in electronics, chemicals, and aviation. A postwar baby boom helped increase the population by almost 30 percent and created great demands for products. The automobile industry produced 8 million cars per year in the mid-1950s, up from 3 million only five years before. Television broadcasting and manufacturing became major new industries. Business organization and consumption habits changed.

[15] closed shop   *A plant or manufacturing shop in which newly hired workers are forced to join a union as a condition of employment.*
[16] cooling-off period   *A set period of time in which an action may not take place while a resolution to the situation is pursued by the parties involved.*
[17] infrastructure   *Those parts of the economy such as roads and highways upon which other industries depend. These are normally paid for by the government.*

Industry turned to conglomerates[18] as a new organizational form. Teenagers became an important consumer group, and advertisers learned to use television to appeal to them. In spite of several mild recessions in the Eisenhower years, the economy essentially boomed. The low inflation rate of roughly 2 percent and the steady growth in the gross national product (GNP)[19] of over 3 percent, made it a time of affluence for many.

> A postwar baby boom increases the population and creates a great demand for products.

In those years the road to economic success was the business road and the "man in the gray flannel suit" became the symbol of success of the age. Sloan Wilson in his novel of that title described the conformity needed in the business world.

KENNEDY-NIXON ELECTION

The 1960 election proved to be extremely close. It illustrates the importance of voting, because a shift of one vote in a number of wards in large states such as Illinois could have changed the result. The Republicans had nominated Richard Nixon, Eisenhower's vice president; the Democrats nominated John F. Kennedy. Kennedy chose as his Vice President Lyndon B. Johnson of Texas, the Senate Majority Leader, who had been his leading opponent for the nomination. Kennedy was young, good looking, a naval hero of World War II, a senator, and the son of a millionaire who had supported Franklin Roosevelt and had served as ambassador to Great Britain during the war. Kennedy was an Irish Catholic from Boston—until then the only Catholic except Al Smith in 1928 to win a presidential nomination.

> John F. Kennedy, gaining national recognition in televised debates with his Republican opponent, Richard Nixon, wins the 1960 election.

The campaign is remembered for the first televised debates between presidential candidates. In the first debate, John F. Kennedy's looks and charisma overshadowed Nixon. The debate gave John F. Kennedy the national recognition he needed. Kennedy attacked the military preparedness of the United States and appealed to Cold War fears. He spoke of a "new frontier" for America. Although the campaign lacked real substance, the young Kennedy and his attractive wife, Jackie, inspired enough Americans for him to win a narrow victory and bring the Democrats back to the White House.

SUMMARY

The United States responded dramatically to the attack on Pearl Harbor and quickly organized for total war. The nation looked forward to peace after the victory of the allied forces in 1945. However, disagreements between the Soviet Union and the western Allies soon led to a Cold War. The struggle affected both foreign relations

[18] conglomerate *A form of business organization in which one company owns many companies involved in a diversity of activities. The concept is that if you own companies doing different things, a recession will not hurt the larger corporation because some company will still be prospering.*

[19] gross national product (GNP) *The total production of goods and services in a nation. It has become the major measurement of the economic growth of a country.*

and domestic affairs. Senator Joseph McCarthy reflected the worst qualities that war can bring out in human beings as he accused hundreds of citizens of Communist connections with no proof. On the other hand, both World War II and the Cold War brought forth noble acts by individuals and by the nation. Without the Marshall Plan, the UN Charter, and Truman's Point Four the post World War II world would have been very different. The Cold War even had an impact on the Civil Rights Movement where concern for the treatment of foreign diplomats from newly independent nations had impact on federal government action. The United States responded to the challenges of war, and the nation changed in many ways.

Key Point to Remember
The Cold War had an impact on domestic legislation and McCarthyism illustrates the intolerance and fear of foreigners that appears often in United States history.

People to Remember

Martin Luther King, Jr.   African-American minister; trained at Boston University; became leader of the Montgomery Bus Boycott and one of the founders of the Southern Christian Leadership Conference (SCLC), the most important organization in the Civil Rights Movement in the 1960s; noted for his effective speaking style (*I Have a Dream* Speech) and writing (*Letter from a Birmingham Jail*) by which he captured the attention of the American people; leader of the 1963 March on Washington; assassinated in 1968 while attempting to focus attention on poverty and the bad working conditions in American cities.

Rosa Lee Parks   Civil rights activist; long-time activist in the NAACP (National Association for the Advancement of Colored People), her refusal to give up her seat in the front of the bus led to the Montgomery Bus Boycott; Martin Luther King, Jr. emerged as the leader of the successful boycott—a major step in the Civil Rights Movement.

Joseph McCarthy   Lawyer, judge, U.S. Senator from Wisconsin; responsible for the term *McCarthyism*—indiscriminate attacks, sensationalism, and unsubstantiated accusations directed at opponents; as Chairman of the Senate Subcommittee on Government Operations, first accused the State Department of protecting communists and then attacked the U.S. Army; televised hearings of the case against the army captured the nation's attention; none of McCarthy's charges were ever proven; he was eventually censured by the Senate and lost his influence.

Links from the Past to the Present

1. In times of tension and conflict, scare tactics and the infringement of civil rights (e.g., McCarthyism), are often used by leaders who feel threatened by foreign or domestic opponents.

2. In spite of the advances brought about by the Civil Rights Movement, some racist attitudes still persist.

3. Civil disobedience has been used by other groups to obtain their civil rights.

4. TV debates have become an important part of presidential and other elections.

Dates

1946—*To Secure These Rights* report of Committee on Civil Rights.

1947—Taft-Hartley Act.

1948—Alger Hiss Case.
   Harry Truman elected president.

1952—Dwight D. Eisenhower elected president.

1953—Julius and Ethel Rosenberg executed.

1954—Senator Joseph McCarthy censured by the Senate.
   Atomic Energy Act.
   Brown v. *Board of Education* decision.

1955—Montgomery Bus Boycott began.

1956—SCLC formed.
   Federal Aid Highway Act.

1957—Little Rock Nine failed to integrate Little Rock High School.
   National Defense Education Act.
   Civil Rights Division of Justice Department and Civil Rights Commission
      established by Civil Rights Act.

1960—SNCC formed.
   John F. Kennedy elected president.

Questions
Identify each of the following:

Alger Hiss	*To Secure These Rights*
Montgomery Bus Boycott	Federal Aid Highway Act
McCarthyism	*Brown* v. *Board of Education*
Sputnik	Little Rock Nine

Multiple Choice:

1. Civil disobedience was rooted in the teachings of
   a. Rosa Parks and the Little Rock Nine.
   b. Henry David Thoreau and Gandhi.
   c. Martin Luther King, Jr. and Joseph McCarthy.

2. Joseph McCarthy capitalized on the mood of the country in the early 1950s and claimed he had evidence of Communists
   a. in the State Department and U.S. Army.
   b. in the U.S. Army, the FBI, and colleges.
   c. in the FBI and White House.

Open-ended, Analysis Questions
The following questions require analysis and reflection. You are encouraged to bring to your answer information and ideas from many sources. The answers should be

presented in composition or essay style but they may be used to initiate discussion. The questions put you in the role of the historian, gathering information to support your personal perspective on the question.

1. "Freedom, Individual Rights, and Democracy are the values Americans have traditionally held to be most important." To what extent are these values reflected in the policies and actions pursued to achieve peace after World War I by President Woodrow Wilson and after World War II by Presidents Franklin D. Roosevelt and Harry S. Truman? Use specific examples to make your points.

2. War presents many challenges to a society. What do you consider the major challenges World War II presented to Americans and what did Americans do to meet them? Be specific in your answer.

3. Pick four of the six items below. In an essay explain how the four are or are not examples of United States policy following the views expressed in the famous "X" Article published in 1947 in *Foreign Affairs* magazine.
   a. Berlin Blockade
   b. Marshall Plan
   c. NATO
   d. Brinkmanship
   e. Korean War
   f. Eisenhower Doctrine

12

Civil Rights, Vietnam, the Cold War, and Watergate: 1960–1976

APPROACHES TO HISTORY

DEFINING WHO YOU ARE

One analysis of human behavior suggests that humans often define who they are by who they are not. As an American, you are not some other nationality. This provides a sense of who you are. The analysis can be applied at many different levels. If you are white, you are not black. If you are a father, you are not a mother. The divisions can go on and on.

This analysis presents a clear but simplistic view of human behavior since we know that all humans share many characteristics and many characteristics are blurred. For instance, at the start of this book, it was pointed out that all Americans are immigrants, so all Americans have their origins somewhere other than in America. Therefore, to say that as an American you are not another nationality is not completely true—it is blurred. Likewise, mothers and fathers share many qualities and responsibilities, but mothers and fathers are taught or learn from society what qualities should be emphasized to make, for instance, an American male a "typical American father."

Even though individuals know the divisions are blurred, humans find it easy to define themselves and others—both friends and enemies—in terms of how they differ from us. This way of thinking leads us to identify others by the fact that they are not "like us." These others are then often seen as a threat or inferior. They are often attacked and become "the enemy."

Can you think of situations in your life where you verbally abused or turned against someone or some group simply because they were not like you?

A simple example is provided by sports contests where fans scream for their team to "kill" the opponent. Fans don't truly mean what they yell, but it allows them to define themselves as different from the opponent. Their opponent is not like them.

Historians often describe situations in history in terms of this concept of enemies, based on those who are not like themselves. Several psychologists have discussed the need to have a devil, someone to hate, in order to identify yourself or your cause. In American history the concept of an enemy or devil can be illustrated by many examples of intolerance or fear of others. The Civil Rights Movement, Vietnam, the Cold War, and Watergate all provide illustrations of this concept of human behavior. In each situation there was a division between us and them, black and white, "gooks"[1] and good Americans, "commies" and freedom lovers, hippies[2] and the "silent majority[3]."

I. The Presidencies of John F. Kennedy and Lyndon B. Johnson

A. DOMESTIC ISSUES

THE NEW FRONTIER

John F. Kennedy brought to the White House an aura of youthful idealism. He surrounded himself with bright young advisors and Cabinet members such as his brother, Attorney General Robert Kennedy; Secretary of Defense Robert McNamara; and Special Assistant for National Security McGeorge Bundy. Kennedy and his wife Jackie exuded charisma, which inspired people and created a surge of purpose and confidence in the nation.

> Kennedy brings a new spirit to the White House but has little success in getting legislation passed for his New Frontier program.

In spite of the new spirit in the White House, Kennedy had little success in getting Congress to pass major domestic legislation that he suggested as part of his New Frontier, including a number of reforms in housing and medical care. Before his assassination in 1963, Kennedy sent to Congress plans for a major

[1] gook   *Derogatory term used by Americans for the Vietnamese.*
[2] hippies   *Members of the counterculture of the 1960s and 1970s who, alienated by bureaucracy and materialism, pursued a different lifestyle based on "love, drugs, and rock 'n' roll."*
[3] silent majority   *Term used by President Nixon to describe those whom he believed supported his conservative views on law and order and did not approve of the hippies and other protest groups.*

tax reduction and an extensive Civil Rights Act, but these, too, were not accepted.

Kennedy's idealism and goals for America are illustrated in his inaugural address and in his establishment of the Peace Corps, in which young Americans worked as volunteers on projects in undeveloped countries to aid the people, not the government, of those countries. Kennedy provided a national purpose when, responding to the Soviet challenge in space, he called on the nation to place a man on the moon by the end of the decade. This goal was achieved when Neil Armstrong took "one long step for mankind" on the moon's surface on July 20, 1969.

In his presidential campaign Kennedy had suggested United States defenses had been weakened under Eisenhower. He was prepared to stand up to the Russians. Under John Foster Dulles' concept of brinkmanship, massive nuclear retaliation was to be the response to Soviet international pressure. Of course, it was not applied because it would have meant nuclear disaster for the world. Kennedy substituted for nuclear retaliation a concept of "flexible response" under which the United States would use different degrees and kinds of force in response to Soviet pressure. Kennedy was a true Cold War warrior who was out to win the war and who saw the Soviets as different, as the enemy. Using the flexible response principle, Kennedy threatened nuclear retaliation in confronting the Soviet Union in Berlin and Cuba and applied a more limited response in Vietnam. The Kennedy policy was still one of containment of the Communists, who were the enemy, who were different from us.

ASSASSINATION OF KENNEDY

On a political campaign trip to Dallas, Texas, Kennedy was assassinated on November 22, 1963. Lee Harvey Oswald was arrested as the suspect but was shot and killed by Jack Ruby while being transferred from jail. TV cameras recorded the shooting of Oswald, and it was shown on national TV, as was Kennedy's funeral. The events of the assassination traumatized the nation and plunged it into a period of grief and mourning. At the time it was not clear if the assassination was part of a major plot or the act of one individual. The nation was put on alert, but, as there were no other actions, quickly returned to former habits. Today it is commonly accepted that Oswald acted alone.

CAMELOT

The 1,000 days of the Kennedy presidency have been referred to as Camelot, the legendary castle of King Arthur of Britain where the king and his Knights of the Round Table fought for good and justice. This Camelot version of the Kennedy years is appealing, but is too idealistic a view. Kennedy supplied the

> The image of Camelot is only one side of the Kennedy presidency.

nation with a new national mood of optimism, signified in his call for the nation to move to the New Frontier, but his presidency also included the brashness and harshness of the frontier as seen in his foreign policy confrontations and his forcing the steel companies and steel union to settle a strike over profits and wages in 1961 simply by "jawboning"[4] the two antagonists. Camelot suggests a mystical world of ideals and good. If the Kennedy presidency had that, it was only one side of those years.

LYNDON BAINES JOHNSON

Lyndon B. Johnson became president on Kennedy's assassination. Johnson had been a senator from Texas and had served as the Senate Majority Leader. He knew the intricacies of Capital Hill. He knew the members of Congress and the way they worked. As president he used this knowledge to get legislation passed. Johnson had great sympathy for people, especially the common people, but was not experienced in foreign affairs. He viewed the world strictly from a Texan, a southern, and an American perspective. His presidency has a tragic quality, in which this man of compassion for and understanding of the average American was forced to devote much of his time as president to the situation in Vietnam.

Johnson was sworn in as president in a dramatic ceremony aboard Air Force One, the president's plane, which took Kennedy's body back to Washington. Kennedy's funeral, viewed on TV by millions, was a time of shared grief. The new president immediately addressed a joint session of Congress and said the best eulogy for the slain president would be to pass his domestic legislative program. Congress soon passed the tax reduction plan and the Civil Rights Act Kennedy had proposed.

Johnson had his own program for domestic legislation, the War on Poverty, the first part of which he introduced in January 1964. The War on Poverty had close links to the major domestic issue of the Kennedy and early Johnson years, the Civil Rights Movement.

> **Congress responds to Kennedy's assassination.**

FREEDOM RIDERS, UNIVERSITY OF MISSISSIPPI, AND BIRMINGHAM, ALABAMA

The Civil Rights Movement gained momentum (see pages 267–269). In 1961 CORE (Council on Racial Equality) founded in 1942, decided to become more active in the Movement. Its new Chairman, James Farmer, determined to test the Supreme Court decision integrating interstate bus travel. He organized the Freedom Riders, groups of young blacks who would ride the buses and test the enforcement of the decision. The Riders were met by mobs that attacked them as local police ignored the situation. The attacks gained national and international attention. Eventually Attorney General Robbert Kennedy was forced to intervene, and the Interstate Commerce Commission issued integrated rules for interstate bus travel but not before many Riders had been injured, two paralyzed, by mob attacks. CORE declared victory. In 1962 Kennedy, who had been slow to act, ordered the Mississippi National Guard into federal service in order to support the federal marshalls who were ordered to enroll James Meredith, an African-American student, at the

---

[4] jawboning   *To influence or pressure through persuasion, especially to pressure for voluntary compliance with official policy or guidelines.*

In this photo, two police officers drag a young African-American student out of the White Only library—a classic view of segregation in operation. Following the SCLC's policy of nonviolence, the young woman is not resisting, yet she is being forcefully removed. She cannot use the resources of the library for self improvement—the goal of Andrew Carnegie when he funded the establishment of hundreds of public libraries throughout the country. Actions of this type shocked northerners and rallied support for the Civil Rights Act desegregating public facilities.

University of Mississippi. James Meredith's enrollment forced the integration of the University.

In the spring of 1963 SCLC organized sit-ins to protest segregation in Birmingham, Alabama. The Chief of Police, "Bull" Connor, used dogs and firehoses on demonstrators, including children. These actions, seen on national TV, gained support for the African-American protesters. Martin Luther King, Jr. was arrested and while in jail wrote *Letter from a Birmingham Jail*, one of the most eloquent statements of the movement's philosophy, explaining why the African-Americans could no longer "wait" for integration and their full civil rights. A settlement was reached between King and the Birmingham city government, which integrated the lunch counters. The TV coverage of the event aroused the public and Kennedy responded.

MARCH ON WASHINGTON

It was then Kennedy called for Congress to pass a Civil Rights Act guaranteeing equal access for all races to public accommodation and withholding federal funds from state-run programs that were segregated. A filibuster in Congress delayed action. Civil rights leaders from SNCC, CORE, SCLC, and other groups organized a March on Washington in support of the Kennedy Civil Rights Bill. A. Philip Randolph of the Pullman Porters Union had suggested such a march in 1940 to call attention to segregation in government. It did not happen then, and it took 23 years before his idea was fulfilled.

Over 250,000 people from all races and all walks of life gathered before the Lincoln Memorial on August 28, 1963, in one of the largest demonstrations held in the Capital. The peaceful demonstrators were thrilled by King's memorable "I Have a Dream" speech, which includes the repeated phrase, "Let freedom ring." It was a masterful appeal to all that was best in America for fairness, for equality, for understanding. It was the high point of the civil disobedience movement led by King.

After Kennedy was assassinated, President Johnson pushed Kennedy's proposal for civil rights legislation through Congress. The Civil Rights Act of 1964 was a major achievement for Johnson, the Movement, and the nation. Many believe it could not have happened if Kennedy had not been killed. The Act forbids segregation in schools, public places, and employment thus ending Jim Crow. Enforcement aspects were comparatively weak, but they were strengthened in succeeding years. The Act did not address voting rights, and they became the focus of attention for the Civil Rights Movement.

Unfortunately, the mood of optimism and hope generated by the March on Washington and The Civil Rights Act did not last. In September in Birmingham, Alabama, four African-American girls were killed while at Sunday school by a bomb thrown at their church by white extremists. 1964 was to be a year of confrontations, as groups of Americans who defined themselves as different from other groups became more violent as they demanded their rights or defended their position.

THE CIVIL RIGHTS MOVEMENT EXPLODES

In 1964 CORE and SNCC organized the Mississippi Summer Project to register African-Americans to vote. Three civil rights workers were murdered by a group of whites that included deputy sheriffs who were supposed to be protecting the civil rights workers. Federal Bureau of Investigation (FBI) investigators were aiding white extremists. The long-time head of the FBI, J. Edgar Hoover, ordered King's telephones tapped, and he leaked uncomplimentary stories about King. Some accused Hoover of being a racist. By keeping African-Americans "in their place," Hoover helped define his own place and identity. Hoover did not use the FBI to support the Civil Rights Movement—a clear demonstration of the power and influence one man can have on history.

BLACK MUSLIMS

In the meantime, new leaders were emerging in the ghettos of the North, where almost three-quarters of African-Americans lived. The most prominent was Malcolm X, a leader of the Black Muslims. Malcolm X and other Black Muslim leaders were preaching a new approach to gaining equality. They called on African-Americans to be sober and thrifty and to seize freedom. They inspired and encouraged self-awareness and a sense of self-respect and power for people in the ghettos. There was much that was good in their message. However, there was a negative side as they spoke of using violence as a legitimate response to oppression rather than using civil disobedience.

> Malcolm X presents a new approach to gaining equality for African-Americans.

Violence did erupt in the Harlem ghetto of New York City and in Rochester, New York, in the summer of 1964—violence directed at a society that appeared insensitive to African-American needs. A government commission that investigated the riots said they were the result of a social system that provided little opportunity and few jobs for African-Americans. Other city ghettos erupted in riots in the 1960s.

While conditions for African-Americans improved considerably during the prosperity of the 1990s, the problems still exist in the inner cities where opportunities are often less than in the suburbs or small towns. A similar problem exists worldwide. There is a great discrepancy between opportunities available in the industrialized nations and in undeveloped regions that creates tension between them. Also, there are extremes of wealth and opportunity both within the industrialized nations and within the undeveloped nations. These discrepancies often lead individuals to attack those who have more—who are different from them because of wealth or opportunities.

MISSISSIPPI FREEDOM DEMOCRATIC PARTY

Meanwhile, the Mississippi voter registration drive resulted in the formation of the Mississippi Freedom Democratic Party (MFDP), which elected representatives to the Democratic Party Convention of 1964 in Atlantic City. Denied the vote in the Democratic Party all-white primary in Mississippi, the MFDP claimed that they were the true representatives of the state's

The Civil Rights Movement puts pressure on the Democratic Party.

Democrats because their primary was open to all. President Johnson, who was assured of his party's nomination, was in a political squeeze. Although he advocated civil rights legislation, he dared not lose the support of the South in the 1964 election. Following the rules of political life, a compromise was offered, but the MFDP through its spokesperson, Fannie Lou Hamer, refused the compromise. The Democratic Party did, as a result of the MFDP, change the rules for representation at the 1968 convention. It made that convention much more representative of the American people, with quotas for women and minorities established. Still, the lack of support for the MFDP by the Democratic Convention was a blow to the leaders of nonviolent civil disobedience.

SELMA, ALABAMA

In the spring of 1964 SNCC began a campaign to register voters in Selma, Alabama. It was not going well, and they asked King and SCLC for support. The city's white mayor was inexperienced. The city sheriff, Jim Clark, blocked the

Violence in Selma leads to the Voting Rights Act.

registration attempts. In early 1965, a white minister supporting King was killed by whites in Selma. The African-Americans refrained from violence but organized a march of protest from Selma to the state capital at Montgomery. The march was blocked by Sheriff Clark and the state National Guard under orders of George Wallace, recently elected Governor of Alabama and at that time an intense segregationist. Again, national television recorded the incident on the Pettus Bridge during which police on horseback attacked the marchers and threw tear gas at them. Again, national reaction was strong. A court decision granted the right to march and forbid interference by the city or state.

Responding to the Selma March and the events in Mississippi, the Congress passed the Voting Rights Act of 1965, which gave authority to the United States Attorney General to appoint officials to register voters in states where only a small percentage of minorities were registered. In the next few years voter registration increased dramatically, providing African-Americans with the power of the ballot box as a way to implement change.

The Voting Rights Act was a great achievement of the movement brought about by civil disobedience. Unfortunately, it was the last major achievement. The movement dissipated, and the leadership went in different directions as the nation focused more and more on the Vietnam War.

EMERGENCE OF BLACK POWER

Building on the idea of "the other" and the uniqueness of one's own group, in 1964 SNCC's Stokely Carmichael declared that SNCC should not include whites. The next year he spoke of the need to achieve Black Power. While achieving successes through the political process, the Civil Rights Movement had not achieved many economic changes. The goals and organizing methods of the movement's leaders became fragmented as they sought ways to gain more economic power for the African-American community. CORE and SNCC demanded Black Studies in schools and colleges. Adding to the mood of violence was the assassination of Malcolm X in 1965. He was assassinated by fellow Black Muslims who disagreed with his positions. In 1965 the ghetto of Watts in Los Angeles erupted in a riot in which 34 were killed and 810 wounded. In 1966 there were riots in New York and Chicago and in 1967 in Newark and Detroit.

The Black Panthers were organized in 1966 to patrol the streets in the ghettos. They quickly became urban revolutionaries and used violence to call attention to the conditions in the ghetto. In 1968 Stokely Carmichael joined the Black Panthers organization as the Prime Minister.

Martin Luther King, Jr. was still advocating peaceful confrontation, but the level of frustration in the ghettos could not be held in check. King and the SCLC saw the Vietnam War taking the money and attention needed to address the poverty of the African-Americans. King protested the United States' involvement in Vietnam, not yet a popular stand, and he began to organize a poor people's march on Washington to focus on the issue of poverty in America, which persisted in spite of Johnson's declared War on Poverty. In 1968, while in Memphis to support garbage workers who were striking for higher wages, Martin Luther King, Jr. was assassinated. King's assassination touched off rioting in over 150 cities—not the memorial celebration this great leader of peaceful change through civil disobedience should have had, but a clear indication of the anger of the African-American urban population who were now demanding Black Power—both political and economic. However, the turn to violence and confrontation to achieve goals was not confined to African-Americans in the mid-1960s.

THE STUDENT PROTEST MOVEMENT

In 1964 white, middle-class students who had participated in Mississippi Summer began the Free Speech Movement at the University of California at Berkeley. As the baby boomers headed to college, universities grew rapidly. Clark Kerr, chancellor of the University of California, compared the university to a business. Students at the university were concerned by the school's bigness and lack of individualism and personal attention reflected in this attitude of college education as a business. They felt they were merely numbers. The students organized peaceful protests, and when Chancellor Kerr ordered the square in Berkeley where students had gathered to argue and debate closed to them, students defied the order. Arrests and riots resulted. To call attention to their concern that the university pay more attention to the individual, in keeping with the American ideals of individualism and democracy, the students seized the administration building. The Governor sent in state police. More arrests were made.

> University students organize to protest limitations on freedom, equality, individualism, and democracy.

Berkeley stands as the symbol of student protests of the 1960s, but protests and building seizures occurred at many other campuses as college students attracted to the American ideals of freedom and equality were frustrated by the limitations they found both in United States society and on college campuses. The Students for a Democratic Society (SDS), a group organized to give leadership to the student movement, articulated these frustrations in their Port Huron Statement. The Port Huron Statement condemned racism and poverty amidst plenty, the power of corporations and the military/industrial complex, and the Cold War. The Port Huron Statement called for a return to the great American ideals of freedom, equality, and democracy. The student movement that became identified with the New Left was active on the college campuses, in the anti-Vietnam protests, and in the political campaigns of 1968 and 1972. While student protests led to violence at times, the movement at first was modeled on the work of Dr. Martin Luther King, Jr. Like the Civil Rights Movement, it fragmented in the late 1960s, and some factions turned to violence. Student protests are another reflection of the fragmentation of society into "we" and "they." The movement lost influence in the 1970s.

THE WAR ON POVERTY

It was not only African Americans and students who were concerned about poverty in America. President Johnson was also. In 1962 Michael Harrington published a book, *The Other America*, in which he documented the prevalence of poverty in the United States. According to Harrington and government statistics, over 20 percent of the population lived in poverty. Kennedy, the millionaire, read the book and was ready to address the issue when he was assassinated. Johnson did address the issue with a comprehensive legislative program. Johnson's War on Poverty and related legislation provides another one of those reform periods that occur with cyclical regularity throughout American history.

The War on Poverty began with the Economic Opportunity Act of 1964, which established a job corps for training those without skills and a work experience program for unemployed parents. Project Headstart which prepared children of low income families for school, and Upward Bound, which helped prepare bright but impoverished and poorly prepared high schoolers for college. Project Headstart is considered the most successful program of the War on Poverty. Volunteers in Service to America (VISTA), a domestic Peace Corps, was established for those who wished to work with the poor to help alleviate problems of rural and urban poverty. Other acts came after Johnson's election as President in 1964.

In the 1964 election Republicans nominated Barry Goldwater, Senator from Arizona, who represented the very conservative side of the party. Johnson chose as his running mate the liberal Senator Hubert Humphrey of Minnesota. They won a one-sided victory, carrying forty-four states. Johnson then introduced his Great Society Program, which incorporated the War on Poverty.

> **Johnson overwhelmingly wins election in 1964.**

THE GREAT SOCIETY

Legislation rolled through Congress in 1965, all aimed at creating what President Johnson called the Great Society. In addition to the Civil Rights Act and the Voting Act, there were environmental, educational, and cultural laws passed. The first Water Quality and Air Quality Acts establishing federal clean water and air standards were passed in response to the first burst of environmental awareness the nation experienced.

An elementary and secondary school act, the first providing direct aid ($1.3 billion) to this age group, and a higher education act providing federally funded college scholarships were passed. Education in America had always been supported and operated by local authorities, and the federal government except for the 1957 National Defense Education Act had not been involved in direct financing until the Great Society legislation.

The National Foundation for the Arts and Humanities was established to provide funding for artists, writers, musicians, and scholars in the humanities as opposed to the sciences. The National Science Foundation had previously been endowed by the government to support scientists.

An Omnibus Housing Bill (OHB) provided support for home building. The establishment of the Cabinet-level Housing and Urban Affairs Department (HUD) was an acknowledgment that our cities were as important as our agriculture. The Department of Housing and Urban Affairs was to administer the government housing and urban programs designed to solve urban problems such as the lack of affordable housing.

A new immigration law abandoned the national quota system established after World War I. It set a total number for immigrants from the Western Hemisphere (120,000) and the rest of the world (170,000) with no more than 20,000 from any one country. The dislocations caused by wars since 1965 have led to many more immigrants coming to America than set in the law.

Finally, in 1965 the first national health insurance measure, the Medicare Act, was passed. It combined hospital insurance for retired people with a voluntary plan to cover doctors' bills.

> **The Medicare Act establishes the first nationally funded health insurance measure.**

Medicaid was established to give grants to the states to administer medical aid to the poor who were not retired. Medicaid was another part of the War on Poverty.

In the next three years Congress passed other legislation including the Highway Safety Act and National Traffic and Motor Vehicle Safety Act, both of them inspired by Ralph Nader, who became the nation's most articulate spokesperson for national consumer rights[5]. Also passed was a raise in the minimum wage, the establishment of a Cabinet Department of Transportation, and a Clean Water Restoration Act.

However, the war in Vietnam became more and more the focus of the nation, and Johnson was faced with the economic dilemma of how much more could be spent on domestic policies when money was needed to fight the war. The dilemma has been described as "deciding between guns and butter." Johnson's response was to keep domestic programs but to create no new ones. Fortunately, the gross national product (GNP) grew rapidly, stimulated by the 1964 tax cut, and government revenues increased. These revenues helped finance the War on Poverty.

The expanding economy provided jobs that helped reduce the number living in poverty. Both the absolute numbers and the percentage of those living below the poverty line decreased dramatically, from almost 25 percent in 1962 to less than 12 percent ten years later, but the War on Poverty put a strain on the economy.

In retrospect, some scholars question its effectiveness, suggesting that it was the improving economy that changed the situation for the poor, and that legislation aiding impoverished families has perpetuated the pattern of poor education and adolescent pregnancies. Others praise the success of some programs such as Project Headstart. However it is judged, the War on Poverty was motivated by those American values of concern for others and a desire for equality. It reflected the attitude we all must work together and not the we versus they attitude.

Meanwhile, during the Kennedy and Johnson years the Cold War continued, and money had to be spent on United States defense.

B. FOREIGN POLICY ISSUES

KENNEDY AND CUBA

Kennedy inherited from the Eisenhower administration a new situation in Cuba. In 1959 after years of guerrilla warfare, Fidel Castro defeated the Cuban dictator, Batista. Castro had received some of his education in the United States, and it was hoped he would establish a democratic government for Cuba. Instead he moved to break the power of American business over the Cuban economy by nationalizing foreign industries and establishing a Communist government. Eisenhower authorized the CIA to train Cuban refugees for invasion of their country. Kennedy accepted the CIA plan to have the refugees land at the Bay of Pigs on the southern coast of Cuba in April 1961, only three months after his inauguration.

The Bay of Pigs invasion was a disaster—the Cuban people did not rise up to support the invaders. The planning had been poor, and the invaders were captured. Castro turned to the Soviet

> The Cuban Missile Crisis brings the world to the brink of nuclear war.

[5] consumer rights *The rights consumers have to good quality, safe products. Several laws have been passed since 1964, protecting consumers from the workmanship of manufacturers.*

Union for support. The CIA then planned to assassinate Castro, but the plots failed. The Soviet Union agreed to send missiles and nuclear weapons secretly to Cuba. On October 14, 1962, a U2 spy plane spotted missile sites being set up in Cuba.

The administration saw the missiles as a threat to United States security. As a response to the Soviet show of force, Kennedy's advisors suggested everything from a United States invasion of Cuba to peaceful negotiation in response to the threat. A naval blockade of Cuba was decided upon to prevent Russian ships from delivering missiles. Kennedy announced this decision on national television on October 22 as ships went into position and planes loaded with nuclear weapons circled the sky. It has been said that Kennedy and Nikita Khrushchev, leader of the Russians, were eyeball to eyeball and Khrushchev blinked. When the United States stopped a Soviet ship, Khrushchev offered to withdraw the missiles if the United States would guarantee Cuba's sovereignty. Later he added the United States should remove United States missiles from Turkey.

Kennedy agreed to guarantee the sovereignty of Cuba; Khrushchev removed the missiles; the United States ended the blockade; nuclear war was averted. Later the United States withdrew its missiles from Turkey.

A telephone hotline between Moscow and Washington was agreed upon soon after the crisis to aid communication between the two capitals in case of another crisis. It is generally agreed that, in the last two weeks of October 1962, the world came closer to a nuclear war than at any other time in the Cold War.

The Cuban Missile Crisis was considered a great success for Kennedy. In the 1980s, as the Cold War ended, Russian, Cuban, and United States scholars of the crisis discussed their findings together. The Cuban scholars said their research showed Castro would not have asked for missiles if there had been no Bay of Pigs or CIA attempts on his life. It is clear United States reliance on military force to counter Communist force bears some responsibility for the Cuban Missile Crisis. Likewise, Khrushchev and Castro share responsibility for their collaboration on missile placement and their testing of the United States' resolve to stand up to a Communist threat in the Western Hemisphere.

The crisis showed that the young Kennedy, a Democrat, could be tough on Communism, as tough as the Republicans. Kennedy had stood up to those people who were different. He had confronted the devil. The Russians, however, felt humiliated and increased their arms buildup.

A debate still continues on whether the United States should have taken the world to the brink of nuclear war over the Cuban missiles. What do you think? There is a large amount of information on the topic if you wish to pursue the issue.

THE BERLIN WALL

Prior to the Cuban Missile Crisis there had been another crisis in Berlin. With the election of Kennedy, the Russians asked for new negotiations on the status of occupied Berlin. The United States declined, and Kennedy called up the National Guard for federal military service. The Russian reaction to this show of force was to build a wall separating their sector of Berlin from the area occupied by

> The Berlin Wall intensifies the Cold War and symbolizes the division of Europe.

the three Western Allies. The wall went up essentially overnight in August 1961. The wall confirmed the separation of Europe into East and West.

NUCLEAR ARMS

In 1958 the United States and the Soviet Union had both stopped nuclear testing, but in 1961, after the Berlin crisis, the Russians resumed testing. Then the United States also resumed underground testing. The arms race was on again. In July 1963, a treaty banning atmospheric testing was finally signed by the major powers except France and China, who were still developing their nuclear capacity. This was the first agreement to begin reduction on nuclear weapons.

THE PEACE CORPS AND ALLIANCE FOR PROGRESS

Kennedy's idealism and desire to have Americans "ask what they can do for their country," as he stated in his inaugural address, led to the establishment of the Peace Corps. Young Americans volunteered to use their skills in Third World countries. After brief orientation they worked on projects designed to help local conditions in rural and some urban settings abroad. Thousands of Americans served. The Peace Corps was an excellent example of the good heartedness and concern for others of the average American.

Kennedy's policy toward Central and South America was to have the nations of the Western Hemisphere work together in an Alliance for Progress in the hemisphere. The concept of the Alliance for Progress was excellent, but the funding, $20 million, was inadequate to address the hopes raised by the project. As has happened often in United States relations with its southern neighbors, good intentions were not fulfilled. In the 1960s the southern neighbors of the United States were not considered central to the Cold War as was Vietnam.

KENNEDY AND VIETNAM

Kennedy, in his years in office, increased the number of United States troops in Vietnam from approximately 2,000 to 16,000. However, the history of United States involvement in Vietnam begins long before Kennedy. Vietnam is the most important single issue the United States faced in the 50 years after the end of World War II and ranks with the Depression and World War II for its impact on 20th-century American history.

> Kennedy increases United States involvement in Vietnam.

Key Point To Remember

John F. Kennedy brought idealism and youthful vigor to the nation but achieved little in domestic legislation and was slow to embrace the Civil Rights Movement. After his assassination, Lyndon B. Johnson led the nation into another great period of reform with his War on Poverty and concept of the Great Society.

People To Remember

Stokely Carmichael   A leader of the Civil Rights Movement, organizer of the Student NonViolent Coordinating Committee; later accepted the need for violence to achieve full rights for African Americans; joined the Black Panthers.

Malcolm X   Most noted spokesperson for the Black Muslim movement; assassinated by fellow Black Muslims in 1965; inspired inner-city African-Americans with a sense of purpose and self-confidence. His approach to civil rights was very different from that of Martin Luther King, Jr.

John F. Kennedy   Naval war hero; Senator from Massachusetts; as President during the Cuban Missile Crisis he led the United States in a confrontation with the Soviet Union that came close to nuclear war; began the escalation of the war in Vietnam; his youth and charisma inspired confidence; he instituted the Peace Corps; he called for civil rights legislation before his assassination in 1963.

Links From The Past To The Present

1. Relations with Cuba continue to be a foreign policy issue for the United States.
2. Legislation has provided important guarantees of civil rights.
3. The problem of poverty in America remains unsolved.
4. United States involvement in Vietnam led to a war that still affects American society.

Dates

1961—Freedom Riders organized.
   Bay of Pigs.
   Berlin Wall built.

1962—Cuban Missile Crisis.
   The Other America published.

1963—*Letter from a Birmingham Jail* published.
   Civil Rights March on Washington.
   Treaty bans atmospheric testing of nuclear weapons.
   Assassination of John F. Kennedy, Johnson becomes President.

1964—Economic Opportunity Act.
   Civil Rights Act.
   Mississippi Freedom Democratic party (MFDP).
   Riot in Harlem.
   Selma march.
   Berkeley Free Speech Movement.
   Johnson elected President.

1965—Voting Rights Act.
   Immigration Act.
   Water Quality Act.
   Riot in Watts. Malcolm X assassinated.
   Great Society legislation passed.

1966—Black Panthers organized.

Questions

Identify each of the following:

Civil Rights Act of 1964	Peace Corps
SCLC	Cuban Missile Crisis
Black Muslims	Economic Opportunity Act
Watts	Medicare

Multiple Choice:

1. The following organizations provided important leadership of the early, nonviolent Civil Rights Movement:
   a. NAACP and the Black Muslims.
   b. SCLC and SNCC.
   c. CORE and the Black Panthers.

2. The main purpose of the Civil Rights Act of 1965 was to guarantee the right to
   a. vote in federal elections.
   b. access to accommodations in hotels and restaurants.
   c. sit-in at lunch counters and on buses.

3. Kennedy's relations with Cuba included all of the following except
   a. U2 spy plane finding missiles and a blockade of Cuba.
   b. sending U.S. troops to attack the Bay of Pigs.
   c. allowing the CIA to plot attacks on Fidel Castro's life.

4. The Cold War continued under Kennedy and Johnson with incidents such as
   a. the Cuban Missile Crisis and the escalation of the war in Vietnam.
   b. the Cuban Missile Crisis and the Alliance for Progress.
   c. the Berlin Wall and the War on Poverty.

II. The Vietnam War

BACKGROUND

United States interest in Vietnam did not begin with Kennedy or even Eisenhower. United States interest in Vietnam, then French Indochina, was one of the reasons the Japanese attacked Pearl Harbor in 1941. After the fall of France in 1941, the United States had warned the Japanese to stay out of the French colony. Negotiations got nowhere, and the Japanese seized the colony. United States–Japanese relations deteriorated and led to Pearl Harbor.

During World War II the Office of Strategic Services (OSS), the United States intelligence service, aided the Vietnamese nationalists led by Ho Chi Minh in their attacks on the Japanese. After the war Ho Chi Minh asked for United States support in establishing an independent Vietnam, but he was ignored. The United States officially supported the French as they tried to reestablish control over all of Vietnam.

War broke out between the French forces and Ho Chi Minh's Vietminh Movement. Ho Chi Minh had studied in Moscow, and, in the context of the Cold

War, the United States saw the Vietminh as another manifestation of the devil, the Communists, who were slowly taking over all of Asia.

The Communists under Mao Zedong had just gained control of mainland China, and the Korean War began in June 1950. Following the containment policy, Truman determined to block the Vietminh from gaining control of Indochina and sent military aid but not troops to support the French in their war.

In retrospect Ho Chi Minh appears first a nationalist fighting for independence and secondly a Communist, but it was difficult to make such distinctions in 1950. The French, even with United States aid, were unable to defeat the Vietminh, and when in 1954 French forces at the mountain outpost of Dien Bien Phu were surrounded and captured, the French began negotiations at Geneva for a peaceful settlement.

> The French fail to defeat Ho Chi Minh and the Vietminh.

The Geneva Accords granted independence to Vietnam as well as Laos and Cambodia. Vietnam was "temporarily" divided at the 17th Parallel into a North Vietnam ruled by Ho Chi Minh's Vietminh and a South Vietnam ruled by Ngo Dinh Diem. The Communists supported the North, and the United States supported Diem in the South. The Geneva Accords called for elections to unite the nation. Diem, supported by the Eisenhower administration, rejected that provision in 1955.

In 1956 Diem began a crackdown on those in the South who questioned his authority. In 1957 those opposing Diem began terrorist attacks on his troops, and in 1959 North Vietnam began sending aid to them. In 1960 Diem's opposition organized as the Vietcong or National Liberation Front. In the meantime Eisenhower sent military advisors to support the Diem government.

> The Vietcong are organized to fight the government of Ngo Dinh Diem.

By the time Kennedy became President, the United States had been involved directly or indirectly in Vietnam for 20 years. We were giving military aid and had 2,000 advisors there. As a Cold War warrior who was determined to win the war, Kennedy decided to increase United States aid. He sent more advisors to help the Diem government in what had become a war against the terrorist attacks of the Vietcong.

Before Kennedy was assassinated, it became clear that the Roman Catholic Diem did not have the support of the South Vietnamese people. In 1963 several Buddhist monks protested Diem's undemocratic tactics by immolating[6] themselves. The incidents were shown on United States television.

Television in the 1950s and 1960s became a very important factor in American politics as Americans viewed incidents such as the attack of police dogs on civil rights workers or Buddhist monks burning themselves alive and reacted with horror. The public's reaction as they saw freedom-loving people like themselves being attacked had to be considered by political leaders.

Kennedy's response to the South Vietnam situation was to approve a coup organized by the CIA to overthrow Diem. It was successful, but the United States was now committed to finding

> A coup supported by the United States overthrows Diem.

---

[6] immolate   *To kill as a sacrifice; the Buddhist monks set themselves on fire as a public sacrifice.*

Vietnam

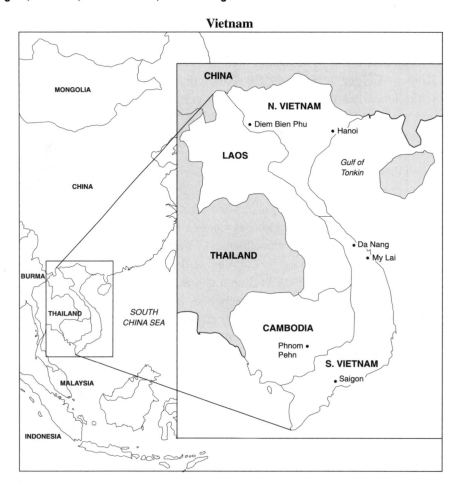

a successor to Diem who could rally the South Vietnamese people and defeat the Vietcong. The United States was never able to do so, and that was the tragedy of Vietnam. The North Vietnamese and the Vietcong were fighting for their freedom and independence from oppression from the other. No South Vietnamese leader could inspire his people the way Ho Chi Minh did. When the United States sent massive aid to the South, it was to support a regime that never won the masses to its side. The South Vietnamese government was seen by many Vietnamese as a puppet of the United States and not a national government. This was the situation Johnson faced when he became president.

AMERICANIZING THE WAR

With South Vietnam in turmoil after the Buddhist protests, there were calls for compromise and a coalition government of Vietcong and United States supported groups. Like Kennedy, Johnson, a novice in foreign affairs, saw the war in Vietnam as a Communist threat. Johnson would not compromise. Johnson adhered to the Domino Theory first expressed during the Eisenhower administration in the 1950s. The Domino Theory held that if one Southeast Asian nation fell to Communism, the others would all fall like a line of dominos.

Johnson wanted victory in Vietnam and in 1964 began a huge buildup of

American forces. In August it was reported that a United States destroyer in the Tonkin Gulf off North Vietnam had been attacked by small North Vietnamese gunboats. No clear evidence was submitted, but Johnson went to Congress with a request to use force against any North Vietnamese attacks. In the emotion and confusion of the moment, the Gulf of Tonkin Resolution was overwhelmingly passed by Congress. While not a declaration of war, Johnson used it as a justification for Americanizing the war. More troops were sent and became actively involved as the fighting escalated[7], and the bombing of Vietcong supply routes in Laos and of North Vietnam was begun.

> Congress passes the Gulf of Tonkin Resolution, and Johnson increases America's involvement in the war.

Johnson overwhelmingly won the 1964 presidential election, which seemed an endorsement of his Vietnam policy. After the Vietcong won a victory in February 1965, the Joint Chiefs of Staff asked Johnson for more military forces. This meant further escalation. After discussions, the decision was made to increase American forces rather than negotiate. Assistant Secretary of State George Ball, who in all the consultations had supported negotiations, declared in his memoir, *The Past has Another Pattern,* "our protracted involvement in the Vietnam War was an authentic tragedy—perhaps the most tragic error in American history."

JUNGLE FIGHTING

Fighting conditions in the jungles of the South and the hills of central Vietnam were horrible. There was no battle line. The Vietcong enemy could be anywhere or anyone. The United States dropped a defoliation agent, Agent Orange, to kill forest growth that hid the Vietcong camps, but this did not help and only harmed the agriculture of the South Vietnamese. Few United States troops spoke Vietnamese, and many Americans viewed them as ignorant peasants. Americans' feelings of superiority and intolerance for others not like themselves were manifested. American troops found their identity in priding themselves on being different from the Vietcong, the "gooks." In frustration, the United States forces committed atrocities both against their own officers who might force them into combat and against Vietnamese who might be an enemy.

THE MY LAI INCIDENT

The most shocking incident took place at My Lai, where troops on a search and destroy mission against the Vietcong massacred men, women, and children in the village of My Lai. The incident was not reported in the United States press for over a year, but when it was, it shocked the American nation. Yet it merely reflected the horrors and frustrations of a war where there was no clear line between the enemy and the defenders.

> The massacre at My Lai shocks Americans and makes clear the horrors of jungle warfare.

United States television reported daily on the war, which seemed to be getting nowhere. More troops were being sent; more bombs dropped—by the end of the Vietnam War more bomb tonnage was dropped on Vietnam than had been dropped

[7] escalate   *To increase or intensify; steady escalation of the United States war effort became the Johnson policy in Vietnam.*

throughout the world in World War II—yet the enemy would not surrender. Finally, Undersecretary of State George Ball and Secretary of Defense McNamara realized there was no way to victory, but they could not persuade the President of that. They resigned from the Johnson government in protest over the continued policy of escalation.

THE TET OFFENSIVE

By the start of 1968 the United States could claim a few minor successes, but the Vietcong forces still occupied almost half of South Vietnam as they had in 1964. After three years of fighting, the United States seemed to be nowhere. Then in January the Vietcong launched a nationwide offensive, the Tet Offensive, that rocked United States forces.

While the cities lost to the Vietcong were recaptured, the Tet Offensive showed how vulnerable United States forces were. The Joint Chiefs asked for 200,000 more troops but would not promise victory with them.

In early March Senator Eugene McCarthy, who ran as an anti-war candidate, made a surprisingly strong showing in the New Hampshire Democratic primary. The Senate Foreign Relations Committee held hearings on whether the war should continue. Antiwar protests were increasing. Some 500,000 protesters had gathered in New York City in the spring of 1967, and many of them burned their draft cards. Young men were leaving the country to avoid the draft. The mood of the nation, which had been strongly supportive of the Tonkin Gulf Resolution in 1964, was shifting.

Those opposing the war were called doves; those in favor, hawks. It was reminiscent of 1812, when the War Hawks from the West wanted war with England. At the end of March 1968, President Johnson announced he would not be a candidate for

> Hawks and doves express different opinions on the war.

reelection and that he was stopping the bombing of North Vietnam and would seek a negotiated settlement. Johnson had come to see the war was unwinnable by military effort but was not prepared, nor were the American people prepared, to simply withdraw and let the Vietnamese people negotiate their future.

The Vietnam War had taken Johnson's time and the government's money away from his plans for the Great Society and the War on Poverty. The Vietnam War had tragic consequences for the United States.

1968: PROTESTS

1968 is one of those years that can be viewed as a watershed in history. The Tet Offensive signaled that the United States would eventually withdraw from Vietnam. In April Martin Luther King, Jr. was assassinated, marking an end to one phase of the Civil Rights Movement. Rioting followed in over 150 cities. The race for the Democratic Party's presidential nomination was full of protest and violence. College youth had become active antiwar protesters, and many of them supported Eugene McCarthy's campaign. When Johnson withdrew, the race was wide open. Robert Kennedy, former Attorney

> 1968 stands as a watershed in American history.

General and brother of President John F. Kennedy, entered the race. He had strong support from African-Americans and former Kennedy supporters. He became the leading contender but was assassinated in June on the eve of his victory in the California presidential primary. He was shot by a young Palestinian upset by Kennedy's pro-Israel position.

With two political assassinations in three months, with riots in the inner cities, with antiwar protests growing, the nation seemed to be falling apart. Student protests, which had begun at Berkeley with the Free-Speech Movement, continued. Students at Columbia University, protesting the university's support of military-oriented research and the recruitment of students by such industries, the CIA, and the military, seized the administration building. Police forcefully removed them, and 150 were injured. Protests occurred at other colleges.

1968: ELECTIONS

Then at the Democratic Party convention in August in Chicago, antiwar student protesters, poor people led by Ralph Abernathy, Martin Luther King, Jr.'s successor as head of SCLC, and Yippies from the Youth International Party, all gathered to express their views before the Democrats. The contest for the nomination was between Eugene McCarthy, the antiwar liberal Senator from Minnesota, and Hubert Humphrey, Johnson's vice president.

The Democratic Convention in Chicago is besieged by protesters but nominates Hubert Humphrey, Johnson's Vice President.

Humphrey carried the stigma of having been in the administration that had escalated the war. In spite of his liberal record on domestic issues, there was no indication he had ever opposed the war. The situation around the convention hall was tense. Finally, the police and National Guard were called in to disperse the protesters, and fighting broke out. Again Americans watched the actions on television.

Humphrey won the nomination but in the campaign was unable to separate himself from Johnson's war. George Wallace, Democratic Governor of Alabama and a strong segregationist, ran as a third party candidate opposing the Democrat's stand on civil rights. The Republicans nominated Richard Nixon, Eisenhower's vice president. Nixon and his vice presidential candidate, Spiro Agnew of Maryland, won the election but with a minority of the popular vote as Governor Wallace received 13 percent of the votes cast—a strong showing for a third party and a clear indication there were still strong anti-civil rights feelings in the nation.

Nixon had first gained prominence with his anti-Communist positions. He was prepared to negotiate a Vietnam settlement, but he was not prepared to "lose the war." As a minority President, Nixon in his victory speech called on the country to come together. 1968 had revealed a great split in the nation. It took a long time for the division to heal, and the scars are still there.

VIETNAMIZATION

Nixon and his Foreign Policy Advisor, Henry Kissinger, began secret negotiations with the North Vietnamese and announced a slow withdrawal of United States forces. Nixon's policy was to train the South Vietnamese army to take over the war. It met

Nixon orders an invasion of Cambodia and provokes more student protests.

with limited success since the South Vietnamese were not fully behind their government. In 1970 Nixon ordered the invasion of Cambodia where the Vietcong had established safe camps and supply bases. Students on college campuses staged protests. At Kent State University in Ohio, National Guard forces fired on the student protesters and killed four. Protests erupted on over 500 college campuses. The CIA undertook assassinations of South Vietnamese civilians who supported an immediate end to the war.

THE END OF THE WAR

The war and negotiations dragged on. Congress repealed the Gulf of Tonkin Resolution, yet Nixon and Kissinger were convinced they had to apply military pressure on Vietnam to prove the United States would not simply withdraw. They mined the harbor of Haiphong, a major port, and resumed the bombing of the North in 1972. After years of private talks during which thousands more Americans were killed, formal negotiations began in 1972 and a cease fire was reached in January 1973, soon after Nixon had won reelection. The negotiated terms called for a coalition government in South Vietnam including the Vietcong.

If the Geneva Accords had been adhered to in 1956, the government that would have been established by elections most likely would have been a coalition government for all Vietnam, but Dulles and Eisenhower saw the North Vietnamese as the enemy and would not compromise. A coalition government could also have been had in 1963 if Kennedy had undertaken negotiations and again in 1969 if Johnson had done so. Part of the tragedy of the Vietnam War is that what it achieved could have been achieved years before through negotiation and without war. It suggests the importance of understanding your capabilities and the history of your allies and enemies. This is one of the great challenges of any war situation.

> An end to the war is negotiated, and its terms suggest the tragedy of the Vietnam conflict.

The 1973 agreement also called for the withdrawal of all United States troops as soon as all United States prisoners of war were released. Prisoners were released, though some soldiers are still listed as "Missing in Action" (MIA) and the last United States forces were withdrawn on March 29, 1973.

There were violations of the cease fire on both sides. The new President, Gerald Ford, asked Congress for more arms for the South, but Congress refused. The Communists mounted an attack on the Saigon government. In April 1975 South Vietnam's capital, Saigon, fell to the Communists and was soon renamed Ho Chi Minh City after the North Vietnamese leader. The war was over.

The strains the war placed on American society are still felt. The cost of the war in killed and wounded (over 350,000 Americans and many thousands of Vietnamese) and money (over $150 billion to the United States alone) was staggering, but the cost of the war cannot be measured only in those terms. The division the war created between hawks and doves, the disillusionment it created in the young, the anger it created among African-Americans and poor, many more of whom fought in Vietnam than did wealthy whites, the horror and terror of the fighting conditions, and the lack

> The Vietnam War still affects us today.

of appreciation felt by disillusioned veterans are still part of the American experience and affect life in the United States.

Today whenever the United States government considers major foreign policy decisions, especially ones that might involve military forces, the "Lessons of Vietnam" affect the decisions. One lesson is that military force alone cannot establish viable governments—the support of the people is essential. This was true in Vietnam, Somalia, and Yugoslavia at the end of the 20th century. With easy access worldwide to weapons and to information from television, the Internet, and other technologies, local leaders and the people are aware of events and can participate in them. The fact that outsiders cannot impose effective democratic governments is another lesson from Vietnam, one that has been hard for American policy makers to learn.

Some historians and political leaders suggested that the successful United States actions under George H. W. Bush that forced Iraq out of Kuwait in 1990 counteracted the failure in Vietnam and marked a new beginning for United States foreign policy and self-image. However, the Iraq War under George W. Bush turned into a situation in many ways similar to that of Vietnam, as did the war in Afghanistan.

Key Point To Remember

United States involvement in Vietnam was an "authentic tragedy" that divided the United States and achieved little for the Vietnamese people. The tragic consequences and "lessons" of Vietnam continue to be important in the development of United States domestic and foreign policy.

People To Remember

Lyndon Baines Johnson   United States Senator from Texas, Senate Majority Leader, vice president under John F. Kennedy; became president after Kennedy's assassination; declared a War on Poverty and set the goal of a Great Society, both to be achieved through legislation and the leadership of the federal government; the success of his domestic programs was jeopardized by the increasing involvement of the United States in the Vietnam War, which led to his decision not to seek reelection in 1968.

Links From The Past To The Present

1. The "lessons" of Vietnam for foreign policy makers still affect decisions.

2. The strengths and limits of bombing to bring victory is one "lesson" of World War II, Vietnam, and the Iraq War.

3. It is always important when conducting foreign policy to have an understanding of your enemy, as the Vietnam War clearly illustrates.

Dates

1941—United States warned Japan not to seize Vietnam.

1953—United States aided French in Vietnam.

1954—Fall of Dien Bien Phu.
    Geneva Accords.

1955—South Vietnam rejected elections.

1960—Vietcong organized.

1963—Buddhist monks opposed Diem.

Coup overthrew Diem.

1964—Massive buildup of U.S. forces began.

Gulf of Tonkin Resolution.

1967—Draft card burning protest in New York City.

1968—Tet offensive.

Martin Luther King, Jr. assassinated.

Johnson withdrew from presidential race.

Robert Kennedy assassinated.

Protests at Democratic Party Convention.

Riots in cities.

Richard Nixon defeated Hubert Humphrey for presidency.

1970—Cambodia invaded.

1971—Kent State killing.

1972—Nixon won reelection.

1973—Cease-fire signed.

U.S. forces withdrawn from Vietnam.

1975—Saigon captured by the Communists.

Questions
Identify each of the following:

Geneva Accord 1954	My Lai	Viet Minh
Vietcong	Tet Offensive	Ho Chi Minh
Tonkin Gulf Resolution	Kent State	George Ball

Multiple Choice:

1. The Geneva Accords in 1954 called for
   a. withdrawal of United States forces after prisoners of war were returned.
   b. division of Vietnam at the 17th Parallel and later elections to unite the country.
   c. the French to remain in the country to preserve order.

2. The Diem government lost the support of the United States government when
   a. it attacked North Vietnam.
   b. it turned to Russia for aid.
   c. it attacked Buddhist monks who responded by burning themselves to death.

3. The United States escalated the war by bombing
   a. North Vietnam and Vietcong supply lines in Laos.
   b. Saigon, the capital of South Vietnam.
   c. Vietcong bases in Southern China.

4. After the United States withdrew its forces from South Vietnam
   a. the South Vietnamese invaded North Vietnam.
   b. Saigon fell to the North Vietnamese in April 1975.
   c. peace reigned throughout South Vietnam.

III. The Presidencies of Richard Nixon and Gerald Ford

THE COLD WAR AND DETENTE

After years of brinkmanship and containment, President Nixon and Henry Kissinger, at first Nixon's National Security Advisor and later Secretary of State for both Nixon and Ford, began a new approach to the Communist world known as détente[8]. The policy of détente acknowledged the differences between the United States and the USSR but sought through negotiations and meetings to achieve limited agreements on issues of common concern. Nixon had gained his reputation as an anti-Communist Republican Congressman from California in the late 1940s even before the era of McCarthyism. As a result, he was able to conduct negotiations with both the People's Republic of China and the Soviet Union without the threat of being called "soft on Communism"—a charge often leveled by American conservatives at Democrats.

Negotiations led to a trade agreement that provided for large amounts of surplus grain to be sold to the Soviets at low prices. The agreement helped United States farmers and helped the USSR feed its people. It was mutually beneficial. It was another approach to the perpetual farm problem of overproduction in America. Negotiations on arms control led, in 1972, to the signing of the Strategic Arms Limitation Treaty (SALT), which limited the number of antiballistic missiles (ABMs) each side could have. Negotiators also agreed to a freeze on the number of offensive weapons each side would hold.

RELATIONS WITH CHINA

The most dramatic move made by Nixon and Kissinger as part of détente was to open talks with the Communist leaders of the People's Republic of China, often referred to in the United States as Red China in order to distinguish it from "Free China," established on the island of Taiwan by Jiang Jieshi (Chiang Kai-shek) and recognized as the government of China by the United States. After the Chinese Communist victory in 1949, the United States had refused to recognize the government of Mao Zedong and both the Korean and Vietnam wars strained United States-China relations.

Although China and the Soviet Union were Communist nations, they had many differences, and these became intensified in the 1960s. By negotiating with the People's Republic, Nixon hoped to encourage the split. The Chinese welcomed United States support and more particularly the opportunity to trade with the United States. Henry Kissinger conducted secret negotiations with the Chinese leaders for several years, culminating in a visit by Nixon to Beijing, the capital of the People's Republic of China, in 1972. The United States agreed to support the entry of the People's Republic into the United Nations and its taking over the Security Council seat reserved for China. In 1979 formal relations between the two nations were established with the exchange of ambassadors.

[8] détente   *A relaxing and easing of tensions between nations.*

While détente did not end confrontations between the Soviets and the United States, relations seemed less tense. Nixon visited Moscow and Leonid Brezhnev, the new Soviet leader, came to the United States for summit meetings. President Ford continued the Nixon policies of détente and kept Henry Kissinger on as Secretary of State. Ford went to China, held two summit meetings with the Soviet leaders, and agreed to further arms limitations. Kissinger clearly believed the United States-Soviet relations were at the center of international affairs, yet there were other international crises to be handled in the Nixon years.

AFRICA AND SOUTH AMERICA

As African nations became independent in the 1960s and South Africa intensified its enforcement of Apartheid, the United States sought allies and attempted to block any possible Soviet influence in the area. President Ford supported anti-Communist guerrillas in the civil war that broke out in the Portuguese colony of Angola. United States investments abroad were large and, according to the Nixon-Kissinger policies, had to be protected. Aid, both economic and military, continued to be sent abroad, but the former did little to redress the greatly increasing gap between the poor nations, referred to as the Third World[9], and the traditionally rich, industrialized nations of Europe, North America, and Japan. Rapid population growth contributed to the gap and stimulated government support for research in contraceptives. One result was the pill that had little impact on Third World population growth but greatly affected moral and cultural attitudes in the United States.

> Ford militarily supports anti-Communist forces in spite of détente.

When a Marxist, Salvatore Allende, was elected President of Chile, the CIA intervened, and a military junta overthrew Allende. The United States government was not going to tolerate another potential Castro in the Americas in spite of détente.

THE MIDDLE EAST

After the Suez crisis of 1956, peace did not come to the Middle East. In 1967 Israel successfully attacked its Arab neighbors in a dramatic Six Day War. Israel more than quadrupled its size. The Arabs were shocked. They refused to sign a peace treaty. Under the leadership of Yassir Arafat, the Arabs who had fled Israel during the 1948 and Six Day wars organized the Palestine Liberation Organization (PLO), pledged to retaking their homeland and destroying Israel. In 1973 in the Yom Kippur War, Egypt and Syria attacked Israel. To support the Arabs, the recently formed Organization of Petroleum Exporting Countries (OPEC) placed an embargo on their exports of oil to the United States.

Nixon sent Kissinger to the Middle East to find a peaceful solution. A cease fire was put in place, and then Kissinger undertook for the United States a year of "shuttle diplomacy," flying frequently between Middle Eastern capitals seeking

---

[9] Third World   *Undeveloped or developing countries that are not aligned with either the Communist or non-Communist blocs; first used in the 1950s by French President de Gaulle.*

agreements between the Arabs and Israel. This approach continued under President Ford. The result was that in 1975 Kissinger finally got Egypt and Israel to agree to a United Nations peace-keeping force in the Sinai Peninsula. The United Nations force separated the two armies, but Israel refused to withdraw from the territories she occupied in 1967. Since 1948 the Arabs and Israelis have defined themselves in we/they terms which made Kissinger's task particularly difficult. Neither side was then ready to find a mutually satisfactory win/win solution. As a result, Kissinger's diplomacy failed to bring a peace agreement.

OPEC ended its oil embargo in 1974, but not before oil prices had more than tripled worldwide and inflation began. The resulting impact on the world economy was widespread—a foretaste of the oil crisis of 2008 that was rooted in the rising

> The world economy is affected by OPEC.

demand for oil and the falling value of the dollar. OPEC still exercises some control over world oil prices. All industrialized nations, especially the United States with its powerful economy, depend on a steady supply of oil. Many foreign policy initiatives of the United States in recent years are connected to this dependency.

NIXON'S DOMESTIC POLICIES

Nixon's view of domestic government was clearly that of a conservative who did not want innovations and preferred the way things were in the past. Nixon attempted to block the renewal of the Voting Rights Act of 1965 and to delay integration of the Mississippi school system ordered by the federal courts. He supported an antibusing law to block the use of buses to integrate schools, but Congress failed to pass the legislation. When Chief Justice Earl Warren retired, Nixon appointed a more conservative Chief Justice, Warren Burger. Later two of Nixon's very conservative, southern Supreme Court appointees were rejected by the Senate.

Nixon introduced a program, the New Federalism, to give more power to the states. He asked Congress to revise the way federal programs were financed by distributing $30 billion to the states for their use without the federal government prescribing

> Nixon presents a conservative program of New Federalism.

how the money should be spent. Nixon also proposed that states take responsibility for most welfare payments, but the proposal was not pushed through Congress.

In 1969 Nixon persuaded Congress to cut spending and raise taxes. The economic situation in the United States had deteriorated due to growing international competition, the cost of the Great Society, and the Vietnam War. Federal deficits had grown in order to finance both guns and butter. Congress gave Nixon authority to regulate prices and wages, but he was reluctant to enforce strong measures. The rate of inflation grew and the situation worsened after the OPEC oil embargo in 1973.

During the Nixon years Congress passed several laws not supported by the administration. These included the strengthening of the Clean Air and Water Pollution Acts in response to growing environmental concerns exemplified by the organization of Earth Day 1970. Congress also extended the vote to 18-year-olds by passing a constitutional amendment, which the states quickly ratified. Proponents argued if 18-year-olds could serve in Vietnam, they were old enough to vote.

DOMESTIC PROTESTS AND THE 1972 ELECTION CAMPAIGN

During Nixon's first term, the 1968 mood of protest continued. Radical groups bombed business offices. African-American protests increased. The crime rate, particularly of violent crimes, grew dramatically. In spite of his statements that he wanted to bring the country together, Nixon's policies and views of government increased the divisions. Students rallied against the escalation of the Vietnam War. The death of four students at Kent State symbolizes these divisions.

Nixon planned a reelection campaign for 1972 based on a southern strategy, designed to attract traditionally Democratic voters to the Republican Party. His civil rights proposals and conservative, southern Supreme Court appointees were part of this strategy. Nixon appealed to what he termed "the silent majority" of middle America who wanted "law and order" and not the permissiveness he claimed was the policy of the Democrats, who were "soft on crime and drugs," and who supported civil rights, black militancy, and student radicals. The strategy worked, and Nixon and Spiro Agnew won an overwhelming victory over the liberal Democratic candidate George McGovern. Nixon and Agnew got over 60 percent of the popular vote compared to the 43 percent they received in the three-party election of 1968.

> In spite of continuing antiwar and student protests, Nixon appeals to "the silent majority" and wins reelection in 1972.

THE WATERGATE BREAK-IN

In spite of his brilliant moves in foreign policy, Nixon did not trust either the American people or his own abilities to appeal to them. He resorted to underhanded and illegal measures, apparently convinced they were the only way to protect the nation from those he perceived as radicals and un-American—the student protesters, the civil rights leaders, the hippies, and those not part of the "silent majority." Nixon even had an "enemies" list—a classic example of dividing the world into us and them.

On June 17, 1972, during the beginning of the presidential campaign, five men were caught after breaking into the Democratic Party headquarters at the Watergate apartment complex in Washington. On June 22, Nixon said his administration was in no way involved in the Watergate break-in. Thus began the Watergate scandal and cover-up. It unwound slowly over the next two years and culminated in the resignation of President Nixon.

After the break-in, Nixon ordered his Chief of Staff, H. R. Haldeman, to keep the FBI from investigating. At first the cover-up worked. Little attention was paid to the Watergate break-in during the campaign, and the voters ignored it. However, President Nixon's cover-up was investigated and a grand jury was eventually established.

THE WATERGATE CASE

In March 1974 the Watergate case reached its climax. The Watergate grand jury handed down indictments against White House staffers Haldeman and John

Ehrlichman, former Attorney General John Mitchell, and four White House aides. President Nixon was named a co-conspirator, but he was not indicted. During the investigation, it was learned that Nixon had tape recordings of all conversations in his office. Nixon at first refused to release the tapes. When he was forced to do so by court orders, the tapes—despite an eighteen-minute blank—revealed White House involvement in the cover-up. Calls for impeachment grew.

> Tape recordings of conversations in Nixon's office reveal White House involvement in the Watergate scandal.

Before impeachment proceedings could begin, on August 8, 1973, Richard Nixon announced his resignation as president of the United States effective the next day. He is the only president to be forced to resign his office. President Gerald Ford in September 1974 pardoned Nixon, believing it was time to put Watergate behind the nation. Nixon was never indicted for a crime and never admitted any wrongdoing. In the years until his death he regained some stature as historians acknowledged his important foreign policy contributions.

Watergate ranks as one of the worst scandals in the history of the nation. The reaction of Congress to Watergate and the Nixon resignation was to pass legislation to address the perceived reasons for the Watergate scandal. Congress acted to limit presidential power with the War Powers Act in 1973. This controversial act required Congressional approval if combat troops are committed for longer than 90 days in any situation. Congress also set limits on the amount of financial contributions and expenditures allowed in presidential campaigns—remember, Watergate began as a campaign issue. Congress also extended the Freedom of Information Act, requiring the government to act promptly when information is sought by the public and to prove the need on national security grounds whenever classifying information as secret.

> Congress moves to limit presidential power.

Whether the measures addressed the true reasons for Watergate is debatable. The mood of the nation as a result of the Vietnam War, the frustrations over the failure to attain the Great Society, the deterioration of the economic situation, and the personality of President Nixon were all factors in the Watergate scandal. No legislation could address these issues. While Watergate dragged on for two years, it weakened the President's credibility and effectiveness as leader of the nation. Before the Watergate case was closed, twenty-nine members of Nixon's administration were indicted, pleaded guilty, or were convicted for their part in the Watergate scandal.

RESIGNATION OF VICE PRESIDENT AGNEW

While the Watergate cover-up was being exposed, Vice President Spiro Agnew resigned his office after he was accused of taking bribes while serving as an official in Maryland. He was also accused of income tax illegalities. Following the provisions of the recently adopted Amendment XXV on presidential succession, Nixon nominated and the Senate confirmed Congressman Gerald R. Ford of Michigan as vice president. At the same time Nixon was assessed $500,000 in back taxes by the IRS for failure to pay all his taxes between 1969 and 1972 and for using federal money to improve his private homes. The government appeared bogged down in scandals and disgrace.

THE FORD PRESIDENCY

When Nixon resigned, Gerald Ford became president, the first not elected by the Electoral College. He nominated Governor Nelson Rockefeller, long time spokesperson of the more liberal wing of the Republican Party, as his vice president. Ford continued Nixon's domestic policies.

> President Ford continues Nixon's domestic policies.

The economy worsened and unemployment rose. The OPEC oil embargo pushed inflation from 3 percent in 1972 to 11 percent in 1974. Baby boomers needed jobs at a time when Americans were rejecting gas-guzzling cars made in Detroit because of high oil prices. Increased foreign competition, particularly from Japan in autos and electronics, hurt the economy. Many new jobs were added, but they were in service industries—restaurants and selling—rather than in heavy manufacturing. American productivity, the amount an individual produced, did not keep pace with the Japanese and Europeans. As a result, profits did not rise as wages did. The economic picture of the nation was changing.

Ford's response, Whip Inflation Now, or WIN, called for voluntary restraints on wages and price increases to combat inflation. He did not want the government to set wage or price controls, but he did call for tax cuts, which, according to theory, would stimulate industry. Ford tried to cut spending for the programs of the Great Society, but with limited success.

Ford's policies were not successful. The nation was in an economic recession—the post-New Deal term for what had been termed panics or depressions. The New Deal had ended laissez-faire as a federal government economic policy and had established that the federal government should act to affect economic conditions of inflation and recession. The Kennedy/Johnson tax cuts had stimulated the economy, but conditions were different in the mid-1970s, and it was not until the Reagan presidency that inflation was reduced and the economic situation improved.

President Ford continued the policy of détente begun by President Nixon. Henry Kissinger remained as Secretary of State. Ford visited China, following Nixon's policy of seeking understanding and trade, and he held summit meetings with the leaders of the Soviet Union. Further arms limitations were agreed to with the Soviets. The major foreign policy issues of Ford's administration focused on the aftermath of the Yom Kippur War and the OPEC embargo (see above).

ELECTION OF 1976

Governor Ronald Reagan of California, a strong conservative, contested the Republican primary with Gerald Ford. Ford won the nomination. Jimmy Carter, Governor of Georgia, worked hard for over two years to win name recognition. In the Democratic Party primaries he did well enough to gain his party's nomination. He ran as an outsider—one who was not linked to Washington

> Jimmy Carter, an outsider, wins the Democratic nomination and the presidency.

and so would bring a new spirit and integrity to the presidency. Carter and his vice president, Walter Mondale of Minnesota, defeated Ford and Bob Dole, who was chosen as the Republican vice presidential candidate replacing Rockefeller. Ford had supported this to appeal to the more conservative members of the party.

To suggest the new spirit and mood he would bring to the nation, Carter and his wife, Rosalynn, after his inauguration at the capital, walked at the head of the traditional parade down Pennsylvania Avenue from the Capitol to the White House. The nation was ready for this new spirit. Unfortunately, the Carter presidency for many reasons was unable to achieve its goals of a more democratic and just society.

SUMMARY

In the period from 1960 to 1976, the United States had to focus on major domestic changes brought about by the Civil Rights Movement. These changes forced Americans to consider who they were as a people and to face the issue of defining who is an American. Is America to be a pluralistic society, accepting all people as citizens or simply those people who share certain traits or characteristics? The many movements that grew out of the Civil Rights Movement emphasized this need for new understandings.

In foreign affairs the continuing Cold War emphasized the differences between peoples, and while Presidents Nixon and Ford attempted through detente to bring the opposing Western and Communist views together, Presidents Kennedy and Johnson re-inforced the we/they mentality in their commitment to the war in Vietnam. The war not only reinforced the differences between the Vietcong and the Americans fighting for the South Vietnamese but created divisions within the American people between hawks and doves, the older citizens and the young, the wealthy and the poor. These divisions forced Lyndon Johnson not to seek a second term and led Nixon into the Watergate fiasco. It is important that people know who they are and what they stand for, but overzealous commitment to an extreme position can lead to decisions that benefit no one. Students of American history can clearly see the dangers of such zealous commitment in the actions and statements of presidents and ordinary citizens in the period 1960–1976; and these dangers can be found at other times in our history.

Key Points To Remember

Nixon's policy of detente relaxed Cold War tensions and led to agreements with the Soviet Union and the recognition of the People's Republic of China. Domestically, the Watergate break-in and resulting scandal destroyed Nixon's credibility and forced his resignation.

Equality and Freedom—The Basis of America's Ideology
Equality
The Declaration of Independence states that "all men are created equal" and throughout American history some people have struggled to make this literally true. Many others have interpreted the phrase to mean all men (and women) should have an equal *opportunity* in life. These two views of equality are often in conflict. To achieve either view of equality, laws are needed and these laws restrict the freedom of individuals.

Freedom
Throughout American history many individuals have emphasized freedom as being the basis of American life. They emphasize that we fought England in the Revolution to defend our freedom and have continued the struggle to the present. While many would support equality as an ideal, they love their freedom more and so oppose laws and other methods used to create equality of all people or situations of equal opportunity. They believe that only by allowing full freedom for individual actions can we achieve our best in society.

People To Remember
Richard Nixon   Congressman from California, vice president under Eisenhower, 37th president of the United States; he was forced to resign the presidency as a result of the Watergate break-in and resulting scandal; he negotiated an end to the Vietnam War and achieved major foreign policy successes through his policy of detente with the USSR and by his recognition of the People's Republic of China; his policy of "New Federalism" attempted to give more power to the individual states.

Links From The Past To The Present
1. Scandals in the federal government recur periodically and have an important impact on the nation.
2. Disarmament negotiations have been an aspect of United States foreign policy since the first Hague Conference in 1899.
3. It is always important to be prepared to negotiate with "the enemy" regardless of who it is.
4. The importance of the American legal system for maintaining honesty and integrity in government has been important in our history from the *McCulloch* v. *Madison* decision to the Watergate Case to the Iran-Contra Affair.

Dates
1967—Six Day War between Israel and her Arab neighbors.
1970—First Earth Day Celebration focused attention on environment.

1972—SALT Treaty signed.
   Nixon visited Beijing, People's Republic of China. Watergate break-in.
   Nixon reelected President.

1973—Yom Kippur War; OPEC Oil Embargo.
   Vice President Spiro Agnew resigned; Gerald Ford named vice president.
   Nixon resigned presidency; Gerald Ford became 38th president; Nelson
   Rockefeller named vice president.
   War Powers Act.

1974—OPEC Oil Embargo ended.

1975—Peace-keeping force sent to Sinai after Kissinger's Shuttle Diplomacy.

1976—Jimmy Carter elected 39th president.

Questions

Identify each of the following:

OPEC	SALT
Southern Strategy	Watergate
Gerald Ford	Yom Kippur War
People's Republic of China	War Powers Act

Multiple Choice:

1. Henry Kissinger undertook shuttle diplomacy in the Middle East in order to bring
   a settlement to
   a. the Six Day War.
   b. the OPEC embargo and the Yom Kippur War.
   c. the poverty in the area.

2. The Nixon concept of government was called
   a. the New Frontier.
   b. the New Federalism.
   c. the Pentagon Papers.

3. Gerald Ford was the first President
   a. to travel to China.
   b. to have Henry Kissinger as Secretary of State.
   c. not to be elected by the Electoral College.

Open-ended, Analysis Questions

The following questions require analysis and reflection. You are encouraged to bring
to your answer information and ideas from many sources. The answers should be
presented in composition or essay style, but they may be used to initiate discussion.
The questions put you in the role of the historian, gathering information to support
your personal perspective on the question.

1. "A belief in freedom and equality define who Americans are yet these beliefs are
   often in conflict."

Pick four examples from United States history of an event, incident, or legislation in which freedom and equality were in conflict. In an essay describe the conflict in each situation and whether the resolution was more in favor of freedom or of equality. *(Note: McCarthyism (an event), Anthracite Coal Strike of 1902 (an incident), and Alien and Sedition Acts (legislation) are examples of what is meant by an event, incident, or legislation which might be considered in this essay.)*

2. In an essay, trace the history of the Civil Rights Movement from its beginnings to 1976. Would you have tried to actively participate in the movement if you had been alive? Why or why not?

3. Which of the following three presidents do you consider the most successful? Why? Use specific information to support your answer. *(Note: In your answer you must explain your understanding of successful. In proving that one was more successful, you can discuss the reasons the other two were less successful. As a review, you might consider other presidents in terms of your definition of successful.)*
   a. John F. Kennedy
   b. Richard M. Nixon
   c. Lyndon B. Johnson

4. How do you explain the failure of the United States in the Vietnam War? Present your views in an essay.

The Presidencies of Carter, Reagan, and George H. W. Bush: 1977–1993

APPROACHES TO HISTORY

HISTORY SEEN AS DRIVEN BY BIOLOGICAL NEEDS OR DRIVES

In the past one hundred years, many psychologists, biologists, social scientists, and others have presented theories about the biological needs or drives of human beings. You may have heard of Sigmund Freud and his theories on the importance of the sexual drive. Other theories have suggested that the need for food and shelter drive human behavior or the need to defend one's territory is basic to human behavior. (See Robert Ardrey, page 241.) Recently, Paul Lawrence and Nitin Nohria, professors at Harvard Business School, have published a book, *Driven: The Four Key Drives To Understanding Why We Choose To Do What We Do*. Rather than focus on one drive as others have done, they suggest humans have four basic drives or needs: to bond—to have long-term, caring relations with others in part to continue the species; to learn—to gain knowledge and try new things as we attempt to make sense of the world; to acquire—to acquire possessions whether they be essential, such as food and housing, or nonessential, such as diamonds and experiences, both of which provide us status; and to defend—to protect ourselves, our family, possessions, home, land, and beliefs.

Over the years, some historians have used the idea of human biologically driven needs to help them interpret and explain the actions of humans.

Can you relate to this approach? Do you ever have an urge to go to the mall just to buy something you can show to others? Are you attracted, sexually or otherwise, to other people, or do you remember happy times with parents or friends? Are you upset and feel like pushing someone away when they come too close to you and move into your space? Do you argue and feel like fighting when someone disagrees with ideas that are important to you? Does learning a new way to solve a problem excite you? If you can relate to any of these examples, then you might interpret it as your response to one of the four drives—to bond, to learn, to acquire, and to defend. You could explain your behavior as driven by a biological need, just as some historians explain history.

The need to defend territory is a popular explanation behind many conflicts in history (see Chapter 11). However, the need to acquire basic food and shelter or wealth, the desire to perpetuate the race, and the urge to experiment and try new things have all been used by historians in explaining the actions of humans in the past. Does this approach appeal to you? Can you see any basic biological needs driving the actions of leaders and the public in recent years? In the more distant past? Might the appeal of capitalism and tax cuts be rooted in the biological drive to acquire?

I. Domestic Policies of Carter, Reagan, and George H. W. Bush

DOMESTIC ISSUES UNDER CARTER

Carter was the "outsider" in Washington. He was a "born again" Christian and wished to conduct the government on moral principles. He introduced legislation to deal with complex energy and economic problems but failed to push his programs consistently. It was said Carter became entrapped in the details of issues and was unable to focus on the broad goals. Carter had no named "program" such as the New Deal or War on Poverty for his presidency but did act in several areas.

Carter began the move toward deregulation of industry, which was accelerated by Reagan. Environmental legislation under Carter included the creation of a "superfund" to clean up hazardous toxic waste dumps and the establishment of a wilderness area of 100 million acres in Alaska, an act some environmentalists have praised as the most important conservation act since Theodore Roosevelt. A Department of Energy and a Department of Education were added to the Cabinet, thus acknowledging the changing role of the federal government in these two areas.

In response to continuing concerns about United States use of oil and the power of OPEC, Carter attempted to establish an energy policy, but oil pressure groups in Congress and Carter's own lack of consistency on what he wanted made the attempt unsuccessful. Carter was no more successful than his predecessors in combating the economic problems of inflation and recession. Carter continued the voluntary approach to wage and price control. The Federal Reserve Board, exercising its control over monetary policy, tightened the money supply, which increased interest rates. High interest rates reduced car and house sales, which affected employment levels. By the time of the 1980 election, the annual inflation rate was 12 percent, interest rates were 21 percent, and unemployment levels were high.

ELECTION OF 1980

The Republicans nominated Ronald Reagan, former movie star and former Governor of California, as their candidate. As an actor in Hollywood, Reagan had been a Democrat and expressed liberal ideas, but his views changed, and as Governor of California he became a spokesperson for the conservative wing of the Republican Party. Reagan believed less government was better. He advocated deregulation of industry, less government expenditure on social welfare, lower income tax rates, and the buildup of United States military defenses. What seemed to

> Ronald Reagan, espousing traditional American values, wins the presidency, and the Republicans gain control of the Senate.

appeal most to the American public were Reagan's sincerity and his appeal to the traditional values of American life—religion, family, and patriotism. Do the needs to bond and to defend appear related to this appeal?

Reagan chose as his Vice President George H. W. Bush, a New Englander by birth who had made a fortune in Texas oil before turning to government service. Bush had served as Congressman from Texas, director of the CIA, United States liaison officer in the People's Republic of China, Ambassador to the United Nations, and head of the Republican Party. He was one of the most qualified candidates on the basis of offices held who had ever run on a national ticket.

John Anderson of Illinois, a more liberal Republican, had contested the primaries against Reagan and ran as an Independent. Carter and Mondale were renominated. They went into the campaign handicapped by the Iranian hostage crisis (see page 320) and the economic situation. Reagan and Bush won overwhelmingly in the Electoral College, and the Republicans gained control of the Senate and made gains in the House of Representatives.

REAGAN'S ECONOMIC POLICY

Reagan was ideologically committed to conservatism. He believed in "supply-side" economics. Supply-side theory holds that if taxes are reduced, people will not spend the extra money for goods but will invest the extra money. These investments will create new jobs in industries. Everyone will benefit, the nation will prosper, and thus the government will collect more in taxes in spite of the lower tax rates. To many, supply-side economics was a new way of describing the old 19th-century "trickle down" theory that held that helping the rich will ultimately help the poor.

Following supply-side economics, in 1981 Reagan pushed through Congress two major bills reforming the tax code. The graduated income tax[1] was an important part

---

[1] graduated income tax   *An income tax policy in which there is a different tax rate for different levels of income, with rates as high as 95 percent on the highest incomes and no tax on the lowest incomes. The opposite policy is to have a flat rate, which all people pay regardless of income level.*

of New Deal social policy, by which the gap between the rich and the poor was to be narrowed by using income and inheritance taxes to take money from the wealthy for the government to spend on programs to benefit the poor and less wealthy. Reagan's new tax code cut the top tax rate from 70 percent to 28 percent, greatly benefiting the wealthy and providing more opportunities for them to acquire more wealth. An increase in deductions helped middle class families, but the middle class as a whole benefited very little. Many poorer Americans paid no taxes as a result of the changes. At the time the Reagan policy was widely acclaimed. It has been referred to as Reaganomics. The Regan philosophy of government dominated American policy until the election cycle of 2008.

Some saw his program as an attack on the whole New Deal and its restructuring of United States society, but Reagan made no changes in the New Deal's Social Security legislation and promised to maintain a "safety net" of welfare benefits for the most needy. Congress did, however, pass massive budget cuts affecting all types of domestic programs from food stamps to college loans.

THE ECONOMY IN THE 1980s

The economy, battered by high interest rates and the oil crisis at the end of Carter's administration, was in recession by late 1981. Blue collar workers of the "old" industries and African-Americans were hardest hit. Slow improvement came as non-OPEC oil-producing nations increased supplies and the rate of inflation declined to 4 percent. The Federal Reserve responded by lowering interest rates, and economic conditions improved, helped by the tax cuts that gave people money to spend. However, the rise in government revenue expected after the tax cuts never occurred. The federal deficit grew tremendously. It reached $195 billion in 1983, and it continued at very high levels during the Reagan administration. In an agreement attempting to deal with the deficit, President George H. W. Bush finally agreed to some tax increases on gasoline and liquor in late 1990 but the agreements did not include the cost of the Savings and Loans "bailout" (see page 313) or the Gulf War. This tax increase went against his campaign promise of "no new taxes" and some believe it cost him reelection in 1992.

> The country emerges from recession.

Making the economic situation more complex was the huge trade deficit that developed in the 1980s as Americans bought more goods from overseas than they exported. During the Reagan presidency the United States became a debtor nation, owing more to foreign nations than it earned from exports for the first time since World War I.

> The trade deficit turns the United States into a debtor nation.

During these Reagan-Bush years the gap between the rich and poor widened. The pay of top business executives grew on a percentage basis much more rapidly than did that of daily wage earners. Much of the money released by the tax cut found its way into the stock market and other speculation and not into new industry. Established companies bought other companies in a great wave of consolidation and takeovers. All of this buying and selling of corporations did not

> The stock market and business takeovers attract large sums of money.

The cartoonist Marland comments on the growing recession in the New England states in this 1989 cartoon. What "line" are the man and woman in? Since the New Deal, the states and the federal government have provided unemployment payments for those who are out of work. It lasts for a limited time, but it provides some help to those who lose jobs when recessions occur.
Reprinted with permission of the artist, Mike Marland, Concord Monitor, Concord, New Hampshire.

address the basic problems of American industries: lack of efficient productivity, aging plants, and foreign competition. It also did not create new jobs in manufacturing, which led to rising unemployment during George H. W. Bush's presidency.

UNEVEN PROSPERITY

While some enjoyed prosperity under Reagan, it was not evenly distributed. Farmers, who had suffered so often in the United States' history, had borrowed heavily in the Carter years and

> Prosperity is unevenly distributed.

were unable to repay loans when farm prices fell in the 1980s. The oil industry in Texas was hard hit by the drop in oil prices in the mid-1980s, and the region experienced a recession that led to the bankruptcy of many Savings and Loan Associations (S&Ls). By 1990 Texas had recovered somewhat, but the northeast was hurt by a decline in the computer industry and a major drop in real estate prices, which led a number of banks in the region to declare bankruptcy in the early 1990s. The American economy was not healthy and slipped slowly into recession, another one of those cyclical economic downturns.

S&Ls

Government deregulation is considered in part responsible for the Savings and Loan problems. S&Ls are like banks and receive from the public deposits that the owners and administrators of the S&Ls invest. They had been under federal government regulation. With deregulation many S&Ls speculated with loans, and when the recession hit Texas in the mid-1980s many S&Ls went bankrupt because their loans could not be repaid. The government then appropriated billions of dollars to buy the bankrupt S&Ls, reorganize them, and return money to creditors. The S&L "bailout" by the Federal government became a major contributor to the federal deficit. The situation has many parallels to the financial crisis of 2008.

> Deregulation allows S&L managers to speculate. This leads to many bankruptcies.

STRATEGIC DEFENSE INITIATIVE

Reagan cut back government-funded social programs and at the same time increased spending for the United States armed forces. This military buildup included new missiles and planes, more aircraft carriers, and the Strategic Defense Initiative (SDI), popularly called "Star Wars." SDI was to provide a shield over the United States against any possible Soviet nuclear attack. Some scientists claimed it was a daydream; others claimed laser technology could achieve it. Congress partially funded the plan, and SDI became an important issue in arms negotiations with the Soviet Union, which saw it as a way for the United States to destroy the Soviet Union without being destroyed itself. As the Soviet Union collapsed and tests of SDI technology failed, suggesting the complexity of the concept of SDI, interest in SDI faded, but Congress continued to appropriate funds for research during both the George H. W. Bush and Clinton presidencies. The concept became an important issue in George W. Bush's presidential campaign in 2000 and in his presidency when he supported the development of the SDI.

ENVIRONMENTAL POLICY

Reagan believed the environmental legislation establishing water and pollution controls saddled American industry with unnecessary expenses. Congress overrode Reagan's veto of a Clean Water Act, but Secretary of the Interior James Watt and others responsible for enforcing environment regulations often ignored them. Scientists warned of the dangers of acid rain, and at the end of Reagan's administration they began speaking of global warming, of the "greenhouse effect" created by increasing carbon gases, and of a hole in the ozone layer. However, under Reagan and George H. W. Bush the United States gave limited support to moves for international cooperation to control the greenhouse effect. President George H. W. Bush refused to support the Rio de Janiero Treaty establishing international guidelines. (See page 366.)

THE SUPREME COURT

Perhaps the greatest impact Presidents Reagan and George H. W. Bush will have on United States' history is through their Supreme Court appointments. Reagan's appointees, including Sandra Day O'Connor, the first woman appointed to the court, were conservatives and reversed what had been a liberal court under Earl Warren

and Warren Burger. Reagan raised conservative Associate Justice
William Rehnquist to be Chief Justice. George H. W. Bush's
first appointee was conservative David Souter, who turned out to
be less conservative than many expected. His second appointee
was conservative Judge Clarence Thomas, an African-American.

> Appointments appear to create a more conservative Supreme Court.

At his Senate confirmation hearing he was accused of sexual harassment by a young
lawyer and former employee, Anita Hill. After very extensive and emotional
hearings before the all-male Senate Judiciary Committee, Judge Thomas was
confirmed as the last of the Reagan/Bush appointees. Since Supreme Court justices
serve for life, the impact on history of presidential appointments lasts long after their
time in office.

The Rehnquist Court has limited the extent of some previous
decisions but did not fully reverse them. On the most
controversial issue before the Court in the Reagan/Bush years,
abortion, the Court upheld laws narrowing the *Roe* v. *Wade*
decision but, in spite of the opposition to the decision by both

> Supreme Court limits but does not overrule *Roe* v. *Wade.*

presidents and the conservative right, the Court did not reverse *Roe* v. *Wade.*

REAGAN'S POPULARITY

Like Nixon, Reagan opposed renewal of the Voting Rights Act. He was also opposed
to NOW's (National Organization of Women) goal of "equal pay for equal work."
Reagan did not appoint as many minorities and women to positions in his
administration as had Carter. Over 100 Reagan appointees, including his Attorney
General, Edwin Meese, were accused and indicted on charges of corruption and
misuse of power, but these accusations did not affect Reagan's popularity. Reagan
was an excellent communicator, and the public supported this man who came to
symbolize all the good and traditional values of America—family, religion, and
patriotism.

In 1984 Reagan and George H. W. Bush overwhelmingly defeated Democrats
Walter Mondale and Geraldine Ferraro, the first woman to run for the vice
presidency as a candidate of a major political party. The Republicans carried every
state except Minnesota and the District of Columbia. The nation had voted for
Reagan's economic policies and conservatism. The nation continued to swing
dramatically from one party to the other and from liberal to conservative.

ELECTION OF 1988

With the approach of the election of 1988, it appeared the Democrats would have a
good chance for victory given the economic situation, the disaffection of women and
African-American voters, and the problems created by the Iran-Contra Affair.

Senator Gary Hart of Colorado, a married man and a top candidate in 1984, was
leading in the polls until a report in the *Miami Herald* reported he had spent a
weekend with a model. The news reporters on a tip had staked out the house. Hart
withdrew but later reentered the race but was ineffective. The "character issue" thus
entered the political scene. Previously the press had not reported on candidates'

"indiscretions," but Hart had almost dared the press to report. The character issue has added a new dimension to American politics.

Michael Dukakis, governor of Massachusetts, and the Reverend Jesse Jackson emerged through the primaries as the leading contenders. Jackson was the first African-American to attain such national prominence in a presidential campaign. Dukakis finally won the nomination and, to appeal to the southern voters, picked Lloyd Bentson, senator from Texas, as vice president. George H. W. Bush won the Republican nomination easily and picked Dan Quayle, a young, little-known but conservative congressman from Indiana as vice president. Dukakis, far ahead in the polls at the start, ran a poor campaign while George H. W. Bush made Dukakis' liberalism an issue. Bush promised "no new taxes." Some analysts deplored the negative campaigning[2] in the election, but American politics has been full of such tactics through the years. Bush and Quayle won a strong victory. The Democrats retained control of both the House and the Senate.

GEORGE H. W. BUSH'S ECONOMIC POLICIES

George H. W. Bush continued Reagan's economic policies. In 1990 he was forced, as a result of the continuing huge budget deficit, to break his "no new tax" pledge, infuriating the strong conservative Republican Right. In spite of the new taxes the deficit grew, and the economy slowed, sliding into a moderate recession in 1992. Congress approved a program, the Gramm-Rudman Plan, for reducing the deficit, but Congress was unable to abide by it because of many pressures such as the S&L bailout and the rising cost of unemployment benefits created by the recession.

There was little agreement between the Republican president and the Democrat-controlled Congress as to what domestic policies should be followed. The result was a gridlock in government. The Democrats in Congress approved a number of

> Gridlock develops in Washington as Bush and the Congress disagree on legislation.

laws, which the president vetoed. Congress did not overturn any of the president's many vetoes until 1992 when his veto of the Cable Television Deregulation Act was overturned. Acts dealing with many different issues ranging from trade—the 1990 Textile, Apparel and Footwear Act set quotas on the growth of these imports—to Civil Rights—the 1990 Act changed provisions of laws as interpreted by the Supreme Court—were vetoed. In 1991 a new version of the act was signed by the president. George H. W. Bush thus used his veto power to force the Democratic-controlled Congress to accept certain Republican points. He used the veto more than any previous president. In 1992 among others he vetoed acts dealing with abortion counseling, campaign financing, family leave—the latter for the second time. When a similar bill was submitted to President Clinton in early 1993, he immediately signed it. These measures reflect the different positions of the two parties.

Among the measures supported by George H. W. Bush and passed by Congress were an extension of the Clean Air Act (1990) and a new crime bill focusing on

---

[2] negative campaigining   *The use of political ads and announcements that emphasize the opponent's weaknesses and points they believe the voters will dislike rather than emphasizing their own candidate's positions on issues.*

white collar crime (1990), an overhaul of the banking system and Federal Deposit Insurance Corporation (1991), and a National Energy Policy (1992), which eased the licensing procedures for nuclear plants and promoted the development of non-gasoline-fueled cars.

ELECTION OF 1992

At the time of the First Iraq or Gulf War in 1991 (see pages 328–330), President George H. W. Bush's popularity reached an all-time high. In spite of the legislative gridlock, it appeared he would win reelection easily. No nationally known Democrat announced for the party's presidential nomination. Bill Clinton, Governor of Arkansas, who had little name recognition on the national scene, although he had served as Governor since 1982 and had chaired the National Governors Council, mounted a campaign that won him the Democratic nomination. Clinton had grown up in the small town of Hope, Arkansas. He was named after his father, William Jefferson Blythe, who died in a car crash before he was born. His mother later married Roger Clinton, but home life was difficult. Clinton went to Georgetown University, was a Rhodes Scholar, and graduated from Yale Law School. Clinton's style was to listen and work for compromise. He had successfully reformed the schools in Arkansas and stimulated its economic growth. His wife, Hillary Rodham Clinton, was a lawyer who had a national reputation for her work on children's issues and worked with her husband as a partner.

Clinton chose Al Gore of Tennessee as his vice president. Al Gore had sought the presidential nomination, was knowledgeable on military issues, and was known for his commitment to environmental issues about which he had published a book, *Earth in the Balance*. His wife, Tipper, had run a national campaign to have all popular music labeled as to the suitability of the lyrics for young people. The Clintons and Gores were of the baby boom generation, the first major party ticket consisting of candidates born after World War II.

The press, following its new role as examiner of candidate's morals, confronted Clinton with questions about his use of marijuana (he admitted smoking as a graduate student in England but stated he did not inhale), his handling of the issue of service in Vietnam, and his suspected infidelity, which he and Mrs. Clinton confronted and denied in a national news broadcast. Clinton's campaign focused on the economy and health care. He effectively used talk show appearances on TV and an informal "town meeting" approach of responding to questions from his audience to get his message across.

By the spring of 1992 George H. W. Bush's popularity had plummeted. The gridlock in Washington seemed to make him ineffective in domestic policy, and the recession was being felt throughout the country. In the campaign Bush seemed insensitive and out of touch with the needs of the average wage earner. However, it is likely he would have won the election as the hero of the Persian Gulf War if a third candidate, H. Ross Perot, had not entered the race.

H. Ross Perot was a Texas billionaire who spent his own money to get his views before the American people. His focus, like Clinton's, was the economy and the need to reduce the deficit. Perot was included in the national televised presidential debates where his humor and direct, simple answers appealed to many people. The press gave Perot good coverage. Many worried about his simplistic solutions, arrogance, and ignorance of the political process, but he won 19 percent of the popular vote.

> H. Ross Perot enters presidential race and offers simplistic solutions to economic problems.

Clinton won the election with 43 percent of the popular vote. For the first time in twelve years, the president and Congress were of the same party, and there was hope the gridlock would end.

Key Point to Remember

In spite of tax cuts, lower inflation, lowered interest rates, and apparent prosperity in the Reagan years, the United States economy was not healthy, as farmers faced foreclosures, the Texas oil industry suffered from a recession, S&Ls failed, trade deficits increased, and the national debt grew dramatically.

Links from the Past to the Present

1. Recent United States attitudes toward taxes and tax policy have their roots in the pre-Revolutionary cry of "No Taxation Without Representation."
2. Issues of recession and what government spending policy should be began with the Panic of 1819 and continue in spite of the New Deal legislation.

Dates

1976—Jimmy Carter elected president.
1980—Alaska Wilderness Act.
　　　Ronald Reagan elected president.
1981—Reagan Tax Reform Bills.
1982—SDI proposed.
1984—Reagan and George H. W. Bush defeated Mondale and Ferraro for presidency.
1988—George H. W. Bush elected president.
1991—Cable Television Deregulation Act.
1992—Bill Clinton elected President.

QUESTIONS
Identify each of the following:

Supply-Side Economics	S&Ls
Greenhouse Effect	NRA
"No new taxes"	SDI

Multiple Choice:

1. Supply-side economic theory holds that if taxes are reduced
   a. the money saved will be invested to create new jobs.
   b. companies will consolidate and small companies will be bought.
   c. the poor will be helped, and ultimately this will help the rich.

2. President Reagan pushed through Congress two tax reform bills that
   a. increased the top tax rate from 28 percent to 70 percent.
   b. ended the New Deal use of income tax rates to make social policy.
   c. created special loopholes for the rich.

3. In the election of 1992
   a. Ross Perot had no impact on the voters.
   b. George H. W. Bush replaced Dan Quayle as the vice presidential candidate.
   c. Bill Clinton won but had less than 50 percent of the popular vote.

II. Foreign Policy Under Carter, Reagan, and George H. W. Bush

CARTER'S FOREIGN POLICY

President Carter had won his election victory as an outsider in Washington politics, but he was also an outsider in foreign policy. His approach to foreign policy was grounded in his belief in peace, democracy, and human rights for all people, but he was inconsistent in its application. In calling on the Soviet Union to allow free emigration of its Jewish population and to release all dissidents and political prisoners, he antagonized Lenoid Brezhnev and détente lost its momentum. A second Strategic Arms Limitation Treaty (SALT II) was signed but never approved by the Senate after the Soviet Union sent troops into neighboring Afghanistan to support its communist government against guerrilla attacks. Carter responded by stopping grain shipments and barring United States athletes from competing in the 1980 summer Olympic Games in Moscow. These actions worsened relations but had little impact on Soviet policy. The United States sent aid to the guerillas, including Osama bin Laden and other non-Afghans who came to Afghanistan to fight a jihad, or holy war, for Islam against the Soviet Union. After eight years of inconclusive warfare an agreement was reached among the warring factions in Afghanistan. The Soviet Union withdrew from Afghanistan, dubbed the Soviet's Vietnam since Afghanistan had the same impact on the USSR as Vietnam had had on the United States. The United States soon abandoned its support for the Afghans. The peace agreement broke down and tribal warfare broke out, creating chaos.

> Carter responds to invasion of Afghanistan by the Soviet Union.

Carter completed the process of recognition of the People's Republic of China begun by Nixon. Ambassadors were exchanged, and the official recognition of the government of Taiwan was ended. Carter resolved growing conflicts with Panama by negotiating a treaty that transferred the United States owned and operated Panama Canal to the Republic of Panama in 1999. Over strong opposition from conservatives, Carter gained Senate approval of the treaty, thus reversing the results of the big stick diplomacy of Theodore Roosevelt.

CAMP DAVID ACCORDS

The high point of Carter's foreign policy was the Camp David Accords. To address the issue of peace in the Middle East, Carter invited President Anwar Sadat of Egypt and Prime Minister Menachem Begin of Israel to the presidential retreat, Camp David, in Maryland, for negotiations. Israel agreed to return the Sinai Peninsula to Egypt, and in return, Egypt officially recognized Israel as a nation, the first Arab country to do so. The 1978 Camp David Accords were a major breakthrough in the slow movement toward peace in the Middle East. Carter's successors in the White House continued to address the issue, but a peaceful solution has not yet been found. The issue is now deeply entangled in the War on Terrorism (see pages 415–419).

IRANIAN HOSTAGE CRISIS: 1979–1980

The low point of Carter's presidency was the Iranian hostage crisis. In 1953 the CIA had arranged the overthrow of a popular nationalist government in Iran, which had deposed the Shah (King) and moved to seize control of foreign oil companies. The monarchy under the Shah was restored. Ignoring the oppressive methods used by the Shah to stay in power and adhering to the containment policy, the United States sent Iran large amounts of military aid to help the Shah maintain stability in the area on the southern border of the USSR. In 1978 a popular uprising forced the Shah to flee Iran, and a Muslim religious leader and nationalist, the Ayatollah Khomeini, established an Islamic Republic based strictly on the laws of the Koran[3]. Khomeini opposed communism and was very anti-American. He deplored the influence of western cultures on Iran and the support the United States had given the Shah. Iran was thus the first nation in the modern era to embrace Islamic fundamentalism and establish a nation based on the concepts of *sharia* law. This idea has had appeal to some Muslims and provides one dimension to the political tensions in the Middle East and the War on Terrorism.

> United States supports the Shah of Iran to maintain stability in the area.

When the Shah became ill with cancer, Carter allowed the Shah to come to the United States for medical treatment. In anger young Iranian militants broke into the United States embassy in Teheran, took the staff hostage, and demanded the return of the Shah for trial. Carter refused, and the resulting 444-day crisis captured the attention of the American people and almost paralyzed the Carter presidency. An attempt to rescue the 52 male hostages—the Iranians had released women and African-American hostages—failed when helicopters malfunctioned.

> Iranian militants seize United States embassy and take hostages.

Carter seized Iranian assets and appealed to the UN. The Shah died of cancer, but the crisis continued. Finally, negotiations did take place, and Carter agreed to release Iranian assets in return for the hostages. However, they were not released until Reagan's inauguration day in January 1981, and accusations were later made and investigated by Congress that the Republican Party held up the release to help defeat Carter. No clear proof was presented to support the accusations.

---

[3] Koran *The holy book of Islam, the religion of which Muhammad is the prophet.*

During the crisis the television news each night had a special report and counted the days since the crisis began, thus keeping the issue before the public as a current event with little time for analysis or reflection. Iranian students carrying signs in English demonstrated before TV cameras in what sometimes looked like an international advertising campaign to convince the world of the evils of the United States, which Khomeini declared to be Satan[4]. The crisis again illustrated the power of television, the growing use of terror and hostages to achieve goals in international affairs, and the difficulty a great power has imposing its desires on small nations. It was a major factor in Carter's failure to win a second term, as he was preoccupied by the crisis and refused to leave the White House to campaign as long as the hostages were held.

> Television plays an important role in the Iranian Hostage Crisis.

IRAN-IRAQ WAR

In 1980 war broke out between Iraq and Iran. The origins were complex. They go back centuries, involving both the history of Islam and the region, the differences between a fundamentalist, Islamic state such as Iran and a socialist, dictatorial state such as Iraq, the struggle to modernize while maintaining adherence to traditional religious practices, and the disparity between rich and poor in the region. A victory for either side would upset the balance of power in the Middle East, which the United States opposed.

> Iran and Iraq are bitter over the policies of the United States.

While the United States did not want to become involved, aid was given to Iraq and negotiated during a visit to Saddam Hussein by then Secretary of Defense and later Vice President Dick Cheney. The war continued for eight years and ended with an armistice that left the situation as it had been at the start of the war but with thousands dead. Both Iran and Iraq believed the United States should have supported them wholeheartedly. The result was strained relations among the three nations that provide an important background to the situation in the Middle East and the Iraq War.

RELATIONS WITH THE SOVIET UNION UNDER REAGAN

Reagan came to the White House convinced the Soviet Union was an "evil empire." His view reflected the attitude of many Americans who were frustrated that the world was not just like America, whose values of freedom, equality, and democracy were obviously good. These views illustrate the nationalistic interpretation of history and the sociological understanding of gaining identity for yourself by being different from and better than "the others."

Reagan was convinced United States military weakness encouraged Communist aggression and that by strengthening United States defenses, he could defeat the "evil empire" around the world. In spite of his views of the Soviets, the Reagan administration began talks on arms limitations, but these collapsed in 1983.

[4] Satan   *Another term for the devil, used particularly in the world of Islam.*

In the early 1980s the Soviet Union was moving through a period of transition as the older generation of leaders died. A rapid turnover of leadership among old and ailing men provided little direction for the USSR as the nation struggled with economic problems.

GLASNOST AND PERESTROIKA

In 1985 Mikhail Gorbachev took control of the government of the USSR and introduced domestic reforms and shifts in foreign policy in an attempt to address the problems of a stagnating economy. Gorbachev's policy of glasnost[5] and perestroika[6] changed Eastern Europe and ended the Cold War. Reagan and Gorbachev met several times, their personal relationship grew warm, and they agreed to talks on arms control.

As the Soviet and Eastern European economies worsened in the late 1980s, Gorbachev made it clear the USSR would no longer force the Eastern European nations to remain Communist or members of the Warsaw Pact. The Soviet-occupied Baltic States—Lithuania, Estonia, Latvia led by Lithuania, declared their independence of the Soviet Union. While this was not then granted by Moscow, the Soviet Union was on the verge of disintegration. This was a challenge for United States policy. Should the United States encourage the breakup of the USSR or was it better to help maintain its integrity?

> Soviet domestic crises present a new challenge to the United States.

George H. W. Bush had won the presidency in 1988 indicating he would pursue Reagan's foreign policy. He enjoyed personal diplomacy and developed close relations with Gorbachev. The United States government therefore decided to support Gorbachev and encouraged his introduction of a capitalist, free market economy and the continuation of the Soviet Union. In return, as Communist regimes fell in Eastern Europe in 1989, the Soviets negotiated withdrawal of their troops, and in August 1990 the Soviet Union supported the United States policy in the Kuwait crisis.

Conditions, however, worsened within the USSR. In 1990 Soviet farmers withheld food from the very poor Soviet distribution system waiting for prices to rise on the free market. The situation was becoming desperate. Gorbachev asked the United States and Western Europe for food aid. The United States offered $1 billion in credit for technology and food purchases. United States-Soviet relations had dramatically reversed themselves in the ten years since 1980. The Republicans claimed the changes in the Soviet Union were the result of Reagan's military buildup. A more realistic analysis would suggest it was the result of years of internal decay and an inability to organize a huge domestic

> Bush supports Gorbachev and the Soviet Union's move toward a free market economy.

---

[5] glasnost   *An opening up; it has been used to describe both the economic and political opening of the Soviet society and the opening in foreign policy which affected Eastern Europe and ended the Cold War.*

[6] perestroika   *A rebuilding; it has referred to the rebuilding of the Soviet economic system; it does not imply a movement in the political area toward democracy but a restructuring of the economy.*

economy by a small group in Moscow. The USSR was a country rich in resources, but the Communist system was unable to tap them for the benefit of the people.

1989 IN EUROPE

Since the start of the Cold War, Eastern European nations had been ruled by Communist governments with Soviet backing. The USSR used its army to crush revolts in Hungary in 1956 and in Czechoslovakia in 1968. Matters changed when Gorbachev indicated the USSR would not use troops to stop change in Eastern Europe.

> **Communist governments fall in Eastern Europe.**

In 1989 Czechoslovakian students protesting their oppressive Communist government were joined by workers and intellectuals, and the Communist government fell. East Germans were allowed to cross the border into neighboring Communist countries from which they went on to West Germany. Thousands left. In November 1989, East Germany opened the Berlin Wall, which had stood as a symbol of divided Europe and the Cold War. In October 1990, less than a year after the fall of the Berlin Wall, Germans in East and West Germany voted for union, and the Chancellor of West Germany became the leader of a new German state with its capital in Berlin. Change was coming more rapidly than anyone could have imagined. While there was opposition to unification among some citizens of the World War II allies, it was impossible to stop the momentum. Germany became the largest single economic power in the European community. The hope for a strong economic future for the new Germany sank as the costs of unification mounted. The economy of Germany and all of Europe entered a recession.

> **The Berlin Wall is opened, and Germany is united.**

New non-Communist governments were established in other Eastern European countries. Vaclav Havel, the new president of Czechoslovakia, had been in prison six months earlier. Lech Walesa, leader of the previously banned Solidarity Union, was elected president of Poland. President George H. W. Bush promised economic aid to Poland and Hungary, but the amount was small. The United States could do little more, considering its own huge budget deficits. By the end of 1990 the last Communist nation in Europe, Albania, was subjected to student protests and riots calling for change. These new governments of Eastern Europe did not find adjustments to capitalism easy to make. Old nationalist feelings emerged.

> **Non-Communist governments are established in Czechoslovakia, Poland, and Hungary.**

THE COLLAPSE OF THE SOVIET UNION

Meanwhile, in the Soviet Union, Gorbachev, supported by the United States, struggled to introduce capitalist economic reforms while maintaining the Communist political organization. It became an impossible task. The Soviet Union began to dissolve into its separate states. Russia, the largest, elected Boris Yeltsin as its president. Gorbachev tried to create a new constitution to hold the Soviet Union together. In August 1991 conservative leaders who wished to maintain the old Communist system attempted a coup putting Gorbachev under house arrest. Boris Yeltsin, now president of the Russian Republic, rallied support for Gorbachev and arrested the coup leaders. This event sealed the fate of the USSR. In December Gorbachev resigned, and the Soviet Union dissolved. A loose confederation, the Commonwealth of Independent States (CIS), replaced the USSR. It remains essentially a powerless structure. Boris Yeltsin, as president of Russia, emerged as the most powerful figure in the former Soviet Union, but the United States now had to deal with the many successor states to that Union.

CONTROL OF NUCLEAR WEAPONS

Of major concern to the United States was who would control the huge nuclear arsenal built by the USSR. These weapons were divided among four nations: Ukraine, Belarus, Kazahkstan, and Russia. All four nations accepted the disarmament agreements signed by the USSR and United States, but questions of compliance were an issue. The Ukraine, Belarus, and Kazahkstan agreed to send their weapons to Russia for disposal. The United States Congress appropriated money to aid the nuclear states in disarming, but the issue of the disposal of former Soviet nuclear weapons remains a major concern for all nations.

ETHNIC RIVALRIES IN THE FORMER USSR

The break-up of the Soviet Union gave victory in the Cold War to the United States and appeared to justify the years of supporting the containment policy and the huge expenditures on military equipment. While the victory was real, it brought with it many new problems beyond concern over the proliferation of nuclear weapons. Strong nationalistic sentiments are held by many ethnic groups in the former Soviet Union and Warsaw Pact nations of Eastern Europe. These sentiments added to the many problems faced by these nations.

Fighting broke out in several of the Soviet Union's successor states. Georgia, home of former dictator Joseph Stalin, erupted in violent warfare.

The breakaway of Chechnya from Russia and the resulting civil war remain a major threat to stability. Chechnya is an Islamic nation, and deep historical antagonisms exist between the two countries. Some Chechnyans have been trained by al-Qaida, which makes the situation even more complex.

ECONOMIC STRUGGLES

All the new nations created from the breakup of the Soviet Union faced major economic problems as they struggled with disbanding the old Communist system. While many former Communist leaders denounced the party, they lacked experience

> Economic reforms in the USSR bring new challenges.

in democratic government and some were committed to maintaining their power within a totalitarian system. Challenges to United States policy makers were great as they too had to shift from their old view of the monolithic Soviet empire to the new situation of dealing with nineteen separate nations.

Boris Yeltsin continued economic reforms. There was a major opposition in his Parliament and Yeltsin was forced to change his policies, moving away from the rapid establishment of capitalism, yet the state-owned industries were sold creating a new class of extremely wealthy owners. A Russian "mafia" emerged, adding to the economic confusion.

YUGOSLAVIA DISINTEGRATES

Yugoslavia was created after World War I as a collection of several different nationalities with separate interests. During World War II there was unusually bitter fighting between two of the nationalities—the Croats and the Serbs. After the war the country was held together under the dictatorial leadership of Marshall Tito, who was a Communist but not under Soviet domination. Marshall Tito ruled by suppressing opposition. As a result, no one emerged as his successor, and upon his death the nation came under considerable stress as the separate nationalities asserted their particular interests. As the Communist control of Eastern Europe ended in 1989, the Yugoslav nation came under greater economic and nationalistic stress. Each ethnic group organized to defend its beliefs as the people bonded together. Finally, Slovenia, a Roman Catholic region bordering Austria, declared independence. Germany recognized Slovenia, and the disintegration of Yugoslavia began.

The largest part of the country, Serbia, followed the Greek Orthodox religion and historically had dominated a large section of the region. As Croatia, with a Roman Catholic majority, and Bosnia/Herzegovina, with a large Muslim population, tried to withdraw from the national union, warfare began as the Serbs within these areas supported by the national government fought to keep the parts together in a greater Serbia. Serbs conquered parts of Croatia and Bosnia where they followed a policy of "ethnic cleansing." As the warfare began, the United States was busy with the Gulf War (see pages 328–330) and did not believe that the United States national interests were involved. After Clinton's election, U.S. policy slowly changed.

> Fighting erupts as Serbs attempt to create a greater Serbia and practice "ethnic cleansing."

INTERNATIONAL TRADE

During the decade of the 1980s Western Europe moved closer to economic unity and set 1992 as the date for all tariffs and other economic barriers to disappear among the European Community (EC). The European Community became one of the largest trading blocks and economic powers in the world. Many United States companies bought European companies during the 1980s to be sure of access to this European market in case the EC established tariff barriers against nonmembers.

From World War II until 1995, the General Agreement on Tariffs and Trade (GATT) guided world trade policy. The GATT agreements led to lower tariffs, more trade, and helped to stimulate economic development, but not always worldwide. There were negotiations over the years to improve the agreements and make trade freer. Finally negotiations began for a new trade agreement. There was disagreement on a number of issues, especially government subsidies paid to European, particularly French, farmers and the accessibility of the European Market to United

States-produced music and films. In 1993, President Clinton applied pressure, and several all-night negotiation sessions led to an agreement on a new trade organization—the World Trade Organization (WTO). The WTO was accepted by the United States Congress and took effect on January 1, 1995. WTO has stimulated and encouraged economic globalization.

In 1987 the Reagan Administration negotiated a free trade treaty with Canada, which opened up the borders beginning January 1, 1989. Many Canadians believed the agreement favored the United States. Canada, however, joined the United States under the leadership of President George H. W. Bush to expand the agreement by negotiating with Mexico a North American Free Trade Agreement (NAFTA). In spite of opposition expressed by Clinton in the 1992 campaign to the environmental and other clauses of NAFTA, Clinton supported NAFTA. The Senate approved it in 1993. NAFTA creates the largest and potentially strongest economic region in the world.

> Congress approves the North American Free Trade Agreement.

A major trade concern of the United States since it became a debtor nation during the Reagan presidency has been the unequal trade balance with several nations, particularly Japan and China.

EL SALVADOR AND NICARAGUA AND IRAN-CONTRA

Under both Reagan and George H. W. Bush, the "we-they" perspective of the Cold War dominated foreign policy decisions in Latin America. In 1980 in El Salvador, revolutionaries were challenging the military dictatorship supported by large landowners. Reagan believed the rebels were agents of Cuba and the USSR and asked Congress to aid the government. He based his argument on the old domino theory used to justify intervention in Vietnam. Congress sent aid but often attached conditions. Some Americans urged negotiation. They saw the rebels as nationalistic, democratic liberals who were trying to achieve a better life for the poor people of El Salvador. The guerilla war dragged on for ten years. Finally, with the support of George H. W. Bush's administration, a cease-fire was arranged and elections were held.

In neighboring Nicaragua, the military dictator had been overthrown by a group called the Sandinistas before Reagan was elected. The Sandinistas asked for help from Cuba to improve health and education in the country. Reagan believed the Sandinistas were committed Communists. He ordered the CIA to train a group of Nicaraguans who became known as the Contras, to attack the Sandinistas, an example of a "we-they" struggle.

> Reagan orders CIA to train Nicaraguans to fight the Sandinistas.

After Congress cut off aid to the Contras, members of Reagan's administration developed a secret plan to aid the Contras. It linked operations in the Middle East involving Lebanon, Israel, and Iran with events in Latin America. In the early 1980s there was an outbreak of international terrorism. Many of the perpetrators were Shiite Muslims inspired by the Islamic fundamentalist regime established in Iran. In Lebanon, where a civil war was being fought, Islamic fundamentalists seized hostages to achieve their goals. While Reagan declared he would never deal with terrorists, members of his administration—including CIA Director William Casey, National Security Advisor John Poindexter, and White House Aide Lt. Colonel Oliver North— arranged to sell arms to Iran in return for Iran's support in obtaining release of American hostages. The money made from the sale of arms was to be used to support the Nicaraguan Contras. Thus began the Iran-Contra Affair, that made headlines for the next three years. American opinion was split over the affair, with many viewing Lt. Colonel North as a hero and patriot and others seeing him as one who ignored the basic concept of constitutional government. The Iran-Contra Case raised important issues over the power of Congress to hold hearings on matters under investigation by the Justice Department. The Iran-Contra investigation lasted seven years and was very inconclusive because the Supreme Court overturned the convictions of North and Poindexter on the issue of self-incrimination—they had testified before a Congressional committee. Lt. Colonel North became a hero of the Republican right wing. North sought and won the Republican Party nomination as candidate for the United States Senate from Virginia in 1994, much to the dismay of many liberals, but lost in the November election.

> The Iran-Contra Affair divides the country.

Throughout the investigations and trials, Reagan maintained he knew nothing of the plan. Some saw parallels between Watergate and the Iran-Contra Affair and the unconstitutional use of executive power, but Reagan's great popularity with the voters kept all suggestions of his involvement from sticking.

In spite of the aid to the Contras from the Iran-Contra Affair, they were unable to defeat the Sandinistas. United States popular support for the Contras waned. Although Nicaragua's neighbors sought a negotiated solution, Reagan preferred a military victory.

Finally, however, in 1988 a cease-fire was signed and elections held, which the Sandinista government lost. The transition of power was successful, economic conditions improved, and a fragile two-party democratic political system established.

INVASION OF GRENADA AND PANAMA

The United States intervened militarily in two Latin American nations, Grenada and Panama, in the 1980s. Reagan invaded the island of Grenada in October 1983, ostensibly to protect United States medical students from internal political strife. The Leftist government of Grenada was friendly to Cuba, and there were rumors it was building a large airstrip that bombers could use. After the invasion, a new government friendlier to the United States was established, and United States troops were slowly withdrawn. Many Americans responded favorably to this show of strength and patriotism but the UN passed a resolution condemning the United States' intervention.

In 1989 President George H. W. Bush ordered United States troops into Panama to seize the dictator, General Manuel Noriega, who was accused of aiding drug smugglers. He was captured, brought to the United States for trial, found guilty, and put in a United States federal prison. This was one aspect of the war on drugs as fought by Reagan and George H. W. Bush. The two presidents worked to control the supply of drugs much of which came from South America through the Caribbean and Latin America. The domestic war on drugs, in spite of publicity and Mrs. Reagan's campaign to "just say no," met with limited success. The failure to successfully reduce demand for drugs has made the curtailing of the supply very difficult. It is an excellent example of supply-demand economics.

THE UNITED STATES AND SOUTH AMERICA

While the United States paid little attention to South America in the 1980s except to wage a war on the drug trade, there was a trend in the region toward democratic governments and away from military dictatorships. The United States encouraged this movement but did not have the funds to make large economic grants to South American countries. Most nations had heavy foreign debts. Many, including Brazil and Argentina, were able to negotiate a lowering of their debt payments, which aided stability and democracy.

CUBA AND HAITI

Two Caribbean nations, Cuba and Haiti, did not follow the progression toward democracy seen in the rest of the Western Hemisphere at the end of the 20th century. With the large Cuban and Haitian immigrant populations in the United States, Cuba and Haiti illustrate the great impact public opinion can have on foreign policy decisions.

In spite of the collapse of the Soviet Union and the discrediting of communism in Eastern Europe, Fidel Castro in Cuba maintained his commitment to communism and governed Cuba as a dictator. Cuban immigrants put pressure on the United States to increase sanctions and force Castro to abandon communism.

> **Castro remains as Communist dictator of Cuba.**

Haiti had been ruled by dictators since before World War II. With the overthrow of Jean-Claude Duvalier in 1986, it appeared as though Haiti would establish a democratic government. Elections were held and Auguste Aristide, a former priest, was elected president with over 60 percent of the vote. He ruled briefly, attempting to change the established ways. The military then intervened, overthrew the elected president, and established a military dictatorship.

First the George H. W. Bush and later the Clinton administrations sought ways to restore President Aristide. Haitians in the United States pressured the U.S. government to intervene. The UN placed an oil embargo on Haiti. While many Haitians suffered, the military junta prospered. Many poor Haitians fled their country. Finally, former President Carter negotiated the end of the military dictatorship. United States troops landed to keep order, and President Aristide was returned to power with their support.

GULF WAR

The Gulf War developed against a background of tension and conflicts going back to the end of World War I when the boundaries of new states were drawn with little attention to history, Islamic traditions, or tribal affiliations. With the discovery of oil in the Middle East and the establishment of Israel in 1948, conflicts increased.

When the Iran-Iraq War ended in 1988, Iraq had a huge debt. To pay the debt, Iraq needed to keep oil prices high. Iraq's dictator, Sadaam Hussein, believed that OPEC was not doing so and that Iraq's neighbor, Kuwait, was both overproducing and pumping oil from an Iraqi-owned field. Iraq claimed independent Kuwait was a province of Iraq. When negotiations between Kuwait and Iraq broke down in July 1990 and when the United States, implied through its ambassador that the United States had no special interest in the issue, Iraq invaded Kuwait. Within three days Kuwait was occupied, and President George H. W. Bush reacted by sending troops to defend Saudi Arabia, whose oil was essential to the economies of United States allies. Osama bin Laden described this act as a desecration of the Islamic Holy Places, and it is considered the origin of his anti-Americanism.

> **Iraq invades Kuwait.**

Bush turned to the United Nations for support, and the world came together to condemn the Iraqi aggression, to establish sanctions stopping all trade with Iraq, and finally to support the use of force by a coalition of nations to push Iraq out of Kuwait if Iraqi troops were not withdrawn by January 15, 1991. As the deadline neared, many nations attempted to negotiate an end to the crisis. There was concern that President Bush had not clearly articulated all of America's goals. Administration leaders gave as reasons for their position the need for oil, the protection of American jobs, the need to stop Hussein, who George H. W. Bush described as "another Hitler," and the creation of a "new world order" where "aggression would not pay." The president received the support of the American people, but there were strong antiwar sentiments expressed illustrating the continuing antiwar feeling as a result of Vietnam. After heated debate, Congress supported the president's policy.

> **Bush creates a coalition through the UN to attack Iraq.**

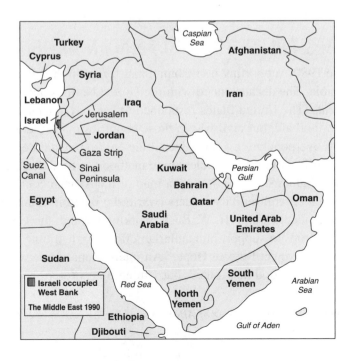

Iraq failed to meet the UN deadline. The UN coalition of nations began heavy air attacks, which were the most successful air strikes ever undertaken, but they failed to destroy all of Iraq's missiles, some of which were launched against Israel. The UN coalition armies attacked and liberated Kuwait. The retreating Iraqi armies set fire to the Kuwaiti oil wells creating a potential ecological disaster. However, it was avoided and the wells were restored to production within a year.

The UN Security Council resolution called for the liberation of Kuwait and not for the overthrow of Saddam Hussein. Therefore, when Kuwait was freed a cease-fire was signed. The terms called for a UN inspection team to assure the destruction of Iraq's weapons of mass destruction, curtailment of Iraqi air space, and an embargo on oil exports until all terms were complied with. With the cease-fire in 1991, many in the world community hoped Iraqis would remove Saddam Hussein from power. Instead, he tightened his grip on Iraq and found ways to bypass the oil embargo.

The Gulf War, called Operation Desert Storm, pulled together the many strands of the complex issue of peace in the Middle East. These issues include: the tension between the rich and poor Arab nations; the size of each nation's armaments including their nuclear and biological arsenals; the antagonisms between the

> The Gulf War pulls together many complex issues in the Middle East.

different Islamic sects especially the Shia and Sunni; the growth of Islamic fundamentalism since Iran's 1979 revolution; the struggle to modernize the political and economic institutions of various nations in the region; the need by Japan, the European nations and the United States for a stable supply of oil; the struggle of the Palestinians, represented by the PLO, for a homeland; the future of Jerusalem and the recognition of Israel by all the Arab nations. Compounding the crisis is the Islamic belief in Jihad[7]. Jihad was used by Saddam Hussein to describe the conflict with the United Nations coalition, by many Arabs to describe the conflict with Israel, and by Osama bin Laden and al-Qaida to describe their attacks on the United States and its allies.

UNITED STATES POLICY TOWARD AFRICAN NATIONS

Reagan began the 1980s supporting non-Communist forces in the civil wars in Angola and Namibia. The decade ended with the United Nations negotiating tentative settlements. The United States responded to severe famines in the Sudan and Ethiopia with food aid, but civil war in those countries made the delivery of aid difficult. Drought, overpopulation, and the resulting environmental degradation made the problems appear insurmountable unless new methods of food production could be developed and taught. (See page 500 for a map of the African continent.)

Civil war between several military leaders (warlords) raged in Somalia and lead to famine. In 1992 President George H. W. Bush, working through the UN, reached an agreement to send troops to support humanitarian efforts to distribute food. The operation was called "Project Restore Hope." An international force was sent and was successful in getting food distributed, but United States forces became involved

---

[7] Jihad   *A Holy War fought in the name of Allah to support the Koran and the teachings of Islam.*

in capturing one of the warlords. Several soldiers were killed, and the American people and Congress forced President Clinton to withdraw United States forces in 1994.

A world outcry led by the United States against the policies of Apartheid[8] in South Africa led to international sanctions. This led to the release from prison of the opposition African National Congress (ANC) leader Nelson Mandela who negotiated with the government. The white government agreed to a new multiracial constitution and voting on a one person-one vote basis. Mandela

> The United States support to end Apartheid in South Africa leads to election of Nelson Mandela and a multiracial government.

and the ANC won the election, and a new multiracial government was established. Democracy came to South Africa as a result of the United States working with the international community—a combination that can bring success.

UNITED STATES POLICY TOWARD ASIAN RIM NATIONS

In China a crackdown on dissident students and workers in June 1989 ended an attempt by them to bring greater democracy to that Communist nation. Protesting unarmed students were attacked by tanks in Tiananmen Square, and the United States Congress responded by passing moderate sanctions against China. President George H. W. Bush ignored the Congressional pressure because he did not want to disturb United States-China trade.

Unlike the other Pacific Rim nations, the former United States colony of the Philippines did not benefit from economic growth in the 1980s. A popular revolution in 1987 overthrew the dictator, Ferdinand Marcos, whom the United States had

> The United States agrees to withdraw from bases in the Philippines.

supported. His popular successor, Corazon Aquino, could not resolve the many economic and political problems she inherited from Marcos. The United States had large military bases in the Philippines that were considered vital to the defense of United States interests in the Pacific. The bases were not supported by the Philippine people. President George H. W. Bush negotiated a withdrawal of United States forces from them in 1992. With the collapse of the Soviet Union, the United States defense policies throughout the world had to be redefined and the withdrawal from the Philippines was one aspect of a much larger issue.

The aftermath of the Vietnam War continued to affect United States relations with Vietnam. Concern over the fate of those missing in action (MIAs) became the focus of activity of several members of Congress. Vietnam began to cooperate in the search for the remains of MIAs. This led to improved relations between the two nations, including trade and diplomatic exchanges.

THE "NEW WORLD ORDER"

As the Soviet Union dissolved, the Cold War ended, and the Gulf War was fought, President George H. W. Bush spoke of the "new world order" that would follow. It was an optimistic

> Bush's concept of a new world order fades rapidly.

---

[8] apartheid   *The policy of legalized race separation practiced in South Africa.*

perspective, which was quickly dampened by the outbreak of conflicts between different nationalities within the Soviet Union and the disintegration of Yugoslavia. Under Clinton, there was less talk of a new world order.

SUMMARY

Many topics and issues presented in this chapter are still in the daily headlines. This fact should help us to realize how important many of the events recorded here are for our lives and how past events affect the future. To understand today's world, one must have a background that includes events such as the Reagan tax cuts, the reasons for the involvement of the United States in the Middle East, the beginnings of the deregulation of U.S. industry, and globalization. How these events will be understood in thirty years is not clear. However, they are clearly impacting our lives today, and that is one important reason for studying history. Whether you believe these actions were responses to basic biological needs and drives or a result of other factors, these actions need to be understood.

Key Point to Remember

As the Cold War ended and Communist governments fell in Eastern Europe, the tensions of the Cold War disappeared, but they were quickly replaced by other international tensions and threats to peace. Events in all parts of the globe affect the United States, and the United States has not been able to exercise total control over any of them.

People to Remember

Jimmy Carter   Peanut farmer, Governor of Georgia, 39th president of the United States; he achieved the Camp David Accords which brought peace to Egypt and Israel; his ideals of international human rights led to tensions with the Soviet Union and the Iranian hostage crisis prevented his focusing on domestic issues; after his defeat in 1980 he established a foundation that deals with international peace and homes for the homeless; winner of Nobel Peace Prize in 2002.

Ronald Reagan   Radio broadcaster, Hollywood movie star, Governor of California, 40th president of the United States; believed in supply-side economics and put through two major tax reforms; cut back on the New Deal and social programs; built up United States defenses; saw the Soviet Union as an "evil empire" but ended his presidency by negotiating arms and trade agreements with the USSR.

George H. W. Bush   New Englander, pilot in World War II, founder and President of Zapata Petroleum Corporation, Congressman from Texas, United States Ambassador to the UN, Chairman of the Republican National Committee, head of the United States Liaison Office in Beijing, head of the CIA, vice president under Ronald Reagan, 41st president of the United States; made a fortune in Texas oil; began his presidency promising no new taxes but as the budget deficit grew, he accepted limited tax increases; committed United States troops to the Gulf War, and worked to create an international coalition against Iraq.

Links from the Past to the Present

1. The Cold War began immediately after World War II with the division of Europe into East and West blocs and ended with the fall of Communist governments in Eastern Europe in 1989, but its effects are still important.

2. The spread of nuclear weapons is a matter of international concern.

3. Tariffs and trade policies can have a major impact on the world economy and have led the international community to establish many different trade groupings such as NAFTA and the EC (European Community).

4. United States armed interference in Latin American nations is still an important element in U.S. policy as seen in Grenada, Panama and Haiti.

Dates

1979—Iran Hostage Crisis began.

1980—Iran-Iraq War began.

1985—Gorbachev attained power in USSR.
      Iran-Contra Affair revealed.

1988—Cease-fire signed in Nicaragua; elections held.

1989—Bush invaded Panama to seize General Noriega.
      Berlin Wall fell.
      Students fired on by Chinese government in Tiananmen Square.

1990—Germany reunited.
      Iraq invaded Kuwait.

1991—Soviet Union collapsed.
      Yugoslavia breakup begins.
      Gulf War (First Iraq War).

1992—U.S. troops to Somalia.

1993—Siege of Sarajevo began.
      NAFTA approved by U.S. Senate.

Questions
Identify each of the following:

SDI	Contras
European Community (EC)	Kuwait
Sandinistas	Apartheid
Sarajevo	Berlin Wall
GATT	WTO

Multiple Choice:

1. President Carter reacted to the invasion of Afghanistan by the USSR by
   a. signing SALT II.
   b. sending grain to Afghanistan.
   c. boycotting the 1980 summer Olympics in Moscow.

2. Changes in Eastern Europe were helped by
   a. Gorbachev's statement that the USSR would not stop them.
   b. the strength of United States forces in Europe.
   c. the crisis over Kuwait.

3. President George H. W. Bush invaded Panama because of
   a. a need to keep the canal open.
   b. attacks on the government by Communist rebels.
   c. General Noriega's involvement in drug traffic.

4. The United States sent forces to Somalia under UN auspices in order to
   a. bring humanitarian aid, especially food, to the starving population.
   b. capture the local warlords.
   c. impose a peace settlement on the warring factions within the nation.

Open-ended, Analysis Questions

The following questions require analysis and reflection. You are encouraged to bring to your answer information and ideas from many sources. The answers should be presented in composition or essay style but they may be used to initiate discussion. The questions put you in the role of the historian, gathering information to support your personal perspective on the question.

1. Explain the connections between the following events:
   a. Iran-Iraq War
   b. Iranian Revolution of 1979
   c. Iranian Hostage Crisis
   d. U.S. Marines in Lebanon 1982–84
   e. Aid to Contras cut by Congress

2. To what extent were the economic problems faced by President Reagan similar to those faced by Presidents Ford and Carter? How were they different? Briefly describe the solutions President Reagan offered to deal with the economic problems of his presidency.

3. The United States claims to have won the Cold War. Describe the actions taken by the United States which led to this victory and explain how the actions led to victory.

4. "The Cold War had a major impact on the United States both politically and socially." Do you agree or disagree? Why? Pick specific examples of political or social impact to support your view.

Social Change: 1945–1992

APPROACHES TO HISTORY

SOCIAL HISTORY AS THE KEY TO THE PAST

History has often been written to trace the political developments of a society focusing on the leaders and the policies they set forth in the areas of economics and foreign policies, military activity, and government performance. We know that throughout history these policies and leaders have affected the lives of the ordinary people. Traditionally, historians largely ignored the history of the "common man and woman." They have recently been referred to as the "voiceless" since they have left few records of their lives. In the past fifty years more and more attention has been paid to the way the policies of the leaders have affected the lives of all people and, in return, how the voiceless have impacted the decisions of the leaders. This has added an important dimension to the study of history and made it much richer and much more reflective of what really happened in the past. It is clear that a leader who wishes to go to war cannot do so unless the people—his followers—are ready to fight. People acting together can have a great effect on leaders and national policy as many protest and liberation movements of the late twentieth century illustrate. As more historians focus on the ordinary people and their social interactions, we are gaining better understandings of the past and of the actions of leaders. These social historians investigate everything that happens in social relations.

Social historians record many different aspects of our lives. For instance, some social historians focus on great social movements such as the Civil Rights or Women's Movements to show how the people acted to gain a more significant role in the life of the nation. Other historians have paid particular attention to where people live and where they have come from explaining the changes in society through the study of population. Others have studied the development of artistic expression in music or literature to illustrate the changes in the way people view the world. Some historians, referred to as oral historians, have collected data through interviews and questionnaires, which they have then used to explain behavior and provide insights into decision-making.

What we do each day and how we feel and think provides social historians with the material they investigate. Their sources from the more distant past are usually paintings, letters and diaries. These sources are hard for the social historian to find since many have been destroyed over the ages. Therefore, they must also interpret artifacts such as clothing and house plans to deduce living patterns and styles. Besides these sources, social historians studying the recent past have many new sources, such as photographs, films, recordings, videos, and e-mails to get information about the lives and feelings of ordinary people. This information provides a different perspective than using only the lives and records of the leaders. The perspective of the common people provide a context in which to place the major political and economic events of the present and recent past. It enriches our understanding and provides a richer account of the history of nations.

Think how much richer our lives are when we share what we think and feel with others and we, in turn, listen to their ideas and feelings. When we read letters, look at paintings, or watch films we gain perspectives on the creators, which provide us with new ideas. When we consider all aspects of the lives we and our friends lead, we have a much better understanding of what is happening. In the same way, the social historian broadens our understanding of the past and therefore of ourselves.

I. Social Aspects of the American Economy

THE ECONOMY IN THE IMMEDIATE POST-WORLD WAR II PERIOD

After World War II there was no major recession. The G.I. Bill aided the transition to civilian life of the large numbers who had served in the military. Demand for consumer goods not available during the war spurred the economy. The "good life," measured by the acquisition of consumer goods, seemed available to most people in the United States. There were only minor economic adjustments during Eisenhower's presidency.

In 1958 John Kenneth Galbraith, one of the leading economists of the time, wrote a book, *The Affluent Society*, describing this postwar phenomenon of apparent affluence. He claimed that there was overexpenditure on private consumption and underexpenditure on the public sector, i.e., schools, state hospitals,

The United States becomes the "affluent society."

transportation. He believed the public sector was underfunded because Americans pursued the good life for themselves in the suburbs.

This was seen in the boom in personal house building. What had been open country around cities became endless acres of similar suburban housing. Ranches, garrisons, and capes as well as shopping centers and acres of asphalt for parking and roads dominated the landscape outside cities, while little money was spent on improving public services or transportation in the cities. Work for many individuals was still in the city centers and commuting, usually by car and often for an hour or more, became a way of life for many individuals. Many women, "moms" in the terminology of the 1950s, ran the home and chauffeured children to activities. After the progress in job opportunities for women during the war, a reaction set in, and the ideal woman portrayed in many articles and ads was the good mother, a stay-at-home "mom."

The United States emerged as the great consumer society using more resources and goods per capita than any other nation. Consumer credit grew, and savings dropped in the 1950s, all of which stimulated the growth of the affluent society. A postwar "baby boom" pushed up demand. Increasingly affluent parents

> A baby boom increases demand for manufactured goods.

wanted to provide goods for their children, which they, as children, had not been able to have in the Depression years. Toy fads, such as hoola hoops, coonskin caps, and G.I. Joes, swept the country. This phenomenon continues to the present.

Overseas markets expanded, adding to America's prosperity. Industrial production to meet military needs grew under stimulus of the Cold War. In his farewell address to the nation, President Dwight Eisenhower warned of the power and potential danger of this "military-industrial complex," which could dominate the United States' economy. Overall the 1950s were a time of prosperity and hope for many Americans.

BUSINESS DEVELOPMENTS OF THE 60s, 70s, AND 80s

Postwar prosperity continued through the 1960s, stimulated by the Kennedy/Johnson tax cut and the spending for both the Great Society and the Vietnam War. While business and economic growth was not entirely untroubled during the 1960s, the federal government through its fiscal and monetary policies seemed to have control of the business cycle. Fiscal policy is controlled by Congress under the president's leadership and involves government spending and the raising and lowering of taxes at the proper moment. Monetary policy is controlled by the Federal Reserve Board and government agencies and involves increasing and decreasing the amount of money in circulation and controlling the interest rate. At times the president and Congress disagree, and both may disagree with the Federal Reserve Board, but overall until the 1970s the system worked quite effectively.

The spending on the Great Society and Vietnam War created economic problems for Nixon. He asked for price controls and a tax cut, using the traditional techniques to combat recession. While the economic situation was not good in the Nixon years, it was the OPEC oil embargo of 1973 that brought an end to

> The OPEC oil embargo brings an end to the postwar boom and begins a period of high inflation.

postwar growth. The economic situation was different from the usual recession, when jobs were lost and prices fell. As a result of the embargo, jobs were lost, but prices rose. Ford and later President Carter struggled with the situation, but neither was able to stop effectively the inflationary cycle. The auto industry suffered and pulled other industries down with it. As the price of gas dropped and remained low in the 1990s, the automotive industry recovered but rather than concentrate on alternative fuels and high mileage vehicles, they turned to producing gas-guzzling SUVs and other heavy vehicles.

FOREIGN COMPETITION AND SERVICE INDUSTRY JOBS

In the 1970s, foreign competition became more and more a factor in the United States economy. Competition from Japanese cars and electronics were particularly worrisome to business leaders. Jobs, many of which were in industries where unions had become strong in the 1930s, were lost. The power and strength of labor unions began a decline. The most important area of economic growth became the service industries of which McDonald's, representative of the fast food business, is an outstanding example. McDonald's golden arches became a symbol of the United States worldwide. Service industries pay lower wages, employ many part-time workers, provide few benefits such as health care, and are nonunion for the most part.

The election of Ronald Reagan reflected a major shift in the mood of the nation to the extent it has been referred to as the "Reagan Revolution." A generation of young people who fought for civil rights and rejected the establishment was replaced by a generation dubbed the Yuppies, who worked within the system to make as much money as possible. Donald Trump, who made millions in real estate and Atlantic City casinos, and Michael Milken, who made billions in junk bonds[1], exemplify the values and goals of the Yuppies. New York and Wall Street became their mecca.

Illegal dealings by Michael Milken and Ivan Boesky, two symbols of the business opportunities and ethics of the age, were uncovered by the Securities and Exchange Commission. Boesky was a stock speculator who used illegal insider trading[2] knowledge of coming takeovers to make millions. He was exposed and sent to jail.

> Failure of S&Ls reflect the economic situation of the 1980s.

Milken used high-yielding junk bonds to get money to use in the taking over of companies by other companies. Milken was considered the most successful businessman of the time. He was finally sent to prison for stock fraud and insider trading. These operations on Wall Street did not help American businesses to become more productive or competitive.

As part of Reaganomics, S&Ls (Savings and Loan Associations) were deregulated. Later many of these S&Ls failed after using funds for speculation in real estate. This speculation after being freed of regulation was reflective of the

[1] junk bonds   *A corporate bond having a high yield and a high risk because its security is based on the prospect of profits not on assets.*
[2] insider trading   *Using information the general public does not have about business changes that would affect the price of stocks and bonds to make money; the practice is illegal under federal law.*

period. Heavy industries did not grow and the productivity of the United States worker dropped, hurting the competitive situation in relation to foreign nations. Millions of dollars were spent buying, selling, and consolidating companies rather than addressing the issue of productivity. As a result, the job outlook worsened for many Americans. The worsening economic outlook affected the lives of millions of people who saw the American dream becoming more unattainable as long-term high-paying job opportunities declined.

While many businesses had good profits and cash flow, their good position was often the result of debt manipulation or restructuring and not increased productivity. Reaganomics reinforced this approach to the detriment of the nation. The goal of restructuring is often higher profits for the stockholders and company executives whose compensation includes stock options. However, restructuring can lead to greater productivity and a better competitive position in world trade.

> **Companies are restructured to improve their competitiveness.**

The Regan tax cuts stimulated the economy, but it became apparent the national debt was growing. By the end of the Reagan presidency, the economy was becoming less prosperous, and during George H. W. Bush's presidency it turned into a recession. His actions were unable to restore confidence by the 1992 election and the economy became the primary issue of the campaign. While most Americans benefited from the growing postwar economy, throughout the period prosperity was not evenly distributed. As today, pockets of poverty could be found throughout the nation in the postwar period.

URBAN WEALTH AND POVERTY

Few people living in the inner city slum areas benefited from the affluent society. The gap between the urban rich and the urban poor widened because, in spite of the move to the suburbs, some wealthier individuals remained in the cities. The general affluence and the Civil Rights Movement raised the expectations for those in the inner cities, but the expectations were not realized. Conditions actually worsened. Under President Lyndon Johnson these expectations were addressed in the War on Poverty but with limited success due to the escalation of the war in Vietnam. The growth in wealth actually widened the gap between the rich and poor.

> **The gap between the urban poor and the rich widens.**

DECLINE OF THE INNER CITY

As suburbs grew in the period after World War II, the more affluent city dwellers moved away from the city. The poor remained as did the need for services—fire, police, trash collection, good roads, education—supplied by the government. Yet the tax base of the cities declined. Property was not as well maintained and dropped in value, reducing income from property taxes. Businesses left sections of the inner cities, reducing job opportunities as well as the income available to deal with the needs and problems of those areas, which became the ghettos and slums where the poor lived. Education declined in quality. Welfare, begun under the New Deal, enabled the poor to survive. By the 1980s it was obvious a whole class of impoverished city dwellers existed who were, and whose parents had been, recipients of welfare. This was an urban underclass who were unable to break the cycle of welfare. Many were young 15- or 16-year-old unwed mothers who lacked skills. In the 1960s and later, many turned to drugs and drug dealing, which supplied the only possible escape from poverty for many as jobs did not exist. The frustration and alienation suffered by these welfare-dependent individuals was a major factor in the urban riots that occurred sporadically in major American cities from the 1960s on. How to break this cycle of welfare became a major political issue.

> Problems of the inner city increase.

DRUGS

Drug use became an aspect of poverty in the inner cities, and drug-related killings have skyrocketed as young inner-city dwellers fought for a piece of the illegal drug business that offered one of the few hopes for wealth and escape from the cycle of poverty. Statistics in the 1990s indicated that one out of every four inner-city young males could expect to be shot. Car accidents, usually connected with alcohol, were the largest killer of adolescents living in the suburbs. These differences in the causes of death between urban and suburban youth reflect the continuing separation of America into rich and poor, suburb and city. Each president after Johnson tried to solve the problems of the cities with welfare reform and, as drug use and violence increased, with antidrug and anticrime legislation.

President Nixon first referred to a War on Drugs and initiated a program of cooperation with foreign governments to reduce production of drugs and enforcement of the prohibition of their use, distribution, and production in the United States. Mandatory prison terms were introduced and led to the incarceration of many citizens on very flimsy charges. The proportion of African-Americans incarcerated was extremely high. Each president extended the War on Drugs, but little success was achieved in reducing consumption or violence in the cities. Slowly the drug culture spread to suburbs and rural America. In the 1960s the Haight Asbury district of San Francisco became symbolic of the use of drugs, and marijuana was widely used by all economic classes.

HOMELESSNESS

Another great problem of urban life is the number of homeless people in America. At one time Americans thought only drunks and mentally disturbed individuals lived on the street without homes, but increasingly people became aware that at least some of the homeless were simply poor. Homeless families were found in communities and rural areas throughout the nation. They worked, sent their children to school, but slept on streets, in cars, or in shelters. The number of homeless fluctuated with the strength of the economy rising in times of unemployment and recession. However throughout the post-war period there were homeless people reflecting the unequal distribution of the benefits of the affluent society. It became an issue affecting the economy as many were on welfare and not

> Homelessness illustrates the gap between rich and poor.

productive. During Johnson's War on Poverty, homelessness received more attention and became a political issue as well as an economic one. In spite of welfare reforms, it continues as an important issue closely related to the lack of low-cost housing.

The history of the homeless would not have been of interest to most historians, but the social historian focuses on the plight of the voiceless and tries to explain how conditions such as homelessness arise and how they affect the lives of all people.

NATIVE AMERICAN POVERTY

As we have seen, there were many who did not share in the affluent society. As a group, the Native Americans benefited less from postwar prosperity than any other single group in American society. Under Eisenhower an attempt was made to close the Indian reservations and integrate those living there into the mainstream of American rural and urban life. It was unsuccessful, and more Native Americans entered the ranks of the poverty stricken. The economic problems were compounded by problems with alcoholism. Many white Americans held stereotypes of the alcoholic, non-working, poverty-stricken Native American, a stereotype that allowed the white American to ignore the situation or blame the Native Americans themselves for their condition. After the success of the Civil Rights Movement, a few Native American leaders organized the American Indian Movement (AIM) (see page 362) to create an awareness of problems and to gain a better place for Native Americans in American life. For many reasons progress was very slow.

> Native Americans do not share in the prosperity.

One way Native Americans have achieved success in combating poverty is to open gambling casinos on their lands—lands where state laws against gambling do not apply according to a Supreme Court Decision in 1976. In 1988, following another Supreme Court decision affirming the 1976 one, Congress passed a law regulating the establishment of casinos on Reservation lands. Since then, many tribes have opened casinos, and some, especially near large cities, have prospered and created wealth for the tribes allowing them to move out of poverty. Casinos were built throughout the west, and two in Connecticut have been very successful allowing the tribes to pump large amounts of money into the state economy and to build an excellent museum. However casinos have not been the solution for many tribes, and the percentage of Native American living in poverty remains high.

WOMEN IN POVERTY

As a result of the Women's Movement, which began in the 1960s, many more women entered the legal and medical professions, government, and business. Still the number of women and children living in poverty increased. Statistics on poverty exhibit an increase in the number of women living in poverty compared to men. The increasing number of unwed mothers, teenage mothers, and mothers who get the children after divorce and are unable to collect support payments; the number of jobs available to women with children; and the limited number of day care facilities all contributed to this

> Number of women living in poverty increases as the disparity in wage payments between men and women continues.

situation. Also, the salary of women and men doing similar jobs continued to favor men. This disparity in wage payments between men and women was a major factor in keeping women in poverty and was one of the most difficult problems to address. The future of these women and their children became a major concern of those wishing to reform welfare and of social workers.

RURAL POVERTY

Rural poverty was widespread in the postwar period. Because it was not as concentrated, rural poverty was not as obvious as urban poverty. Yet in absolute numbers there were more poor in the country than in the cities.

Areas of rural poverty could be found throughout the nation, particularly in the tenant farms of the South and the few remaining small farms of the Midwest and West, in New England, and in the Appalachian Mountains of the South. Appalachia in the mountains of West Virginia, Kentucky, and Tennessee became a synonym for rural poverty in America at the time of the New Deal. In spite of efforts to change conditions, it remained an area of rural poverty in the postwar period. In these same regions there were poor in small towns. Often in these towns neighbors helped neighbors, and on the farms there was often some food, but living was bleak and opportunities for change almost non-existent without government assistance. It was these conditions of poverty that President Johnson addressed in the 1960s. Johnson's policies met with some success, and the numbers living in poverty declined. Nevertheless, rural poverty appears as persistent an issue for the United States as does urban poverty. It strains the economy and makes the nation less productive than it might be.

> **Rural poverty persists throughout the nation.**

AMERICAN AGRICULTURE AND THE ECONOMY

Agriculture has been a major aspect of the United States economy throughout the nation's history. However, throughout the 19th and 20th centuries, it has rarely prospered as industry grew. This has created many social and economic problems.

The New Deal began subsidizing American agriculture, and subsidies continued in the postwar period. Farms were consolidated and more and more run like businesses, designated agribusinesses.[3] Small farmers suffered as a result. Many were forced to sell their farms to the large conglomerates. Nixon's grain deals with the USSR benefited the large wheat farmers of the Midwest. The government acquired large amounts of food in paying subsidies and these farm surpluses were distributed to needy countries as part of Cold War policy to win them to the American side.

In spite of increasing mechanization, farm workers were needed at harvest time. Migrant workers, many of them illegal immigrants, filled this need and were often exploited. Their living conditions were as poor as any in the country.

In California during the 1960s Cesar Chavez organized agricultural workers in the United Farm Workers to gain for them greater economic power and human dignity.

---

[3] agribusinesses *Large-scale farms run by corporations.*

Chavez's work on behalf of the poor migrant farm worker parallels the work done by the civil rights leaders. Chavez created a greater awareness of the lot of the farm workers by organizing boycotts of produce produced on non-union farms. The nonviolent technique proved successful. Working conditions and pay scales did improve. U.S. agriculture is still dependent on migrant workers.

> Agriculture becomes a large business, and Cesar Chavez organizes agricultural workers to gain economic advantages for them.

FARMING AND THE ENVIRONMENT

Scientific development increased farm production after World War II, but the use of pesticides created environmental hazards of which most people were unaware. Rachel Carson in her book *The Silent Spring* reported on pesticide use, and the environmental awareness movement began. The Environmental Protection Agency (EPA) was established in 1970 and gradually grew in significance. The issues raised by environmental, marketing, and scientific developments helped push the growth of agribusiness since it became more and more costly and complicated to respond to all the laws and new scientific information available.

> Rachel Carson's *The Silent Spring* calls attention to the dangers of pesticides and leads to great environmental awareness and the establishment of the EPA.

Farming, which had been the dominant occupation of Americans, provided jobs for fewer and fewer people, yet production increased throughout the 20th century. The small farm has almost disappeared. Many Americans romanticize the life of the farmer, but few are ready to pursue it in the age of TV and suburban malls.

GROWTH OF SUBURBS

Suburbs grew rapidly in the postwar years. The growth of suburbs meant the end of open spaces near cities. The growth was seen as urban sprawl by many, and in some regions such as the eastern seaboard from Boston to Washington and the Los Angeles and Dallas-Fort Worth areas, what were separate metropolitan areas grew together to form megapolises. One could drive from city to city on the new highways built during the Eisenhower years without ever seeing farmlands. The character of the American landscape was thus greatly changed as was the character of the urban centers.

The growth of the suburbs greatly affected the economy. The growth was driven in part by the postwar Baby Boomers—a population spurt that greatly affected the economy and put heavy demands on housing and other consumer goods. Housing starts

> Suburban lifestyle differs from that of the city.

are considered one measure of economic vitality because building a house impacts so many different businesses from lumber to plumbing. New housing developments also require roads and sewers, electric power, and telephones. Schools and other services, many of which must be supported by taxes, are also needed. As the population spread out, public transportation was unable to expand to keep up with the spread of population, forcing the residents to depend on automobiles. Mass housing projects forced builders to offer limited house plans, which made many suburbs monotonous and unattractive. Pete Seeger in a popular song of the 1960s protest period referred to them as "little boxes on a hillside." Suburbs tended to be isolated communities of like individuals that do not reflect the great diversity found in America. The growth of suburbs provided comfortable living areas for many but presented new problems for those who lived there.

The lifestyle of Americans living in suburbs was different from those living in small towns or in cities. Someone had to transport the children to all activities except when the school bus picked them up. Jobs were usually in nearby cities, and the commute to work became the norm for suburbanites. Relaxed time at home except on weekends became a luxury. As a social historian how do you think these changes might have affected the American family?

Suburban malls assembled together a variety of stores under one roof creating an artificial environment. "Going to the mall" became one of the most accepted adolescent activities as malls sprang up in suburbs throughout the nation. Many older people went to the mall, where they could exercise in air-conditioned or heated spaces without concern for the weather. Parking was available. The commercial downtown areas of many cities both small and large suffered as a result of the growth of suburban malls, creating major problems for the local government, which had to maintain services in spite of the drop in tax revenue as downtown businesses failed.

In the farm states small towns lost population and declined as small farms were sold and people moved to the larger cities or suburbs. In areas of economic growth such as Silicon Valley, the managers who ran the plants producing the new microelectronics tended to live in one area while the usually nonunion, poorly paid production line workers lived in others. These suburban areas tended to have some of the problems of the inner city—poor schools with high dropout rates, disillusioned young people, drug problems. Social historians bring such issues and their social and economic consequences to the attention of all historians. It gives the student a much fuller picture of the past.

Key Point to Remember
The economic growth after World War II that produced the affluent society did not spread affluence evenly, and the gap between rich and poor widened as many of the affluent left the cities for the suburbs.

People to Remember
Cesar Chavez   Founder of United Farm Workers; organized migrant farm workers in California and other regions; started a national, nonviolent boycott of California grapes to force farm owners to improve conditions and wages for migrant workers.

Rachel Carson   Author, researcher, environmentalist; in *The Silent Spring* brought to the public's attention the dangers of pesticides; created an environmental awareness, which led to federal legislation for clean air and water, Earth Day celebrations, and various action groups.

Links from the Past to the Present

1. Economic growth was uneven in the years after World War II with numerous recessions and adjustments, just as it had been in the first 150 years of the nation's history.

2. Despite efforts to combat poverty, divisions of wealth in the nation remained.

Dates

1958—John Kenneth Galbraith wrote *The Affluent Society.*

1970—Environmental Protection Agency founded.

1973—OPEC oil embargo.

1976—Supreme Court decision, *Bryan* v. *Itasca County*, states Native-American reservations not subject to state gambling laws.

1988—*Indian Gaming Regulatory Act* (IGRA).

Questions
Identify each of the following:

Baby Boom   Appalachia
McDonalds   War on Drugs
The Affluent Society   Homelessness
The Silent Spring

Multiple Choice:

1. Symbols of the business ethics and opportunities of the 1980s were
    a. Michael Milken and Donald Trump.
    b. Cesar Chavez and Ivan Boesky.
    c. Ronald Reagan and George H. W. Bush.

2. *The Silent Spring* by Rachel Carson called attention to
    a. the economic conditions of the inner city.
    b. the danger of pesticides used in farming.
    c. the problems of single mothers on welfare.

3. Cesar Chavez is particularly connected with
    a. the Hispanic community of Los Angeles.
    b. organizing itinerant farm laborers.
    c. building low-cost housing through Habitat for Humanity.

4. An indication of the decline of the inner city is
    a. the growth of suburbs.
    b. the fact one of every four inner city youths can expect to be shot.
    c. both of the above.

II. Diversity in American Life: Changing Social Patterns

The United States from the beginning has been a nation of diverse peoples and interests. For many this diversity has been the strength of the nation. Since World War II greater attention has been given to the different groups that make up the United States. The traditional concept of the nation as a mixing bowl[4] has been replaced by the idea of the nation as a mixed salad[5]. Social historians helped precipitate this change in concept because they are interested in recording the voice, the history, of all people within society. The Civil Rights Movement and the War on Poverty focused attention on this diversity.

IMMIGRATION PATTERNS

Since World War II, the United States continues to be a nation of immigrants. Immediately after the war large numbers of Displaced Persons[6] (DPs) came to settle in this country, escaping from Communism in Europe. Many of these white immigrants came from eastern and southeastern Europe.

As political disruptions occurred abroad, America gave asylum to many peoples. Often they arrived with skills and training that benefited the country and made it comparatively easy for them to find a job and fit into society. Political unrest, poor economic conditions, and the pressure from a rapidly increasing population led many from Central and South America and the Caribbean to immigrate to the United States. They added to the rapid growth of the Hispanic population. Many of these immigrants arrived with limited skills having grown up in rural areas or slums.

After the Vietnam War large numbers of immigrants came to the United States from Southeast Asia. They have been joined by Asians from South Korea, Taiwan, Hong Kong, India, and Pakistan. Each group has brought its cultural identity adding to

Asian immigrants adapt to American life.

the nation's diversity. Many arrived with impressive skills and found work in hi-tech industries. Others became inner-city shopkeepers, which increased tensions in places such as Los Angeles.

Unrest in Africa after the movement to independence in the 1960s also added to the growing mix of peoples immigrating to the United States. Civil War (Congo 1960–65, Sudan 1955–72 and 1984 on), famine (Ethiopia 1984), genocide (Rwanda 1994), and political unrest became widespread and brought refugees, often with little

---

[4] mixing bowl   *The concept that when people from different cultures arrive in the United States they are blended together losing their own cultural identity and all become the same— an American. The idea is also captured in the United States Latin motto, e pluribus unum— from many, one.*

[5] mixed salad   *The concept that when people from different cultures arrive in the United States they come together in a bowl, the United States, but each remains separate with his own cultural identity just as the lettuce, carrots, and tomatoes in a mixed salad remain separate. The vegetables all share the salad dressing just as all Americans share certain ideas and experiences that make them different from citizens of other nations.*

[6] displaced person—*often abbreviated as DP. An individual who is forced to flee his homeland because of political unrest, pressure, or conflict.*

education and suffering from exposure to traumatic events, seeking asylum. The government, aided by many nongovernment organizations (especially churches), struggled to make the resettlement of these new immigrants easy. Certain communities were chosen as settlement centers for different groups with the idea that immigrants with shared cultural backgrounds might make the transition to their new lives easier. Continuing warfare in the Middle East and the outbreak of Civil War in Yugoslavia (1990) added to the mix of peoples arriving in the United States during the years of the Cold War. The numbers continue to grow.

These new immigrants illustrate how diverse and complex American society has become. As the variety of cultural backgrounds of citizens expanded, social scientists introduced the concept of pluralism[7] (mixed salad) to explain the new complexity and to replace the previous concepts of the mixing bowl or melting pot[8] and to describe a new understanding of *e pluribus unum* as the motto of the nation. Some political leaders have argued pluralism is a polite word for separatism and have not accepted pluralism. They fear pluralism will allow all ethnic groups to express their separate identities at the expense of the united nation. The political debate over accepting Spanish as a language equal to English illustrates this fear. The issue of pluralism and the use of the Spanish language became part of the "culture wars."

THE AMERICAN YOUTH CULTURE EMERGES IN THE 1950s

The postwar Baby Boom affected not only the economy but also the culture. One of the most popular books of the period was Dr. Benjamin Spock's *Baby and Child Care*, published in 1946. A whole generation was raised according to Dr. Spock's principle that the child was to be the center of a mother's life. Fathers were essentially ignored in Dr. Spock's book, which called on the mother to meet the child's needs. Prospective parents studied Dr. Spock's work and referred to it often as their children grew. Whether it was Dr. Spock's teachings or a combination of factors including the sheer numbers of children, by the 1950s a youth culture dominated America, and many aspects of it are still present. Youth presented a huge market, and fads swept the nation as they still do. As mentioned previously, everything from coonskin caps made popular by a TV program on Davy Crockett to hoola hoops and Frisbees had to be had by young people if they were to be an accepted member of their group. Expenditures by the young as well as money spent by their parents on them became and remains an important part of the American economy.

> The Baby Boomers begin to have an impact on American life.

By 1959 it was estimated teenagers were spending $10 billion a year on themselves. Advertisers appealed to this market. Magazines such as *Seventeen*, aimed exclusively at teenagers, were started. Articles described how they should dress and behave. The concept of the adolescent years—the teenage years—as being a separate

[7] pluralism   *each individual's cultural background is respected under the umbrella of American democracy.*

[8] melting pot   *all immigrants are Americanized through education and lose their cultural identity.*

time with its own culture, needs, and wants originated in the United States and was emphasized after World War II. Sociologists have analyzed teenagers, and books have been written for parents on how to deal with their teenage children and their rebellious behavior. In recent years other affluent nations, especially western nations, have accepted adolescence as a separate time, but it is not a universal idea.

Parents worried about threats to their authority and the traditional understanding of the family. The term *juvenile delinquent* became popular in the United States, and articles were written deploring the rise in crime among suburban youth. In the mid-1950s Congress held hearings on juvenile delinquency and its causes, which focused attention on the issue but probably exaggerated its occurrence. Teenagers were struggling to establish a place and identity for themselves in those years when anticommunism, as seen in McCarthyism, the Korean War, and the conformity of the Eisenhower years were the prevailing values of the nation.

Teenagers in rebellion turned to new heroes from the movies and music. In 1955 James Dean in *Rebel Without a Cause* caught the imagination of many teens and the birth of rock 'n' roll opened a whole new world of expression. Teenagers particularly responded to rock "n" roll while many parents and religious leaders condemned rock for its words, beat, and style of dancing. It accentuated the alienation of youth from their parents.

> Teenagers struggle to establish their identity under the conformity of the Eisenhower years.

The alienation of youth has manifested itself in many ways. Drug and alcohol abuse, dropping out of school, running away from home, suicide and violence from teasing and bullying in schools to shootings of fellow students are all considered aspects of alienation. They all provide major challenges to society. They affect education and create an atmosphere in which teaching becomes even more difficult.

TEENAGERS AND EDUCATION

American education felt the impact of the growing numbers of teenagers. Schools have been given more and more tasks from driver education to mainstreaming all children. In the late 19th century public schools provided a basic elementary education for most children who then went on to work on farms or in industry. Many left school to learn skills on the job as interns or apprentices. In the 20th century more and more students were forced to stay on in high school as the minimum age for leaving school was raised. After World War II young people who wanted decent jobs were expected to get a college degree even if it was not what the student wanted. There were few apprenticeship opportunities, and the curriculum became very standardized with tracks leading to college or the workplace. Keeping large numbers of adolescents together in school where many did not want to be and where the curriculum was not appealing intensified the sense of conformity and frustration for the teenager. This reinforced the idea of the youth as a threat to authority as they complained or dropped out of school. As new schools were built to house the growing numbers, too little attention was paid to what should be taught. This situation led to calls for reform and since the 1960s many different solutions to the "problem of education" have been offered.

> A college degree becomes an expectation for a decent job.

After the Soviet Union launched Sputnik into space, the Federal Government made its first move to support education. Traditionally in the United States education has been the responsibility of local government with some state government taking an active role. Therefore, this act was a major shift in national policy. By law, federal funding was made available for science, math, and language teaching, considered "needs" in the Cold War. Since then more and more federal funds have been directed toward education through various laws.

Unfortunately, there are as many solutions to the "problem of education" as there are students. No single solution will fit all students. Flexibility in programs and approaches appears the best solution. More and more research by scholars, such as Harold Gardner at Harvard University's School of Education, indicate the multiplicity of learning styles and intelligences humans have. The more closely curriculum can reflect this multiplicity, the more likely students will learn. With the growing complexity of an electronic world, education becomes more crucial for all people.

> No single solution to the "problem of education" will fit all students.

HOME AND FAMILY PATTERNS

As after every war, the immediate post–World War II years saw changes in American life styles. Several of these changes have been mentioned, including the emergence of a teenage culture and the growth of the suburbs. The number of families classified in government statistics as middle class grew from roughly 5.5 million to over 12 million during the Truman and Eisenhower presidencies. The Eisenhower years have been considered years of conformity, in part because of those attitudes summarized in the word *McCarthyism*.

> The middle class grows dramatically.

In those years the road to economic success was the business road, and the "man in the gray flannel suit" became the symbol of economic and, in that era, personal success for men. Sloan Wilson in his novel *Man in the Gray Flannel Suit* described the conformity needed in the business world.

There were critics of the postwar society. John Keat's *The Crack in the Picture Window* criticized the suburban mass-produced communities where all houses were the same, stores sold the same goods, and members of the middle class lived lives of smugness, indifferent to or unaware of how homogeneous[9] their suburban life was.

Another type of critic was Dr. Albert Kinsey, founder of the Kinsey Institute for the Study of Behavior of American Sexuality. In 1948 Dr. Kinsey published his first study, *Sexual Behavior of the American Male*. Using the statistical methods of sociology, he interviewed American males about their sexual habits. Almost all reported some experimentation or practices that went against the traditional moral and ethical teachings of the society—premarital or extramarital affairs, homosexual encounters, masturbation. A later publication described similar but not as widespread behavior among American females. Kinsey's work suggested that the conformity of

> Kinsey Reports document the sexual practices of Americans.

[9] homogeneous   *Appearing the same with all parts blended into a single consistency or type.*

the 1950s did not mean personal conformity to the established teachings of sexual morality.

Although Kinsey's research methods have been criticized, his reports were widely read and discussed. In spite of Kinsey's reports, or perhaps in reaction to them, the traditional values of family and home were given publicity reflecting society's expectations. This also reinforced the conformity of the 1950s and has become an issue in political life in the United States since then. The nuclear family of parents and two or three children, a home in the suburbs, a job for father in the city, and a wife at home caring for the children established the "American dream." A revolution against these traditional attitudes burst forth in the 1960s. However, the "American dream" is still an important political issue as seen in the 2008 election, and many conservatives still adhere to the 1950s model of the American family.

THE NEW LEFT

Two movements, the New Left and the counterculture, best represent the changing expectations and lifestyles of the 1960s and early 1970s. The New Left—in which the Students for a Democratic Society (SDS) founded at Port Huron, Michigan, in 1962, was most significant—believed in changing the political system. Members of the New Left believed their goal of a more democratic society would best be achieved through participatory democracy, in which all members of society—rich and poor; African-American, Hispanic, Native American, white—would be heard in any decision making.

Members of the New Left strongly opposed the intense anti-Communism expressed by most Americans. Many were committed to the teaching of Marxism and the antiwar radicalism that had been first expressed in Europe in the 1920s. The New Left began using nonviolence as did the Civil Rights Movement, but it slowly slipped into the use of violence, especially after 1968. At the same time, many New Left members, especially those in SDS, became more radical, founding groups like the Weathermen, committed to the violent overthrow of existing institutions. When several of the founders abandoned the New Left, it quickly lost political impact.

THE HIPPIES AND THE COUNTERCULTURE OF THE 1960s

The counterculture movement was not only nonpolitical but also antipolitical. Those who were part of the counterculture are known as Hippies. They were mainly young people. As a result of the postwar Baby Boom, by the mid-1960s over half the United States population was under 30. The counterculture was another manifestation of the youth culture of the post World War II years.

> The Hippies reject bureaucracy and materialism and protest the Vietnam War.

The Hippies were alienated by bureaucracy, materialism, and the Vietnam War. They encountered bureaucracy in the ever-growing size of universities and the government that was conducting the war. They agreed with the New Left that all people should participate in decision-making—decisions should not be made by bureaucrats or established government. Hippies were exposed to materialism in the lives of their parents, who had lived and often suffered as youngsters in the Depression years and had become adults during the war and postwar years of conformity and business success under Eisenhower. The Hippies accused this older generation of measuring success in materialistic terms of what they could acquire rather than in more personal terms of sharing or giving. The Hippies saw themselves in these latter terms. It was another case of identifying yourself as what the others were not.

Hippies were angered by the Vietnam War, in which they were expected to fight and of which they disapproved. The New Left and the counterculture united in opposition to the Vietnam War. In 1965 the largest antiwar rally organized that year brought together only 80,000 people in New York; two years later 500,000 members of the New Left and counterculture gathered in Central Park in New York City for an antiwar rally. These figures illustrate the growing strength of the counterculture and the opposition to the Vietnam War. Draft resisters were supported by the counterculture movement. Over 30,000 young men went to Canada. In 1968 what for most began as peaceful demonstrations at the Democratic Convention turned into riots. Some of the more violent leaders had planned for violence from the start, and this helped split the New Left. After 1968 the New Left became more and more violent and essentially died out. The Hippies of the counterculture continued. Charles Reich, a university professor, in *The Greening of America* (1970) explained the counterculture as an attempt to create a new community in which cooperation would replace competition.

> Antiwar protests grow and young men flee to Canada to escape the draft.

To achieve this goal, some Hippies set up communal living arrangements or communes on farms in some ways reminiscent of those of the Transcendentalist movement of the 1830s and 1840s. Large numbers settled in cities. San Francisco and its Haight Ashbury district was the mecca for many. During the summer of 1967, proclaimed a "Summer of Love," long-haired, flower-bedecked Hippies camped in the city's parks where they experimented with drugs and love. Many citizens were frightened and concerned over the experimentation and this "new morality," which rejected their learned values.

While the Hippies were antiwar, they were nonpolitical; however, many college students were not. In 1964 students returning to the University of Berkeley in California from the Civil Rights Freedom Summer were stopped from distributing information on the college campus. Their protest became the Free Speech Movement and was the first of many protests on college campuses during the decade. Some focused on the university size and the resulting isolation of students from faculty; others focused on war-related issues such as ROTC (Reserve Officer's Training Corps), which prepared officers for the military service, or campus recruitment for the CIA. Colleges had been viewed by conservatives as centers of Communist activity and subversion in the 1950s. By the late 1960s the situation reversed itself, and liberals viewed college administrations as supporters of the establishment and the Vietnam War.

THE SEXUAL REVOLUTION OF THE 1960s

Another aspect of cultural change in the 1960s is seen in the so-called Sexual Revolution of which the Hippies were one part. The Sexual Revolution, however, was much more widespread. The awareness that sexual patterns differed and many men and women experiment with premarital sex, combined with the

> Several factors lead to an apparent sexual revolution.

attitudes expressed by the counterculture, laid the foundation of the Sexual Revolution. The availability of "the Pill," an effective female contraceptive, affected the changing moral and ethical behavior of young Americans who saw themselves as "liberated" from the "old morality." Many young people lived together as their attitudes toward premarital sex changed.

Alex Comfort's, *The Joy of Sex*, became a best-seller in 1972 and reflected the openness of sexual discussion at the time. Such openness and the publicity given to sexual behavior may be responsible for its seeming to be a revolution because there had always been several standards for morality in America. While female promiscuity was frowned upon in the past, male infidelity and loose behavior had been tolerated. It was only with the publicity given to sexual behavior of males and females by the Kinsey reports and the availability of the Pill that a new morality was shared by both sexes and was seen as a revolution.

Sexual behavior became a major social and political issue with traditional churches taking stands against promiscuity and homosexuality. The call for "family values" became a rallying cry for conservatives and a major issue of the cultural wars of the 1980s and after. The identification of the AIDS virus in 1984 added a new factor to the sexual revolution bringing changes in behavior especially among the homosexual population. However, while the "Summer of Love" has not been repeated, many of the attitudes expressed in that summer became part of the social life of the nation. This was seen in the increasing use of sexual innuendoes in advertising where women in bikinis sold everything from automobiles to beer, in the stage actions of musicians and the lyrics they presented, in movies and TV, and in literature. The increasing use in public of vocabulary that had for years been considered suitable only for use in locker rooms also reflects changing attitudes.

RELIGIOUS DIVERSITY

In the 1960s members of the counterculture became interested in eastern religions. To them the teachings of the Buddha provided support for their less competitive view of society. Eastern gurus[10] developed large followings. Groups such as Hare Krishnas and the Unification Church founded by the Reverend Sun Myung Moon from Korea, whose members were referred to as Moonies, grew rapidly. Traditional churches introduced folk masses using guitars and popular music to appeal to those disillusioned with the emphasis on the traditions of the church.

At the same time interest in revivalist religion grew with the beginning of television evangelism. Pat Robertson, who was a political candidate in the 1980s, and Jim Bakker, who later admitted to an extra-marital affair, began their ministries, which reached

---

[10] guru   *A teacher, particularly one who has special insights into religious understandings.*

thousands of people who were exhorted to be "born again." Billy Graham, a revivalist speaker, who held meetings throughout the world including Moscow, a frequent White House guest, and the most noted evangelist of the postwar era, published *How to be Born Again* in 1977. Revivalist preachers deplored the use of drugs,

condemned the counterculture, and preached the values of the traditional American family at the time these values were changing rapidly. These preachers supported the anti-abortion movement after the *Roe* v. *Wade* decision in 1973. Together these conservative, fundamentalist, and tradition-oriented preachers with mega-churches and/ or TV congregations and their followers were soon referred to as the Religious Right. They became a significant part of the diversity of the United States. Jesse Helms, Senator from North Carolina, became the spokesperson in the United States Senate for the views of the Religious Right. The Religious Right clearly showed the counterculture reflected only one aspect of American society and during the Reagan years was a significant political force.

Another aspect of American society that other religious leaders addressed in the Cold War years was civil rights. The Southern Christian Leadership Conference (SCLC) headed by Martin Luther King, Jr. was organized in Birmingham, Alabama, in 1957 to address the issue. In the later 1960s the SCLC shifted its focus to address the issue of poverty in America. Self-help plans and reform efforts were made in many cities to try to bring hope to the dispossessed. The Rev. Jesse Jackson began his work to empower the poor in Chicago in the mid-1960s.

These varying religious groups—the eastern religions supported by the counterculture, the traditional churches, the Religious Right and the civil rights leadership—illustrate the

Religious attitudes reflect the diversity in America.

great diversity in religious patterns and understandings that developed in the 1960s and 1970s. The Sexual Revolution, the breakdown of the family with the growing divorce rate, the increasing poverty, and the Vietnam War led many Americans to reject the old ways. In spite of many efforts to, in President Nixon's words, "bring America together," the diversity increased in the 1980s.

THE YUPPIES

The diversity in America is well illustrated by the changing attitudes of young adults. It is another example of the cyclical patterns of history. The Yuppies—young urban professionals—replaced the 1960 Hippies who in turn had replaced the conservative young adults in gray flannel suits of the 1950s. The Yuppies were the leaders of what the novelist Tom Wolfe dubbed the "me" generation. Wolfe described the life style of the Yuppies in his novel *The Bonfire of the Vanities*. Yuppies focused on themselves. As already mentioned, Donald Trump and Michael Milken epitomized their goals of making money and finding success and economic well being. They also sought personal well being and emotional security turning to a variety of self-help programs to achieve these goals. TM (Transcendental Meditation) in which meditation techniques from eastern religions were drawn upon to achieve mental tranquillity and balance, and EST (Erhard Seminars Training), which taught self esteem and the importance of "power relationships," were among the most popular. Yuppies thought in terms of self-improvement. Books on the topic as well as on special diets were often at the top of the best seller lists. Another aspect of the Yuppie lifestyle was a concern for health, and jogging and health clubs became part of the American scene.

Many Yuppies were attracted to the cities with their cultural opportunities. In the 1970s government and local efforts led to the revitalization of certain residential areas in the inner cities, and projects, such as Lincoln Center in New York, provided new support for the arts. Yuppies moved into neighborhoods of restored homes originally meant for lower or middle income families and gentrified[11] these neighborhoods. The presence of the Yuppies in the city accentuated the split between rich and poor. Few minorities were accepted into Yuppie ranks, and those who were found their loyalties torn between their race and their financial success.

Social historians and commentators then replaced the term, Yuppies, with "Gen-X" as a term used to categorize young, twenty- and thirty-year-old college graduates who form an important economic and cultural group within society. Each change in term has meant a change, often slight, in the way these historians understand the shifting values, interests and priorities of this younger group. Except for the Hippies, there has been very little interest in politics and government by these designated groups and, of course, not all twenty and thirty year olds fit in the group.

THE CONTINUING FIGHT OVER TRADITIONAL VALUES

Beginning with the Civil Rights Movement in the 1950s, different groups have followed the lead of that movement to seek their rights and recognition within the American democratic framework (see pages 358–366). As these groups obtained success, the diversity within the United States has been clearly demonstrated. Some leaders and groups have embraced the pluralism thus represented. They have emphasized the word *pluribus* (many) in the motto of the United States—*e pluribus unum*, i.e., from many, one—found on the shield of the United States, which appears on every dollar bill. Opposing groups and their leaders have emphasized the word *unum* (one). These leaders deplore the acceptance of lifestyles and traditions that they term different from those of the United States. They fear that without an acceptance of one set of values for all, the country will fragment and become weak. Republican presidents have tended to proclaim the "traditional values" of the United States as the values of the Republican Party and to accuse the Democratic Party leaders of being liberal or willing to accept change and diversity. President Nixon was convinced there was a "silent majority" who endorsed what he and his supporters saw as the traditional American values at the time the Hippies were active and the opposition to Vietnam War was increasing. Nixon believed the base of these values was the traditional family—two or three children, a mother who cared for them, a father who supported them, all of whom attended church, would not divorce, believed in hard work, supported the government, and held a steady job. It was an ideal to which many might subscribe,

> The motto of the United States, *e pluribus unum*, is interpreted differently by different groups.

---

[11] gentrified   *From gentrification, the restoration of urban, especially working class, neighborhoods by middle and upper classes.*

but this ideal was difficult to obtain given the economic situation, the changing attitudes toward sexuality, the drug culture, and the increasing disparity between rich and poor. President Reagan, in spite of his divorce and remarriage, made support of "traditional family values" an important part of his campaign and repeated the phrase throughout his presidency as a statement of his most basic belief.

In 1988 at the Republican Presidential Convention, George H. W. Bush indicated his adherence to the values endorsed by Reagan and the Republican Party by picking the relatively unknown, young, conservative Dan Quayle for vice president. Throughout Bush's term and the elections, Dan Quayle spoke for the "traditional values" strongly supported by the conservative, often referred to as the "Right Wing," of the Republican Party. In the 1988 election Bush and Quayle labeled their opponents, Michael Dukakis and Lloyd Bentsen, as liberals. Dukakis stood for help for all elements in society—for the pluralistic and diverse society America had become.

This help would include a "safety net" of government-supported programs that more conservative Republicans considered socialistic and against the American way of rugged individualism. The Republicans used the word "liberal" to describe those they considered un-American, and the word has been used by them since then to rally conservatives to the Republican Party. For years "liberal" was a positive term with roots in the reform traditions of the nation. The change in use of the word by Republicans is an excellent example of how the meaning of words changes through history.

URBAN RIOTING AS A RESPONSE TO ECONOMIC AND SOCIAL ISSUES

Throughout United States history, groups within cities have responded to changing social or economic conditions or government policies with which they disagreed by rioting. Gang action against immigrants in the 19th century, anti-draft riots during the Civil War, and an anti-Greek immigrant riot in Omaha, Nebraska, in 1909 are examples. However, with population growth and inner city decline after World War II, urban riots became more destructive. The first large postwar riot took place in the Watts district of Los Angeles in 1965 after a state law requiring equal access to housing for blacks was repealed. Blacks in Watts burned buildings and looted shops in protest over the racist attitude reflected in government policy. The Watts riot was another aspect of the Civil Rights Movement as African-Americans outside of the South sought equal rights, but economic rather than political rights. The riots also reflected the growing divide between rich and poor and changing attitudes toward poverty and welfare. New leaders, such as Malcolm X and Stokely Carmichael, were not committed to nonviolence and "Black Power" became a rallying cry for many frustrated African-Americans. These leaders and the Vietnam conflict, in which a disproportionate number of African-Americans fought, slowly forced King to shift the focus of the SCLC to poverty and economic issues and to take his campaign to northern cites. In the two years after Watts, there were riots in many cities from Omaha to Detroit, from Minneapolis to Washington, D.C., all with roots in racism and the failure of governments to meet the needs of the inner cities. After the assassination of Martin Luther King in 1968, another wave of rioting swept the nation, reflecting frustration at the slow speed of economic change. Many northern liberals, who had supported the Civil Rights Movement as it worked to end segregation in the South, were shocked by these riots. The Movement was never again as cohesive as it had been before passage of the Civil Rights Act of 1964 and the Voting Rights Act of 1965— acts that northerners thought took care of African-American concerns. Riots, often in reaction to racist behavior, occurred occasionally in the years after King's death, most notably the Rodney King riots in Watts in 1992. It started in reaction to police brutality toward an African-American.

> The police beating of Rodney King was recorded on video, and acquittal of the officers involved provoked the most destructive riot in United States history.

Changing sexual values and attitudes led to numerous cases of violence against abortion clinics and homosexuals but only to one riot, the Stonewall Riot in New York City in 1969. Police had been harassing gays in the city bars for years, and when they entered the Stonewall Bar, gays battled back. The riot crystallized the Gay Rights Movement. Social historians have studied these riots and found all have common roots in frustration and the failure of society to respond to changing conditions. As the struggle over changing values continues, there is always the danger of some groups turning to violence to support their positions.

> Stonewall Riot focuses Gay Rights Movement.

Key Point to Remember

The United States is a powerful nation composed of individuals with a great diversity of attitudes and values which is one of its great strengths as seen in its motto—*e pluribus unum*, from many, one.

People to Remember

James Dean   Movie hero; starred in rebellious roles in *East of Eden* and *Rebel Without a Cause*; became a hero to 1950's teenagers; his early death in a car accident made him a cult hero and symbol of rebellion against established values and traditions.

Links from the Past to the Present

1. Periodic swings in American attitudes from idealism to personal concerns is reflected in the Hippies and Yuppies.

2. Revival religion in America began with the first Great Awakening in the 18th century and continues with TV revivalist preachers and born-again Christians.

3. Racism has been a factor in American life throughout our history.

Dates

1946—Dr. Spock wrote *Baby and Child Care.*

1948—Dr. Albert Kinsey published *Sexual Behavior of the American Male.*

1955—James Dean starred in *Rebel Without a Cause.*

1962—Students for a Democratic Society (SDS) founded. Michael Harrington wrote *The Other America*.

1964—Free Speech Movement begun at Berkeley.

1965—Watts Riot in Los Angeles.

1967—500,000 attended anti-war rally in New York City.
    "Summer of love" in San Francisco proclaimed by Hippies.

1968—Martin Luther King, Jr., assassination riots.

1969—Stonewall Riot in New York City.

1970—Charles Reich wrote *The Greening of America*.

1977—Billy Graham wrote *How to be Born Again*.

1980—Reagan campaigned on adherence to traditional values.

1988—Quayle picked as Vice President, reinforcing Republican campaign for traditional values.

1992—Rodney King riots in Los Angeles.

Questions

Identify each of the following:

Counterculture	Hippies	Yuppies
Religious Right	Teenagers	New Left
Juvenile Delinquent	*E pluribus unum*	ROTC

Multiple Choice:

1. The changing attitudes of young American adults is illustrated by the social historian's use of the terms
   a. Moonies and Religious Right.
   b. Hippies and Yuppies.
   c. McCarthyism and Sexual Revolution.

2. Television evangelists and members of the Religious Right opposed
   a. situation ethics and the Sexual Revolution.
   b. abortion.
   c. all of the above.

3. The counterculture and the New Left were united in their attitudes toward
   a. the Vietnam War.
   b. the importance of rock 'n' roll and the SDS.
   c. violence.

4. The Kinsey reports revealed that
   a. Americans strictly adhered to the teachings of all churches on morality.
   b. American women were more promiscuous than American males.
   c. neither of the above.

III. Social Movements and Social Protests

CONFORMITY IN THE 1950s

The 1950s have been characterized as years of conformity in which the American Dream of a house in the suburbs and a job in the city was held by all Americans; in which one attended church on Sunday and adhered to the moral principles set forth in churches—no premarital sex or divorce, marriage until death,

> McCarthyism typifies the emphasis on conformity and anticommunism.

abortion and homosexuality were crimes; in which students accepted what was taught; in which patriotism came first, the government was honest, and the country must unite behind stopping communism. McCarthyism typified this attitude. Senator Joseph McCarthy's attacks on Communists in the State Department and military frightened many and stamped protest as un-American and the period established what later were referred to as America's "traditional values." Actually this period was much more complex and diverse than it appears at first look, and the roots of several movements of social protest were cultivated in the 1950s. These movements accelerated change in American society creating the diversity and complexity of life today. Social historians have analyzed these movements providing a clearer understanding of the United States in the 1950s and 1960s.

THE CIVIL RIGHTS MOVEMENT

The Civil Rights Movement began with legal cases brought by the NAACP in the 1930s but the landmark *Brown* v. *Board of Education* in 1954 gave it momentum as did the Montgomery Bus Boycott in 1957 (see pages 267–268). In the bus boycott individuals such as Rosa Parks and Martin Luther King, Jr. emerged as leaders, and the people—the voiceless—felt empowered. The first actions were directed toward gaining social rights such as the right to equal education and access to lunch counters and buses, changing the face of cities and institutions throughout the nation. Later, political empowerment became the goal.

The Voting Rights Act of 1965 marked a major success in gaining political power. After the passage of the act, African-American voters became important to both Republican and Democratic parties. Eventually as the African-Americans dominated the Democratic Party in the south, whites turned to the Republican Party. They replaced the Democrats as the dominant party in the south, reversing a hundred year pattern and providing the base for conservative Republican power until 2008. Slowly, more and more African-Americans gained elected office, and by the late 1980s several major cities—Detroit, New York, Los Angeles—had African-American mayors and Virginia elected an African-American governor, Douglas Wilder. In 1992 the first African-American woman, Carol Moseley-Braun (Illinois), was elected to the U.S. Senate.

The Civil Rights Movement inspired and gave momentum to other protest and empowerment movements. The Free Press Movement at Berkeley was begun by students who had been involved in the Civil Rights Movement.

The SDS (Students for Democratic Society) took inspiration from it. With the emergence of Malcolm X as a spokesman of the Black Muslims and the call of the Student Non-Violent Coordinating Committee's (SNCC) founder, Stokely Carmichael, for "Black Power," the Civil Rights Movement offered both the nonviolent approach of Martin Luther King, Jr. and the violence-prone approach of Black Power as models.

Carmichael, King, and the emerging leader, Jesse Jackson, began to focus the Civil Rights Movement on economic issues in the mid-1960s. With the assassination of King in 1968, the leadership of the movement became fragmented. It was less successful in attaining economic equality for African-Americans than it had been in obtaining social and political empowerment. However, its successes in the 1960s did much to change the structure of American society.

WOMEN'S LIBERATION MOVEMENT

The Civil Rights Movement not only provided a model for the SDS, it awakened other minorities to their subordinate status. The largest group so inspired were women, who actually formed a slight majority of the population but who shared with ethnic minorities a place in the economic and political structure subordinate to the white male.

There had been women's movements in the 19th century, and the suffrage movement had gained the vote for women in 1919, but neither economic nor political equality followed. More women joined the work force in both world wars but in the postwar periods numbers of those working declined as, in the 1920s, the "flapper" and then, in the 1950s, the "mom" became the model for feminine behavior and soldiers returned to the civilian work force. There were always women concerned with the place of women in society, and President Kennedy early in his presidency appointed a Committee on the Status of Women to consider what issues needed to be addressed by the government.

Betty Friedan in her 1963 book *The Feminine Mystique* first expressed views that became the focus of the Women's Liberation Movement. Friedan claimed middle class values stifled women who were expected to spend their days with children with no stimulation from other adults. A woman was to fill the position of housewife and companion to her husband, who left home daily to meet the challenges of the world. Many women agreed with Friedan's criticism, and in 1966 the National Organization for Women (NOW) was organized.

Unfortunately for the effectiveness of the Women's Movement, the focus of NOW was blurred in 1969 when lesbians, who were organizing for their rights, were kept out of the organization. Also, the abortion issue split women into two camps on that very personal and emotional topic, and African-American women were torn between commitment to the white led NOW and the Civil Rights Movement. These differences raised the question, "Should NOW support only political and economic rights or all rights of women?" In 1971 the antilesbian policy was reversed and NOW accepted all women without regard to sexual preference. Society's values were changing.

EQUAL RIGHTS AMENDMENT

NOW focused its attention on equality and an Equal Rights Amendment (ERA) to the Constitution. They began by calling attention to the job discrimination women faced in companies run by white males where women rarely had executive positions. NOW argued for equal pay for equal work done by men and women, for greater job opportunities, and for day care facilities. In 1972 Congress passed and sent to the states for ratification the ERA, which would guarantee equality of the sexes. First Ladies Lady Bird Johnson, Betty Ford, and Rosalyn Carter all spoke in favor of ERA, and it was endorsed by groups as varied as the AFL-CIO and Girl Scouts. The New Right opposed ERA. Although 35 states ratified ERA, the needed three-fourths of the states (38) failed to ratify the amendment within the ten-year time limit. The time was extended three years in 1982, but the amendment was not ratified. NOW leaders suggest this failure confirms their analysis that white men in position of power discriminate against women.

ERA is defeated.	

The debate over ERA and women's liberation was intense and raised such questions as, "Would women be drafted into the armed services if the ERA were passed?" This and similar questions seemed to go against the traditional value of the male as defender of the home and the perceived role of women in society. The male-dominated legislatures of the more conservative states were unable to accept this change in role.

CONSCIOUSNESS RAISING

The Women's Movement addresses primarily issues of concern to middle-class Americans.

The Women's Movement created a greater awareness of the place of women in American society and raised the consciousness level of both men and women. CR (consciousness raising) groups brought women together to discuss their frustrations and shared experiences, and many men in the 1960s were forced by their wives and female friends to reconsider the role of the male in society. For many men it was a troubling time. By the 1980s a backlash had set in, and men's groups developed their own CR programs. Robert Bly with his book *Iron John* and in his work with men's groups became a spokesman in the mid-1990s for men working on their identity and the issue of masculinity.

OPPORTUNITIES FOR WOMEN

In the 1960s NOW's membership and the concerns it addressed were largely middle-class issues, which limited its success and appeal. However, in the 25 years after NOW was founded, job opportunities for women greatly increased, and some progress was made in equal pay and in the availability of day care. All three issues became very important for all American women as the divorce rate climbed and more single women became heads of families.

The Women's Movement gave publicity to the issue of sexual harassment in the workplace and at home. Shelters for battered women were established in cities throughout the country. Date rape was discussed openly on college campuses. Sexual harassment policies were developed in schools, colleges, and work places and widely publicized.

The Clarence Thomas Supreme Court hearings in which Anita Hill accused the nominee of sexual harassment electrified the nation in 1992. He was confirmed by the Senate. After the Anita Hill incident, more women were elected to the male-dominated U.S. Senate.

One most important measure that opened opportunities for women was Title IX of the Education Amendments of 1972 known as the Mink Equal Opportunity in Education Act. Title IX of the act stated that "No person . . . shall on the basis of sex be denied the benefits of, or be subject to discrimination under any education program or activity receiving Federal financial support." While the act covered all educational activities from dormitory arrangements to lab access, the aspect gaining most public attention was athletics. High schools and colleges receiving any federal aid, from school lunch money to research grants, had to provide equal access to athletic opportunities. The result was a surge in women's athletic programs and highly visible female athletes. This built confidence, provided economic opportunities, and helped change attitudes toward the role of women in society.

ABORTION RIGHTS: PRO-CHOICE AND PRO-LIFE MOVEMENTS

NOW's fight for a woman's right to abortion in cases of unwanted pregnancy was won in the Supreme Court decision of *Roe* v. *Wade* in 1973. The Roe decision expanded the Court's interpretation of the right to privacy and removed state restrictions on abortion during the first three months of pregnancy.

The abortion decision created great controversy in America and split the Women's Movement. A pro-life group emerged claiming abortion was murder because the fetus was a human life; a pro-choice group countered that until the fetus could survive outside the womb, it should not be considered a person and that a woman should be in charge of her own body—not a man, a court, a church, or the legislature. The Pro-Life Movement wished to overturn the Supreme Court decision and fought for state and federal laws restricting the right to an abortion. Although the United States Supreme Court upheld several state laws restricting the government's need to pay for abortions and setting conditions for underage women to obtain them, it did not override the original decision to the dismay of members of the New Right who were vehemently pro-life and anti-abortion. Since *Roe* v. *Wade* according to polls, the majority of Americans favor a woman's right to an abortion, but they also approve various restrictions on it.

> The *Roe* v. *Wade* decision by the Supreme Court makes abortion a major controversy in America.

GAY RIGHTS MOVEMENT

Homophobia[12] is another way fear of others who are different is manifested in society. For years it kept homosexuals "in the closet," afraid to admit publicly their sexual orientation.

> The Gay Rights Movement achieves some results.

Throughout United States history until the 1960s, there was very limited acceptance by the American people of homosexuality, and homosexual practices were criminalized. Every state had antisodomy laws until 1962 when Illinois became the first state to repeal its law, and the medical profession viewed homosexuality as abnormal and many psychologists classified it as a mental illness. During the ferment of the 1960s, gay communities emerged in New York, California, and elsewhere. Then when the police clashed with the frequenters of a gay bar in New York in 1969, the resulting Stonewall Riot led to the organization of the Gay Liberation Front in which lesbian and homosexual Americans organized to secure their rights as minorities who shared a different lifestyle. The Gay Liberation Movement reflected another aspect of the Civil Rights Movement.

As did that movement, the Gay Rights Movement in the 1970s and 1980s produced many local leaders who focused on achieving social and political rights for the gay community as American citizens. Harvey Milk, the first openly gay man to be elected to a major political office—San Francisco Board of Supervisors—is an example. He left a job in investment banking in New York, moved to San Francisco, started a camera business, and coming out of the closet, announced that he was gay. He ran for office three times before being elected—each time widening his appeal in the straight community. When a California legislator put a Proposition on the ballot that would forbid any positive mention of homosexuality in schools, Milk organized the gay community and campaigned against it. In the 1970s several communities (e.g., Dade County, Florida) passed ordinances giving civil rights to gays. There was a backlash led by the Religious Right. Anita Bryant, a pop singer, became a spokesperson for this anti-gay backlash and spoke in favor of the California Proposition, but with gays and the Democratic Party opposed, it lost overwhelmingly. Milk was then elected as Supervisor in 1978 but was assassinated by a conservative, anti-gay fellow supervisor. Milk became a martyr for the gay cause and illustrated clearly "that a gay person can live an honest life and succeed." Several of his close friends went on to important roles in the gay community including the creation of the AIDS quilt. Many other individuals had similar impacts on the Gay Rights Movement, and by the end of the 1970s, seventeen states, largely in the northeast and west, had repealed laws criminalizing sodomy between consenting adults. However, it was not until 2003 in the *Lawrence* v. *Texas* case that the Supreme Court declared all such laws unconstitutional.

AMERICAN INDIAN MOVEMENT

In the 1960s following the example of the African-American community, Native Americans organized the American Indian Movement (AIM) in 1968. From the start,

---

[12] homophobia   *Fear of homosexuals or homosexuality.*

the goal of the movement was to call attention in the media to the problems of Native Americans. To achieve this the leaders adopted a more aggressive, violent approach then that of the SCLC. In 1970 AIM members seized the replica of the *Mayflower* during the celebration of the 350th anniversary of the establishment of the Plymouth colony. In 1971 they seized

> The American Indian Movement uses violence to call attention to the status of Native Americans.

Mount Rushmore, and in 1973 members of AIM took hostages and seized a trading post on the Pine Tree reservation at Wounded Knee, South Dakota, site of a massacre of Native Americans by the United States Cavalry in 1890. After a two-month siege the United States government agreed to examine the treaty signed with the Sioux. Such actions continued through the 1970s and gave AIM leaders publicity and an opportunity to explain their issues on TV and in the press, but their tactics alienated many and their success was limited. However, through cases brought in the federal courts, Indian groups have been able to get native tribal lands returned, to gain hunting and fishing rights, and to have museums return sacred objects to tribal ownership.

In spite of the efforts of AIM, the majority of the Native American population remains the most depressed group in the country.

OTHER MINORITY MOVEMENTS

During the 1960s and early 1970s other groups organized to gain power and/or claim their rights as citizens of the United States. Hispanics and Asians organized but did not gain the national attention achieved by African-Americans, women, or gays. However, they benefited from the success of the other movements, and their contributions to the pluralism of American life has been recognized.

THE NEW RIGHT MOVEMENT

The New Right emerged in the late 1960s in part in opposition to the many liberation movements of the period. The New Right brought together different groups that held to the traditional values and attitudes of Americans as they understood them. Many were threatened by the changes that were occurring.

> New Right emerges as a conservative force after the defeat of Republican presidential candidate Barry Goldwater in 1964.

Senator Barry Goldwater, Republican candidate for president in 1964, was a conservative and reflected these views. After his defeat the more conservative of his supporters coalesced as the New Right. Senator Jesse Helms of North Carolina was one spokesperson. His comments against homosexuality, against government support for art that had any pornographic cast, against abortion, and in favor of prayer in the schools summarize the program of the New Right. President Nixon appealed to the votes of the New Right when he referred to the "silent majority," whom he believed supported the values voiced in the 19th century and did not support the changes advocated by the various liberation movements. It was in these circumstances that the Republican Party began to gain strength in the formerly solidly Democratic south laying the foundation for the Reagan Revolution and the strength of the Republican Party until 2008.

Phyllis Schlafly emerged as one leader of the New Right. She fought the ERA in a STOP-ERA campaign in several crucial states where the amendment was narrowly defeated. Another leader was Anita Bryant who campaigned against homosexual rights in the 1970s. Television evangelists Pat Robertson and Jerry Falwell were considered spokespersons for the movement. In the 1970s, they spoke of themselves and their followers as the Moral Majority, and organized a political action committee with that name. It publicized political campaigns in churches and gave support to many Republican candidates. The name implied that the majority of Americans supported their views on morality and the future of the nation. It implied they were the only ones with true morals. The Moral Majority campaigned against homosexuality, premarital sex, abortion, and pornography and in favor of reduced welfare payments for the poor and a stronger military.

In the Reagan years the views of the New Right helped guide policy as Reagan spoke of family values, being tough on crime, a return to prayer in schools, and the repeal of *Roe* v. *Wade* by appointing conservative justices to the Supreme Court. The New Right clearly illustrates that all Americans did not favor the liberation movements changing moral values and attitudes of the 1960s. The tensions between the views of the Moral Majority and the liberation movements illustrate the complexity of American society and how difficult the role of the social historian is in determining the forces that influence political and economic leaders.

After the Republican Convention of 1992 there was a slight backlash at the views of the New Right. Clinton, in his campaign, opposed their position on several important issues such as gay rights and abortion. The overwhelming Republican victory in the Congressional elections of 1994 again placed the agenda of the New Right at the forefront of political controversy.

THE ANTI-NUCLEAR AND PEACE MOVEMENTS

Throughout the Cold War there was deep concern about nuclear war. The concern was expressed in different ways. In the 1950s some individuals built bomb shelters. A major effort to organize civilian defense in case of war occurred at the time of the Cuban Missile Crisis. During the Vietnam War a peace movement developed but its main focus was anti-Vietnam War not anti-nuclear war. In the 1960s and 1970s there was concern that the fear of nuclear destruction was affecting the way youth behaved. Statistics suggested juvenile delinquency was increasing. Some psychologists indicated adolescents and young adults were seeking instant gratification rather than plan for a long life. There were studies that suggested this might be true, but it was hard to prove a correlation between adolescent behavior and a fear of nuclear destruction.

> Concern about nuclear war is expressed in different ways.

There were often rumors of nuclear disasters but until the Three Mile Island, Pennsylvania, nuclear power plant nearly had a meltdown in 1979, there was no public acknowledgment of any accident by either the government or private industry. The destruction of the nuclear power plant at Chernobyl in the Soviet Union in 1986 dramatically illustrated the destructive power of nuclear energy. It helped to reactivate anti-nuclear protests and reignited the fear of a misguided reliance on nuclear power to produce electricity and on nuclear weapons for defense.

Since the dropping of the first atomic weapon on Japan in 1945, there were groups that opposed the use of nuclear weapons and stood for peace and disarmament. The strength and activities of the groups varied over the years. Then in the 1980s a strong peace movement developed in opposition to Reagan's defense buildup and the Chernobyl incident. The Reagan administration suggested the United States could fight and win a nuclear war and advocated the Strategic Defense Initiative (SDI) or "Star Wars" program. Focusing on the threat of a "nuclear winter"[13] following any use of nuclear weapons, there were protests around the country. The Peace Movement grew quite spontaneously. What impact the movement had on national policy cannot be determined, but in the mid-1980s Reagan began negotiating arms reduction with the Soviets. The Peace Movement was another of those outpourings of the people concerned with issues of change and reform we have seen so often in American history. As with the movements for liberation, the Peace Movement changed attitudes of some Americans and was led by relatively unknown citizens who stepped into leadership positions.

ENVIRONMENTAL MOVEMENT

Throughout the Cold War there were people who expressed concern about environmental issues. As with the Peace Movement, its strength varied over the years. The Environmental Movement in the United States has had a long history. It began as a conservation movement at the start of the 20th century and was led by people like John Muir who founded the Sierra Club as an environmental group in 1897 and President Theodore Roosevelt who established the first national parks. Over the years it has included diverse groups who have focused on issues from saving the rain forests to the clean up of toxic waste dumps. After World War II, the primary focus was on restoring and maintaining a clean environment. Groups as diverse as the World Wildlife Fund and Greenpeace were formed to call attention to various aspects of environmental concerns. Rachel Carson in *Silent Spring* (1962) called attention to the use of pesticides in agriculture and the damage they had done. It was a stimulus to the growth of environmental awareness.

In 1970 the first Earth Day was organized to draw attention to the environment and the need for actions to protect it. Many individuals and organizations participated, and the celebration received extensive press coverage. A greater personal awareness of environmental issues resulted. Congress responded to the concerns expressed by the movement by passing the first Clean Air and Water Quality Improvement Acts during Nixon's presidency, although he personally opposed such legislation. In 1987 Congress overrode President Reagan's veto of the Clean Water Act showing Congress can act on environmental issues (see page 314).

---

[13] nuclear winter   *The concept supported by many scientists that after a nuclear war the fallout dust would shield the earth from the sun and create permanent winter conditions on the earth.*

In April 1990, on the 20th anniversary of the first Earth Day, Denis Hayes, one of the organizers of the first Earth Day, organized the second Earth Day. It was celebrated throughout the world and is now celebrated annually. Earth Day calls people's attention to various environmental concerns from toxic waste dumps to destruction of the rain forest to the greenhouse effect and global warming.[14] By the end of the Reagan/Bush terms, the environmental discussion was shifting from cleaning and protecting the environment to the impact of and causes of climate change. Scientists were becoming more aware of dramatic changes, and laboratory modeling suggested major impacts on climate and weather were rapidly approaching. In 1992, the UN Framework on Climate Change held a meeting in Rio. The resulting treaty was implemented by the 1997 Kyoto Protocols setting guidelines for reducing greenhouse gases. Neither Clinton nor Bush asked the Senate to approve them. In 2009, a conference on climate in Copenhagen will address the next steps. How the U.S. will respond is not clear.

However, in the more narrow area of environmental protection, progress was made. By the 1990s many cities had adopted recycling programs to reduce the need for landfills. The federal government had undertaken to clean up toxic waste dumps and passed domestic Clean Water and Air legislation. Cleaner running car engines, but not for SUVs or trucks, were required by federal legislation. Environmental awareness became a part of American life.

> **Environmental cleanup becomes government policy.**

THE SUPREME COURT SUPPORTS INDIVIDUAL RIGHTS

The Supreme Court under Chief Justice Earl Warren, who was appointed by Eisenhower, handed down several significant decisions in the area of civil and individual rights. Besides the *Brown* v. *Board of Education* decision in 1954, which declared unconstitutional "separate but equal" schools and stimulated the Civil Rights Movement, the Warren Court upheld the civil rights legislation of the 1960s. It also supported the legal actions of the SCLC, which helped it win successes in the Montgomery Bus Boycott and the Selma March.

In three important cases, *Gideon* v. *Wainwright* in 1963, *Escobedo* v. *Illinois* in 1964, and *Miranda* v. *Arizona* in 1966 the Warren Court interpreted the Constitution to give protection to the rights of individual criminal suspects. In the *Gideon* case the Court held that a lawyer must be supplied for any accused prisoner who could not afford a lawyer. In the *Escobedo* case the Court declared the police had to inform a suspect of his or her legal rights, and in *Miranda* that a suspect had the "right to remain silent" to avoid self-incrimination. If this were not done, the case could be dismissed. These Supreme Court cases illustrate that the Court shared the 1960s concern for the poor.

Some Americans reacted that the Court was "soft on crime." This became an issue in Nixon's 1968 election campaign when he appealed for "law and order" in America. When Earl Warren retired, Nixon

> **The Burger Court declares quotas unconstitutional.**

[14] greenhouse effect and global warming   *The scientific concept that our pollution traps heat and creates a greenhouse-like warm atmosphere, which will increase the temperature of the earth. This temperature increase is referred to as global warming.*

appointed a more conservative Chief Justice, Warren Burger, but the Court under Burger continued to interpret the Constitution to extend an American's right to privacy and to protect the rights of individuals and especially of the poor. The most important and still controversial decision of the Burger Court was the *Roe* v. *Wade* decision on abortion in 1973 (see page 361). In another controversial decision, the Bakke case, the Burger Court declared unconstitutional quotas that were used to establish equal opportunities for minorities in hiring and schooling. Quotas had been established by federal legislation to gain greater access for minorities to the business and economic life of the nation. The decision supported the rights of the individual, yet it was not supported by leaders of several liberation movements who viewed quotas as a way for members of their group to gain access to education and jobs.

The Supreme Court throughout American history has interpreted the Constitution. Some groups are always pleased with decisions; others are not. Over the years, as membership in and leadership of the Court change, the Court's interpretation of the meaning of the Constitution changes. This can be illustrated by the Court's interpretation of the death penalty. For centuries

> The Supreme Court interprets the meaning of "cruel and unusual punishment."

societies have used death as the ultimate penalty for crime. In the 1960s the Court ruled against the death penalty as a "cruel and unusual punishment," which was forbidden by the Eighth Amendment to the Constitution. By the 1990s the death penalty was again in wide use, supported by the Court and Congress, which continually expanded by legislation the crimes for which death would be an acceptable penalty. In 1994 Justice Harry Blackmun, previously a supporter of the death penalty, stated he believed it could not be imposed fairly, and he opposed its use. The issue is not settled.

Another area where the changing views of the Court on the meaning of the Constitution can be illustrated is the Court's decisions on prayer in the schools, an issue of great interest to conservatives, members of the New Right, evangelical Christians, and Christian Fundamentalists. In 1962 the Warren Court declared prayer in public school classrooms unconstitutional. They based their decision on the so-called separation of church and state clause of the First Amendment. The issue became an important aspect of the debate over traditional values and was argued in political campaigns at all levels. President Reagan was a strong advocate for prayer in schools and the individual's right to free expression. In 1992 the Rehnquist Court declared a prayer offered by a student at a public school graduation to be constitutionally acceptable because the individual student not the government-supported school introduced the prayer. The Court also said moments of meditation are acceptable if they are not designated for prayer. While school prayer may seem a minor issue to many, the right of the individual to act according to one's conscience and not be coerced by the government is at the heart of individual liberty. Some social historians saw the conservative support of school prayer as hypocritical since conservatives who supported the individual's right to prayer in school also opposed an individual woman's right to an abortion. Others saw the latter as an issue of the individual fetuses right to life. In decisions involving moral and ethical issues, the Court often found itself the center of controversy. However, throughout the period of social movements and social protests of the fifty years after World War II, the

Supreme Court played a very significant role supporting individual rights and the changes that were taking place in American society.

Key Point to Remember

The Civil Rights Movement inspired many other minority groups to organize to seek recognition and rights, and they achieved considerable success; however, they created a backlash from the New Right. The tensions created by these two opposing perspectives are an important part of present day American society.

People to Remember

Betty Friedan   Reformer; founder and president of National Organization for Women and National Woman's Political Caucus; author of *The Feminine Mystique*, which analyzed the role of women in American society.

Links From the Past to the Present

1. The various minority movements for civil rights—Gay Rights, NOW, AIM, Farm Workers—reflect Americans' concern for individual rights.

2. The Supreme Court has always reflected the changing attitudes of the American people.

3. Abortion, first raised as an issue by the Women's Movement, continues as a major issue in American politics.

Dates

1954—*Brown* v. *Board of Education.*

1957—Montgomery Bus Boycott.

1962—*Silent Spring* published.

1963—*Gideon* v. *Wainwright.*
  The Feminine Mystique by Betty Friedan published.

1964—*Escobedo* v. *Illinois.*

1965—Voting Rights Act.
  Civil Rights Act.

1966—NOW founded.

1969—Stonewall Riot in New York City led to organization of Gay Liberation Front.

1970—First Earth Day celebration held.

1970s—New Right and Moral Majority represent conservative backlash to 1960s.

1972—ERA passed by Congress.

1973—*Roe* v. *Wade.*
  Wounded Knee Confrontation organized by AIM.

1978—Harvey Milk assassinated.

1979—Three Mile Island near nuclear meltdown.

1990—Second worldwide celebration of Earth Day.

1991—Anita Hill accused Supreme Court nominee Judge Clarence Thomas of sexual harassment.

Questions
Identify each of the following:

ERA	Pro-Life Movement
AIM	Pro-Choice Movement
Escobedo v. *Illinois*	New Right
Roe v. *Wade*	Moral Majority

Multiple Choice:

1. In *Roe* v. *Wade* the Supreme Court stated women have a right to privacy and permitted abortion
   a. at any time.
   b. under orders from a doctor.
   c. during the first three months of pregnancy.

2. Among the groups formed to advance their rights as minorities were
   a. the Gay Rights Movement.
   b. AIM.
   c. both of the above.

3. The American Indian Movement out of frustration turned to violence and seized hostages at
   a. Wounded Knee, South Dakota.
   b. Three Mile Island, Pennsylvania.
   c. Miami, Florida.

4. Among the leaders of the New Right and Moral Majority were
   a. Barry Goldwater and Cesar Chavez.
   b. Jerry Falwell and Rachel Carson.
   c. Phyllis Schlafly and Pat Robertson.

IV. Culture and Society

TELEVISION

The most significant developments in American culture in the immediate postwar years resulted from the growth of the television industry. The changes were as significant and complex as were those stemming from the introduction of the automobile in the first half of the 20th century and of the computer in the last quarter of the century. Everyone has heard statistics of how many hours of television high school graduates have seen or children have viewed before entering kindergarten. Specific

> Television becomes a major factor in the daily lives of the American public.

numbers vary, but they are always staggering and in the thousands of hours. Yet in 1945 there were only 7,000 TV sets in the nation, illustrating how different were the experiences of childhood and adolescence of those born before World War II and those born after. By 1960 there were 50 million television sets in the country. TV reinforced the conformity that was a hallmark of the Eisenhower years as the limited number of television stations provided standardized entertainment for the American people. Frozen TV dinners became a part of American life eliminating meal preparation time and allowing the family to quickly heat a frozen meal to be eaten on a tray while watching the prime-time programs.

Television provided shared experiences for Americans, as it still does. The first such event, the investigation of the U.S. Army by Senator McCarthy, was watched by thousands and revealed to viewers the personality of McCarthy. The decline of his influence can be traced to that televised hearing. The assassinations and funerals of J. F. Kennedy, M. L. King, Jr., and

> Television provides instant, shared experiences, often tragic, for the American people.

Robert Kennedy provided shared tragic experiences for those living in the 1960s. The first landing on the moon provided Americans with a shared triumph as millions watched the event. The instant presentation of events to millions, whether it be a scheduled Presidential Debate, unexpected tragedy or Super Bowl, provides shared experiences for discussion, bonding and a sense of unity. However, it can also stifle dissent and isolate or alienate those who do not choose to participate. Whatever one's personal reaction is, the sharing of national events through television coverage is a recent phenomenon and one of interest to the social historian.

As the industry grew, afternoon programming was quickly filled with soap operas similar to those heard on radio. Evening time, prime time for the advertising industry that paid for TV programming by running commercials, was filled with news broadcasts and comedy shows such as the very popular and successful *I Love Lucy* starring Lucille Ball, which provided laughs for the nation. In the 1970s *MASH* with its setting of the Korean War followed as the most popular and successful comedy. *MASH*, starring Alan Alda as "Hawkeye,"

> Crime dramas and sitcoms dominate prime-time television after the success of Dallas in 1978.

set a tone of humor against the horrors of war—a good combination for the Cold War years. Ed Sullivan found a niche early in the history of TV, and for over twenty-five years Americans saw the stars of the day including the Beatles on the Ed Sullivan Show. *Saturday Night Live* debuted in 1975 offering a sense of what vaudeville shows might have been like with skits, solos, and music. In 1978 *Dallas* brought afternoon soap opera to prime time. Crime dramas and sitcoms came to dominate evening TV, with each episode complete in the 30- or 60-minute time period. Some psychologists have suggested the easy resolution of difficult problems, usually personal as in *The Cosby Show*, have led Americans to expect instant solutions to problems. They also suggest that continual interruptions for advertising have had a negative impact on people's attention spans. It is an important issue to consider as the social historian reflects on the impact of TV on society and the changes it has brought to American life.

In the early years of TV, families portrayed were middle-class and white. Archie Bunker in *All in The Family*, and later *Roseanne*, expanded the images portrayed as did the long-running *The Cosby Show* (1984–1992). In 1990 the new FOX network introduced a cartoon sitcom, the first successful one since the *Flintstones* in the 1960s. *The Simpsons* caught on immediately, and Bart Simpson T-shirts were seen throughout the country. Compared to the sweetness portrayed in the early Disney full-length cartoons, *The Simpsons* gave a cynical yet cartoon perspective on real-life situations that were often unpleasant yet laughed at by the people. Some critics have suggested the popularity of *The Simpsons* reflected the cynicism of the 1990s.

> The Simpsons on the FOX network introduced a new type of cartoon show.

CHILDREN'S TELEVISION

Sesame Street, one of the first and most successful children's shows, has had mixed reviews because, as it attempts to reach children at their level, to prepare them for school, and to teach about cultural diversity, the lessons have used pratfalls to teach numbers and loud music to attract attention. However, it has been a most important show for generations of young Americans, some of whom received their first exposure to Hispanics on the show. *Mr. Rogers Neighborhood* was an attempt to provide children TV entertainment without violence. These programs illustrate what can be done with TV to teach children. In contrast, prime-time shows with their violence and sex were not appropriate for children, yet many children viewed them. While political leaders discussed traditional values, the advertising and TV industries found traditional values did not attract viewers to TV. The social historian must ask whether the advertising and TV industries push programming with violence and sex on the public including children or whether the public only wanted to watch such shows.

> Child-oriented programs provide educational opportunities but are not broadcast on prime time.

TV introduced many fads to young people. Youngsters have been intrigued by everything from the coonskin caps inspired by *Davy Crockett* to the dinosaurs of the *Barney* craze of 1994.

TELEVISION AND THE POLITICAL PROCESS

Three commercial networks, which got their revenue from advertising, and one public network, which got its revenue from public and government contributions and corporate grants, dominated the television industry until the 1980s. The start of cable programming transformed TV. Cable News Network (CNN), founded by billionaire Ted Turner in 1980, captured thousands of viewers who got their news only from the networks. Availability of round-the-clock news forced changes on the newspaper industry and led to the establishment of single-topic cable programming. Music Television (MTV) founded in 1981 is an early example. Originally it was to play music videos, but in the 1990s MTV expanded its coverage to other programming. Its appeal has been to a young audience and has had

> Cable channels provide increased opportunities in viewing.

an important impact on the development of pop culture. Not only have new cable stations focused on single topics, they have also been found to present a particular viewpoint on news and society. As television became ever more popular, newspaper and magazine reading declined, as did the appeal of radio. Both cable and network TV have affected the political process. The earliest major example is the presidential debates between John F. Kennedy and Richard Nixon in 1960. Since that 1960 debate, which some believe lost Nixon the presidency because of his personal appearance—he had a 5 o'clock shadow—not because of his ideas, TV election debates have been used at every level of the electoral process from local school board to president. In the 1960s news coverage of both the Civil Rights Movement and the Vietnam War informed the public of those events and helped shape their reactions. A TV image of a Vietnamese girl in flames from a napalm bombing horrified viewers and encouraged anti-war protests. TV pictures of white police attacking African-American children with fire hoses and dogs focused attention in favor of civil rights. TV images of the 1968 Democratic Party Convention in Chicago made Americans wonder if a civil war was about to happen and helped elect Nixon. At the time of the first Iraq War, CNN gained an international reputation. It became the chief source of information for everyone from the common person to the presidents of the United States and Iraq.

MOVIES

Long before TV, movies provided an outlet for American creativity. Hollywood and movies became synonymous before World War II. Ever since the invention of the motion picture, movies have provided insights into American life and culture as well as escape and entertainment for millions. Movie stars are icons for many Americans. People follow the personal lives of the stars. In turn, the stars have become role models for many. After her very successful performance in *Gentlemen Prefer Blondes* (1953), Marilyn Monroe emerged as the female sex symbol of the 1950s. Cary Grant and John Wayne provided the male symbols.

Alfred Hitchcock directed a series of mystery films such as *To Catch a Thief* (1955) that still rank among Hollywood's best. Katherine Hepburn gave several memorable performances including *The African Queen* (1951) with Humphrey Bogart and *State of the Union* (1948) with Spencer Tracy. *Casablanca* (1944) with Humphrey Bogart and Ingrid Bergman confirmed the two leads as top box office stars. It became one of the most popular films for the Baby Boomers in the 1950s and established itself as one of the first "cult" films—films that have a particular audience who like to see the film over and over again. A few movies revealed memorable developments in technique and set the direction for the future. Orson Welles' *Citizen Kane* (1940) and Walt Disney's *Fantasia* (1940), a full-length animated cartoon illustrating the artists' responses to several classical music scores, are two examples.

Several of the more distinguished movies of the 1960s reflected the changing values of society. The life of the counterculture was portrayed in 1969's *Easy Rider*, the story of a drug-using motorcycle rider who travels the country with no

Films reflect the views of the counterculture.

particular goals. *Who's Afraid of Virginia Woolf* with Elizabeth Taylor and Richard Burton in 1966 and *The Graduate* with Dustin Hoffman in 1967 were brilliantly acted. Both stories questioned the traditional social and sexual values of America.

From 1977 to 1983 George Lucas produced the first three *Star Wars* films. They captured the public's imagination with their combination of science fiction, morality play, and extraordinary special effects. Twenty years later when Lucas returned to the *Star Wars* theme to produce a "prequel" of three films, they were less effective. Public expectations and values had changed. Another science fiction film, Steven Spielberg's *E.T.*, was designed to make one feel good. *E.T.* broke all box office records. Spielberg emerged as one of Hollywood's finest directors and money makers with his films *Jaws* (1975), *Close Encounters of the Third Kind* (1977), *Raiders of the Lost Ark* (1981), which made Harrison Ford a male sex symbol for the 1980s, and *Empire of the Sun* (1987). Spielberg's films took many Oscar Awards in Hollywood, but he did not win the directors award until 1994 for *Schindler's List*, a telling story of the Holocaust filmed in black and white. *Schindler's List* brought the Holocaust home to viewers by personalizing it at a time when ethnic cleansing was being practiced in the former Yugoslavia. It clearly illustrated the power of film. Movies like *The Deer Hunter* (1978), *Apocalypse Now* (1979), *Platoon* (1986), *Good Morning Vietnam* (1987), and *Born on the Fourth of July* (1989) addressed the issue of the Vietnam War and its effects on the individuals who had been involved in it. These films helped Americans to understand and come to grips with the way that war affected the nation.

MUSIC AND THE 1940s

Humans have always expressed themselves through music, instrumental or vocal, that clearly reflects aspects of the culture that has produced it. One can trace in the music of the years since World War II the changes in values and concerns of Americans as well as the continuity in America's view of life. It

> Music reflects aspects of the culture that produces it.

is most clearly revealed in popular music, but composers of classical music have responded in their own way. Aaron Copland, one of America's best-known classical composers, used jazz and American folk tunes in his best-known works such as *Appalachian Spring*. Leonard Bernstein bridged the gap between the classical and Broadway in several works including *West Side Story*, which reflected the diversity and violence of postwar society. To reflect diversity, musicians used different scales, instruments from traditions other than the European, and greater dissonance to illustrate changing interests.

As with any war, World War II produced its own ballads from the German *Lily Marlene* to America's *Praise the Lord and Pass the Ammunition*. Big bands were popular in the 1940s and the Glenn Miller sound of *In the Mood* expressed the wartime excitement. In the immediate postwar period, musicals such as Rogers and Hammerstein's *Oklahoma* kept America singing, but other styles were popular with different ethnic and age groups. Jazz, popular in the 1920s, was still popular. The trumpeter Miles Davis was an outstanding jazz musician who influenced many others with his blend of jazz and rock. Bebop became popular among African-American musicians in the 1950s and had an impact on the development of American popular music. The music of the African-American cultural tradition has been a very important part of the American musical scene throughout American history as seen in spirituals, soul, jazz, blues, gospel, and rap.

As the price of phonographs and 78-rpm records fell after World War II, popular music was easily available for anyone to purchase. Songs heard on the radio could be bought and listened to repeatedly. This appealed particularly to America's teenagers and opened up a huge new market. Radio and records and later TV and CDs made it possible for new groups and individuals to win popularity. Agents became important as competition for a top-selling record increased. Hitting the top-ten charts could make a fortune for a singer.

ELVIS PRESLEY AND ROCK 'N' ROLL

The first great cultural development in popular music after World War II was the start of rock 'n' roll. It had a great impact on youth and American culture. Rock 'n' roll had its roots in rhythm and blues, bebop, and the American musical tradition, yet it was different. Its new sound and approach is best personified by Elvis Presley, who sang and gyrated through many movies in the 1950s and became the first rock 'n' roll superstar. His records sold in huge numbers. Although he did not originate rock 'n' roll, Elvis Presley made it the new music of America. Youth responded, and rock 'n' roll became the music of the young.

Dancing to rock 'n' roll required an entirely new approach with loose joints and individual actions. It was a perfect style for a generation raised on Dr. Spock's theory that the individual child was the center of attention. Many parents were shocked by Elvis Presley's gyrations, which were considered lewd, but they became incorporated in American dancing and in performances of American musicians. They have been exported around the world.

> Rock "n" roll and folk artists express the sentiments of the counterculture movement.

Music in the 1960s, especially rock "n" roll, provided an outlet for the ideas of the counterculture. The tour of the United States by the English rock group the Beatles illustrated the popularity of rock and its international following. The rock music of stars such as Janice Joplin and Jimi Hendrix appealed to both Hippies and teenagers. The rock concert at Woodstock, New York, in August 1969 brought over 400,000 members of the counterculture together in an atmosphere of rock, joy, love, and drugs. Their emphasis on love and peace earned them the name of "flower children." The lyrics of folk artists Bob Dylan and Joan Baez expressed the concerns and alienation of the Hippies, and popular lyrics of the day reflected the counterculture's interest in drugs, sex, and love.

Woodstock and the music presented became synonymous with the counterculture and its values, which American traditionalists viewed as dangerous and subversive. This split over popular music reflects the split in society in the Nixon years which led Richard Nixon to fear for his reelection. It led to his concern about loyalty, patriotism, and support for his Vietnam policy which eventually led to Watergate. The social historian is particularly interested in exploring the popular expression of culture and its connections to the more traditional history, which records the political life of the nation.

THE EVOLUTION OF ROCK 'N' ROLL

Rock 'n' roll evolved into several different forms that appealed to different groups, reflecting the diversity within the nation and within popular culture. In the mid-1970s the Sex Pistols from England introduced "punk" rock. Later "hard" rock arrived. In

> Variety of popular music reflects the diversity of America.

1975 Bruce Springsteen's *Born to Run* announced a new and radical star who by 1994 was so accepted by the main musical tradition that his song, *Philadelphia*, won an Academy Award. In the 1980s Michael Jackson emerged as one voice of rock. In 1982 his album *Thriller* sold 40,000,000 copies, and he had seven of the ten top singles. His income soared. In the same decade Madonna typified the materialistic desires and self-focus of the "me" generation, ignoring accepted dress and lyrics to promote herself and her music.

RAP AND OTHER POPULAR MUSIC

In 1986 *Raising Hell* became the first rap "platinum" recording, and rap, born in the inner cities, became the new musical rage. Cities epitomized the changing styles of rock with Memphis (Presley) in the 1950s, Liverpool (Beatles) in the 1960s, and Seattle (Nirvana) in the 1990s. In the 1990s rap broke into several styles as popular music continued to evolve. Whatever becomes popular next will both reflect interests of the young and make a fortune for the stars.

In 1981 MTV debuted. Music was no longer only for listening, it was accompanied by the visual, which reflected the needs of the generation brought up with television. Listening to the popular music of the last half of the 20th century gives one a sense of the tremendous changes and vitality in American society. Rock 'n' roll was not the only popular music. Disco swept the country in the 1970s with the movie *Saturday Night Fever*. Gospel, Western, and country music all had large followings as did folk music, which illustrates the great diversity of American life. Orchestras playing classical music and opera houses had loyal followings as did classical stars such as the cellist Yo-Yo Ma and tenor Luciano Pavarotti. Music is a social phenomenon, and its changes and popularity provide the student of history important insights into a nation's culture.

DANCE IN AMERICA

What has been reported concerning popular music could also be said of dance in America. There has been a great growth in popularity and styles from western to classical ballet. In the post-war years ballet in America became as fine as that offered anywhere in the world. The Joffrey Ballet Company founded in 1956 led the way. The defection of Rudolf Nureyev and later Mikhail Baryshnikov from the Soviet Union focused attention on ballet as an art form. The growth of ballet enriched lives and provided channels of expression for talented young people. At the same time other American companies pursued modern dance, whose best-known American advocate was Martha Graham. The diversity and increasing support for dance in the United States was another reflection of cultural growth and diversity.

Styles of popular participatory dancing changed dramatically in the post–World War II years. The fox trot, polka, and waltz dominated the prewar era until the introduction of the jitterbug, also known as the "swing," by Cab Calloway's 1935 recording, *The Call of the Jitterbug*. "Swing" was spread worldwide by United States troops during the war. After the war, dances of South American origin such as the rumba were introduced. They all were couple based with the male leading his partner in often very complex steps requiring a good deal of skill and athleticism. "Swing" was danced to the first "rock 'n' roll" music but a new style quickly evolved involving partners dancing apart but doing the same or similar steps. The "Twist" is one early example of what became the dominant popular dance style in the nation. In 1957 *American Bandstand* began on ABC TV and popularized quickly new music and new dance styles. As with music, dance style is a reflection of the values and attitudes of society.

AMERICAN LITERATURE SINCE WORLD WAR II

Literature, especially novels, gives great insights into society and its problems. Most students have not had the time to read extensively, and so music and movies, both readily available, are a more accessible primary source for understanding society of the recent past. It is important to realize, however, that American authors have produced books of major significance in the period since World War II. They reflect the changing values and concerns of society as seen through the eyes of very perceptive individuals. Among the noteworthy books and authors of the Truman and Eisenhower years were Jack Kerouac's *On the Road* (1955), Joseph Heller's *Catch 22* (1961), and Ralph Ellison's *Invisible Man* (1952). The latter is autobiographical and tells of the experience of being an African-American in America. Heller's *Catch 22* is a vivid anti-war novel. Kerouac is a member of a group of authors, the Beat Generation, who rebelled at the middle-class values and conformity of the Eisenhower years. The Beat Generation experimented with and wrote about drugs and their own sexual experiences. They, as did Elvis Presley, appealed to the younger generation of Americans. These works are still widely read in the United States by those wishing to understand the post-World War II era, and the Beat authors again became very popular in the mid-1990s. One of the most popular works of the 1950s for younger readers, which is still widely read in schools, was J. D. Salinger's *Catcher in the Rye* (1951), which told the story of an affluent yet alienated adolescent.

As the counterculture emerged, it produced several writers of note. One with a particularly keen eye was Tom Wolfe. His novel, *Electric Kool Aid Acid Test* (1968), questioned the traditional social and sexual values. Wolfe's later work, *Bonfire of the Vanities* (1984), exposed the values of the "me" generation and the conflicts within New York City. At the same time John Updike commented on the spiritual malaise and sexual adventures of middle-class suburbanites in works like his Rabbit series:

> **Authors reflect different aspects of the American experience.**

Rabbit Run (1960), *Rabbit Redux* (1971), and *Rabbit Is Rich* (1981). Thomas Pynchon's *Gravity's Rainbow* (1973) explored new areas of literary understanding and gained a wide following.

American literature became more and more diverse. More and more women and ethnic writers have been recognized. Among the many works produced, Erica Jong's *Fear of Flying* (1973) is noteworthy as a reflection of the Women's Liberation Movement. Jong explored a woman's sexuality from a woman's perspective. Amy Tan in *The Joy Luck Club* (1989) and *The Kitchen Gods Wife* (1991) presented the Chinese American experience. Annie Dillard emerged as one of the most thoughtful and expressive writers of the late 1980s, and won a Pulitzer Prize for her book, *Pilgrim at Tinker Creek*, in 1974.

> Women authors add to the diversity found in American literature.

While all of these works gained wide recognition and appeared on best seller lists, the reading habits of Americans were much more varied. Each year many new science fiction, mysteries, westerns, and romances were published. Many of the stories all share an element of escape. The popularity of such works suggests they fill an important need for Americans to find romance and excitement beyond their daily lives. In spite of TV, computers, and the Internet, Americans continued to read with hundreds of new books published each year.

NEWSPAPERS

The growth of television changed the reading habits of America. The paperback revolution of the 1950s reduced the cost of books and increased sales, but newspapers were not as successful.

> Publishing companies eliminate many local papers.

There was consolidation as newspaper publishing companies bought out local papers, and by the 1990s most cities had only one paper. Ownership of TV networks, radio stations, and newspapers by large companies gave considerable control over American citizens' access to news to a few executives.

USA Today, introduced in 1982, became a national paper. It is a smaller paper with few in-depth stories but lots of color and news briefs. The way it digests the news, as does television, into small bits without great analysis worries critics who believe the people in a democracy need more information to make wise decisions. However, the trend to small news bites and less analysis continued, and many papers cut their reporting staff.

AMERICAN PAINTERS

American artists of the 1950s painted in many styles, reflecting the diversity of American culture and views. Without visual access to the works, it is hard to judge them. Jackson Pollock worked in an abstract style in which he dropped paint onto canvasses, while Andrew Wyeth painted in minute detail realistic and personal scenes of individuals in the farmland country southwest of Philadelphia and in Maine. Other artists painted in every style between these two extremes. Andy Warhol and Roy Lichtenstein used items from the popular culture—tomato soup cans and comic strips—to create a new world of art in the 1960s. Their art reflected the same questioning of materialism and its values seen in the counterculture and the Sexual Revolution. While some critics deplored the quality of popular culture as seen in art, television, movies, and music, major contributions were being made by Americans in these areas.

The United States government had not subsidized the arts until establishment of the National Foundation for the Arts (NFA) in 1965. Through this federal government organization some funding became available to help art organizations and museums. It was a controversial move but was welcomed by the arts community. Then in 1989 the Corcoran Gallery in Washington organized a show, partially subsidized by the NFA, of Robert Mapplethorpe's photographs. Senator Jesse Helms of North Carolina, a member of the New Right, criticized the photographs as homoerotic and said the government should not subsidize such pornography. Some saw the works as those of a sensitive individual using life in America as his subject. Since this incident, there have been arguments nationally on what control, considered censorship by more liberal individuals, the government should have over federal money appropriated to support the arts. The issue became embroiled in the controversy over traditional values and political arguments. The issue is complex and suggests the struggle artists face as they reflect on American society in their works. It also reflects the diversity in American values and what is accepted. Because artists have always been considered at the forefront of change, their presentations of society have often been controversial.

> National Foundation for the Arts is criticized for its support of some artists and museums.

ATHLETICS

Professional sports have a long history in America. With the advent of television, and of cable channels devoted to sports, the organized professional sports leagues—baseball, basketball, football, and hockey—all expanded. Names of professional athletes from Ted Williams in 1950s baseball to Wayne Gretsky in 1990s hockey have become household words. Few American males, whether in the inner city or the suburbs, did not have their sports heroes and teams. With increasing coverage and more opportunities for women to play sports, both as amateurs and professionals, more and more women are becoming sports fans.

> Professional athletes and teams provide heroes for Americans.

As suburban America grew in the post-World War II years, parents in the suburbs organized athletic opportunities for their children. Little League baseball became part of the childhood experience of most white middle-class males. The Pop Warner football league introduced that extremely popular and uniquely American male sport to youngsters. With the impetus of Women's Liberation and the government's Title IX, many teams were open to or organized for girls. In the suburbs, soccer was organized for children, and both sexes played. For inner city youngsters the streets provided the play areas and basketball was popular. Americans, especially in white upper class, suburban areas, pursued physical fitness well beyond adolescence as seen in the "me" generation's involvement in jogging and health clubs.

As sports coverage on TV increased, many youngsters set their hopes on gaining a place on professional teams. In spite of expansion, places were very limited for males and, almost nonexistent for females, except for the individual sports of golf and tennis.

With the breaking of the color barrier in baseball by Jackie Robinson in 1946, opportunities slowly became available in all sports for talented players regardless of race. Professional sports have provided great opportunities for minorities. Together with television, which has brought their achievements into every home, professional sports helped to modify society's attitudes toward race.

THE BEGINNINGS OF THE ELECTRONIC REVOLUTION

The most significant developments in American culture in the late 20th century were the introduction of the personal computer and the Internet. (See pages 463–465) Together they were to transform America's lifestyle and make "the global village" described by Marshall McLuhan in 1964 a reality. Computer literacy became essential. Every aspect of living, from banking to design to research to writing, was affected.

> Personal computers and the Internet transform America's lifestyle.

Since World War II, changes in communications were steady and often dramatic. For instance, consider the changes in the music recording and listening industry. In 1945, phonographs played 78-rpm[15] records, then came 45-rpm records in the 1950s, to be quickly replaced by $33\frac{1}{3}$-rpm "long-play records." Those were followed by audiotapes and then CDs in the late 1980s. By 2002 new digital technology (DVD) was providing another method of recording music and other information. Thus there were six different methods of recording and listening to music in just over fifty years. Consider the cost of replacing an entire music collection every ten years. This is only one example of how technological change has affected society's habits and impacted on the economy.

> The rapidity of change in American life today is illustrated in the recording industry.

Other electronic changes have been as profound. In the 1980s, VCRs added a new dimension to America's culture and TV-viewing habits. VCRs allowed individuals to record TV programs for viewing at their leisure without seeing the commercials. The effect on advertising is hard to estimate. Video rental stores, renting both movies and games on video, proliferated—another example of the growth of a service industry. Videos made the archives of movie studios highly desirable as old films were re-issued as videos and new ones were made available quickly often affecting movie house attendance and changing viewing habits. As the 20th century ended, the pace of the electronic revolution intensified creating new industries overnight and producing an economic boom.

THE PACE OF LIFE AT THE END OF THE 20TH CENTURY

The many labor-saving and entertainment-oriented inventions of the last half of the 20th century increased the pace of American life dramatically, changing the way Americans live. The VCR made movies of your choice a nightly possibility. Cable

---

[15] rpm *revolutions per minute.*

television companies offered more than 100 channels from which to choose. Channels devoted to one subject—sports, news, or weather—made such information instantly available at all times to everyone. Satellites allowed for live radio and television broadcasts from anywhere in the world as well as for telephone communication. Home video cameras allowed for instant replay of what one has recorded. The fax machine and Internet allowed the immediate sending of printed information around the world. Computers, laptop or desktop, instantly provided access to publishing, editing, game playing, or personal banking. Microwave ovens permitted each family member to prepare a hot meal almost instantly, making it possible for each family member to eat what he or she wanted when he or she wanted it, thus eliminating family meals together. Some psychologists expressed concern as to how this ability to achieve instantly whatever one wants will affect the American values of hard work and effort.

> New inventions and the goals of the "me" generation increase the pace of life in the nation.

American homes are filled with devices to make life easier and more comfortable. Washing machines and dryers cut down on time spent washing clothes, but an emphasis on cleanliness require clean clothes every day, increasing rather than reducing hours spent washing. The list of time-saving devices is great, but statistics show that the number of hours available each week for leisure in the average American home dropped in the last thirty years of the 20th century from 26 hours to 19. The Yuppies of the "me" generation jogged and did aerobics to improve their health, taking time away from home life. Because of poor economic conditions and low salaries especially in service industries, many workers had to moonlight[16], putting an added burden on them, reducing their leisure hours, and increasing the pace of their lives. The reasons for less leisure time are many and complex, but they clearly indicate a major change in society's style of living. Many political analysts expressed concern that the lack of time for personal reflection would affect personal and national affairs.

> Leisure time declines in spite of new time-saving devices.

The above examples illustrate how home conveniences have affected the pace of life. In addition, there are changes in the speed of travel—from propeller planes of 1945 to supersonic jets; developments in medicine—from polio shots to artificial hips; and in many other areas that allowed Americans to move faster, live longer, and perhaps worry more. As the 21st century approached, there was every indication that the pace of life in America and ultimately throughout the world would continue to increase as new inventions became available and Americans placed more demands on themselves.

SUMMARY

The last half of the 20th century were years of tremendous change in American society. Change manifested itself in everything from economic conditions to protest movements, from popular music to personal computers. People were continually forced to adjust their lifestyles and adapt what they had been taught to new

---

[16] moonlight   *Work at a second job, often at night, in order to make extra money.*

situations. The result for individuals was often stressful and uncertain. The trend continues.

The social historian must take note of all these changes within society and analyze them to discover possible trends and the effect they have on the people living within the society. One suggestion has been that change has created stress, and stress has led to violence within society. Political leaders must then address the violence. Some social historians and psychologists have suggested political leaders should address causes rather than the manifestations of stress. Can the pace of life for a society be changed by government action? Would a change make life more interesting? More rewarding? Whatever your point of view, history illustrates that it is not only the actions of leaders that affect history. How the people behave and what issues concern them affect society as a whole. Change can be created by the common people and must be understood if one is to understand the past—to understand history.

> The social historian analyzes the changes taking place in society to discover possible trends.

Key Point to Remember
The fifty years since the end of World War II saw great change in the way Americans live and view themselves, which is reflected in everything from the advent of computers to changes in popular music. As a result, it is impossible to speak of an American culture except in terms of its diversity.

People to Remember
Elvis Presley   Popular singer, musician; symbolizes the power and variety of popular music in the age of television; raised on Gospel music, he dominated rock music until the Beatles; he was comfortable in country and western, rhythm and blues, and rock 'n' roll, and impacted them all musically; his loose hips and gyrations incurred the wrath of many, but he headed American popular music in new directions.

Miles Davis   Jazz musician, trumpeter; one of the great jazz musicians of the mid-20th century, producing a blend of jazz and rock that influenced many later musicians.

Aaron Copland   Composer; in his use of jazz and American folk tunes, he was the best-known and, in many ways, most influential American classical composer of the 20th century; his ballets *Billy the Kid*, *Rodeo*, and *Appalachian Spring* are the best known of his works.

Martha Graham   Dancer, choreographer, teacher; noted for her stark and angular style, she gave American dance its own personality; as teacher and choreographer *(Phaedre* and *Appalachian Spring)* for her own company, she affected many of the finest American dancers of the 20th century.

Jack Kerouac   Author; a leading spokesperson of the post-World War II "Beat Generation"; *On The Road* has been read by and influenced millions; it exemplifies "Beat" literature of the 1950s and 1960s, restless, seeking new sensations while disdaining conventional economic and social success.

Tom Wolfe   Author whose journalistic style combines personal impressions and reconstructed dialogue and is used in all his work; *The Electric Kool Aid Acid Test* (1968), *The Right Stuff* (1975), and *The Bonfire of the Vanities* (1987) all make strong comments about contemporary society; Wolfe, noted as a commentator on the social condition, has had wide influence on teachers and students influencing many writers of the late 20th century.

Links from the Past to the Present

1. Television has played a major role in the life of Americans since 1950, affecting everything from the conduct of politics to eating patterns.

2. Movies, television, and popular music have reflected and continue to reflect the changing values of society with more sex and violence portrayed over the past fifty years.

3. The values of the young are expressed through popular music.

Dates

1951—J. D. Salinger wrote *Catcher in the Rye.*

1953—*Gentlemen Prefer Blondes* made Marilyn Monroe a star.

1955—Jack Kerouac published *On the Road.*

1956—Elvis Presley revolutionized American popular music.

1960—Kennedy-Nixon television debate.

1965—National Foundation for the Arts established.

1979—*Apocalypse Now* portrayed the Vietnam War.

1982—*USA Today* first published.
   Michael Jackson's album *Thriller* released.

1984—*The Cosby Show* began.

Questions
Identify each of the following:

Sesame Street	CNN
Kennedy-Nixon Debate	Elvis Presley
The Simpsons	*USA Today*

Multiple Choice:

1. Woodstock became synonymous with
   a. the Gay Rights Movement.
   b. Women's Liberation.
   c. the counterculture movement.

2. Andy Warhol and Roy Lichtenstein found inspiration for their art in
    a. tomato soup cans and comic strips.
    b. movies.
    c. stories from Tom Wolfe's *Electric Kool Aid Acid Test.*

3. Examples of the youth culture of the postwar period are
    a. the appeal of Elvis Presley and rock "n" roll.
    b. sitcoms on evening TV.
    c. the popularity of opera and classical music.

4. Among the important novels of the post-war period were:
    a. Ralph Ellison's *Invisible Man.*
    b. Orson Welles' *Citizen Kane.*
    c. John Kenneth Galbraith's *Affluent Society.*

Open-ended, Analysis Questions

The following questions require analysis and reflection. You are encouraged to bring
to your answer information and ideas from many sources. The answers should be
presented in composition or essay style but they may be used to initiate discussion.
The questions put you in the role of the historian, gathering information to support
your personal perspective on the question.

1. "In the 20th century inventions greatly changed the lifestyle of Americans."

    From the following list pick the one invention that you believe changed American
    lifestyle the most. In an essay explain what these changes were.
    a. automobile
    b. movies
    c. television

    *(Note: In the essay you may refer to other inventions than the one you pick and
    explain why you did not pick them.)*

2. Social historians record many different aspects of our lives. Pick three examples
    of aspects of the social life of Americans that are included in this chapter that you
    believe are important to know. In an essay explain why you believe they are
    important to include in a history book.

    *(Note: Examples of aspects you might consider range from urban growth to
    music.)*

3. In an essay explain the impact of the "new morality" on American social and
    political life.

15

The Recent Past: Clinton, G. W. Bush, Obama: 1993–2009

APPROACHES TO HISTORY

CURRENT EVENTS OR HISTORY AND THE NEED FOR REVISION

As you are aware, historians interpret history in many different ways. No matter what perspective an historian takes, all historians deal with events in the past, events that can be investigated and analyzed over time, events that can be shown to have had significance. As historians study events closer to the present, they gradually lose that historic perspective. Historians are called upon to make decisions about what current events are significant without experiencing and studying the impact of an event over a period of years.

All people face a similar problem in their own lives. How do you decide in your own life what is important in a given year? If you look back to when you were five or ten, you will recall a few events you can say were important in making you who you are today, but how do you decide what events of the past year will be included in your biography written 30 years from now? An athletic victory, ending a close relationship, an illness, may all seem very important now and you may be able to give a clear statement of why it is important, but time may change that understanding. So it is with recent events with which historians must deal. It would appear certain that September 11, 2001, will be in history texts thirty years from now, but will historians then describe the event in the same way we do? Probably not, because they will have more information on what happened both before the event and after. Their perspective and analysis will be different from ours.

Because of this lack of perspective, some historians suggest that the events of the most recent ten to twenty years should be considered current events and not history. They suggest that only with time will we truly understand what events were significant and be able to analyze them effectively. To illustrate this, these historians refer to "revisionist" history, i.e., the reinterpretation of past events giving them different meaning or emphasis and providing additional understanding of the past. While some interpretations of events from the distant past are revised, it is more common to have revisions made of recent history—of the last 100 years.

In the past few years, historians have presented revisions of the formerly accepted views of the origins of the Cold War, the 1950s, and the Cuban Missile Crisis, all because they had gained a perspective on those times and had access to new information. Earlier explanations no longer appeared valid. The historian recording recent events and the students of them must realize they are dealing with current events. What events of the past twenty years will prove to be of real significance in the chronology of cause and effect relationships? What actions of Clinton George W. Bush, and Obama will be included in history texts in fifty years?

To illustrate this point consider two recent events: the Monica Lewinsky scandal under Bill Clinton and the Enron bankruptcy under George W. Bush. At the time of each event, there was extensive coverage in the press, books were quickly written about each event, and they were included in history texts. In fact, several very detailed paragraphs on each event were included in the last edition of this text. Note, however, how they are covered in this edition. How will they be treated in the future?

As you read the following pages, keep in mind that many historians would consider this chapter an account of current events, which will require careful analysis by historians in the years ahead to determine just how significant they are in the long history of the United States. Perhaps you will be one of those historians.

I. DOMESTIC ISSUES DURING CLINTON'S TWO TERMS

RESPONSE TO THE RECESSION

During the 1992 campaign, candidate Bill Clinton had a sign at his headquarters saying, "It's the economy, stupid." As one of his first actions after his election, he held an economic round table to listen to various proposals and concerns in order to draft legislation to deal with the economy. The round table suggested ideas and Clinton presented an Economic Stimulus Package to Congress. The Republicans filibustered the measure. He eventually dropped the $12 billion economic stimulus proposals and settled for $4 billion for unemployment compensation. The fighting over the stimulus package indicated gridlock had not been overcome with the election of a new president. The economy, with interest rates dropping, began to

> Clinton offers Economic Stimulus Package that Congress rejects.

improve by the beginning of 1994, and strong economic growth, referred to as the dot-com boom, continued until the end of Clinton's second term.

GAYS IN THE MILITARY

One of Clinton's first actions as president backfired and lost him support and momentum. After that he relied heavily on opinion polls before announcing policies. During the campaign, Clinton had promised to remove the ban on homosexuals in the military forces. His attempt to achieve this met with strong opposition in the Defense Department and Congress. A compromise, "Don't ask, don't tell," allowing gays to serve if they do not reveal their sexual preference was finally accepted. This policy is still being debated.

Clinton quickly issued several executive orders that reversed Reagan/Bush policies and antagonized conservative right wing elements and antiabortion groups. One permitted research on fetal tissue. Another allowed for privately funded abortions at U.S. military medical facilities. A third allowed patients at federally funded family-planning clinics to receive information on abortion. President George W. Bush reversed the Clinton policies as one of his first actions, and President Obama returned to the Clinton policies as one of his first actions. He also appointed a committee to consider the issues and make recommendations for consistent policy. The issues are key issues in the traditional values debate, and both sides are deeply committed to their positions. Any compromise on the issues will indicate a major shift in cultural attitudes.

> Abortion policy continues to be an issue.

EARLY LEGISLATIVE SUCCESSES

In 1993, Clinton signed the Family and Medical Leave Act, which had been vetoed by his predecessor; a National Service Act, which paid up to $4,725 a year to selected young people who did community service projects before, during, or after college; a Voter Registration Act, which required states to provide the opportunity for people to register to vote when they get a driver's license or other public document; and the Handgun Waiting Period Bill, the so-called Brady Bill, which requires a five-day waiting period during which the police are to check the purchaser's criminal record before handguns may be purchased. The rich and powerful National Rifle Association (NRA) had lobbied against any restrictions for years, and passage of the Brady Bill was a major breakthrough. The bill passed largely in reaction to the increase in incidents of random violence taking place throughout society. Also passed was another crime bill that included a ban on the sale of several assault weapons and put more police onto the streets. Some suggest these bills helped reduce the crime rate in the 1990s.

Education has traditionally been a local matter in the United States, but over the years states have become more involved in education financing with the control that comes with money. Since Sputnik in 1957, the federal government has become more and more involved in education. George H. W. Bush had a Goals 2000 program. The goal was to get states to redesign and update school curriculum to prepare for the 21st century. Clinton fine-tuned the program as Goals 2002. Educational reform has

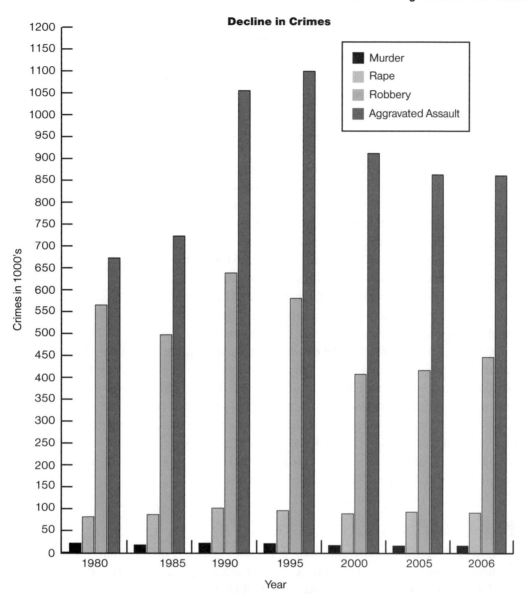

Crime declined in the 1990s. Federal legislation had increased the number of police officers available and prosperity had created more opportunities for work.
Source: U.S. Census Bureau, *Statistical Abstract of the United States: 2008.*

always come slowly. Neither of these programs brought about real change in student test scores, and neither had any incentives except monetary support. George W. Bush made education reform a major campaign issue and addressed it in his Education

> Education bill, No Child Left Behind, focuses on accountability and testing.

Bill known as No Child Left Behind of 2002. After extensive debate, a bill requiring annual testing of math and English in grades 3 through 8 to assure "accountability" of schools and providing federal aid tied to performance/accountability was passed. Senator Ted Kennedy, leader of the liberal wing of the Democratic Party, led the Democratic support. Congress never fully funded the bill, but states were expected to follow all its directives creating a financial burden on the states. Several aspects of the bill have created controversy including the exclusion of testing of history/social studies and the arts and the emphasis on multiple-choice questions to determine the level of a child's understanding. In the campaign, President Obama indicated he would ask Congress to review No Child Left Behind. Education continues to be a high priority for both parties and the American public.

THE HEALTH CARE ISSUE

Clinton referred to himself as a "new democrat," a democrat who did not believe that bigger government could solve all social problems. He even proclaimed in a speech, "The era of big government is over." However, Clinton clearly believed in a more active and more regulatory federal government than did Reagan and G. H. W. Bush. This is seen in the Clinton health care proposal.

Clinton appointed his wife, Hillary Rodham Clinton, to chair a task force to study the health care issue and make recommendations for legislation. Clinton believed two concerns had to be addressed: the lack of universal health care and the rapid increase in health care costs, far higher than the overall

> Clinton sets goal of universal health care and control of health care costs, but is defeated.

inflation rate in the 1980s and 1990s. After exhaustive study, pursued in some secrecy, the task force submitted a complex proposal guaranteeing health care to all, mandating that employers finance health care for their employees, and establishing a government-run mechanism to control prices and insurance companies. After being submitted to Congress, the proposal drew criticism from many quarters. Campaigns on television were mounted against the proposal, and competing proposals were introduced in Congress. Finally, compromise became impossible due to the complexity of the issues. No legislation was passed.

1994 CONGRESSIONAL ELECTIONS

In spite of the growing economic recovery and the passage of important legislation, Clinton's popularity in the polls hovered at around 50 percent. The Republicans, led by House Minority Leader Newt Gingrich, announced a *Contract with America* as the platform for a "national election approach" to the Congressional elections. The contract called for, among other things, less government, reduced taxes, welfare reform, and more spending on a stronger defense of the nation.

With less than 40 percent of the registered voters voting, in 1994 the Republicans gained control of both the House and Senate. Many Democrats who were running in the election separated themselves from President Clinton, claiming he had abandoned the "new democrat" approach of less government in his health care proposals. In actuality, Clinton had asked Vice President Al Gore to head a program on reducing the size of government. During the Clinton years, government did shrink in size. The new Congress followed a confrontational approach to the Democratic White House. The House quickly passed the essentials of the *Contract with America*, but Senate Majority Leader Robert Dole was unable to get the program through the Senate with one exception. After years of struggle, a Line Item Veto Bill, a favorite of conservatives, giving the president the power to eliminate specific items from any departmental budget was passed. Clinton used it in 1997 before it was declared unconstitutional by the Supreme Court—a decision that added to the political frustration in Washington.

WELFARE REFORM

Welfare reform had been a major issue for the Republicans since Reagan's presidency. Clinton accepted the need for reform, and in 1996, a major overhaul of the welfare system was signed. The goal was to reduce the number of people on welfare and limit the time one could collect welfare payments. The new law set a limit of five years for payments and included job training to help people stay off welfare. Greater authority was given to the states to administer the law under federal guidelines. With the prosperity of the late 1990s, the reforms worked well and welfare roles were reduced dramatically. However, many worried what would happen in less prosperous times. Clinton was committed to a "safety net" for the poor, but not all politicians were. In 2002, President George W. Bush and the Republicans pushed for tighter requirements for work.

> Welfare Reform offers job training and sets limits on benefits.

BUDGET CRISES

Reagonomics of the 1980s led to large budget deficits that worried the political leadership of both parties. The *Contract with America* called for a balanced budget. Budget spending priorities differed between Republicans—more for tax cuts and higher defense spending—and Democrats—more for social services and less on defense. In 1995, no agreement on the budget was reached. With no appropriations, Clinton closed down the government except for the most essential services. The Republicans got most of the blame from the public. The situation was repeated to a lesser extent in 1996 and, in spite of prosperity, deficits grew. Finally, in 1997 a compromise, the Balanced Budget Agreement, was reached. It included some tax cuts, prioritized spending, and established a balanced budget. Helped by the booming economy, in 1998 the federal government reported the first budget surplus in thirty years. By 2000, the surplus for the year was a phenomenal $237 billion. The political struggle then became one of determining what to do with the surplus.

> Balanced Budget Agreement reached after Clinton closes down government operations.

In the 2000 election, George W. Bush and the Republicans proposed large tax cuts, stating the money was the people's and should be returned to them. Democrats supported paying off the national debt and increasing social services in areas such as education and health care. With Bush's election, a tax cut was passed. Within a year the surpluses had disappeared as the War on Terrorism began.

CONGRESS AND TRADE

Clinton was an advocate of freer trade and early in his administration saw NAFTA (North American Free Trade Act) through Congress. The act essentially established a free-trade zone between the three largest nations in North America—Canada, the United States, and Mexico.

In 1993, Clinton invited the leaders of the Pacific Rim[1] to meet in Seattle, Washington, to discuss matters of trade. A formal agreement, APEC, the Asia–Pacific Economic Cooperative, was eventually established. It included annual meetings and consultations among these nations on issues of trade and other matters. The organization cooperated in the 1997–1998 economic crisis in Asia and developed plans to combat the financial crisis of 2008. In 2007 it was reported that the 21 nations of APEC held 41 percent of the world's population and created 56 percent of the world's GDP. Cooperation on trade issues among the members can have a major impact on the world economy and Clinton saw an important role for the United States in the region.

TRADE WITH CHINA

Throughout the Clinton years, trade with China was of great concern to business and political leaders. Congress wanted to link trade with China on a "most favored nation" (MFN) basis to an improvement in China's treatment of its political prisoners and an end to China's human rights abuses. Business leaders wished to offer China MFN status with no strings attached as China provided a huge market. Clinton's secretary of state, Warren Christopher, visited China in 1994 to negotiate the issue. The Chinese leadership rebuffed him, stating that the condition of human rights in China was their affair and not that of other nations. Congress renewed trade with China on a yearly basis. Clinton eventually sided with the business community on MFN status and accepted the Chinese view on human rights. After struggling with the issue throughout the 1990s, in 2000 Congress finally approved more permanent trade relations with China. This prepared the way for China's admittance in 2001 into the World Trade Organization (WTO) that oversees the operation of international trade according to negotiated rules and regulations.

OTHER CLINTON LEGISLATION

In 1998, the Senate rejected a $526 billion settlement worked out between the states and tobacco companies that would eliminate lawsuits against the tobacco companies. For years, controversy had raged over the responsibility of the companies for smoking-induced deaths. When juries in lawsuits accusing tobacco companies of causing the death of individual smokers began to side with the individuals raising the possibility of industry bankruptcies, the government and industry began negotiations. A settlement was reached subject to Senate approval, but it was rejected by the Senate. This led to 46 individual states negotiating agreements for less money but still billions of dollars. In theory, the compensation to states was to be used to treat smoking-related illnesses and run

> Senate rejects tobacco settlement and States negotiate their own arrangement.

---

[1] Pacific Rim   *Those nations such as South Korea, Japan, Taiwan, Singapore, Indonesia, Australia, the United States, Mexico, and Chile that border the Pacific.*

antismoking campaigns, but some states used the funds for general expenses. In these years smoking declined and a movement for clean air environments led to the banning of smoking in many work places, schools, and places of public entertainment. Still, the cost to the nation in health care and lost work due to smoking is tremendous and will continue to be as long as people smoke.

> **National Drunk Driving Law sets alcoholic level at 0.08.**

After a number of irregularities were identified in the work of the Internal Revenue Service (IRS), reforms were passed in Congress in 1998. In 2000, a national Drunk Driving Law was passed, denying federal highway funds to any state that did not set 0.08 as the level of alcohol in the blood to define driving while intoxicated.

The issue of abortion came before Congress a number of times in the Clinton years. A law banning partial birth abortions was passed several times but vetoed by Clinton, who supported abortion rights and *Roe* v. *Wade*.

The number of troops on active military duty was reduced, as were military expenditures. SDI was not canceled, but spending for it was reduced. The United States Information Agency (USIA) was incorparated into the State Department, thus

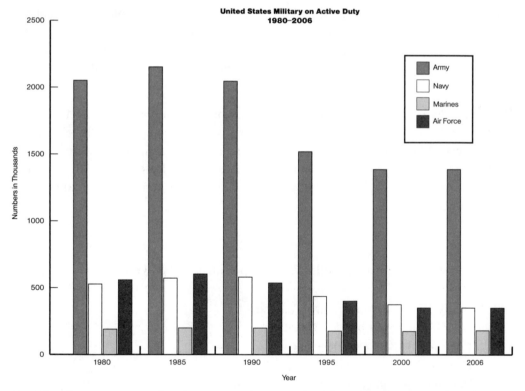

President Reagan supported an increase in the strength of the military and President Clinton has been accused of letting the military become weak. This chart illustrates how the Reagan military buildup was not concentrated on manpower as much as on weaponry and nuclear strength. It does illustrate that the manpower available for combat dropped considerably during the Clinton years. However, one must remember that the Cold War had ended before Clinton became president and the need for large numbers of troops had declined.
Source: United States Defense Department, Selected Manpower Statistics, *Statistical Abstract of the United States: 2008.*

eliminating the one government group that had effectively represented the United States to the world. Throughout the Clinton years, Congress and the executive branch were involved with accusations of scandal, corruption, and impeachment. These were all time consuming and distracting. They intensified the gridlock in Washington and set a tone of character assassination that was detrimental to the functioning of government and soured many Americans attitude toward government officials and both political parties.

Key Point to Remember
The Clinton years were ones of economic growth and prosperity, with the first budget surplus in thirty years.

Links From Past to Present
When different political parties control Congress and the White House, potential exists for political gridlock.

People to Remember
William (Bill) Jefferson Clinton   Rhodes Scholar, lawyer, elected governor of Arkansas at the age of 33 in 1978 and reformed education and encouraged economic growth; styled himself a "new democrat"; in 1992 presidential campaign used TV for town meetings where he directly responded to questions from live audiences; elected to two terms as 42nd president; presidency was plagued by scandals and impeachment trial.

Hillary Rodham Clinton   Lawyer, First Lady, senator from New York, Secretary of State, defended her husband through all the sex scandals; she and Bill Clinton were at the center of Whitewater, Filegate, and Travelgate investigations and were acquitted of all charges; chaired Committee of Health Care Reform; elected senator from New York in 2000; lost Democratic Party presidential nomination in 2008 in very tight primary race.

Dates
1992—Election of Democrats Bill Clinton as president and Al Gore as vice president.
1993—Brady Bill (hand gun control) passed.
    NAFTA approved by U.S. Senate.
1994—Failure of Health Care Reform.
    Contract with America.
    Republicans win control of House and Senate.
1995—Budget crisis, and government shut down.
1996—Welfare reform instituted.
1997—Budget compromise reached.
1998—First budget surplus in thirty years.
    Senate rejects tobacco settlements.
2000—Drunk Driving Law.

Questions

Identify each of the following:

"It's the economy, stupid."   *Contract with America*
"Don't ask, don't tell."   Brady Bill

Multiple Choice:

1. During Bill Clinton's administration, he shut down government operations because
   a. there was a $237 billion budget surplus.
   b. Reagonomics had created large deficits.
   c. Congress could not agree on the budget.

2. Bill Clinton was a supporter of freer trade as indicated by his support of
   a. NAFTA.
   b. an economic stimulus package.
   c. welfare reform.

3. President Clinton asked his wife, Hillary Rodham Clinton, to chair a committee on
   a. welfare reform.
   b. health care reform.
   c. budget reform.

II. Other Domestic Issues: 1993–2001

SUSPICION OF SCANDAL

Suspicion of wrongdoing and the implication of scandal overshadowed many other issues throughout Clinton's eight years. During his first presidential campaign, accusations of sexual misconduct were raised and confronted in a television interview. Suggestions of illegal actions in real estate development on the Whitewater River in Arkansas were voiced but not resolved.

WHITEWATER

The scandal that ran through all eight years of Clinton's presidency was Whitewater—a land development scheme on the Whitewater River in Arkansas. During 1993, reports began to appear linking the land development plan, a failed Saving & Loan (S&L) Association in Little Rock, Arkansas, with which

> Whitewater real estate deal becomes focus of investigation.

Mrs. Clinton's law firm did business, possible illegal monetary transactions including misuse of tax revenues, and the granting of special privileges by Governor Clinton. While no one accused the Clintons of criminal actions, a feeding frenzy of suggestion, innuendo, and "revelations" began among the press and the Republicans.

The White House responded slowly and guardedly adding to the frenzy of speculation.

In 1994, a special prosecutor, Kenneth Starr, was appointed to investigate the Whitewater real estate plan. Five years of investigation resulted in a guilty plea on two counts by Webster L. Hubbell, Mrs. Clinton's law partner who had worked on the real estate deal, and a jail sentence for perjury for the bank president's wife, Susan MacDougal, who refused to answer Starr's questions. In 1999 Starr resigned but the Whitewater investigation continued until March 2002 when the Clintons were cleared of all possible charges in the case. The Whitewater case was costly and distracting for the Clintons, and it cost the taxpayers over $64 million.

> A conservative lawyer, Kenneth Starr, is appointed to head investigation. Clintons cleared of wrongdoing.

In 1993, several employees of the Senate Travel Office were dismissed, and Mrs. Clinton was accused of wrongdoing. Starr included this "Travelgate"[2] case in his investigation. Later he did the same with "Filegate"—the suggestion of illegal action when some FBI files, several dealing with prominent Republicans, disappeared at the White House. In 2000, the Clintons were both cleared of all possible charges of wrongdoing in these two cases.

MONICA LEWINSKY

The scandal that drew the most attention began when Paula Jones, an Arkansas State employee accused Clinton of sexual misconduct in 1991 and sued him while he was president. The Supreme Court rejected Clinton's plea to postpone the case until the end of his term and required that he give testimony. In the course of the investigation information emerged concerning a possible sexual affair between Monica Lewinsky, a former White House intern, and the president. The information was given to

> Starr gives Congress a report setting forth grounds for impeachment of President Clinton. House votes to accept two articles of impeachment.

Starr. He immediately asked the attorney general to add Monica Lewinsky to his investigation. After eight months of investigation, in September of 1998 Starr gave his report to Congress accusing Clinton of wrongdoings including obstruction of justice, and setting forth a case for impeaching the president. The House Judiciary Committee, under Republican leadership, accepted the report and voted along party lines to accept four articles of impeachment against the president. The Republican-controlled full House voted on December 19, 1998, to accept Articles I and III. Five Democrats joined the Republicans. Article I, accused Clinton of "perjurious, false and misleading testimony" involving Monica Lewinsky before Starr's grand jury. Article II accused Clinton of "obstructing justice" in the Paula Jones grand jury probe. Some Republicans joined the Democrats to defeat Articles II and IV. The vote totals demonstrated that impeachment was a heavily partisan issue.

---

[2] Travelgate   *Since the Watergate scandal of the Nixon years, the press and commentators have used the suffix "gate" to describe any possible political scandal in Washington, coining words like "Irangate," "Travelgate," and "Filegate."*

IMPEACHMENT

The Senate trial was set for February 1999. The case against Clinton was argued before the Senate by selected members of the House. Clinton had to hire lawyers to defend himself. On

Clinton found not guilty by Senate.

February 12, 1999, the Senate voted "not guilty" 55 to 45 on Article I and "not guilty" 50 to 50 on Article II (formerly referred to as Article III). To find Clinton guilty, a two-thirds vote (67 senators) was required. The Senate Democrats all voted not guilty. Thus, as in the first impeachment in U.S. history (of President Johnson in 1868), the president was acquitted.

PUBLIC SUPPORT

Throughout the Lewinsky scandal, Clinton's public opinion ratings remained high. In February 1999, 60 percent of the public believed he should stay in office and 35 percent felt he should resign. Fifty-two percent believed Clinton was able "to

Public support for Clinton remains positive during impeachment.

get the job done" better than Republicans, who got 35 percent support. However, a majority of Americans had a negative view of Clinton as a person. The public was clearly able to separate Clinton's ability to govern from his personal morality. However, his lack of sexual control tarnished his presidency.

OTHER EXECUTIVE DEPARTMENT INVESTIGATIONS

Bruce Babbitt, secretary of interior, was investigated for possible wrongdoing involving his handling of an application for a Native American casino. Mike Espy, secretary of agriculture, was investigated over an issue involving acceptance of gifts. Henry Cisneros, secretary of housing, was investigated over issues concerning a mistress and money. After extensive, costly, and distracting investigations, all three were cleared of any wrongdoings, and no charges were brought. Such investigations and the impeachment trial distracted government officials and the public.

ETHICS AND CONGRESS

Speaker of the House Gingrich found guilty of ethics violations.

Not all scandals during the Clinton years involved the executive branch. Newt Gingrich, Speaker of the House of Representatives and organizer of the 1994 Republican congressional election victory, was investigated by the House Ethics Committee in 1995, and, after two years, charges of ethics violations involving fund-raising were brought against him. The House found him guilty of the violations. He was fined $300,000. Gingrich decided not to run for Congress in 1998.

1996 PRESIDENTIAL FUND-RAISING

Democratic Party fund-raising methods for the election of 1996 also were investigated by the Department of Justice. Attorney General Reno cleared Gore and

Clinton of misusing government phones and the White House in fund-raising. Several Democratic fund-raisers were indicted, and one of them, Yah Lin (Charlie) Trie, pleaded guilty to illegal fund-raising from foreign nationals. Although never indicted, Gore's involvement in possible wrongdoing clouded his image in the 2000 election.

The fund-raising scandal illustrated the power and need of money in politics. The Democrats feared Republicans could raise more money than they. The 1996 irregularities clearly illustrated the need for campaign finance reform—a popular issue with voters but not with elected officials who feared a loss of campaign funds. Senator John McCain was its primary supporter in the Senate. Although passed by one house of Congress or the other over a seven-year period, reform was not made law until 2002 after the collapse of the Enron Corporation in 2001 showed how pervasive corporate gifts were for both parties.

> Money is important in politics as fund-raising scandal illustrates.

PRESIDENTIAL PARDONS

One final scandal occurred as Clinton left office. As have many presidents, he exercised his power of pardon to release a number of prisoners. There were cries that several of them had used bribes to obtain the pardons. After being investigated, Clinton was again cleared of wrongdoing, but this added another shadow to his presidency.

How important the scandals of the Clinton years will prove to be in the future cannot be determined. Clearly, however, they captured the attention of many in the government, the press, and the country. When compared with the number of executive branch members found guilty of misconduct during Reagan's eight years in the White House, the number during the Clinton years was negligible. However, the press coverage was greater because the president himself was under the cloud of investigation.

Political scandals have occurred throughout American history. However, the gridlock in Washington in the 1990s and early 21st century and deep divisions over values between the two major parties, the size of government, the growth of the news media and round the clock news broadcasting, as well as the breakdown of the wall of privacy around politicians personal lives that began with the exposure of an affair by Senator Gary Hart (see pages 315–316) have created a climate of accusation and suspicion in Washington. While it is crucial for a democracy that government officials be kept honest, it is important that a system of investigation be in place that permits the government to operate effectively and smoothly.

ELECTIONS: 1996, 1998

In the presidential election of 1996, Clinton and Gore ran for a second term. Robert Dole, Senate majority leader, won in the Republican primaries and chose Jack Kemp, a former Reagan cabinet member and strong supporter of supply-side economics, as the vice presidential candidate. Their campaign never caught fire, and the Democrats again won the presidency, but the Republicans retained control of the Congress.

Commentators suggested the public wanted this divided government that assured there would be no major changes in policy. Their interpretation was that the public was satisfied with the growing economy, and, with no apparent threat to America's security, they did not want changes. This may have been true, but it does not explain the poor turnout in elections. Just over 50 percent of the people eligible to vote bothered to do so.

The 1998 election was considered to be very close. The Republicans lost some congressional seats but retained control of both the Senate and the House. This may confirm the commentators' interpretation. It also meant that the extensive acrimony and gridlock in Washington would continue.

> In 1998 Democrats are unable to regain control of Congress.

THE ECONOMY

Clinton came to office with a mild recession underway. He left office after eight years of phenomenal economic growth. For instance, in one year alone, 1995, the Dow Jones Industrial Average grew 33.5 percent, making millionaires of many executives and founders of dot-coms. It also broadened the gap between rich and poor. With the prosperity, everyone's financial position was apparently improving to some extent. One aspect of the economic prosperity that affected many was the decline in violent crime in the 1990s and the drop in the number of people on welfare.

MICROSOFT

The computer dot-com sector grew very quickly in the 1990s. A driving force behind computers was Microsoft, a company founded by Bill Gates. Following the traditional Democratic approach to business and monopoly, the Justice Department began an investigation of Microsoft, whose software essentially controlled the computer revolution. To the surprise of some who believed a monopoly of operating systems would benefit the industry and allow all computers to communicate, the Department of Justice brought a suit against Microsoft accusing the company of violating the antimonopoly laws. In 2000, the federal courts ruled against Microsoft, finding the company displayed anticompetitive behavior and later ordered the company be split. On appeal after the election of George W. Bush, the decision was reversed. Some controls were established for the future activities of Microsoft. What impact this case had on the slowdown within the computer industry at the end of the Clinton years can be determined only by future historians.

Y2K—THE MILLENNIUM

As the nation approached the end of the second millennium, A.D. 2000, many were concerned that computers were not properly programmed to handle the change in year from 1999 to 2000. This was called the Y2K problem. They believed that computers would read the year 2000 incorrectly and as a result, many records would be lost and perhaps entire systems controlling crucial operations such as electrical power would shut down. Millions of dollars were spent checking computers, and this gave a temporary boost to the economy. The new millennium arrived with only very minor computer problems. The new millennium was greeted by worldwide celebrations covered by around-the-clock television.

GROUP ACTION

In 1995, Hillary Rodham Clinton published a book, *It Takes a Village*. It set out the ideal that everyone, each individual, has responsibilities for others and that only by cooperating can we successfully raise our children or achieve progress. Some found the message went against the ethos of American individualism and denounced it as socialism and the reason people remained on welfare, expecting others to take care of them. Others believed the book truly addressed the role of government. These two views are representative of the two views of government and society that were dominating the political debate in the United States.

> It Takes a Village set forth ideal of responsibility and cooperation.

The same year, Louis Farrakhan, leader of the Nation of Islam, staged a "million man march" on Washington, D.C. Farrakhan wished to illustrate the power of the Black Islamic community and the need for every African-American man to be a leader. The message, as was Mrs. Clinton's, was sound, but it frightened some to see African-Americans so organized.

> "Million man march" illustrates importance of Black Islamic community.

RACISM—THE O. J. SIMPSON TRIAL

Clinton appointed a cabinet that reflected the racial mix of the country. He appeared comfortable with people of all races and set an example for the nation. However, racism remained an issue as several situations illustrate.

In 1995, the "trial of the century" took place in Los Angeles. O. J. Simpson, a football legend, was on trial for murdering his estranged white wife, Nicole Brown Simpson, and her friend, Ron Goldman. The trial, as did O. J. Simpson's arrest, created a media-frenzy of television coverage. Simpson was acquitted to the delight of many in the African-American community and to the surprise of many in the white community—an indication of the split in perception of the same information by the two communities. Clinton saw this as a threat to the nation. He began a series of roundtable discussions around the country that brought together members of all racial groups. It was an attempt to address the continuing issue of racism in America.

> O. J. Simpson acquitted of murder in the "trial of the century."

ELIAN GONZALEZ

In 1999–2000, a case illustrating racial tension of another type—that between the Cuban immigrant community in Florida, the federal government, and the fear of communism—gained national prominence through TV coverage. Elian Gonzalez and his divorced mother were fleeing communist Cuba when their boat capsized, the mother drowned, and the elementary school student was picked up by the United States Coast Guard. The boy had relatives in Miami who befriended him, but his father in Cuba requested his return. Federal marshals seized the boy from his relatives at gunpoint. The federal courts ruled in favor of the father, and Elian Gonzalez was returned to Cuba.

The incident split the country. Some saw police brutality; others saw issues of illegal immigration; others saw discrimination against Cubans; some saw United States support for a Communist government. The Clinton administration was following the law in supporting the father, but it cost the Democrats support from Cuban exiles in Florida. The case illustrated the complexity of dealing with issues involving immigrants and minorities. It also illustrated how TV coverage can bring any case into every home. While many situations, such as shootings in schools, are local, TV makes them national, forcing the president and federal government to be prepared to react to them before the cameras. This has created a new dynamic in politics since the Vietnam War.

THE SUPREME COURT

The appointments to the Supreme Court by Ronald Reagan and George H. W. Bush, moved the court in a more conservative direction. President Clinton reversed the trend. His first

> Clinton appoints two Supreme Court justices.

appointment in 1993, Ruth Bader Ginsburg, the second woman on the court, had a reputation of commitment to individual rights. In 1994, Justice Harry Blackmun, author of the *Roe* v. *Wade* decision and many others defining rights to privacy, resigned. Clinton appointed Stephen Breyer, a circuit court judge appointed by President Carter to the court.

In 1992, the Court by a 5–4 vote in *Planned Parenthood* v. *Casey* upheld *Roe* v. *Wade* and continued to uphold the landmark abortion decision in other cases. The outcome of other cases concerning privacy, rights of the accused, school prayer, and individual rights were decided by narrow margins. The

> Supreme Court is essentially evenly divided as seen in many 5–4 decisions.

Court was essentially evenly divided. Many decisions became 5–4 with Justices O'Connor and Souter shifting back and forth from the more conservative four to the more liberal three members. This made it hard to predict outcomes of cases, but it reflected the political reality of the nation.

In *Romer* v. *Evans*, the court struck down 6–3 a voter-approved amendment to the Colorado Constitution that barred local communities from passing laws to protect the rights of gays.

In *Boy Scouts* v. *Dale* in 2000 the Court 5–4 ruled that requiring the Boy Scouts to admit a homosexual as troop leader violated the organization's First Amendment right of association to choose only those members who subscribe to its stated values.

In spite of its conservative leaning, the Court declared unconstitutional the Line Item Veto Act and the Decency Act (regulation of pornography on the Internet), both of which had strong support from conservatives. The most important case heard during the Clinton years was the one determining the result of the 2000 presidential election.

THE 2000 ELECTION

Al Gore was the leading candidate for the 2000 Democratic Party nomination, which he easily obtained. He picked Senator Joseph Lieberman of Connecticut, the first Jew to be named to a national ticket, as vice presidential candidate. As a result of the Lewinsky scandal, Clinton's participation in the campaign, was limited as Gore attempted to establish his own identity. Gore attempted to use the economy as an issue, but prosperity was identified with Clinton, and Gore's campaign never captured the imagination of the voting public.

The Republicans had several state primary battles between leading candidate Governor George W. Bush of Texas, son of former President George H. W. Bush, and Arizona Senator John McCain, a Vietnam War hero who had been a prisoner of war. McCain raised several issues that resonated with the voters—particularly campaign finance reform and prescription drug coverage through federal subsidies. In spite of McCain's openness and his appealing issues, the money and organization of Bush overwhelmed McCain in the later primaries. Bush's "compassionate conservatism" appealed to the core of conservative Republican voters. Bush was nominated and chose Dick Cheney as vice president. Both candidates had strong connections to the oil industry.

To complicate the race, Ralph Nader, a noted defender of the public interest, ran as a candidate for the Green Party—an environment-focused party quite strong in Europe. He appealed to many young voters, especially on college campuses.

CLOSEST PRESIDENTIAL ELECTION IN HISTORY

The 2000 election proved the closest in U.S. history. On election night it was clear that Gore had carried the Northeast (except New Hampshire) and Pacific Coast and scattered states in the Midwest. He was ahead in the popular and electoral votes, but three states were too close to call—Oregon, New Mexico, and Florida. Bush had won the entire South and many states in the Mountain West and the large states of Missouri, Ohio, and Indiana. Finally, the election depended on who carried Florida and its 25 electoral votes.

U.S. SUPREME COURT DECIDES ELECTION IN *BUSH* V. *GORE*

On November 8, Bush led in Florida by 1,784 votes. However, a recount of machine-cast votes cut the lead to 327. There appeared to be some irregularities in ballot design and punching of ballots. The two candidates then resorted to lawsuits to seek

> Gore concedes the election.

recounts or to block them as seemed best for their side. The process became ever more complicated. The press and television news channels gave minute-by-minute coverage to the unresolved election. The Florida Supreme Court became involved. Finally the U.S. Supreme Court took the case and on December 12 voted 5–4 in *Bush* v. *Gore* to end the Florida recount. In effect, this gave Florida's electoral votes to Bush, for a total of 271 to Gore's 266. Thus Bush was elected president although

Popular Vote for President by Major Political Party; 1972 – 2000

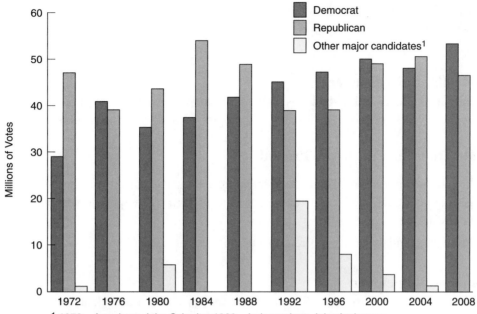

¹ 1972 – American, John Schmitz; 1980 – Independent, John Anderson;
 1992 – Independent, Ross Perot; 1996 – Reform, Ross Perot; Green, Ralph Nader;
 2000 – Reform, Pat Buchanan; Green, Ralph Nader
 2004 – Green, Ralph Nader

Source: U.S. Census Bureau, *Statistical Abstract of the United States: 2000;*
 Internet, U.S. Elections, 2000, ABC News. Internet, U.S. Elections,
 2004, 2008, CNN.

Gore had won the popular vote. Gore conceded the election. After five weeks of uncertainty, the nation had a new president.

Ralph Nader won only 2 percent of the vote, and there were suggestions he took enough votes away from Gore to deny him the election. Nader won 100,000 votes in Florida. There were those who believed the resolution of the election crisis and the Supreme Court decision were determined by politics and not the people's voice. Bush's brother was governor of Florida, which added to their concern. Many were concerned that only 50.7 percent of the people voted, meaning only a quarter of eligible voters had voted for Bush. However, the election was a triumph for the American democratic process. The Court's decision was accepted; there was no violence. After September 11, the issue of the election was forgotten as the nation rallied behind President George W. Bush.

CONGRESSIONAL ELECTION

The closeness of the election and the political division of the country was also seen in the congressional election. The Senate was split 50–50, which gave Republicans control since vice president, Dick Cheney, as presiding officer of the Senate, would vote as a Republican to break any tie vote. There were arguments between the parties as to how the Senate committees should be organized. The Republicans insisted on control.

The Republicans retained control of the House by only six votes. The Republicans controlled both the executive and legislative branches. One historic result of the election was former First Lady Hillary Rodham Clinton was elected as Senator from New York.

Key Point to Remember
In spite of scandals and budget crises, the Clinton years were peaceful and prosperous years for most Americans, who approved of Clinton as president.

Links from the Past to the Present

1. In spite of impeachment, scandals, budget crises, and a close election the federal government continued to operate and was supported by the people without riots or revolution.

2. Political scandals have occurred throughout American history.

People to Remember
Albert (Al) Arnold Gore, Jr.   Senator from Tennessee, vice president, presidential candidate, lecturer, college professor, filmmaker, Nobel Peace Prize winner 2007; a student of the environment and military policy; as vice president he worked on government reform and environmental issues; separated himself from Clinton in the 2000 presidential campaign in which he won the popular vote but lost the Electoral College vote by decision of the Supreme Court; became spokesperson on environmental and global warming issues; Gore's documentary film, *An Inconvenient Truth*, was widely viewed and won an Oscar in 2007.

Dates

1994—Kenneth Starr appointed independent counsel to investigate the Whitewater real estate plan.

1995—Dow Jones industrial average rises 33.5 percent.
    O. J. Simpson "trial of the century."

1996—Clinton and Gore win second terms, the first Democrats to do so since Franklin Roosevelt.

1997—Monica Lewinsky scandal.

1998—Republicans retain control of Congress.
    U.S. House votes to impeach President Clinton.

1999—President Clinton acquitted in impeachment trial before U.S. Senate.

2000—Microsoft found to be a monopoly in a court trial.
    Elian Gonzalez returned to Cuba.
    Bush and Cheney declared winners of presidential election by the Supreme Court in a 5–4 vote.

2002—Clinton pardons are investigated.
    Campaign finance law approved.

Questions

Identify each of the following:

Kenneth Starr	Y2K
Whitewater	Newt Gingrich
Ralph Nader	*Bush* v. *Gore*

Multiple Choice:

1. Responding to the requests for information and documents by the independent counsel while he investigated matters of possible wrongdoing
   a. was done by the counsel's staff and not by the one being investigated.
   b. could be ignored by the one under investigation.
   c. cost money and took time away from one's job while being investigated.

2. Joseph Lieberman, vice presidential candidate in 2000, was the first member of what religious faith to run as a national party candidate?
   a. Roman Catholic
   b. Jewish
   c. Islamic

3. President Clinton made two appointments to the Supreme Court:
   a. David Souter and Ruth Bader Ginsburg.
   b. Sandra Day O'Connor and Clarence Thomas.
   c. Ruth Bader Ginsburg and Stephen Breyer.

III. Domestic Policies and Issues During Bush's Two Terms

George W. Bush campaigned strongly in favor of budget cuts to return some of the budget surplus to the people, for modernization of the military, for market-based reform of social security, and for education reform. Bush chose several individuals from his father's administration for key positions, including General Colin Powell as secretary of state, former Secretary of Defense Donald Rumsfeld to fill that post again, and Condoleeza Rice as national security advisor. He also chose former Senator John Ashcroft, a very conservative member of the Republican right, as attorney general. The appointments worried all liberals.

LEGISLATION

With the cabinet in place, Bush focused on the tax cut issue. A budget surplus of $5.6 trillion was projected over ten years. It was merely a projection. However, Bush proposed a $1.35 trillion tax cut spread over ten years. With strong Democratic objection, the proposal became law. Top tax rates were to be gradually reduced from 39.6 percent to 35 percent. The inheritance or estate tax was to be gradually lowered. These changes appeared to benefit the wealthy. This was the major Democratic objection to the cuts. The tax cuts expire in ten years unless Congress acts to extend them. While some cuts have been extended, what to do about the remaining taxes must be addressed early in President Obama's term.

Early in his presidency, Bush appointed Cheney chair of a committee to develop an energy policy for the nation. Democrats in Congress argued the report emphasized use of oil and natural gas rather than conservation and renewable energy sources, such as sun and wind. Conservation-minded individuals, especially those concerned with global warming—a concern that grew throughout the Bush presidency—were disappointed. Democrats demanded the committee records, and Cheney refused to provide them, claiming executive privilege. The federal court ruled in favor of Cheney, and most of the information was never released. It was the start of a running battle between the executive branch under the vice president's leadership and the Congress on the issue of executive power and privilege. The situation was reminiscent of the deadlock and acrimony in Washington during the Clinton years.

> Cheney chairs committee to develop an energy policy and creates controversy.

Energy was an issue in Congress throughout the Bush presidency. There was a bill in 2002, and in 2005 a comprehensive bill was signed that included tax subsidies to oil companies, tax breaks for work on alternative energy sources, extension of daylight saving to cut power use in the evening, and a tax cut for buying hybrid cars. It did not include oil drilling off shore or in Alaska's wilderness and did not mandate lower gas consumption engines for SUVs. Energy use and global warming were issues in the 2008 campaign, and Obama in the first days of his presidency ordered lower gas emission standards for cars and approved a new look at oil and gas leases of federal lands. Energy will continue as a major issue for years as oil reserves decline and worldwide demand increases.

Harry Truman first brought the issue of universal health care to Congress, but no legislation was passed. The Medicare/Medicaid program, providing medical benefits for many poor and for retirees who met certain age requirements and/or other criteria, became law as part of Lyndon Johnson's Great Society Program. Jimmy Carter presented health care reform proposals, but Congress did not act on them. Clinton's attempt failed. The United States is the only major industrialized nation without universal health care. To many Americans, any government health care is a form of communism or socialized medicine. Government-subsidized health care appears to some to be in opposition to the American ideal of individual responsibility. Because of these attitudes and the complexity of the issue, health care reform has been difficult.

However, in 2003 Bush signed a Medicare Modernization Act (MMA; Prescription Drug Benefit) that had passed Congress by a narrow margin after

> Medicare Part D adds drug coverage for seniors.

considerable debate and compromises that resulted in a very complex law. It reflected the complexity of the medical services in the United States. Rather than following most other developed nations with a straight government paid drug allowance for seniors, in the MMA participation in Medicare Part D is voluntary. Private insurance companies that provide a variety of options provide drug coverage. Payment is complex. It was a major breakthrough in health coverage.

CAMPAIGN FINANCE REFORM

Senator John McCain had made campaign finance reform a key issue of his 2000 presidential primary campaign. Bush, who had broken all records for money raised for a presidential campaign, wished to ignore the issue but it had great popular appeal.

The collapse of Enron and the revelations of its political contributions focused public attention on the issue. Finally Congress passed a Campaign Finance Reform Law that Bush signed in March 2002. The law increased the amount of hard money[3] donations to candidates. It changed the rules for raising and spending soft money[4]. The Supreme Court has overturned several aspects of the law, but it is in effect.

After initially saying he would accept government financing for his 2008 presidential campaign, on winning the nomination, Obama, the Democratic nominee, did not accept federal funding leaving him free to raise millions largely in small donations. Senator McCain, the Republican nominee, did accept it, and the disparity in amount of money available to the two candidates certainly had some impact on the campaign. Whether to accept federal funding will an issue for every future candidate.

OTHER LEGISLATION

In 2006 Bush pushed for a major overhaul of immigration policies and failed to gain congressional support. After long and and often heated debate, a compromise focused on border security measures. Increased patrolling and some fencing were approved for the Mexican border.

> **Bush fails to achieve overhaul of immigration policy.**

Other important legislation passed by Congress under Bush were the Patriot Act (see pages 418–419), and other anti-terrorism measures, the Election Reform Bill, a Corporate Governance Reform Bill, the No Child Left Behind Education Bill, welfare reform that also included healthy marriage and responsible fatherhood measures, and the Partial Birth Abortion Bill (2003) that was later declared unconstitutional by several federal judges but whose opinion was reversed by the Supreme Court in a 5–4 decision, *Gonzales* v. *Carhart*, in 2007.

STEM CELL RESEARCH

After months of consideration and extensive press coverage, Bush issued an executive order declaring the federal government would support limited embryonic stem cell research. It would make illegal the creation of new embryo stem cells but would permit research using established stem cell lines. Embryo stem cell research is a complicated issue. The potential for cures of inherited disease appears great, but the creation and destruction of embryos hits at the heart of pro-life beliefs. This tension

> **Bush compromises on embryo stem cell research.**

[3] hard money *Money raised for political campaigns that is given directly to a candidate.*
[4] soft money *Money raised for political campaigns that is given to local and state parties to spend as they see fit to support candidates.*

led some antiabortion people to support stem cell research. Because of the federal restrictions on research, several states developed their own stem cell research projects creating new stem cell lines. In 2006 Congress passed a bill removing restrictions on federal funding, but Bush vetoed the measure—the first veto of his presidency. In 2007 researchers discovered a way of creating stem cells from adult cells meaning embryos might not need to be created for research. In one of his first acts as president, Obama reversed Bush's executive order thus permitting federal support of research funding. While research appeared promising, researchers warned that cures for specific diseases were not imminent. Stem cell research and cloning of humans, as well as questions of who should receive the benefits of new medical technology raise many ethical questions that society has not addressed. They will be important issues in the 21st century.

ABM TREATY

Bush and his secretary of defense, Donald Rumsfeld, were committed to the concept of a missile shield to protect the United States—similar to Reagan's Strategic Defense Initiative (SDI). After two unsuccessful and one successful test, Bush decided to build the shield. To continue testing, the Antiballistic Missile (ABM) Treaty of 1972 had to be either amended or abandoned. Russia refused to amend the treaty. Bush announced to the dismay of the NATO allies on December 13, 2001, that the United States would withdraw from the treaty, claiming its restraints on the power of the United States were "not appropriate" after the attacks of September 11, 2001. Many nations perceived this act as arrogant unilateralism (see page 448). It marked a major shift in U.S. foreign policy and the rejection of an internationalist approach that had been followed since Franklin Roosevelt's presidency. Bush had appointed a number of individuals referred to as neo-cons (neo-conservatives)[5] to important positions in the administration and their view's were strongly supported by Vice President Cheney.

THE BUSH DOCTRINE

Incorporating views of neo-cons, in September 2002, the Bush Doctrine of preemptive war was issued. It formalized the new approach to foreign relations stating that the "even if uncertainty remains as to time and place of the enemy's attack . . . the United States will attack preemptively." It reflected the attitude of the neo-cons and the Bush administration that the United States had to go out and attack the terrorists. At the time this unilateral position was being presented, Bush was attempting to organize a coalition of allies to attack Iraq. The two actions reflected the concerns of Americans after the 9/11 attacks.

---

[5] neo-conservative   *The first expression of the neo-conservative view came in the 1970s. With the fall of the Soviet Union, their views became more popular as the United States was the only super power. Neo-cons believed that power should be used to obtain goals without concern for other nations or treaties.*

SENATOR JEFFORDS LEAVES REPUBLICAN PARTY

Senator Jeffords of Vermont, a liberal Republican, announced on May 24, 2001, that he was leaving the Republican Party. He became an Independent, voting with the Democrats. This changed the Senate alignment from 50–50 to 51–49 in favor of the Democrats and created an entirely new political dynamic. Democrats became chairs of all committees, and the legislative agenda for the Senate was in the hands of the Democrats. Divided government had returned to Washington, and this meant Bush would have to work with Democrats to achieve his political goals as occurred with the Education and Campaign Finance Bills.

ELECTION 2002

With the Democrats controlling the Senate by one vote and the Republicans controlling the House by six, much attention was devoted to the election of 2002. After September 11, Bush's popular support was extremely high and Democrats sought ways to establish positions without appearing to criticize him on foreign policy. Democrats tried to focus on prescription drug coverage and social security reform. Their campaign did not appeal to a public that seemed more concerned with terrorism than the economy. The Democrats lost two Senate seats and several in the House, and the Republicans recaptured control of Congress. With control of Congress, the White House, and a conservative leaning Supreme Court, the Republicans anticipated advancing their agenda in the years ahead.

ELECTION OF 2004

In the 2004 presidential primary Bush was unopposed, and Senator John Kerry of Massachusetts, a decorated Vietnam War hero who had later opposed the war, emerged from the Democratic field as the nominee. He picked former Senator John Edwards of North Carolina as his running mate. After the debacle in Florida in 2000, there were concerns of a repeat. Congress had passed an Election Reform Bill calling for extensive updates of voting methods, and many states expanded their use of electronic voting machines, which caused some controversy, but the voting took place with only minor difficulties. Karl Rove, the political consultant who had master-minded Bush's 2000 victory and who served in the White House until 2007, again set strategy. When the race appeared very close, an ad questioning Kerry's war participation turned some voters against Kerry. The election results were close, but Bush and Cheney won a second term. The Republicans retained control of the Congress. Among the campaign issues were the conduct of the war in Iraq and reform of Social Security.

After the election Bush made cabinet changes replacing Secretary of State Powell with former Security Adviser Condoleezza Rice and Attorney General Ashcroft, who had refused to agree to the administration demands for wiretapping authority, with Alberto Gonzales, a lawyer working in the White House. He was more subservient to the administration's wishes; he became a very

> **Bush replaces Cabinet members and attempts to reform Social Security.**

controversial figure and was a factor in the 2006 defeat of the Republicans. He then resigned from the cabinet. Bush made Social Security reform, which would include partial privatization of the program, a top priority for Congress but failed to find support in spite of the Republican majorities.

ELECTION OF 2006

By 2006 dissatisfaction over the conduct of the war in Iraq and with the Republican administration became the top priority for voters. The Democratic Party won a landslide victory recapturing the Senate and House and a number of governorships from the Republicans. Nancy Pelosi, Representative from California, was elected Speaker of the House, the first woman to hold the position—the highest position ever achieved by a woman in the federal government. Secretary of Defense Rumsfeld resigned his cabinet post after the election. With strong neo-conservative views, he had been a strong supporter and the chief architect of the the war in Iraq. The Democrats addressed the war issue by proposing timetables for withdrawal of troops but were unable to get the measure passed in spite of controlling both houses. Democratic suggestions for stopping funding appropriations got nowhere as Congress would not abandon support for the troops. The Congressional session was bitter until the financial crisis overwhelmed the war issue, and action was taken to address the banking crisis.

SUPREME COURT

Bush made two conservative appointments to the Supreme Court continuing its conservative disposition. In 2005 Sandra Day O'Connor resigned and was replaced by Samuel A. Alito, an Appeals Court judge who has a strong conservative record. When Chief Justice Rehnquist died later that year, John G. Roberts, lawyer in the Reagan administration and later Appellate Court judge, was appointed Chief Justice.

The Court during the Bush years made several decisions limiting the use of the death penalty—banning the execution of retarded convicts and the execution of convicts who committed crimes before they were 18 and requiring that only juries, not judges, can impose the death penalty. The Court also struck down the federal sentencing guidelines passed by Congress in its

> Court decides on death penalty, race, and same sex relations.

attempt to be hard on criminals, but left them as advisory guides for judges. On the issue of race, the Court accepted race as one of many factors to be considered in college admission but declared unconstitutional the mechanical use of racial preference that did not consider all the qualifications. In the most important case dealing with traditional values, the Supreme Court in *Lawrence* v. *Texas* declared unconstitutional the Texas law banning sodomy between consenting same sex adults.

Many cases continued to be decided by 5–4 majorities reflecting the split between conservative and liberal viewpoints on the Court. This also reflects a division in the nation as seen in the closeness of elections in the 20 years since the end of Reagan's presidency.

ENVIRONMENTAL ISSUES

Environmental and conservation organizations described the Bush administration's environmental polices as the worst in recent history. His appointment of Gale Norton, an attorney representing mining, logging, oil and gas companies in the west, as secretary of interior set the tone for the administration. The Cheney energy plan confirmed that there would be strong support for these industries. One of the first acts of the administration in 2001 was to move to rollback the Roadless Rule of the Clinton era. Bush wished to open millions of acres of national forest for roads supporting logging, mining and gas, and oil leasing, and one of the last acts in December 2008 was the statement of the EPA (Environment Protection Agency) administrator that the EPA would not regulate CO_2 pollution from power plants. In the eight years in between, the Clean Air Act, Clean Water Act, and the Endangered Species Law were all weakened by decisions of the administrators of those agencies, and research and development funding was cut by 27 percent.

> Bush Administration gets poor grades on environmental policies according to environmental groups.

The administration failed to accept the scientific community's evidence on increasing global warming and the impact of human activity on it until the end of Bush's term, and then took no action. Bush rejected the Kyoto Accords on global warming, which committed three dozen industrialized countries to cut their greenhouse gases an average of 5 percent below 1990 levels by 2012, because the accords did not require developing nations, such as China and Brazil, to reduce their levels. In 2007, at the U.N. Conference on Global Warming in Bali, the United States lost support of allies by insisting on that position, and China refused to accept limits until the United States did. The issue appeared at an impasse, but efforts continued to develop an international plan to address global warming.

Former Vice-President Al Gore spent the years after his defeat in 2000 calling attention to global warming. For his efforts, he won the Nobel Peace Prize in 2007, and his documentary, *An Inconvenient Truth*, was seen by millions around the world and won an Oscar. The work of environmental groups also publicized issues of global warming and harm to the environment. President Obama made it clear that his administration would acknowledge the research of scientists when he appointed a Nobel Laureate in Physics, Stephen Chu, as Secretary of Energy. To quickly establish that the Democratic administration would pursue a new direction in environmental policy, among the first acts of the Obama administration were the dropping of the Bush administration court challenge to mercury emissions policy under the Clean Air Act and the canceling of leases for oil and gas drilling in National Forest lands in Utah signed in the final days of the Bush administration.

> Obama Administration quickly reversed Bush environmental approaches.

SCANDALS

As in the case of all recent administrations, several scandals surfaced during the Bush presidency. Several involved the Congress. In 2002 Trent Lott, Republican Majority Leader, was forced to resign as a result of comments about Strom

Thurmond's presidential race in 1948 that were considered racist. Then in 2005 then Republican Majority Leader Tom De Lay was forced to resign his position when accused by a Texas Grand Jury of conspiring to violate campaign finance laws. He resigned from Congress in 2006. Also in 2006 Jack Abramoff, a high-profile lobbyist, pleaded guilty in three cases involving political lobbying misconduct, bribery, and fraudulent dealings. He was sentenced to prison, but the investigation of the case led to the conviction of two White House aides, a Congressman, and nine congressional staff members. Voters' response helped defeat the Republicans in 2006, and in 2007 the Democratic-controlled Senate passed changes to the Ethics rules on lobbying and related matters. The need to curtail the power of lobbyists was an important message in the Obama campaign.

> Scandalous conduct forces two Republican House Majority Leaders to resign.

The first major scandal of the Bush executive department involved the leaking of the name of a covert CIA agent, Valerie Plame, to the press allegedly in retaliation for her husband, former Ambassador James Wilson, publishing that he found no evidence of shipments of uranium from Nigeria to Iraq, a claim the president had made in his justification for war against Iraq. A Grand Jury indicted no one in connection with the leak but indicted Vice President Cheney's former Chief of Staff, I. Lewis Libby, for obstuction of justice. He was found guilty, sentenced to 30 months in jail, but President Bush immediately commuted the sentence.

In 2006 seven state federal prosecutors were dimissed in the middle of their terms by the Justice Department in an unprecedented move. It quickly became a scandal. Investigated by the inspector general of the department, the dismissal was called fundamentally flawed. A special federal prosecutor was appointed to pursue the case. Rumors suggested the dismissals came at the request of the White House under the direction of Karl Rove and involved possible voter fraud cases the White House wanted investigated. Karl Rove who had previously pleaded executive privilege in the case and refused to testify reversed his position after the election of Obama. After the revelation of the use of torture by the government, there were cries of misues of power, but no cases had been brought against administration members by the end of Bush's presidency.

> Investigation of dismissal of state Federal Prosectutors.

ECONOMIC DEVELOPMENTS: 2001–2007

As Bush took office, there were signs of an economic downturn, which led to a recession in 2001–2002 as the dot-com boom ended. The Federal Reserve Board responded by cutting interest rates to the lowest level in years. Bush argued his tax cut would help the economy, but two years later the economy had not recovered. The attack of September 11, 2001, complicated the issues. Bush asked Congress for an economic stimulus package, but as under Clinton, Congress could not agree on its terms. Congress did pass an extension of unemployment benefits as it had under Clinton. By July 2002 the stock market had fallen to its lowest level in five years.

Enron, a company created in the 1980s to sell natural gas, grew dramatically to become one of the ten largest companies in the nation. Its approach of contracting for, rather than owning, assets was hailed as the business approach of the future. Executives received high salaries, and stock in the company rose rapidly. The company and its executives became big contributors to both political parties, especially to the Republicans and to Bush's gubernatorial and presidential campaigns. However, Enron's bookkeeping was deceitful, and the company declared bankruptcy on November 28, 2001. It was the largest bankruptcy in the nation's history to that time. A large telecommunications company, Global Crossing, also declared bankruptcy in late 2001. The bankruptcies slowed economic recovery. Investor confidence was shaken, and the stock market dropped.

The bankruptcies had repercussions for the accounting industry.

> **Accounting firms come under scrutiny.**

Congress began over a dozen investigations. CEO, Kenneth Lay, sold over $100,000,000 in stock just before Enron's collapse while employees were not allowed to sell stock and lost their life savings. In early 2002, several other highly respected companies including Xerox and WorldCom revealed their accounts had not been kept correctly, resulting in billions of dollars of false profits. The Bush administration had favored deregulation, and many members of Congress received large campaign contributions from businesses, yet it was clear something had to be done. In

> **Corporate Governance Bill (Sarbanes-Oxley Bill) passed in response to auditing fraud.**

mid-2002 Congress passed a Corporate Governance Bill (Sarbanes-Oxley Bill) that tightened oversight of auditing practices and made CEOs and CFOs financially responsible for the company's financial reports. In 2006 Kenneth Lay was found guilty on eleven counts of securities fraud but died before he was sentenced for his role in the corporate abuse and accounting fraud scandal.

Bush requested a third tax cut of $350 billion to combat the recession, and economic recovery began in 2003. However, scandals continued to emerge in the business world. Federal and state regulators settled civil law suits against ten Wall Street firms over bias in stock research for $1.4 billion. The New York

> **CEOs sentenced to prison over fraud in their business operations.**

Stock Exchange chair was forced to step down over a pay scandal involving $139.5 million, and the founder of Health Source Corp. resigned over a $2.7 billion accounting fraud. In 2006 New York State authorities charged the CEO and CFO of AIG, a global insurance company, in a scheme to misrepresent the company's financial condition. World Com Inc. CEO was sentenced to twenty-five years in prison for fraud in the company's bankruptcy and Tyco CEO was sentenced to eight to fifteen years for looting $600 million from the company. Fraud appeared widespread in the business world.

Personal spending drove the recovery. It included a boom in housing as financial institutions developed new types of mortages. Home ownership was a part of the American Dream and had been encouraged by the government over the years.

> **New mortgage offerings support housing boom.**

Bush referred to his ideal for the nation as an "ownership" society in which every individual would own a home, own his own social security by being able to invest in the stock market, and control his own health insurance. The administration therefore supported the new mortgages. There were government oversight agencies, but under the Republican philosophy of less government and deregulation, several agencies were lax in their oversight. Many other factors contributed to the start of a finacial crisis that became a major economic decline in 2008. (See page 451.)

The 2001–2002 recession, combined with the federal expenditures necessitated by the September 11 attacks and Bush's tax cut, wiped out the projected budget surplus and led to renewed budget deficits. A deficit of over $140 billion was predicted for 2002. The budget surplus had lasted only four years.

> Economic crises lead to end of surplus and return to government deficits.

RESPONSE TO HURRICANE KATRINA

On August 29, 2005, Hurricane Katrina hit the Louisiana coast and floodwaters breached the levees at New Orleans creating one of the worst natural disasters in United States history. Federal, state, and local responders worked to avert disaster, but

> New Orleans, in spite of promises, has not recovered from the effects of Hurricane Katrina.

coordination was poor between them and the needs overwhelming. Over $81 billion in damage was done by the storm, many lives were lost, and thousands suffered loss of property. Rescue plans moved slowly in part due to floodwaters. The president appeared slow to react. Blame was distributed widely. In spite of many announced efforts to speed reconstruction including the efforts of former Presidents George H. W. Bush and Clinton to raise funds, New Orleans still suffers from the impact of the hurricane. While the levees were repaired by the end of Bush's presidency, many homes had not, and thousands had not returned to the city. No comprehensive plan for the future of New Orleans was developed—one that addressed the issue of rebuilding a city below sea level in a storm-threatened region in the time of global warming. The response to Katrina cost Bush much support and damaged the image of his administration and of the United States.

CULTURE WARS AND TRADITIONAL VALUES

With Republicans in control of Congress and the White House, the conservative wing of the party believed they could advance their social agenda—a part of the culture wars and struggle over

> Same-sex marriage becomes a major political issue.

the meaning of traditional values of the previous thirty years. The first law restricting abortion since *Roe* v. *Wade*, appointment of conservative judges to the Supreme Court, passage of laws defining marriage as between a man and a woman, and state constitutional amendments banning same-sex marriage were examples of their success. However, on other issues there was greater acceptance of new attitudes and values. The Episcopal Church in 2003 accepted Gene Robinson of New Hampshire as the first openly gay bishop in the church. That year the Massachusetts Supreme Court struck down a ban on same-sex marriage, and since 2004 such marriages have been performed in that state. Later the California court declared a ban on same-sex marriage unconstitutional. The voters overturned the decision in 2008, and the issue is back before the courts.

In 2005 Congress intervened in the Schivao case in Florida that involved life support for a woman in a vegetative state. Her husband asked for removal of the machines, her family supported by pro-life groups asked to keep them. Congress supported the family, but the federal courts refused to order them reinstated. The case illustrated the continuing struggles over traditional values involving life, euthanasia, medical practices, and choice—issues that have become more complex with medical advances and must be addressed by society.

In spite of the Scopes Trial in the 1920s, controversy continued over the teaching of evolution. Fundamentalists who read the Bible literally were opposed to it. They proposed the idea of Intelligent Design as the explanation for the creation of the universe and found supporters including President Bush who advocated its teaching as an alternative to evolution. The local school board of Dover, Pennsylvania, required its teaching as had boards in other states, and the state of Louisiana passed a law that allowed it to be taught as an alternative to evolution. A lawsuit was filed against the Dover district, and a federal court declared promoting Intelligent Design over evolution in the schools was unconstitutional as the theory lacked any scientific evidence. The controversy over Intelligent Design continues. It reflects another aspect of the culture wars.

Roman Catholic clergy in Massachusetts and later in many other states had been accused of sex abuse scandals involving children as early as the late 1980s. The accusations spread, lawsuits were filed, and in the first diocese-wide settlement in 2003 the Boston diocese agreed to pay $85 million to victims. Cases and settlement agreements continue to be made. In a visit to Boston in 2008, the Pope met victims and apologized. The church banned homosexuals from admission to seminaries. Public outrage at the abuse by priests, over the acts of sexual offenders throughout the country, and the passage of strict laws requiring released sex offenders to register to be tracked for life suggest traditional values in this area remain strong.

> Roman Catholic church faces charges of sex abuse by priests.

Key Point to Remember

In spite of the 9/11 attack on the United States, the Bush administration faced many unrelated domestic issues during its eight years.

Links from the Past to the Present

1. As after every election when the party holding the White House changes, a new mood and a new set of political priorities were introduced in Washington by the Bush administration.

2. Economic issues of business bankruptcies and corruption by CEOs created uncertainties that eventually led to another recession after a short period of growth indicating the capitalist business cycle still operated.

People to Remember

George W. Bush   Oil executive, owner of Texas Rangers baseball team, governor of Texas, 43rd president of the United States; son of 41st president George H. W.

Bush, called himself a "compassionate conservative"; won the presidency in a disputed election settled by a Supreme Court ruling 5–4; declared a War on Terrorism after the September 11 attacks on the United States; invaded Afghanistan in pursuit of al-Qaida after 9/11 and Iraq seeking destruction of weapons of mass destruction that were never found.

Dates

2000—November 7, Election Day
    December 12, Supreme Court 5–4 decision in *Bush* v. *Gore* settles the election in favor of Bush, although Gore wins popular vote.

2001—Tax Reform Act, $1.35 trillion tax cut spread over 10 years.
    Senator Jeffords leaves the Republican Party.
    Enron Corporation declares bankruptcy.

2002—Education Reform Bill (No Child Left Behind)
    Campaign Finance Reform Bill.
    WorldCom bankruptcy.
    Supreme Court declares unconstitutional the execution of retarded convicts.

2003—Medicare Modernization Act adds Prescription Drug Benefit to Medicare.
    Space shuttle *Columbia* disintegrates as it enters earth's atmosphere.
    Roman Catholic Diocese of Boston settles priest's sex abuse scandal for $84 million.
    Massachusetts Supreme Court declares state ban on same-sex marriages unconstitutional.
    Partial Birth Abortion Bill signed.

2004—George Bush and Dick Cheney defeat John Kerry and John Edwards to win second presidential term.
    Reform of Social Security fails.

2005—Texas Grand Jury indicts House Majority Leader Tom Delay for campaign finance violations.
    John G. Roberts appointed Chief Justice of Supreme Court.
    Hurricane Katrina.

2006—Samuel A. Alito appointment to Supreme Court approved.
    Democrats sweep elections winning control of Senate and House.
    Secretary of Defense Rumsfeld, Iraq War architect, resigns.
    Major immigration reform fails in Congress.

2007—Attorney-General Gonzales resigns amidst controversy over firing of federal state attorneys-general.

2008—Subprime mortgage and Housing Crisis extends to financial markets worldwide.

Questions

Identify each of the following:

Stem cell research	Bush Doctrine	Kyoto Accords
Global warming	Enron	Medicare Modernization Act
Hurricane Katrina	Budget surplus	ABM Treaty

Multiple Choice:

1. When Senator Jeffords left the Republican Party
   a. the Senate defeated the Patriot Act.
   b. Republicans refused to finance the government.
   c. the Democrats became the majority party in the Senate.

2. During the Bush administration
   a. the economy remained stagnant for eight years.
   b. government regulation of financial institutions and business increased.
   c. several large corporations were forced to declare bankruptcy.

3. Bush's withdrawal from the ABM Treaty upset
   a. the Russians and NATO.
   b. the Republican conservative right.
   c. the pro-choice lobby.

4. Bush named to positions in his administration
   a. George H. W. Bush and Dick Cheney.
   b. Donald Rumsfeld and Condoleezza Rice.
   c. Hillary Rodham Clinton and John Ashcroft.

IV. Bush Undertakes War on Terrorism

SEPTEMBER 11, 2001

On the morning of September 11, 2001, in a tightly organized plan, nineteen terrorists hijacked four planes, and successfully crashed two into the Twin Towers of the World Trade Center in New York City, one into the Pentagon in Washington, D.C., and one crashed in a field in Pennsylvania after the passengers foiled the hijackers. The hijackers' fourth destination is still unknown. The buildings attacked were symbols of the financial and military power of the United States. The event had a profound impact on United States domestic and foreign policy and continues to affect many policy decisions.

The Twin Towers of the World Trade Center collapsed with the loss of almost 3,000 lives. Despite the confusion and uncertainty, the national response was an instant outpouring of grief and support for all those affected, fully documented by around-the-clock television coverage. The U.S. air space was closed, the military was put on alert, the stock market was closed, and the nation waited.

World Trade Center collapses on September 11.
Courtesy: Associated Press

Central and Southern Asia and the Middle East—2008

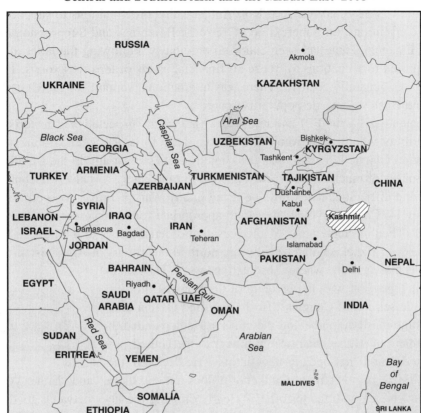

President Bush addressed the nation, calling the three attacks "acts of war" and declaring the nation was embarking on a "monumental struggle of good versus evil," an idea that he pursued for the remainder of his presidency.

The nation went on war alert, and Vice President Cheney went to a secret location where a shadow government was set up, and Bush began building an international coalition to combat terrorism.[6] The world response was supportive. NATO declared it would support the United States if it took military action. The United States focused on Osama bin Laden then living in Afghanistan and the al-Qaida terrorist[7] network as the probable perpetrators of the attacks.

> Bush builds international coalition against terrorism.

[6] terrorism   *The unlawful use of violence and intimidation against civilians in order to obtain a political goal. It may be exercised by a government, often a threatened one, as in the Reign of Terror during the French Revolution, or by groups or individuals opposing an established authority. Terrorism is not a new phenomenon and has been used throughout modern history.*

[7] terrorist   *One who uses terrorism (i.e., unlawfully uses violence against civilians).*

The United Nations had scheduled a Conference on Terrorism for October. At the conference, UN Secretary-General Kofi Annan called on all nations to support the two UN conventions, on Suppression of Terrorist Bombings and Suppression of Terrorist Financing, that had been endorsed previously. Following the latter idea, Bush appealed to all nations to freeze all financial assets of terrorist groups. The response was generally positive. There was international support for the United States, and Bush's domestic popularity soared.

By September 14, the FBI had released 19 names of suspected 9/11 terrorists, the majority of whom were from Saudi Arabia. Next to Israel, Saudi Arabia, an authoritarian Islamic kingdom, was the United States closest ally in the Middle East and the source of much of the world's oil. This immediately revealed the conflicting interests and difficulties that would be faced in any War on Terror. Also on September 14, Congress voted "to use all appropriate force" necessary to deal with the attack. Then on September 19, the president ordered forces to the Persian Gulf and to bases in Uzbekistan and Tajikistan, northern neighbors of Afghanistan. Few Americans had any idea where these nations were. They had become independent with the breakup of the Soviet Union.

In a joint session of Congress, Bush identified Osama bin Laden as the mastermind behind the attacks. He demanded the Taliban rulers of Afghanistan turn him over to the United States—a demand "not open to negotiation." He declared, the

> Al-Qaida and Osama bin Laden identified as organizers of the attacks.

"War on Terror begins with al-Qaida but it does not end there," and "Either you are with us or you are with the terrorists," clearly drawing the lines between good and evil. This view was reinforced in his 2002 State of the Union Address. In it he referred to Iraq, Iran, and North Korea, as an "Axis of Evil" and accused them of supporting the use of terrorism, and implied that the War on Terrorism would be carried to these countries.

CONGRESS ACTS

Besides its declaration on the use of force, Congress quickly approved $40 billion for disaster relief and recovery and military operations. Congress approved $15 billion to help the airlines avoid financial disaster as a result of the closure of the air space and the drop in passenger numbers.

An anti-terrorism bill, referred to as the Patriot Act, was passed. The bill gave intelligence agencies new powers such as making it easier to obtain search warrants and warrants to tap all phones and computers. Sharing of information between intelligence agencies and the criminal justice system was made

> Anti-terrorism bill, the Patriot Act, passed by Congress.

easier. Defenders of the Bill of Rights argued that provisions in the bill encroached on the basic rights of citizens and would destroy American liberties as the terrorists desired. However, the majority of the people supported the limited curtailment of liberties to gain greater security.

In November, Congress passed an Airlines Security Bill. It created a new federal force to handle security at airports. Plans to tighten security on both the Canadian and Mexican borders were endorsed.

By mid-2002 it was clear that there had been intelligence information available relating to a possible attack on September 11, but government agencies had not shared it effectively. In June, Bush requested that Congress create a new cabinet department bringing intelligence agencies and others involved with security together in one new Department of Homeland Security. There were Democratic objections, but after the 2002 election, Congress established the department. Overall, Congress was very supportive of the War on Terrorism.

> Congress establishes cabinet-level Department of Homeland Security.

ANTHRAX SCARE

As the nation struggled with the aftermath of the terrorist attacks, a new threat appeared as spores of anthrax, a deadly disease adaptable for use in biological warfare were found in Florida at American Media Publishing House, at newscaster Tom Brokaw's office in New York City, at ABC, NBC, and CBS news offices, and at New York Governor Pataki's office.

A letter sent to Majority Leader Senator Tom Daschle's office contaminated the Senate Office Building that took two months to clean indicating the severity of the threat and how biological warfare can affect a nation. Several individuals died; thousands were put on antibiotics. The first reaction was these were terrorist attacks. Press coverage was intense. Panic was avoided and slowly the issue died down as the War in Afghanistan and the move toward war in Iraq took the headlines.

Investigation of the case continued with several suspects but no convictions. In 2008 the FBI was closing in on a suspect, Dr. Bruce Ivins, who worked at the Army Medical Institute for Infectious Diseases at Fort Detrick in Maryland. He had worked at the biodefense lab for 18 years and received the highest honor given to Defense Department civilian employees for helping solve technical problems in the manufacture of the anthrax vaccine. He cooperated with the investigation and had been informed of the impending prosecution. He committed suicide without confessing to being the one behind the 2001 scare. However, the FBI believed the case was settled.

> Anthrax case investigation chief suspect commits suicide.

WAR IN AFGHANISTAN: 2001–2008

The Bush administration focused its attention on Osama bin Laden and al-Qaida as the perpetrators of the 9/11 attack. They had been accused of attacks on U.S. embassies in Africa and the U.S. Naval destroyer *Cole*. Osama bin Laden and al-Qaida were based in Afghanistan, then ruled by an extremely conservative Islamic fundamentalist group known as the Taliban.

> Al-Qaida based in Afghanistan.

Afghanistan had been involved in war for over twenty years. The United States was involved in the 1980s, supporting anti-Soviet forces including Osama bin Laden, but had withdrawn support after the Soviets withdrew. The Taliban then gained control of most of the country, establishing an oppressive regime that followed an extreme interpretation of the Koran, the Muslim holy book. One group of warlords, the Northern Alliance, still held territory in northern Afghanistan and was fighting the Taliban. When President Bush demanded the Taliban hand over bin Laden, the Taliban refused unless specific evidence of his guilt was presented. There was none. No peaceful resolution was possible to the impasse. On October 7, the United States and Great Britain launched air strikes against Afghanistan.

MAJOR ATTACKS BY TERRORISTS ON UNITED STATES TARGETS
A TWENTY-YEAR RECORD

Date	Target	Location	Accused or Guilty Group	Number Killed
April 1983	U.S. Embassy	Beirut, Lebanon		63
October 1983	U.S. Marine Compound	Beirut, Lebanon	Islamic Shiites	241
September 1984	U.S. Embassy Annex	Beirut, Lebanon	Hizballah	16
December 1988	Pan Am flight	Lockerbie, Scotland	Libyan Abdel al-Megrahi (found guilty 2001)	270
February 1993	World Trade Center	New York City	Muslim Cleric Sheik Omar Abdul Rahman	5 (1,000 injured)
April 1995	Alfred P. Murrah Federal Building	Oklahoma City, Oklahoma	Timothy McVeigh (executed) and Terry Nichols (imprisoned)	168
November 1995	Saudi Arabian military facility with U.S. troops	Riyadh, Saudi Arabia	Movement for Islamic Change and Tigers of the Gulf	7
June 1996	U.S. military housing complex	Dahran, Saudi Arabia	Not Determined	19
July 1996	Summer Olympics	Atlanta, Georgia	Not Determined	1
August 1998	U.S. Embassies	Kenya and Tanzania	al-Qaida	224
October 2000	USS *Cole*	Aden, Yemen	al-Qaida	17
September 2001	World Trade Center Twin Towers and Pentagon	New York City and Washington, D.C.	al-Qaida	WTC: 2,830±* Pentagon: 189 Total: 3,019±

As one considers this list in light of September 11, it is clear Americans have been the target of many terrorist attacks. In spite of presidential commissions recommending antiterrorism actions, Congress and the American people ignored these proposals and in essence forgot the attacks soon after the events.

*Estimate as of June 2002.

At first the war was fought from the air with everything from old bombers to new unmanned spy drones. Special forces of the United States and of other nations infiltrated Afghanistan, and cooperation was established with the Northern Alliance. Their forces, with supplies and air support from the United States and Britain, advanced. By the end of November, the Taliban government had collapsed, the capital—Kabul—was captured, and discussions began on the formation of a new government. Many al-Qaida supporters and Taliban troops fled into Pakistan's mountainous border regions where they regrouped and from where they organized the resurgence of the Taliban that threatened by 2009 to overwhelm the democratic government established in 2002 after complex negotiations among all the many tribal, military, and political factions in Afghanistan.

> **War against Taliban waged from the air leads to collapse of Taliban.**

Some fighting continued while nation building and the establishment of a democratic government progressed. United States and Allied troops from a coalition built by the Bush administration supported the efforts to end the fighting and capture Osama bin Laden. Fighting decreased but never ended, and bin Laden was not captured. With the invasion of Iraq, troops and attention were diverted from Afghanistan. In his campaign, Obama promised more troops for Afghanistan and destruction of al-Qaida bases in the Pakistan border region. The establishment of a democratic Middle East became one of the goals of Bush's War on Terrorism, and the return of the Taliban and failure of the elected government of Afghanistan would be a major defeat for the policy.

In recent years, the United States, sometimes working with the UN, has not been very successful at nation building, as seen in Somalia, Haiti, and the former Yugoslavia, and its success in Afghanistan is uncertain.

> **Nation building undertaken in Afghanistan as democratically elected government is established in Kabul.**

BUSH ADMINISTRATION REDEFINES "ENEMY COMBATANT"

The War on Terrorism, as revealed in Afghanistan, created a special problem as the enemy was not just the armed forces of a nation-state but also the informal fighters of a terrorist group that was responsible to no nation and did not fight in uniform. Also, individuals from many nations including Osama bin Laden had come to Afghanistan to fight the Soviet invasion in the 1980s. Some went on to join the Taliban. The United States in the War on Terrorism referred to all terrorists as "enemy combatants," a term that traditionally meant an enemy soldier subject to the Geneva Conventions. The Conventions provide protections to captured soldiers in time of war. Another term, "unlawful combatant" traditionally meant a fighter who did not qualify for the provisions of the Geneva Convention. The Bush administration greatly confused matters by classifying al-Qaida and other terrorists as enemy combatants and then denying them the rights of the Geneva Convention. Therefore, in seeing the term today, one must know the context of its use and whether the captive is from a terrorist network or national army.

Identifying who is the enemy has become very complex in the War on Terrorism. An example is John Walker Lindh, an American interested in Islam, who joined the

Taliban and was captured and brought back to the United States. In a plea bargain, Lindh, 20 years old, pleaded guilty to two charges—serving in the Taliban army and carrying weapons. He was sentenced to prison for twenty years. In return he agreed to cooperate with government interrogations, not to write or publish

> Enemy combatants denied protection of Geneva Convention by Bush administration.

anything about his capture and interrogation, and not to speak concerning charges of torture in his handling by U.S. forces. A photograph of Lindh naked, blindfolded, and strapped to a board shocked many Americans. Rumors suggested he had been tortured. It was one of the first instances of many involving possible torture of prisoners by United States military personnel. In the preceedings, Lindh was identified as an enemy combatant and traditionally would have had the protection of the Geneva Convention but these were denied him. The case illustrates the complexity of the appeal of the Islamic fundamentalist cause to the Muslim world—a factor Americans found hard to understand as they raised the question, "Why do they hate us?"

SPECIAL PRISONS ESTABLISHED

As the war was extended to Iraq, there were more and more cases involving captives, especially those suspected of involvment with al-Qaida, who were denied the protection of the Geneva Conventions. The government did not want to hold them on U.S. soil where the courts might decide they were protected by the Constitution. Therefore, they established a prison at the United States Naval Base at Guantanamo Bay in eastern Cuba where the administration believed U.S. law would not apply. Other prisoners were held in secret CIA prisons abroad, some at U.S. bases in Iraq and Afghanistan, and some in foreign nations where they were allegedly tortured to get information. Under the Bush administration, the treatment of enemy combatants existed in a vacuum without protection of the laws of their nation, of their captor, the United States, or of international law as found in the Geneva Conventions. The United States established Special Military Tribunals that were subject to their own rules. The Supreme Court intervened and Congress rewrote the law, but Tribunal procedures were not required to follow the tenets of the U.S. court system with its protections of the rights of individuals. The situation was unclear. Eventually some prisoners were released after being held without charges for years. A few were brought to trial. One group of Uyghurs were kept without charges for more than seven years. Fellow countrymen in the United States agreed to be responsible for them but the Defense Department refused to let them enter the country. The issue of treatment of prisoners became a political issue in the country, and Obama ordered the closure of Guantanamo as soon as possible as one of his first acts as president, but issues of fair trials, release and acceptance of prisoners by other nations make the closure complicated. Questions concerning how the United States treated prisoners will continue for years to come.

THE IRAQ WAR: 2003–2009

President Saddam Hussein, dictator of Iraq, defied terms of the truce that ended the Gulf War of 1991. These included adhering to an embaro that limited Iraqi oil producion to the cost of food imports, and welcoming UN arms inspectors that conducted searches for weapons of mass destruction (WMD)—chemical,

> The Bush administration, certain Iraq possessed WMDs, invaded the country.

biological, nuclear—and no-fly zones for Iraqi military planes that protected the territory of minority groups such as the Kurds in the north. The Bush administration was convinced Iraq possessed WMDs and, after 9/11, focused attention on getting rid of them. The administration was certain Hussein would use them to support terrorists and perhaps to attack Israel. Hussein had used chemical weapons in attacks on Iraqi minorities and against Iran in the Iran-Iraq War—1980–1988. Even as the war in Afghanistan began, neo-cons in the administration were pushing for an attack on Iraq to eliminate WMDs. Bush included Iraq in his "Axis of Evil." Presenting the argument to Congress, Bush won overwhelming support for a resolution to attack Iraq unilaterally if Hussein refused to destroy all WMDs. Secretary of State Colin Powell presented the case to the UN Security Council. It was based on U.S. intelligence that included photos interpreted to illustrate that Hussein had WMDs. Hussein readmitted UN inspectors who found no evidence of WMDs, but the United States, Britain, and Spain insisted they were there. Finally, frustrated by the slowness of the UN actions, in March 2003 the United States and Britain launched massive air strikes against Iraq followed by a ground invasion planned largely by the civilian leaders of the Pentagon under Defense Secretary Rumsfeld. The result was a quick military victory that Bush proclaimed from the deck of a navy carrier onto which he had flown a fighter jet reminding the public of his service in the National Guard. It was an act that came to haunt the administration as sectarian violence broke out and racked Iraq for years.

It was soon clear that the war had been well planned and executed but little planning had been done for the occupation. The neo-con assumption had been the Iraqis would welcome the U.S. "liberation" and would quickly establish a democracy modeled on that of the United States. The neo-cons believed in the use of U.S. power and that the world would embrace U.S. democracy and values when given the opportunity. This proved a wrong asumption. The United States disbanded the Iraqi army removing the only effective security force in the country. The United States had fought a streamlined war with limited troops, and few allies had joined the "coalition of the willing"—Bush's attempt to make the invasion an international effort. Bureaucrats belonging to Hussein's Baathist Party were removed leaving leadership gaps in the government administration. Rioting erupted in Baghdad, destroying more infrastructure in the city. The UN was largely ignored by the United States and, after their headquarters in Baghdad was bombed, withdrew from the country. A coalition government was set up that slowly began to function, but sectarian differences slowed the process. The Arab population was divided. The minority Sunni Muslims had run the country under Hussein suppressing both the Shia majority and Kurdish minority who dominated the oil-rich north and who had been supported by U.S. and British control of the air over Iraq since the end of the Gulf War. Many Iraqi loyalties were to tribal leaders. Hussein had controlled these factions by the use of force, imprisonment, and torture. Each group had its own agenda for the future of Iraq and had loyal militias ready to fight to achieve them. On top of all this, the U.S. government never found any WMDs, and, in the chaos, al-Qaida established a strong foothold in the country.

While a unified government was formed and elections were held giving encouragement to the Bush administration, violence that many considered a civil war, continued. Car bombings and roadside bombs (IEDs—improvised explosive devices) killed hundreds of civilians and many U.S. troops. Shia attacked Sunni; Sunni attacked Shia; Kurds attacked both. Caught in the middle were U.S. occupation forces. Baghdad was divided by violence into separate enclaves with a special area of high security for the U.S. headquarters and the Iraqi government. The U.S. death toll rose. Bush's 90+ percent post-9/11 approval rating plunged. The war became a national political issue with calls for withdrawal of U.S. troops and comparisons to Vietnam. Democrats won control of Congress in 2006, but their efforts to set deadlines for withdrawal from Iraq were frustrated by the Republicans. No one was willing to end monetary support for the troops thus forcing their recall. Rumsfeld resigned in 2006, and Bush looked for a new policy. He turned to General David Petraeus, who had been successful in creating small, secure areas in Iraq, to plan the next steps. A temporary increase in troops—referred to as the "Surge"—was recommended. The Petraeus policies were quite successful in reducing violence in 2008, but the democratically elected government struggled to make major decisions. The neo-cons had assumed Iraqi oil profits would pay for the occupation, but terrorists' attacks kept production down. The war cost fell to the U.S. taxpayer. In late 2008 a Security of Forces Agreement (SOFA) was reached by the Iraqi government and the United States, calling for withdrawal of combat troops from cities by the end of 2009 and from the country by 2011. Car bombings of Sunnis and Shia were increasing again in 2009 and the national infrastructure was still not back to its prewar operation level. In 2008, Iraq ranked fifth on the Failed State Status Index. However, Iraqi troops were taking over more responsibility for security including the Green Zone—the highly protected area in Baghdad that housed the U.S. headquarters. What the final resolution of the War in Iraq will be is not clear, but President Obama announced U.S. combat troops would be withdrawn within eighteen months as his administration focused on the War in Afghanistan.

> General Petraeus's plan for a "surge" reduces killings and allows announcement of U.S. troop withdrawal.

ABU GHRAIB, TORTURE, AND THE IMAGE OF THE UNITED STATES

After the attack of 9/11, the Bush administration made the prevention of another terrorist attack on the United States the top national priority. All of the acts in the War on Terror had that as the ultimate goal. This included domestic matters such as the

> War on Terrorism produces new type of enemy.

Patriot Act that curtailed individual freedoms to protect the common good, as the administration saw it, to foreign initiatives from the War in Iraq to the interrogation of prisoners and the rejection of the protections of the Geneva Conventions for them. Since the enemy in the War on Terror was not identifiable by uniform, intelligence on who and where the enemy was became crucial, as enemy combatants were captured, getting information from them seemed essential to the Defense Department, the intelligence agencies, and the administration. The result led to the United States abandoning its high moral and ethical positions and using torture that was unacceptable according to the Uniform Code of Military Justice, Art. 93, and to international treaties.

> Photos from Abu Ghraib prison confirm use of torture by U.S. troops.

How this use came to be approved is a murky story involving shaky legal advice and directives from the administration to get information from prisoners at Guantanamo Bay. While there were many rumors of torture, the first evidence came from Abu Ghraib prison where captured Iraqi insurgents were held. Intelligence interrogators wanted help in getting prisoners to talk. They were desperate for information to prevent attacks on allied troops by the insurgents. Ill-trained U.S. military guards interpreted this need to mean softening prisoners up by abuse— torturing them, forcing them into sexual behavior, and beating them. The situation was revealed when soldiers circulated a number of photographs showing the mistreatment of prisoners. The revelation of the torture was met with shock in the United States and horror throughout the Islamic world. Several guards were court-martialed, the commander of the prison was reduced in rank, but no one in the Pentagon was punished in spite of later evidence that directives approving torture had been issued at the highest level.

> In 2008 CIA Director admits use of water boarding; President Obama rejects its use.

The use of torture, the value of information obtained by its use, the legal arguments, and the moral and ethical issues all surfaced in the discussions following the revelations of abuse at Abu Ghraib. There was major controversy over the government's use of torture revealing different ethical perspectives. One technique that was discussed widely was water-boarding[8]. The Bush administration refused to admit it was used or that it was torture. Later in 2008 the CIA director admitted the use of water-boarding on prisoners but justified it because of the information attained. The CIA never released what that information was. The damage done to the United States' reputation throughout the world as the leader in the battle for human rights was tarnished, and it may take years to recapture the high moral ground. President Obama began the effort. As one of his first acts as president, he forbade the use of torture by the United States thus reversing the Bush administration policy and ending the long running controversy over its use.

---

[8] Water-boarding *An individual is strapped to a board and tipped feet up. Sometimes he is gagged and/or blindfolded. Sometimes a cloth is placed over the face. Water is poured over his head and the victim feels he is drowning. The gag reflex kicks in. It has a traumatic psychological effect. It is a technique that dates back hundreds of years.*

This photograph of an Iraqi prisoner being subjected to torture at the Abu Ghraib prison is one of the vivid ones of the many photos taken by United States guard and distributed worldwide when the torture scandal was revealed. It shocked the world as it confirmed the many rumors of torture by the United States in the War on Terror. It undercut the nation's reputation as a defender of human rights and lost the nation support particularly among the people in Islamic countries. How long do you think a person could stand blindfolded on top of such a small box? Would you consider it torture if you were told the electric wires would kill you if you fell off?
Courtesy: Associated Press

NEWS COVERAGE OF THE WAR ON TERRORISM

During the fighting in Iraq, news reporters were embedded in military units to report on the action. The Defense Department carefully monitored what was reported. They often underestimated Iraqi casualties. With U.S. cable news, information was available 24/7. However, a new dimension was added with Arab cable news broadcasts such as al-Jazeera based in Doha, Qatar, where United States headquarters was located. They broadcast news and photos that often contradicted U.S. news reports. The Islamic world was more inclined to believe al-Jazeera and saw U.S. reporting as hypocritical and self-serving again damaging the nation's reputation among Muslims. The United States lost the worldwide support and sympathy it had gained after the 9/11 attacks and even support among European allies dropped below 40 percent in France and Germany by 2004. This loss of support, while intangible, made United States leadership as the only superpower much more difficult. It was one of the legacies of the Bush administration that may be difficult to overcome. However, the election of Obama was greeted with enthusiasm by most nations.

IRAN

Iran, Iraq's neighbor and a Shiite Muslim but non-Arabic country, had fought a war with Iraq in the 1980s. In 1979 the first successful Islamic fundamentalist revolution took place in Iran establishing a government that was anti-American. Bush included Iran as part of the "Axis of Evil." The nation's president was anti-Israel and apparently supported both Hezbollah and Hamas, Palestinian organizations identified by the United States as terrorist groups. Thus Iran became a possible target in the War on Terrorism. When the Bush-led coalition invaded Iraq, Iran felt threatened and became involved supporting their fellow Shiites and, according to many reports, the insurgents. Iran embarked on a nuclear program claiming the need for new sources of electric power, but the United States and allies believed Iran was building a nuclear weapon. If this proves true, it would change the military balance in the Middle East. Negotiations for controlling Iran's nuclear program have begun but without results to this date. It is one indication of how complex the War on Terrorism is.

PAKISTAN

Pakistan is another area where the complexity of the War on Terrorism is evident. After 9/11 the government supported the Afghan War, but there was strong support for the Taliban in the Northwest Territory along the Afghan border where strong tribal loyalties crossed the border. The Pakistan secret service was also divided in its loyalties. They had originally supported the Taliban as an agent for stability in Afghanistan at the time of the Soviet invasion. The Afghan–Pakistan issue was compounded by three factors: first, long standing animosity between Muslim Pakistan and Hindu India; second, sporadic fighting between those two nations over the province of Kashmir; third, the fact both nations possessed nuclear weapons. As the War in Afghanistan dragged on, it was clear the Taliban were using areas of

Pakistan as a base. Pakistan military action proved weak and the United States undertook attacks on al-Qaida and Taliban safe havens in Pakistan's border regions killing civilians and angering the Pakistani population. A new, more popular government in Pakistan seemed unable to change the status quo. In 2009 the Pakistan government undertook military actions against Taliban forces. In retaliation there was an increase of terrorist attacks throughout Pakistan. How this will impact fighting between the Afghan, Taliban, Pakistan, and allied forces (since 2003 under the command of NATO) is unclear. It is clear that Afghanistan continues to be a hot spot in the War on Terrorism and Pakistan's role in it as a supply base for NATO forces is crucial. President Obama has indicated the area is a top priority for his administration. He appointed a special envoy, Richard Holbrooke, veteran diplomat and negotiator of the Dayton Peace Accords in 1995, to resolve the many issues and bring peace to the area.

> Pakistan illustrates the complexity of the War on Terrorism and its many issues.

NORTH KOREA

President Bush included North Korea in the "Axis of Evil." Autocratic dictators have ruled one of the last remaining communist countries, North Korea, since its establishment. The nation is still technically at war with South Korea as no peace agreement was ever reached after the Korean War (1951–1953), although a few steps toward reconciliation were taken in the 1990s. The communist government has destroyed the economy for the average person while seeking nuclear weapons. The first crisis involving their development came under Clinton when the nation refused to accept UN weapons inspectors. Former President Carter resolved that crisis but several since have led to alternating agreements and provocative actions by the North. President Bush refused to negotiate directly with the North—a position he reversed. Six-nation negotiations were begun with North Korea in an attempt to have the nation end its new program and destroy the weapons—estimated at as many as ten—it has built.

Korea is on the edge of the War on Terrorism. The greatest concern has been that it might supply terrorist groups with a nuclear weapon or at least nuclear information and materials. There has not been a clear link with al-Qaida or Islamic Fundamentalists—Korea is outside of the Islamic world—but according to the Bush administration, it has been a supporter of terrorists. Whether a permanent agreement that will assure the destruction of North Korea's nuclear and missile capacity can ever be reached is uncertain. The record is not encouraging, and the issue provides another challenge for the Obama administration.

> North Korea is on the edge of the War on Terrorism, but nuclear weapons provide a special threat.

TERRORIST ATTACKS: 2001–2008

After 9/11 the administration of George W. Bush was successful in avoiding new terrorist attacks on the United States. Preemptive attacks on al-Qaida leaders in several parts of the world, the use of the provisions of the Patriot Act to survey actions of U.S. citizens, and information gained from enemy combatants were given as reasons for the success. The level of threat of another attack was color-coded by the Department of Homeland Security, and different color threats were announced from time to time—often just before elections or Congressional votes on war-related issues. The administration suggested many plots had been foiled, but full details were never revealed. A sense of security settled on the country.

Other allies were not as fortunate. On March 11, 2004, just before a national election in Spain, terrorists trained in Morocco coordinated an attack on trains in Madrid killing 191 and wounding more than 2,000. The Spanish government, an early

Terrorists attack Madrid and London.

ally of the United States in the Iraq War, was voted out, and the new government withdrew its troops from Iraq showing the power of the terrorist to impact national policy. No link was ever established with al-Qaida. In London on July 7, 2005, four suicide bombers exploded bombs that interrupted public transport, killed 56 people, and injured over 700. Investigations focused on educated Muslims of Pakistani origin living in England. No direct link was made to al-Qaida, but disaffection with the Iraq War was a motivation as revealed in videos made by the bombers. Plots were uncovered in Germany and France. It was clear that the United States was not the only target for terrorists.

THE IRAQ WAR AND U.S. POLITICS

As the War in Iraq continued, domestic opposition grew. News reports in the *New York Times* and *Washington Post* revealed the government was tapping phones of U.S. citizens bypassing the Foreign Intelligence Surveillance Act (FISA). The Act established a special court that had the authority to approve wiretapping under special circumstances. The administration pleaded the need for speed and secrecy and that revelation of techniques being used, such as listening in on cell phone calls from overseas to U.S. citizens, would aid al-Qaida. Revelation that libraries under provisions of the Patriot Act were being required to reveal the reading habits of users to intelligence agencies created reactions against the Act and some of its more intrusive aspects. Also, it was revealed that communication between police, fire, and government agencies had not improved in many areas and that many first responders were not receiving the training needed. While the public continued to give strong support to the troops, there was rising dissatisfaction with the administration and its handling of the War in Iraq and the War on Terrorism.

By 2006 opposition to the Iraq War led to a victory for the Democratic Party, giving it control of Congress. Unsuccessful in getting troops withdrawn, the war became the major issue of the early 2008 presidential primary season. The leading Democratic antiwar candidate, Senator Barack Obama, won the nomination. Elected in the fall of 2008, after his inauguration he immediately addressed many issues of the War on Terrorism and began a reversal of many of the Bush administration policies. Just how successful the Obama administration will be in fighting the use of terrorism will not be determined for some years, but it was immediately clear that a new direction would be followed.

SOMALIA AND PIRACY

Somalia on the eastern tip of Africa is another example of how complex, widespread, and involved the War on Terrorism is. Civil War in the early 1990s destroyed the central government's control. The UN sent a humanitarian mission with strong military support from the Clinton administration, but attacks by

> Failed state of Somalia supports piracy and may provide a haven for terrorists.

warlords forced the withdrawal of U.S. troops. The strongest forces in Somalia were Islamic fundamentalists, and Osama bin Laden had spent time in the country. Ethiopia intervened to pacify the nation but was forced to withdraw. Since the early 1990s pirates based in Somalia attacked international shipping in the Gulf of Aden. By 2008 the attacks were affecting the shipping lanes, and the UN called for an international fleet to stop the pirates. Throughout this period Somalia was considered a failed state. Islamic groups in the country supported al-Qaida; pirates seized ships with arms that might reach terrorists; the lack of central authority made the nation a potential haven for terrorist groups. Under these circumstances, what should the United States and the international community do about Somalia? Is it a training area for terrorists? Do the warlords and pirates supply them with funds and arms? Somalia is not alone among nations that have potential to be supporters of terrorists. In waging a War on Terrorism, where and how extensive must the battlefield be? Is there a better approach to controlling and ultimately eliminating the use of terror as an instrument to attain political goals for nonnational groups and even nation states? It is questions of this type that must be faced by the citizens, the Congress, and the new administration in 2009.

THE ISRAELI/PALESTINIAN CONFLICT AS ONE ROOT CAUSE OF TERRORIST ACTIVITY

One issue, the Israeli/Palestinian conflict, links many of the issues mentioned in this section on the War on Terrorism. The conflict has deep roots that can be traced back to the Old Testament story of Abraham a version of which appears in the Koran, the Muslim holy book. According to Jewish faith, God gave the land claimed by both Palestinians and Israelis to Abraham. His oldest son by the servant Hagar, Ishmael, is considered the ancestor of the Arab peoples and heir to the land of Abraham. They believe he was the child offered as a sacrifice by Abraham. Jews and Christians believe the child, Isaac, Abraham's first child by his wife, was the child offered as a sacrifice and the legitimate heir. He is considered the ancestor of the Jewish peoples. Thus the conflict between Jews and Arabs began.

In the 19th century, many oppressed European Jews were attracted to the political philosophy of Zionism. Zionism called for a return of the Jewish people to the land of Abraham. Unfortunately, Arab Palestinians already inhabited the "promised land" along the eastern coast of the Mediterranean. However, Jewish immigrants settled in the area and set the stage for the current Arab/Jewish conflict. During World War I,

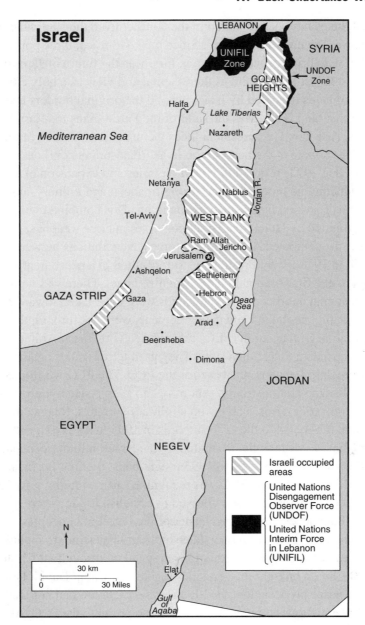

to gain support of both the Arabs and Jews, the British promised the region to both. The land was actually part of the Ottoman Empire. Under Hitler's persecutions, some Jews were able to escape to the region, and conflicts broke out in the land then under British supervision as a League of Nations mandate. After World War II the British wished to withdraw from the region. In 1947 the UN proclaimed a state, Israel, for the Jewish peoples on part of the land. War immediately broke out between Israel on one side and the Palestinians and the surrounding Arab nations on the other. The Israelis won, and a truce was agreed to in 1948. The terms of the truce enlarged the state of Israel. Many Palestinians were driven from their homes by the Israeli victory. Jerusalem was occupied by Israel and became its capital. No peace treaty has been signed to end the conflict.

State of Israel established in 1947 by United Nations.

The United States has been involved in the conflict from the start when President Truman supported the creation of Israel. Since the 1948 truce, three points have needed resolution to bring peace to the area. First was the future of Jerusalem which both Israelis and Palestinians claim as their capital and view as a holy city. Second was the future of lands occupied by Israel beyond the original borders and Jewish settlements on that land. Third was the right of the Palestinians to return to their original homes. As a new U.S. president faces the unsettled situation in the region, these three issues remain at the heart of the Israeli/Palestinian conflict. Several wars (in 1956, 1967, and 1973) resulted in Israeli victories and expansion of the state but no peace. Compounding the problem is the strong financial and military support the United States has provided Israel since its founding. This combined with the fact, although not admitted by Israel, that Israel possesses nuclear weapons, gave Israel an advantage over the combined Arab fighting forces. Negotiations between the two sides at Camp David in 1978 led by President Carter resulted in a peace treaty between Israel and Egypt, the first Arab nation to recognize Israel. There was no resolution to the Israeli/Palestinian conflict, but several steps were to be taken toward peace. Tensions and conflict continued and the agreements were not fully implemented. The Palestine Liberation Organization (PLO) was formed with Yassir Arafat as head to fight for an independent Palestinian state. They used terror tactics against Israel who retaliated by invading Lebanon, the base for the PLO. The PLO was forced to withdraw. The Reagan administration sent troops to keep peace in Lebanon but was forced to withdraw after terrorists blew up a military barracks. Reagan then agreed to negotiations that finally led to the Oslo Accords in 1993 that were signed at the White House under Clinton. Meanwhile, frustrated by the Israeli military occupation of the West Bank, Palestinians from 1987 to 1993 fought back, the first Intifada, using stones and terrorist tactics. In 1995 the PLO was recognized as the interim government of any territory ceded by Israel and was allowed to establish headquarters on the occupied West Bank as the recognized leader of the Palestinian peoples in negotiations. The PLO goal was a two-state solution—Palestine (to include Gaza and the West Bank) and Israel. Final negotiations dragged on throughout Clinton's two terms. In 2000 Clinton brought the two sides together at Camp David. Israel offered a comprehensive peace proposal that the PLO rejected. Clinton had not included Arab nations in the negotiations and none were willing to pressure the PLO. As Clinton left office a second Intifada or uprising against the occupation broke out.

The Bush administration decided to stay out of negotiations, but announced support for a two-state solution to the problem. Arafat died and elections were held to create a new Palestinian government. Terrorist attacks by the Palestinian Hezbollah organization against Israel led Israel to again invade Lebanon with little success. Israel withdrew from the Gaza area, but continued to build settlements in the occupied West Bank area. New elections split the PLO and the Hamas faction, an extremist Palestinian group that refused to recognize the existence of Israel that the PLO had done, took control of Gaza. In 2008 Israel invaded the territory killing many civilians but failing to crush Hamas. A truce was made and Israel withdrew. The situation remains fraught with danger.

The Obama administration must deal with the situation, and the president indicated he would take an active role, as have other Democratic presidents. The U.S.

commitment to Israel is longstanding and considered by many Arab and Muslim nations to be one-sided. As a result, U.S. actions have antagonized many Arab and Muslim nations—Iran's president has called for the destruction of Israel. Frustrated young Arabs have turned to al-Qaida and Osama bin Laden. They support Hamas, Hezbollah, and calls for the destruction of Israel. Arabs on the streets throughout the Middle East express disgust with Israel and U.S. support of Israel's actions in destroying the infrastructure of first Lebanon and recently Gaza. Until a settlement can be reached of the Israeli/Palestinian conflict and U.S. policies in the area are viewed as more evenhanded, success in the War on Terrorism in the region will not be achievable.

> Israeli/Palestinian conflict fuels the War on Terrorism.

Key Point to Remember
The terrorist attacks on New York and Washington dramatically changed the dynamics of political life in the nation and affected the world.

Links from the Past to the Present
When the country is under attack from foreign forces, as it was on September 11th, 2001, the nation rallies to support a united response as it did in World Wars I and II.

People to Remember
Osama bin Laden   Terrorist leader, Islamic fundamentalist, head of al-Qaida; born in Saudi Arabia, son of a Yemeni billionaire; graduated from King Abdul Aziz University; fought against the Soviet Union in Afghanistan with U.S. support; founded al-Qaida in 1987; developed a hatred of the United States reinforced by the U.S. role in the Persian Gulf War; accused of planning attacks on U.S. embassies in Kenya and Tanzania, the USS *Cole,* the World Trade Center, and the Pentagon; the United States attacked the Taliban in Afghanistan in an attempt to capture him.

Dates

1947—State of Israel established by United Nations.

1948—Truce ends first Arab/Israeli War

1978—Carter negotiates Camp David Accords; Egypt recognizes nation of Israel.

1993—Oslo Agreement restarts Arab/Israeli peace negotiations.
    Clinton sends troops to support UN humanitarian mission in Somalia.

1994—Clinton withdraws troops from Somalia.

2000—PLO's Arafat rejects terms for PLO–Arab Peace Agreement.

2001—U.S. announces withdrawal from ABM Treaty.
    September 11, terrorists attack World Trade Center and Pentagon.
    War on Terrorism announced.
    Airline Bailout Act.
    Anti-Terror Bill—Patriot Act
    Airlines Security Act.
    War in Afghanistan.

2002—Department of Homeland Security established.

President Bush names Iraq, Iran, and North Korea as an "Axis of Evil" claiming they all have or seek nuclear weapons and support terrorists.

2003—United States invades Iraq; President declares victory; insurgency begins.

Iran admits having a nuclear program and invites UN inspectors to observe the nuclear program.

2004—Caretaker government set up by United States in Iraq.

Terrorists bomb railroads in Madrid, Spain.

Photos of abuse and torture of Iraqi prisoners by U.S. guards released.

2005—New constitution approved in Iraq; elections held.

Terrorists attack London transport system.

2006—New government established in Iraq.

Iraq insurgency considered a civil war by many observers.

Democrats gain control of Congress.

2007—U.S. military "surge" reduces insurgency activity in Iraq.

2008—United Nations calls for multinational naval force to control pirates off African coast.

CIA director admits agency used water-boarding to get information from prisoners.

Iraq—U.S. Security of Forces Agreement to withdraw U.S. forces by 2011.

Antiwar candidate Barack Obama wins Democratic Party presidential nomination and the general election.

2009—Pakistan army attacks Taliban-related forces in northern Pakistan.

Obama inaugurated; reverses Bush policies on torture; appoints special envoys to Afghanistan/Pakistan and Israel/Palestine.

Questions
Identify each of the following:

Saddam Hussein	World Trade Center
Hamas	Osama bin Laden
Water-boarding	Taliban
Axis of Evil	Anthrax
Enemy combatant	al-Qaida

Multiple Choice

1. Terrorist plane attacks on New York City destroyed the
   a. Empire State Building.
   b. Pentagon.
   c. Twin Towers.

2. A combination of events including September 11 and the Bush tax cut brought an end to
   a. budget deficits.
   b. budget surpluses.
   c. economic recession.

3. As a response to the September 11 attacks, Congress
   a. declared war on al-Qaida and Osama bin Laden.
   b. passed no legislation to support the War on Terrorism.
   c. voted $40 billion for disaster relief and military operations.

4. The War in Afghanistan was waged
   a. entirely by air power.
   b. using only Afghan soldiers.
   c. by an international coalition.

5. A prison was built at Guantanamo Bay
   a. to house members of al-Qaida found guilty of attacking the World Trade Center.
   b. as a holding place where intelligence officers could question enemy combatants.
   c. where the leaders of the Iraqi army could be held until the end of the Iraq War.

6. The most difficult issues to resolve in the Israeli/Palestinian conflict have been the
   a. future of Jerusalem, removal of Israeli settlements, and right of return of Palestinians.
   b. successor to Yassir Arafat, the disarming of Hezbollah, and future of Jordan.
   c. destruction of Israel's nuclear arsenal, future relations with Lebanon, and disbanding of Hamas.

V. Foreign Policy Issues: 1993–2009

A SENSE OF PERSPECTIVE

With the end of the Cold War, the United States became the only superpower in the world. Some Americans saw the Cold War victory as an endorsement of U.S. values and sought to impose American democracy and its values and culture on the world. This unilateralist view has been best expressed by the those referred to as neo-cons (neo-conservatives). Others saw victory as an endorsement of international cooperation and multilateral pursuits best illustrated by the U.S. Cold War policies of containment and participation in NATO. Presidents George H. W. Bush and Bill Clinton pursued the latter approach. President George W. Bush and his advisers reversed the sixty-year tradition of internationalism followed throughout the Cold War and declared a new doctrine based upon the

> President George W. Bush abandons internationalist approach for neo-con supported unilateralism.

military and economic strength of the United States. The Bush approach, referred to as the Bush Doctrine, called for preemptive war, that is, the United States would strike first, even with nuclear weapons, if our security was threatened. The War in Iraq and the failure to build a more than a token multinational force to fight that war, illustrate the Bush Doctrine and the Bush administration shift in approach to foreign policy.

Since the end of the Cold War, the United States has remained the sole superpower, but shifting conditions have continually challenged that position. Both President Clinton and George W. Bush had to respond to a number of situations that illustrate the emergence of new power centers around the world. In few cases was the nation able to control the situation. For example, the development of nuclear weapons by India and Pakistan has affected the power balance in southern Asia and the long history of conflict between those two countries makes the possibility of nuclear conflict a possibility yet the United States cannot control the situation. The emergence of China as an economic power and the development of the strength of the EU and of the OPEC nations are other examples. While the United States remains the only superpower for the moment, history is dynamic and illustrates that situations are continually changing.

At least since the end of World War II, the history of the United States has been part of world history. Before then, the United States sometimes reacted to events, but isolation dominated the nation's reactions. The perceived threat of communism after 1945 changed the nation's attitude. Gradual economic globalization reinforced the involvement of the nation in the world. However, it is only one aspect of this involvement. In politics, culture, religion, science, environmental concerns, and social mores, all peoples in all nations have the capacity in some degree to be aware of these issues. As attitudes are expressed, defended, or changed as a result of rapid developments in transportation and communication, peoples and nations everywhere can react. What happens in one area affects other regions quickly. Even though the War on Terrorism dominated U.S. foreign policy after 2001, there were other issues that should be noted. There are over 190 independent nations and the United States and its policies affect them all to some degree. Likewise, from time to time, any nation on earth can act in a way to impact the United States and its citizens.

> Today the world is interconnected.

THE EVOLUTION OF NATO: 1985–2009

NATO symbolizes the multilateral approach of the United States to the Cold War. Since joining the first foreign military alliance signed by the United States in its history in 1949, NATO remained the cornerstone of United States policy toward Europe. Although at times there were calls for new arrangements and the withdrawal of large numbers of military forces, U.S. commitment remained strong. With the collapse of the Soviet Union, the original purpose of NATO—to confront the Soviet threat to Western Europe—disappeared. As the alliance groped for a new identity, the disintegration of and outbreak of war in the former Yugoslavia provided a new direction for NATO. In 1992 NATO offered support to UN operations in Yugoslavia, and in 1995 NATO forces entered combat against the Bosnian Serbs for the first time in the alliance's history and suggested there might be a peacekeeping role for NATO in response to fighting within Europe. This concept led to the Partners for Peace offer to the former states of the Soviet Union under which they would cooperate with NATO in assuring peace in Europe. NATO with the urging of the Clinton administration then decided in the mid-1990s to offer full membership in NATO to Poland, the Czech Republic, and Hungary. These countries all accepted.

> NATO takes on a new role after the end of the Cold War.

RUSSIA AND NATO

The admittance of former Warsaw Bloc nations into NATO appeared a threat to Russian independence, but negotiations resolved most issues and gave Russia a special relationship to NATO headquarters. However, the admittance of former Soviet bloc nations Lithuania, Latvia, and Estonia in 2004 strained relations with Russia. Invitations to the Ukraine and Georgia in 2005 and 2006 created further tensions. When in 2008 Russia, because of ethnic differences, invaded Georgia, a former state in the Soviet Union on Russia's present border, the United States voiced support for Georgia. Several Senators visited and declared friendship for Georgia. The United States declared it would protect Georgia and wanted it to join NATO immediately. Under Bush the United States appeared ready to include all former Soviet republics in NATO and to support their independence—a position Russians viewed as a threat to their hegemony in the region. This attitude greatly increased the tensions between the two former enemies and the Bush administration's unilateralism did not help. Russian–U.S. relations became more strained over the years as President Putin reasserted federal authority in Russia and oil resources provided prosperity. The U.S. plan to install new missile sites in the Czech Republic and Poland, ostensibly to protect the United States and Europe from any attack from Iran, was considered a provocation by the Russians.

CHECHNYA

Another disagreement centered on the Russian province of Chechnya. Since the early 1990s, Russia faced the attempt of the province to become independent. A two-year war was fought, a brief peace was established, and then war began again in 1999. Complicating the situation is religion. Chechnyans are Muslim. Islamic fundamentalism has appeal, and some Chechnyan fighters have been trained by al-Qaida. Human rights have been violated on both sides, and Chechnyans have been accused of terrorist attacks in Moscow.

> Russia views war in Chechnya as a war on terrorism.

Chechnya was granted quasi-independence, warlords exercised control, and elections were held. In 2007 the elected leader declared the area an Islamic Emirate with him as Emir. Accusations of torture and human rights violations continued but, as an isolated area to which neither NATO nor the United States can gain access, Chechnya was not high on the Bush administration's agenda; nevertheless, it added to tensions between Russia and the United States. The Russians consider Chechnya their part of the War on Terrorism. Chechnya presents an excellent example of the complex forces that must be considered when making foreign-policy decisions. Chechnya will remain an issue in U.S.–Russian relations for some time.

RUSSIA AND THE WAR ON TERRORISM

After the attacks of 9/11, Russia offered support in the War on Terrorism, but differences in approach to it as well as the growing tensions between the United States and Russia has made Russian support appear only half-hearted. In the 1990s Russia sold a nuclear reactor to Iran and has been slow to support the U.S.-led attempt to stop Iran's development of nuclear weapons. Likewise Russia has not been involved in the Wars in Iraq or Afghanistan. How the Obama administration will address the issues between Russia and the United States remains to be seen. However, as one of his first foreign policy announcements, Obama put on hold the development of missile sites in Poland and the Czech Republic, suggesting a willingness to discuss matters of sensitive military nature with the Russian government.

YUGOSLAVIA: BOSNIA AND KOSOVO

In 1993, as fighting continued in Bosnia (see page 325), there were numerous stories of atrocities and ethnic cleansing. As a result, President Clinton suggested the western allies might intervene in Bosnia. With U.S. troops already committed to Somalia, this stand was not popular. However, by early 1994, the United States, NATO, and the UN intervened to bring about an uneasy truce to areas within Bosnia. NATO planes shot down four Serbian fighter-bombers, the first time NATO forces were involved in combat. The Dayton Peace Accord was negotiated in Dayton, Ohio, under the leadership of the United States.

In 1998, tensions developed in Kosovo, another part of Yugoslavia, where the majority were Albanians. As the Serbian government refused to allow Kosovo's Albanians to establish an independent nation and began a program of ethnic cleansing, NATO intervened in 1999 with a United States led bombing

> NATO bombing forces Serbia to change Kosovo policy.

campaign against Serbia to halt the ethnic cleansing. Damage to Serbia was great. Slobodan Milosevic, dictator of Serbia, accepted NATO's terms, and NATO and Russian forces entered Kosovo.

In 2000, the Serbians overthrew Milosevic. In 2001, he was extradited to the Netherlands and tried for crimes against humanity before a UN established War Crimes Tribunal. He died before a verdict was reached, but others, both Serbs and Bosnians, have been tried and found guilty of ethnic cleansing and crimes against humanity suggesting that there is a growing desire in some areas to punish perpetrators of such crimes.

Today the former Yugoslavia consists of seven independent nations. Their economic and political strengths vary, but there is peace between them. Slovenia has already joined the EU and NATO. Bosnia expects to join NATO in 2009. The use of NATO forces in the Balkans prepared NATO to act militarily in pursuit of peace. In 2003 NATO took a leadership role in the War in Afghanistan.

The Balkans–2008

EUROPEAN UNION (EU)

The European Union (EU) traces its beginnings to the post–World War II European Coal and Steel community consisting of six nations—West Germany, France, Italy, Belgium, the Netherlands, and Luxembourg. The original goal of the community in 1951 was to prevent war among the members. The same is true today and in the post–Cold War era, as former Soviet bloc nations have joined the EU and it has expanded to include twenty-seven nations, a European War appears less likely. However, as the dissolution of Yugoslavia indicated, war within Europe is possible. Over the years the economic power of the EU has made it an important part of the world economy. With the introduction in 2001 of a common currency, the Euro, the currency for sixteen of the EU nations, the economic power has become even greater.

Throughout the postwar era, U.S. administrations have supported the growth and economic development of the EU viewing it has a force for stability. As trade barriers among the members fell, Europe became a large common market for goods

> EU has economic power that must be considered in foreign policy decisions.

produced throughout the world, and its exports formed a high percentage of world trade. While each nation of the EU preserves its own culture and language, travel between them is open. Whether the EU will evolve into a unified political bloc or remain essentially an economic common market is not clear. In 2004 a Constitution for EU was not ratified. However, the EU in the 21st century has become an important economic factor. The United States continues to support its expansion, and the EU has become a factor in U.S. foreign policy decisions.

**Europe in 2008 showing Members
of and Candidates for Membership in the European Union**

NORTHERN IRELAND

Because of the large numbers of U.S. citizens that trace their ancestry to Ireland, the country has always held an interest for the nation. For centuries there has been conflict between Ireland and Britain and after World War I the island of Ireland was divided into two parts—an independent and Catholic south (Eire) and a British-occupied and dominantly Protestant north (Northern Ireland) in an attempt to stop the conflict. It was unsuccessful. The Irish Republican Army (IRA) increasingly used terrorist tactics against the British forces and they retaliated. It was Britain's own War on Terrorism. Attempts at peace failed, but in 1998 President Clinton intervened and appointed former Senator George Mitchell to lead a peacekeeping mission to

Ireland. An agreement (signed on Good Friday) worked out power sharing and, although outbreaks of violence occurred after the signing and there were major disagreements on details, the peace has held. The agreement was one of the successes of Clinton's administration.

CIVIL WARS AND GENOCIDE IN AFRICA: SOMALIA, RWANDA AND BURUNDI, THE CONGO, SUDAN

After the failure of the United States-UN effort to restore peace and build a new national government in Somalia, the Clinton and Bush administrations decided not to become militarily involved in conflicts in Africa. These conflicts are largely rooted in ethnic tensions, overpopulation, climate issues, and economic stagnation. Civil war began in 1994 in Rwanda and Burundi, and it led to mass killings and genocide. The UN supported by the United States established a war crimes tribunal regarding Rwanda, which pleased those Americans who felt frustrated by the failure of the United States to become involved.

Both the Clinton and Bush administrations supported efforts by the Organization of African Unity (OAU) and its successor in 2002, the African Union (AU), to oversee the end of military conflicts in Africa. The United States has also supported the UN

> The African Union (AU) has limited success in peacekeeping.

in its efforts but has shown no interest in sending troops since the 1994 disaster in Somalia. The OAU arranged a truce in 2002 between military factions fighting for control of the Congo (formerly Zaire), but it broke down, and fighting especially on the eastern border continues sporadically. The Congo is rich in resources and home to different tribes all of whom want to exploit the resources for their own advantage. Refugees from Rwanda and Burundi compound the situation. It is one of several continuing conflicts in Africa.

Darfur in the western Sudan is another. The African Union organized a peacekeeping force, but it was ineffective in restoring peace, and the AU turned Darfur over to the UN in 2008. The UN is still struggling to bring in enough peacekeepers to end the genocide. The AU has also sent peacekeepers to Somalia with little impact.

The African Union is an ambitious undertaking bringing together fifty-three African nations in one organization. It has undertaken several economic and human rights initiatives, which hopefully will have an impact on the continent. Some AU members wished to intervene in Zimbabwe after the corrupt election of 2008, but all they could achieve was a resolution for the two parties to work together. This was more than the United States was able to do; quiet efforts to end the dictatorship of Robert Mugabe were undertaken, but the United States was not ready to take the lead in the effort.

Besides population, poverty, and general lack of economic development, African nations have the highest incidence of HIV in the world. On the average, 20 percent of the sexually active population of Africa has AIDS, and in South Africa it is reported to be 33 percent. One of President George W. Bush's most successful foreign policy efforts was to address the African AIDS crisis. He asked Congress for over $15 billion to be spent on drugs and, working with several nations such as

Uganda that had developed effective attacks on the epidemic, achieved some success, but it is a massive problem affecting economic, social, cultural, and political life. While there is no cure, drugs can control the disease. Drugs are produced by companies, often based in the United States, that want to make a profit and that too complicates the issue.

> Each African nation has its own problems.

Home to over fifty independent nations, Africa cannot be viewed as a bloc although that has been the tendency in schools in the United States and often in policy discussions. Each nation has its own needs and history. With so much attention given to the War on Terrorism, it has been difficult to respond to the individual concerns of each African nation.

ECONOMIC CRISES IN CENTRAL AND SOUTH AMERICA

During the Clinton years, democratically elected governments came to power throughout Central and South America except in Cuba. Economic development varied, and in 1995 the United States loaned Mexico $20 billion to support the peso and worked with the International Monetary Fund (IMF) to support the Brazilian real in 1998. No action, however, was taken by the Bush administration to support Argentina in an economic crisis in 2001.

> Economic crises bring different responses from the United States.

All three nations recovered, but there were calls for the revision of the Bretton Woods Economic polices including the International Monetary Fund (IMF) established after World War II. As the world entered the financial meltdown of 2008, there were further calls for such revisions. It is an item that must be addressed by the Obama administration.

MOVE TO POPULAR, LEFTIST GOVERNMENTS IN THE AMERICAS

In 1998 Hugo Chavez was elected president of Venezuela on a platform calling for greater aid to the poor. With increasing wealth from the nation's oil resources, Chavez became more vocal in opposition to U.S. policies in the region and used oil revenues to support Cuba, Brazil, and Argentina. In 2008 he won a referendum ending presidential term limits suggesting he will remain in power. He has found allies in Cuba and Bolivia where Evo Morales, a socialist, was elected president in 2006. Morales, the first Bolivian Indian president, in 2008 pushed for a new constitution giving the president two five-year terms, greater government control of the economy, and more power to indigenous peoples and provinces. Bolivia is the poorest nation in South America and is divided in many ways. Morales is reported to receive help from Chavez. In neighboring Peru in 2008 there were protests against the government and demands by the Andean peoples for a greater share in the wealth of the nation. It was reported in Washington that the Bush administration believed Chavez was behind these developments and was supported by Cuba. How widespread this call for more socialism will be is uncertain as is how South and Central America will survive the financial crisis of 2008.

> Socialist presidents elected in Venezuela and Bolivia.

Fidel Castro overthrew the Cuban dictator, Batista, in 1959. He introduced a program of support for the poor and land ownership reform. The United States saw this as socialism, and relations with the United States rapidly deteriorated. In 1961 Castro declared Cuba a communist nation and became an ally of the Soviet Union. The United States responded with an embargo that is still in effect. Every president since has isolated Cuba. Fidel Castro resigned the presidency in 2008 turning power over to his brother, Raul. There was some hope this might bring an improvement in relations, but the Bush administration made no gestures. In the 2008 election, Obama promised to open personal contacts and Raul Castro in 2009 acknowledged change might come. The United States may be ready to accept socialism as one type of economic system in the Americas.

INTERNATIONAL TRADE AGREEMENTS

With the establishment of the North American Free Trade Agreement (NAFTA) in 1993, trade has flourished between Canada, the United States, and Mexico. Not everyone in the United States was pleased by the agreement. They feared the exploitation of workers and resources by huge multinational corporations over which the workers will have no control. Protests at world economic meetings became commonplace at the end of Clinton's administration and continue. While some concerns may be legitimate, in the early years of the 21st century, globalization, freer trade and lower tariffs, and large multinational corporations controlling manufacture and distribution dominate the world economy. What impact the financial crisis of 2008 will have on these corporations, on world trade, and on the average worker is unclear, but free trade and globalization were the national goals of most nations in the early 21st century.

The formation of free trade areas was widely discussed. The first moves for reduction of tariffs in the Americas came in the 1960s with limited results, but after NAFTA several nations in the Americas pursued the idea of regional trade pacts. Then in 2003 the first discussions about a Free Trade Area of the Americas (FTAA) were held with limited progress as several nations were opposed.

> The United States is involved in discussions concerning membership in several free trade groups.

Talks continue. In the meantime, in 2006 a P4 Agreement—Brunei, Chile, New Zealand, Singapore—was reached, and in 2008 the United States indicated an interest in joining. Talks on membership began in 2009. The United States became involved in discussions in 2008 concerning an Asia-Pacific Economic Cooperation agreement among twenty-one nations that control over half the world's economy and half its population. It would create another free trade zone. Negotiations may take years, and again the financial meltdown of 2008 may end interest in free trade zones. Certainly the U.S. government has been interested so far.

PANAMA CANAL

In 1999, a momentous change occurred in U.S. relations with Central America when the Panama Canal, at one time considered the United States' trade lifeline, was taken over by Panama under treaty terms negotiated by President Carter. The changeover was barely noticed in the United States. Larger ships, new shipping lanes, and other means of transportation had reduced the significance of the canal.

THE WAR ON DRUGS

Throughout the Clinton and Bush years, the illegal drug trade was a major concern. The War on Drugs began years ago and has had only limited success. Drug use, like capitalism, is linked to a supply and demand cycle. The War on Drugs, as is seen in U.S. action in Colombia, in the golden triangle of Southeast Asia, and now in Afghanistan, is based on destroying the supply. Our allies in these areas suggest we must also reduce demand in the United States. Both supply and demand must be addressed if the War on Drugs is to be won.

> Demand as well as supply must be attacked to achieve success in War on Drugs.

United States involvement in Colombia provides evidence of lack of success in the War on Drugs. For over twenty years, the United States has supplied military and economic support to the Colombian government to suppress a rebellion led by drug lords. Still, drugs are grown and smuggled into the United States. Several other nations including Panama, Haiti, and Mexico have been involved in the smuggling. Neither alone nor with the support of the United States with all its military potential have these countries been able to stop the smuggling. As long as there is demand for illegal drugs in the United States, someone will find a way to get them into the country.

Warfare among Mexican drug gangs is a major threat to the stability of Mexico and the United States. In 2009 drug gang killings occurred daily, and the Mexican government has been powerless to stop them. President Obama announced greater cooperation with Mexico to attack the problem. As the U.S.–Mexican border comes under tighter control, the efforts needed to get drugs, as well as illegal immigrants, across will grow greater. Drug lords will up the ante to maintain the movement of drugs. It is a complex problem with high stakes for both nations, public safety, and security.

In Afghanistan poppies are the primary cash crop. The Taliban almost destroyed the heroin trade as the Koran opposes drug use, but under the weak government in Kabul, the poppy trade flourished and the resurgent Taliban allowed it as the profits help finance their antigovernment attacks. Thus, in Afghanistan, the War on Drugs has become entwined with the War on Terrorism. Victory in either war will not be easy and the Drug War cannot be won by following present approaches. A new effort is required that addresses supply, demand, allies, and enemies.

JAPAN

Trade issues and the perceived lack of openness of Japanese markets to U.S. exports provided the background for United States–Japanese relations since the 1970s. The Japanese economy was in recession during the Clinton and Bush presidencies. It had not fully recovered by the time the worldwide financial crisis of 2008 began. Successive Japanese governments, often plagued by scandals, were unable to take the drastic measures needed for recovery—drastic measures many economists believe all nations involved in the 2008 financial crisis must take. Trade with the United

States continued strong, and Japanese carmakers found an important market in the United States—a market now being shared with South Korea and even India. For years the balance of trade favored Japan and concerned U.S. economists, but as China replaced Japan as the United States' chief trading partner, the concern and negotiations with Japan became secondary to relations with China.

Japan remains a strong U.S. ally. The United States maintains military bases there. Criminal acts by a few military personnel over the years created several crises in relations. The Japanese government has given support to the War on Terrorism. Japan lost over two dozen citizens in the 9/11 attack. Reversing its Constitutional requirement of no international military involvement, the Japanese supplied logistical support (navy) to the War in Afghanistan joining President Bush's "coalition of the willing." Japan also continued its high level of contributions to international relief especially targeting the rebuilding of Afghanistan. In 2008 the Japanese Parliament debated continuing its logistical support and approved its continuation. Japan has also joined the United States in negotiations with North Korea to end its nuclear program. U.S. bases in Japan are potential targets of North Korea as is Japan itself. This fact supports a close relationship between the United States and Japan.

> Japan sends logistical support for the War in Afghanistan.

INDIA AND PAKISTAN

United States relations with India and Pakistan have followed an erratic course. Pakistan has had an unstable government for many years, alternating between elected governments supported by the United States and military governments established by military coups that the United States condemned. This changed after September 11 when Pakistan gave its support to the War in Afghanistan (see page 419) and the United States supported the military government of Pakistan.

India, the world's largest democracy, like China, has the potential to become a superpower. Its economy grew rapidly in the early 21st century, a large middle class emerged, although there are still millions living in poverty—a huge potential market—and India's presence has been evident worldwide in trade missions. India has maintained an independent foreign policy, and its support for U.S. policies has varied.

U.S. relations with both India and Pakistan and peace in the entire region of South Asia is complicated by the dispute over the region of Kashmir, which both India and Pakistan claim. Compounding the problem of Kashmir are several matters. First, India is predominantly Hindu, and Pakistan is predominantly Muslim, with an Islamic fundamentalist minority. Kashmir is predominantly Muslim. Second, India accuses Pakistan of terrorism in Kashmir, and clashes occur regularly. India believes it is waging a war on terrorism there. Third, terrorist attacks have taken place periodically in India both against the Muslim minority by Hindus and against the government by Islamic extremists. In November 2008, an attack—a multipronged coordinated attack led by Islamic extremists trained in Pakistan on tourist hotels, a railroad station, and a Jewish center in Mumbai—killed and wounded over 300. Both

> Dispute over Kashmir creates tension between India and Pakistan.

nations remained calm, but troops were sent to the border. Pakistan arrested leaders of the terrorist group and promised cooperation with the Indian investigation, but the attack illustrates the fragility of the peace between India and Pakistan. Fourth, both nations have nuclear weapons. The war effort in Afghanistan depends on the support of Pakistan and peace in South Asia. The importance of the region was illustrated by President Obama's appointment of a special envoy to negotiate a coordinated approach to peace. However, it is important to note that Kashmir was left out of the charge given to the envoy, Richard Holbrooke. The issues he faces are complex, but an overall peace settlement for South Asia depends on his efforts. The United States is deeply committed to the region.

SOUTHEAST ASIA AND INDONESIA

In the early Clinton years, Southeast Asia, a largely Islamic region, was prospering. In 1997 an economic crisis that began in Thailand hit the region. Action by world monetary organizations slowly reversed the situation. The economies of the Pacific Rim nations rebounded, but prosperity was not evenly distributed. This has created a situation in which Islamic fundamentalism has become appealing to some people.

The Philippines illustrate this. Guerilla forces fighting the government on the southern islands were linked to al-Qaida by the United States. The United States and the Philippine government launched an attack against these guerillas in early 2002. The guerilla forces were largely destroyed, and humanitarian aid given to the population has hopefully removed support for the Islamic fundamentalists. The Philippine attack demonstrated that Bush was serious in his intent to root out terrorists worldwide.

> Bush sends troops to Philippines as part of War on Terrorism.

The Bush administration found evidence in captured al-Qaida bases in Afghanistan that al-Qaida has links to groups in Singapore and Indonesia, which has the largest Muslim population of any nation. Bombings on the tourist island of Bali in 2002 and 2005 and at the Australian embassy in Jakarta in 2004 seemed to confirm the connection. However, the emerging democratic government of Indonesia reacted by tracking down the bombers and punishing them in spite of relying on political support from Islamic parties in parliament. Secretary of State Hillary Clinton visited Jakarta on her first trip abroad in 2009 and praised the nation for its progress toward democracy, for its illustration that Islam and democracy are compatible, and for its cooperation in the War on Terrorism.

Not all links between Southeast Asia and the United States during the Clinton and Bush administrations involved the War on Terrorism. Twenty years after the fall of Saigon to the communist North Vietnamese, normal diplomatic relations were established by the Clinton administration in 1995. President Bush visited Vietnam on his Asia trip in 2006. High-level visits including military commanders continue. The Defense Department has received cooperation in the location of the remains of U.S. soldiers, a high priority for the U.S. Agreements ranging from antinarcotic cooperation in 2006 to trade agreements in 2007 have been signed. Relations between the two enemies illustrate what can be accomplished in reconciliation when it is in the interest of both countries.

Cooperation in time of natural disaster has also driven U.S. policy toward Southeast and South Asia as well as other regions of the world. Responses to massive earthquakes in Turkey in 1999 and in China and Pakistan in 2008 are examples. The massive tsunami caused by an underwater earthquake off the island of Sumatra, Indonesia, in 2004 affected all the nations bordering the Bay of Bengal, created massive destruction as fifteen-foot-high walls of water poured ashore, killed over 200,000 people, and destroyed the livelihood of thousands. The United States mobilized quickly to send aid to the hardest hit areas. Cell phones and blogs kept the world abreast of the situation.

OPPOSING TRENDS IN FOREIGN POLICY

GLOBALIZATION

Two trends have appeared in U.S. foreign policy since the end of the Cold War. The first, internationalism, of which globalization[9] is one aspect, and has brought nations together in cooperative organizations (e.g., NAFTA, the United Nations, NATO). Each example brings nation states together to achieve mutual

> Globalization makes national boundaries less important.

economic, political, or military goals. Globalization on the other hand is more economically driven and has made national boundaries less significant. Large corporations with no commitment to a nation state act independently or in cooperation place factories in nations with few environmental controls and low pay scales. This increases profits. The United States and a few other national economies boomed. Globalists believe the trend toward globalization will increase trade, world prosperity, and understanding between nations. Those opposing globalization fear exploitation of labor and the environment by organizations that are not responsible to any authority greater than a board of directors. They fear the loss of control over their future, and they fear we will become slaves to technology. There have been protests, especially at meetings of international bankers and the Group of Eight. With an international financial crisis facing the world, it is unclear how globalization will be impacted. During the Great Depression of the 1930s, the United States and other nations turned inward in an attempt to save jobs within the country. Tariffs were raised and local industries subsidized. The stimulus signed by President Obama at first included a clause that required companies getting stimulus aid to "buy American." In Canada, on his first trip outside the country, President Obama disavowed the idea. In his first address to Congress he also opposed a nationalistic, America first approach to the economic crisis. Whether this approach will be continued will not be answered for some time.

[9] globalization *The movement toward a global economy, ignoring national borders. It is driven by the Internet, elimination of tariffs, and multinational corporations that have control of business and banking worldwide.*

UNILATERALISM

The second trend, unilateralism,[10] was especially strong in the Bush administration before 9/11 and continued even as he organized an international response to terrorism. Unilateralism can also be seen in several actions of the Clinton administration. Clinton, under pressure from the Pentagon, did not sign the Ottawa Treaty known as the Land Mines Treaty banning the use of land mines in military conflict. Clinton signed the 1995 UN Convention on the Rights of Children, but Congress failed to ratify it. Opponents claimed it would supersede state law, infringe on family rights, and possibly subject parents to lawsuits for failure to comply in every detail. The United States and Somalia were the only nations not to sign the convention. Clinton signed the Kyoto Accord on Global Warming in 1997, but neither his administration nor Bush's would submit it to the Senate for approval, and Bush withdrew the president's signature from the accord and protocols in 2001. The Kyoto Accord was signed by 178 nations. The Senate under Clinton rejected the Comprehensive Test Ban Treaty on nuclear weapons in 1999.

Bush refused to sign the treaty establishing a permanent war crimes tribunal under the UN. Bush withdrew from the Anti-Ballistic Missile (ABM) Treaty—the first time the United States withdrew from a negotiated and Senate-approved treaty. The administration argued that these treaties were not in the "best interest" of the country. Bush also pushed for a missile defense shield (SDI) for the

> United States refuses to sign treaties that are not in "best interest" of the United States.

United States. The Bush administration support for unilateralism is most clearly illustrated in the Bush Doctrine supporting preemptive war and its use in the Iraq War. Many nations saw unilateralism as self-serving and lost faith in the United States. Support for the Bush government dropped as allies urged the administration to support the Kyoto agreements and other UN treaties. However, as the world's only superpower, the United States could act as it wished. The administration declared that U.S. troops would not be subject to the new International War Crimes Tribunal. President Bush refused to attend the UN World Summit on Sustainable Development where over 100 leaders of nations signed an agreement to address poverty and growth. The United States disagreed with several clauses.

After two months in office, it is too early to be certain what policies the Obama administration will ultimately support. First indications from his pronouncements on torture, the closing of Guantanamo Bay, and the appointment of special envoys to work for solutions to difficult international issues suggest a return to internationalism.

CLINTON AND BUSH—A COMPARISON

While Clinton and Bush were from opposing parties and appear very different, there are several striking similarities between the two men. Both came to the presidency

[10] unilateralism *An approach to foreign policy and international affairs based on the theory that what is in the best interest of the United States is best for the world. Concerns of other nations and international cooperation are ignored by unilateralists. It is seen as extreme nationalism and a new expression of the concept of isolationism pursued by the United States after World War I only now it includes an interventionist, usually military, component.*

with experience as governors and little foreign policy experience. Both were forced to become active leaders in the international field—Clinton in Yugoslavia, Northern Ireland, and the Middle East; Bush in the War on Terrorism. Both administrations supported globalization. Both committed U.S. forces to nation building—Clinton in Somalia (a failure), Bosnia, and Kosovo (partial successes); Bush in Afghanistan and Iraq (question marks as of this writing). The greatest difference between Presidents Clinton and Bush was the latter's adoption of a unilateralist, preemptive war as an approach to foreign relations and concentration on a War on Terrorism. These conflicting trends, unilateralism and internationalism, have been in tension for many years and will continue to be. Perhaps the inclination of the American people not to be involved in foreign affairs while at the same time desiring to do good and correct wrongs is driving U.S. foreign policy.

Key Point to Remember
Since World War II, U.S. foreign policy has been part of world history and U.S. actions affect, to some degree, every nation in the world, and their actions affect the United States.

Links from the Past to the Present
The United States, the world's only superpower, is a crucial player in world affairs and has been since World War II.

Dates

1993—NAFTA approved.
   U.S. sends troops to support UN humanitarian mission in Somalia.

1994—Dayton Peace Accords.
   United States withdraws from Somalia
   Rwandan genocide

1995—WTO comes into existence.
   NATO forces enter combat in Bosnia.
   Vietnam–U.S. relations normalized; embassies opened.

1997—Asian economic crisis begins.

1998—Good Friday Peace Accords in Northern Ireland.
   Hugo Chavez elected president of Venezuela.

1999—Panama Canal under control of Panama.

2001—September 11 attacks on the World Trade Center and Pentagon.
   EU introduces common currency, the Euro.

2002—Bush labels Iraq, Iran, North Korea an "Axis of Evil."
   African Union (AU) formed replacing Organization of African Unity (OAU).
   First terrorist bombing on Bali.

2003—NATO takes leadership role in War in Afghanistan.
   Discussions begin on creation of a Free Trade Area of the Americas (FETA).
   Rebellion in Darfur leads to genocidal acts.

2004—Latvia, Estonia, and Lithuania join NATO.

Massive tsunami hits coastal regions of Bay of Bengal and Indian Ocean.

2005—NATO invites Ukraine to join NATO.

2006—Bolivia elects socialist, Evo Morales, president.

President Bush visits Vietnam.

2008—Russia–Georgia military conflict.

Financial crisis becomes worldwide as United States and other nations enter recession.

Questions
Identify each of the following:

Bush Doctrine	Internationalism	AIDS
Unilateralism	African Union	NAFTA
War on Drugs	Globalization	EU
International War Crimes Tribunal	Dayton Peace Accord	NATO

Multiple Choice:

1. Response to natural disasters has driven U.S. foreign policy as can be seen in the nation's response to
   a. the situation in Darfur.
   b. Russia's invasion of Georgia.
   c. earthquakes in Turkey and China.

2. Among the major problems facing African nations is
   a. rapid economic growth.
   b. AIDS.
   c. a low birth rate.

3. Many people believe the United States has not been successful in its War on Drugs primarily because it has failed to
   a. reduce the demand for drugs in the United States.
   b. supply enough arms to Colombia.
   c. legalize the use of all drugs.

4. Which nation did not test nuclear weapons in the 1990s?
   a. India
   b. Iraq
   c. Pakistan

5. Examples of U.S. unilateralism in recent years is its refusal to support the
   a. Land Mines Treaty and Kyoto Accords.
   b. UN Document on the Rights on Children and International War Crimes Tribunal.
   c. all of the above.

VI. Financial Crisis, Election of 2008, and President Obama's First Two Months

FINANCIAL CRISIS: THE COLLAPSE OF THE HOUSING MARKET

Owning one's own home has been part of the American Dream at least since the Homestead Act in 1862. Starting with the New Deal, government housing policy was designed to encourage ownership. Looking back from 2005, Clinton proudly stated that under his presidency there was the highest rate of home ownership among the lower income groups in the history of the nation. Home ownership was a part the goal—creating an "ownership society"—that Bush set for his second term. To encourage this, low interests and new types of mortgages were developed. Under first the Clinton and then the Bush administrations, Fannie Mae and Freddie Mac, both quasi-government agencies, were encouraged to lower the personal financial requirements for mortgages. This attitude reflected the assumption that, over time, the value of houses rose. However, a close study of house prices shows they fluctuate over the years. Overlooking this fact and providing low adjustable rate mortgages (ARMs) allowed many to buy homes they could not afford when the adjustable rates rose. These buyers could not make the mortgage payments, and banks foreclosured. House prices declined. This simple situation is at the base of the ensuing financial crisis of 2008–2009 that began with the collapse of the housing market in 2007.

> Home ownership is part of the American Dream and has been encouraged by government policies.

Fannie Mae and Freddie Mac were affected first, but it soon became evident that other lending institutions were involved. To make the risky mortgages—referred to as sub-prime mortgages[11] more attractive to the large financial institutions that bought them from issuing institutions, mortgages that were known to be risky were bundled (i.e., sold together). The companies whose business it was to analyze the risk of stock offerings and other securities gave a low risk rating to these bundles because they assumed that if there were many poor risk mortgages together, somehow the risk was reduced. Investment houses bought these bundles, referred to as SPIs or SIVs.[12] SPIs and SIVs, supposedly were supporting the policies of the Clinton and Bush administrations. As a new financial concept, there was no government regulation of this bundling. Since the Reagan years, regulation was viewed as restricting business and the overall economic growth of the nation. Even Democrat Clinton espoused this attitude, and the Republicans under Bush stressed it. As a result, even those long established agencies that were meant to oversee the financial markets failed to do so. A few whistle blowers were ignored, and the economy slid into recession in 2008.

[11] Sub-prime mortgage   *A risky mortgage because the borrower has a low credit rating.*
[12] Special Purpose Entity (SPI) and/or Structured Investment Vehicle (SIV)   *A bundle of sub-prime mortgages in which the risk is supposedly reduced by the number of mortgages included. Banks that issued sub-prime mortgages sold them to large financial houses where they were bundled and sold to other entities both in the United States and worldwide. When mortgage interest payments could not be paid by the borrower, the value of the SPI or SIV declined, and financial institutions were left with nearly worthless paper.*

FINANCIAL CRISIS: THE COLLAPSE OF THE BANKING INDUSTRY

Home ownership in the United States peaked in 2004. By the end of 2005, the number of new houses being built and the price of houses dropped, the first signs of trouble ahead. Sub-prime mortgages were still being offered by Fannie Mae and Freddie Mac but there were signs of trouble if one was astute. In February 2007, the consumer confidence rate reached its lowest level in twenty-five years. The economy for years had been driven by consumer spending. In April the largest sub-prime bank declared bankruptcy, and in May the chairman of the Federal Reserve Bank, which had begun dropping prime rates to address mortgage and credit concerns, declared the "sub-prime mess" had been contained, and in July the Dow Jones reached its highest point, over 14,000. The economic signals were very mixed. Looking back, economists say the nation had entered recession during the last months of 2007.

In March 2008, in the middle of the presidential primary campaign, Bear Stearns, one of the giant Wall Street investment firms was bailed out of bankruptcy by the federal government working with another firm, J. P. Morgan. The banking crisis was in full bloom, and the Bush administration was responding, but there appeared to be no clear policy as seen in July when the seventh largest sub-prime bank in the nation was allowed to declare bankruptcy. Then in September three events shook the markets: the government allowed another large investment bank, Lehman Brothers, to go bankrupt; the government intervened to have another investment bank, Merrill Lynch, bought by Bank of America; and the government arranged to have Washington Mutual, a savings and loan association that was a symbol of excesses in the sub-prime market, bought by J. P. Morgan. The banking industry was in collapse. President Bush called an economic summit and presidential candidates McCain and Obama attended. McCain had said previously that the economy was strong, and then he announced he would suspend his campaign to help solve the crisis. At the President's summit his comments proved unfocused. Obama was more reserved.

> **Purchase of financial giant Bear Stearns arranged by federal government.**

FINANCIAL CRISIS: TARP

A policy was emerging as the president signed the Emergency Economic Stabilization Act, creating a $700 billion Troubled Assets Relief Program (TARP) to purchase the assets of failing financial institutions. Immediately the government announced the use of $250 billion of this public money to acquire equity in those banks that chose to participate in the program. There would be certain restrictions on the banks, but it would not be nationalization. Consideration was given to buying the bad assets of banks, but it was abandoned. In mid-October several European nations and China in a joint effort cut interest rates indicating the financial crisis was worldwide. The Federal Reserve had been dropping U.S. rates since 2006. The financial situation continued to deteriorate in the last two months of Bush's term. The new administration inherited the worst financial crisis since the Great Depression of the 1930s plus wars in Iraq and Afghanistan. History's final judgment on the presidency of George W. Bush may well rest on how quickly the nation can recover from the financial crisis.

PRESIDENTIAL PRIMARY CAMPAIGN

In 2008 for the first time since 1928, there was no sitting president or vice president seeking the presidency, and the race was wide open. The primary campaign began in January 2007 when New York Senator and former first lady Hillary Clinton, announced her candidacy. Six other Democrats soon entered the race including Senator Joe Biden of Delaware and Senator Barack Obama of Illinois. Clinton immediately took a lead in the polls and established herself as the strongest woman presidential candidate in U.S. history. Barack Obama, son of a white mother from Kansas and a black father from Kenya, had opposed the War in Iraq and soon became her chief rival. At that stage, the campaign centered on the war and foreign policy. As the year progressed, the economic situation became more and more important. Obama won the first caucus in Iowa in January, and Clinton the first vote in New Hampshire. Obama had first gained national recognition with a speech at the 2004 Democratic convention, and his power as an orator was clear throughout the campaign drawing crowds of thousands to his rallies. The issue of race surfaced several times particularly involving the pastor of Obama's church whose derogatory comments about the United States were quoted widely. He decided in March to address the race issue. He did so at Independence Hall in Philadelphia in a speech that he wrote. It was hailed as one of the finest statements on race in U.S. history and one the finest campaign speeches ever delivered. After that the campaign was essentially fought on the issues of the wars in Iraq and Afghanistan, health care, a green economy, jobs, and the economy. The Obama campaign was highly organized and focused on the caucus states. They made use of the Internet to raise money in small amounts—a record $32 million in January 2008. He had a million Internet donors by February and used YouTube and Facebook to gather young supporters. The race remained tight until the end of the primaries in June when Clinton, trailing in convention delegates, withdrew from the race—the longest Democratic primary ever.

> Obama and Clinton contest Democratic primary.

The Republican campaign also began in early 2007. Senator John McCain of Arizona, who had run against George W. Bush in 2000, was the leading candidate. Polls showed he was losing strength to former Mayor of New York City, Rudy Giuliani. He reorganized his campaign and went on to win a majority of the convention delegates in March.

PRESIDENTIAL ELECTION

During the primaries Obama had been accused of lacking foreign policy experience. At the convention, he chose Senator Biden, an expert on foreign policy, as his vice presidential running mate. Senator McCain chose the somewhat unknown governor of Alaska, Sarah Palin, as his running mate. She was the first woman chosen to run on the national Republican ticket. She held

> Obama and Democrats win 2008 election and control White House and Congress.

This cartoon, produced by two Australian high school students, Rachael Blackwell and James Fenton, illustrates the worldwide interest in the U.S. election of 2008. What is the point being made? At the time of the election, George W. Bush's popularity was at a near record low. Is it possible even his wife, Laura, could have voted for Obama?

very conservative views and appealed to the right wing of the party. The economic crisis of September changed the dynamics of the race. Foreign policy became less and less of an issue. President Bush's popular support was under 30 percent. McCain kept away from the president whose only participation in the election was as a fund-raiser among the Republican right wing. Obama with his Internet fund-raising refused to accept federal funding, an issue that McCain had focused on for years. The Democrats outspent the Republicans—a somewhat unusual situation. Obama contested the election in all states not ceding the traditional Republican states to McCain. While he did not win in the Deep South, Obama won 53 percent of the popular vote and the Electoral College, 365–173. The Democrats increased their majorities in the House and Senate. They held fifty-six seats in the Senate with one Senate seat being contested in the court in Minnesota. The two Senate independents have voted with the Democrats. The Republicans held forty-one seats, a loss of eight but enough, if they vote as a block, to keep the Democrats from ending a filibuster.

THE TRANSITION PERIOD

Between election and inauguration there are two and a half months in which the new president can organize his administration. Immediately the president-elect is given highly classified intelligence information. Outgoing presidents issue Executive Orders that continue the administration's policies, do not need the approval of Congress, and are often controversial. Bush issued several involving the environment. Outgoing presidents also have a last chance to issue pardons. Bush did not pardon J. Gordon Libby, which apparently widened the rift between Bush and Cheney that had developed during the second term. The defeated administration is in charge during the transition, and there were both domestic and international decisions that were Bush's alone to make. These involved the worsening worldwide financial crisis, a terrorist attack on Mumbai, India, that brought Pakistan and India close to war and diverted Pakistan's attention from the struggle against the Taliban and elections in Iraq. Obama worked to put together his cabinet and economic and foreign policy teams.

> Obama's appointments confirm a pragmatic and centrist approach to government.

In recent years usually the key figure at the White House has been the Chief of Staff. Obama chose Rahm Emanuel, a Congressman from Illinois. Other appointments indicated a centrist approach not moving to the Left or Right of the Democratic Party. Obama in the campaign advocated a pragmatic approach to problems identifying them and finding solutions rather than following strict party ideology. His cabinet reflected this. He stated that, "I need mechanics who can get the job done." His appointments—Hillary Clinton, his rival for the nomination, as secretary of state; Republican Robert Gates as secretary of defense, the post he held in the Bush administration; and Leon Panetta as director of the CIA and Timothy Geithner as secretary of the Treasury, both experienced members of the Clinton administration—indicated he was surrounding himself with experienced leaders. The appointments met with approval and quick confirmation in the Senate. However, as had happened in other transitions, several appointees were not approved because of failure to pay taxes. Former Senator Tom Daschle was one. A close friend of Obama, he was asked to lead the Department of Health and Human Services and be in charge of the reform of health care. Health care was a top priority for Obama, and Daschle's withdrawal was a disappointment. The economic and security teams were mainly in place by the inauguration and signaled a smooth transition. In foreign policy, Obama appointed three experienced negotiators to be responsible for policy development in three crisis areas: Richard Holbrooke for Pakistan and Afghanistan; George Mitchell for Palestine and Israel; and Dennis Ross for Iran. Full reviews of policies in these areas were begun.

INAUGURATION OF PRESIDENT OBAMA

A presidential inauguration is a great American spectacle celebrating over 220 years of peaceful transition between administrations that may differ extensively on many points. It illustrates the strength and greatness of the American democratic

> Presidential inaugurations celebrate American democracy.

system. The day is full of pageant, poignant moments, and events that symbolize the nation and the passing of power. The inauguration of Barack Obama as 44th president was of unusual significance—the first African-American president. As he stated, his family is scattered over three continents and comes in many colors. His half-sister's father is Indonesian and that is only a small part of the diversity in the family. The nations of the world did not fail to note the significance of this background.

Traditionally, Inauguration Day begins for the president-elect with a church service, then a meeting with the retiring president at the White House, and a trip together to the capitol for the swearing-in ceremony that marks, at noon on January 20, the transition of power. A parade and balls follow. The Obama inauguration followed this outline and included a walk along Pennsylvania Avenue by President and Mrs. Obama. A mother of pre–teen daughters, lawyer, youthful, and stylish, Michelle Obama was compared to Jackie Kennedy and was expected to bring a new and fresh presence to the White House. The Obama inauguration was viewed by over 37 million homes in the United States, millions more abroad, and over two million on the Mall—the largest crowd ever in Washington.

FINANCIAL CRISIS: FIRST RESPONSE OF THE OBAMA ADMINISTRATION

The nation in January 2009 was in full recession. The Treasury Department was using $350 million of TARP funds to support banks, but there was no increase in the availability of credit as banks used the government funds to address issues of debt. Government oversight of TARP had been limited. In the final quarter of 2008, the economy shrank at the fastest pace since 1982. Consumer spending was down 3.5 percent and purchase of durable goods including cars was down 22.8 percent. Unemployment rose to 7.6 percent—for blacks it was 12 percent and for teenagers 20 percent.

Talk of the need for a stimulus package to jump-start the economy was widespread during the transition. Driving the idea was the need to create jobs by funding infrastructure needs. Congress addressed the issue immediately. In spite of unusual efforts by Obama, the Republicans in the House refused to vote

> Economic Recovery Act passes with support of only three Republicans.

for the stimulus insisting that tax cuts and not spending were the way to stimulate the economy. Both Clinton and Bush had asked for a stimulus package to address economic problems when they became president. Both failed to get it passed. Three Republicans in the Senate joined the Democrats to pass the $787 billion Economic Recovery Act (ERA) signed on February 17. Infrastructure improvements were underway almost immediately. The bill included large sums for support of green technology, health record improvements, and other issues Obama had called for in his campaign. Republicans saw it as a big giveaway of tax payers' money. However, almost one-third of the money went for direct tax cuts and more for indirect ones such as credits for college tuition. How effective the stimulus will be is not clear. It follows Keynesian economic principles used in the New Deal. Some economists believed a larger amount was needed. Others were satisfied, and some deplored the amount to be spent. Obama's pragmatism showed in his appeal to try something.

The Treasury addressed the banking crisis using TARP funds while promising more oversight. AIG, an insurance company that had created a new way to insure SPIs and SIVs, had been on the verge of collapse in

> Financial Stability Plan introduced to aid banks; auto makers given deadline for restructuring.

President and Mrs. Obama walk down Pennsylvania Avenue as part of the Inauguration Day Parade.
Courtesy: Associated Press

2008 and was rescued with federal funds. In February 2009 they received more government funds. AIG proceeded to pay top executives large bonuses, and there was public outrage saying taxpayer money was being used to reward those who had brought on the financial crisis by their policies. It was an example of the complexity of the crisis and the need for oversight. A new approach to saving banks, the Financial Stability Plan, required that they pass a "stress test" to determine their stability before receiving funds. There was extensive talk of temporarily nationalizing the banks, but it was labeled socialist, and the nation has a long history of opposing anything socialistic. Eventually it may be necessary, if the economy does not improve by 2010. Finally a plan to buy the bad debts—referred to as toxic assets—was discussed as a way to revitalize the banking industry.

In February the situation in Europe deteriorated confirming the recession was worldwide and worldwide cooperation would be necessary to solve the many problems. Prime Minister Gordon Brown of Great Britain was calling for such an approach and a restructuring of the world economic system established after World War II at Bretton Woods. The Group of 20 (G20)—the twenty nations with the largest economies—were to meet April 1 to address the issue. Meanwhile, the daily news, the current events of the time, brought in more and more bad news. The Big Three auto makers had been in deep financial trouble for several years. The Bush administration had provided some temporary funding and required a restructuring of GM and Chrysler. The plans submitted were rejected by the Obama administration who gave them weeks to produce new plans or face bankruptcy. The failure of the industry would have a huge impact on the nation's economic strength and recession. The Obama economic team was working on a variety of approaches to deal with the economic crisis.

THE FIRST TWO MONTHS

President Obama stated in a news interview, of which he held several in the first days of his presidency, that it would have been nice to be able to face one crisis at a time but that was not the situation. In an address to Congress and the nation in February, he set the tone for his administration indicating health care reform, education improvements and increased funding, movement toward a greener society, changes in Social Security, and tax cuts for all but the wealthiest earning over $250,000 would be addressed with proposals being presented during his first term. He argued these reforms would make the nation more competitive and ultimately help end the recession, and all were included in his first budget. Immediately there was Republican objection stating it was too much and too costly. They opposed raising taxes on wealthy Americans to pay for health care reform. The response was that in 1980 at the start of Reagan's terms, the wealthiest 1 percent of Americans held 8 percent of the total wealth of the nation. In 2006, the top 1 percent held 23 percent of the wealth. Obama indicated that fairness suggested that taxing this increased wealth to support the common need for better health care was fair.

> Obama calls for a multipronged attack on needs of the nation.

Announcements came daily from the White House reversing Bush policies on issues from torture to birth control funding. The president announced all combat troops would be withdrawn from Iraq within eighteen months—two more months than he had stated in his campaign—and he announced more troops would be sent to Afghanistan. After his security team reviewed the War in Afghanistan in consultation with allies, a new plan incorporating both military and civilian changes was announced. Secretary of State Clinton made two overseas trips immediately, the first, symbolically, to Asia, not Europe. In the first few days Congress passed two major acts, one expanding health care insurance for children and the other providing women greater legal support in the fight to end pay discrimination against women. The financial crisis worsened, but there was a sense of purpose and direction coming from Washington. It was a period in which history was being made, events came rapidly, but how they will all fit into the large picture of U.S. history will take years to determine. As with every lifetime, current events provided excitement, but, in spite of endless commentary on news channels, there was no time for historic analysis. That will come with the next generation.

CONCLUSION

From the perspective of the Western-oriented historian, there is no conclusion as history is a continually unfolding pattern of cause and effect instituted by human actions and influenced by nature and past events. How that pattern will play out during the Obama presidency is to be revealed. In recent U.S. history, the political process has often stalled as individuals in each party find commitment to the common cause less important than commitment to a set of beliefs, an ideology. Whether Democrats or Republicans have been in charge, change has come slowly. Obama based his campaign on the need for change and that "Yes we can" achieve it. The multiple crises facing the nation cannot be solved by one party, by one person, but only by the efforts of a united people. President Obama with his pragmatic approach has called for this. Within two weeks he had visited Republicans at the capitol and entertained them at the White House in an effort at bipartisanship and dialogue. He has indicated, in spite of getting no votes from Republican House members for his stimulus package, he will continue the efforts. What the Republican response will be is uncertain. Just what is compromise cannot be agreed upon, but it is essential to bring about change. Compromise at the Constitutional Convention created this nation. Compromises have held it together through much of its history. Does compromise require that the opposition write half of each law, or does it mean the party with a large majority has the responsibility to lead presenting legislation, listening to the minority, incorporating some of their suggestions to improve the law after debate and discussion so that the voice of the minority is heard? In 2008, with many new, young voters participating, the American people voted for Obama and his call for change. The first two months introduced some changes. Unfortunately, it did not seem to end commitment to ideology, nor did it create an atmosphere of compromise.

One example of that was seen in Obama's appointment of a secretary of commerce. Senator Judd Gregg, a leading fiscal conservative from New Hampshire, indicated an interest in the position. Obama asked him to serve thus increasing the number of Republicans in the cabinet. Gregg accepted. Several days later he withdrew. Gregg was complimentary of the president and said he had not thought the issues through enough. He added he was used to being his own man and realized he could not compromise on basic issues over which he disagreed or give his support to them as a member of the cabinet. The comments were revealing of an attitude that appears to be widespread in Washington. "Me and my ideology" comes first over any consensus as to what is needed for the common good. Some commentators suggested that what Gregg heard from Republicans determined his action. The situation was a sad comment on bipartisanship and compromise. For the sake of the nation, let us hope it does not prevail as the nation faces momentous problems.

Key Point to Remember
The greatness of the Constitution and the American political system is seen in the peaceful transition of power from one elected president to the next.

Links from the Past to the Present
The pageantry of the inauguration is seen every four years.

People to Remember
Barack Obama   Chicago community organizer, lawyer, civil rights attorney, Constitutional law professor, U.S. Senator, 44th president of the United States; son of a white American and a black father from Kenya, he is the first African-American elected president; raised in large part by his mother and his white grandparents after his father returned to Kenya; stepfather was Indonesian; graduate of Columbia University and Harvard Law School where he was the first African-American head of the Law Review.

Dates

2004—Home ownership peaks.

2007—Presidential primary campaign of 2008 begins with Hillary Clinton. Housing market collapses.

2008—Financial crisis; recession begins. Democrat Barack Obama elected president with Senator Joe Biden as vice president.

2009—Economic Recovery Act.

Questions
Identify each of the following:

Economic Recovery Act (ERA)	Inauguration Day	SPI and SIV
Financial Stability Plan	TARP	Sarah Palin

Multiple Choice
1. Among his first acts in office, President Barack Obama
   a. gave an excellent speech on race.
   b. made a visit to Iraq.
   c. signed an Economic Recovery Act.

2. The financial crisis of 2008 can be traced to
   a. the collapse of the housing market in 2007.
   b. Obama's centrist approach to governing.
   c. support for the Iraq War.

Open-ended, Analysis Questions
The following questions require analysis and reflection. You are encouraged to bring to your answer information and ideas from many sources. The answers should be presented in composition or essay style, but they may be used to initiate discussion. The questions put you in the role of the historian, gathering information to support your personal perspective on the question.

1. "Since World War II, U.S. foreign policy has been part of world history."

Do you agree or disagree? Pick three examples of U.S. foreign policy and illustrate how these actions have or have not affected the world.

2. Presidents Clinton and George W. Bush are more similar than different in both their domestic and foreign policies. Do you agree or disagree?

   Explain your view. Pick at least one example from domestic policy and one from foreign policy to support your position.

3. Pick two presidents elected since 1900 and show how their policies, both domestic and foreign, were either similar or different and explain why they were. Be specific in describing their policies giving at least two examples from domestic and foreign events.

4. Based on the year you are writing your answer, what would you leave out of Chapter 15 and what information would you add? Give your reasons based on the significance of the information at the time you are writing.

16

Social Trends and Developments: 1993–2009

APPROACHES TO HISTORY

EVERYONE'S STORY IS PART OF HISTORY

History is made up of the stories of individuals. Since the advent of recording devices, it has become possible to include more and more information about the average individual. Historians who emphasize these personal stories are considered social historians as was discussed in Chapter 14. In recent years with the development first of cameras, radio, TV, and recording devices and more recently the web, computers, and other electronic technology, it has become easier for average individuals to tell their stories thus making them available to the professional historian. Today with blogging, personal web sites, and e-mail, we can all tell our own stories and put our personal views out for all to see and read. The result is a more personal world, but also one in which it becomes more difficult for everyone to identify the accurate from the fiction, the balanced presentation from the biased ranting of angry individuals. It is all part of our world, but what should we believe? And what is and will ultimately be important? This forces everyone to make decisions as to what he or she believes, and where information will be obtained to support, as well as question, those beliefs. Educated judgments become more important as more information is available.

However, as more sources of information become available, more and more sources are being presented that focus on a particular philosophy or point of view. An individual today can obtain all his or her information from radio broadcasts, TV channels, blogs, or friends who agree with them. We each have our own biases and stories that we choose to remember because we agree with them. This is human and has always occurred, but today the number of opportunities to find sources that affirm our views and fail to present alternatives is greater than ever. We feel comfortable when all we hear is what we already believe. Unfortunately, this is not healthy for us, the nation, or the world.

Partisanship and commitment to ideologies and particular views of life and values have come to dominate both our social and political lives. Compromise is hard to achieve, yet our nation was created through compromises embedded in the Constitution. To achieve change, one must hear the other view and seek those areas where there can be steps taken toward agreement. Without this skill, government cannot function effectively because to do so both majority and minority opinions must be heard. We must tell our own stories, but we must hear the stories of others. If one's source of news is only Fox or MSNBC, if one only talks to friends, if one never seeks the views and stories of others, one will not hear the other side, the many other stories that together with ours make history. How often have you viewed the BBC channel or al-Jazeera—English? What we choose to remember is what we believe—it can lead to partisanship, social separation, the ranting of ideologues. On the other hand, seeking as many stories as possible, evaluating them, and taking what is reasonable and can be incorporated in your story is another approach and resembles what the historian attempts to do. History is the sum of all our stories. The writer of history brings together as many of those stories as possible to create his or her account of the past. Perhaps you will be the author that synthesizes all the stories of the Clinton, Bush, and Obama years.

I. The Impact of Business and Industry on Social Patterns

GROWTH OF THE COMPUTER INDUSTRY

The electronics industry grew in the 1970s, bringing rapid growth to some regions such as the peninsula south of San Francisco, California, dubbed Silicon Valley because of its heavy concentration of electronics companies, Route 128 around Boston, Massachusetts, and northern Virginia. There are now pockets of computer and Internet-driven industry in many

> Silicon Valley and Route 128 are centers of growth of the electronics industry.

regions. The computer industry has had a profound impact on our lives. Computers and the Internet have changed the way we think and communicate. Computers have made vast amounts of information available to everyone who can afford it whether via CDs and DVDs or by accessing the web originally called the Information Highway. The impact of computers on education, business, entertainment, and warfare has been profound. Computers also underscore the split between have and have-nots since without a computer, you are excluded from many opportunities in today's world. America led the world in computing, but worldwide competition has increased.

The phenomenal growth of the computer industry together with service industries drove the prosperity of the Clinton years. The miniaturization of computers, the increasing speed and access to the Internet, the founding and selling of both manufacturing and Internet companies such as *amazon.com* allowed many fortunes to be made apparently overnight. The stock market drove up the value of many dot-coms even though no profits were made. Inevitably by the end of the 1990s, the growth began to slow, and stock prices dropped. This led to the end of rapid growth and the beginning in 2001 of a recession.

As the nation recovered from the recession of the early years of the Bush administration and the attacks of 9/11, the economy grew. The computer/electronic industry was again a major factor in the growth with the introduction of new devices each year. Behind many of these was increasing miniaturization of electronic chips and the number of transistors that could be put on each chip. One handicap to the process was heat generated by the amount of information being included. Scientists addressing the issue focused on the "spin" or orientation of the electron. They believe increased miniaturization can be achieved by capitalizing on that spin, opening up ever-new possibilities for development of electronic devices.

The miniaturization of computers has had a great impact on social patterns. The first computers, large, bulky, heavy and expensive, were placed in a separate air-conditioned room to be shared by all. By 2009 hand-held computers in cell phones were available. Individual desktop computers allowed each person in a company access to a computer and printer and affected communication and business operation dramatically. The advent of the Internet and e-mail changed communication patterns and quickly replaced the phone, copying machine, and fax in many businesses. With the introduction of laptops, business people were freed from a desk, and work could be continued on the train during commutes and at home. The computer drastically changed the concept of working in offices, and the virtual office—meaning any place you were as long as you owned or had available for use a cell phone, laptop, copying machine, and access to the Internet—became the work place for many individuals. Cell phones along with laptops allow business to be done twenty-four hours a day. A business can as easily be run from a vacation house in the Caribbean as from an office cubicle in Boulder, Colorado.

> Use of the virtual office becomes commonplace.

Computers did more than impact office workers. For example, the functions of automobile engines were computerized, and auto mechanics became dependent on computer technology. Hospitals and doctors computerized medical records so that all medical professionals had to be computer literate. The impact of the computer on society has been pervasive, and the computer illiterate individual is being pushed out of the work force except for the most menial of jobs. Even there, computers have a place as there are robot-like, computer-run vacuum cleaners that can replace the menial worker. Almost every restaurant and market uses digitalized, computer-driven registers. Shopping and personal banking using the web are becoming standard practice. Many computer users access blog reports and newspapers on the web. As a result, many newspaper have stopped publishing hard copies or gone bankrupt, and the number of reporters has been reduced—a clear impact of the computer on previous social patterns. Without access to a computer, one's participation in society is reduced, as is one's ability to hear other's stories.

THE CELL PHONE SOCIETY

The first use of radiotelephony was in Europe in the 1920s when communication between stations and trains was established. In the 1940s, Motorola, a U.S. company, developed a walkie-talkie for two-way communication and developed efficient devices for the military. In the 1950s in Sweden, a 90-pound mobile phone was in use. In 1971 AT&T applied to the Federal Communication Commission for permission to operate an analog Advanced Mobile Phone Service (AMPS). It was finally approved in 1982. The system was digitalized in 1990, and the industry took off. In the 1990s, cell phones of the second generation were in wide use. In many cases, families bought the first phone for safety reasons to be able to call if in a highway accident, but their use rapidly become part of the life style of the nation. Phones were continually made smaller with more features such as cameras, computers with access to the web, and Global Positioning Systems (GPS) were added. During the Bush presidency, a third generation of phones and a new telecommunication support system was developed. It was rapidly replacing the older system. The cell phone phenomenon illustrates clearly the relation between industry/business and social patterns.

Today not being part of the cell phone society isolates you. Many families have abandoned landlines for total reliance on communication via airwaves. A teenager without a cell phone cannot be part of the group. Elementary school children are given them so parents can track their activities. Text messaging and e-mail have replaced personal contact and face-to-face conversation for thousands who spend the day texting friends and following their every act.

The evolution of computer networking changed during the Clinton and Bush years. In the 1990s blogging emerged as a replacement for networking forums on the web devoted to exchanges on a given topic. Blogging began as a web log in 1994 when a student at Swarthmore began keeping a journal on

> Blogging becomes important tool in networking.

the web. It grew to 112 million recorded sites in December 2007. Blogs are personal and can include everything from personal journals to commentary on current politics. It has become competition for traditional journalism with thousands expressing their personal views. There is a danger in this as people reading blogs may not be aware of the writer's personal view. Use of the web for personal contacts has a negative side as it has been used for solicitation of sex and display of pornography.

As part of the recovery of the early Bush years, new dot-coms were founded. Facebook, which was started by a Harvard undergrad in 2004, became an instant success among college students seeking friends. The idea behind Facebook was introduced at colleges where, on administration-controlled sites, information on the student body was made available to all students. All types of information can be posted on one's site. In 2008 a fad developed among high school students of posting nude pictures of themselves on their sites to the concern of police authorities and many parents. What appears on sites can affect an individual's future as business firms check out Facebook sites before interviewing candidates for jobs. New sites such as Twitter are constantly being developed. Blogging and Facebook both illustrate how young people have affected the development of the web. They also illustrate the impact the individual can have on business and society.

COMPUTER GAMES AND MUSIC

For years pinball machines provided entertainment for Americans. Too large and expensive for most homes, they were played in arcades, amusement parks, bars, and many other places. With the advent of computer gaming consoles in the

> The Wii introduces a new type of interactive, computer-driven game.

early 1970s, a whole new industry developed. At first, most games were played at public locations as were pinball machines. Then in the 1980s a new generation of smaller, less expensive console games were introduced, and the industry grew to the point that Nintendo and Sony Play Station became household words and youngsters had to have the latest generation. Games became more and more sophisticated with graphics and stories that gripped the imagination. Violence prevailed, and youngsters were killing and shooting their way through challenges that became more complex. Games were interactive in that the player had buttons to push and the game had built-in responses. In 2006 with the introduction of the Wii (pronounced we, symbolizing the inclusiveness of the new game)—the seventh generation of computer based game in thirty-five years—a new approach was established in which the player could compete while in their home against a fellow human player in games such as boxing or golf. Finally, there was a computer game in which the players could get exercise while in the comfort of their home. Wiis were introduced to retirement communities where they changed the health of many by allowing physical activity indoors and at the participant's own speed. Between its introduction in 2006 and the end of 2008, 20 million Wiis were sold in the United States illustrating the importance of the industry to the economy of personal consumption.

Likewise, computers transformed the music industry. Since Thomas Edison patented the phonograph in 1877, sound reproduction has been available. Improvement came steadily and by 1980 analog reproduction achieved the highest quality possible. A new approach, the digital, was introduced in 1982 with CDs and CD players. The quality was high, and by the 1990s, CDs became the medium of choice for music reproduction. CD players were somewhat bulky, but some were designed for portability, replacing the old "boom boxes." Earlier in 1979 Sony had introduced the "Personal Stereo" known as the Walkman. It played tapes (music cassettes), had earphones, and could be attached to a belt or hung around the neck. It provided the individual with a personal choice of music wherever he went. In 1984 a Walkman using mini-CDs was introduced and changes came rapidly including video. Sony dominated the market until the introduction in 2003 of the iPod by Apple Computer. New technology allowed hundreds of songs to be stored, and the iPod was flexible in its operating systems unlike Sony's Walkman. The iPod swept the market and brought Apple Computer back as a major player in the computer industry. iPod technology grew rapidly to include a phone and other personal items, and the prices dropped.

The iPod has further isolated individuals from each other as everyone listens to their own music. Since the first use of headphones, doctors have worried that the level of sound pouring into the ears of youngsters will lead to early deafness. Because the iPod allows for accessing music from the web, it intensified the conflict between the traditional music publishing companies and the listening public that no longer needed to buy recordings. The conflict including lawsuits had been underway since music was first accessible on the web. Like newspaper publishing, music publishing had been deeply affected by the Internet, new technology, and new personal behavior. How all the electronic-based changes of the past two decades—iPods, laptops, texting, e-mail, cell phones, blogs, and personal web sites—will affect social relationships is of interest to the social scientist and historian. Are we at a major changing point in the evolution of human relations?

THE COMPUTER AND POLITICS

Computer technology and the web were used very effectively by Barack Obama in his primary and presidential campaigns. Howard Dean, a Democratic candidate in 2004, used the web as

> Obama uses Internet as a fund-raising device.

a fund-raiser. Obama built on this and out-raised his opponents by concentrating on the web and small donations. He had over two million donors of less than $250, and these funds helped him to contest every state in both the primary and presidential campaigns. As president, Obama has continued to use the web to inform his supporters of his actions.

In a move followed by many younger candidates, Obama produced a Facebook page illustrating his campaign's understanding both of the web and the need to appeal to young voters in new ways. What was cause, and what was effect, is difficult to determine, but Obama obtained a large proportion of the youth vote (18–34) and the numbers of young voters increased. The use of the web transformed the election process and the economics of campaigning. As president, Obama continued to use the Internet. Messages were sent daily to those supporters who had funded his campaign. A lottery was held among these supporters with the prizes being invitations to the inauguration. Obama had promised a new style of presidency with transparency in which he would explain policies frankly and discuss both good and bad news. His first weeks in office reflected this and an understanding of the new information technology. Appearances on Jay Leno's evening TV show (the first sitting president to appear), news conferences, interviews with chosen reporters including a first one with an Arab news channel, traditional TV news conferences, and a virtual town meeting to which the public was invited to submit questions illustrated this. The questions submitted for the town meeting were voted on the web, and Obama answered the most popular in an hour-long interactive webcast. Each presentation was directed at a different audience to avoid danger of overexposure.

Effectively used by Obama and a few other candidates in 2008, this use of the web and all aspects of the new computer technology created the possibility for a new era of participation in politics and social activism. The technology opens up communication worldwide and suggests that there may be a way in the future for oppressed individuals to organize and become a force in social and political reform.

FARMING AND BUSINESS

Since the New Deal, the federal government has subsidized agriculture in the United States. During those years agribusiness has become the standard of agricultural life replacing the small farm. Debate over whether multimillion dollar agribusinesses should be subsidized has occurred over and over. With globalization, small farmers in developing nations have been hurt by subsidies paid to farmers in developed nations. Subsidies allow developed nations to undersell local farmers. Large agribusinesses can change prices to impact different areas at different times thus driving local farmers out of business. The result is unemployment, growing slums in Third World cities as displaced farmers flee to urban centers, and a general displacement of agricultural efforts. Globalized agribusinesses have changed local production so that farmers grow food for export. The United States and other developed countries enjoy fruits, vegetables, and flowers in the off-season, while these poorer countries must import basic food. For example, Haitians rarely raise chickens since U.S. producers flood the market with cheap chicken parts rejected by the American market. In a country such as Afghanistan the local farmers have turned to poppy growing for the world drug market since on the world market they could not compete with subsidized crops from developed nations. The development of agribusiness has provided the nation with wide choices of food while drastically affecting world food production and social patterns in small countries. Social patterns were also affected in the United States where inexpensive food, fast food chains, and a more sedentary lifestyle led to an epidemic of obesity. On the positive side, as a result of the subsidy program in which the federal government bought surplus production, the United States was able to supply food as foreign aid to drought and famine stricken areas of the world. There are at least two very different stories to hear when investigating agriculture.

> Subsidized agribusinesses affect agriculture production worldwide.

In 1996 Congress passed a Farm Bill reducing government subsidies to farmers. It was hailed as a breakthrough, a response to the new World Trade Organization. For years farm subsidies, particularly in France, had held up (WTO) negotiations. The Farm Bill was another aspect of freer trade and globalization. It was hoped the European market would help U.S. farmers. It did not, and in 2002 a Farm Bill, supported by Republicans who for years had opposed subsidies, reinstated and increased them. The Bill went against the WTO goal of eliminating farm subsidies. Our European allies saw this as another example of unilateralism.

The question of government support for farming will continue to be an issue. Some politicians follow Thomas Jefferson's argument that the small, independent farm is the base upon which American democracy was built, and they must not be allowed to disappear. They believe subsidies will keep the small farm going. The reality is that government subsidies help the agribusinesses.

IMMIGRANTS, MINORITIES, AND THE JOB MARKET

The American Dream of economic success still attracts many immigrants both legal and illegal. Quota systems in place since the 1920s, were abandoned in 1986, but restrictions control immigration. The 1986 law granted amnesty to illegal immigrants in the country before 1982. An attempt at reform in 2006–2007 failed to grant amnesty to later illegal immigrants, intensified border patrols, and provided for a wall to be built on large sections of the Mexican border. Immigrants provide an important part of the United States labor force often filling low-level jobs scorned by citizens. In 1996 the law put restrictions on the hiring of illegal immigrants and fined businesses guilty of doing so, but this failed to reduce illegal immigration. Because of their illegal status, working conditions for these immigrants are often poor. Legal immigrants, on the other hand, often arrive with academic credentials that allow them to find places in the medical, computer, and other professions. In fact, foreign-trained immigrants founded half of the technology and engineering companies started between 1995 and 2005 in the Silicon Valley area of California.

> Immigrants supply an important part of the U.S. labor force.

The African-American, Hispanic, and recent immigrant population in the inner city ghettos continue to suffer from poor education and lack of jobs. After World War II, the Mexican-American population in the Southwest and in California began to increase, and many of them found homes in the inner cities. Most of them were recent immigrants from Mexico, who had left impoverished conditions to find a better life in the United States. Instead they met with racist attitudes and lived in urban poverty. Some Mexican-Americans found work as itinerant farm laborers. While these migrant workers had jobs and food, the living conditions were often as bad as those in the inner cities. Also settling in the inner cities especially after the Vietnam War were immigrants from Southeast Asia and Korea. Many operated small stores with some success. This added to the tensions as evident in the riots in Los Angeles in the 1990s in which Korean stores in the ghetto areas came under particular attack.

Absorption of the immigrant population appears to follow the pattern established in the 19th century. Recent immigrants usually settle in urban centers in blocks where they find comfort from fellow countrymen. Education makes life more comfortable for the second generation and those with academic records move on joining the mainstream of society while those who fail academically struggle. Educated first-generation immigrants are more quickly absorbed.

As civil war and famine have hit different areas of Africa, the United States has accepted immigrants from those areas. Government policy has been to settle political asylum seekers throughout the country, and many small towns have found they have large immigrant populations for the first time. Racial tensions have surfaced in some communities, but most immigrants have been accepted often through the efforts of local churches. Immigrants, both legal and illegal, are important to business in this country. However, there are many who oppose immigration and wish to return all illegal immigrants to their own countries. How these two perspectives will evolve is an important question for the future of the country, its tradition of welcoming the oppressed of the world, and the needs of the business community.

WEALTH AND INCOME DISTRIBUTION

With the financial crisis of 2008–2009 and the bailout of financial institutions, the issue of CEO compensation became a major political and social issue. During the Clinton and especially the Bush administrations, the distribution of wealth and compensation of CEOs was a continual topic as the Bush tax cuts took effect. The Democrats argued they favored the wealthy and statistics confirm this. From 1990 to 2005 the income of CEOs rose 300 percent, while the average worker's yearly earnings rose 4.3 percent. At the same time the purchasing power of those earning the minimum wage decreased 9.3 percent as Republican congresses refused to raise the minimum wage. In 2007 the average salary of the CEOs of the fifty largest corporations was $14 million a year including cash, bonuses, stock options and perquisites, while that of the CEOs of the smallest corporations averaged $4.7 million. The average American workers salary was $28,000—less than a day's pay for the top CEOs. When insurance giant AIG, which had been rescued from bankruptcy in 2008 by the government's TARP program (Troubled Assets Relief Program) paid millions in bonuses to its top executives in 2009, public outrage exploded at the arrogance shown and the disregard for taxpayers' money. It was the

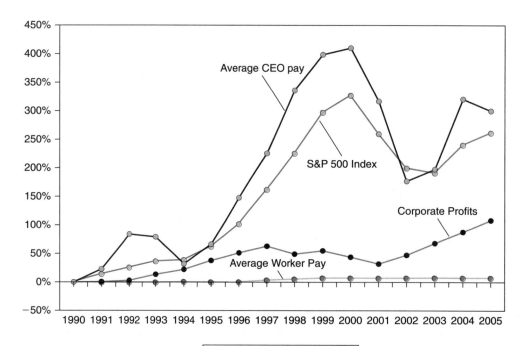

culmination of two decades of growing resentment at the rising disparity between income of workers and managers and the focus on dividends and higher stock prices rather than on the workers and their productivity. The scandals surrounding the bankruptcy of Enron and other companies at the turn of century had prepared the public to distrust business leaders. The rise in CEO salaries supported this distrust as these salaries paralleled the rise of the S&P 500 on the stock market. Globalization, endorsed by CEOs seeking these higher returns for shareholders, had sent jobs overseas. Many workers were laid off while others increased their productivity helping to create the booms of the 1990s and 2003–2006. While consumption increased and most Americans were enjoying the benefits of the computer revolution, the distribution of wealth was changing, and savings of average families fell. Again, CEOs and workers have very different perspectives and stories to tell.

Starting in the Reagan years, the brightest business school graduates headed for Wall Street and the financial markets where the idea of managing money challenged them. It shifted the emphasis of the American economy. Previously the best MBAs had pursued new businesses and the improving of old companies and that drove the economy. These factors all helped contribute to the financial breakdown and the public protests of 2009. President Obama during the campaign called for a change in the tax structure with higher taxes for those earning over $250,000 in order to pay for health care reform. Republicans saw this as socialism and a forced redistribution of wealth. Whether Congress and the people will support Obama's approach is not clear, but it is clear that the growth and distribution of wealth in the country since the start of the Reagan Revolution was dramatic. It greatly affected social patterns in the country.

THE HEALTH CARE ISSUE AND THE ECONOMY

There have been remarkable improvements in health care in the years since World War II. Childhood diseases such as measles have almost been eliminated by programs of vaccination of babies. The government and the philanthropic March of Dimes organization supported research on another dreaded disease, polio, which affected children and left them paralyzed. President Roosevelt was a victim in his early 40s. Dr. Jonas Salk in 1955 developed a vaccine based on a killed virus, which eliminated polio and led to other vaccines for viral diseases. Smallpox was wiped out worldwide and malaria and tuberculosis reduced. Foundations supported research on many illnesses, and with the establishment of the National Science Foundation more government funds became available. Major efforts have been made to find cures for heart-related diseases, cancer, and AIDS (Acquired Immune Deficiency Syndrome). In spite of exciting diagnostic developments such as CAT scans, access to facilities where the latest technology is available varies greatly depending on the community and one's ability to pay.

During the 1980s and early 1990s the cost of health care in the United States increased rapidly, outpacing inflation every year. The result was devastating for many Americans who could not afford health care. During these decades new approaches to health care financing were developed. The old concept was "fee for service" where patients and their insurance companies paid the doctor/hospital the

fees they charged. A new idea, managed health care run by
HMOs (Health Management Organizations), was introduced.
HMOs signed up doctors to work for a particular plan. The
HMOs set fees, reviewed patient records and approved or
rejected treatment ordered by doctors, and set fees for and the length of stays at
hospitals, all in an attempt to control rising costs. HMOs were successful for a few
years in reducing the rate of increase of medical services, but many believed the
reduction was a result of both efficiency and curtailing of needed services.

> HMOs achieve limited success in reducing health care costs.

Widespread complaints that non-professionals were determining treatments and
destroying doctor-patient trust were heard. When it became standard practice of
many HMOs to cover only one day in the hospital for new mothers, states intervened
and passed laws controlling the HMOs. Without full control, HMOs were unable to
keep costs down and by 2001 health cost inflation was again in double digits.

In 2003 Congress passed the Medicare Modernization Act (MMA) to provide
prescription drug coverage for retirees and some disabled Americans. The bill passed
the house by one vote, and later it was revealed the government withheld information
on the actual cost of the bill in order to win the votes of conservative Republicans.
In 2005 the ten-year cost estimate was $1.2 trillion, three times the original estimate
given Congress. The bill was a patchwork reflecting the complexity of health
insurance in the United States.

Health care reform was again a major issue in the 2008
election with candidates presenting plans to achieve coverage for
all Americans. In 2008 the Census Bureau reported that 47
million Americans, 15.8 percent of the population, were without
health care—an increase of 4.9 percent since 2005. While U.S.
costs were higher than those in any industrial nation, health

> Obama puts health care high on his agenda, linking reform to ending financial crisis.

standards in many rural areas and inner cities of the United States were well below
those of other countries. U.S. health care was considered the best in the world, but
only for those who could afford to pay the high costs. In his first address to
Congress, President Obama put health care reform high on his list of priorities. The
president had presented a plan during the campaign but, learning from the Clinton
administration's failure to achieve reform, he organized a task force to seek ideas
from the people and encouraged Congress to design its own plan in a move toward
full transparency. What the results will be are not clear, but any proposal will, no
doubt, be built on the existing system and not introduce an entirely new one of
government insurance.

PERSONAL INCOME AND ITS USE: 1990–2007.*

Item	1990	1995	2000	2005	2007
Total Personal Income in the U.S.	4,879	6,152	8,430	10,301	11,660
Total Personal Taxes Paid in the U.S.	593	744	1,236	1,209	1,483
Total Personal Savings	299	251	169	45	43
Savings as a Percentage of Disposable Income (i.e., Income less Taxes)	7.0%	4.6%	2.3%	0.5%	0.4%

Source: U.S Bureau of Economic Analysis, *Survey of Current Business*, April 2008.

* In billions of dollars (i.e., 4879 means $4,879,000,000,000).

President Obama stated in 2009 that reform was necessary not only for ethical considerations but to help recover from the recession. No matter what the motivation, reform of the health care system in the United States will be very difficult as there are so many with vested interests in the system. Costs of health care outpace inflation and put a great burden on businesses and industries that want costs reduced. Most workers have their health insurance paid for by their employer, and it forms an important part of their compensation. Private health insurance companies make profits by insuring thousands and make large contributions to political candidates to maintain political control over the regulation on the industry. Drug and medical supply companies as well as HMOs have a stake in reform, as do hospitals and doctors. The general public has a variety of needs. Congress has its own, very extensive, government-paid health care plan they do not want to lose. Since Clinton's 1993–1994 attempt at reform, Congress has been unable to prioritize all the needs and create a major overhaul of the system. Whether the Obama administration can achieve reform will be a major test of his political skill.

> Healthcare reform is a very complex issue.

Health care was also impacted by the electronic revolution of the late 20th century. New methods of diagnosis of illness aided the profession but increased the cost of providing care. Everything from CAT scans to the miniaturization of intrusive processes such as knee and heart surgery changed the need for long hospital stays and created new industries. The pharmaceutical industry underwent extensive growth producing new medications that helped heart and diabetic patients among others. Firms combining new technology with new understandings of biology increased research efforts and provided a whole new set of biotech industries. The cost of these medical breakthroughs added to the inflationary rise of health care costs.

AIDS AND THE ECONOMY

Besides urban problems of poverty, homelessness, drugs, and crime, the rise of AIDS put great pressure on city budgets. AIDS is a fatal disease and was first diagnosed in 1981. Transmitted only through the exchange of bodily fluids, AIDS first appeared in the United States among intravenous drug users and the homosexual population of the major cities. As the homosexual population shifted its sexual practices, the spread of AIDS slowed within that group, but little impact has been made on the drug-using population with particularly disastrous results for their babies, for themselves, and for the health care programs for the urban poor.

> AIDS becomes a major health problem.

As the AIDS epidemic grew in the 1990s with no cure in sight, public awareness increased. However, there were strong objections when communities undertook publicity campaigns very frankly discussing the cause and spread of AIDS. Some cities tried to institute needle exchange programs and to distribute condoms in schools, but there were objections from those who claimed such programs encouraged drug use and promiscuous sex. There is evidence that such programs decrease the spread of AIDS, but the possibility of it being a national policy, as it is in some European and African nations and Australia, is slight with the great diversity of attitudes about AIDS held in the United States. These attitudes range from those who see AIDS as a punishment from God for improper sexual behavior to those who view it as a scientific phenomenon.

Announcements of the death from AIDS of well-known individuals such as Arthur Ashe, the first African-American to win the famous Wimbledon tennis tournament, and the open discussion about AIDS as seen in the film *Philadelphia* made America aware AIDS is not a disease of drug addicts and homosexuals only. Worldwide, AIDS has been and is a heterosexual disease. The epidemic is rampant in Africa and Southeast Asia. AIDS is found everywhere. In the United States and many other areas, many cases of AIDS are being found among the college-age population, suggesting adolescents are exposing themselves to this disease, which has a long incubation period. Drugs that delay the impact of AIDS and can protect babies born of infected mothers have been developed, but there is no cure. The number of potential victims and the cost of caring for them is staggering. Without inexpensive treatment or a cure, AIDS will be among the greatest health and economic problems of the 21st century.

While the federal government has funded research and appropriated over $15 billion to fight AIDS in Africa, local communities in the United States bear most of the cost of expensive treatment for the uninsured. The epidemic has multiple effects on business and government and on social activity. Education helped reduce its spread, but drug use and unprotected sex still make thousands vulnerable to the disease.

GOVERNMENT SUPPORT OF NEW INDUSTRIES

Many changes have come about by private industry competing to produce better products. Some have come from individuals who have dreams and follow them, such as Bill Gates of Microsoft. The NASA space program is another example of how new inventions have occurred. NASA is a government program that was organized to keep the United States ahead of the Soviet Union in space exploration. While putting a man on the moon and exploring the universe, the NASA space program developed many items, from double-sided tape to Teflon, that the have come into common use. NASA's most significant influence came in electronics. The development of miniature computer chips transformed everything.

NASA also illustrates the role the federal government can play in stimulating economic development in a capitalist society. Government expenditures for space exploration did for late 20th-century economic growth what government subsidies for the railroads did for the 19th century. The Internet developed by the government for military purposes is another example of how government expenditures and research can affect economic growth. When the Internet was opened to the public, it quickly changed ways in which communication, research, and business were operated.

POPULATION SHIFTS AFFECT THE ECONOMY

During the last fifty-five years a number of important changes in American population patterns have had an economic impact on the nation. The movement of

African-Americans from the South to the cities of the East Coast and Midwest such as New York and Chicago, which was accelerated by World War I, continued throughout the century. The shift from city to suburb by affluent white Americans has already been mentioned. The problems of the inner city that resulted have also been discussed.

The growth of population in Florida, California, and the Southwest (called the Sun Belt) after World War II have made those areas increasingly important both economically and politically. These population changes will be of major significance as the Sun Belt states continue to grow and as New England and the Midwest continue to shrink in relative population. The Sun Belt states tend to be politically conservative with their relatively older population of retired persons. As the number of representatives from states is changed after each census, this population shift may have an important impact on the United States House of Representatives and its voting patterns on economic and other issues.

After the postwar surge in the birth rate, which aided the economy and produced the Baby Boom generation, the birth rate slowed. Then after a brief increase the birth rate declined in the 1980s, and as the Baby Boomers aged, so did the average age of Americans. Social Security will be affected as there are fewer young workers to pay Social Security taxes to support older, retired workers. The birth rate drop was particularly sharp among middle- and upper-class whites, where women, enjoying the liberation gained in the 1960s and early 1970s, followed careers and had fewer children or had children later.

On the other hand, the Hispanic population, which increased 61 percent in the 1970s, continued to grow rapidly through births and immigration, both legal and illegal. Illegal immigrants came to escape revolution, poverty, or both in Central America. The Hispanic-American population will soon become the largest minority group in the United States. It will form a majority of the population of California. A disproportional number of Hispanics and African and Native Americans live in rural or urban poverty. This economic disparity must be of prime concern to the United States.

> **The Hispanic percentage of the population grows rapidly.**

As population shifted to the Southwest, cities grew creating new business opportunities and problems such as issues of water supply. The climate attracted many retirees. They looked for new lifestyles to fill their time and also increased the need for health care facilities.

The American population from the days of settlement has been a mobile population. It continues as was suggested by a Pew Research Center poll in 2009. Nearly half of those polled indicated they would rather live in another location. Of people between 18 and 34, 45 percent would like to live in New York City, while families and older citizens find cities unattractive. The West proved most appealing and seven of the ten most popular metropolitan areas were in the West with Denver heading the list. The accuracy of such polls is always questionable, but if accurate, it suggests current trends of population movement will continue. The poll also revealed an interesting aspect of 2009 social patterns. Asked if they would rather live in a community with a McDonalds or a Starbucks, McDonald's won 43 to 35 percent.

AFRICAN-AMERICANS AND WOMEN IN THE WORK FORCE

African-Americans and women have always been an important part of the work force but usually in menial and low-paying positions. That began to change with the Civil Rights Movement of the 1960s. Slowly professional and business opportunities began to open for African-Americans both men and women as education improved and racial barriers fell. During the Clinton and Bush years, the African-American middle and upper classes grew, and individuals rose to become CEOs of large corporations, presidents of major universities, doctors, lawyers, politicians, and president of the United States.

> Title IX ends discrimination of women in educational institutions accepting federal funds.

Since the pre–Civil War period, rights for women and blacks have been intertwined. In 1870 in spite of the active women's suffrage movement whose leaders had supported voting rights for blacks, Amendment 15 to the Constitution granted voting rights to all males but not females, the first time gender had been mentioned in the Constitution. It wasn't until Amendment 19 in 1920 that the Constitution stated that voting "could not be denied or abridged . . . on account of sex." Again, the Civil Rights Act of 1964 ended discrimination on the basis of race but not fully on the basis of sex, an interesting comment on the values held by the members of Congress and the nation at that time. It wasn't until seven years later in 1972 after the creation of NOW and the organization of an active women's movement that discrimination against women was specifically addressed. The Education Amendments to the 1965 Act denied federal funding to any education program or activity that discriminated on the basis of sex. Title IX of the act slowly impacted women's education in many ways. By the 1990s women were entering the professions, politics, and business world in ever-increasing numbers. Poorer and minority women had for years been forced to work outside the home to support families. After Title IX and the founding of NOW, more and more women from the middle and upper classes joined the work force and the definition of the "role of women" changed rapidly. While pay discrimination remained an issue, women in leadership roles became common. As stated earlier, the first legislation signed by President Obama addressed the equal pay issue.

Key Point to Remember
Business, industry, and social changes are closely connected and should be considered together.

Links from the Past to the Present

1. Women and minorities have had to struggle to obtain equal opportunities.
2. Inventions have changed American social patterns throughout history.

Dates

1972—Title IX of Education Amendments to Civil Rights Act of 1965.

1979—Sony Walkman introduced.

1981—AIDs first diagnosed.

1982—Cell phone technology approved by FCC.

1986—Immigration Act.

1990s—AIDS reaches epidemic proportions.

1994—Clinton Health reform fails.
    Blogging begins.

1996—Farm Bill cuts subsidies.

2000—Dot-com boom ends.

2002—Farm Bill reintroduces subsidies.

2003—iPod introduced.

2004—Facebook.

2006—Wii introduced.

2007—Immigration Reform Bill fails to grant amnesty to illegal immigrants.

2008—47 million Americans lack health insurance—Health Care reform becomes a campaign issue.
    Financial Crisis—TARP.

2009—AIG Bonus scandal.

Questions
Identify each of the following:

Title IX	iPod
HMOs	Wii
AIG	Blog
TARP	Virtual office

Multiple Choice:

1. According to a Pew Research Center poll the most popular metropolitan center in the United States in 2009 was
   a. Denver.
   b. Los Angeles.
   c. Seattle.

2. The economic prosperity of the Clinton years was a result of
   a. large tax cuts for the wealthiest Americans.
   b. the rapid growth of dot-coms throughout the country.
   c. the actions of CEOs of large corporations such as Enron.

3. Many illegal immigrants come to the United States
   a. to escape poverty at home.
   b. for the excitement of crossing the border.
   c. to get a free college education.

II. Values, Diversity, and Changing Cultural and Social Patterns

RELIGION, TRADITIONAL AND FAMILY VALUES, AND SOCIAL CHANGE

Since the founding of Plymouth Plantations in 1620, religion has played an important role in American history sometimes dominating the political life and, more often, simply a factor in social behavior. Since the Nixon presidency, religion has played a more political role as televangelist spokesmen such as Pat Robinson, candidate for the Republican Party's nomination in 1988, dominated conservative, evangelical Christianity with talk of family values and opposition to any change in gender roles and gay and lesbian behavior. At the start of the 21st century, new, less political televangelists such as Mark Driscoll of Seattle, with mega churches and thousands of followers, continued to preach the conservative, social message of family values and the submission of women to their husbands. Driscoll used YouTube as many of his fire and brimstone sermons would not get through the censorship of religious TV stations. His appeal has been strong to young men, as have others who preach these family values and portray Jesus as a fighter. The message of these religious leaders is far from that of the more liberal elements found in Seattle and cities throughout the country. They suggest the "culture wars" are still being fought in 2009.

The most significant social issue that separates the country into groups that rarely listen to the other's story is the meaning of traditional values. When conservatives refer to the family, they appear to mean the "traditional, church-going, happy family" of the 1950s with a salaried father, a stay at home mother, and two children. Unfortunately, that is an idealized family that few Americans experienced even in the 1950s. Research shows that poverty, two working parents, single-parent homes, unhappy marriages often the result of a pregnancy from premarital sex, and extramarital affairs, were as prominent in the 1950s as today when even more issues—divorce, same-sex unions, unemployment, homelessness, single-teenage parents—impede on the idealized family. When liberals speak of values, they often have in mind ideas also grounded in Christian belief—take care of the poor, the uneducated, the oppressed, the widow, and the outsider. This view of traditional values leads them to respond to societal issues in ways quite different from the average conservative—increase minimum wages, put money into schools, treat women as equal under the law and in education, provide health insurance, accept minorities of all color and sexual persuasion. They are often accepting of changing patterns of sexuality and social patterns. Conservatives and liberals have their own perspective on traditional values: both perspectives are grounded in religious teachings; both have individuals committed to actively defending their ideological viewpoint. When and if conservatives and liberals will be able to agree on any common approach to the multiplicity of social changes facing the United States in the 21st century will be closely watched by social historians.

> Two views of traditional values are both founded in religious beliefs.

CULTURE WARS AND TRADITIONAL VALUES

Since the rise of the highly conservative Religious Right, there has been a struggle over so-called traditional values regarding home, gender roles, sex, and morality. Rooted in the Nixon years, the politicization of the arguments intensified especially under Presidents Reagan and George W. Bush.

At the 1992 Republican Presidential Convention, members of the conservative wing of the party made traditional values a major issue. Pat Robertson, TV evangelist of the Religious Right, praised traditional values, implying they were the only way to be a true American. Pat Buchanan, a conservative news analyst who had run against George H. W. Bush in the primaries, attacked the gay community and other groups who did not fully ascribe to his definition of traditional values. It appeared to be the ultimate statement of the "unum" perspective and denied the diversity, the pluralism, which had become a part of United States culture and society in the years since World War II. Although George H. W. Bush did not support the extremism of Buchanan, he did not reject him outright. He went on to lose the election to Bill Clinton and Al Gore. Both Clinton and Gore spoke in favor of family and of traditional values, but they acknowledged diversity and pluralism. Clinton gained strong support from the gay community. The struggle over and the definition of values—both traditional and changing—is far from over.

The struggle appears in many areas. For instance, in March 2009 the head of the Catholic Church, Pope Benedict on a tour of Africa where the AIDs epidemic rages and the use of condoms has been proven to reduce its spread, condemned their use while insisting abstinence was the only Christian method of birth control. The message appalled many African and world leaders who have been fighting AIDS in their countries. In the United States, conservative Protestant churches support the Pope's stand and Congressional conservatives following George W. Bush's lead have supported abstinence-only sex education in the public schools, and in some communities have stopped the distribution of condoms in public high schools to sexually active teenagers. More liberal groups believe that to reduce teen pregnancy, which did decrease slightly during the prosperous years of the Clinton and Bush presidencies, information on birth control and sexually transmitted diseases must be made available to young people. President Obama has endorsed "age appropriate" sex education for the public schools. This is just one area where value differences have been incorporated into the political dialogue.

> Republican-controlled Congress supports abstinence-only sex education.

Another is abortion where the pro-life/pro-choice struggle continues with pro-life advocates holding vigils outside abortion clinics throughout the country, both sides organizing parades on January 22, the anniversary of the *Roe* v. *Wade* Supreme Court decision, and pro-choice legislators introducing bills that require pharmacists to provide birth control information even if the individual pharmacist is religiously opposed. States struggle with the abortion issue. The South Dakota legislature passed a total antiabortion law in 2006 that the voters overturned in a referendum that fall. Voters rejected another attempt to ban abortion in 2008. That year voters in Colorado rejected a pro-life referendum that defined the fertilized egg as a person with full constitutional rights, and California rejected a referendum that would require 18-year-old women to get parental permission for an abortion and to wait 48 hours. In 2009 the North Dakota legislature passed a bill bestowing "personhood" on the fertilized egg. The conflict over abortion and the start of human life will continue as both sides are committed to their positions and rarely hear the other's side. Polls suggest that the majority of Americans support abortion in particular circumstances.

THE DEATH PENALTY

Another area where the value of human life enters the debate centers on the use of the death penalty. The Supreme Court has handed down conflicting opinions over its constitutionality as a "cruel and unusual" punishment ending its use for two years in the 1970s. During the George W. Bush years, the court limited the death penalty use. No longer may the death penalty be used in cases involving minors (2005) or mentally retarded individuals (2002) even in cases where they are found guilty of murder. Reversing the position they hold on abortion, many conservatives support the death penalty as a deterrent, while liberals view it as unnecessary and cruel.

States have control over the use of the death penalty but must follow the Court's interpretation of its use under the Constitution. Since 1970 Texas has executed four times more individuals as the next state, Virginia. Two states, New Jersey (2007) and New Mexico (2009) have eliminated the death penalty. Recently the cost factor—because of the cost of appeals, it is much more expensive to execute people than to imprison them—has entered the argument along with the moral and ethical issues. The European Union considers the death penalty a violation of human rights and refuses to extradite to the United States any criminal or terrorist accused of crimes for which they might receive the death penalty in a U.S. trial. The arguments will continue and reflects the complexity of the "culture wars" and the meaning of the value of life.

VALUES AND INTERNATIONAL RELATIONS

The Universal Declaration of Human Rights includes both political and civil rights particularly supported and valued by the United States and economic and cultural rights supported by many developing nations. The UN adopted declaration on

> **UN Declaration of Human Rights includes both civil and economic rights.**

Human Rights was a compromise between the Soviet Union and the United States in which the views of each on human rights were included in one document. The United States continues to support those rights that came from the English tradition while often ignoring other rights in the UN declaration.

Values, civil rights, and international relations became entwined in the United States in the 1960s when African nations were achieving independence, while segregation prevailed in much of the South. They continue to be interconnected. The United States has supported human rights, particularly political and civil, throughout the world. Part of the neo-con rationale for the War in Iraq was to bring democracy and human rights to Iraq and to end the use of torture by Saddam Hussein as a way to deny human rights to his people. This was in keeping with the position the United

States had long supported. The revelation of the use of torture by the Bush administration in Iraq and in the War on Terrorism shocked most Americans and diminished America's image abroad. It appeared a denial of a fundamental American value. Yet two views were expressed by the people—the U.S. must protect itself at any cost, and the United States must not abuse human rights any where at any time. These conflicting positions revealed another aspect of the argument over traditional values and their meaning.

The United States in the War on Terrorism supports human rights but continues to debate what that means. Islamic fundamentalists offer an entirely different perspective on the world—one tied to the Koran, Sharia law (or law as interpreted by early Islamic scholars), and male dominance. In this global context, Americans appear to be united in their view; nevertheless, the religiously driven culture war presents a less than unified vision to the world.

RACISM, SEXISM, AND GENDER

The election of an African-American as president of the United States was haled as an indication that racism was ended. It was a hopeful sign, but comments heard on the campaign trail and elsewhere clearly indicated many Americans still did not accept the equality of the races. Racism has roots that go deep and that provide different manifestations in different areas and among different groups. For instance, the case of black football star O. J. Simpson accused of the murder of his white wife and her boyfriend reflect how differing groups interpret race-based information. An all-black jury in 1995 Los Angeles acquitted Simpson. In a civil trial for damages, and all-white jury found him guilty. One can find similar incidents involving other races and other incidents. By 2009, the situation for African-Americans had improved tremendously since the 1960s. The same was true for women, but not for all minorities. In 2009, the gay community was still involved in a fight for their rights.

In 1987 Boulder, Colorado, site of the University of Colorado, passed the first in the nation public ordnance giving rights to gays, but there was a backlash. The voters approved a

> Homophobic attacks on gays continue.

constitutional amendment denying civil rights to gays. The state earned the title the "hate state." The state Supreme Court in 1993 declared the amendment unconstitutional—an infringement on the rights guaranteed by the U.S. Constitution. In 2004 voters in Colorado approved a referendum banning gay marriage and the expansion of any rights for gays. In 1994 Irish-Catholic organizers of the Boston St. Patrick's Day parade refused to allow a gay group to participate, and the courts upheld them as the parade was considered a private not a public event. In 1998 in Wyoming two men chained a gay young man to a fence, beat him, and left him to die. The cruelty horrified many, but attacks on gays continue. While discrimination against and fear of homosexual males has received publicity throughout much of American history, lesbian, bisexual, and transgender individuals have experienced the same attitudes.

In the 1970s gays and lesbians began to organize and speak out. Formed in 1987 to combat AIDS, ActUp caught public attention. Support groups for gays in different businesses and organizations formed including one of West Point graduates in 2009 to support gays in the military.

Gay and lesbian groups formed at many colleges, and schools and support groups can be found throughout the country. Attempts by young people to explain their sexuality and avoid a life "in the closet" adds a new dimension to society.

In the 1992 election, the gay community exercised its political power by supporting Clinton, who actively sought their support. In return, as one of his first actions, Clinton tried to change the law that forbid homosexuals to serve in the military (see page 386).

> Clinton is forced to compromise on the issue of gays in the military.

While homophobia is still prevalent in American society, as a result of the Gay Rights Movement, it is now possible for gays in many communities to work openly and to live productive and fruitful lives. It clearly reflects the diversity in America today and the acceptance by some of new attitudes.

GAY MARRIAGE, ADOPTION, AND DIVERSITY

As society has slowly become more accepting of diversity, the entire GLBT (gay, lesbian, bisexual, transgender) community has found greater acceptance. However, two issues, adoption and marriage rights, became divisive social and political issues during the Clinton and Bush administrations and continue to illustrate the national conflicts over traditional and family values, gender roles, and sexuality.

As gay individuals applied to adopt children, there was a backlash centering on the definition of male/female roles and the suitability of gays as parents. The belief that gay parents would teach their adopted children to be gay underlay the debate. It was based on the widely asserted assumption that homosexuality was a choice. An idea the medical profession had rejected as research indicated homosexuality was determined by the genetic code. Other arguments such as children of gay parents would be discriminated against in school were rejected. With a few exceptions gay individuals have been allowed to adopt children, but there are those who still strongly disapprove. However, in 2008 a federal court ruled that the equal protection clause of the federal Constitution applies to adoption and that any adoption permitted in one state is legal elsewhere and must be recognized under federal law. The same is not true of gay marriage.

The same-sex or gay marriage issue began quietly in 1970 when a gay couple in Minnesota was denied a marriage license. They appealed to the U.S. Supreme Court, but the Court refused to hear the case. In 1975 in Colorado the Boulder County clerk issued a marriage license to a male couple—an American and an Australian—who were married. When the Australian applied for citizenship as a spouse, it was denied, and the courts upheld the decision. Cases continued during the 1980s with gays continually losing. Then in the 1990s, a case centering on the interpretation of Hawaii's marriage laws caught national attention, and the issue of same-sex marriage exploded. Conservatives rallied around traditional family values arguing that same-sex marriage would destroy the family. Congress under Republican control passed in 1996 the Defense of Marriage Act (DOMA) defining marriage as between a man and a woman. President Clinton signed it indicating the issue crossed party lines. Congress debated a constitutional amendment on the topic.

In 1999, the Vermont Court declared the Vermont marriage law discriminatory and left it up to the state legislature to give gays equal rights to all the legal benefits that go with marriage. This had been at the heart of the issue for many as marriage conveys rights of inheritance, hospital visitation, family insurance, and many other civil rights denied to unmarried couples. Vermont in 2000 approved a civil union law conveying on participants all the civil privileges of marriage but not calling a same-sex union a marriage. In 2003 the Massachusetts Supreme Court declared that the state's marriage law was unconstitutional and that civil unions would not create equality. Same-sex marriage therefore became legal. There was a rush of weddings in the state. Again family values appeared threatened. The Religious Right, the Focus on the Family group, and other such organizations, as well as many churches, such as the Mormons and Catholics, and conservatives coalesced to protect marriage as they understood it—an institution based on the Bible whose purpose was procreation and the creation of a family. The result was a series of state constitutional amendments either banning same-sex marriage or defining marriage as between a man and a woman. By 2009, twenty-nine states had such amendments. However, there were eleven states that had passed civil union laws giving civil rights to same-sex couples. In 2008 Connecticut and California, where same-sex marriage had been an issue for a decade, allowed same sex marriage. Voters overturned the law in a California referendum.

> **Massachusetts declares state marriage law discriminatory and allows gay marriage.**

The issue split the country and the split illustrates the complexity of reaching agreements where differences are rooted in views of traditional values. If marriage is a religious commitment as tradition suggests, it raises the question of the separation of church and state. Should the government provide licenses for a religious event or should it only provide the legal rights of a civil union to all who wish to live together? Religious bodies would determine who might participate in the religious ceremony of marriage. While a solution of this type has been discussed, it is hard for both sides to hear the other's story. Partisanship and arguments over family values drive the debate. Resolution may not come until the next generation controls the political structure.

In general, the younger generation appeared more open to changes in family structure and acceptance of gender differences. The Sexual Revolution of the 1960s affected their upbringing by the Baby Boomer generation. During the Clinton and Bush presidencies high school and college age students lived a much freer and more relaxed lifestyle that continued in adulthood. Advertising, TV programs, movies, the Internet, magazines, and the openness of the gay community made young people more aware of the diversity in the nation, and in most cases, young people were more accepting than their parents of this diversity. In spite of the AIDS epidemic, sexual relations were more open, co-habitation was common starting with mixed gender dormitories in college and continuing until marriage, and the opportunity to meet and socialize with gays and lesbians was much greater than in earlier years.

> **Younger generation appears more tolerant than older individuals.**

Many in the generation had never experienced the "traditional family of the 1950s" having lived with single or divorced parents.

GLOBAL WARMING AND SOCIETY

Another issue that has separated conservatives and liberals, Republicans and Democrats, is the environment. Beginning with Nixon, the government has passed laws concerning cleaner air and water, pollution control, and automobile emissions. The question of global warming became an international issue with the signing of the United Nations Convention on Climate and Development at the Earth Summit in Rio de Janeiro in 1992. The Kyoto Protocols to that treaty signed in Japan in 1997 provided details to which the United States objected. Neither Clinton nor Bush presented the Protocols to the Senate for approval, Bush argued against their provisions calling them anti-economic growth and unfair to developed nations. Only the United States, Zimbabwe, Chad, Somalia, Iraq, and Afghanistan have not signed the Protocols. Negotiations for international agreements continue.

Al Gore, after his defeat for the presidency, became a strong spokesman for action on global warming. (See page 409.) The George W. Bush administration's policies and manipulation of scientific data defeated efforts to address the matter. President Obama's announced policies suggest a new U.S. approach to science and global warming. By 2009 most scientists believed the earth was warming, that part of the cause was due to human activity, that change in the use of fossil fuels would slow

This cartoon, again produced in Australia, shows the universal concern with global warming. It suggests people need to be really shocked and personally touched by events before they take action. In this case, the couple sees a chicken laying an egg that fries on the highway— an indication of the increasing warming of the earth.

the warming over time, and that research into new sources of energy could produce alternatives and new industrial developments. Whether societies can respond and address global warming together is far from clear as the world moves into economic recession.

NUCLEAR ISSUES

One alternative to burning fossil fuels is the use of nuclear power to create electric power. Its appeal is the lack of carbon emissions. The negatives include cost and the failure to agree on a plan for the storage of nuclear waste. As the George W. Bush administration warned, terrorists could do great damage if they got a nuclear bomb from a rogue nation or from poorly secured weapons in Russia or elsewhere. They could also attack a nuclear power plant.

> Nuclear power considered as a clean alternative to fossil fuels.

Throughout the Cold War, nuclear weapons treaties were signed with the Soviet Union. Negotiations continued after the war's end and agreements on the storage and reduction of nuclear arsenals were signed. However, the announcement of the Bush Doctrine and withdrawal from the Anti-Ballistic Missile Treaty created tensions with the Russian leadership and opened the possibility of the creation of a new generation of nuclear weapons and defense. In the meantime, the number of nations with nuclear weapons increased. Negotiations with North Korea, who has tested weapons, and Iran, who in 2009 clearly was building a nuclear capacity, were not just issues of foreign policy but of the future state of the planet.

EDUCATION

The No Child Left Behind Act was considered a major achievement of the George W. Bush administration. It was meant to bring accountability and improvement to education. The Act was never fully funded so its effectiveness cannot be truly evaluated. Improvements were to be measured by tests, which easily lead to teaching to the test—a method that often limits effective education. American education, as measured by test scores, lags behind that of many developed nations and, in math, remains behind China. Changes are needed as a lack of education condemns a person to a lower economic status in this computer age. Often the poorest schools are in minority areas perpetuating a gap between the economic level of whites and minorities. High school dropout rates in these areas remain high. The solution is complex, but one element must include the latest educational research. Such research supports the idea there are different learning and teaching styles and to reach all children, the different styles must be employed. Also research shows that parental involvement and a safe environment for students are essential for the most effective learning to take place. The Obama administration announced it wanted to address educational change, but whether it will be successful depends on many variables including the state of the economy and the willingness of teacher unions to address tenure, evaluation, salary scales, and different teaching styles. Reform also involves issues of traditional values.

COLLEGE ENROLLMENTS* 1980–2006

Gender Race	1980	1990	2000	2006
Male	5,430	6,192	6,683	7,427
Female	5,957	7,429	8,631	9,593
White	9,925	11,488	11,999	13,112
Black	1,163	1,393	2,164	2,304
Male	476	587	815	886
Female	686	807	1,349	1,418
Hispanic	443	748	1,426	1,914
Total	11,387	13,621	15,314	17,020

Source U.S. Census Bureau: *Current Population Reports—2009*.

* 5,430 means 5,430,000.

One area of success in education in recent years is in the number enrolled in college. The success of Title IX can be seen in the numbers of women, both minority and white, now in college. They account for almost 60 percent of those enrolled. This high rate raises a sociological question for the future. For years African-American women have achieved higher educational levels than African-American men, which has affected the family structure and the role of women as the source of higher earnings. As the population of educated white women grows, how will it affect their earning power and their social relations with men?

> More women seek college education.

SUPREME COURT DECISIONS AND SOCIAL CHANGE

The Supreme Court was considered a conservative court under Chief Justices Rehnquist (1985–2005) and Roberts (2005–), yet many decisions were decided by 5–4 margins suggesting the Court reflected the political and social divisions in the country. The 2000 5–4 decision in *Bush* v. *Gore* that determined the 2000 election was probably the most important case settled by the Rehnquist Court and will rank among the most important in U.S. history. The decision reflected the social divisions in the nation.

The Rehnquist Court reaffirmed *Roe* v. *Wade* in *Planned Parenthood* v. *Casey* (1992) supporting the woman's right to abortion in the first trimester. In *Lawrence* v. *Texas* (2003) the court declared in a 6–3 decision that a Texas law restricting specific individual sexual acts among gays was unconstitutional. Thus homosexual sex was decriminalized. The decision stated, "Our laws and tradition afford constitutional protection to personal decisions relating to marriage, procreation, contraception, family relationships, child rearing, and education." The breadth of the statement led some to believe the court might support a same-sex marriage law. Clearly these court decisions were supportive of changing sexual and moral behavior in the country (see page 399).

In the Roberts Court, in *Gonzales* v. *Carhart* (2007), the Court upheld the federal ban on partial birth abortions reversing a previous decision. The Court stated the difference in the two cases was that the federal law allowed for the procedure's use to

> Roberts Court restricts abortion rights.

protect a woman's life. Where the Court might go in future decisions is uncertain, but the Court, with its two new Bush appointed members, is considered more conservative learning than the Rehnquist Court.

The Roberts Court also upheld an Indiana law requiring a photo I.D. before voting. Opponents of the law argued that minorities and the poor were less likely to have such I.D.s and thus the law was discriminating against them, another example of the social/political division in the country. The Court also upheld lethal injection as an acceptable way of carrying out the death penalty. However, the Court rejected the death penalty in the case of the rape of a child in which the child did not die. These varied decisions affirm the importance of the Supreme Court as citizens seek to change social patterns through the courts.

TELEVISION AND SOCIETY

Television continued to be a major source for entertainment with A. C. Nielson, the TV rating organization, reporting that 99 percent of homes had at least one TV set, and the average viewer watched twenty-eight hours of TV a week, the equivalent of approximately two months a year. The report stated the average 8 to 18 year old watched four hours of TV a day, and by 18 had seen 200,000 acts of violence. Starting in 2000 TV manufacturers were required to include in each set a V-chip that allowed parents to control the amount of violence seen, but there was no control over news and sports programs or commercials. There was continuing debate as to the impact on children's behavior of watching violence on TV and in movies. And there was a strong disagreement between producers and parent organizations. Studies showed that children watching over four hours of TV were apt to be overweight and that TV watching contributed to the epidemic of obesity in the nation. The American Academy of Pediatrics acknowledges the educational and entertainment benefits of TV but recommended only one or two hours of quality TV viewing be allowed children. TV obviously has both good and bad features for society.

The television coverage of the destruction of the World Trade Center on September 11, 2001, created a unity among the American people that could not have been achieved in any other way. The attack on Pearl Harbor in 1941 brought the nation together, but the lack of the immediate visual experience made it less of a shared emotional event.

With more than 800 channels to choose from and competition from computers, videos, and movies, TV industry profits were threatened. Compounding the problem were increasing costs of salaries for stars of TV shows such as *Seinfeld* and *Friends* and of contracts for sporting coverage such as the NBA, NFL, and the Olympics.

Beginning in the late 1970s, salaries of professional athletes skyrocketed, as did those of movie and rock stars, all of whom justified their salaries by the fact their earning period was "limited" and they had to make their money fast. Professional baseball salaries reached such levels that the owners attempted to cap the salaries, which led to strikes stopping the season several times for this all-American game. More and more, five- to seven-year contracts for over $100,000,000 are offered, which compares very favorably to the salaries plus stock options for top

> High salaries and celebrity status of sports stars attract young people.

CEOs. Television coverage has made such sports salaries possible. And the seasons of the professional clubs are now determined by the TV networks. Sports seasons no longer run by the seasonal calendar. Football runs from summer to winter on TV. In ice hockey, originally a winter sport, the NHL ends its season in June after an endless playoff series. All of this is geared to gaining audiences, especially 18- to 35-year-old males, who have great potential spending power.

Sports coverage was not limited to professional sports as television covered college football and basketball. The hype for the final four in college basketball rivaled that for the professional football Super Bowl, all reflecting the fanaticism of sports fans. Golf, sparked by the magnetic Tiger Woods, and NASCAR racing gained fans and extensive TV coverage. Even soccer, the world's most popular sport but never very popular in the United States, was getting TV coverage.

At the start of the 21st century, reality TV became a craze with shows such as *Survivor*. Reality TV shows were much cheaper to produce. They placed people, not actors, in a variety of challenging or embarrassing situations that entertained

Reality shows proliferate on TV.

millions. By March 2009 more than 450 reality TV series had appeared and 20 were still on the air competing with sports channels devoted to a team or sport, news channels, and traditional sitcoms, dramas, and police shows. Talk shows, such as Oprah Winfrey's, had many viewers both overseas and at home. Her endorsement of books had great affect on their popularity. Her endorsement of Obama for president encouraged the African-American community to support him. Both endorsements illustrate the impact of TV and TV celebrities on U.S. society.

In 1996 two new cable news channels were created, the FOX Newspaper chain of Rupert Murdoch started the FOX TV news channel. It has a more conservative approach than MSNBC founded by Microsoft and NBC news in the same year. Individuals can pick their source of news and entertainment based on their personal views and interests isolating themselves from other's stories and points of view.

In 2009 all analog TV broadcast was to stop, converting the nation to digital broadcast only. The former analog wavelengths were needed for new computer-driven technology.

American shows have long dominated international TV programming. The culture and values presented in these shows are what most people identify as American. Consider what impressions of American life and values foreigners get as a result of seeing them. This is the culture for which the United States is known worldwide. Is it representative of what we are as a nation? Do *Dallas*, *ER*, *Seinfeld*, *Friends*, *American Idol*, or *NYPD Blue*, reflect real life in America as you live it? When foreign leaders or individuals denounce America, too often all they have learned about the United States has come from TV, popular music, the Internet, and movies.

With the advent of around-the-clock news coverage, the educational potential of television grew as people throughout the world had instant access to fast developing news stories. There were negatives to this instant access. News channels rushed to present the breaking news with little time for analysis, and the same pictures were repeated over and over. This opening of information became a factor in the War on Terrorism as Arab TV channels presented news that differed from the U.S. news channels. Great Britain and China both offered international news broadcasts.

RADIO TALK SHOWS

Radio talk shows are another popular source of information for Americans. The format gives control to the hosts, who introduce a topic and then invite listeners to call in with comments on local issues ranging from taxes to sports, but many are nationally syndicated. Like blogs and the Internet talk shows provide an opportunity for the public to express personal opinions regardless of their source or accuracy. Some talk show formats bring to the air well-qualified experts on topics and allow listeners to call in with questions. Such shows were more likely to provide information than opinion.

> Radio talk shows are both local and national.

After the 1994 election, analysis showed that many of the radio talk shows were very conservative, and many continue to be. For years, conservatives accused the press of being controlled by liberals—the press claims the talk shows are controlled by conservatives. Several hosts gained a large national following.

Limbaugh's show began in 1988 and during the Clinton presidency became popular as he bashed the president and Democrats on over 600 stations. Under Bush he supported all his actions and was the voice of the conservative Republicans. After McCain's defeat, opponents labeled Limbaugh the "voice of the Republican Party" as he bashed Obama's policies and wished him failure. In 2004, Al Franken, former *Saturday Night Live* writer, became a voice for more liberal views as Democrats fought back on the airwaves. Again one could listen to the story he or she preferred.

THE MOVIE INDUSTRY

Movie production both in the United States and abroad has increased greatly in recent years. The quality of films varies widely, but paralleling or reflecting the increase in violence and the more open expression of sexuality in American society, movie makers included increasing amounts of violence, sex, and nudity in their films since the 1960s. Many critics abhorred the increasing portrayal of violence and sex, but it sold movies. Film makers claimed there was no proven connection between violence shown on the screen and violence in society. However, several studies indicate there is a correlation. The controversy over the impact of movie and TV violence on human behavior continues.

From the early days the movie industry developed ways to police itself and control what was portrayed, thus avoiding government censorship. After World War II, rating standards were developed. In 1990 a new listing was added, "R-17"—no one under 17 admitted—to identify movies that were sexually explicit and violent but did not deserve the "X" rating given to pornographic movies. Previews are often rated "approved for a general audience" but show uninterrupted violence, leading some to question the standards of the movie industry.

> Films are increasingly more explicit in portraying crime and sexual violence.

Generally Hollywood has avoided the controversial issues of the day. An illustration of Hollywood's sensitivity to the mood of the viewing public is its reaction to the destruction of the World Trade Center in 2001. Several studios held up the release of films for months because they contained material or presented

> Occasionally, films deal with controversial issues of the day.

a story line that might remind viewers of the destruction. Occasionally issues such as interracial dating explored in *Guess Who's Coming to Dinner* (1967), AIDS shown in *Philadelphia* (1993), schizophrenia, the theme of *A Beautiful Mind* (2001), homosexual love, the story line of *Brokeback Mountain* (2006), and gay activism portrayed in *Milk* (2008) have been presented. Such films help society to gain a better understanding of social issues. Occasionally, Hollywood has produced films based on a true situation that provides the public insights into political and social issues. *Erin Brockovitch* (2000) showed how a persistent woman was able to bring a large polluting power company to justice. Julia Roberts, possibly the most popular actress of the 1990s, starred. The theme had appeal to an environmentally concerned public and illustrated the potential power of Hollywood to publicize causes. The film won several Oscars.

The large Hollywood companies produce mainly films considered safe as box office hits. Robert Redford, a star since *Butch Cassidy and the Sundance Kid* (1969), organized a film festival, Sundance, to showcase films by independent producers. This provided an outlet for low-budget and experimental productions to get attention.

Animated movies became more sophisticated and popular as computer technology improved. Topics ranged from light entertainment, *Shrek* (2001) the story of an ogre, to serious social issues, *Waltz with Bashir* (2008) concerning the Israeli/Palestinian conflict.

Fantasy, whether science fiction or earthly as in the hugely popular *Lord of the Rings: The Fellowship of the Ring* (2001), has been popular for years, as have films based on best-selling novels. However, too often readers are disappointed with the film version. *Harry Potter and the Sorcerer's Stone* (2001) was a particularly successful adaptation. Successful films like *Spiderman* (2002), *Harry Potter*, and *Lord of the Rings* can make millions of dollars in the opening weekend and then look forward to later income from TV showings and sales of DVDs. The film industry is a major export industry for the United States and brings in large amounts of foreign currency. In 2008 the Batman movie, *The Black Knight*, and *Indiana Jones and the Kingdom of the Crystal Skull* each earned over $460 million overseas and the entire film industry earned $9.9 billion. Movies provide entertainment, role models in their stars, insights into the current culture, and escape from daily concerns as seen in the increase of ticket sales in 2009 as the financial crisis worsened.

LITERATURE, MUSIC, AND THE ARTS

In 2007 in spite of the appeal of the Internet, TV, DVDs, and the availability of e-books and Kindle, libraries were still checking out roughly 3 million items a day. American authors wrote on every topic, and readers with favorite authors, such as John Grisham and David Baldacci, put their newest novels on

> Toni Morrison wins Nobel Prize for Literature for her works on African-American life.

the best-seller lists. The Pulitzer Prize Committee awards identified noteworthy books and often introduced new authors to the American public. Many awards went to established writers such as John Updike in 1991 for *Rabbit at Rest*. Updike for fifty years recorded the lives of ordinary Americans living in New England. Toni

Morrison, one of the finest living American writers, was the winner for *Beloved* in 1988. She won the Nobel Prize for Literature in 1993 for her works on African-American life. Cormac McCarthy, the Pulitzer Price winner for literature in 2007 for *The Road*, is a younger writer noted for his sparse tales of the West. American authors, while sometimes criticized by foreigners for being "too provincial," continued to provide important insights into the changing diversity, values, and culture of the nation.

The Pulitzer Committee occasionally gives awards to recognize special contributions to American culture by individuals. Two musicians, Duke Ellington in 1999 and Bob Dylan in 2008, received recognition. Both men's careers spanned years, and both had profound impact on the musical world. Even though there was much popular music during the Clinton and Bush years, no one affected the music scene as had Elvis Presley and the Beatles. A few individuals and bands from the 1960s, 1970s, and 1980s continued to perform supported by the Boomers. Computer-generated changes in the music scene made it possible for any high school student to organize a band and put music on YouTube. The TV reality show, *American Idol*, the most popular TV show for four years, produced a new star each year and many runners-up broke into the music scene. The quality and lasting power of popular stars changed as a result.

> Duke Ellington and Bob Dylan are acknowledged for their many contributions to American music.

The music industry continues to adapt as new electronic devices enter the market. Since *The Chorus Line* on Broadway in 1975, it has been possible to individually amplify the stage voices of actors and singers. Now instant corrections can be made to a singer's pitch so the listener no longer hears the true voice of the performer. One must therefore question the quality of today's stars when compared to those of the past. Music has always been a part of American culture and will be in the future; however, how the music will be produced and how it will be delivered to the public will change.

Broadway for years had been the goal of actors and, in spite of rising costs of production and changing tastes, continued to be their mecca. However, local theater groups throughout the nation provided high-quality theater and opportunity to aspiring actors. The same held true for classical musicians. Local orchestras increased in quality, and summer festivals brought musicians together from all over the country. Even though they are a minor part of the entertainment world, theater and concert have been part of American culture since colonial days. Minstrel shows, vaudeville, Shakespeare productions, and opera, were part of 19th and early 20th century America. Many western mining towns boasted opera houses and a few still exist. Live productions provide an experience different from that of radio, movie, or TV.

The art scene in the United States at the beginning of the 21st century was as diverse as the population. Artists representing every school from extreme abstraction to detailed realism could be found and were popular. Prices for art works of familiar painters soared, and works of famous photographers were popular. Many middle- and upper-class individuals enjoyed painting for pleasure. The art world may be hurt by the financial recession, but there are those who use art as an investment. Computer-generated enhancements and creations added a new dimension to works of traditional art reflecting the impact of the computer on all areas of life.

CONCLUSION

As President Obama entered his third month in office, the financial crisis continued to dominate the news. How it will appear in the long sweep of history will not be clear for a generation. However, it is clear that even though there is great diversity and different perspectives on economic policy, social mores, and values, there is strength in the American people. While each individual has his or her own story, the nation together has moved through crises before as the people came together to solve problems as a united country. While daily activity in Congress and the fluctuations of the stock market make headlines, underneath there appeared a willingness to come together, guided by fairness and hard wok, to create the next period of the nation's history.

The computer and electronic industries revolutionized life for the individual at the end of the 20th century. New challenges in green technology and the reconstruction of financial organizations have the potential to change life in the 21st century. As the people of the nation live their stories, share them, and learn from others, the future will unfold. Readers like you will do the writing of that history.

Key Point to Remember

Both conservative and liberal American values that were defended in the culture wars of the late 20th and early 21st centuries had roots in American history, traditions, and religious understandings.

People to Remember

Bob Dylan   Singer-songwriter, author, poet, social critic, "guiding spirit of the countercultural revolution (of the 1960s)"—*Time*; combined rock and folk music; produced lyrics that were political, social, philosophical, and literary over five decades; awarded special Pulitzer Prize for his "profound impact on popular music and American culture marked by lyrical compositions of extraordinary power."

Rush Limbaugh   Host of *Rush Limbaugh Show* on AM radio; conservative political commentator; called "leader of the opposition" during Clinton presidency and "voice of Republican Party" at start of Obama's presidency; best-selling author.

Links from the Past to the Present

1. Government support of research and industry from railroads to the Internet has aided the growth of the American economy.

2. From the founding of Plymouth to the present, religious-based values have dominated America's social life.

3. Economic crises have occurred periodically throughout U.S. history.

Dates

1992—*Casey* v. *Planned Parenthood.*

1993—"Don't ask; don't tell" compromise for gays in the military.

1996—Defense of marriage Act (DOMA).

      Fox News and MSNBC cable news channels started.

1997—Kyoto Protocols agreement.

1999—Vermont Court declares state marriage law is discriminatory.

2000—Vermont introduces civil unions for same-sex couples.

2002—No Child Left Behind Act.

2003—Massachusetts Supreme Court decision permits same-sex marriages.

2007—*Gonzales* v. *Carhart* accepts federal law banning partial birth abortions.

2009—All analog TV broadcasts replaced by digital broadcasts.

Questions
Identify each of the following:

DOMA

GLBT

Lawrence v. *Texas*

Televangelist

Universal Declaration of Human Rights

Kyoto Protocols

Bush v. *Gore*

Civil Union

Multiple Choice:

1. An illustration of the influence of TV on Americans is the TV talk show hosted by
   a. Rush Limbaugh.
   b. Oprah Winfrey.
   c. Bob Dylan.

2. According to recent decisions of the United States Supreme Court concerning the death penalty, it may not be used to punish
   a. military officers.
   b. women.
   c. mentally retarded.

3. Neither President Clinton nor President George W. Bush was prepared to submit to the Senate for a vote the
   a. Kyoto Protocols.
   b. Anti-Ballistic Missile Treaty.
   c. Universal Declaration of Human Rights.

Open-ended, Analysis Questions and Review

At the end of each chapter throughout the book several questions requiring reflection and analysis have been included. As a review of your study, it would be helpful to review those questions at this time. That will remind you of the important issues and themes that occur throughout American history.

    The following two questions are based on themes that are important in this chapter but that run through all of United States history. As a review in addition to considering these two questions, your study would benefit by some time spent listing major themes that you have studied and then writing or asking yourself questions that involve those themes. Making up your own questions for a test is an excellent way to review history.

1. To what extent have religion and religious values been of significance in the making of political decisions throughout United States history?

   Suggestion: First, consider what you believe is meant by "religion and religious values" and then pick several periods in United States history in which you believe they were important or not important in making political decisions. Among the times you might wish to consider are the writing of the Constitution; the abolition movement; Reconstruction; the Spanish-American War and the start of the "American Empire"; entry into World War I; The Great Depression and New Deal; attitudes toward the Soviet Union (or communism in general) during the Cold War; the Reagan presidency; George W. Bush's "compassionate conservatism."

2. "United States history is nothing but a history of economic crises."

   Evaluate the above statement drawing on your knowledge of United States history since 1789.

Appendix

Twenty-four Significant Dates

Twenty-three of the dates included in this list of twenty-four significant dates in American history appeared on the majority of the responses of over fifty high school and college teachers to the following request made in 1991: "Please list the ten most significant dates in American history." While the dates listed at the end of each section provide important chronological information, as do the years of presidents' terms in office, these dates, because of the general agreement on their importance, should be learned by all students.

| *Dates* | *Significance* |

1492—First voyage to America by Columbus.

1607—Founding of the first English settlement at Jamestown.

1620—Pilgrim's arrival at Plymouth in New England.

1763—Peace of Paris ends French and Indian War.

1776—Declaration of American Independence.

1789—Ratification of United States Constitution and start of new government.

1800—Election of Thomas Jefferson transfers power to new political party for first time.

1850—Compromise of 1850 delays Civil War for ten years.

1860—Election of Lincoln; secession of states of the deep South and establishment of CSA.

1861—Start of Civil War.

1865—End of Civil War; assassination of Lincoln; Reconstruction begins.

1896—Election of McKinley marks end of Populist Movement.

1898—Spanish-American War.

1914—World War I begins in Europe; United States neutrality.

1917—United States enters World War I.

1929—Wall St. Stock Market Crash starts the Great Depression.

1941—Pearl Harbor; United States enters World War II.

1945—V-E and V-J Days end World War II in Europe and Pacific.

1954—Armistice ends fighting in Korean War.

1968—Tet Offensive in Vietnam; antiwar demonstrations; riots at Democratic Convention.

1974—Resignation of President Nixon after Watergate scandal.

1980—Election of Reagan marks conservative political swing.

1989—End of Cold War; fall of Berlin Wall and political changes in Eastern Europe.

2001—World Trade Center Twin Towers in New York City destroyed by terrorists and Pentagon damaged; War on Terrorism declared.

The United States with Date of Entry into the Union

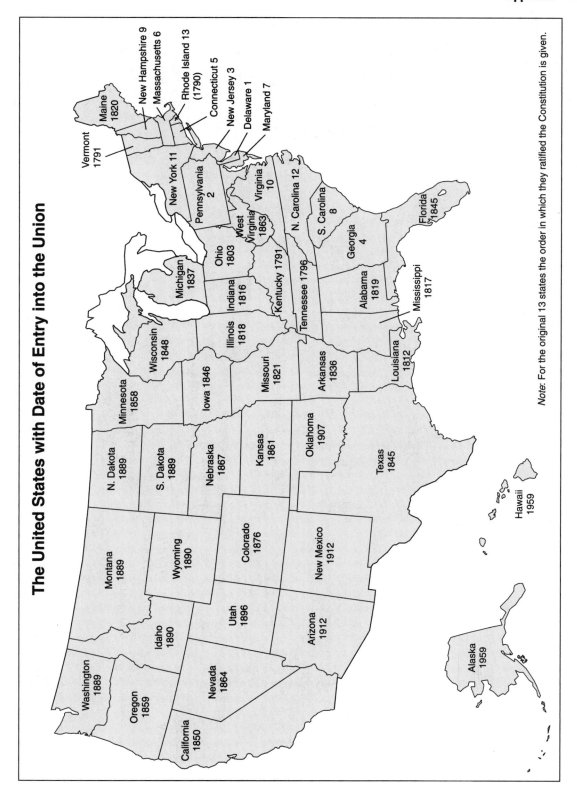

New Hampshire 9
Massachusetts 6
Rhode Island 13 (1790)
Connecticut 5
New Jersey 3
Delaware 1
Maryland 7

Maine 1820
Vermont 1791
New York 11
Pennsylvania 2
West Virginia 1863
Virginia 10
N. Carolina 12
S. Carolina 8
Florida 1845
Ohio 1803
Kentucky 1791
Tennessee 1796
Georgia 4
Alabama 1819
Michigan 1837
Indiana 1816
Illinois 1818
Wisconsin 1848
Missouri 1821
Arkansas 1836
Mississippi 1817
Louisiana 1812
Minnesota 1858
Iowa 1846
Oklahoma 1907
Texas 1845
N. Dakota 1889
S. Dakota 1889
Nebraska 1867
Kansas 1861
Montana 1889
Wyoming 1890
Colorado 1876
New Mexico 1912
Idaho 1890
Utah 1896
Arizona 1912
Washington 1889
Oregon 1859
Nevada 1864
California 1850
Hawaii 1959
Alaska 1959

Note: For the original 13 states the order in which they ratified the Constitution is given.

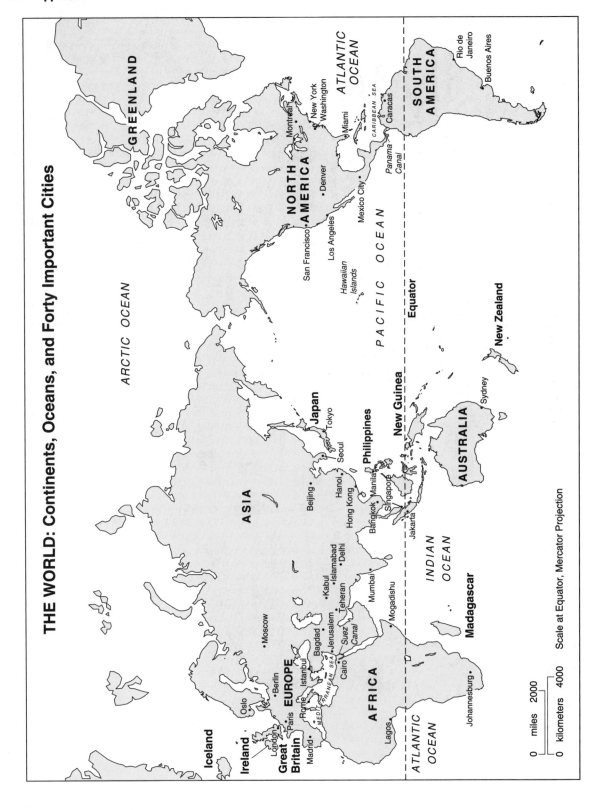

THE WORLD: Continents, Oceans, and Forty Important Cities

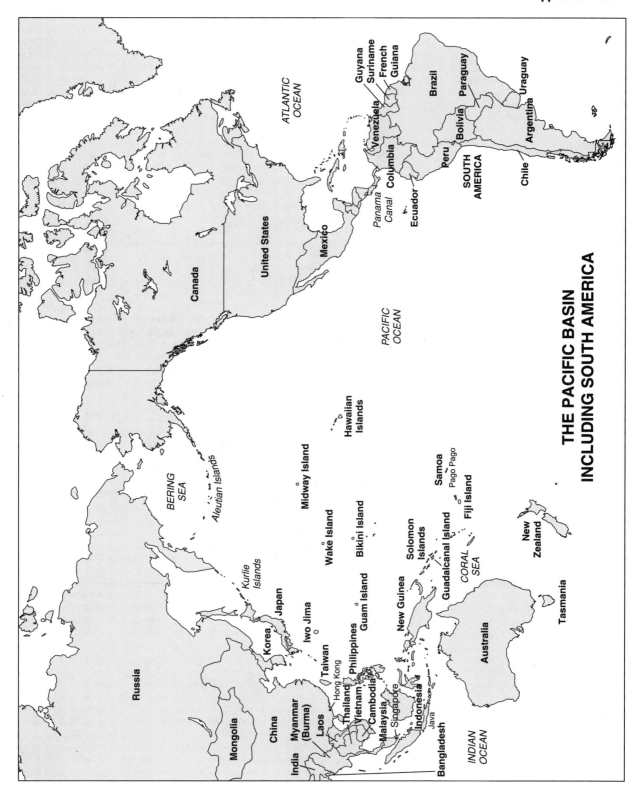

**THE PACIFIC BASIN
INCLUDING SOUTH AMERICA**

The African Continent

List of Presidents

President	Years in Office	Political Party
George Washington	1789–1797	not affiliated Federalist leanings
John Adams	1797–1801	Federalist
Thomas Jefferson	1801–1809	Democractic Republican
James Madison	1809–1817	Democratic Republican
James Monroe	1817–1825	Democratic Republican
John Quincy Adams	1825–1829	National Republican
Andrew Jackson	1829–1837	Democrat
Martin Van Buren	1837–1841	Democrat
William H. Harrison	1841	Whig
John Tyler	1841–1845	Whig
James K. Polk	1845–1849	Democrat
Zachary Taylor	1849–1850	Whig
Millard Fillmore	1850–1853	Whig
Franklin Pierce	1853–1857	Democrat
James Buchanan	1857–1861	Democrat
Abraham Lincoln	1861–1865	Republican
Andrew Johnson	1865–1869	Republican
Ulysses S. Grant	1869–1877	Republican
Rutherford B. Hayes	1877–1881	Republican
James A. Garfield	1881	Republican
Chester A. Arthur	1881–1885	Republican
Grover Cleveland	1885–1889	Democrat
Benjamin Harrison	1889–1893	Republican
Grover Cleveland	1893–1897	Democrat
William McKinley	1897–1901	Republican
Theodore Roosevelt	1901–1909	Republican
William Howard Taft	1909–1913	Republican
Woodrow Wilson	1913–1921	Democrat
Warren G. Harding	1921–1923	Republican
Calvin Coolidge	1923–1929	Republican
Herbert Hoover	1929–1933	Republican
Franklin D. Roosevelt	1933–1945	Democrat
Harry Truman	1945–1953	Democrat
Dwight D. Eisenhower	1953–1961	Republican
John F. Kennedy	1961–1963	Democrat
Lyndon B. Johnson	1963–1969	Democrat
Richard M. Nixon	1969–1974	Republican
Gerald R. Ford	1974–1977	Republican
James Carter	1977–1981	Democrat

Ronald Reagan	1981–1989	Republican
George H. W. Bush	1989–1993	Republican
William J. Clinton	1993–2001	Democrat
George W. Bush	2001–2009	Republican
Barack H. Obama	2009–	Democrat

Answers

Chapter 1

I. NATIVE AMERICAN IMMIGRANTS
Multiple Choice: 1. c   2. b   3. a   4. c

II. EUROPEAN IMMIGRANTS
Multiple Choice: 1. c   2. a   3. c   4. a

Chapter 2

I. THE SPANISH IN THE AMERICAS—THE EARLY YEARS
Multiple Choice: 1. b   2. c   3. a

II. EUROPEAN COLONIES IN NORTH AMERICA
Multiple Choice: 1. c   2. a   3. a

III. THE ENGLISH COLONIES TO 1763
Multiple Choice: 1. b   2. c   3. b

Chapter 3

I. STEPS LEADING TO THE AMERICAN REVOLUTION
Multiple Choice: 1. c   2. a   3. c

II. THE BEGINNING OF VIOLENCE

Multiple Choice: 1. b   2. c   3. c   4. b

III. THE AMERICAN REVOLUTION

Multiple Choice: 1. c   2. a   3. b

Chapter 4

I. POST-REVOLUTION GOVERNMENT UNDER THE ARTICLES OF CONFEDERATION

Multiple Choice: 1. c   2. a   3. b

II. THE NEW GOVERNMENT

Multiple Choice: 1. a   2. b   3. b

III. THE FRENCH REVOLUTION'S IMPACT ON AMERICA

Multiple Choice: 1. c   2. a   3. a

Chapter 5

I. THE REVOLUTION OF 1800 AND JEFFERSON'S PRESIDENCY

Multiple Choice: 1. a   2. c   3. b

II. THE ERA OF GOOD FEELINGS AND THE JACKSON PRESIDENCY

Multiple Choice: 1. c   2. a   3. b   4. b

III. NATIONALISM AND TERRITORIAL EXPANSION

Multiple Choice: 1. c   2. b   3. a

Chapter 6

I. EARLY SUPREME COURT DECISIONS

Multiple Choice: 1. b   2. a   3. c

II. RELIGION AND REFORM: 1800–1850

Multiple Choice: 1. c   2. b   3. c

III. SOCIAL CHANGES IN AMERICA

Multiple Choice: 1. a   2. b   3. c

Chapter 7

I. THE FAILURE OF COMPROMISE

Multiple Choice: 1. a   2. c   3. b

II. THE CIVIL WAR

Multiple Choice: 1. a   2. c   3. a   4. b

III. THE PERIOD OF RECONSTRUCTION

Multiple Choice: 1. b   2. a   3. a

IV. FOREIGN POLICY ISSUES

Multiple Choice: 1. a   2. c   3. c

Chapter 8

I. THE FRONTIER AND AMERICAN HISTORY

Multiple Choice: 1. c   2. c   3. c   4. a

II. REFORM MOVEMENTS

Multiple Choice: 1. a   2. c   3. b

Chapter 9

I. BUSINESS CYCLES

Multiple Choice: 1. b   2. a   3. b

II. THE PROGRESSIVE MOVEMENT

Multiple Choice: 1. a   2. c   3. c   4. a

III. FOREIGN POLICY: 1877–1914
Multiple Choice: 1. c   2. a   3. b   4. a

Chapter 10

I. WORLD WAR I AND THE PEACE
Multiple Choice: 1. b   2. c   3. b   4. c

II. THE COMING OF WORLD WAR II
Multiple Choice: 1. b   2. c   3. a

III. DOMESTIC AND SOCIAL ISSUES: 1918–1932
Multiple Choice: 1. a   2. a   3. a   4. b

IV. THE NEW DEAL
Multiple Choice: 1. c   2. a   3. a   4. c

Chapter 11

I. WORLD WAR II
Multiple Choice: 1. b   2. b   3. c   4. a

II. THE EARLY YEARS OF THE COLD WAR
Multiple Choice: 1. a   2. a   3. c   4. b

III. DOMESTIC AFFAIRS: 1945–1960
Multiple Choice: 1. b   2. a

Chapter 12

I. THE PRESIDENCIES OF JOHN F. KENNEDY AND LYNDON B. JOHNSON
Multiple Choice: 1. b   2. a   3. b   4. a

II. THE VIETNAM WAR
Multiple Choice: 1. b   2. c   3. a   4. b

III. THE PRESIDENCIES OF RICHARD NIXON AND GERALD FORD
Multiple Choice: 1. b   2. b   3. c

Chapter 13

I. DOMESTIC POLICIES OF CARTER, REAGAN, AND GEORGE H. W. BUSH
Multiple Choice: 1. a   2. b   3. c

II. FOREIGN POLICY UNDER CARTER, REAGAN, AND GEORGE H. W. BUSH
Multiple Choice: 1. c   2. a   3. c   4. a

Chapter 14

I. SOCIAL ASPECTS OF THE AMERICAN ECONOMY
Multiple Choice: 1. a   2. b   3. b   4. c

II. DIVERSITY IN AMERICAN LIFE: CHANGING SOCIAL PATTERNS
Multiple Choice: 1. b   2. c   3. a   4. c

III. SOCIAL MOVEMENTS AND SOCIAL PROTESTS
Multiple Choice: 1. c   2. a   3. a   4. c

IV. CULTURE AND SOCIETY
Multiple Choice: 1. c   2. a   3. a   4. a

Chapter 15

I. DOMESTIC ISSUES DURING CLINTON'S TWO TERMS
Multiple Choice: 1. c   2. a   3. b

II. OTHER DOMESTIC ISSUES
Multiple Choice: 1. c   2. b   3. c

III. DOMESTIC POLICIES AND ISSUES DURING BUSH'S TWO TERMS
Multiple Choice: 1. c   2. c   3. a   4. b

IV. BUSH UNDERTAKES WAR ON TERRORISM
Multiple Choice: 1. c   2. b   3. c   4. c   5. b   6. a

V. FOREIGN POLICY ISSUES: 1993–2009
Multiple Choice: 1. c   2. b   3. a   4. b   5. c

VI. FINANCIAL CRISIS, ELECTION OF 2008, AND PRESIDENT OBAMA'S FIRST TWO MONTHS
Multiple Choice: 1. c   2. a

Chapter 16

I. THE IMPACT OF BUSINESS AND INDUSTRY ON SOCIAL PATTERNS
Multiple Choice: 1. a   2. b   3. a

II. VALUES, DIVERSITY, AND CHANGING CULTURAL AND SOCIAL PATTERNS
Multiple Choice: 1. b   2. c   3. a

Index